The Global Arms Trade

The Global Arms Trade

A handbook

Editor: Andrew T. H. Tan

LONDON AND NEW YORK

First published 2010 by Routledge

Published 2014 by Routledge

2 Park Square, Milton Park, Abingdon, Oxfordshire OX14 4RN
711 Third Avenue, New York, NY 10017

First issued in paperback 2014

Routledge is an imprint of the Taylor and Francis Group, an informa business

© Taylor & Francis 2010

ISBN 978-1-85743-497-2 (hbk)
ISBN 978-1-85743-797-3 (pbk)
ISBN 978-0-203-85145-6 (ebk)

Europa Development Editor: Cathy Hartley

The publishers make no representation, express or implied, with regard to the accuracy of the information contained in this book and cannot accept any legal responsibility for any errors or omissions that may take place.

Typeset in 10/11.5pt Baskerville by Taylor & Francis Books

Contents

Figures

Tables

The editor and contributors

Andrew T. H. Tan is Associate Professor and Convenor for International Studies at the University of New South Wales, Australia. His research on defence and security issues is supported by the university's prestigious Strategic Priority Fund. He was previously Senior Lecturer in Defence Studies, King's College London, and taught at the Joint Services Command and Staff College, Watchfield, United Kingdom. Educated in Singapore, Cambridge and Sydney (where he obtained his PhD), his advice on security issues is sought by governments, armed forces, universities and research institutes. His many journal articles and book reviews have appeared in leading internationally refereed academic journals, such as *Contemporary Security Policy*, *Terrorism and Political Violence*, *Studies in Conflict and Terrorism*, *Harvard Asia Review*, *Korean Journal of Defense Analysis*, *Cambridge Review of International Affairs*, *Contemporary Southeast Asia*, *Asia Pacific Review*, etc. He has written or edited 10 books, including: *Security Perspectives of the Malay Archipelago* (Cheltenham, United Kingdom: Edward Elgar, 2004); *A Political and Economic Dictionary of South-East Asia* (London: Europa Routledge, 2004); *The Politics of Terrorism* (London: Routledge, 2006); *A Handbook of Terrorism and Insurgency in Southeast Asia* (Cheltenham, United Kingdom: Edward Elgar, 2007); and *The Politics of Maritime Power* (London: Routledge, 2007). His latest sole-authored book is *US Strategy Against Global Terrorism: How it Evolved, Why it Failed and Where it is Headed* (New York: Palgrave Macmillan, 2009).

Riad A. Attar is Assistant Professor in the Department of Government, Law and International Affairs at Murray State University. Attar obtained a PhD in Political Science from Texas A&M University–College Station, Texas in 2006, and an MA in Political Science from Midwestern State University-Wichita Falls, Texas in 1997. The focus of Attar's research is on international political economy in general, and on the political economy of defence in particular. His region of interest is the Middle East. His publishing activities include: 'Egypt: State, Security, and Human Rights', in a reference work published by Praeger Security International, 2006; *The Political Economy of Military Spending, Freedom, Conflicts, and Economic Growth in Developing Countries* (Palgrave, 2002); and 'The Determinants of the Liberalization Process in the Middle East', delivered at the International Studies Association, New Orleans, 2002.

Desmond Ball is Professor in the Strategic and Defence Studies Centre at the Australian National University, Canberra, and is generally regarded as Australia's leading strategic analyst. He was Head of the Centre from 1984 to 1991, and is the author or editor of some 30 books and monographs on global strategic matters, regional security developments and Australian defence issues. He has served as a consultant to a wide range of Australian government departments and agencies. In the 1970s and 1980s, Professor Ball was one of the key actors in the conceptual transformation in Australian defence policy away from 'forward defence' and dependence upon 'great and powerful friends' to the defence of Australia and self-reliance. He has worked on most aspects of Australian defence policy, including defence decision-making processes, force development methodologies, intelligence capabilities, defence acquisition programmes (e.g. the F/A-18 and Jindalee programmes), Australian Defence Force command and control arrangements, Northern agencies and Australian defence infrastructure, including Australian defence industry. Since the early 1980s, Professor Ball has worked increasingly on security developments in the Asia/Pacific region. In addition to his research and publication activities, Professor Ball has been at the forefront of 'second-track' processes of co-operation in the region. He is a founding member of the Steering Committee of the Council on Security Co-operation in the Asia Pacific (CSCAP).

Sibylle Bauer (Germany) is a Senior Researcher with the Stockholm International Peace Research Institute (SIPRI) and Head of the Export Control Project. Previously, she was a Researcher with the Institute for European Studies in Brussels. She has published widely on European export control and armaments issues, including chapters in *The Restructuring of the European Defence Industry* (Office for Official Publications of the European Communities, 2001), *Annuaire français de relations internationales* (French Yearbook of International Relations) (Bruylant, 2001) and *The Path to European Defence* (Maklu, 2003). She is co-author of *The European Union Code of Conduct on Arms Exports: Improving the Annual Report*, SIPRI Policy Paper no. 8 (November 2004). She has contributed to the *SIPRI Yearbook* since 2004.

Richard A. Bitzinger is Senior Fellow at the S. Rajaratnam School of International Studies, Nanyang Technological University in Singapore, where his work focuses on military and defence issues relating to the Asia-Pacific region, including the challenges of defence transformation in the Asia-Pacific, regional military modernization activities, and local defence industries, arms production and weapons proliferation. Mr Bitzinger is the author of *Towards a Brave New Arms Industry?* (Oxford University Press, 2003); 'Come the Revolution: Transforming the Asia-Pacific's Militaries', *Naval War College Review* (Fall 2005); and *Transforming the US Military: Implications for the Asia-Pacific* (Australian Strategic Policy Institute, December 2006). He has written several monographs and book chapters, and his articles have appeared in such journals as *International Security*, *Orbis*, *China Quarterly* and *The Korean Journal of Defense Analysis*. Mr Bitzinger was previously an Associate Professor with the Asia-Pacific Center for Security Studies (APCSS), Honolulu, Hawaii, and has also worked for the RAND Corporation, the Center for Strategic and Budgetary Affairs, and the US Government. In 1999–2000, he was a Senior Fellow with the Atlantic Council of the United States. He holds a master's degree from the Monterey Institute of International Affairs and has pursued additional postgraduate studies at the University of California, Los Angeles.

Mark Bromley (United Kingdom) is a Researcher with the Arms Transfers Programme at the Stockholm International Peace Research Institute (SIPRI). Within the Arms Transfers Programme, his responsibilities include collecting information on Latin America for the SIPRI Arms Transfers Database, which contains information on all international transfers of major conventional weapons since 1950. His areas of research include defence acquisitions within Latin America, transparency in the field of international arms transfers and the illicit trafficking of small arms and light weapons. His publications include: *The European Union Code of Conduct on Arms Exports: Improving the Annual Report*, SIPRI Policy Paper no. 8 (November 2004); *CBMs in Latin America and the Effect of Arms Acquisitions by Venezuela*, Real Instituto Elcano Working Paper (September 2005); *The Impact on Domestic Policy of the EU Code of Conduct on Arms Exports: The Czech Republic, the Netherlands and Spain*, SIPRI Policy Paper no. 21 (May 2008); and *Stemming Destabilizing Arms Transfers: The Impact of European Union Air Safety Bans*, SIPRI Insights on Peace and Security no. 3 (October 2008).

Michael Brzoska studied economics and political science at the Universities of Hamburg (Germany) and Fribourg (Switzerland), completing a Diploma in Economics and a PhD in Political Science (University of Hamburg) in 1985 and habilitation in 1997. He has been Scientific Director of the Institute for Peace Research and Security Policy (IFSH) and Professor at the University of Hamburg since February 2006. From 1994 until January 2006 he was Director of Research at the Bonn International Center for Conversion, Germany. Between 1987 and 1994 he was Project Leader at the Unit for the Study of Armaments, Development and Wars, Institute for Political Science, University of Hamburg. From 1983 to 1986, he was research member and co-director of the Arms Trade and Arms Production Team at the Stockholm International Peace Research Institute (SIPRI), Sweden. His main fields of research are arms control and disarmament, targeted sanctions and sanction reform, economic actors in internal armed conflicts, Europeanization of arms production, international arms transfers, security sector reform, conflict research and global arms industry. Among recent publications are: *Promoting Security: But How and for Whom?* (Bonn: BICC, 2004; co-edited with Peter Croll); and as co-editor with David Law, *Security Sector Reform in Peace Support Operations* (London: Routledge, 2006).

Malcolm R. Davis, an Australian citizen with United Kingdom permanent residency, is currently employed with the Australian Department of Defence at an APS 6 Level as 'Staff Officer – Strategy' with Directorate of Navy Strategy and Futures, which is part of Navy Headquarters. He has held this post since November 2007. Prior to this appointment, he was employed as a Lecturer in Defence Studies with the Defence Studies Department, King's College London, based at the Joint Services Command and Staff College. His PhD, which examined 'The impact of the RMA in East Asia from a Maritime Perspective', was awarded in Politics from the University of Hull in July 2003. His academic focus is broadly in the 'strategic studies and security futures' realm. Previous research activities have been centred on military 'transformation' and the impact of future military technology on the conduct of warfare, including notions of RMAs, Network Centric Warfare, and the future of Air Power and Seapower, particularly in an East-Asia strategic context. He has developed a strong research interest and expertise in issues related to the military utility of space, and broader strategic aspects of 'spacepower'. He is currently completing a single-authored monograph to be published by Routledge in 2010, entitled *Military Transformation in East Asia – Technology, Warfare and Future Security*.

J. Paul Dunne is Professor of Economics at Bristol Business School, University of the West of England, Bristol and a research affiliate at the Southern Africa Labour and Development Research Unit (SALDRU), University of Cape Town. He was previously Research Professor in Economics at Middlesex University and has held posts at Birkbeck College, Warwick University, Department of Applied Economics and Magdalene College, University of Cambridge, and the University of Leeds. He is an applied economist whose main area of research is the economics of peace, security and military spending, he is chair of the United Kingdom affiliate of Economists for Peace and Security (EPS), and edits the *Economics of Peace and Security Journal* with Jurgen Brauer. His publications include numerous articles in journals, including *Defence and Peace Economics, Economic Journal, Journal of Conflict Resolution, Journal of Peace Research, Cambridge Journal of Economics, Journal of Industrial Economics, European Economic Review* and the *Scottish Journal of Political Economy*. In addition, he is on the Editorial Advisory Board of the *International Review of Applied Economics*, and the Editorial Board of *Defence and Peace Economics* and is an associate editor of the *Cambridge Journal of Economics*.

Iñigo Guevara (Mexico) is currently undertaking a master's degree in Security Studies at Georgetown University; he is a graduate of the Strategy and Defense Policy course (SDP,

2008) at the Center for Hemispheric Defense Studies (CHDS) at the National Defense University in Washington, DC and holds a Diploma in Public Security Administration from the Instituto de Administración Pública del Estado de Querétaro (IAPQ). He has a BA in International Trade from the Instituto Tecnológico y de Estudios Superiores de Monterrey (ITESM). His main research comprises Latin American armed forces, conventional arms transfers, orders of battle and procurement policy analysis. He is a member of the International Institute for Strategic Studies (IISS) and is in regular communication with the department that produces the annual publication *The Military Balance*. He is also a member of the Military Expenditure and Arms Transfers networks of the Stockholm International Peace Research Institute (SIPRI), which contribute to publications such as the *SIPRI Yearbook*. He forms part of the Collective for the Analysis of Security with Democracy (CASEDE), a Mexico-based NGO. He is the consultant on Latin America for Jane's Armed Forces desk and contributes to the Sentinel series country-risk analysis. He is also a regular contributor to several United Kingdom-based specialized publications.

Yong-sup Han is currently Director of the Research Institute on National Security Affairs and a Professor at Korea National Defense University. He was Special Assistant to the Korean Minister of Defence in 1993 and a Senior Staff Member to the South-North Joint Nuclear Control Commission in 1991–92. He was Research Fellow at RAND Corporation from 1999 to 2000 and a Visiting Fellow in 1999 at the Center for Nonproliferation Studies of Monterey Institute for International Studies. He was also Senior Visiting Fellow at the United Nations Institute for Disarmament Research in 1993. Dr Han holds a master's degree in Political Science from Seoul National University, a master's in Public Policy from Harvard University, and a PhD in Security Policy from RAND Graduate School. His publications include: 'Delving into the Lee Myung-bak Government's New Security Policy', *Korean Journal of Security Affairs*, June 2008; 'Applying European Success of Economic and Security Co-operation to the Korean Peninsula and Northeast Asia', *Korean Journal of Security Affairs*, June 2006; *Peace and Arms Control on the Korean Peninsula* (Kyungnam University Press, 2005); *Sunshine in Korea* (RAND, 2002); 'Time for Conventional Arms Control on the Korean Peninsula', *Arms Control Today*, December 2000; 'North Korean Behavior in Nuclear Negotiations', *The Nonproliferation Review*, Spring 2000; and *Nuclear Disarmament and Nonproliferation in Northeast Asia* (United Nations, 1995).

You Ji is Associate Professor in the School of Social Science, University of New South Wales, Australia. He has published widely on the People's Republic of China's political, military and foreign affairs. He is author of three books: *In Quest of High Tech Power: The Modernisation of China's Military in the 1990s* (1996); *China's Enterprise Reform: Changing State/Society Relations after Mao* (1998); and *The Armed Forces of China* (1999); and numerous articles, of which the most recent include: 'The Soviet Military Model and the Breakdown of the Sino-USSR Alliance', in Thomas Bernstein and Hua-yu Li (eds), *The Soviet Influence on China in the 1950s* (Rowman and Littlefield, 2009); 'China's New Diplomacy, Foreign Policy and Defense Strategy', in Stuart Harris, Qin Yaqing and Pauline Kerr (eds), *China's New Diplomacy: Tactical or Fundamental Change?* (Palgrave Macmillan, 2008); 'Beyond Symbiosis: Redefining Civil-Military Relations in China', in Wang Gungwu and Yongnian Zheng (eds), *China's Grand Transformation* (Routledge, 2008); 'Revolution in Military Thinking', in Bo Huldt and Masako Ikegami (eds), *The Strategic Yearbook on East Asian Security* (Swedish National Defence College and the Finnish Defence University, 2008); 'Dealing with Malacca Dilemma: China's Effort to Protect its Energy Supply', *Strategic Analysis*, Vol. 31, No. 3, 2007; 'Unravelling the Myths of the PLA Political Commissars', in David M. Finkelstein and Kirsten Gunness (eds), *Swimming in a New Sea: Civil-Military Issues in Today's China* (M. E. Sharpe, 2007).

Andrew D. James is a Senior Lecturer at Manchester Business School, University of Manchester, United Kingdom, and a Senior Research Fellow at the Manchester Institute for Innovation Research. His research focuses on corporate technology strategy, innovation management and science and technology policy, with a particular focus on the industrial and technological dynamics of the defence, security and aerospace sectors.

Ephraim Kam is Deputy Director of the Institute for National Security Studies (formerly the Jaffee Center for Strategic Studies) in Israel. He served as a Colonel in the Research Division of IDF Military Intelligence. His last position there was Assistant Director of the Research Division for Evaluation. In 1993 he retired from the IDF and joined the Jaffee Center, where he has been deputy director since 1995. Dr Kam took his BA at the Hebrew University of Jerusalem in Middle Eastern Studies and Economics, and his MA and PhD degrees in International Relations at Harvard University. He specializes in security problems of the Middle East and the Arab states, Israel's national security issues, as well as strategic intelligence. During the last 15 years he has specialized in Iranian strategy. His book *Surprise Attack: The Victim's Perspective* (Harvard University Press, 1988) was awarded the National Intelligence Study Center 1988 prize for the best book on intelligence issues. Among his other publications are: *From Terror to Nuclear Bombs: The Significance of the Iranian Threat* (Hebrew, 2004); *The Implications of the Collapse of the Soviet Union on the Middle East* (1991); *The Political Framework of the Palestinian Entity* (1994); and *A Nuclear Iran: What Does It Mean and What Can Be Done* (2007).

Yaacov Lifshitz is currently an independent economic adviser, a member of the boards of various public and private companies, a senior research associate of the Begin-Sadat (BESA) Center for Strategic Studies, and a lecturer at the Ben-Gurion University, in Israel. In recent years his academic interest as a researcher and a teacher has been mainly in the areas of defence economics, economics of terrorism, and social-economic policymaking in Israel. In the past, among other positions in the public and business sector, he served as the Director-General in the Ministry of Finance, the Chief Economic Adviser in the Ministry of Defence, and the Chairman of the Board of Israel Military Industries. He has written the book *The Economics of Producing Defense* (Kluwer Academic Publishers, 2003), as well as articles on defence economics and related issues.

Harsh V. Pant teaches at King's College London in the Department of Defence Studies. He is also an Associate with the King's Centre for Science and Security and lectures at the United Kingdom Defence Academy. His current research is focused on Asia-Pacific security and defence issues. He has published on these issues in a number of academic journals and other publications. His most recent books include *Contemporary Debates in Indian Foreign and Security Policy* (New York: Palgrave Macmillan, 2008) and *Indian Foreign Policy in a Unipolar World* (London: Routledge, 2008).

Malcolm Hugh Patterson graduated with degrees in history, international relations and two law degrees from the University of New South Wales, Australia. He also holds diplomas in legal practice, company direction and financial markets. He is a solicitor of the Supreme Court of New South Wales and the High Court of Australia. In August 2007 Malcolm completed a PhD at the University of Cambridge. His dissertation was entitled 'Private Military Actors in United Nations Peacekeeping and Humanitarian Operations'. An article derived from the dissertation has recently been published in the *Journal of Conflict and Security Law*. A book to be published by Palgrave Macmillan in late 2009 will be based on his Cambridge research. That publication will advance a case for corporate forces to serve in UN operations under a new administrative and criminal justice model. Malcolm

Patterson lives in Sydney where he is a lecturer in the School of Social Sciences and International Studies at the University of New South Wales.

Sam Perlo-Freeman is a Senior Researcher with the Stockholm International Peace Research Institute (SIPRI) Military Expenditure and Arms Production Project, heading SIPRI's work on Military Expenditure. Previously, he was a Senior Lecturer in Economics at the University of the West of England, working in the field of Defence and Peace Economics, in which he is the author of a number of publications, including: 'The Demand for Military Expenditure in Developing Countries', *International Review of Applied Economics*, 2003; and 'Offsets and Development of the Brazilian Armaments Industry', *Arms Trade and Economic Development: Theory and Policy in Offsets* (Routledge, 2004). He has also worked on policy papers for Oxfam and BASIC, contributing to a recent Oxfam report on the impact of arms transfers on the Millennium Development Goals. During his two stints at SIPRI he has contributed to the Yearbooks for 2003, 2004 and 2008, and has co-authored two SIPRI publications: *Armament & Disarmament in the South Caucasus and Central Asia* (SIPRI Policy Paper no. 3, July 2003) and more recently *The Private Military Services Industry* (SIPRI Insight no. 1, September 2008). He is a long-standing member of the United Kingdom's Campaign Against Arms Trade.

Alexander A. Pikayev is Director of the Department for Disarmament and International Security at the Moscow-based Institute of World Economy and International Relations (IMEMO). He is also a member of the London-based International Institute for Strategic Studies (IISS). Dr Pikayev received his MA from the Moscow State University in 1984 and PhD from IMEMO in 1992. He has worked at IMEMO since 1984. From 1994 to 1997 he was a professional staff member of the Russian Duma's Defence Committee. From 1997 to 2003 he directed a Non-Proliferation Programme at the Carnegie Moscow Center and was Editor-in-Chief of the Center's *Nuclear Proliferation Journal*. Dr Pikayev has authored several hundred books, chapters and articles on nuclear disarmament and non-proliferation, Russian foreign and security policy, and military reform. He has spoken to numerous authoritative audiences, including the US Congress, German Bundestag, United Kingdom Parliament and Russian Duma. Dr Pikayev is one of the most frequently cited Russian political experts by international media.

Martin Rupiya is Director of Research (Africa) at the Centre for Security Sector Management (CSSM), Cranfield University, United Kingdom, since June 2008. His portfolio, apart from lecturing on the MSc in Security Sector Management as well as supervising PhD students, includes leading on options for post-conflict recovery, which focus on security sector reform as well as stabilization on the African continent as part of a wider project of stability, peace and development. Before this, he was a Senior Researcher and MilAIDS Project Manager with the Institute for Security Studies (ISS) in Pretoria, South Africa. The move to work in security policy research-oriented establishments followed more than a decade and a half of teaching at various universities, including the Universities of Zimbabwe, Witwatersrand and Rhodes in Grahamstown, South Africa. Rupiya has published extensively on peace and security issues related to conflict and crises on the African continent. His latest work has focused on a region that has turned out to be the most volatile on the African continent: 'A Regional Security Perspective from and for the Horn of Africa', with Alfred G. Nhema, in Hans Gunter-Brauch et al. (eds), *Globalization & Environmental Challenges: Reconceptualising Security in the 21st Century* (Peace Research & Europe Security Studies, AFES-PRESS, 2008).

Elisabeth Sköns is a Senior Fellow at the Stockholm International Peace Research Institute (SIPRI) and the leader of the SIPRI Military Expenditure and Arms Programme. This programme monitors and analyses trends and developments in these two areas and produces annual surveys for the SIPRI Yearbook. It maintains a database on military expenditure for 167 countries and a database on arms-producing companies, covering the largest companies in the main arms-producing countries apart from the People's Republic of China. Sköns has contributed to SIPRI publications since 1983. Her most recent publications apart from the annual surveys on military expenditure and arms production are: *The Private Military Services Industry* (SIPRI Insight no. 1, September 2008, with Sam Perlo-Freeman); 'Analysing Risks to Human Lives', *SIPRI Yearbook 2007*; 'The Economics of Arms Production', *Encyclopaedia of Violence, Peace and Conflict* (Academic Press, 2008, with Paul Dunne); 'In Search of the Peace Dividend', *The Statesman's Yearbook 2007*; papers on 'The Costs of Conflict' and 'Financing of Peace Missions' for the *International Task Force on Global Public Goods* (Stockholm, 2006); papers on the restructuring of the Western European defence industry in *Mot et avnasjonalisert Forsvar?* (*Towards a Denationalized Defence?*) (Abstrakt: Oslo, 2005); and a chapter on defence offsets in Finland and Sweden, in *Arms Trade and Economic Development: Theory and Policy in Offsets* (Routledge, 2004).

Thomas Teichler is a Research Associate at the Manchester Institute for Innovation Research, Manchester Business School. He has a PhD from the European University Institute in Florence on the political, industrial and legal aspects of European armaments co-operation. For this purpose he also spent five months at the European Commission, DG Enterprise and Industry, where he worked with the desk officer 'Defence' in 2005/06. For three years he has extensively worked on matters of European and transatlantic security and defence policy in an academic and policy environment at the Robert Schuhman Centre in Florence and at the University of Bielefeld. He has presented his research results at numerous international conferences in Europe and the USA.

Mehmet Uye is a PhD candidate at the Department of Economics, Bristol Business School, University of the West of England, Bristol.

Brad Williams is a visiting fellow in the Department of Political Science, National University of Singapore. He is the author of *Resolving the Russo-Japanese Territorial Dispute: Hokkaido-Sakhalin Relations* (London: Routledge, 2007) and co-editor of *Japan, Australia and Asia-Pacific Security* (London: Routledge, 2006). His research interests focus on the international relations of the Asia-Pacific and he has published in several internationally refereed journals, such as *Journal of Asian Studies*, *The Pacific Review*, *Japan Forum*, *Non-proliferation Review* and *Europe-Asia Studies*.

Siemon T. Wezeman is a Senior Fellow at the Stockholm International Peace Research Institute (SIPRI) where, since 1992, he has tracked and analysed international arms transfers as part of the Arms Transfers Programme (formerly Arms Transfers Project). Since 2006 he has been the head of the Arms Transfers Programme. He has published on the arms trade, transparency in arms and security, and on developments in military technology. His research field is global but with a specific interest in conflict areas and Asia. He is a Dutch citizen and holds an MA in Contemporary History from the State University Groningen. He has contributed to the *SIPRI Yearbook* since 1992. His latest publications include work on UN embargoes, European UAV developments, the UN Register of Conventional Arms and on cluster weapons.

Lt Col Isaiah (Ike) Wilson, III, US Army, PhD, is an Associate Professor at the US Military Academy at West Point, where he directs the American Politics, Policy and Strategy programme in the Department of Social Sciences. He is a former army aviator and military strategist with peace enforcement and combat experience in the Balkans in the 1990s and in Iraq 2003–04, serving on former Chief of Staff of the Army, Gen. Eric Shinseki's Operation Iraqi Freedom Study Group (OIFSG) and later as chief of plans, 101st Airborne Division (Air Assault). Dr Wilson is an accomplished scholar and published author. His recent book, *Thinking Beyond War: Civil-Military Relations and Why America Fails to Win the Peace* (2007) is considered an important early contribution to the contemporary debates over the US war effort in Iraq. Dr Wilson holds master's degrees in public affairs, political science, strategy and theatre operations, as well as a doctorate in government from Cornell University. He is a life member of the Council on Foreign Relations, holds visiting and adjunct professorships at Cornell University, Columbia University and George Washington University, and has served on the faculty of the prestigious National War College in Washington, DC.

Acknowledgements

The editor wishes to acknowledge the invaluable assistance rendered by several individuals who helped to locate and put the team of writers together. Elisabeth Sköns of the Stockholm International Peace Research Institute (SIPRI) was generous with her time and contacts in locating highly specialized writers for several important topics, and also recommended several of her colleagues at SIPRI to participate in this project. Victor Sumsky suggested Alexander Pikayev to write the important chapter on Russia. Eunsook Chung introduced Yong-sup Han to write the chapter on North Korea. My colleague at the University of New South Wales, Jeffrey Levey was kind with his suggestions and contacts which led to the participation of several top analysts from Israel.

The editor wishes especially to thank Cathy Hartley (Europa Development Editor at Routledge), who has done an immense and superb job in overseeing the editing and production of this important volume. Indeed, this work would not have been possible without Cathy's support, encouragement and vision, which led to the commissioning of this work. The editor also wishes to acknowledge Professor Michael Rainsborough, Department of War Studies, King's College London, for his valuable support and advice for this project, which has been much appreciated.

The most important contribution comes from the writers themselves, who took the time and effort to write superb chapter contributions for this volume. The writers are as follows: Riad A. Attar, Desmond Ball, Sibylle Bauer, Richard A. Bitzinger, Mark Bromley, Michael Brzoska, Malcolm R. Davis, J. Paul Dunne, Iñigo Guevara, Yong-sup Han, You Ji, Andrew D. James, Ephraim Kam, Yaacov Lifshitz, Harsh V. Pant, Malcolm Hugh Patterson, Sam Perlo-Freeman, Alexander A. Pikayev, Martin Rupiya, Elisabeth Sköns, Thomas Teichler, Mehmet Uye, Brad Williams, Siemon T. Wezeman and Isaiah Wilson, III.

The editor also wishes to thank the University of New South Wales for providing the needed support for this project. As recipient of the Strategic Priority Fund, the editor was exempted from teaching in order to undertake projects such as this. The editor wishes especially to thank the following individuals from the university for their invaluable support: Professor James Donald, Dean of the Faculty of Arts; Professor Roger Bell, Convenor for International Studies (until June 2009); Associate Professor Rogelia Pe-Pua, Head of the School of Social Science and International Studies; and Professor Mark Wainwright, former Vice-Chancellor.

The editor wishes to add his personal appreciation to loved ones who have provided so much support and encouragement for his endeavours. They include his mother, sister Lily, and his beloved wife, Angela Wong. Without family and God, we are truly nothing.

Andrew T. H. Tan
University of New South Wales
October 2009

Foreword

The global arms trade is an important, but under-researched, area of academic enquiry. Despite the end of the Cold War, arms expenditure as well as arms procurement have not, as a whole, declined. Instead, the trends suggest that aside from Western Europe, the rest of the world has not reaped a peace dividend from the end of the Cold War. Globally, the increase in military expenditure has led to the procurement of increasingly sophisticated weapons systems as well as the refurbishment of old ones. This has ensured the continuation and expansion of the global arms trade. The international supply of arms is also backed by the existence of a sophisticated arms industry that has gradually become a globalized industry.

Some key questions include: What have been the trends in arms procurement? What accounts for defence procurement? What are the key issues in arms procurement? What are the future prospects for the global arms trade? How has the arms industry adapted to the end of the Cold War and the emergence of globalization? Furthermore, what are the key issues in the global arms trade?

Some key issues that come to mind include: the trade-off between defence spending and development, the undue influence of the 'military industrial complex', the control of the proliferation of conventional arms, insurgencies and their impact on arms procurement, the privatization of force, and future war and weapons systems.

Written by a team of international arms experts, *The Global Arms Trade: a handbook* is divided into sections that examine the demand for arms, the supply of arms and the key issues in the global arms trade. Although this is a refereed volume, its comprehensive and in-depth treatment of the subject will make this a standard reference for years to come. This volume is especially useful to scholars, policy analysts, those in the arms industry, defence professionals, students of international relations and security studies, media professionals, government officials, and those generally interested in the arms trade.

Andrew T. H. Tan
University of New South Wales
October 2009

Abbreviations

AA	anti-aircraft
ACDA	Arms Control and Disarmament Agency
AFCON	Advanced Frigate Consortium
AIFV	Advanced Infantry Fighting Vehicle
AIP	air independent propulsion
AMRAAM	advanced medium-range air-to-air missile
AOI	Arab Organization for Industrialization
APC	armoured personnel carrier
APM	anti-personnel mines
ASAT	anti-satellite
ASEAN	Association of Southeast Asian Nations
ASTOVL	advanced short take-off and vertical landing
ASW	anti-submarine warfare
ATE	Advanced Technologies and Engineering
ATT	Arms Trade Treaty
ATR	Avions de Transport Régional
AWAC	Airborne Warning and Control
BAE	British Aerospace
BBC	British Broadcasting Corporation
BGT	Bodenseewerk Geratetechnik
BMD	ballistic missile defence
bn	billion
BVR	beyond visual range
BWC	Biological and Toxin Weapons Convention
C4ISR	command, control, communications, computers, intelligence, surveillance and reconnaissance
C4ISTAR	command, control, communications, computers, intelligence, surveillance, target acquisition and reconnaissance
CASA	Construcciones Aeronauticas SA
CCM	Convention on Cluster Munitions
CFE	Treaty on Conventional Forces in Europe
CFSP	Common Foreign and Security Policy
CIA	Central Intelligence Agency
COCOM	Co-ordinating Committee for Multilateral Export Controls
COMINT	communications intelligence
COTS	commercial off-the-shelf
CPI	Consumer Price Index
CSIS	Center for Strategic and International Studies (Washington)
CVF	Carrier Vessel Future

CWC	Chemical Weapons Convention
DASA	DaimlerChrysler Aerospace
DEW	directed energy weapons
DIB	defence industrial base
DIO	Defence Intelligence Organisation
DoD	Department of Defense (USA)
DPRK	Democratic People's Republic of Korea
EAC	European Airlift Centre
EADS	European Aeronautic Defence and Space
ECAP	European Capability Action Plan
ECJ	European Court of Justice
ECM	electronic counter-measures
ECOWAS	Economic Community of West African States
ECSC	European Coal and Steel Community
EDA	European Defence Agency
EDC	European Defence Community
EDEM	European Defence Equipment Market
EDSP	European Defence and Security Policy
EEC	European Economic Community
EEZ	Exclusive Economic Zone
EFTA	European Free Trade Association
ELINT	electronics intelligence
EU	European Union
EW	electronic warfare
FCS	Future Combat System
FDI	Foreign Direct Investment
FREMM	Frégates Européennes Multi-Missions
FY	Fiscal Year
GAO	Government Accountability Office
GDP	gross domestic product
GNP	gross national product
HIPC	highly-indebted poor countries
HPW	high power microwave
IADS	Integrated Air Defence System
IAI	Israel Aerospace Industries
ICC	International Criminal Court
IDF	Israel Defence Forces
IDP	internally-displaced persons
IEPG	Independent European Program Group
I&EW	information and electronic warfare
IFSEC	(USA-Japan) Industry Forum for Security Co-operation
IFV	infantry fighting vehicle
IGAD	Intergovernmental Authority on Development
IHI	Ishikawajima-Harima Heavy Industries
IISS	International Institute for Strategic Studies
IMF	International Monetary Fund
IMI	Israel Military Industry
IRBM	intermediate-range ballistic missile
ISI	Inter-Services Intelligence
JADI	Japan Association of Defence Industry
JDA	Japan Defence Agency

JSDF	Japan Self-Defence Force
JSF	Joint Strike Fighter
km	kilometre(s)
LCA	Light Combat Aircraft
LFK	Lenkflugkorpersysteme GmbH
m.	million
M&A	mergers and acquisitions
MANPADS	man-portable air defence systems
MAST	Micro Autonomous Systems and Technology
MBDA	Matra BAE Dynamics Alenia
MBT	main battle tank
MCO	Major Combat Operations
MHI	Mitsubishi Heavy Industries
MIC	military-industrial complex
MoD	Ministry of Defence (United Kingdom)
MRAP	mine-resistant ambush-protected
MRBM	medium-range ballistic missile
NATO	North Atlantic Treaty Organization
NCW	network-centric warfare
NDPG	National Defence Program Guidelines
NGO	non-governmental organization
NIC	National Intelligence Council
nm	nautical mile(s)
NPDO	National Defence Program Outline
NPT	Nuclear Non-Proliferation Treaty
OAS	Organization of African States
OCCAR	Organisation Conjointe de Coopération en Matière d'armement
OMB	Office of Management and Budget
OODA	observe, orient, decide, act
OPEC	Organization of the Petroleum Exporting Countries
OSCE	Organisation for Security and Co-operation in Europe
PAAMS	Principal Anti-Air Missile System
PFI	Private Finance Initiative
PGM	precision-guided munition
PhD	Doctor of Philosophy
PLA	People's Liberation Army
PLO	Palestine Liberation Organization
PMSC	private military and security contractor
PNA	Palestinian National Authority
PPP	purchasing power parity
PSC	Peace and Security Council
QDR	Quadrennial Defense Review
RDT&E	research, development, test and evaluation
RECAMP	Reinforcement of African Capacity to Maintain Peace
RMA	Revolution in Military Affairs
ROK	Republic of Korea
RPV	rocket-propelled launcher
SALW	small arms and light weapons
SAM	surface-to-air missile
SIC	Standard Industrial Classification
SIGINT	signals intelligence

SIPRI	Stockholm International Peace Research Institute
SLBM	submarine-launched ballistic missile
SLOC	sea lines of communications
SLV	space launch vehicle
SME	small and medium-sized enterprises
SRBM	short-range ballistic missile
SRO	stability and reconstruction operations
SRSAM	short-range surface-to-air missile
SSTR	stability, security, transition, reconstruction
TMD	Theatre Missile Defence
TRP	Technology Reinvestment Programme
UAV	Unmanned Aerial Vehicle
UCAV	Unmanned Combat Air Vehicle
UK	United Kingdom
UN	United Nations
UNODA	United Nations Office for Disarmament Affairs
UNSC	United Nations Security Council
US(A)	United States (of America)
WAPT	Wadi-Araba Peace Treaty
WEAG	Western European Armaments Group
WEAO	Western European Armaments Organisation
WEU	Western European Union
WMD	weapons of mass destruction

Part I

Introduction

1 The global arms trade

Andrew T. H. Tan

The global arms trade phenomenon

The global arms trade is a phenomenon that deserves special attention and in-depth analyses. It is a massive global industry that is built on the foundation of strong and continuing demand arising from military expenditure that includes the procurement of new weapons systems and the refurbishment of old ones.

According to the authoritative Stockholm International Peace Research Institute (SIPRI), world military expenditure in 2007 totalled an estimated US$1,339 billion. Over the 10-year period from 1998 to 2007, world military spending increased by 45% in real terms. The biggest increases in military spending occurred in a number of regions: Eastern Europe (particularly Russia), North America (mainly the USA), the Middle East (the Gulf States, Iran, Jordan and Lebanon), South Asia (mainly India), North Africa (led by Algeria), and East Asia (led by the People's Republic of China with its 202% increase, Indonesia and Malaysia). Both Western Europe and Central America recorded the lowest increase in military expenditure over the same 10-year period. Military expenditure by the top 15 countries alone accounted for 83% of total world military spending, with the USA leading the way with 45% of total world military spending (SIPRI Yearbook 2008, 175–8). Excluding domestic sales, global arms exports were estimated at $45.6 billion in 2006 (SIPRI Yearbook 2008, 295). During the period 2003–07, the USA was the world's leading supplier of major conventional arms, with a share of 31% of global arms exports, followed by Russia, Germany, France, the United Kingdom (UK) and the Netherlands. Other significant arms supplying nations during this period included Italy, Sweden, China, Ukraine, Spain, Israel and Canada, all of which exported more than $1 billion in arms over 2003–07. During the same period, the major recipients of conventional arms transfers were, in order of rank, China, India, the United Arab Emirates (UAE) and Greece, which all bought more than $7 billion in arms. This was followed by states that bought more than $3 billion in arms, namely the Republic of Korea (South Korea), Israel, Egypt and Australia (SIPRI Yearbook 2008, 321–5).

What is significant has been the fact that globally, arms expenditure as well as arms procurement have not declined despite the end of the Cold War in the early 1990s. The figures and trends instead indicate that whilst there have been declines in Western Europe, much of the rest of the world has seen increased military expenditure accompanied by the procurement of weapons systems that are also increasingly sophisticated. In turn, this has helped to sustain the global arms trade. A summary of the defence economics of various key regions in the 2008 edition of the authoritative Military Balance, published by the International Institute for Strategic Studies (IISS), reveals the continued salience of arms and military deterrence. The USA has led the way, with a steady increase in military expenditure since 2001. As a percentage of gross domestic product (GDP), defence expenditure increased from 3.02% in 2001 to 4.05% in 2006. The US Congress also approved $459.6 billion for fiscal year (FY) 2008, not counting military construction or the 'war on terror' in Iraq, Afghanistan and elsewhere. If this was counted, the total cost was estimated to be around $695 billion for 2008 (Military Balance 2008, 18–9). Spending on this scale sustains a vast defence industry and it is little wonder that the USA is the world's largest supplier of arms, though it imports comparatively few weapons systems from abroad. The USA is committed to a process of 'military transformation' based on the so-called revolution in military affairs (RMA), in which precision, stealth, information dominance and battlespace awareness would be melded through a systems approach using vast improvements in IT and communications. The RMA has evolved into the direction of 'network-centric warfare', essentially a systems of systems approach that would substitute mass with precision firepower, mobility and reach. However, this process has turned out to be very expensive to implement, relying on expensive electronics and weapons systems.

Moreover, questions have been raised over the long-term sustainability of US defence-related expenditure. The increasing cost of weapons systems, the size of the armed forces and the huge costs associated with the wars in Iraq and Afghanistan, impose a heavy economic burden on the USA, given rising budget deficits and economic recession. According to one study by Joseph Stiglitz, the true cost of the war in Iraq alone would top $3,000 billion, if all war-related costs are factored in (Stiglitz and Bilmes 2008). This suggests a classic imperial over-reach by the world's sole superpower, though the consequences of this on the future of the global arms trade are uncertain.

In contrast, according to *The Military Balance 2008*, military expenditure as a percentage of GDP declined in most parts of the world. This declined from 1.5% of GDP in 1997 to 1.3% of GDP in 2006 for the Caribbean and Latin America. The corresponding figures for Europe (defined as North Atlantic Treaty Organization—NATO excluding the USA) was 2.09% in 1997 and 1.74% in 2006. Non-NATO Europe declined from 1.79% in 1997 to 1.16% in 2006. Russia declined from 5.79% in 1997 to 3.72% in 2005, and then went up again to 4.11% in 2006, although *The Military Balance* noted the special difficulties in estimating Russia's military expenditure (*The Military Balance 2008*, 211). The Middle East and North Africa, too, declined, from a high of 7.73% in 1998 to 5.26% in 2006. In Central and South Asia, this declined from 3.33% in 1998 to 2.38% in 2006. In East Asia and Australasia, in contrast, it held steady at around the 1.5% level from 1997 to 2006.

However, a more accurate picture of regional military expenditure is reflected in SIPRI figures, which strongly suggest that overall, global arms expenditure has increased in real terms despite declining as a percentage of GDP. This can be attributed to the generally stable global economic growth that has been taking place since the end of the Cold War and the gathering pace of globalization. According to SIPRI, military expenditure in Africa, measured in constant 2005 prices and exchange rates, rose from $11.1 billion in 1998 to $16.8 billion in 2007. In North America, it rose from $340 billion to $562 billion over the same period. In South America, this rose from $23.3 billion to $32 billion. In Asia and Oceania, the increase was from $132 billion to $200 billion. Europe as a whole rose slightly from $276 billion to $319 billion, although Eastern Europe showed a marked increase from $15.6 billion to $40.8 billion over the same period. In the Middle East the increase was from $48.8 billion in 1998 to $79 billion in 2007 (SIPRI Yearbook 2008, 208). What these figures and trends tell us is that the world's biggest arms market remains North America. However, it is also clear that Asia and Oceania represent a rapidly developing arms market, whilst the Middle East remains an important market as it continues to maintain the highest burden in military expenditure, at around 5%–6% of overall GDP.

The international supply of arms is backed by the existence of a sophisticated arms industry, which has gradually become a globalized industry just like any other commercialized industry today. This arms industry originated as national defence industries designed to reduce dependence on foreign arms supplies, but the end of the Cold War and the globalization of this industry has resulted in a process of rationalization, consolidation and niche specialization (Bitzinger 2003). According to SIPRI, companies in the USA and Western Europe dominate the list of arms sellers, numbering 76 out of the top 100 if China is excluded (due to the lack of readily accessible information). Of the top 10 arms-producing companies in the world, (excluding China) in 2006, six are US companies with the other four being European companies. They are: Boeing, Lockheed Martin, BAE Systems (UK), Northrop Grumman, Raytheon, General Dynamics, European Aeronautic Defence and Space (EADS, in Europe), L-3 Communications, Finmeccanica (Italy) and Thales (France). SIPRI also confirmed the trend towards further consolidation, which has resulted in the emergence of larger companies at the top through mergers and acquisitions, and a concomitant decline in competition. To sustain expensive defence industries, governments have also had to collaborate on defence projects with other states as well as encourage arms exports. According to SIPRI, arms sales of the top 100 companies increased by 32% over the period 2002–06 if measured at constant 2006 prices and exchange rates (SIPRI Yearbook 2008, 255–77). This confirms the overall global trend towards greater military expenditure and arms procurement, which has contributed to the global arms trade phenomenon.

The study of the arms trade

Given the importance of the subject matter, as the consequence of the arms trade are arms races and conflict in the form of interstate and civil wars, it is surprising how little academic attention is actually paid to it. As the above discussion demonstrates, there are excellent primary resources maintained, on the one side by the IISS in the form of the annual Military Balance and, on the other, by the peace and disarmament institution, SIPRI, in the form of the annual SIPRI Yearbook. Both contain authoritative data, information and analyses on the international arms trade, military procurement and military expenditure.

These two institutions represent different approaches: the IISS takes a state-centric perspective in terms of providing some measure of military power through an assessment of expenditure, procurement and arms transfers. SIPRI assesses the trends in expenditure, procurement and arms transfers with a view to improving the prospects for arms control and disarmament, and generally takes a more human security perspective. Similarly, strategic studies institutes using state-centric realist perspectives, and peace research institutes with a greater focus on human security and peace, are throughout the world churning out studies and volumes focusing on: the use of military power; conflict and the management of conflict, including interstate wars, civil wars, insurgencies and terrorism; and on multilateral mechanisms for arms control. What is interesting, though, is that there has been little competitive analysis of the primary facts and figures painstakingly gathered by both the IISS and SIPRI. A number of questions, arising from the demand and supply of global armaments, for instance, come to mind. What have been the trends in arms procurement? What accounts for defence procurement? What are the key issues in arms procurement? What are the future prospects for the global arms trade? How has the arms industry adapted to the end of the Cold War and the emergence of the global interlinked economy (a process better known as globalization)? What are the prospects for the global arms industry? Furthermore, what are the key issues in the global arms trade? What are the problems and prospects of these issues?

Some key issues that come to mind include: the trade-off between defence spending and development, the undue influence of the military industrial complex (MIC), the control of the proliferation of conventional arms (particularly to non-state actors), insurgencies and their impact on arms procurement, the privatization of force, and future war and future weapons systems.

Where before the end of the Cold War there existed those who studied the arms trade using the methodology of analysing defence expenditure and procurement, these traditional realist-oriented analysts have died a natural death (some literally) and have not been replaced. This can be attributed to the end of the Cold War, which resulted in a refocusing on the expected peace dividends of that seminal event, in the form of the rise of post-positivist approaches and the emergence of human security. Thus, to cite an example from the Asian context, Chin Kin Wah's excellent edited volume entitled 'Defence Spending in Southeast Asia', published in 1987, remains one of the few in-depth analyses of the subject matter and, indeed, has been reprinted several times. Desmond Ball's article 'Arms and Affluence: Military Acquisitions in the Asia-Pacific Region' published in *International Security* in 1993/94 expands beyond defence spending and remains the most thorough analysis of the arms trade in Asia to this day. Other attempts to add to this appeared in a much-cited working paper on 'Force Modernization in Asia: Towards 2000 and Beyond' (Dibb 1997), and the excellent IISS Adelphi Paper entitled 'Arming East Asia' (Huxley and Willett 1999), on defence spending, arms procurement and the defence industry. However, these are sporadic works focusing on a specific region, albeit one of major importance to the arms trade, with no attempt at a comprehensive, in-depth analysis of the global arms trade phenomenon. Instead, the ground in international relations/security studies shifted to post-positivist approaches. Defence spending itself became the domain of Defence Economics and has resurrected itself into a highly specialized field in economics that studies the arms industry from an econometrics perspective, often using quantitative analyses.

There is, thus, a gap in mainstream international relations and security studies, arising from the lack of a more positivist analysis of defence spending, arms procurement and the defence industry, one which will provide a better description of the current phenomenon that is the arms trade, identify practical issues of concern, and assess problems and prospects in a way that will deepen our understanding of the global arms phenomenon. A comprehensive study of this nature, utilizing an empirical focus and written in clear, positivist language, will have a much broader impact and readership than Defence Economics or the post-positivist peace studies literature accessible only to those who can master the specialized language. Such a study, which is the focus of this book, will, therefore, be especially useful to scholars, policy analysts, those in the arms industry, defence professionals, students of international relations and security studies, media professionals, government officials, and those generally interested in the phenomenon that is the global arms trade.

The demand and supply of arms

During the period 2003–07, the top recipient of major conventional arms was China, which imported $13.4 billion worth of weapons systems. This was followed by India, which spent $9.1 billion on foreign arms (SIPRI Yearbook 2008, 321). The global arms trade is to a large degree underpinned by the strong demand for arms in Asia and the Middle East, the two largest arms export markets in the world. Despite major efforts by some developing countries such as China and India in developing their indigenous arms industries in order to ensure greater self-sufficiency, the dependence on imported arms has not decreased. Thus, Herbert Wulf's conclusion in 1985 still holds true: 'for developing countries, the implications of the technological lead of the major industrial countries in arms production are that, for modern sophisticated weaponry, dependence upon one or more of the major arms-producing countries cannot be avoided' (SIPRI Yearbook 1985, 320).

What accounts for the strong demand for imported arms, especially from Asia and the Middle East? Apart from the lack of a technological base to produce the most sophisticated weapons systems, other reasons cited in a vintage 1971 study by SIPRI concluded that there were five factors that explain the demand for arms. The first is conflict, especially in the Middle East and in East Asia (referred to as 'the Far East'); the second is nationalism, which has been a driving force behind the wars for national liberation in an age of decolonization; the third is the role of the armed forces – the armed forces being the most important modernizing force in many Third World societies; the fourth is the size of foreign exchange earnings, which enable the purchase of foreign weapons systems; and finally, the interests of the major powers, which is a major determinant (SIPRI 1971, 41–4).

In 2009, some of these factors remain relevant. For instance, areas of conflict, such as in the Middle East revolving around Israel, the tensions over Iran's regional ambitions, the Indo-Pakistan conflict over Kashmir, the Taiwan Straits, and in the Korean peninsula, continue to underpin a strong demand for military forces and capabilities, which rely on expensive, sophisticated weapons systems, some of which have to be imported, as no single nation can produce a broad range to ensure self-sufficiency. Nationalism continues to be an important force in international relations, in an international system that continues to be in many ways anarchic, in the sense that there is no supra-national authority that can impose law and order on states. The end of the Cold War brought about heightened expectations that global norms and institutions, as well as globalization, would help to usher in a new world order in which the state would be diminished and conflicts ease, but this has not happened. On the contrary, shorn of superpower restraints imposed during the Cold War, there has been a massive outbreak of civil conflict. The emergence of non-state actors, such as al-Qa'ida and global terrorism, epitomized by the seminal terrorist attacks on 11 September 2001 in the USA and the subsequent 'war on terror', has introduced a new global security challenge. The unilateralism of the USA and the subsequent marginalization of the United Nations (UN), particularly in the wake of the 11 September attacks, have resulted in a drift in the international system, which appears to be evolving into a concert of powers with the state still the most dominant player (Bell 2007).

In explaining 'the new Asian arms race', Desmond Ball argued in 1993 that 'military and geostrategic factors, such as threat perceptions or arms race dynamics, have generally been less determinate than other considerations' (Ball 1993, 79). These other considerations or factors include: economic growth and increasing resources for defence; the requirements for enhanced self-reliance; the drawdown of the US presence and capabilities in the region; fears of the increasing power projection capabilities of China, Japan and India; the increasing salience of regional conflict (given the increasing prominence of maritime conflict issues); the requirements for exclusive economic zone (EEZ) surveillance and protection in an era of 200-mile EEZs; the broadening of regional security concerns to include transnational crime and environmental issues, which require better maritime surveillance capabilities; weapons being acquired as symbols of national prestige; technological acquisition and transfer; and corruption, which has been a significant factor behind the arms build up in some Asian countries (Ball 1993, 79–91).

Ball also identified 'supply side pressures' as a significant factor in the demand for arms. The factors influencing the supply of weapons were considered in SIPRI's study in 1971. According to the study, the desire to impose and maintain great power hegemony is a principal factor. The supply of weapons reinforces hegemony in the following ways: first, arms are supplied to enable local forces to perform military tasks that are in the interests of the supplying country; second, the supply of arms serves to strengthen the relationship between the supplying country and the recipient government; third, the supply of arms may provide an opportunity to influence the recipient government, particularly through the military, which tends to be an important and influential institution in many countries. The same study also concluded that 'the importance of exports to the domestic defence industry has been stressed in all European countries'. This was due to a number of advantages, such as economies of scale, lengthening of production runs, reduction in per unit costs of increasingly expensive weapons systems, and the filling of surplus capacity. An alternative to exports would be international collaboration, which, though, paradoxically increases total costs and results in duplication as well as excess capacity since each partner nation would demand delivery priority (SIPRI 1971, 17–31; Buzan 1987, 40–1).

According to Ball, writing in the post-Cold War era in 1993, the end of the Cold War had resulted in arms manufacturers in the West having to seek new export markets in order to compensate for the decline in their home markets. Thus, Russia was 'willing to sell virtually anything to anybody with the cash to pay, or even the products to barter', citing China's purchase of Su-27 jetfighters, and Malaysia's purchase of MiG-29 jetfighters (Ball 1993, 91). The gathering pace of globalization has also resulted in the arms industry gradually becoming a globalized industry just like any other commercialized industry today, as it seeks more capital, cheaper labour and new markets. Thus, arms industries that originated as national defence industries have, in the post-Cold War era, undergone a process of rationalization, consolidation and niche specialization (Bitzinger 2003). This has also included greater international collaboration to increase the economies of scale and to share development costs, the outsourcing of parts production to contractors around the world in a bid to keep costs down, and the search for new export markets. The new economic rationalization that is part of emerging globalization has changed the face of the arms industry. Thus, Wulf presciently observed that 'in a desire to finance arms industries, many countries find it natural to seek markets abroad and to subordinate arms sales policies almost exclusively to economic considerations' (SIPRI Yearbook 1985, 320).

Arms and technology

Another important factor in the global arms trade is the role of technological revolution. According to Barry Buzan, the arms trade is part of the process of the spread of technology around the world (Buzan 1987, 9). He argued that technology has defined much of the contemporary strategic agenda. Pointing out that the increase in firepower has been a historical development, Buzan also noted that this has been enhanced by increases in the range and accuracy of delivery systems. Precision-guided munitions, in particular, have reduced the need for both volume of fire and weight of destructive capability delivered to the target. In addition, there have been enormous advances in mobility, communications and intelligence (Buzan 1987, 17–26). This technological advancement is spread around the world through the global arms trade. Leading powers must keep to the front of technological advance to maintain their rank and status, whilst aspirants to first power must acquire the capability to compete at the leading edge.

Thus, 'because the leading edge of technological advance sets the standard for the international system, its continuous forward movement exerts pressure on the whole process of spread'. Where rivalries exist between states, the level of technology becomes a crucial strategic issue. Thus, states that can afford to do so will attempt to buy modern weapons systems to either maintain parity or gain an edge; those that cannot will have to make do with the second-hand market (Buzan 1987, 37–9). In order to gain advanced military technology, states must buy. In order to sustain domestic arms industries as well as a host of other economic and political reasons, supplier states want to sell. Because of this potent community of interest between suppliers and buyers in maintaining the arms trade, Buzan thus concluded that the trade will remain a durable feature of the international system (Buzan 1987, 42).

However, Martin van Creveld noted the extraordinary complexity of modern warfare compared with all its predecessors. The revolution in military technology gave rise to complexity, particularly the vast amounts of information needed for effective military decision-making. He thus envisaged the emergence of computerized warfare (van Creveld 1989, 235–6). Both Buzan and van Creveld were, thus, in some respects addressing the process of technological transformation known as the RMA. Begun in the USSR as the Military Technology Revolution, the RMA in the USA originated with the concept of the 'systems of systems' developed by Admiral William Owens. Such a new way of warfare would be made possible through a revolution in surveillance and electronic capabilities that could dispense with the age-old problem of the 'fog of war', by providing superb battlefield awareness, thus enabling one to locate the opponent as well as to know the disposition of one's own forces in real time. Together with precision strike capabilities and an integrated systems approach to ensure seamless harmony amongst all the different parts of the vast US military, this would enable devastating precision attacks over long distances, thereby reducing time and space as constraints. The opponent within an expanded battlespace could thus be attacked simultaneously and continuously. As Krepinevich noted, 'the new structure of warfare integrates and synchronizes redundant, multi-service war-fighting systems in simultaneous attacks on the enemy throughout his entire depth and in the space above him as well' (Krepinevich 1994, 30). The Gulf War of 1990–91 appeared to prove the efficacy of the evolving RMA, as a partially RMA-equipped US armed forces took on the Iraqi armed forces and easily overwhelmed it. When the ground offensive began after weeks of massive precision air and missile strikes, Iraqi units disintegrated or simply fled. Fears of being bogged down in a long conflict with Iraq's armed forces, at the time one of the world's largest, did not eventuate as the US-led coalition easily defeated Saddam Hussain's shell-shocked forces.

The RMA captured the imagination of the world's armed forces. Thus, according to Paul Dibb, states in Asia have participated in the RMA to varying degrees. According to him, there are four tiers to RMA participation in Asia. Tier 1 consists of close allies of the USA and is characterized by a high capacity to absorb the RMA. These include Australia, Japan and South Korea. Tier 2 consists of states with a high threat perception and a moderate capacity to absorb the RMA, such as China, Taiwan and Singapore. Tier 3 includes states with a moderate-to-low perception of external threat and/or generally with a low capacity to absorb the RMA, such as Indonesia and Viet Nam. Tier 4 consists of states with a very low capacity to absorb the RMA, such as Myanmar, Cambodia and Laos (Dibb 1997).

However, van Creveld warned that the very concept of technological superiority is misleading when applied to the concept of war. Noting that sub-conventional warfare, such as terrorism and insurgency, is more far reaching in political effects than conventional wars, van Creveld argued that the best military technology is not what is superior in an absolute sense, but what neutralizes the other side's strengths whilst exploiting its weaknesses. He thus warned against the common habit of referring to technology in terms of its capabilities, as what is even more important is what it cannot do (van Creveld 1989, 299 and 311–20). Van Creveld has been proved prescient in the light of the USA's overwhelming conventional capabilities and its demonstrated weaknesses in guerrilla and terrorist theatres in Iraq and Afghanistan after the 11 September attacks.

The arms dynamic, arms races and wars

The arms dynamic is a useful conceptual framework that can be applied to further understand the global arms trade phenomenon. The arms dynamic refers to 'the whole set of pressures that make states both acquire armed forces and change the quantity and quality of the armed forces they already possess'. This exists along a spectrum, with arms racing being the most extreme manifestation of the arms dynamic, when states engage in major competitive expansion of military capabilities. At the other extreme, there is the maintenance of the status quo (Buzan 1987, 73–4).

According to Colin Gray, there are four basic conditions for an arms race: there must be two or more parties, conscious of their antagonism; they must structure their armed forces with attention to the probable effectiveness of the forces in combat with, or as a deterrent to, the other arms race participants; they must compete in terms of quantity and quality; and there must be rapid increases in quantity and/or improvement in quality (Gray 1972, 41). Gray has also pointed out that it is possible for arms races to develop even in the absence of any serious political antagonisms. A fairly autonomous arms increase, undertaken for a variety of reasons, might be matched by a fairly disinterested party solely as a precautionary move, and, thus, spark off a cycle of close or intermittent armament interactions. Previously unacknowledged political antagonisms might then occur. Indeed, while arms races are evidently run between mutually perceived enemies, arms racing behaviour – that is, a process of inter-active or competitive arms acquisitions – can also be discerned among even formal allies, whether out of prestige or the need to maintain a relationship of equality. Interactive arms acquisitions of this nature, coupled with conflicting claims over territory and other issues, could result in the security dilemma, conflict spirals, heightened tensions and eventually lead to conflict, thereby destroying the very security that arms acquisitions were meant to ensure.

Three processes explain the arms dynamic. The first is the process of action-reaction, which rests on the proposition that states strengthen their armaments in response to external threats that they perceive from other states. The second is the domestic process, in which internal domestic factors are important. In this process, the institutionalization of research and devel-opment is one of the drivers for technological innovation, and the arms modernization. Others include strategic doctrine, geographical location, the structure of government and the balance of power between its agencies, and interest, in which major defence decisions are merely rationalizations for the domestic interests of decision-makers (Gray 1972, 74–7). The third is the process of technological change. In this respect, the issue is whether technology drives military expansion or vice versa. Buzan is definitive in his evaluation though, in that 'a large percentage of the behaviour that is commonly identified as arms racing stems directly from the underlying process of technological advance'. According to him, if states do meet the challenge of keeping pace with adversaries, they will embark on a process that produces an endless flow of new weapons. Thus, the technological imperative is an important independent variable that also affects the process of action-reaction and domestic factors, as it forces states to behave in a way that looks like arms racing (Buzan 1987, 105–13).

Finally, there is the ultimate reason for the global arms trade: wars and preparations for war. Why are wars fought? There are political wars, in which war is used as an instrument of state policy in order to accomplish certain political objectives; wars of justice, in order to right a perceived wrong, such as wars fought to restore the status quo; ideological and religious wars; and wars fought for the existence of a state. Thus, van Creveld concluded, there is a plethora of reasons why wars are fought, and not just for policy or interests alone (van Creveld 1991, 124–56). However, often the causes of war are not easy to uncover, given the many cases in which the reasons for war 'were not only hopelessly intertwined but ill understood by the belligerents themselves' (van Creveld 1989, 298). War, whether conventional or non-conventional, is a condition of the anarchic international system. As van Creveld concluded, 'it must be recognised that there exist today, and probably will continue to exist in the future, some states, some groups, and some people, who are not content with the existing state of affairs or, indeed, with any conceivable state of affairs', and who are determined to use force to change the status quo, using whatever means are available (van Creveld 1989, 309).

The global arms trade: demand, supply and key issues

This volume is divided into four sections, and is written by a team of international arms experts. The first section consists of this introductory chapter, which developed the general conceptual framework by providing an overview of the global arms trade and explaining the nature of the arms dynamic. The second section focuses on the demand for arms, namely in terms of defence spending, procurement and modernization. It contains 13 chapters that explore regional arms modernization after the end of the Cold War. The regions covered include: Asia, Europe, the Middle East, Latin America and Africa. The specific countries covered include China, India, Japan, the Democratic People's Republic of Korea (North Korea), Russia and Iran.

The third section, consisting of six chapters, focuses on the supply of arms, i.e. the evolu-tion, development, problems and prospect of the arms industry. Two chapters provide an overview of the global arms trade and industry. Another four chapters focus on the arms industry in Europe, the USA, the UK and Israel.

military-industrial complex

The fourth and final section discusses the key issues arising from the arms trade phenomenon. This section has six chapters, which cover the following issues: the MIC (i.e. the links between government and the arms industry), defence spending and development, the post-Cold War control of conventional arms, the impact of insurgencies on arms procurement, the privatization of force, and future warfare and its impact on the shape of weapons to come.

Bibliography

Ball, Desmond, 'Arms and Affluence: Military Acquisitions in the Asia Pacific Region', *International Security*, Vol. 18, No. 3, Winter 1993–94

Bell, Coral, *The End of the Vasco da Gama Era: The Next Landscape of World Politics*, Lowy Institute Paper No. 21, Lowy Institute, Sydney, 2007

Bitzinger, Richard, *Towards a Brave New Arms Industry?* Adelphi Paper 356, International Institute for Strategic Studies, 2003

Buzan, Barry, *An Introduction to Strategic Studies, Military Technology and International Relations*, London, Macmillan, 1987

Chin Kin Wah, *Defence Spending in Southeast Asia*, Singapore, Institute for Southeast Asian Studies, 1987

Dibb, Paul, 'The Revolution in Military Affairs and Asian Security', in *Survival*, Vol. 4, No. 3, 1991

——*Force Modernization in Asia: Towards 2000 and Beyond*, Canberra, Australian National University, 1997

Gray, Colin, 'The Arms Race Phenomenon', *World Politics*, Vol. 24, No. 1, 1972

Huxley, Tim and Susan Willett, *Arming East Asia*, Adelphi Paper 329, International Institute of Strategic Studies, London, 1999

IISS, *The Military Balance 2008*, London, International Institute for Strategic Studies, 2008

Krepinevich, Andrew, 'Cavalry to Computer: The Pattern of Military Revolutions', *The National Interest*, August 1994

SIPRI, *The Arms Trade with the Third World*, Stockholm, Stockholm International Peace Research Institute, 1971

——*SIPRI Yearbook 1985*, Stockholm, Stockholm International Peace Research Institute, 1985

——*SIPRI Yearbook 2008*, Stockholm, Stockholm International Peace Research Institute, 2008

Stiglitz, Joseph E. and Linda J. Bilme, *The Three Trillion Dollar War: The True Cost of the Iraq Conflict*, New York, W. W. Norton, 2008

van Creveld, Martin, *Technology and War: From 2000 BC to the Present*, New York, Free Press/Macmillan, 1989

——*The Transformation of War*, New York, Free Press/Macmillan, 1991

Part II
Arms modernization after the Cold War

2 Defence spending and procurement trends in South-east Asia

Andrew T. H. Tan

Arms and military revolutions in South-east Asia

In the context of the general post-Cold War reduction in arms spending in Europe, the Asia-Pacific region has become an especially crucial export market for arms manufacturers. Within this vast region, South-east Asia is particularly important despite its comparatively small arms market (around US$3 billion annually), as it is open and competitive compared with the captive markets in Japan and the Republic of Korea (South Korea) (both dominated by the USA), and India and the People's Republic of China (dominated by Russia). Moreover, with its general economic development, strategic waterways (especially the Straits of Malacca) and the desire by states in the region to modernize their armed forces, South-east Asia presents an interesting case study of the promise and potential of an emerging market for the global arms industry.

South-east Asia began to attract attention after security analysts observed in the 1990s that there was a clear trend towards a military build-up in the region (Huxley and Willett 1999). Since the end of the Viet Nam War in 1975, arms modernization and military expansion programmes that were begun as a response to US retrenchment from the region in fact continued in the 1990s despite the end of the Cold War and the rapprochement between the non-communist states comprising the Association of South East Asian Nations (ASEAN) and the communist states of Indochina. Although the Asian economic crisis of 1997–98 affected some states in the region and resulted in a halt to arms modernization and military expansion programmes, this proved to be temporary. Indeed, since around 2001, the region as a whole has resumed procuring modern weapons systems as part of their ongoing military modernization.

The caveat, though, is that defence spending and arms procurement do not equate to military effectiveness, as military power is not merely the sum total of military budgets and weapons systems. As Andy Marshal pointed out in 1966, mere tabulations of military forces are not meaningful estimates of military power, which is always relative to the military posture of some other country or alliance (Marshall 1966). Moreover, as Hans Morgenthau noted, military power is only part of broader political power. According to him, national power is a function of factors such as military preparedness, geography, natural resources, population, industrial character, national morale and diplomacy (Morgenthau 1948). Thus, meaningful estimates using official figures and tables are often difficult. Any quantitative approach will need to be supplemented by qualitative analysis. These caveats aside, though, estimating the military effectiveness of regional armed forces is not within the scope of this study.

Instead, this essay will focus on examining the trends in defence spending and arms procurement in South-east Asia. Whilst defence spending and the numbers of key weapons systems do not equate with military effectiveness, they are indicative of security perceptions and the amount of resources that states in the region are prepared to spend in order to meet perceived security threats and needs. An examination of such trends will give some indication of their future trajectories.

In doing so, this essay also aims to shed light on two key issues in defence spending and procurement in the region. The first of these is whether there is a regional 'arms race'. The answer to this question will indicate the intensity of defence spending and arms procurement patterns. The second is the region's level of participation in the USA-led revolution in military affairs (RMA). The answer to this will indicate the level of sophistication in arms procurement. To assess these two issues, this chapter will use quantitative data to better understand the trends in arms modernization and expansion programmes. However, it will also conclude that although using quantitative data provides useful insights, a more holistic qualitative approach taking into account relevant political, economic and social factors would be required for a more comprehensive explanation and analysis.

An arms race?

There is compelling evidence of an ongoing process of military modernization in South-east Asia since 1975. The military build-ups, particularly on the part of the ASEAN states, increased in the 1980s and 1990s. Although they slowed due to the Asian financial and economic crisis in 1997–98, they have, since around 2001, picked up momentum. This phenomenon, namely the concerted regional arms build-up, has caused some to express concerns about the prospects of an 'arms race' in the region (*The Economist*, 20 February 1993), but is there real evidence for this?

An analysis of the trends in defence spending using local currency (Table 2.1) as published in the SIPRI Yearbook 2007 seems to indicate a general upward trend in defence spending from 1997 to 2006, despite the impact of the Asian financial and economic crisis of 1997–98. The trend appears particularly evident in the case of Myanmar, Indonesia, Malaysia and Singapore, which all appeared to register a steep increase in defence spending. However, as the Stockholm International Peace Research Institute (SIPRI) noted, there are limitations to such data. For instance, there are varying definitions of military expenditure, as important items (such as military construction, and research and development) can be hidden under non-military budget headings or can even be financed entirely from outside the government budget. In some countries, actual expenditure may in fact be higher than the published budgeted expenditure. Indeed, as SIPRI noted, 'the most appropriate use of military expenditure data, even when reliably measured and reported, is therefore as an indicator of the economic resources consumed for military purposes' (SIPRI Yearbook 2006, 338).

Indeed, in the cases of Indonesia and Thailand, the massive devaluation of the rupiah and the baht, respectively, following the 1997–98 Asian economic crisis meant that there was, in fact, a very steep decline in defence spending in the years following 1997.

Table 2.1 Military expenditure by country (local currency) 1997–2006

Country	Currency	1997	1998	1999	2000	2001	2002	2003	2006
Brunei	m. dollars	548	492	438	421	390	405	424	449
Indonesia	bn rupiahs	8,336	10,349	10,254	13,945	16,416	19,291	27,446	40,491
Cambodia	bn riel	447	481	474	455	417	407	411	498
Laos	bn kip	53	66.5	224	278	325	n.a.	n.a.	n.a.
Malaysia	bn ringgit	5,877	4,547	6,321	5,826	7,351	8,504	10,950	11,734
Myanmar	bn kyats	29.4	37.3	43.7	58.8	63.9	73.1	n.a.	n.a.
Philippines	m. pesos	29,212	31,512	32,959	36,208	35,977	38,907	44,440	52,657
Singapore	m. dollars	6,618	7,475	7,616	7,466	7,721	8,108	8,230	9,849
Thailand	m. baht	98,172	86,133	74,809	71,268	75,413	76,724	77,774	85,936
Viet Nam	bn dong	n.a.	n.a.	n.a.	n.a.	n.a.	n.a.	n.a.	n.a.

Source: *SIPRI Yearbook 2007*, p.306

Table 2.2 Military expenditure by country (US$) 1997–2006, in constant US$ m. (2005 prices and exchange rates)

Country	1997	1998	1999	2000	2001	2002	2003	2006
Brunei	334	301	269	254	234	249	260	268
Indonesia	2,653	2,079	1,710	2,242	2,367	2,486	3,319	3,695
Cambodia	147	138	131	127	117	110	110	114
Laos	44.3	29.1	42.9	42.5	46.1	n.a.	n.a.	n.a.
Malaysia	1,858	1,365	1,847	1,677	2,087	2,370	3,020	2,996
Myanmar	n.a.	n.a.	n.a.	n.a.	n.a.	n.a.	n.a.	n.a.
Philippines	828	818	807	853	794	833	920	901
Singapore	4,153	4,703	4,791	4,634	4,745	5,002	5,051	5,868
Thailand	3,006	2,440	2,113	1,982	2,063	2,087	2,077	2,045
Viet Nam	n.a.	n.a.	n.a.	n.a.	n.a.	n.a.	n.a.	n.a.

Source: *SIPRI Yearbook 2007*, p.313

Table 2.2 is more meaningful in that military expenditure is compared using constant US dollars in 2005 prices and exchange rates. Despite variations in exchange rates, this does provide some indication of the trends in defence spending. According to this table, there was a real fall in defence spending in Indonesia following the financial and economic crisis of 1997–98, followed by a gradual recovery and a real increase after 2002. Thailand, too, was severely affected by the crisis and Table 2.2 indicates that in 2006, unlike Indonesia, the defence budget had not recovered and remained in real terms substantially below 1997. Malaysia recovered much quicker from the crisis, with real defence spending in 1999 not dissimilar to 1997, but this reflected the fact that the crisis affected Malaysia much less severely than Indonesia. After 1999, Malaysia's defence spending increased in real terms. Singapore is an interesting case as its defence spending was not affected at all by the crisis, but this reflects the fact that the economic difficulties had only a minor effect on the country. Moreover, defence has been a national priority since it became independent in 1965. The case of Myanmar is difficult, as rampant inflation and the wildly fluctuating exchange rates between the kyat and the US dollar have made any effective comparison almost impossible. One can only examine the size of its armed forces in terms of military personnel and acquisition of key weapons systems to gauge if there has been any increase over the years.

It is, thus, clear that defence spending figures provide a very limited picture. A more useful approach is to ask a different question: has defence spending translated into military personnel and the acquisition of major weapons systems?

Tables 2.3–2.5 examine this question. Table 2.3 comprises key statistics in 1975, at the end of the Viet Nam War. Table 2.4 comprises key military assets in 1990, at the end of the Cold War and the rapprochement in the region between non-communist ASEAN and communist Indochina. Table 2.5 measures the key military assets in 2007.

Table 2.3 indicates that the then-ASEAN states of Singapore, Malaysia, Indonesia and the Philippines could be described as militarily weak, with small numbers of major weapons systems. Thailand was an exception; as the frontline state against communist Indochina, it had the support of the USA, which provided substantial military aid.

Table 2.4 indicates that 15 years after the end of the Viet Nam War, the various states in South-east Asia, especially the non-communist ASEAN states, had made great efforts to develop their own military capabilities. There is a substantial increase in the numbers of key military assets, such as military manpower, tanks, armoured personnel carriers (APCs), long-range artillery, missile-armed naval vessels and combat aircraft. This is particularly evident in the case of Myanmar, which had to deal with ethnic minority insurgencies along the periphery; Indonesia,

Table 2.3 Military assets of the South-east Asian states (1975)

Country	Military Manpower	Tanks	APCs	155mm Howitzer	Missile Craft	Submarine	Combat Aircraft
Brunei	see Note 3						
Indonesia	246,000	125	266	0	9	3	30
Cambodia	80,000	0	0	0	0	0	0
Laos	43,000	—	—	0	0	0	63
Malaysia	62,000	0	940	0	8	0	50
Myanmar	170,000	0	85	0	0	0	10
Philippines	78,000	7	35	5	0	0	56
Singapore	76,000	75	500	20	6	0	97
Thailand	210,000	195	330	12	0	0	179
Viet Nam	615,000	900	—	—	4	0	198

Source: *The Military Balance* 1975–76

Notes:

1 Military manpower does not include reserves, except in Singapore, which adopted the Israeli system whereby reserves are kept trained for frontline roles;
2 APCs refer to armoured personnel carriers;
3 Brunei became fully independent in 1984; in 1974, its defence was still the responsibility of the United Kingdom;
4 In the case of Indonesia, the large Soviet-supplied naval and air force complement existed on paper only, as many were delivered before 1965 and were by 1975 running down or non-operational due to a lack of spares;
5 In the case of Laos, all air assets were inherited from the defeated Royal Lao Air Force, with the degree of serviceability unknown;
6 Viet Nam's military assets in 1975 did not include equipment of the former forces of the defeated South Viet Nam

which rebuilt its Soviet-era armed forces; Singapore, which despite its small size carried out a sustained military build-up based on active reservist forces, armour and air power, after the Israeli model; and Thailand, which as the frontline state against communist Indochina, invested heavily in expanding the size of its armed forces and acquiring sufficient weapons systems particularly on land in order to better defend its borders. In the case of Viet Nam, it continued to maintain large armed forces in view of its occupation of Cambodia and the ongoing anti-Vietnamese insurgency there. Table 2.5 shows the regional balance of military power in 2007.

An overall analysis of Tables 2.3–2.5 provides two sets of interesting conclusions. First, the period from 1975 to 1990 (Tables 2.3–2.4) clearly indicates a dramatic increase in military personnel following the end of the Viet Nam War in 1975. This was especially evident in the case of Myanmar, Malaysia, Singapore and Viet Nam, with more modest increases in all of the other states in South-east Asia. Overall, the number of military personnel rose from 1.6m. to 2.5m. Another feature of this period is the increase in land capabilities, as indicated by the increase in the number of long-range artillery assets and the dramatic increase in armour. In fact, the number of tanks and APCs increased during this period from 3,458 to 8,936, more than doubling. There was also a clear increase in the number of naval vessels armed with anti-ship missiles and a more modest but obvious increase in the overall number of combat aircraft.

The second set of conclusions revolves around the period from 1990 to 2007 (Tables 2.4–2.5). These indicate that the number of military personnel appeared to have stabilized. In the case of Viet Nam, there was a dramatic reduction in the number of military personnel from 1.1m. in 1990 to 455,000 in 2007. This indicates that Viet Nam had reaped a considerable peace dividend from the end of the Cold War, following its withdrawal from Cambodia and its rapprochement with ASEAN. On the other hand, both Myanmar and Singapore appear to

Table 2.4 Military assets of the South-east Asian states (1990)

Country	Military Manpower	Tanks	APCs	152/155mm Howitzer	Missile Craft	Submarine	Combat Aircraft
Brunei	4,200	16	24	0	3	0	4
Indonesia	283,000	171	631	0	10	2	81
Cambodia	112,000	110	170	0	0	0	17
Laos	55,000	55	70	0	0	0	34
Malaysia	130,000	26	1,063	9	10	0	67
Myanmar	230,000	26	85	0	0	0	16
Philippines	109,000	41	455		0	0	26
Singapore	237,000	350	1,000	62	9	0	193
Thailand	283,000	414	935	168	8	0	158
Viet Nam	1,052,000	1,600	1,700	250	8	0	250

Source: *The Military Balance* 1990 91

Notes:

1 Military manpower does not include reserves, except in Singapore, which adopted the Israeli system whereby reserves are kept trained for frontline roles;

2 APCs refer to armoured personnel carriers

Table 2.5 Military assets of the South-east Asian states (2007)

Country	Military Manpower	Tanks	APCs	152/155mm Howitzer	Missile Craft	Submarine	Combat Aircraft
Brunei	7,000	20	39	0	3	0	0
Indonesia	302,000	405	664	5	16	2	94
Cambodia	124,000	170	260	0	0	0	24
Laos	29,000	35	50	12	0	0	22
Malaysia	109,000	32	1,549	34	18	0	68
Myanmar	406,000	255	440	16	14	0	125
Philippines	106,000	65	564	12	0	0	30
Singapore	385,000	546	1,574	106	15	4	102
Thailand	307,000	848	1,039	217	16	0	182
VietNam	455,000	1,935	1,780		21	2	219

Source: *The Military Balance* 2008

Notes:

1 Military manpower does not include reserves, except in Singapore, which adopted the Israeli system whereby reserves are kept trained for frontline roles;

2 APCs refer to armoured personnel carriers;

3 Indonesia has 1,122 artillery pieces but the bulk of these are mortars;

4 In addition to 34 155mm howitzers, Malaysia also has 18 ASTROS II multiple rocket launchers equipped with 127mm SS-30 rockets;

5 Thailand has 2,473 artillery pieces but the bulk of these are mortars;

6 The total number of artillery pieces that Viet Nam possessed in 2007 was 3,040, though the actual number of long-range artillery could not be determined

have continued to build up their armed forces. Myanmar's increase from 230,000 military personnel in 1990 to stabilize at 406,000 in 2007 can be explained by its preoccupation with internal insurgencies and political opposition to the ruling military regime. Singapore's increase of its active and reservist forces from 237,000 to 385,000 over the same period can be attributed to the natural development of its Israeli-style national service system, whereby reservists are regularly trained and kept operationally ready to deploy as frontline troops.

Therefore, an analysis of Tables 2.4–2.5 (1990–2007) indicates that overall the end of the Cold War did bring about an end to dramatic increases in the size of military forces. However, there is also evidence of a determination to maintain key capabilities such as armour and combat aircraft, given no obvious reduction in the numbers of such weapons systems. In addition, there was an effort to improve military effectiveness and to meet emerging security challenges. This is evident from the introduction of new military capabilities which hitherto did not exist or were clearly under-emphasized. For instance, the period 1990–2007 saw a dramatic increase in the number of naval vessels armed with anti-ship missiles, from 48 to 103. The two submarines in the Indonesian navy in 1990 were joined in 2007 by four in Singapore, and two in Viet Nam. There is also evidence of a much greater interest in modern long-range artillery of the 152/155mm calibre, with some countries such as Myanmar and Indonesia acquiring such capabilities where they did not have them, and existing operators such as Singapore, Malaysia and Thailand substantially increasing their numbers.

Is there evidence from the above analysis of regional defence spending and procurement that there is a regional arms race? To answer this question, there is a need for clarity as to what constitutes an arms race. According to Colin Gray, there are four basic conditions for an arms race: There must be two or more parties, conscious of their antagonism; they must structure their armed forces with attention to the probable effectiveness of the forces in combat with, or as a deterrent to, the other arms race participants; they must compete in terms of quantity and quality; and there must be rapid increases in quantity and/or improvements in quality (Gray 1972, 41).

A quantitative analysis based on examining regional defence spending and procurement and measured against these criteria, does not suggest this to be the case. Indeed, it seems that the regional arms build-up stabilized after 1990. In 2007, the region's armed forces deployed a total of about 2.2m. military personnel, compared with about 2.5m. in 1990. The number of key weapons systems deployed after 1990 increased (especially naval vessels with anti-ship missiles and also submarines), but overall the numbers have not gone up dramatically.

Therefore, in summary, there is no regional arms race according to the Gray definition, and this conclusion is supported by the fact that a general state of peace has existed in the region amongst the ASEAN states since the end of the Cold War. However, this conclusion does not rule out arms racing behaviour or a process of competitive arms acquisitions by some states. For instance, the initial acquisition of F-16 combat aircraft by Singapore, then Indonesia and Thailand, as well as Malaysia's subsequent interest in acquiring an advanced strike fighter, point to the need to counter or at least not be left behind by one's neighbours (Cheung 1990, 25–6). Such dynamics are short of an arms race but, if present, indicate the lingering presence of mutual suspicion. However, a more detailed political analysis will be required to better understand these underlying dynamics and is beyond the scope of this essay.

Is there an RMA in the region?

The so-called RMA, has been an ongoing debate in the USA and various aspects have been adopted under Joint Vision 2010. The key to the RMA is the vast improvement in information and information systems technology, which will give the necessary real-time battlefield awareness to lift the 'fog of war' and enable complex, high-tempo precision operations to be conducted over a much wider battle space. The new military technology, for instance, in the form of stand-off precision strike weaponry, stealth capabilities, surveillance systems, and command, control and communications systems, are tremendous force multipliers that can tilt the regional balance of power. The 'Shock and Awe' strategy displayed to such effect in both Gulf Wars by the US armed forces is an indication of the kind of overwhelming conventional military superiority that an RMA could provide.

However, much more than the mere acquisition of modern weapons systems is required for a true RMA to take place. The RMA also includes the development of doctrine, strategies and military organizations that can take advantage of the technological potential (Nye and Owens 1996). There is, thus, also the need for integrated logistical capabilities, joint force doctrines, a very high level of technical support and training, and integrated command, control and communications capabilities.

According to Paul Dibb, however, these are mostly not practised in Asia. Moreover, the RMA might not be entirely appropriate for the Asian context since it may have limited applicability to low-intensity conflict, a prescient observation given the US quagmire in Iraq since invading the country in 2003. Thus, it is evident that few countries in South-east Asia have the technical and economic capacity to implement a true RMA, nor do they all want to, given the local conditions and the continued salience of internal security threats. However, as Dibb also noted, partial or hybrid RMAs may be appropriate to Asian strategic circumstances, given that real-time surveillance and information gathering technologies could improve maritime and border surveillance, for instance, thus improving maritime security, a growing area of concern for the ASEAN states (Dibb 1997).

According to Dibb, there were four tiers to RMA participation in Asia. Tier 1 consists of close allies of the USA and would have a high capacity to absorb the RMA. These would include Australia, Japan and South Korea, though no South-east Asian state had the potential to make it to this level. Tier 2 consists of states with a high threat perception and a moderate capacity to absorb the RMA, such as China, Taiwan and Singapore. Tier 3 consists of states with a moderate-to-low perception of external threat and/or generally having a low capacity to absorb the RMA; in South-east Asia this included Indonesia, Malaysia, the Philippines, Thailand and Viet Nam. Finally, Tier 4 consists of states with a very low capacity to absorb the RMA, such as Myanmar, Cambodia and Laos. Dibb missed out Brunei, which because of its small size, would belong to Tier 4.

A country-by-country assessment could yield a better idea of regional arms dynamics than a more general quantitative analysis. Are states in the region acquiring new capabilities or improving existing ones? Are they seeking an RMA by acquiring RMA-type technologies that would confer conventional military superiority? A brief sketch will give some idea.

Brunei

Brunei is the smallest state in ASEAN, with a population of 379,000 in 2006. However, it does possess oil and natural gas, which has enabled it to build a small military deterrent capability. Indeed, since independence from the United Kingdom in 1984, Brunei has made ongoing efforts to build up its military capabilities, given past tensions with Malaysia and Indonesia as well as past political opposition to the ruling Sultan. In recent years, the Kikeh offshore oil dispute with Malaysia has sharpened concerns over maritime security, particularly its ability to defend its maritime boundaries and its offshore oilfields (Tan 2004, 146). However, Tables 2.1 and 2.2 indicate that Brunei has, in fact, reduced its defence spending from 1997 to 2006, with expenditure falling from B$548m. to B$449m. Measured in constant US dollars (2005 prices), it fell from $334m. to $268m. This could be attributed to the effects of the collapse of the government's investment arm in 1998, in what has become known as the Amadeo crisis, which led to a subsequent clampdown on government spending (Tan 2004, 13).

According to *The Military Balance 2008*, Brunei's land forces totalled 4,900 in 2007, built around three infantry battalions, with a small armoured corps of 20 Scorpion light tanks and 39 APCs. In addition, there are two Ghurkha battalions which protect the oilfields and provide security for the Sultan. The small navy has three Exocet-armed missile boats which were built in Singapore in 1978–79. Their reported replacements, three coastal patrol frigates built by BAE Systems in 2004, were not delivered due to a dispute over their specifications. In 2007 it was agreed that the ships would be sold on (*BBC News*, 29 November 2007). The small air force has some 23 helicopters, six fixed-wing training aircraft and no combat aircraft. It has ordered three CN-235 maritime patrol aircraft, of which one has been delivered.

Indonesia

Indonesia's military modernization has concentrated on improving its maritime security. The declaration of Exclusive Economic Zones (EEZs) in the 1980s and heightened concerns over maritime security, especially terrorist threats and piracy in the Straits of Malacca, following the terrorist attacks in the USA on 11 September 2001 as well as the Bali bombing by Islamist militants in 2002, have resulted in a focus on developing the conventional naval, air force and rapid deployment capabilities to patrol and defend its huge archipelagic waters and its EEZ. The economic crisis of 1997–98 had a severe and negative impact on defence spending and procurement, but this recovered by 2002, with a substantial increase in real defence spending in 2003 (see Tables 2.1 and 2.2).

According to *The Military Balance 2008*, the Indonesian army does not possess main battle tanks, with its current armour consisting of 405 light tanks (comprising mainly outdated AMX 13 light tanks of 1950s vintage) and 664 APCs of a number of different makes. Its acquisition of five FH2000 155mm howitzers indicates a desire to upgrade. The key weapons systems in its air force are: two Su-27 Flanker, two Su-30 MKI Flanker, 10 F-16A/B, 12 F-5E/F, 11 A-4E Skyhawk and 35 Hawk ground attack aircraft. In 1997 an agreement to purchase 12 Su-30K fighter-bombers and eight Mi-17 helicopters was signed with Russia. This was subsequently cancelled due to the economic crisis. In 2003, on a visit to Russia, President Megawati agreed to the initial purchase of two Su-30, two Su-27 fighter-bombers and two Mi-35 helicopters to upgrade the air force (*Jane's Defense Weekly*, 3 September 2003). In August 2007 Indonesia ordered six new Sukhoi jetfighters (three Su-27 and three Su-30) to be delivered by 2010 (*Military Technology*, October 2007). In September 2007 Indonesia also finalized a $1.2 billion arms deal with Russia, for two Kilo-class submarines, as well as tanks and helicopters (*Sydney Morning Herald*, 5 September 2007).

The navy is more impressive, with two German-made Type 209 submarines, 16 frigates (eight armed with Harpoon anti-ship missiles and four armed with Exocet anti-ship missiles), 16 corvettes and four Exocet-armed missile boats in 2007. It has ordered four new Sigma corvettes from the Netherlands (of which two were delivered in 2007), and four new landing ships from South Korea (*Korea Times*, 21 December 2004).

It is clear that Indonesia, given its size, has been relatively relaxed in its arms modernization, as it does not perceive any external threat in the near future. Apart from limited plans and aspirations, funding for any major military modernization programme will remain tight in the foreseeable future. This is due partly to the fact that the military is no longer a central political player in the post-Suharto era. What is likely is that Indonesia will use scarce resources to improve maritime patrol capabilities in the form of acquiring more patrol vessels and maritime patrol aircraft, ensuring that it has the capacity to respond quickly to any crisis in its far-flung archipelago. In addition, it will want to ensure that it follows technological change, by acquiring modern but cheap Russian weapons systems such as the Su-27 jetfighter and the Kilo-class submarine, to at least keep pace with its more sophisticated neighbours, such as Singapore, Malaysia and Australia.

Cambodia and Laos

Cambodia maintains fairly large armed forces, with 124,000 military personnel. However, these are mostly land forces, with a very small coastal patrol force for its navy, and a small air force of which the most prominent assets are 19 MiG-21 jetfighters, some of which have been upgraded by Israel.

Laos has small armed forces of 29,000 and fields obsolescent weapons systems. The army continues to field 170 tanks and 260 APCs, which are old Chinese and Russian models. The air force has an outdated fleet of 22 MiG-21 jetfighters and a small assortment of helicopters (*The Military Balance* 2008, 392). Neither country perceives an imminent external threat and they are, therefore, not active in the global arms market.

Malaysia

Beginning with the PERISTA modernization programme in 1979, Malaysia has made a determined effort to build up its conventional capabilities. Some analysts have commented that this is due to the mutual deterrent postures between Malaysia and Singapore (Huxley 1991).

Malaysia recovered relatively quickly from the 1997–98 Asian financial crisis. According to Tables 2.1 and 2.2, Malaysia recovered its defence spending by 1999–2000. Malaysia thus proceeded to purchase a number of key weapons systems that it had put on hold. In 2002 it announced the purchase of 48 T-91 main battle tanks from Poland (*Straits Times*, 9 April 2002). New APCs were also ordered from South Korea and Turkey. In 2006 the army also deployed very modern artillery, including 18 Brazilian-made Astros II MRLS (multiple-rocket launching systems) and 22 South African-made Denel G5 155mm howitzers (*Straits Times*, 30 October 2000).

The air force has also been upgraded. In May 2003, Malaysia ordered 18 Sukhoi Su-30MKM jetfighters, which were to be delivered by 2008 (*Straits Times*, 20 May 2003). The Su-30 jetfighters would replace the current fleet of 18 MiG29 jetfighters, which would be withdrawn from service. In addition, the air force also deploys eight F-18 Hornet, 23 Hawk and 13 F-5E/F Tiger jetfighters (*The Military Balance 2008*, 394). Significantly, the air force has also deployed the locally built Eagle UAV (unmanned aerial vehicle). In June 2003, Malaysia announced that it would spend $1 billion to acquire at least four Airborne Warning and Control (AWAC) aircraft, although no purchase has yet taken place (*Straits Times*, 3 June 2003).

Malaysia has also made significant efforts to modernize and expand its navy. In June 2002 Malaysia signed an agreement to buy two French-made Scorpene submarines (*New Straits Times*, 6 June 2003). In 2007 the Malaysian navy deployed a modern fleet of two Lekiu frigates armed with Exocet anti-ship missiles and Sea Wolf anti-missile defences, four Laksamana corvettes armed with long-range Otomat anti-ship missiles, two MEKO corvettes armed with Exocet anti-ship missiles (with another four on order) and eight fast missile boats also armed with Exocet anti-ship missiles (Military Balance 2008, 393).

The end result has been more proficient armed forces with enhanced maritime security and power projection capabilities. Indeed, these capabilities are important because patrolling the long coastlines and defending extensive maritime territories has presented daunting security challenges. Malaysia has had boundary disputes with all its neighbours, important offshore oilfields, problems with piracy in the environs of the South China Sea and the Straits of Malacca, as well as refugee and migrant inflows, notably illegal immigrants from Indonesia and refugees from the separatist conflict in the southern Philippines. Despite some evidence of an interactive arms dynamic with Singapore, the many security challenges that Malaysia faces provide a greater impetus for defence modernization than any singular obsession with Singapore.

Myanmar

Myanmar launched a major expansion programme after 1988 when the military took power, in order to redress perceived weaknesses in size and military capabilities. According to *The Military Balance 2008*, Myanmar has 406,000 military personnel, 255 tanks, including 50 T-72 tanks bought from Ukraine, and 440 APCs consisting mainly of Type 85 and Type 90 APCs bought from China. Burma will also assemble up to 1,000 Ukrainian BTR-3U APCs over the next 10 years (McCoy 2006). The army has also acquired 16 Israeli-made Soltam 155mm towed howitzers and unspecified numbers of 122mm BM-21 howitzers. Its small defence industry is today also able to produce light weapons, light armoured vehicles, land-mines, mortars and ammunition (*Asian Defence Journal*, March 2003).

The core of the air force consists of 10 MiG-29 jetfighters, some 50 Chinese-made F-7 (MiG-21) jetfighters and 22 A5M ground attack aircraft, with the F-7 aircraft upgraded with Israeli avionics. The MiG-29s are said to have been acquired to counter Thailand's F-16s, but other reasons advanced include prestige and national pride, the dissatisfaction with the performance of Chinese-built jetfighters and the perceived need to balance China's influence (*Asia-Pacific Defence Reporter*, February 2003, 22–3). There are also 66 helicopters, including 11 Russian-made medium-lift Mi-17 helicopters as well as 10 W-3 Sokol and 18 Mi-2 Hoplite helicopters from Poland. The small navy has six Chinese-made Houxin fast missile craft armed with C-801 anti-ship missiles and eight new missile craft armed with the same missiles. It has been reported that this new class of missile craft were built in Myanmar using Chinese hulls and Israeli electronics (*Asian Defence Journal*, March 2003).

What is obvious is that this has been a quantitative, not qualitative expansion, given the relatively small numbers of major weapons systems employed and their generally low level of technology. Thus, the indications are that Myanmar's defence priorities are mainly aimed at regime survival. Despite economic and arms embargoes by the West, Myanmar is still able to obtain the weapons systems it requires from willing sellers in China, Ukraine, Poland, Israel and elsewhere, proving that the global arms trade today is a buyer's market.

Philippines

The withdrawal of the USA from its huge Subic Bay naval facility in 1992 meant that the Philippines had to provide for the security of a vast archipelagic state. However, the 1997 economic crisis resulted in the abandonment of the planned modernization programme. In 1999 the Philippines resumed large-scale military exercises with the USA, with the ratification of the Visiting Forces Agreement (VFA). With this, the Philippines could access discarded or surplus US equipment under the US Excess Defence Articles (EDA) programme (*Asian Defence Journal*, July 1999). However, the modernization plan has revolved around the refurbishment of already obsolescent naval vessels and the provision of basic equipment such as trucks and communications equipment for land forces.

Since 11 September 2001, US forces have been providing training for counter-insurgency operations against the radical Islamist group, the Abu Sayaff Group in the south, but this excludes the provision of modern weapons systems. In 2007 the army fielded 65 Scorpion light tanks and an assortment of 564 obsolescent APCs. The air force had no fighter aircraft, deploying 15 vintage OV-10 Bronco as counter-insurgency aircraft and operating a number of second-hand UH-1H helicopters, although it did acquire a small number of Blue Horizon UAVs. The navy had no missile-armed naval vessels (Military Balance 2008, 399). This situation is likely to persist for some time given economic constraints and the focus on counter-insurgency operations against the Maoist New People's Army and the Muslim Moros.

Singapore

Modelled after the Israel Defence Forces, the Singapore Armed Forces emphasizes armour, air power and pre-emptive defence, built on a national service system and the active training of reservists for frontline operations. This has resulted in military manpower totalling 385,000 in 2007, most deployable within 12 hours using a well-practised system of recall. Singapore's army deployed a very large number of armour assets, including 546 tanks and 1,574 APCs. In addition, it has a very modern artillery capability, with 106 155mm long-range artillery increasingly dominated by its own indigenously built air-portable Pegasus and the heavy SSPH1

Primus. The army has introduced the locally built Bionix infantry fighting vehicle (IFV), which will eventually replace the obsolescent M113 APCs (*The Military Balance 2008*, 401). In 2006 Singapore announced plans to refurbish 66 Leopard II main battle tanks from Germany (*Channel News Asia*, 11 December 2006). It is also reported to be contemplating the purchase of M142 High Mobility Artillery Rocket Systems (HIMARS) from the USA (Strategic Comments 2007).

In 2007, the air force deployed 60 F-16/D and 37 F-5S Tiger jetfighters, 12 Apache helicopter gunships, 4 Hawkeye AEW (Airborne Early Warning) aircraft, 5 F50 maritime patrol aircraft, a fleet of 9 air refuelling tankers, 10 CH-47SD Chinook heavy lift helicopters and over 40 UAVs (*The Military Balance 2008*, 402). In 2005, Singapore ordered 12 F-15SG Strike Eagle jetfighters and in 2007, ordered an additional 12, making a total of 24 (*Defence Industry Daily*, 22 October 2007). In 2007, Singapore announced that it was converting four Gulfstream 550 jets into AEW aircraft with Israeli-made Phalcon radars, replacing the E-2C Hawkeye (*Forbes.com*, 23 April 2007). In 2007, Singapore unveiled its reported 16 Israeli-made Hermes 450 UAVs which have an endurance of 20 hours (Strategic Comments 2007). In summary, Singapore's air force is by far the most sophisticated in the region.

Its navy has also seen rapid modernization in recent years. In 2007 the navy deployed three Lafayette 'stealth' frigates (with another three on order), six corvettes armed with Harpoon anti-ship missiles and Barak anti-missile defences, six fast missile boats armed with Harpoon anti-ship missiles, four submarines, 11 modern patrol vessels, four modern Endurance-class landing ships, and four minehunters. The new frigates are noteworthy for their sophistication, each deploying eight Harpoon anti-ship missiles, Aster 15 anti-missile defences, anti-submarine torpedoes and a S-70B Seahawk helicopter (*The Military Balance 2007*, 401). In 2005 Singapore also purchased two refurbished Swedish A17 Vastergotland submarines which will enter service in 2010 possibly equipped with the latest Air Independent Propulsion (AIP) systems (*Strategy Page*, 7 November 2005).

Singapore has noted the RMA debate in the USA, which has touted the new information, sensing, precision attack, stealth and aerial warfare technologies employed in the Gulf War as being the precursor of a fundamental change in the way wars will be fought. Thus, it has adopted its own version of the RMA, under the doctrine of IKC2 or Integrated Knowledge-based Command and Control, the goal of which is the superior collection and organization of knowledge that can provide dominant situation awareness and achieve more effective command and control of forces as well as the precise application of force (*Asian Defence Journal*, July–August 2003, 14). Singapore plans to leverage on its strengths, such as its well-educated workforce and its sophisticated information technology, to achieve such an RMA, which it hopes will compensate for its lack of strategic depth.

As Tables 2.1 and 2.2 indicate, the Asian economic crisis in 1997–98 did not affect its military modernization, which has been ongoing since the late 1960s. This reflects Singapore's basic insecurity as a small but wealthy Chinese-dominated city-state in the midst of a potentially unstable Malay Archipelago. Given the lack of strategic depth, the reliance on external markets, the reliance on its neighbours for water and food supplies, Malay-Chinese ethnic animosities in the past, and the sometimes palpable resentment by its neighbours at its economic success, Singapore has developed a fortress mentality in the area of defence. Singapore's economic importance and current military capability rank it among South-east Asia's middle powers despite its small size and population. The trajectory suggests that Singapore will be a keen consumer of cutting-edge Western and US defence equipment for the foreseeable future as it seeks to achieve its own military transformation based on the RMA.

Thailand

Thailand, the so-called frontline state, undertook a comprehensive military build-up in the aftermath of the communist victories in Indochina in 1975 (see Tables 2.3–2.4). Over time, the military build-up achieved a momentum of its own, with attention shifting in the 1990s to maritime security, given growing concerns over piracy, sea lanes of communications and overlapping sea boundary claims. The Asian economic crisis in 1997–98 seriously affected Thailand. Indeed, Thailand lost a $74.5m. deposit on eight F-18 Hornet jetfighters when it was forced to cancel the order (*Air Forces Monthly*, July 1998, 7). Defence spending in real terms fell sharply and Thailand has still not recovered. As Table 2.2 indicates, Thailand's defence spending in 2006 was, in real terms, still one-third less than in 1997. Thus, instead of buying new equipment, it has concentrated on the cheaper option of upgrading existing equipment and buying used weapons systems. Instead of buying the latest F-16C/D jetfighter, Thailand opted for another squadron of the older and cheaper F-16A/B. Seven F-16A/B jetfighters were also given to Thailand by Singapore in exchange for training facilities in the country (Far Eastern Economic Review, April 2006). Elbit Systems of Israel has also upgraded Thailand's F-5 Tiger jetfighters (Asian Defence Yearbook 2000–01, 112).

According to *The Military Balance 2008*, the most significant assets in Thailand's air force in 2007 were 50 F-16A/B and 35 F-5E/F Tiger jetfighters, and 34 L-39ZA Albatros ground attack aircraft. The rest consisted of a large assortment of fixed-wing transport aircraft, utility/ ground attack aircraft such as 22 obsolescent AU-23A Peacemaker, training aircraft including 10 ex-German Alpha jet trainers, and helicopters, including 20 obsolescent UH-1H helicopters (*The Military Balance 2008*, 407).

Since 1998 the army has downsized from 230,000, to 190,000 in 2007 (*Straits Times*, 20 October 2001; *The Military Balance 2008*, 405). In 2007 it deployed a large but obsolescent force of 848 tanks consisting of M60A1, M60A3, M48A5, Scorpion, Stingray, and Chinese-made Type 69, as well as 1,039 APCs dominated by obsolescent US-made M113 and the Chinese-made Type 85. Its navy had 16 vessels equipped with anti-ship missiles, including eight frigates, of which four are Chinese-made and equipped with CSS-N4 missiles and four are US-made equipped with Harpoon missiles. The remaining two corvettes and six missile boats are equipped with anti-ship missiles including Harpoon, Exocet and Gabriel missiles. What is significant is the fact that Thailand is the only state in South-east Asia to operate an aircraft carrier, the Chakri Narvebet, which was delivered in 1997. The aircraft carrier oper- ates nine used AV-8A Harrier jetfighters and six S-70B Seahawk helicopters. However, the lack of spare parts and high operating costs have resulted in the aircraft carrier spending most of its time at port.

The military coup that ousted the Thaksin government in 2006 and replaced it with a military regime led to new orders for weapons systems. In September 2007 it was announced that Thailand would buy 96 APCs from Ukraine and C-802 anti-ship missiles from China. In October 2007, Thailand also announced the purchase of 12 Swedish Gripen jetfighters at a cost of about $1 billion (*Bangkok Post*, 17 October 2007). In November 2007, the military announced that it would be requesting the government for 300 billion baht on arms moder- nization over the next 10 years. The main priority for the navy would be the acquisition of submarines, while the air force wanted new jetfighters (*The Nation*, 26 November 2006). With these developments, it seems that the era of fiscal restraint since the 1997 economic crisis has ended.

Viet Nam

With the end of the Cold War, withdrawal from its occupation of Cambodia in 1991 and rapprochement with ASEAN in 1995, Viet Nam was able to reap a major peace dividend by downsizing its armed forces. Thus, its armed forces were reduced from 1,052,000 in 1990 to 484,000 in 2006 (see Table 2.5).

According to *The Military Balance 2008*, Viet Nam's army continued to deploy substantial armour assets in 2007, including 1,935 tanks and 1,780 APCs, as well as substantial artillery assets numbering over 3,000. However, these are mostly outdated Soviet equipment, with the most modern asset being 70 T-62 main battle tanks. The air force is dominated by 150 MiG21 (many recently upgraded by Russia) and 53 Su-22M jetfighters, but there is an air superiority capability in the form of four Su-30MKK and 12 Su-27 Flanker jetfighters. There are 48 helicopters, including a large contingent of 30 Mi17 medium-lift helicopters. In addition, the air force also deploys 26 Mi-24 Hind helicopter gunships (*The Military Balance 2008*, 409). Its air defence has been bolstered by the deployment of two modern Russian S-300 air defence batteries that cost $300m. in 2003 (*Asia Times*, 5 September 2003). Significantly, Viet Nam reportedly also bought unspecified numbers of Scud C missiles with a range of 550 km from the Democratic People's Republic of Korea (North Korea) in a $100m. deal paid partly with rice (*Asia Times*, 5 September 2003).

The navy has been a beneficiary of limited arms modernization. Its five Petya-class corvettes have been refitted and two small submarines were procured from North Korea (*Naval Forces*, February 2001). The navy currently deploys five patrol frigates, as well as vessels armed with anti-ship missiles. These consist of four Tarantul corvettes and eight Osa missile boats armed with SSN2 anti-ship missiles. Two Svetlyak patrol vessels armed with SSN25 anti-ship missiles (with another two currently on order out of a planned total of 10 vessels) have been delivered from Russia (*Moscow Defence Brief*, May 2002; *The Military Balance 2008*, 409).

The generally diminished state of Viet Nam's armed forces compared to the immediate aftermath of the Viet Nam War indicates the country's current economic priorities and also the generally benign state of its immediate strategic environment. Viet Nam, however, is aware of the need to defend its maritime resources, as it has important offshore oilfields and overlapping maritime boundaries with China in the South China Sea. New Su-27 and Su-30 jetfighters and missile boats have, thus, been procured in recent years. However, it is clear that these are limited measures meant to redress previous neglect and do not amount to a major military expansion. Indeed, the very real poverty of the country, a lack of resources and the absence of any major benefactor means that military modernization will remain fairly modest and will not resemble the more serious expansion in some of the other ASEAN states.

Conclusions

We can, thus, summarize briefly the above analysis. Clearly, South-east Asian armed forces are becoming more technologically sophisticated as states in the region acquire new capabilities and improve existing ones. The post-Cold War proliferation of sophisticated weapons systems have included sophisticated fighter or multi-role combat aircraft (such as the F-15 Strike Eagle, Su-27 Flanker, F-16C Fighting Falcon, MiG-29 and F-18 Hornet), maritime reconnaissance aircraft, modern missiles (including anti-ship missiles, beyond visual range air-to-air missiles, air-to-ground missiles and tactical ground-to-ground missiles), AEW systems, modern artillery systems (such as MRLS), submarines and warships equipped with the latest electronics and anti-ship missiles. They have both changed the strategic landscape as well as raised fears of a regional 'arms race', with negative implications for regional security, as they have provided states in the region with long-range conventional strike capabilities that they did not previously possess.

Yet, regional arms modernization programmes must be seen in proper perspective. It is clear from the above analysis that the military modernization programmes in South-east Asia have been modest and are not aimed at building up large offensive military capabilities. Naval modernization and expansion programmes in Indonesia, Malaysia, Thailand and Viet Nam appear to be aimed at building up capabilities that can protect economic resources, especially offshore maritime resources, which have to be defended against potential rival claimants, and protected against piracy and terrorist threats. Thus, these states today have navies which can perform a variety of functions, including patrol, anti-submarine warfare, surface combat, amphibious operations and mine hunting. Limited numbers of air superiority jetfighters have also been procured by these states, and both Indonesia and Malaysia are also building rapid-deployment forces, which could respond to any crisis throughout the Malay archipelago.

Balanced against this build up of naval and air capabilities is the fact that military manpower levels since the end of the Cold War have generally remained static or have been reduced, as in the cases of Thailand, Malaysia and, more dramatically, Viet Nam. While Myanmar has developed its conventional capabilities, the quantitative approach indicates that they are aimed primarily at ensuring regime survival against domestic opposition and ethnic insurgencies. Lack of funding has also kept the numbers of sophisticated weapons systems small, with the key players such as Malaysia, Indonesia, Thailand, Viet Nam and Myanmar opting for cheaper weapons systems from countries such as Russia, China and Ukraine. Overall, therefore, there does not appear to be strong evidence of a regional arms race according to the Gray definition. The caveat here is that at a more localized level, both Singapore and Malaysia are acquiring quite similar capabilities with some evidence of an interactive arms dynamic at work, given that there is an action-reaction phenomenon in the acquisition of major weapons systems, such as air superiority jetfighters, AEW systems, modern artillery systems, submarines and main battle tanks.

It is also clear that few states in South-east Asia are ready to adopt the RMA, as countries in the region generally do not have the economic resources, military budget, technological capability and trained manpower to acquire the full suite of RMA technologies. To embark on the path of RMA, armed forces must also undergo fundamental doctrinal, logistical and organizational changes, as well as acquiring relevant equipment, which they are in the main not prepared to do. Pragmatism demands the use of limited resources to protect economic resources, especially offshore maritime resources. However, the information collection and surveillance capabilities that are the hallmark of modern RMA technologies may be relevant to countering illegal migration, piracy or even drugs trafficking, problems which are prevalent among some regional countries. Moreover, states in the region are conscious of military technological developments and want to stay on the learning curve. There is, thus, a varying degree of interest in the technological aspects of the RMA.

Among countries in the region, Malaysia has expressed an interest to acquire new information-based systems, but inter-service rivalries and budgetary constraints have impaired the ability of the armed forces to embrace fully the required organizational and doctrinal changes. Still, the Malaysian armed forces have improved steadily and appear determined to at least stay on the learning curve and be able to deploy some RMA-type technologies to meet the varied and complex security challenges that they face.

It is Singapore that has perceived the RMA to be a solution to external conventional threats. RMA-type technologies are seen as a force-multiplier that can offset the country's lack of strategic depth and limited resources. Moreover, Singapore has a population that is literate and technologically disposed to adapt the RMA. Thus, Singapore has formally embraced the RMA with its IKC2 concept, and has a long-term plan to ensure its implementation. Singapore also appears prepared to invest in the latest, expensive Western technology to do so.

In evaluating the region's participation in the RMA, then, the countries occupying Dibb's previous four tiers need to be re-arranged to reflect the situation in 2008 and beyond. Singapore should now be in Tier 1, given its desire to achieve an RMA and that some of its current military capabilities in fact exceed Australia's. Malaysia, in its aspiration to modernize, partly to match Singapore, should now be in Tier 2. Tier 3 consists of Indonesia, Thailand and Viet Nam, countries which, due to funding and lack of technology, can only participate in the RMA in a very limited way. Tier 4 consists of Myanmar, the Philippines, Laos, Cambodia and Brunei. In Myanmar's case, there is a lack of access to the latest technology. The Philippines has been unable to find the resources to move beyond basic weaponry and Brunei is too small. States in Tiers 3 and 4 will remain, at best, industrial-age armed forces.

Finally, it is clear from this case study of South-east Asia, that quantitative assessments based on defence spending and procurement provide some indication as to the current status of military acquisition and modernization in the ASEAN states. However, they do not provide a complete picture as they do not inform about the political, economic and social variables and dynamics that underlie military acquisition and modernization. Therefore, performing analyses using quantitative data is useful, but limited. A more complete assessment will require a holistic approach which would examine such variables and dynamics.

Bibliography

Air Forces Monthly
Asia Times, www.atimes.com
Asian Defence Journal
Asian Defence Yearbook 2000–01, 2000
Asia-Pacific Defence Reporter
Bangkok Post (Thailand)
Ball, Desmond, 'Arms and Affluence: Military Acquisition in the Asia-Pacific', *International Security*, Vol. 18, No. 3 (Winter 1993–94)
BBC News, news.bbc.co.uk
Channel News Asia, www.channelnewsasia.com
Cheung, Tai Ming, 'Shoulder to Shoulder: ASEAN Members Strengthen Ties', *Far Eastern Economic Review*, 22 March 1990
Defence Industry Daily, www.defenseindustrydaily.com
Dibb, Paul, 'The Revolution in Military Affairs and Asian Security', *Survival*, Vol. 39, No. 4, Winter 1997–98
The Economist, 'Asia's Arms Race', *The Economist*, 20 February 1993
Forbes.com, www.forbes.com
Gray, Colin S., 'The Arms Race Phenomenon', *World Politics*, Vol. 24, No. 1, 1972 www.atimes.com/atimes/Southeast _Asia/HJ07Ae01.html
Huxley, Tim, 'Singapore and Malaysia: A Precarious Balance?', *Pacific Review*, Vol. 4, No. 3, 1991
Huxley, Tim and Susan Willett, *Arming East Asia*, Adelphi Paper No. 329, International Institute of Strategic Studies, London, 1999
IISS, *The Military Balance 1975–1976*, London, International Institute for Strategic Studies, 1975
———*The Military Balance 1990–1991*, London, International Institute for Strategic Studies, 1990
———*The Military Balance 2008*, London, International Institute for Strategic Studies, 2008
Jane's Defense Weekly
Korea Times
Marshall, Andy W., *Problems of Estimating Military Power*, RAND, 1966
McCoy, Clifford, 'Myanmar's Losing Military Strategy', *Asia Times*, 7 October 2006, www.atimes.com/atimes/ Southeast_Asia/HJ07Ae01.html
Morgenthau, Hans, *Politics Among Nations: The Struggle for Power and Peace*, New York, Alfred A. Knopf, 1948
Military Technology
Moscow Defence Brief, mdb.cast.ru/mdb/5 2002/ff/atd
The Nation (Thailand)
Naval Forces
New Straits Times (Malaysia)
Nye, Joseph S. and William A. Owens, 'America's Information Edge', *Foreign Affairs*, Vol. 75, No. 2, March–April 1996
SIPRI, *SIPRI Yearbook 2006*, Stockholm, Stockholm International Peace Research Institute, 2006
———*SIPRI Yearbook 2007*, Stockholm, Stockholm International Peace Research Institute, 2007*Straits Times* (Singapore)
Strategic Comments, 'Singapore's Military Modernization', *Strategic Comments*, Vol.13, Issue 10, December 2007
Strategy Page, www.strategypage.com
Sydney Morning Herald
Tan, Andrew T. H., *A Political and Economic Dictionary of Southeast Asia*, London, Europa/Taylor & Francis, 2004

3 Arms modernization in Asia

An emerging complex arms race

Desmond Ball

'Asia is rushing to arm itself as never before' (Sikes 1990); 'Southeast Asian countries have recently gone on a military spending spree' (Clad and Marshall 1992); the People's Republic of China is also now engaged in an 'arms buying spree' (Tai Ming Cheung 1992); 'Asia's armories are bulging … conventional arms abound, and more are flooding in' (*Economist*, 20 February 1993, 19); and there is a 'new Asian arms race' underway which 'bodes ill for a region already racked by ancient animosities and border disputes' (Clad and Marshall 1992). These quotations from press reports in the early 1990s reflect the concerns that were widespread among strategic analysts at that time regarding the sustained build-up of modern conventional weapons systems in Asia, which had been underway since the mid-1980s. I argued then that it was misleading to characterize the robust weapons acquisition programmes as an 'arms race', but that they could be better explained in terms of defence modernization and the new requirements for defence self-reliance in the region (and especially the maritime dimension) (Ball 1993–94).

However, a decade and a half later, the question of whether the Asia-Pacific region is on the verge of an emerging arms race must be reconsidered. Regional defence budgets were hit by the Asian economic crisis in 1997–98, but they mostly rebounded fairly quickly, and a multitude of new weapons systems were soon ordered – dozens of new warships, submarines, hundreds of fighter aircraft and all sorts of infantry weapons. This was particularly the case in North-east Asia, where the growth in China's defence budget has been especially disturbing – it has increased by double digit figures nearly every year since 1988, meaning that it has increased eight-fold over the 20-year period (according to official budget figures). The US defence budget has also increased rapidly since 2002, with significant implications for the strategic balance and security in the Asia-Pacific region. This region is now also subject to the most active proliferation of weapons of mass destruction (WMD), as well as long-range delivery systems, in the world today. Estimates of WMD capabilities must now figure integrally with new conventional weapons capabilities in strategic calculations with respect to this region – and in any discussion of the question of a prospective arms race in the region.

This chapter has five principal parts. The first part discusses the 'arms race' argument of the early/mid-1990s and the conceptual meanings of the terms 'modernization' and 'arms race'. The second part describes the recent trends in regional defence expenditure and acquisitions. It briefly outlines the main new capabilities most commonly being acquired in the region, and shows the preponderance of North-east Asia in the regional military balance. Special attention is drawn to naval acquisitions and the issue of an 'emergent naval arms race' in the region. It also discusses a couple of particular developments, viz: unmanned aerial vehicles (UAVs) and information warfare (IW), the implications of which are relatively unexplored. The third part briefly describes the proliferation of nuclear weapons and associated delivery systems in this region. The fourth reviews Asia's place in the global arms trade and particularly its prominent position with respect to arms importation. Finally, the fifth part argues that untrammelled by any arms control arrangements, 'arms-racing' behaviour is likely to increase over the next one to two decades, with disturbing implications for regional stability.

The 'arms race' argument in the early/mid-1990s

The common characterization of the arms acquisition programmes in East Asia in the late 1980s/early 1990s as an 'arms race' was not based on any systematic analysis. Rather, it reflected astonishment at the rapid increase in Asian defence expenditure, anxiety about China's growing capabilities, and bewilderment about some of the major acquisitions in the region.

From the mid-1980s to the mid-1990s, defence expenditure in Asia increased at an unprecedented rate. Together with a decline in defence spending in the USA, Europe and the former Soviet Union in the late 1980s and early 1990s, this resulted in the Asian share of world military expenditure almost doubling in the decade from 1984 to 1994 – from 11% to 20% (see Table 3.1 – US ACDA 1995).

In the case of arms imports to the region, Asia's share of world expenditure on arms transfers more than doubled from the early 1980s to the early 1990s – from 15.5% in 1982 to 33.24% in 1993 (Anthony et al. 1992, 308; Anthony et al. 1994, 510; Gill 1994, 552).

Any arms race should have two principal features. First, it should involve a rapid rate of acquisitions, with the participants stretching their resources in order to ensure that they remain at the head of the race, or at least are not falling behind; and, with their capabilities increasing, in quantitative and/or qualitative terms. It is commonly presumed that the proportion of gross domestic product (GDP) being allocated to defence expenditure is a good indicator of national commitments to this effort, but this can be very misleading. It is quite possible, given high rates of economic growth, for the proportion of GDP spent on defence to decline while real defence spending and capabilities are being substantially increased.

In most countries in the Asia-Pacific region, the proportions of gross national product (GNP) committed to defence spending were much lower in the mid- and late 1990s than they had been in the early 1980s – typically 30% or 40% lower. China, where the proportion has remained fairly constant, was the only exception to this. However, most countries had much more capable forces in the 1990s than they had in the 1980s.

Second, there should be some reciprocal dynamics in which developments in the defensive and offensive capabilities of one adversary are matched by attempts to counter the advantages thought to be gained by another. Thus, the continued acquisition of new weapons capabilities becomes an interactive process in which the arms requirements of one party depend upon the known, assumed, or anticipated capabilities of the forces of the other party or parties.

However, there was little evidence of these action-reaction dynamics in the regional acquisition programmes of the 1980s and 1990s. Rather, those programmes could best be explained in terms of modernization, or the requirements for enhanced self-reliance in the context of a rapidly changing and increasingly uncertain regional security environment, with the extraordinary rates of economic growth across most of the region providing the largesse for the increasing defence budgets. For many countries, modernization involved the replacement of

Table 3.1 Asia's share of world defence expenditure, 1984 and 1994

	1984		1994	
	Defence expenditure US$b (constant 1994)	*% of world defence expenditure*	*Defence expenditure US$b (constant 1994)*	*% of world defence expenditure*
World	1,251.8		840.3	
South Asia	9.1	0.73	12.5	1.49
East Asia	120.9	9.66	144.8	17.23
Oceania	7.1	0.57	9.0	1.07
Asia	138.1	11.03	166.3	19.79

obsolescent equipment acquired in the 1960s and 1970s. This replacement process often involved substantial increases in qualitative capabilities, especially with respect to weapons, sensors and electronic warfare (EW) systems.

On the other hand, there were two important cautionary points expressed by those who denied the arms race thesis. The first was that many of the new weapons systems being acquired had an 'offensive' character (such as fighter/strike aircraft, modern surface combatants, submarines and long-range anti-ship missiles), which not only made them more likely to generate counter-acquisitions in the future, but which were also disturbing in terms of their implications for crisis stability (Ball 1993–94, 105).

Second, it was noted that the possibility of some regional arms race developing within the next decade or so remained a serious concern. Since the requirements for defence self-reliance cannot be defined without some consideration of the capabilities possessed by neighbours and potential adversaries further afield, there must come a point where further acquisitions begin to stimulate reciprocal or interactive dynamics. By 2010, most countries in the region will face the demands not only of continued force modernization but also of replacement of the weapons systems acquired in such large volumes in the late 1980s. Defence budgets and acquisition programmes may enter another cycle of substantial increase – but this time for a base of higher numbers and more sophisticated capabilities than obtained during the round of the late 1980s and early 1990s.

It is of course possible, region-wide, for modernization and arms racing processes to proceed simultaneously. In this situation, which by and large obtains in Asia today, the analytic task is to locate the presence of arms racing behaviour and to determine the extent to which force structures are being affected by arms race dynamics, i.e. the extent to which equipment is being procured beyond the requirements of modernization, maritime patrol and other identified national purposes, in order to match or counter the acquisitions of notional adversaries.

Defence economic trends, 1996–2006

In 1996, the last full year before Asia was struck by the 1997–98 economic crisis, it accounted for 18.9% of world defence expenditure, with East Asia accounting for 15.8% (Sköns et al. 1999, 270). The high rate of growth in North-east Asia had levelled off in 1993–94 but was resumed in 1995–96, until hit by the regional economic crisis towards the end of 1997. The proportions of GNP being spent on defence in most countries in the region continued to decrease (DIO 1997, tables 24 and 25; DIO 1998, tables 24 and 26; DIO 1999, tables 24 and 26). In 1997 Asia's share of world spending decreased to 17.75% (Sköns et al. 1999, 270). In 1998, when most of the region was suffering economically, Asia's share of world arms transfers reached 41% (Asia-Pacific Economic Update, 2000, 89). It was 45.15% in 2002 (Hagelin et al. 2003, table 13B.1).

US defence expenditure increased dramatically in fiscal year 2002, following the terrorist attacks on the World Trade Center and the Pentagon in September 2001 and Operation Enduring Freedom in Afghanistan, and has been further bolstered by the war in Iraq since 2003. By 2003, when US defence spending increased by 14% over the previous year, and spending in Europe and the Middle East was increasing in real terms, Asia's share of world spending had fallen to 15.67%; it was 15.66% in 2006 (Stalenheim et al. 2007, 299).

Nearly all of the countries that were severely affected by the economic crisis had resumed increasing defence budgets by 2000 – Indonesia being the most important exception to this. In North-east Asia, the Republic of Korea (South Korea), which was hit the hardest by the crisis, increased its defence spending by 6.2% in the fiscal year 2000/01. South Korea's defence budget for fiscal year 2001/02 was a record US$12.72 billion. It included plans to spend $26.5 billion on new weapons systems over the next five years, including the acquisition of 40 new fighter aircraft, manned and unmanned reconnaissance aircraft, the SAM-X air defence system, at least three and perhaps six KDX-III destroyers, and improved command and control systems (Lake 2001a). In 2007, to complete and expand these acquisitions, South Korea announced a defence plan for 2008–12 which included $61 billion for weapons systems. The defence budget in 2007 was 9.9% higher than the previous year, with military spending planned to increase from 2.7% of GDP to 3% over the next five years (*Asian Defence Journal*, September 2007, 55).

Conventional acquisition programmes

Throughout the region as a whole, there have been significant common themes apparent in the acquisition programmes since the late 1980s. Asia is, of course, an extremely diverse region, with extraordinary disparities in national economic resources and military capabilities, and significant differences in security concerns and threat perceptions – in light of which, the degree of consistency in the acquisition programmes is all the more remarkable. The principal common themes involve:

National command, control and communications systems

Since the end of the Cold War and the commitment by most countries in the region to policies of enhanced self-reliance, there have been substantial investments in national command, control and communications (C^3) systems – including the construction of modern HQs and command and control centres, and the procurement of all sorts of communications and data-relay systems. The events of 11 September and the 'war on terror' prompted moves to enhance both the physical and electronic security of key C^3 facilities.

National strategic and tactical technical intelligence systems

The policies of greater self-reliance, together with the continuing prevalence of conflicts and disputes (both inter-state and intra-state) throughout the region, the requirements for maritime surveillance in exclusive economic zones (EEZs), and the need to monitor the details of new weapons systems being acquired by neighbours and potential adversaries, have led to increased investments in technical intelligence collection systems, especially signals intelligence (SIGINT) capabilities. Budgets for new SIGINT systems and expanded collection operations typically doubled during the period from around 1985 to 1995 (Ball 1993). Many countries in the region now maintain ground stations for intercepting satellite communications (i.e. long-distance telephone calls, facsimile traffic, e-mails, computer-to-computer data exchanges, etc.), including the USA, Russia, China, Japan, Australia, Singapore and even Myanmar (Ball 1993, 102–6; Ball 1998, 107–10).

Some countries have also been acquiring extensive airborne SIGINT capabilities. These are very expensive to maintain, but they provide the only means for effective, continuous, real-time surveillance of the electromagnetic emissions across maritime approaches and around areas of interest further afield. Japan now has about 16 dedicated SIGINT collection aircraft, six EW training aircraft with some electronics intelligence (ELINT) capabilities, 13 E-2C Hawkeye and four E-767 airborne early warning and control (AEW&C) aircraft with substantial secondary ELINT capabilities (Ball and Graham 2000). The Chinese Air Force has more than 20 dedicated ELINT collection aircraft – several HD-5s, at least one EY-8, eight HD-6s and five Tu-154M aircraft. In addition, China has also an active ELINT satellite programme, which would be very useful in maritime contingencies (including in the Taiwan Strait) (Ball 2003).

In South-east Asia, Singapore acquired modest but sophisticated airborne SIGINT capabilities in the early 1990s. Two of the Air Force's C-130H Hercules aircraft have been equipped with extensive suites of Israeli-supplied communications intelligence (COMINT), ELINT and EW systems for strategic, operational and tactical SIGINT missions (Ball 1995, 16–7; IISS 2001–02, 207). They have been reported undertaking collection in Australia; over the Andaman Sea and along the western coasts of Malaysia, Thailand and Myanmar, with stop-overs in Rangoon and Dhaka (Ball 1998, 235–7; Karniol 1997; Lintner 1997); and 'as far west as Pakistan' (Ricketts 2002). Singapore also has four Fokker F-50 Maritime Enforcer Mark-2 maritime patrol aircraft, which are equipped with similar Israeli SIGINT systems, and which operate around South-east Asian waters from the Andaman Sea to the South China Sea (Ball 1995, 16; Ricketts 2002).

In 1995–98, the Royal Australian Air Force acquired two EP-3C Orion aircraft which had been specially configured for SIGINT operations (La Franchi 2000; Barker 2000; McPhedran 2000), which were used extensively around Timor in 1999–2000, and which have more recently been used in the Persian Gulf in support of Operations Enduring Freedom and Iraqi Freedom. The RAAF reportedly also operates a SIGINT configured C-130H; the Australian Army has a King Air 200 fitted for ELINT operations; and the Navy has a Learjet specially equipped for ELINT and electronic warfare activities (Ricketts 2002).

Operations Enduring Freedom and Iraqi Freedom undoubtedly stimulated further regional interest in the acquisition of airborne collection systems. The intensity of intelligence collection flights in the region is increasing, but so too are the risks of neighbourly disputes about them (as occurred between Singapore and Australia because of RSAF technical intelligence collection activities in Australia in 1993–94), as well as more serious crises, such as the confrontation between the USA and China occasioned by China's shooting down of a US EP-3 SIGINT aircraft near Hainan Island on 1 April 2001 (Ball 2004).

Multi-role fighter aircraft, with maritime attack capabilities as well as air superiority capabilities (e.g. F-16s and F-18s)

During the decade from around 1987 to 1997, Asian countries procured about 3,000 new fighter and strike aircraft, and about an equal number of existing aircraft were upgraded with new mission avionics and armaments. By 2000 Asia accounted for about 60% of world holdings of combat aircraft. A somewhat smaller number of more advanced and more expensive fighter aircraft were procured during the decade from 1997 to 2007.

China has developed a new multi-role fighter aircraft called the Jian-10, which entered service in 2003. It is said to be 'superior to the Su-27 but inferior to the Su-30'; as many as 300 may be produced (Asian Defence Journal, January/February 2007, 38). In April 2002, South Korea announced that it had decided to buy 40 new Boeing F-15K (designated Slam Eagle) fighter jets, at a cost of $4 billion. Deliveries began in October 2005, with all 40 expected to have arrived by the end of 2008. Another 20 were ordered in January 2008, to be delivered from 2010 to 2012 (Fong 2007; Asian Defence Journal, January/February 2007, 40). In October 2007 South Korea also announced plans to purchase about 60 fifth-generation fighters (such as the F-22 Raptor and the F-35) from 2014 to 2019 (Asian Defence Journal, December 2007, 74). Japan has identified a requirement for a 'stealth' fighter, and has decided to develop a prototype for test flight by 2012, in addition to seeking procurement of F-22 Raptors from the USA (Asian Defence Journal, September 2007, 55). Taiwan decided in mid-2007 to buy 66 F-16C/D fighters from the USA, to complement the 146 F-16A/B versions that it acquired in 1996–99. A prototype upgraded version of Taiwan's Ching-Kuo Indigenous Defence Fighter (IDF-II) had its first test flight in early 2007.

Australia has embarked on the process to replace its F-111 strike aircraft and its F/A-18A Hornet fighters in the 2010s. In 2007 the government decided to purchase 24 F/A-18F Super Hornets, at a cost of $5.6 billion; already on Boeing's production line in St Louis, they are to be delivered from early 2010 to late 2011. The Super Hornets are intended to prevent the emergence of any 'air combat capability gap' following the retirement of the F-111s in 2010 and the introduction of the new J-35 Joint Strike Fighter (JSF) later in the decade. Australia plans to acquire 'up to 100' JSFs by 2020, with the first scheduled to enter service in 2013. There is also considerable interest in Australia in the acquisition of a number (perhaps 10–12) of F-22 Raptor 'stealth' fighters.

In 2007 India signed an agreement with Russia for 40 Su-30MKI multi-role fighters, in addition to 140 ordered in 2000. India has also reportedly reached agreement with Russia for the provision of some 126 fifth-generation fighters, to begin entering service between 2012 and 2015 (*Asian Defence Journal*, December 2007, 62).

In September 2005 Singapore decided to procure the F-15SG, a variant of the F-15E, as its next-generation fighter, with the intention of initially acquiring 20–24 new fighters to replace its highly-upgraded A-4s, but the final total requirement may be for as many as 80 (Fong 2007). Malaysia ordered 18 Su-30MKM multi-role fighters in May 2003; the first two were delivered in May 2007 and the rest by the end of 2008. The Royal Malaysian Air Force has expressed a desire to procure a number of 'fifth generation fighters like the … Super Hornets' in 2010–15 (*Asian Defence Journal*, June 2007, 10). Myanmar has acquired 10 MiG-29 fighters from Russia (Lintner 2001). In August 2003 Indonesia took delivery of two Su-27 Flanker fighter-bombers and two Su-30 fighter aircraft from Russia (Tjahjadi 2003). It planned to have a squadron of 10 Sukhoi fighters operational by 2009.

A significant feature of the current fighter programmes is the acquisition of new air-to-air missiles, such as the US AIM-20 Advanced Medium Range Air-to-Air Missile (AMRAAM), which has a range of more than 40 km and uses active radar guidance for interception. Australia, South Korea, Taiwan and Japan have already taken delivery of AMRAAMs; missiles reportedly purchased by Thailand and Singapore 'are held in the US on 48-hour call'; and the USA is considering supplying them to Malaysia, Indonesia and the Philippines (Kerr 2002).

Unmanned aerial vehicles (UAVs)

Throughout Asia there have been substantial investments in the acquisition of unmanned aerial vehicles (UAVs) for surveillance, targeting and fire support, especially since around 2001. It is the main sort of defence equipment needed for the 'war on terror'. The regional interest was palpably quickened by the capabilities demonstrated in the UAV operations in Operation Enduring Freedom in Afghanistan in 2001–02.

In North-east Asia, China is the only country with an extensive operational UAV capability, including ELINT and EW systems. The Chinese Air Force's primary long-range UAV is the WZ (Wu Zhen, or unmanned reconnaissance)-5, better known as the Chang Hong-1, based on US reconnaissance drones shot down over China in the 1960s. Production began in the late 1970s and some were used in the Sino-Viet Nam border conflict in 1979. The latest version of the Chang Hong is a prospective ELINT platform (Fisher 2001, 7–8). In addition, according to a report by the US Department of Defense, 'China already has a number of short-range and longer-range UAVs in its inventory for reconnaissance, surveillance, and electronic warfare roles', and has 'several developmental UAV programs underway related to reconnaissance, surveillance, communications, and EW' (US Department of Defense 2002, 18).

South Korea has recently deployed several indigenously-designed Night Intruder 300 UAVs, which have a range of up to 120 km from their ground station using a line-of-sight data link and 200 km using a relay system. South Korea also plans to acquire four Global Hawk high-altitude UAVs for broad-area surveillance purposes by 2012 (*Asian Defence Journal*, October 2007, 53).

Australia plans to acquire six Global Hawk UAVs, at a cost of $200m. A Global Hawk UAV flew to Australia from California in April 2001, the first non-stop flight across the Pacific Ocean by an autonomous aircraft, and was tested in several roles over the next month (Nelson

2001). Australia is also acquiring about 16 tactical UAVs for focal-area surveillance (Bostock 2001). In August–September 2003, four Project Nervana UAVs were deployed to the Solomon Islands as part of Operation Anode, and were used to provide real-time video imagery for the Regional Assistance Mission (RAMSI) (Liebelt and Burton 2003; Air Force News, 11 September 2003, 6). Boeing ScanEagle UAVs were used by the Australian Army in southern Iraq in 2006–07 (*Asian Defence Journal,* January/February 2007, 44).

Singapore is the only country in the region that had hitherto invested in a substantial UAV capability. The Singapore Air Force currently has a Squadron with several Blue Horizon 'stealth' or 'penetrator' UAVs, with an endurance of more than 16 hours, 40 Searcher Mark-2 and 24 Chukar 111 UAVs (IISS 2007, 371). Singapore Technologies has also been working on the development of larger UAVs, such as the Firefly, which could carry a warhead rather than sensor payload (Eshel and Kemp 1998).

Thailand has a single Searcher UAV. In the early 2000s it was mainly used for surveillance flights along the northern Thailand-Myanmar border in support of counter-narcotics operations. In March 2001 the Thai Army released images, taken by the Searcher, of opium crops and methamphetamine laboratories in Myanmar. Thailand has also produced a small indigenously-designed UAV for reconnaissance purposes, 10 of which were delivered to the Royal Thai Army in 2007. These are to be mainly used for monitoring violent activities in the south (*Asian Defence Journal,* September 2007, 53).

In 2001 the Philippines acquired two Blue Horizon UAVs from Singapore for use against Abu Sayyaf and other Muslim rebel groups. The Philippines Army has also developed its own unmanned surveillance aircraft to support its counter-terrorist programme, including especially locating Abu Sayyaf units (*Straits Times,* 31 January 2002). The Malaysian Ministry of Defence has begun flight testing a locally-produced Eagle UAV system, complete with a ground control station and a remote receiving station, and with a 60 kg payload capacity for carrying various sensors or EW equipment (*Jane's Defence Weekly,* 24 April 2002, 13).

Maritime surveillance aircraft (e.g. P-3 Orions)

About 120 new maritime reconnaissance aircraft were acquired by East Asian countries during the 1990s, and a similar number is likely to have been acquired during the 2000s. In February 2008 the USA agreed to sell Taiwan 12 P-3C Orion long-range maritime patrol aircraft (LRMPA), at a cost of $1.9 billion for the aircraft and $272m. for missiles. The P-3Cs are able to carry eight AGM-86 Harpoon anti-ship missiles (with a range of 120 nm or 225 km) as well as surface search radar, SIGINT/ELINT/EW equipment, and anti-submarine warfare (ASW) systems.

Anti-ship missiles (e.g. Harpoon and Exocet)

Since the mid- to late 1980s, East Asian defence forces have acquired more than 3,000 modern anti-ship missiles, such as Harpoons and Exocets. More than 2,000 are deployed aboard surface combatants and more than 1,000 are for use by maritime strike aircraft. These numbers could well double through the coming decade as a consequence of the acquisition of new submarines, surface combatants and maritime strike aircraft (including maritime reconnaissance aircraft with anti-ship missile capabilities).

Modern surface combatants – destroyers, frigates, ocean patrol vessels

More than 200 new major surface combatants were acquired in East Asia through the 1990s, ranging in size and capability from the 13,000-ton light aircraft carrier acquired by Thailand and the four 7,200-ton DDG-173 Kongo (US Arleigh Burke)-class Aegis destroyers acquired by Japan, through about 100 new frigates, to more than 100 corvettes and ocean patrol vessels in the 1,000–1,500-ton range.

Since 2000, similar numbers have been acquired or ordered. China has acquired four Sovremenny-class destroyers and several variants of its Luhai/Luzhou destroyers. It has also begun deployment of its Type 054A or Jiangkai-II frigate; some 28–32 are expected to be produced to replace obsolescent Jiankai-1 vessels (Jacobs 2007). In 2000 Japan decided to build two 7,700-ton DDG-177 Atago-class destroyers, larger and more capable than the Kongo-class; they were commissioned in March 2007 and March 2008. It is likely that a further two will be ordered in the next few years. South Korea decided in 2002 to build three KDX-III (King Sejong the Great) Aegis-equipped destroyers, with a full-load displacement of 10,290 tonnes. The first of these (DDH-991) entered service in December 2008, with the second expected in 2010 and the third in 2012. The ROK Navy hopes to procure another three.

Singapore has acquired six Formidable-class frigates (3,200 tonnes), the last of which was launched in May 2006 and which will all be in service by 2009. They are nominally replacements for the six Sea Wolf missile gunboats which entered service in 1972, but carry Harpoon missiles and a helicopter, as well as modern sensors and electronic countermeasures (ECM) systems, providing a small-scale illustration of the qualitative advances incorporated in replacement processes (*Asian Defence Journal*, May 2007, 12).

Several countries in the region have acquired or are in the process of acquiring Standard SM-2 (Block IVA) and even SM-3 capabilities. With a range of 400 km, the Aegis/SM-2 (Block IVA) system provides air defence and limited ballistic missile defence over areas of fleet operations, amphibious landings, ports and support facilities, etc. Japan's four Kongo-class and two Atago-class destroyers are equipped with a mixture of SM-2s and SM-3s. In December 2007 an SM-3 (Block 1A) launched from the Kongo (DDG-173) successfully intercepted a ballistic missile in a test exercise in the mid-Pacific. South Korea's new KDX-III destroyers, the first of which entered service in December 2008, are also being equipped with SM-2s. In June 2007 Australia announced its decision to acquire 'at least three' Hobart-class anti-air warfare destroyers from Spain's Navantia, at a cost of $6.7 billion, with the first to be delivered by late 2014 and the third by mid-2017; they are to be equipped initially with SM-2 missiles.

Submarines

East Asian navies currently possess more than 100 submarines and, although many of the Romeo-class boats possessed by China and the Democratic People's Republic of Korea (North Korea) are no longer operational, more than 36 new boats were acquired during the 1990s. Most of these were in North-east Asia, where Japan acquired seven Harushio-class boats and began the eight-boat Oyashio project, South Korea acquired eight Chang Bogro (Type 209) boats, and China acquired four Song-class (Type 039) and four Russian Kilo-class submarines. Australia produced six Collins-class boats, the last of which was commissioned in March 2003, which are among the most capable conventional submarines in the world.

Since 2000, Asian countries have acquired or signed contracts for the delivery of about 30 new submarines, with orders for a further 20 expected in the next several years. China purchased eight more Project 636 Kilo-class submarines in 2002. South Korea has three 1,800-tonne Type 214 Sohn Won II-class submarines which should be ready to enter service in 2010, and has announced plans to procure six more between 2012 and 2020. Taiwan is seeking to acquire eight new boats. In early 2008 India ordered six Scorpene submarines from France, the first of which is to be delivered in 2012 and the rest over the next five years (Asian Defence Journal, March 2008, 47). India is building two prototype nuclear submarines, the first of which is expected to be commissioned in 2011–12 (*Asian Defence Journal*, May 2007, 52). Several more are likely to be procured in South-east Asia.

The role of submarines is being revolutionized. In Australia's case, for example, the Collins-class submarines will operate very differently from submarines in the past. Their primary roles are no longer anti-submarine warfare (ASW), convoying, or supporting battle groups in large-scale open ocean engagements. Rather, they will operate primarily in joint or combined operations in littoral regions, and in the new theatre of IW or Network-enabled Warfare. The submarines will remain an indispensable element of the RAN's fleet operations, but the chains of command, the range of information being distributed to the submarines, the recipients of information disseminated from the submarines, and hence the contribution of the submarines to Australian Defence Force (ADF) operations more generally, will be very different (Ball 2001, 7–10).

Electronic warfare capabilities

Most countries in East Asia are rapidly developing their electronic warfare capabilities, including their maritime EW capabilities. This reflects the widespread efforts in the region to achieve national self-reliance, the general recognition of the value of EW as a 'force multiplier', the defence modernization programmes (which necessarily include significant electronic components), and the ability of many countries in the region to produce advanced electronic systems for the desire to promote the development of indigenous electronic sectors through local design and production).

EW operations require full and real-time intelligence concerning the adversary's electronic order of battle (EOB) – that is, catalogues of the plethora of communications systems, radars and other electro-magnetic emitters which might be expected in area of operations. Electronic support measures (ESM) systems, including electronic counter-measures (ECM) and electronic counter-counter-measures (ECCM) systems, have to be carefully tailored to an adversary's EW systems and techniques. It is a highly interactive process which presumes identification of particular possible adversaries. In North-east Asia, there is evident action-reaction with respect to naval EW capabilities (Ball 2004, 76–7).

Rapid deployment forces, special forces, amphibious landing capabilities

Many countries in the region have either recently established or are in the process of developing some form of rapid deployment force, typically of brigade or light divisional size, designed to be deployed to possible areas of operation (AOs) at short notice and to fight as more or less self-contained units. Some of these forces are specially equipped and trained for amphibious assault operations.

Several countries are acquiring large amphibious landing ships (around 20,000 tons and heavier), described in one report as 'the real Asian arms race' (Stratfor 2007). These ships are able to carry 15–24 helicopters, a handful of transport hovercraft, heavy battle tanks, hundreds of troops, dozens of vehicles and tons of supplies for a variety of expeditionary missions. South Korea is producing four Dokdo-class LPX (Landing Platform Experimental), the first of which was commissioned in July 2007 and named after the Dokdo islets in the Sea of Japan, which South Korea contests with Japan. Its logo is inscribed with the words (in English): 'Project Power'. In November 2007 during a joint South Korean-US amphibious landing exercise, the Dokdo served as the exercise's command vessel with the landing force operation centre (LFOC) on board (Mingi Hyun 2007). Japan is building two Hyuga-class 16DDH helicopter-carrying destroyers, the first of which was laid down in May 2006 and is scheduled for commissioning in 2009. In June 2007 Australia decided to buy two 27,000-ton Spanish Navantia-designed LHDs, also called 'strategic projection ships', at a cost of $2.6 billion.

Information warfare capabilities

Although the investments have been too small to figure in defence budgets, and are generally covert anyway, many countries in the region have been acquiring IW capabilities – from internet monitoring and manipulation to strategic deception, to capabilities for destroying or incapacitating the critical information infrastructure of notional adversaries (including their defence C^3I systems).

China began to implement an IW plan in 1995, and since 1997 has conducted several exercises in which computer viruses have been used to interrupt military communications and public broadcasting systems. In April 1997 a 100-member élite corps was set up by the Central Military Commission to devise 'ways of planting disabling computer viruses into American and other Western command and control defence systems' (Dawnay 1997). In 2000 China established a strategic IW unit (which US observers have called 'Net Force') designed to 'wage combat through computer networks to manipulate enemy information systems spanning spare parts deliveries to fire control and guidance systems' (Sherman 2000). In August 1999, following a spate of cross-Straits attacks against computer networks and official websites in Taiwan, the Minister for National Defence in Taipei announced that the Ministry had established a Military Information Warfare Strategy Policy Committee and noted that 'we are able to defend ourselves in an information war' (ADJ News Roundup, August 1999, 14). In December 2000, this committee was expanded and converted into a battalion-sized centre under the direct command of the General Staff HQ, with responsibilities for network surveillance, defence and countermeasures (Minnick 2000; Lake 2001b). In May 2000 Japan announced plans to establish a research institute and an operational unit for fighting cyber-terrorism.

The 'war on terror' has added further impetus to these IW developments. In addition to forming IW units for conducting defence operations, there has been more intrusive monitoring of domestic electronic communications and transactions in many countries.

IW and related cyber-warfare or Network-centric warfare (NCW) activities are intrinsically target-specific. They require detailed knowledge of the telecommunications architectures of selected prospective targets, as well as the pro formas they use for computer-to-computer data exchanges, and identification of the 'back door' access points for insertion of viruses and 'Trojan horses'. These activities also involve action-reaction phenomena, as an intruded party takes measures to address its vulnerabilities and the intruder responds with new viruses and insertion techniques (Ball 2008, 138–42).

The predominance of North-east Asia and the rise of China

Northeast Asia accounts for the great bulk of the total defence expenditure and acquisitions in the region, including most of the more disturbing new capabilities. Japan, China, Taiwan, and North and South Korea account for more than 80% of East Asian and Australasian defence expenditure ($108.7 billion, or 83% in 2001; and $196.83 billion or 83% in 2006), and about three-quarters of total Asian defence expenditure (i.e. including South Asia) – 73% in 2001 and 74% in 2006. According to International Institute for Strategic Studies (IISS) estimates, China accounted for about 46% of total Asian expenditure in 2006 (see Table 3.2). An overview of defence capabilities in North-east Asia (in 2001 and 2006) is given in Table 3.3.

There is enormous uncertainty about Chinese defence expenditure. The official budget was $17 billion in 2001 and $35.3 billion in 2006, but this includes only a part of the funds spent on defence. Outside estimates vary widely, with some as high as $140 billion as far back as 1999 (Shaoguang Wang 1999). The IISS has long produced estimates of Chinese defence expenditure which include estimates of the extra-budgetary military expenditure. In 2001, for example, it estimated that actual expenditure was $47 billion and in 2003, when the official budget was $22.3 billion, it estimated that actual expenditure was $55.9 billion. Since 2004

Table 3.2 East Asia, South Asia and Australasia: defence budgets 1998, 2001 and 2006 (US$)

	1998	*2001*	*2006*
North-east Asia			
China, People's Republic	37.5 bn	47.0 bn	122.0 bn
Japan	37.66 bn	40.4 bn	41.1 bn
South Korea	9.9 bn	11.8 bn	23.7 bn
North Korea	1.3 bn	1.3 bn	2.3 bn
Mongolia	24 m.	30.2 m.	17 m.
Taiwan	8.3 bn	8.2 bn	7.73 bn
	94.62 bn	*108.73 bn*	*196.83 bn*
South-east Asia			
Brunei	357 m.	348 m.	343 m.
Cambodia	75 m.	128 m.	123 m.
Indonesia	939 m.	1.27 bn	2.59 bn
Laos	33 m.	15.8 m.	13.4 m.
Malaysia	1.2 bn	1.9 bn	3.08 bn
Myanmar	1.7 bn	1.7 bn	6.23 bn
Philippines	1 bn	1.1 bn	909 m.
Singapore	4.4 bn	4.3 bn	6.4 bn
Thailand	2 bn	1.7 bn	2.13 bn
Viet Nam	924 m.	1.8 bn	3.43 bn
	12.63 bn	*14.26 bn*	*25.24 bn*
Australasia			
Australia	7 bn	6.6 bn	15.1 bn
New Zealand	860 m.	678 m.	1.31 bn
	7.86 bn	*7.278 bn*	*16.41 bn*
South Asia			
Bangladesh	612 m.	692 m.	843 m.
India	10 bn	15.6 bn	22.3 bn
Pakistan	3.2 bn	2.6 bn	4.14 bn
Sri Lanka	733 m.	700 m.	686 m.
	14.55 bn	*19.59 bn*	*27.97 bn*
	129.71 bn	**149.86 bn**	**266.45 bn**

Source: IISS 2000–01; IISS 2001–02; IISS 2007

Note: Official budget figures, except for China (IISS estimates)

the IISS has adopted a 'purchasing power parity' (PPP) approach to estimating Chinese spending, which has produced figures more than three times as high as the official budget. In 2004, when the official budget was $25 billion, the IISS estimate jumped to $84.3 billion. In 2006 the IISS estimate was $122 billion (see Table 3.4). The Stockholm International Peace Research Institute (SIPRI), on the other hand, estimated that actual expenditure was $49.5 billion in 2006 (Stalenheim et al. 2007, 289), while the US Defense Intelligence Agency (DIA) estimated it to be $80 billion–$115 billion (Maples 2007).

China has now clearly overtaken Japan (which spent $41.1 billion in 2006, essentially stagnant since 2001) with respect to defence expenditure, making it the largest defence spender in Asia. According to IISS figures, this happened in around 2001, while SIPRI reckons it occurred in 2006 (Stalenheim et al. 2007, 289). According to the IISS figures, China is now the second-largest defence spender in the world (after the USA), while Japan ranks fifth (after the United Kingdom and France). Both China and Japan are now well ahead of Germany and Russia, the sixth- and seventh-largest spenders in the world. South Korea ranks eleventh in the world (see Table 3.5).

Table 3.3 The military balance, North-east Asia, 2001 and 2006

	Japan		China, People's Repub.		Taiwan		North Korea		South Korea		USA	
	2001	*2006*	*2001*	*2006*	*2001*	*2006*	*2001*	*2006*	*2001*	*2006*	*2001*	*2006*
Defence Budget (US$ billion)	40.4	41.1	47	122	10.9	7.73	2.1	2.3	12.8	23.7	310.5	559
Total Armed Forces (Active)	239,800	240,000	2,310,000	2,255,000	370,000	290,000	1,082,000	1,106,000	683,000	687,000	1,367,700	1,506,757
Army (Active duty)	148,700	148,300	1,600,000	1,600,000	240,000	200,000	950,000	950,000	560,000	420,000	477,800	488,944
Navy												
Aircraft carriers	–	–	–	–	–	–	–	–	–	–	12 (6)	12 (6)
Submarine	16	16	69	58	4	4	26	22	19	20	55 (30)	58 (27)
Destroyers	42	44	21	28	11	11	–	–	6	6	71 (38)	72 (37)
Frigates	12	9	41	48	21	22	3	3	9	9	35 (18)	31 (15)
LRMPA	90	80	4	7	–	–	–	–	8	8	260 (73)	174
Combat Aircraft	297	280	2,900	2,643	482	479	621	590	555	518	3,939 (657) (CINCPAC)	4,199

Source: IISS 2001–02; IISS 2007

Table 3.4 Estimates of the People's Republic of China's defence expenditure, 1991–2007 (US$ bn)

	Official	*IISS*
1991	6.1	18.8
1992	6.8	24.3
1993	7.3	27.4
1994	6.7	28.5
1995	7.5	33.0
1996	8.4	35.4
1997	9.7	36.6
1998	11.0	37.5
1999	12.6	39.5
2000	14.5	42.0
2001	17.0	47.0
2002	20.0	55.3
2003	22.3	55.9
2004	25.0	84.3
2005	29.5	103.0
2006	35.3	122.0
2007	46.7	

Source: IISS

Table 3.5 World's top 12 defence spenders, 2006

	Country	*Defence expenditure (US$ bn)*
1	USA	535.0
2	China, People's Republic	122.0
3	United Kingdom	55.1
4	France	45.3
5	Japan	41.1
6	Germany	35.7
7	Russia	24.9
8	Saudi Arabia	25.4
9	India	22.3
10	South Korea	23.7
11	Italy	15.5
12	Australia	15.1

Source: IISS 2007

The emerging naval arms race

The naval acquisitions have become especially disturbing, with undeniable signs of action-reaction dynamics. East Asia is now embroiled in a serious maritime strategic competition. Highly capable 'blue-water' navies are being developed, with modern surface combatants (destroyers and frigates), aircraft carriers (euphemistically called 'air defence ships' or 'sea control ships'), and new submarines, as well as land-based aircraft for both maritime surveillance and strike. Maritime surveillance and ELINT collection operations are being conducted with increasing intensity and intrusiveness. Hundreds of long-range anti-ship missiles (e.g. Harpoons and Exocets), which require over-the-horizon targeting capabilities, are being acquired. The proliferation of submarine- and ship-based land-attack cruise missiles is also underway.

According to an analysis by Sam Bateman, the current naval acquisition programmes have overtones of arms racing, which were not present in the acquisitions prior to the economic downturn in 1997–98. As he has wrote in 2001:

> The 'first round' of naval expansion was argued away on the basis that it was part of an understandable non-threatening process of modernization. This does not appear to be the case with this 'second round' of naval expansion which appears to be much more clearly posited on assessments of threats posed by other regional countries.
>
> (Bateman 2001, 85)

The expansion of naval forces has been particularly rapid, and the evidence of reciprocal dynamics most apparent, in North-east Asia. As Bateman concluded in 2001 with respect to this sub-region:

> Unfortunately [there is now] an element of acquiring new capabilities competitively to keep up with other navies. Certainly a strong element of technical modernization is present but there is also a large element of competitiveness.
>
> (Bateman 2001, 90)

The Japanese Maritime Self-Defence Force is the most powerful Navy in the Asia-Pacific after the US Navy. Its recent acquisitions include four Kongo-class and two Atago-class Aegis destroyers, the three Osumi amphibious assault ships commissioned between 1998 and 2003, with at least two new Hyuga-class 16DDHs planned, and 10 Oyashio-class submarines. The acquisitions of the Aegis-equipped destroyers have been determined in large part by Chinese and North Korean ballistic missile developments, while other elements are indubitably intended to offset China's growing maritime capabilities.

The Chinese Navy has more than 75 major surface combatants (destroyers and frigates), 62 submarines (including one Xia-class SSBN and six Han-class/Type 091 and Shang-class/Type 093 SSNs), and aspirations to acquire an aircraft carrier capability. Its recent acquisitions include two 8,000-ton Sovremenny-class destroyers purchased from Russia in 2000, with another two ordered in January 2002. Two more 6,000-ton Luhai-class DDGs, as well as two Type 051C Luzhou-class destroyers, were built in the early 2000s. Numerous Type 054A or Jiangkai-II frigates are under construction.

There has been speculation about China's interest in the acquisition of an aircraft carrier since at least the 1980s, usually misinformed and invariably premature, but some such capability now seems fairly close. In 1998 China purchased the former Varyag, a Soviet Kuznetsov-class multi-role carrier (with a displacement of about 33,000 tons) that was only 70% complete when the Soviet Union collapsed. It was delivered in 2002 to the Dalian Shipyard in northern China, where refurbishment of the deck was completed in late 2006, and where it was renamed the Shi Lang (after the mainland Chinese general who conquered Taiwan in 1681). However, whether this will become an operational aircraft carrier or serve as a training and transition platform for an indigenous design yet to be constructed remains unknown (Goodman 2008). In late 2008 Chinese government spokesmen suggested that China would soon proceed with construction of its 'first aircraft carrier'. Defence Ministry officials said that carriers were 'a reflection of a nation's comprehensive power', that China would use any such carrier to 'safeguard its shores and defend sovereignty over coastal areas and territorial seas', that 'the navy of any great power … has the dream to have one or more aircraft carriers', and that 'the question is not whether you have an aircraft carrier, but what you do with your aircraft carrier' (*Straits Times*, 18 November 2008; Wong 2008). In October 2006 China reportedly signed a deal with Russia for the supply of up to 48 Sukhoi Su-33 Flanker-D carrier-capable fighter aircraft. In September 2008 the PLA Daily announced that the first batch of 50 pilot cadets had been inducted at the Dalian Naval Academy to undergo training on 'ship-borne aircraft flight', while other training has reportedly recently also been conducted in the Ukraine.

Taiwan has recently acquired eight Cheng Kung (US Perry)-class frigates (the eighth entered service in 2004), six Kang Ding (French La Fayette)-class frigates, and four refurbished Kidd-class guided missile destroyers. US President George W. Bush announced in April 2001 that the USA would sell Taiwan 'up to eight' conventional submarines; the project made no progress for several years, but in December 2007 Taiwan's legislature approved funding to begin the design process, with at least one US submarine builder eager for the construction contract (Hamilton 2007). Taiwan's acquisitions are avowedly intended to offset China's growing capabilities.

In March 2001, South Korea's President Kim Dae-jung said that 'our navy will have a "strategic task force" for protecting the national interests and international peace [on a] blue water scale' (cited in Bateman 2001, 86). South Korea has constructed the first of at least three KDX-111 Aegis-equipped destroyers; its ninth Chang Bogo submarine was delivered in 2001; it has announced that it will build nine advanced German-designed submarines by 2020; and it is acquiring four Dokdo-class LPX amphibious transport ships. While North Korean capabilities obviously figure centrally in South Korea's force development, it is also clear that there is an element of competitiveness with Japan with respect to its major naval systems.

The situation is rather different in South-east Asia, where the maritime capabilities have been improving significantly both quantitatively and qualitatively, but from a much lower base. South-east Asian countries are acquiring new maritime surveillance and maritime strike capabilities, modern surface combatants (frigates and ocean patrol vessels) and, perhaps most disturbing and reaction-provoking, submarines. Singapore has procured four Challenger-class (refurbished Swedish Sjoormen-class) submarines, the first of which was delivered in 2000 and the fourth (RSS Chieftain) in mid-2001 (Kockums 2001). In late 2000 Malaysia received two submarines from the Netherlands for 'training purposes'. It reportedly now plans to purchase four submarines (*Financial Times*, 27 August 2000; *Straits Times*, 22 April 2001). In 2002 it ordered two French/Spanish Scorpene boats, which were launched in 2007 and 2008 and were to enter service in 2009 (*Asian Defence Journal*, July/August 2007, 23). Some Asian diplomats have characterized Malaysia's move as a response to Singapore's Challenger programme (*Financial Times*, 27 August 2000). The Royal Thai Navy has also proposed the lease of one or two second-hand submarines from Germany 'to keep up with the underwater ambitions of neighbours Malaysia and Singapore' (*The Times of India*, 10 January 2001), but these plans have not been accepted by the government (Wassana 2001). These naval developments in South-east Asia are not significant enough to affect the balance of power in East Asia, but they could easily prove to be destabilizing within the sub-region itself.

Furthermore, there is a real risk of the maritime strategic competition in East Asia 'spilling over into the Indian Ocean' (Bateman 2001, 139).

The proliferation of nuclear weapons and long-range delivery systems

The proliferation of WMD and long-range missile systems is now proceeding much more rapidly and extensively in Asia than in any other part of the world. It is both a much more complicated and a potentially more volatile process than the bipolar superpower strategic nuclear arms race of the Cold War. The proliferation process that is developing in Asia involves multidimensional dynamics. There are several bilateral competitors, some of which are engaged in multiple pairings. The most obvious direct nuclear competition is between India and Pakistan. A nuclear arms race between India and China, which is a real possibility, would be especially disturbing. The expansion of China's nuclear arsenal could also cause other countries in North-east Asia to exercise their own nuclear options. Moreover, the dynamics now involve not only comparative nuclear capabilities, but interactive connections between nuclear postures and developments in other WMD areas (i.e. chemical and biological weapons), and between WMD and conventional capabilities. The situation is further complicated by the possibilities for access to WMD by non-state actors, such as terrorist organizations.

Five of the world's nine nuclear countries (see Table 3.6) are in Asia, including Russia, which still maintains hundreds of nuclear weapons in the Far East, China, India, Pakistan and North Korea (designated by President Bush as a member of 'the axis of evil'). The USA also maintains hundreds of nuclear weapons in the Pacific, as well as hundreds of others based in the USA itself but targeted on China, North Korea and the Russian Far East.

China is the largest nuclear power in Asia, with a stockpile of about 400 nuclear weapons and an active development programme. Official US estimates credit China with only about 150 weapons, but this comprises only deployed 'strategic' missile- and bomber-delivered weapons, with no allowance for tactical weapons (including short-range missiles such as the DF-18) or non-deployed weapons held in reserve. It is likely that China has now overtaken the UK and perhaps even France to become the world's fourth- or even third-largest nuclear power.

Nuclear proliferation has become overt in South Asia since the flurry of Indian and Pakistani tests in May 1998. India might now possess some 120–125 plutonium-based weapons, although some estimates are as low as 50–75. Its current production capability is 6–10 bombs per year. The USA-India agreement on civil nuclear co-operation, approved by the US Congress in October 2008, would allow diversion of India's uranium to reactor fuel and allow production of several dozen weapons a year. Pakistan has produced a substantial stockpile of highly-enriched uranium (HEU)-based weapons; estimates range from about 30 to 60 weapons (Kile et al. 2007, 543).

North Korea conducted its first nuclear test on 9 October 2006 and may have a stockpile of more than 10 weapons, although some estimates credited it with as many as 20 by the end of 2005 (Pike 2005). It is likely that it produced sufficient plutonium for two weapons in the early 1990s, before acceding to the agreed framework in 1994, although some estimates range up to five to six weapons. Another four to six could have been produced with plutonium obtained with the removal of fuel rods from the 5 Mw reactor at Yongbyon from 1994 to 2005, and

Table 3.6 Nuclear weapons inventories, 2007

	Country	Number of weapons	Comments
1	USA	5,045	First detonation in 1945. US stockpile peaked at 32,500 in 1967.
2	Russia	5,614	First detonation in 1949. Stockpile reached 45,000 in 1986.
3	China, People's Republic	490	First detonation in 1964. Inventory includes about 160 IRBM and ICBM warheads, some 50 short-range ballistic missile warheads, 12 SLBM warheads, 150 air-deliverable warheads and some 120 tactical weapons.
4	France	470	Inventory includes 384 SLBM warheads and some 80 air-deliverable weapons.
5	Israel	200	Production began in 1968. More than 25 bombs in September 1973 (Yom Kippur War).
6	United Kingdom	185	160 SLBM warheads (and approx. 25 spares). Had 350 warheads in 1975–81.
7	India	125	First detonation in May 1974. More than 24 weapons in 1990. Five detonations in May 1998.
8	Pakistan	60	Produced first bomb in 1984. Had about eight (unassembled) weapons in 1990. First tests in May 1998.
9	North Korea	10	First detonation 9 October 2006. One to five weapons produced in 1993–94; five to six in 2004–05; and two to three in 2005–06.

Table 3.7 Ballistic missile proliferation in Asia

Country / system	Type	Maximum range (km)	Status
China, People's Republic			
CSS-2 (DF-3/3A)	IRBM	2,800	In service
CSS-3 (DF-4)	IRBM		In service
CSS-4 (DF-5/5A)	ICBM		In service
CSS-5 (DF-21)	MRBM		In service
CSS-8 (M-7)	SRBM	160	In service
CSS-N-3 (JL-1)	SLBM		In service
DF-11 (CSS-7/M-11)	SRBM	300	In service
DF-15 (CSS-6/M-9)	SRBM	600	In service
DF-25	MRBM	1,700	Development
DF-31	ICBM	8,000	Tested
JL-2	SLBM	8,000	Development
India			
Prithvi 1 (SS-150)	SRBM	150	In service
Prithvi 2 (SS-250)	SRBM	250	In service
Prithvi 3 (SS-350)	SRBM	350	Development
Sagrika	SLBM	300	Development
Agni 1	MRBM	1,500	Tested
Agni 2	IRBM	2,500	Production
Agni 3	IRBM	3–5,500	Development
Surya	IRBM	5,500	Development
ASLV	SLV	4,500	In service
GSLV	SLV	14,000	Development
PSLV	SLV	8,000	Development
Japan			
M-3	SLV	4,000	Capability
H-1	SLV	12,000	Capability
H-2	SLV	15,000	Capability
North Korea			
Scud Mod B	SRBM	320	In service
Scud C	SRBM	550	In service
Nodong 1	MRBM	1,000	In service
Nodong 2	MRBM	1,500	Development
Taepodong 1	MRBM	2,000	Tested
Taepodong 2	IRBM	4–6,000	Development
South Korea			
NHK-1	SRBM	250	In service
KSR-1	SRBM	150	Development
NHK-A (Hyon Mu)	SRBM	180	Development
Pakistan			
Hatf 1	BSRBM	100	In service
Hatf 2	SRBM	300	In service
Hatf 3	SRBM	600	Development
M-11 (CSS-7)	SRBM	300	In service
Shaheen 1	MRBM	750	Development
Ghauri (Hatf 5)	MRBM	1,000+	Tested
Taiwan			
Green Bee (Ching Feng)	BSRBM	130	In service
Sky Horse (Tien Ma)	MRBM	950	Development
Viet Nam			
SS-1 Scud B (R-17)	SRBM	300	In service

Source: ACA 2002

Notes: BSRBM is Battlefield Short-Range Ballistic Missile; SLV is space launch vehicle; SRBM is Short-Range Ballistic Missile; MRBM is Medium-Range Ballistic Missile; IRBM is Intermediate-Range Ballistic Missile; SLBM is Submarine-Launched Ballistic Missile; ICBM is Intercontinental-Range Ballistic Missile another two or three after the April 2005 shut-down of the reactor (Niksch 2006). North Korea may also have produced a few uranium-based weapons.

There is also considerable proliferation of ballistic missile technology in the region, or at least in the North-east and South Asia sub-regions (see Table 3.7). China has produced a full suite of intercontinental ballistic missiles (ICBMs), submarine-launched ballistic missiles (SLBMs), intermediate-range ballistic missiles (IRBMs), medium-range ballistic missiles (MRBMs), and short-range, tactical ballistic missiles. Two new road-mobile ICBMs are being developed – the Dong Feng-31 (DF-31), which is likely to have now entered service and which 'will be targeted primarily against Russia and Asia'; and a longer-range solid-propellant ICBM, which will primarily be targeted against the USA (and which replaces the aborted DF-41 programme). China has also exported some short-range ballistic missiles elsewhere in the region (e.g. M-11 missiles, with a range of some 300 km), to Pakistan. China now has some 1,320 ballistic missiles facing Taiwan (Reuters, 1 January 2008), a rapid increase from around 800 in 2006. They comprise DF-11, DF-15 and DF-15A medium-range missiles, with conventional warheads and are based mainly in Fujian Province. North Korea has some 30 Scud B/C and perhaps 15 Nodong missiles. South Korea has some 12 NHK (250 km) ballistic missiles. Taiwan is developing the 950 km range Tien Ma ballistic missile. India has a comprehensive development programme which includes the short-range (150–250 km) Prithvi, the Agni IRBM, and several possible ICBM launchers. Pakistan has flight-tested the short-range Shaheen I and the medium-range Ghauri (1,300 km) ballistic missiles. The dual-capability of many of these missiles would greatly complicate any notional arms control processes.

The relationship between these nuclear weapons and ballistic missile programmes on the one hand and the conventional weapons acquisition programmes on the other hand is difficult to ascertain. At a minimum, they compete for budgetary resources, requiring some trade-offs. None of the Asian nuclear countries have clearly articulated policies for the employment of their nuclear weapons, at least not publicly available, which might illuminate the point in their strategic policies where reliance on conventional weaponry would give way to employment of their nuclear forces.

China, India and Pakistan have each effectively declared their adoption of nuclear 'no first-use' policies, suggesting a requirement for robust conventional capabilities able to balance those of notional adversaries in order to forestall pressures to 'go nuclear' in plausible contingencies.

Cruise missile proliferation

There is a serious danger of cruise missile proliferation in this region. Cruise missiles are technically easier to produce and cheaper to acquire than ballistic missiles. Enabling technologies such as anti-ship cruise missiles (e.g. Exocets and Harpoons), UAVs, GPS satellite navigation systems and small turbojet engines are now widely available. However, the development and deployment of cruise missiles are also more difficult to monitor.

Several countries in East Asia have either begun to indigenously design and develop long-range, land-attack cruise missiles (e.g. China), or to seriously consider the acquisition of such missiles (e.g. Australia). China's Hong Niao family of cruise missiles is armed with both nuclear and conventional warheads, with ranges up to 1,500 km–2,000 km (in the case of the HN-2, which entered service in 1996) and 4,000 km (in the case of the HN-2000, a supersonic version which is currently in development) (Lennox 2000a; Lennox 2000b). Taiwan tested a Hsiungfeng 2E cruise missile in 2007; it may have a range of about 1,000 km, enabling it to reach Shanghai (*Asian Defence Journal*, October 2007, 53).

The US Navy, of course, maintains about 4,000 Tomahawk land-attack cruise missiles, which it has used against six countries since 1991. In August 2000 the US Air Force confirmed that it had moved 'an unspecified number' of conventional air-launched cruise missiles to Guam, which USAF officials said 'will allow the USA to respond more quickly to crises, particularly in the Asia-Pacific region' (*Jane's Defence Weekly*, 6 September 2000, 22).

In South Asia, India is in the process of developing and producing a variety of cruise missiles, with co-operation from Russian defence industries. These include the Kh-35 Uran anti-ship cruise missile, the 3M-54E Klub anti-ship missile, and the PJ-10 supersonic medium-range cruise missile (which was first successfully tested in June 2001). Both the Klub and the PJ-10 could be redesigned to serve as long-range (3,000 km) land-attack cruise missiles, and can potentially carry nuclear as well as conventional warheads (Raghuvanshi 2001; Jasinski 2002).

Asia and the global arms trade

Since the Asian defence build-up began in the mid-1980s, Asian countries have accounted for a higher proportion of global arms purchases than their share of global expenditure – 20% of transfers compared to 11% of expenditure in 1984, about 33% of purchases compared to 20% of world expenditure in 1994, 41% of transfers compared to 17.75% in 1998, and 45.15% of purchases compared to 18.7% of expenditure in 2002. Many countries in Asia have substantial indigenous defence industries, but they are still much more dependent on foreign purchases than the world's other major defence spenders. Within Asia there are, of course, significant sub-regional differences, particularly with respect to the arms exports side of the ledger. South Asia does not figure among the world's suppliers of defence hardware, and neither does Japan. On the other hand, there are voracious importers in each sub-region.

Asian countries, with the exception of China, are not major arms exporters. China is the only Asian country in the world's top 10 exporters. There are only six Asian countries in the world's top 40. A ranking by SIPRI of arms exporters in the five-year period 2002–06 placed China eighth, with exports amounting to $2.134 billion (in constant 1990 terms) over that period; this is about 6.6% of the US figure, and less than half the UK figure. South Korea is the second highest Asian arms exporter, but ranks only 19th in the world, with sales of $262m. over the five-year period. Australia is ranked 27th, with exports amounting to only $126m. Indonesia ranks 32nd, Singapore 36th and North Korea 37th, but their exports each amounted to less than $100m. over that same five-year period (Wezeman et al. 2007, 422–3).

On the other hand, Asian countries dominate the lists of the world's major arms importers. China and India are the world's first and second arms importers by a large margin. Over the five-year period 2002–06, China's imports amounted to $14.6 billion and India's were $10.15 billion (in constant 1990 dollar terms). Together, they accounted for nearly a quarter of the world total (23.24%). In addition to China and India, six other Asian countries are in the world's top 20 importers: South Korea ($3.884 billion) ranked fifth in 2002–06 and Australia ($3.461 billion) came sixth, with Taiwan ($2.17 billion), Pakistan ($2.038), Japan ($2 billion) and Singapore ($1.295 billion) ranking between 12th and 20th. Together, the eight countries accounted for nearly half (46.6%) of the world total (Wezeman et al. 2007, 418).

In North-east Asia, Japan and South Korea get most of their imports from the USA. Given their strong ship-building sectors, the major imports are aircraft and missile systems. Japan, for example, acquired its F-16 and F-15 fighters from the USA. South Korea's nine Chang Bogo (Type 209) have been built and its nine Type 214 submarines are being built in South Korea under licence to a German company.

Taiwan gets virtually all of its major capital equipment from the USA (including its F-16 fighters, its six E-2C Hawkeye AEW aircraft, 12 P-3C Orions, eight Cheng Kung or US Perry-class frigates, and its six Patriot PAC-3 air/missile defence batteries), although it has indigenously produced several significant weapons systems, including the Indigenous Defence Fighter (IDF) and various missile systems. There have been no major non-US foreign sales to Taiwan since France supplied six La Fayette-class frigates and 60 Mirage 2000–5 fighters in the early 1990s.

China's principal supplier of weapons systems continues to be Russia, which has supplied Su-27SK fighters, Su-30MKK fighters, Sovremenny-class destroyers, and Project 636 Kilo-class submarines. In the decade from 1991 to 2001, more than 90% of China's imports were from Russia, but in more recent years China has also acquired important weapons systems from Ukraine (especially missile-related systems), Israel, France, Italy, Germany and the UK.

Asian countries figure even more prominently in lists of arms transfers to 'developing countries', where the relative economic burden is greatest, and where there are human security concerns as well as arms race issues. The US Congressional Research Service regularly produces reports on arms transfers to 'developing nations', which in Asia means every country except for Japan, Australia and New Zealand. Six Asian countries were in the top 10 'developing country arms importers' in 2002–05: China, Taiwan, India, South Korea, Malaysia and Pakistan (Grimmett 2006, 67). Four Asian countries were in the top 10 in 2004–07: India, Pakistan, China and South Korea; the other six were all in the Middle East, which in recent years has outpaced Asia in terms of arms imports. In 2007 India, Pakistan, South Korea, China and Taiwan were in the top 10 (Grimmett 2008, 54–5).

The prospects

Asia has now been involved in a sustained build-up of defence capabilities for two decades, hardly affected by economic tribulations. However, the character of the acquisition dynamics began to change around the end of the 1990s. Whereas the acquisitions in the first decade could be explained by and large in terms of modernization, they have in some places in the past decade involved substantial competitive elements. This combination of increasing capabilities and action-reaction is the essence of arms-racing. It may still not be the dominant driver of the acquisitions throughout the region, but it is playing an increasingly significant role in some sub-regions, most especially with respect to naval acquisitions in North-east Asia. Even in South-east Asia, arms-racing behaviour has been manifest in a couple of areas (fighter aircraft and submarines) in Singaporean and Malaysian acquisitions (Tan 2004, 4 and 28).

It is likely that over the next one to two decades, the role of arms-racing will continue to increase. Action-reaction generates its own momentum. Further, there are no arms control regimes whatsoever in Asia that might constrain or constrict acquisitions. Moreover, prospective regional security dynamics, including prospective arms racing, will be much more complex than those which obtained in the old bipolar Cold War situation. There are none of the distinctive categories, milestones and firebreaks which were carefully constructed during the Cold War to constrain escalatory processes and promote crisis stability. Now, there are also interactions between conventional weapons acquisition programmes on the one hand and developments with WMD and long-range delivery systems on the other hand. South Korea and Japan have responded to the development of ballistic missiles by China and North Korea by greatly enhancing their airborne intelligence collection and early warning capabilities and their land- and sea-based theatre missile defence (TMD) capabilities. US nuclear strategy is moving to permit virtually commutual employment of nuclear forces, precision conventional capabilities and information operations (IO), and to permit the use of nuclear weapons in otherwise non-nuclear situations. In this environment, with many parties and many levels and directions of interactions, the possibilities for calamity are high.

Bibliography

Anthony, Ian, Paul Claesson, Gerd Hagmeyer-Gaverus, Elisabeth Sköns and Siemon T. Wezeman, 'Volume of Imports of Major Conventional Weapons', for Table 13B.1, in *SIPRI Yearbook 1994*, Oxford, Oxford University Press/ Stockholm International Peace Research Institute, 1994

Anthony, Ian, Agnes Courrades Allenbeck, Paolo Miggiano, Elisabeth Sköns and Herbert Wulf, 'The Trade in Major Conventional Weapons', in *SIPRI Yearbook 1992*, Oxford, Oxford University Press/Stockholm International Peace Research Institute, 1992

Arms Control Association (ACA), 'Missile Proliferation in South Asia: India and Pakistan's Ballistic Missile Inventories', March 2002, www.armscontrol.org/factsheets/agni

Ball, Desmond, *Signals Intelligence in the Post-Cold War Era: Developments in the Asia-Pacific Region*, Singapore, Institute of Southeast Asian Studies, 1993

——'Arms and Affluence: Military Acquisitions in the Asia-Pacific Region', *International Security*, Vol. 18, No. 3, Winter 1993/94

——*Developments in Signals Intelligence and Electronic Warfare in Southeast Asia*, Working Paper No. 290, Strategic and Defence Studies Centre, Australian National University, Canberra, December 1995

——*Burma's Military Secrets: Signals Intelligence (SIGINT) from the Second World War to Civil War and Cyber Warfare*, Bangkok, White Lotus, 1998

——*The New Submarine Combat Information System and Australia's Emerging Information Warfare Architecture*, Working Paper No. 359, Strategic and Defence Studies Centre, Australian National University, Canberra, May 2001

——'China Pursues Space-based Intelligence Gathering Capabilities', *Jane's Intelligence Review*, Vol. 15, No. 12, December 2003

——'Intelligence Collection Operations and EEZs: The Implications of New Technology', *Marine Policy*, No. 28, 2004

——'An Australian Cyber-warfare Centre', in Gary Waters, Desmond Ball and Ian Dudgeon, *Australia and Cyber-warfare*, Canberra, ANU E Press, Australian National University, 2008

Ball, Desmond and Euan Graham, *Japanese Airborne SIGINT Capabilities*, Working Paper No. 353, Strategic and Defence Studies Centre, Australian National University, Canberra, December 2000

Barker, Geoffrey, 'RAAF Spy Planes Secretly Watch Indonesia', *Australian Financial Review*, 11 May 2000

Bateman, W. S. G., *Strategic and Political Aspects of the Law of the Sea in East Asian Seas*, PhD Dissertation, Australian Defence Force Academy, University of New South Wales, Canberra, 2001

Bostock, Ian, 'ADF Launches Search for TUAV', *Jane's Defence Weekly*, 10 January 2001

Clad, James and Patrick Marshall, 'Southeast Asia's Quiet Arms Race', *Chicago Tribune*, 23 May 1992

Dawnay, Ivo, 'Beijing Launches Computer Virus War on the West', *The Age* (Melbourne), 16 June 1997

Defence Intelligence Organisation (DIO), *Defence Economic Trends in the Asia-Pacific 1997*, Canberra, Australian Government Publishing Service, 1997

——*Defence Economic Trends in the Asia-Pacific 1998*, Canberra, Australian Government Publishing Service, 1998

——*Defence Economic Trends in the Asia-Pacific 1999*, Canberra, Australian Government Publishing Service, 1999

Eshel, Tamir and Damian Kemp, 'Singapore Company in UAV Deal With Israel', *Jane's Defence Weekly*, 2 December 1998

Fisher, Richard D., Jr, 'PLAAF Equipment Trends', paper presented at the National Defense University Conference on PLA and Chinese Society in Transition, 30 October 2001, www.ndu.edu/inss/China_Center/RFischer.htm

Fong, Kelvin, 'Export Fighters for Asia-Pacific Air Forces', *Asian Defence Journal*, June 2007

Gill, Bates, 'Trends in the Import and Licensed Production of Major Conventional Weapons in East Asia, 1984–93', for Table 13E.1, in *SIPRI Yearbook 1994*, Oxford, Oxford University Press/Stockholm International Peace Research Institute, 1994

Goodman, David J., 'A Chinese Aircraft Carrier: Not If but When', *New York Times*, 17 November 2008, thelede.blogs.nytimes.com/2008/11/17/a-chinese-aircraft-carrier-not-if-but-when

Grimmett, Richard F., 'Conventional Arms Transfers to Developing Nations, 1998–2005', Congressional Research Service, Library of Congress, Washington, DC, 23 October 2006

——'Conventional Arms Transfers to Developing Nations, 2000–2007', Congressional Research Service, Library of Congress, Washington, DC, 23 October 2008

Hagelin, Bjorn, Pieter D. Wezeman, Siemon T. Wezeman and Nicholas Chipperfield, 'International Arms Transfers', in *SIPRI Yearbook 2003: Armaments, Disarmament and International Security*, Oxford, Oxford University Press/Stockholm International Peace Research Institute, 2003

Hamilton, Jesse, 'Taiwan OKs Sub Money', *The Hartford Courant*, 21 December 2007, www.ct.gov/oma/cwp/view.asp?q=411616&a=3422

IISS, *The Military Balance*, International Institute for Strategic Studies (IISS), London, successive annual editions

Jacobs, Keith, 'PLAN: Rapid Frigate Growth', *Asia-Pacific Defence Reporter*, April 2007

Jasinski, Michael, 'Russia and India Step up Cruise Missile Co-operation', *Jane's Intelligence Review*, March 2002

Kaplan, David E. and Andrew Marshall, *The Cult at the End of the World: The Incredible Story of Aum*, London, Arrow, 1996

Karniol, Robert, 'Singapore Boosts SIGINT Using C-130 Transports', *Jane's Defence Weekly*, 17 September 1997

Kerr, Julian, 'AMRAAM Release Nears', *Asia-Pacific Defence Reporter*, March/April 2002

Kile, Shannon N., Vitaly Y. Fedchenko and Hans M. Kristensen, 'World Nuclear Forces, 2007', in *SIPRI Yearbook 2007*, Oxford, Oxford University Press/Stockholm International Peace Research Institute, 2007

Kockums, *Some Brief Facts About the Riken Project*, May 2001, www.kockums.se/News/oldnews/riken.html

La Franchi, Peter, 'Australian Orion Spy Exposed', *Flight International*, 9–15 May 2000

Lake, Darren, 'South Korea Announces Record High Budget', *Jane's Defence Weekly*, 4 July 2001a

——'Taiwan Sets Up IW Command', *Jane's Defence Weekly*, 10 January 2001b

Lennox, Duncan, 'China's New Cruise Missile Programme "Racing Ahead"', *Jane's Defence Weekly*, 12 January 2000a

——'More Details on Chinese Cruise Missile Programme', *Jane's Defence Weekly*, 6 September 2000b

Liebelt, Simone and Sean Burton, 'Video Link: Our Analysts Assess UAV Images', *Air Force News*, 28 August 2003

Lintner, Bertil, 'Burma Road: China's Economic Push Southward Worries Neighbours', *Far Eastern Economic Review*, 6 November 1997

——'Burma MiGs Spell Trouble', *Far Eastern Economic Review*, 2 August 2001

Maples, Lt Gen. Michael D., 'Current and Projected National Security Threats to the United States', Statement for the US Senate Armed Services Committee, Washington, DC, 27 February 2007, armed-services.senate.gov/statement/2007/February/Maples%2002-27-07.pdf

McPhedran, Ian, 'RAAF Sends Spy Planes Over Timor', *The Courier Mail* (Brisbane), 12 May 2000

Mingi Hyun, 'LPX Dokdo Leads US-ROK Exercise', 2 December 2007, maritimeasia.blogspot.com/2007/12/lpx-dokdo-leads-us-rok-exercise.html

Minnick, Wendell, 'Taiwan Upgrades Cyber Warfare', *Jane's Defence Weekly*, 20 December 2000

Nelson, Brendan, 'Aviation History as Global Hawk Completes US-Australia Flight', *Media Release*, 24 April 2001

Niksch, Larry A., *North Korea's Nuclear Weapons Program*, Congressional Research Service, Library of Congress, Washington, DC, 5 October 2006

Pike, John, 'Nuclear Weapons Program – North Korea', 28 April 2005, www.ct.gov/oma/cwp/view.asp?q=411616&a=3422

Raghuvanshi, Vivek, 'Secret India-Russia Pact Produces Cruise Missile', *Defense News*, 18–24 June 2001

Ricketts, Peter, 'Special Mission Aircraft: Same Result, Lower Cost', *Asia-Pacific Defence Reporter*, March/April 2002

Shaoguang Wang, 'The Military Expenditure of China, 1989–98', in *SIPRI Yearbook 1999*, Oxford, Oxford University Press/Stockholm International Peace Research Institute, 1999

Sherman, Jason, 'Report: China Developing Force to Tackle Information Warfare', *Defense News*, 27 November 2000

Sikes, Jonathan, 'Asia Puts its Wealth in Military', *Washington Times*, 12 February 1990

Sköns, Elisabeth, Agnes Courades Allebeck, Evamaria Loose-Weintraub and Peter Stalenheim, Petter, 'Military Expenditure', in *SIPRI Yearbook 1999*, Oxford, Oxford University Press/Stockholm International Peace Research Institute, 1999

Stalenheim, Petter, Catalina Perdomo and Elisabeth Sköns, 'Military Expenditure', in *SIPRI Yearbook 2007*, Oxford, Oxford University Press/Stockholm International Peace Research Institute, 2007

Stratfor, 'Amphibious Warships: The Real East Asian Arms Race', Stratfor, 5 April 2007

Tai Ming Cheung, 'Loaded Weapons: China in Arms Buying Spree in Former Soviet Union', *Far Eastern Economic Review*, 3 September 1992

Tan, Andrew T. H., *Force Modernisation Trends in Southeast Asia*, Working Paper No. 59, Institute of Defence and Strategic Studies (IDSS), Singapore, January 2004

Tjahjadi, Victor, 'Russian Arms Delivered to Indo', *Herald Sun* (Melbourne), 27 August 2003, www.heraldsun.news.com.au/common/story_page/ 0,5478,7081820%255E1702,00.html

United States Pacific Command, *Asia-Pacific Economic Update, January 2000*, Honolulu, United States Pacific Command, 2000

Arms Control and Disarmament Agency (US ACDA), *World Military Expenditures and Arms Transfers 1995*, 1995, dosfan.lib.uic.edu/acda/wmeat95/wmeatcov.htm.

US Department of Defense, *Annual Report on the Military Power of the People's Republic of China: Report to Congress Pursuant to the FY2000 National Defense Authorization Act*, 12 July 2002, www.defenselink.mil/news/Jul2002/d20020712china.pdf

Wassana Nanuam, 'Navy Proposal on Subs Sunk', *Bangkok Post*, 6 March 2001

Wezeman, Siemon T., Mark Bromley, Damien Fruchart, Paul Holtman and Pieter D. Wezeman, 'International Arms Transfers', in *SIPRI Yearbook 2007*, Oxford, Oxford University Press/Stockholm International Peace Research Institute, 2007

Wong, Edward, 'China Signals More Interest in Building Aircraft Carrier', *New York Times*, 23 December 2008

4 Friends in need or comrades in arms

The dilemma in the Sino-Russian weapons business

You Ji

The People's Republic of China's military acquisition from the international arms market has declined steeply in the last two years: from the peak of US$2.2 billion in 2002 to $100m. in 2006, and $170m. in 2007. Since 90% of China's foreign purchase comes from Russia, this has raised the world's attention to the problems of Sino-Russian arms trade (SIPRI 2008). In contrast, Russia's sustained increase in overall arms sales in the world market, with minimum Chinese contribution, testifies that it has successfully found alternative markets. The question is then a strategic one: does this represent a hiccup or a pattern of future developments? This chapter argues that there are structural attributes to the slowdown; therefore, it is not just a hiccup. The primary reason is that the overall Sino-Russian relations have been strongly influenced by factors of expediency that have impacted on bilateral arms relations since they began in 1991. When the conditions upon which this expediency rests change substantially, the arms trade will reflect this change, especially in terms of altered supply and demand relations. This is what has happened in the last few years. This chapter will present a detailed analysis of the changing conditions for the Sino-Russian arms trade.

On the other hand, this chapter also argues that it is too early to predict that the current sluggish Sino-Russian arms trade constitutes a pattern of future development. Clearly both countries value their arms business. At the political level it has become a symbol of the Sino-Russian strategic partnership, something Beijing cherishes in offsetting Western pressure (Pan Guang 2008, 239). Technologically, China's R&D and innovative capability remains weak, despite the visible improvement. The People's Liberation Army (PLA) still needs Russian weaponry in key defence areas. However, it has adopted new approaches to obtain it. Instead of focusing on hardware acquisition, it will more vigorously seek technological transfers. The nature of change can be seen from China's effort to facilitate a fundamental shift from the current pattern of one-way arms purchase to multiple ways of co-operation, including joint research and development. In the final analysis, Sino-Russian military co-operation will continue with arms trade as a key component.

Foreign acquisition: addressing the transitional vacuum

China's abrupt halt on arms purchases from Russia has caught many analysts by surprise. In fact there has been virtually no major arms deal between the two countries since 2006 (*Huanqiushibao*, 27 May 2008; *ITAR-TASS*, 26 May 2008). The reasons are manifold. The most important one is that China sees foreign procurement as a quick fix, not a solution. It is used to address a transitional vacuum in the PLA's transformation, which means that the bulk of the inventory has become obsolete but it takes years for self-developed replacements to enter service. In the meantime, security threats or challenges are mounting. Today, with decades of concentrated research and development efforts, the PLA has effectively tackled this transitional challenge and the need to buy more Russian arms is no longer as pressing.

Russian arms as a quick fix measure

China's military equipment policy has long been defined as a middle course: most weaponry is upgraded through generational change but its research and development targets technologies of one or two generations ahead (You 1999a). This is a rational strategy for a backward military facing multiple security challenges, especially the prospect of a war with a superpower. However, this strategy is inherently risky. Transformation through generational change is slow and may leave the PLA lagging further behind its rivals. The generation leap in research and development can be risky due to China's weak technological foundation. In addition, the first Gulf War instilled in the PLA high command a huge sense of urgency to catch up with the global trend of military transformation, or revolution in military affairs (RMA), based on the acquisition of high-tech arms (Cheng Bojiang and Perry 1998, 50).

Under the circumstances, foreign arms procurement becomes a crucial measure for the PLA in bridging the gap between a zero stock of high-tech weapons and a long lead time for indigenous development. Indeed, when the PLA started to import Russian weaponry in 1991, it was at a dangerous transitional vacuum, as mentioned earlier.

Moreover, the US show of force close to the Taiwan Strait in March 1996 and its bombing of the Chinese embassy in 1999 added a military dimension to the already tense Sino-US relations. Taipei's push of independence since the mid-1990s under successive pro-independence leaders further highlighted Beijing's perceived threat of war and the urgency for advanced weapons. In 1999 China's top leadership took a strategic decision to 'accelerate war preparation' (Qian Guoliang 2000, 6). The upsurge of weapons acquisition from Russia in the first half of this decade should be seen in this context, as Beijing's military response to Taiwan's opposition DDP's call for a statehood referendum in 2008 (You Ji 2006b, 237).

Russia was the only country from which China could obtain such weapons, although very limited weaponry leaks to China from other sources, such as from the European Union (EU) states and Israel. Yet China is always wary of dependence on any foreign power for its military modernization. Beijing's great push on the EU to lift the arms embargo is aimed at diversifying its sources of weapons procurement from the world market, which would help reduce its reliance on Russia for advanced hardware. Moreover, the economic cost would be prohibitively high if modernization of a force of 3m. were based on foreign purchases. Technologically, the difficulty of integrating the various foreign components into complete and effective weapons systems is tremendous. In short, the PLA cannot afford to count on any overseas supplier to improve its overall capabilities.

Therefore, China saw Russian weaponry as a quick fix from the very beginning, despite the importance it attaches to them (Yao Yanjin and Liu Jingxian 1995, 159). At the time the PLA's top priority was to have them so it could learn to handle high-tech weapons a decade earlier than if it had to develop them indigenously (Liu Huaqing 2004). For instance, the significance of the Su-27 deal to the PLA lies less in obtaining a better aircraft than in the unprecedented opportunity of operating a third generation weapons system. Without a platform like the Su-27, the PLA Air Force (PLAAF) could only explore in books the theory of long-range air control missions and the importance of avionics in modern air warfare.

The specific functions of Russian arms

In practical terms, Russian weapons serve several functions. First, they help the PLA tackle its weakest link in war preparation against high-tech military powers. For instance, all of China's potential adversaries had third-generation combat aircraft before the PLA acquired similar ones in the 1990s. This 'time lag' means that the PLAAF could not attain air control vis-à-vis its enemies, as its obsolete aircraft (without BOR capabilities) were able to engage the enemy only long after being already a perfect target of the adversary. This is also true of the PLA Navy (PLAN).

Until recently, all the indigenously developed destroyers had no area air defence systems. This cast serious doubts about the Navy's blue water strategy and capabilities. The Russian destroyer, Sovremenny, was the first warship that gave the PLAN limited area air defence capabilities.

Secondly, Russian weaponry provides hardware for reverse technological engineering and shortens the lag time for China's own research and development. Although most weapons that China bought from Russia were vintage 1980s technology, they served as the best prototypes for the PLA to emulate when it attempted to develop its own third-generation systems. For instance, the licensed production of the Su-27 has offered a valuable opportunity for the Chinese to learn how to design and produce the most sophisticated modern combat aircraft by itself. The J-10 is a success story of the Chinese producing a 3.5 generation combat aircraft indigenously while absorbing the best foreign technologies. As all the Western militaries are still operating similar weapons systems, China has narrowed its technological gap with the West in this respect.

The third function is that the weapons improve the PLA's combat readiness, with its elite units equipped and trained with advanced Russian weaponry. China's war preparation has realistic objectives: it will not fight an all-out war with the major powers. The strategy is designed to create conditions for a political resolution to protect China's sovereignty (Zhang and Shi 2002, 43). Since the most likely form of PLA military action would be limited regional wars, it is not necessary for the entire force to go high-tech in one stroke. Only a proportion of its best troops need to be equipped with the best available weapons in order to deal with the worst-case scenarios. These so-called 'fist units' would be ready for actions that are perceived to be limited in scale and duration and thus buy time for the PLA to transform in its entirety in a gradual manner. Therefore, Russian arms help the PLA reconcile the dilemma of being unable to modernize the whole of its forces. Selectively adding crucial foreign offensive capabilities is the most cost-effective way to address the PLA's obsolescence. Foreign purchase thus gives China time to concentrate on building a powerful economic base for its future overall military modernization.

Russian arms sales and PLA transformation

Russian arms have significantly contributed to the PLA's transformation, especially to that of the special services of the PLAAF and the PLAN. The overwhelming proportion of Russian procurement has gone to these two services and this shows where the priority for foreign purchase is. Indeed, the PLA has a clear vision of its most likely war actions: maritime operations in the West Pacific that require both air and naval superiority (Yang Jinshan 2004, 31). It is largely due to Russia's weaponry that the two services achieved the initial change in their force structure, deployment posture and training reforms in the 1990s.

The Russian contribution to PLAAF modernization

Before the PLAAF obtained the Su-27 jetfighters and Il-78 in-flight refuelling tankers, it was a typically inland air force for the mission of territorial defence. Except for obsolete H-6s (a medium-range semi-strategic bomber with 1960s Soviet technology), the radius of all other aircraft in the PLAAF's inventory was no more than 500 km (Allen and Pollack 1995, 123). This means that the depth of China's air defence was extremely shallow. Moreover, it had virtually no platforms to deliver ordnance beyond the country's immediate land and maritime borders.

This posture of defensive defence is completely out of the step with the age of high-tech and information warfare. In time of war, the enemy's aircraft and naval vessels can approach China's key political and military targets without worrying about being intercepted from a distance by China's jetfighters, which could only engage their counterparts close to home airports due to their lack of beyond horizon combat capabilities and their limited flying radius. The PLAAF substantially revised its doctrine in the late 1990s, stipulating that it should be transformed from a homeland tactical force to a strategic force capable of launching offensive operations against the enemy's defence depth (You Ji 1999b).

Thus, an extended radius of operations is the key for the PLAAF to realizing this strategic change from a defensive air force to an offensive one. This has been the main reason why the top PLA command opted for the Su-27 instead of buying the MiG-29 that was proposed to Chinese leaders at the beginning of Sino-Russian arms trade in 1990 (Taylor 1995, 213). Another important consideration for PLA commanders was the need to dispatch the combat aircraft to potential war zones in the South China Sea and waters to the east of Taiwan island, which requires the air force to operate at a distance of about 1,500 km. If not for the importation of the Su-27s and Su-30s, China would have to wait for another 15 years before it could operate at this distance. The advanced avionics and the superb manoeuvrability of the two aircraft filled a huge vacuum in China's aviation technology. Their on-board medium- and long-range air-to-air missiles partially rectified the PLAAF's weakness in that it had no over-the-horizon capability to defend itself if attacked over distance.

More importantly, the Russian aircraft helped the PLAAF realize its force restructuring, which suits its doctrine of launching both defensive and offensive air campaigns (Liu Guangzhi 2003, 49). With newly gained capabilities, the PLAAF has visibly altered its emphasis on homeland defence to engage in 'outside territorial attacks'. The large transport airplanes of Il-76 and the refuelling tankers of Il-78 have substantially improved the PLAAF's strategic lift capability. The PLAAF today has the largest number of third-generation combat aircraft in Asia, owing to about 350 Russian aircraft plus over 100 J-10s and FC-1s. By 2020, the number of modern combat aircraft will increase to the level of all Asian air forces combined.

Russian arms and PLAN modernization

The same can be said about PLAN modernization. For a long time, the Navy's 1987 blue water strategy was just a set of abstract concepts, without real capabilities to sustain it (You Ji 2006a, 71–94). In fact, a strategy does not drive force transformation; only technology does. Therefore, the PLAN's real transformation towards an IT-RMA force did not get started until it procured Sovremenny destroyers and Kilo submarines in the second half of the 1990s. Indeed, it is quite fortunate for the Chinese that the St Petersburg Shipyard was also desperate to sell, as it was in huge need of new orders that the Russian military could not place. This made it easier for a deal to be struck in 1996. The PLA acquired two Sovremenny destroyers at $400m. apiece. Sovremenny is a specialized surface warfare ship the displacement of which, at 7,900 tons, is comparable to the US Navy's Arleigh Burke-class (8,300 tons) and the Japanese Kongo-class (8,400 tons). As described by the US Department of Defense, it is the best destroyer the Soviet Union has ever made. Its impressive firepower includes eight supersonic, active homing, medium-range SS-N-22 Sunburn anti-ship missiles (speed mach 2.5, range 90–120 km), which have a downlink terminal seeker that can be programmed to manoeuvre and select a carrier in a naval battle group, and can evade the US Aegis/Standard RIM-67-equipped cruisers and destroyers that protect US carriers. Sovremenny deeply impressed the Chinese also because of its integrated air defence system, which is a significant weakness in PLAN major surface combatants. The system can deal with multiple air threats simultaneously, with a digital fire control system and 44 short-to-medium range SA-N-7 Gadfly SAM missiles and two fast-reload launchers (Kintworth 1997, 6).

China bought four Sovremenny destroyers not just for its supersonic Sunburn anti-ship missiles (designed to strike aircraft carriers), but also to serve as a high-tech platform for the PLAN to learn how to handle a large multi-purpose warship. The latter purpose was actually the primary rationale for the deal. The Sovremenny destroyer was the first PLAN warship that had area air-defence missiles, comprehensive command, control and radar systems, and sophisticated anti-submarine warfare (ASW) facilities. She thus fulfilled the dual role of filling a capability gap against potential adversaries as well as functioning as a training tool for the PLAN to acquire basic skills in order to manage its future indigenous heavy destroyers.

The Kilo submarines serve similar dual purposes. They are so quiet that they pose a realistic threat to US carrier groups within the second island chain in the West Pacific. Deploying just eight of them in waters east to Taiwan island, the PLAN could mount a seamless blockade against the two international ports there. The level of deterrence is thus very high (Liao Wenzhong 2002). Kilo technology has also helped the PLA to manage its new 039 submarines, especially in terms of mastering Air Independent Propelling systems.

The PLAN has positioned itself as a regional navy but with beyond-region power projection capabilities (Liu Yijian 2004, 233). This means that the normal area of PLAN activity is within the first island chain in the West Pacific, but it should have the capability to engage the enemy fleet in other parts of the world, especially for sea lines of communications (SLOC) operations in the Indian Ocean. The key to realizing this goal is to form a number of ocean-going fleets centred on warships with large displacements and supported by specialized vessels such as area air defence destroyers or ASW destroyers. To achieve this objective, the first step in force transformation is to change the currently light structure of the navy. Before the incorporation of the Sovremenny in 1999, the PLAN had only one destroyer with a displacement exceeding 5,000 tons. In combat terms, the entire navy could only operate in coastal waters. With the rapid addition of major combatants into the force structure since this decade, at no fewer than 12, the PLAN has made visible progress in this regard. All of these ships have incorporated Russian weaponry. The PLAN's Somalia escort operations in 2008 shed light on the basic flotilla formation upon which larger expedition fleets are to be built.

The ultimate symbol of the PLAN becoming a true blue water power is, however, carrier battle groups. Beijing's political leadership froze the Navy's aircraft carrier proposal in the 1990s, as it believed that the issue of building a carrier was not just about adding a piece of naval equipment. It was related to China's overall foreign policy and defence strategy. For instance, Beijing has to consider the responses of regional countries.[1] However, upon entering the new century, there have emerged many official confirmations of such a project. Lieutenant-General Zhang Yuanchuan, head of China's defence industry in charge of the carrier project, told the media on 15 March 2008 that China was developing an indigenous carrier and that the research and development was being smoothly carried out (*Strategic Observer* 2008, 15). Qian Lihua, director of the foreign affairs office of the Ministry of Defense, made it clear that any major power in the world should have the natural right to build an aircraft carrier. A few years earlier, several Chinese generals had also revealed to the media that the PLA was busy with the research and development of aircraft carriers and it had already made technological breakthroughs for the projects.[2]

China is studying key carrier technologies, such as elevator, landing arrester and steam catapults, by itself. However, it has benefited considerably from studying Russia's carrier design, structure and other related technologies starting from the four carriers acquired by China for the purpose of scrap (Story and You Ji 2008). The conversion of the Russian carrier Voyage into a trainer platform (to be completed before the end of the decade) has been particularly useful for China's eventual operation of a carrier (*Jane Defense Weekly*, 5 November 2008, 32). Thus, without Russia's contribution in this regard, the PLAN's carrier programme would have experienced further delays. Indeed Russian technology has helped the PLAN transform itself into a high-tech navy at least one decade earlier than otherwise would have been the case.

Russian arms sales and Sino-Russian military co-operation

It is apparent that China and Russia entertained different goals for the arms trade when it began in 1991. Yeltsin's Western-leaning policy was a concern to Beijing, and the Cold War legacy still influenced Moscow, which saw China as an adversary. There was virtually no shared political and ideological foundation for military co-operation. Yet a solid relationship of convenience began smoothly owing to their shared perception of the Western threat (Menon 1997). This relationship may be long-lasting if the international environment remains suitable. NATO's diminution of Russia's strategic space through its eastward expansion and Russia's entry into Georgia in August 2008 have helped change the nature of its relations with the West. Moscow needs support from other non-Western powers. China itself has had an uneasy relationship with the West and increasingly faces a long-term concerted reaction of the West toward its rise in the 21st century (Ikenbery 2008). This indicates that Sino-Russian military co-operation will continue both in depth and breadth in the years ahead.

Saviour of the Russian defence industries

Russian arms were certainly a windfall for the PLA in the early 1990s amidst its transitional vacuum and Western arms embargo, as discussed above. For the Russians, the newly found Chinese market was also a windfall. Following the demise of the USSR, the Russian Defence Industries (RDI) in 1993 could only operate at 10% of its capacity due to a lack of domestic orders. Half the defence firms were closed due to bankruptcy. International orders from traditional buyers disappeared almost completely (*ITAR-TASS*, 7 December 1993). The Chinese monetary transfusion was essential for the RDI to survive and revive. In that decade, China alone provided half of all sales income for the RDI.

The Chinese arms purchase also provided essential funds to help fund Russia's programme of converting defence production into civilian production through arms sales. Russia's dominant share in the Chinese market and the seemingly insatiable Chinese demand encouraged the RDI to set exports to China as a top priority to stimulate its recovery. After years of hard promotion, the RDI achieved overall overseas arms sales of $7.5 billion in 2007, reaching the average annual sales of the USSR era (Abdullav 2008). In 2008 Russia further increased its global arms sales. According to Russian Deputy Prime Minister Sergei Ivanov, Russia's arms sales exceeded $8 billion in 2008, up nearly 15% on 2007. Ivanov stated that the growth of this sector of the economy showed no sign of slowing down, despite the on-going global economic meltdown. Presently, Russia has over $33 billion in orders for various weapons systems. It has targeted developing countries for the promotion of its arms. For instance, Moscow announced it would give Lebanon 10 MiG-29 fighter jets, apparently as a gift (*New York Times*, 16 December 2008; *The Guardian*, 18 December 2008). Arms sales are part of Russia's long term strategic considerations vis-à-vis the West (Blank 1997). Without China's large orders at the beginning of the 1990s, the RDI would not be prospering today.

Arms sales – a mechanism of influence

There is no doubt that the arms trade has helped to consolidate overall Sino-Russian relations. Moscow has benefited significantly more from this co-operation than Beijing. Through defence co-operation with China, Russia has gained influence in regional affairs. Arms sales have played an important role in helping the two countries forge a strategic relationship that has a significant military component. The idea of establishing the Shanghai Co-operation Organization was embedded in the initial negotiation process of various arms deals. The Sino-Russian annual joint military exercises have also become a platform for Russia to demonstrate its weapons for potential sales. The significance of Sino-Russian arms trade is not confined to the two countries. For instance, Moscow intentionally fans a competition for arms between China and India and has placed itself in a favourable position in the tripartite interaction.

More importantly, as the sole supplier of advanced weaponry to China, Russia's influence on the PLA, the most important political institution in the country, should not be underestimated. Now that Russia provides the principal weapons systems for the PLAAF and the PLAN, it is in a position to affect the level of the PLA's readiness for action. For instance, during the Wenchuan earthquake rescue operations in May 2008, the lack of parts for Il-76 transports hampered the movement of badly needed relief material that had to be sent to the disaster zones in Sichuan. The fear of Russia's influence can clearly be seen by China's worry over Russian control of the supply of parts in a crisis. This was one of the main reasons why Beijing insisted on acquiring assembly rights of the Su-27 in 1993 during tough negotiations between the two countries over the Su-27 package.[3]

Russia's influence on China through arms sales is not limited to its control over supply of important parts and hardware. Every year, the PLA sends up to 800 officers to Russia to study military science and learn how to operate the Russian arms it has bought.[4] A good example is the training of the Shenzhou personnel (the PLA's manned space project), which so far has been based on Russian protocols and literature. The PLA's space programme largely follows the Russian model. It is logical to assume that some of the PLA trainees would develop pro-Russia sentiments or a favourable view of the Russian model of military transformation vis-à-vis the West. This may have fostered a kind of personal affinity of PLA commanders who once studied in Russia. Generals Liu Huaqing (top PLA soldier 1989–97) and Cao Gangchun (defence minister 2002–07), who studied in Russia in the 1950s and 1960s, respectively, were strong advocates of importing more Russian arms (Liu Huaqing 2004). Moreover, education experience in Russia has become a useful credential for promotion.

The barriers to the Sino-Russian arms trade

Despite the importance both sides attach to the arms trade, problems have never failed to surface. The dichotomy in objectives constantly creates challenges. In 2007 Russia's arms sales climbed to a post-USSR peak with minimum Chinese contribution. This indicates two significant developments in the Sino-Russian arms trade. First, Russia has successfully found alternative markets that can sufficiently compensate the loss of Chinese orders. Secondly, this shows that although there are still many problems, the Russian RDI has basically returned to normal production and exportation. It fulfils a demand gap in the developing countries, which cannot afford expensive Western weaponry. Moreover, the unexpected upsurge of oil income has substantially reduced Russia's need for hard currency from arms sales. With $630 billion at its peak in reserves, it was among the top five countries with the most US dollar reserves in 2008. All this means that Moscow is in a stronger position to bargain for higher prices for arms intended for export to China, often more than Beijing is willing to pay. This has been another reason for the slow-down of the bilateral arms trade.

The weakening Chinese demand

On the part of China, its ability to develop current generation weaponry has reached new heights given the long period of technological accumulation. This visibly reduces its dependence on foreign procurement, especially from Russia. For instance, the Heilongjiang Heavy Machinery Firm has developed computer-aided high-precision tool machines capable of making sophisticated propulsion blades for very quiet submarines. This will reduce the PLA's incentive to import additional Kilo submarines. The series production of the J-10s (a 3.5 generation multiple-purpose combat aircraft that is considered better than the F-16 in mechanical performance) will also gradually meet the PLAAF's basic needs for advanced combat aircraft. China's new Aegis destroyers and the Yuan class submarines with air independent propulsion (AIP) systems exceed the general combat capabilities of Russia's Sovremenny and Kilos. PLA Major-General Xu Yan thus asserted that the era of the Chinese buying spree of Russian arms is essentially over (Xu Yan 2008, 2). With Chinese defence industries gradually maturing, China is increasingly moving to equip the PLA with the best weapons systems that have been indigenously developed (*The PLA Daily*, 18 November 2008).

Secondly, after years of equipping its elite units with advanced Russian weapons, the PLA has completed the mission of establishing a core force to fight a medium-scale intensive regional high-tech war, the only likely scenario for the PLA for the foreseeable future. The level of mobility, fire power and information warfare capabilities of this elite force have reached parity with that of other major world powers. The PLA currently has the largest number of third-generation combat aircraft in Asia. Its navy is about to achieve anti-access capabilities within the first islands chain in the West Pacific. The PLAN's Somalia escort mission shows that it has, for the first time in its history, become confident enough to dispatch task fleets to assume limited combat missions in waters far away from home. Beijing is thus assessing where to go from here in terms of foreign acquisitions.

Russia's control over China's shopping list

With its economic recovery, Russia has shifted its preoccupation with commercial gains from arms sales to more comprehensive considerations based on national security. This does not mean that Russia will lessen military co-operation with China, given its tense relations with the West. A militarily weak China would not effectively offset Western pressure on Russia. However, Moscow's perception of China as a potential rival has never failed to influence its arms sales decisions to China (Rangsimaporn 2006). It has thus attempted to establish control over China's shopping list from the beginning of the bilateral arms trade. For instance, Russia's early agreement to sell the Su-27s in 1991 was conditional upon Beijing's promise not to deploy the aircraft north to the Yellow River. With its long-range combat radius of Su-27s, this deployment would pose a threat to Russia's far east. This was changed only at the beginning of the new century, as China deployed J-11B (the Su-27 assembled in Shenyang under licence). China's continued rise in economic and military power has enhanced a sense of nervousness among some of Russia's security experts, who have advised the government to exercise more effective control over China's shopping list (Rangsimaporn 2006). Russia's control over Sino-Russian arms trade lies in its status as the primary seller of hi-tech weapons to the Chinese. This has deeply frustrated the Chinese buyers and planted the seeds for today's decline in China's enthusiasm to buy. The problem of the discrepancy in the selection of weapons systems between the buyer and the seller can be traced to the early 1990s when Russia only agreed to sell its second line of equipment to China. When China received the first Sovremenny destroyer, they found that the updated command and control systems were removed from the ship. In contrast, Moscow has been much more accommodating to Indian requests for more sophisticated hardware (Bersert 2008, 12).[5] Russia's strategic sensibility to long-term Sino-Russian relations is channelled into three sales restrictions. First, Russia is determined to sell hardware, not associated technology. Secondly, it is vigilant not to sell equipment that China can use to make other weapons platforms for export. Thirdly, Russia has been resistant to China's demand for the latest version of the classes of weapons that Moscow agrees to sell, e.g. Sovremenny I rather than Sovremenny II destroyers. In recent years, Beijing has responded to these restrictions with a simple countermeasure: forget about the orders.

Persistent thorns

This two-way mistrust is not far beneath the surface of Sino-Russian military co-operation and defines the relationship of convenience that constantly impacts on the arms trade. From Russia's perspective, the three restrictions are reasonable, as it has to factor in scenarios in which the two states may again enter into a relationship of confrontation. Technological superiority is Russia's only trump card, but the effect of this is quickly exhausted due to its relatively rapid obsolescence. At the same time, China's own research of current generation military technology is making visible progress. The transfer of technology will help China's strategy to catch up. There is another concern over technological transfers: China's vigorous efforts at reverse engineering Russian technology helps it to produce its own weapons for export and thus undermines Russia's shares in global arms trade. This conflict of interests is obvious but Russia's insistence on control erects obstacles for the sustained growth in the bilateral arms trade.[6]

Since 2002 both Russia and China have tried to overcome this barrier in order to move their arms business to a new stage of development. One major bilateral initiative is to sign an intellectual property agreement as part of a regulatory regime to safeguard Russia's interests and narrow the grey areas in technological transfers. For instance, when China acquired the production licence to assemble Su-27s, it was not clarified whether the aircraft engines that China would produce under the agreement could be used for other Chinese aircraft, still less, for Chinese export of its aircraft with the engines produced under the licence. This has been a persistent dispute in the Sino-Russian arms trade. In December 2008 the two countries finally signed an intellectual property rights (IPR) agreement that imposes restrictions on Beijing's export of arms originating from Russian models, but does not prevent China from producing them for its own use. This agreement has lessened Russia's concerns that potentially China may copy Russian weapons without prior Russian consent and Chinese military hardware may flood the global marketplace, eroding Russia's hard-won market share (*Defense News*, 15 December 2008). Apparently, the agreement has cleared a major obstacle to further military co-operation between the two countries.

New challenges

One new challenge to Sino-Russian arms business is China's changed military transformation path, which requires a different type of weapons development and equipment strategy (You Ji 2004, 97). The hardware-driven Russian arms exports are increasingly a mismatch to the PLA transformation that is shifting from mechanization (hardware upgrading) to informatization, i.e. network-centric warfare equipment (You Ji 2008). This exposes the limitations of Russian arms that are good at the former but not good enough for the new forms of warfare. From the Chinese perspective, the Russian defence industries have not made any major technological breakthroughs since the end of the USSR, especially in the area of information warfare. Depending on Russian arms amounts to freezing PLA transformation at the era of mechanization. This means that China can only break this cycle through developing its own advanced weapons systems, especially sensor platforms. The PLA believes that with strong state financial support, it can achieve this goal in a not too distant future (Zhang Sheng 2008, 2).

The quality of Russian arms often falls far below China's expectations. For instance, the life span of Russian aircraft engines is far below Western standards. Many of the PLAAF's flight accidents are due to engine failures, which have cost the PLA dearly. The rate of recalls is also high. For example, the PLA discovered that the Russians used many second-hand parts to build the Sovremenny destroyers. Upon Beijing's protest, the Russians replaced them, but this seriously disrupted the PLAN's training schedule.[7] In addition, the delivery is seldom punctual, to the annoyance of the purchaser. This results in cancellations of the agreed deals worth billions of dollars, such as the Il-76 deal in 2007.

In the past, Beijing preferred not to press the issue too hard. Recently, however, it has become increasingly strict on quality and delivery control. If in the past, it had to make do with one badly needed weapon system, even if it was not satisfactory according to its technological criteria, it is no longer the case, and will be still less so in the future. China has stopped producing J-11B (Su-27K) half way through the programme due to its obsolescent avionics. It cannot launch R-77 anti-aircraft (AA) missiles and KH-31 anti-ship missiles, and has no beyond-visual-range (BVR) capability. J-11B avionics are inferior to J-10 but are a lot more expensive.[8]

Finally, China's need for emergency capabilities to deal with a sudden crisis has been eased with the regime change in Taipei in May 2008. In fact, the biggest driver for the PLA to purchase Russian arms in recent years has been its preparation for an anti-independence war in Taiwan. Now that cross-Strait relations have visibly improved, the PLA has once again freed itself from the pressure of an imminent war. The last time it was under such pressure was during the Sino-Soviet confrontation in 1969. It was then forced to equip its troops with a great deal of otherwise unnecessary and costly weapons. Four decades later, the PLA has once again reoriented its modernization in the direction of gradual transformation, a departure from adding quick-fix equipment that quickly becomes obsolete.[9]

A future trend assessment

It is too early to determine if the current sluggishness of the Sino-Russian arms trade is a hiccup or a pattern of future development. Yet if one looks closely at the nature of Russia's recent large orders, e.g. aircraft sales to Algeria and Venezuela, they appear to be one-off deals. The West is trying to penetrate Russia's traditional arms market through aggressive marketing. The USA has been successful in capturing India's orders for expensive weapons systems. Thus, Russia cannot afford to lose the Chinese market. Eventually it has to return to the Chinese, by which time Moscow may find that it has to play a different game with Beijing, given the changed circumstances noted above.

Playing by different rules of the game?

Some analysts claim that it is a buyer's market for the Sino-Russian arms trade (Tsai 2005, 2). This is true to some extent, but the fact is that Russia achieved $7.5 billion in sales in 2007 with little Chinese contribution. This demonstrates that the RDI's dependence on Chinese orders for survival is a thing of the past. Others argue that the Chinese arms market has become saturated (Kommersant, 27 May 2008). Again, this is not an accurate claim. The PLA is still in its initial stage of transformation, which requires an enormous amount of advanced weaponry to replace its current obsolete equipment. There is a long list of key items the country cannot produce in the near future. The latest SIPRI prediction that China would be rid of dependence on Russian arms in a decade is the logical conclusion, but needs to be qualified (SIPRI 2008). By then, China will still need Russia's weaponry in key areas, although it may adopt new means to obtain it.

There are new signs of interaction between the two militaries in pursuit of the arms trade. First, the PLA will be more selective in identifying and buying key capabilities. This means Beijing will only buy the capabilities it regards as most urgent and absolutely necessary. The list of these items has become shorter and shorter, as the country is under no imminent threat of war. Moreover, the quantity for each deal will become smaller. This would alter the PLA's past practice of acquiring sizable amounts of Russian equipment to equip several campaign level units (divisions) in one go.

Secondly, the PLA's newly enlarged bargaining power in choosing what to have and in what sequence allows it to redefine the nature of the arms trade vis-à-vis the Russians. The first rule it hopes to revise is the previous one-way direction of 'you sell and we take', to a two-way co-operation with a calculated emphasis on technological transfers. Russia is seriously short of financial resources to develop the next generation of principal weapons systems. It has, therefore, proposed to China a number of joint research programmes, including the fourth generation of combat aircraft. The two countries have already signed deals to jointly develop military micro-electronics facilities and embark on new aerospace research, i.e. the GLO-NASS/Beidou GPS systems (*Huanqiushibao*, 31 May 2008). Clearly, China does not only want new hardware, but technology as well.

62   *You Ji*

Importing key capabilities

There is good potential for the long-term Sino-Russian arms trade. One key reason is NATO's continued arms embargo on China. Had the PLAN procured German 212 submarines, it would have been happy to drop the Kilos from its shopping list in the 1990s. As long as the Western embargo is in place, China will be technologically tied to Russia one way or another.

China's need for emergent capabilities has not disappeared altogether. Since it cannot get them from elsewhere, Beijing will continue to buy Russian arms well into the next decade. The following is casually selected and covers the items the PLA would likely acquire from Russia in the immediate future. Each of these items would affect the arms trade within a timeframe of a decade or more.

The Su-33s carrier aircraft

If Beijing gives the green light to the carrier project, the Navy must have at least two of them to meet the minimum operational requirements. Among the challenges to this project is the carrier aircraft that China cannot develop by itself, at least for the time being.[10] Therefore, the procurement of Su-33s may have become inevitable. It has been reported that the two militaries are close to ending the negotiation on this deal, with deliveries of up to 50 planes worth $2.5 billion in the next decade (*Jane's Defense Weekly*, 28 October 2008).

Il-76 transport planes

China's 'large aircraft project' will not yield real results until at least 2025.[11] The Wenchun earthquake revealed how weak China's strategic lift capabilities are. This played a part in the renegotiation of the cancelled deal that China would buy 38 Il-76 transports from Russia, a deal that was signed in 2005 but cancelled two years later.[12] Even if China becomes able to produce large aircraft, it is unlikely that it could fully meet the domestic and military demand any time soon. Therefore, it may be a foregone conclusion that China will continue to buy Russia's large transport aircraft for the foreseeable future.

Helicopters for military and civilian use

The Wenchun earthquake also revealed the inadequacy in the number of helicopters. Compared to the large aircraft project, the domestic helicopter research and development capability is very weak, if not weaker. This means that China will continue to import helicopters from overseas and Russia would be the primary supplier, especially for military use. So far, fewer than half of the PLA's group armies have aviation units. If they all have at least one helicopter regiment according to the army transformation plan, there is a minimum of 330 helicopters required to equip 10 regiments in the Army, not to mention the requests from other services.[13] The demand from the civilian sector is even bigger.

Conclusion

The current sluggishness of the Sino-Russian arms trade may not represent a future pattern of development. China still needs Russian weaponry in key defence areas. However, as China continues to improve its capability in technological research and development and as it faces the reduced possibility of war around its borders, it can afford not to acquire large quantities of emergent weaponry to prepare for a sudden crisis. Therefore, it has adopted new approaches to obtaining it, such as being more selective in purchasing Russia's advanced arms, and it will more vigorously stress technological transfers. As both countries are adjusting policies to the new situation in the bilateral arms trade, it is likely that the two-way arms trade will remain stagnant before it is revitalized.

On the other hand, there is still much potential for Sino-Russian military co-operation, including in the arms trade. It is mutually beneficial and the Chinese demand is still relatively strong, as discussed in the last section of the chapter. Yet, as considerations of expediency in the two countries often clash, the bilateral arms trade relationship will continue to encounter difficulties. Clearly, the pattern of frequent large deals that characterized Sino-Russian arms business over the last 15 years seems to have become a thing of past.

Both countries value the arms trade. At the political level it has become a symbol of the Sino-Russian strategic partnership, something Beijing cherishes in countering Western pressure. Without substantial arms transactions, the foundation of Sino-Russian military co-operation would be eroded. Technologically, there is a long way for China to go in order to catch up with the West. The PLA's transitional difficulties will persist for one or two decades, during which time Russia can provide valuable help for the Chinese to redress the gap. Sino-Russian military co-operation will continue, although it may not follow a straight course.

Notes

1 Liu Huaqing strongly pushed for the carrier project but until his retirement in 1997, he was not successful in getting the civilian approval (see Liu Huaqing 2004, 481).
2 Ukraine / China: 'Ukraine to help train China's navy pilots', UPI Asia, 5 December 2008.
3 According to this agreement China could assemble up to 200 Su-27s, which the PLA has named J-11.
4 This is stipulated in the Sino-Russian Military Co-operation Treaty – 2000–2015, signed by General Chi Haotian, Chinese defence minister during his visit to Moscow in January 2000 (*China Times*, 8 February 2000).
5 For instance, Russia refused China's request for Su-30MK2, and was only willing to provide a less-sophisticated version of the Su-30. However, Moscow was forthcoming to India's request for the Su-30MK2 (Bursert 2008, 12).
6 One typical example was Russia's initial refusal to sell RD-93 aircraft engines to China, which uses the engine in its FC-1 fighter-bomber earmarked for export to Pakistan. Russia changed its mind only after China pointed out that this rejection would threaten the overall bilateral arms trade.
7 From the author's conversation with PLAN officers in the East Sea Fleet in Shanghai, 2001.
8 The PLA Air Force conducted a combat exercise using a J-10 equipped with indigenous avionics against a Su-27. The J-10 proved to be superior by key criteria such as finding the enemy earlier, engaging it from a longer distance and achieving the kill with more accuracy.
9 An important consideration for the PLA in purchasing Russia's strategic bombers was to employ them in sea battles east to Taiwan island, where the PLAN fleets would have weak air cover. The prospects of such a campaign are now virtually non-existent. Therefore, China can afford not to acquire this obsolete aircraft and to wait for its own large-aircraft project to deliver the indigenous strategic bombers in the third decade of the century.
10 Although the design of the J-10 leaves room for carrier aircraft development, it would take a long time to materialize and it would still be a light jetfighter with limited capabilities (see Jianchuanzhishi, no. 8, 2008, p.23).
11 This project is about China's effort to make its own aircraft for civilian and military purposes, including principal civil aircraft and strategic bombers.
12 In 2005 China signed a deal with Russia to buy 38 Il-38 worth $1.5 billion, but Russia later informed China that it had facility and labour shortages so it could not fulfill the contract.
13 The PLA's Chengdu helicopter maintenance factory has been designated to be upgraded to a helicopter factory. It will produce M-171 helicopters in sizeable quantities and this will be the first major Russian transfer of assembly rights since the Su-27SK (J-11B) project in the early 1990s (Central News Agency, 1 October 2008).

Bibliography

Abdullav, Nabi, 'Russia Sets Post-Soviet Arms Sale Record', *Defense News*, 19 February 2008
Allen, Kenneth and Jonathan Pollack, *China's Air Force Enters the 21st Century*, Santa Monica: RAND, 1995
Blank, Stephen, *The Dynamics of Russian Weapons Sales to China*, Carlisle, US Army War College, 1997
Bursert, James, 'China Copies Russian Ship-building Technology', *Signal*, No. 6, translated and published by *Junshiwenzai* (Military Digest), No. 7, 2008
Cheng Bojiang and William Perry, 'RMA and US Defence Development in the Century', *The Journal of PLA National Defence University*, No. 12, 1998
Huanqiushibao, www.huanqiushibao.com
Ikenbery, John, 'The Rise of China and the Future of the West: Can the Liberal System Survive', *Foreign Affairs*, January/ February 2008

ITAR-TASS, www.itar-tass.com

Kintworth, Gary, 'The Chinese Navy to Get Some Big Guns, At Last', *Asia-Pacific Defence Reporter*, April–May 1997

Liao Wenzhong, 'System Integration and Upgrading Combat Capabilities', in Chong-Pin Lin, ed., *Strategizing the Military Stance of the Taiwan Strait*, Taipei, The Student Publishing Bureau, 2002

Liu Guangzhi, 'Air-space War – the Strategic Goal of the PLAAF Transformation', *Military Art*, no. 9, 2003

Liu Huaqing, *The Memoirs of Liu Huqing*, Beijing, PLA Publishing House, 2004

Liu Yijian, *The Command of Sea and the Strategic Employment of Naval Forces*, Beijing, The PLA National Defence University Press, 2004

Menon, Rajan, 'The Strategic Convergence between Russia and China', *Survival*, Vol. 39, No. 2, 1997

Pan Guang, 'China in the Dhanghai Cooperation Organization', in Wang Gungwu and Yongnian Zheng, eds, *China and the New International Order*, London, Routledge, 2008

Qian Guoliang, 'Implement the Guideline of Headquarters Construction in Earnest', *Journal of the PLA National Defence University*, no. 6, 2000

Rangsimaporn, Paradorn, 'Russia's Debate on Military-Technological Cooperation with China', *Asian Survey*, May/June 2006

SIPRI, *Annual Report on the World Arms Trade*, Stockholm International Peace Research Institute (SIPRI), 31 March 2008

Story, Ian and You Ji, 'China's Aircraft Carrier Ambitions: Seeking Truth from Rumours', *The Naval War College Review*, Vol. LVII, No. 1, 2003

Strategic Observer, No. 5, 2008

Taylor, John, 'The Su-27 Flanker Series', *Jane's Intelligence Review*, No. 5, Vol. 7, 1995

Tsai, Ming-yen, 'Russian-Chinese Military Ties: Development and Implications', *Journal of Russia Studies*, No. 5, 2005

Xu Yan, 'China No Longer Needs to Import Russian Arms in Large Quantities', *Bingqizhishi* (Journal of Arms), No. 12, 2008

Yang Jinshan, 'The Form of Joint Campaigns in the Future Warfare', *The Journal of PLA National Defence University*, No. 1, 2004

Yao Yanjin and Liu Jingxian, *Study of Deng Xiaoping's Military Theory*, Beijing, The PLA Academy of Military Science Press, 1995

You Ji, *The Armed Forces of China*, Sydney, London and New York, Allen and Unwin, and I. B. Tauris, 1999a

——'Adding Offensive Teeth to the PLA Air Force', *Issues & Studies*, Vol. 35, No. 2, 1999b

——'Learning and Catching Up: China's RMA Initiative', in Emily Goldman and Tom Mahnken, eds, *The Information Revolution in Asia*, New York, Palgrave Macmillan, 2004

——'China's Naval Strategy and Transformation', in Lawrence S. Prabhakar, Joshua Ho and Sam Bateman, eds, *The Evolving Maritime Balance of Power in The Asia-Pacific*, Singapore, World Scientific Publisher, 2006a

——'The Anti-Secession Law and the Risk of War in the Taiwan Strait', *Contemporary Security Policy*, Vol. 27, No. 2, 2006b

——'Revolution in Military Thinking', in Bo Huldt and Masako Ikegami, eds, *The Strategic Yearbook on East Asian Security*, Swedish National Defence College and the Finnish Defence University, 2008

Zhang Sheng, *Dialogue between Soldiers of Two Generations*, Beijing, Chinese Youth Publication House, 2008

Zhang Youxia and Shi Xiangyuan, 'Zhuquan kongzhizhan: xianshi junshi douzheng ni ke caiyongde yizhong zuozhan xingshi' [War for protecting sovereignty, a realistic method of operations in preparing military struggle], Junshixueshu [Military Studies], Vol. 29, No. 11, 2002

5 India's arms acquisition

Devoid of a strategic orientation

Harsh V. Pant

In November 2008, the financial capital of India, Mumbai, was struck by terrorists that Indian (as well as American and British) intelligence later confirmed had received extensive training from the Pakistan-based group, Lashkar-e-Taiba, or Army of the Pure. Given the sophistication of planning and execution involved, it soon became apparent that this was a commando-style operation that possibly had the involvement of a state actor. As physical evidence mounted in terms of satellite phone calls, equipment and boats used for the attack, Pakistan's hand was perceived as being smeared all over the operation. Though India conceded that probably the new civilian administration of Asif Ali Zardari was not behind the attacks, the army and the ISI were seen as the main culprit (Chengappa 2008).

The public outcry after the Mumbai attacks was strong enough for the Indian government to consider using the military option vis-à-vis Pakistan. However, it soon turned out that India no longer had the capability to impose quick and effective retribution on Pakistan and that it no longer enjoyed the kind of conventional superiority over its regional adversary that it had enjoyed for the past five decades (Gupta 2009). This was a surprising conclusion for a nation that the international community regarded as a major global economic and military power, which is pursuing a defence modernization programme estimated to be over US$50 billion over the next five years. Yet in many ways, it underlined fundamental weaknesses in Indian defence policy, especially its ad hoc attempts at arms procurement and defence modernization. This chapter examines the trends in defence spending and arms procurement in India since the early 1990s, a period that has seen India rising in the global hierarchy. It argues that a lack of strategic orientation in Indian defence planning will make it difficult for the country to effectively use its resources and this will circumscribe India's rise as a global military power. First an overview of trends in Indian defence spending is presented, followed by a discussion of the drivers of the Indian defence modernization programme. Subsequently, India's ties with its major defence partners – Russia, Israel and the West – are examined. Finally, the constraints that will continue to prevent India from emerging as a major global military power are examined.

India's rise: economic and military

Sustained rates of high economic growth over the last decade have given India greater resources to devote to its defence requirements. India's real gross domestic product (GDP) has surged by an annual average of nearly 9% in the last five years, and it is on track to emerge as the fastest-growing economy in the world in 2008–13, with an average annual expansion of 6.3% (Economist Intelligence Unit 2008). India has emerged as one of the largest arms buyers in the global market in the last few years and is expected to make more than $435 billion of arms purchases in 2009–13 (IISS 2009, 334). In the initial years after independence in 1947, India's defence expenditure as a percentage of GDP hovered around 1.8%. This changed with the 1962 war with the People's Republic of China, in which India had to suffer a humiliating defeat due to its lack of defence preparedness and Indian defence expenditure came to stabilize at around 3% of GDP for the next 25 years (Singh 2001, 22–23). Over the past two decades, the military expenditure of India has been around 2.75%, but since India has been experiencing significantly higher rates of economic growth over the last decade compared to any other time in its history, the overall resources that it has been able to allocate to its defence needs have grown significantly. The armed forces have long been asking for an allocation of 3% of the nation's GDP to defence; this has received broad political support in recent years. The Indian Prime Minister has been explicit about it, suggesting that 'if our economy grows at about 8 percent per annum, it will not be difficult for [the Indian Government] to allocate about 3 percent of GDP for national defense' (AFP 2005). The Indian Parliament has also underlined the need to aim for the target of 3% of GDP.

India's rise as a global economic power has also transformed the global defence market where it has emerged as one of the most proactive buyers. India, with the world's fourth-largest military and one of the biggest defence budgets, has been in the midst of a huge defence modernization programme for nearly a decade, which has seen billions of dollars spent on the latest high-tech military technology. This liberal spending on defence equipment has attracted the interest of Western industry and governments alike and is changing the scope of the global defence market.

It is not surprising, then, that India is viewed these days as the new centre for defence procurement. Defence companies looking to sell 'big ticket' items have made India their favoured destination. The spending is diverse across all three services branches. Items such as fighter planes and bombers, transport aircraft, missile systems, aircraft carriers, helicopters and tanks are all on the list of items India has been buying over the last few years.

During the 10-year period between 1996/97 and 2005/06, the average share of the expenditure on the army, navy and air force was 57%, 15% and 24%, respectively. Though the navy's share is the smallest, it has been gradually increasing over the years, whereas the share of other services has witnessed great fluctuations. The Indian Navy saw its allocation going up by 10.5% and procurement spending rising by 17% in 2007 (IISS 2008, 336). In 2008/09 the Navy's share of total defence allocation was 18.47% compared with 46.62% for the Army and 53% for the Air Force (Government of India, Ministry of Defence 2007/08, 14). On the revenue side of the budget, pay and allowances including those of personnel, civilians and reservists account for the second-largest expense, which is nearly 40% of the revenue budget and 22% of the total defence budget (Behera 2007). The capital expenditure side of the defence budget has grown considerably from nearly 25% in 2000/01 to over 45% in 2008/09, reflecting the growing emphasis of the Indian armed forces on modernization (Behera 2008). As for overall defence expenditure, it is the ratio of revenue to capital expenditure that is the most significant factor in assessing how the services are utilizing their allocated resources, as capital expenditure is the one that is directed towards building future capabilities. While the ratio of revenue to capital expenditure has been around 70:30 for the defence forces as a whole, there is a huge variation among the services, with the ratio of the Navy being 48:52 and that of the army and the air force being 85:15 and 55:45, respectively.

Of the three services, the Indian Navy is the only service that is investing in future capabilities more than it is spending on operational expenditure (Srinivas 2006, 64–73). Capital expenditure determines the trend of modernization and with 52% of its allocation going towards capital expenditure, the Indian Navy is ahead of the other two services in its endeavour to modernize itself. Three key acquisitions by the Indian Navy – long range aircraft, aircraft carriers and nuclear submarines – are intended to make India a formidable force in the Indian Ocean. While India's global aspirations are clearly visible in the modernization activities of the Indian Navy, non-conventional threats to Indian and global security have also risen in recent times, which might result in a change of priorities for the defence forces. The Indian Air Force is attempting to build up an effective capability with the induction of force multipliers and a growing emphasis on its strategic thinking on core competencies, joint operations and the asymmetric nature of modern warfare. The Indian Army is continuing with its efforts to modernize and upgrade its weapons systems to prepare it to address the requirements of modern day warfare and to enhance its combat capability.

Drivers of India's arms build-up

India's drive towards arms acquisition in recent years can be attributed to several factors. The process was ignited in the 1990s by a combination of the end of the Cold War and the growing threats from Pakistan and China. India's close ties with the Soviet Union during the Cold War made the Soviet Union India's primary supplier of defence equipment. The West could only make small inroads into India's defence market during that time. When the Cold War ended and with the demise of the USSR, India and Russia maintained their relationship. Gradually the government found itself with old and outdated weapons technology. Russia was and still is a huge seller of defence equipment to India, but the government's newly re-established relations with the USA and Europe allowed for a diversification of arms suppliers.

The rapidly evolving security environment facing India continues to pose challenges to Indian defence planners. A combination of internal and external, as well as state- and non-state-based threats have emerged, which have made the Indian security scenario more chal-lenging in recent years. Internally, Indian security is challenged by a plethora of insurgencies which are a product of a range of factors including a desire for greater autonomy, left-wing radicalism and prevailing socio-economic inequities. As a result, the authority of the Indian State has seen a progressive weakening over the last few years. Externally, India's immediate neighbourhood continues to pose challenges to its statecraft. India is witnessing rising turmoil all around its borders. The instability in Pakistan, Afghanistan, Bangladesh, Nepal, Sri Lanka and Myanmar is a greatly inhibiting factor for India to realize its dream of becoming a major global player. India is surrounded by several weak states that view New Delhi's hegemonic status in the region with suspicion. A policy of 'splendid isolation' is not an option and Indian strategic elites recognize that India's desire to emerge as a major global player will remain just that—a desire—unless it engages its immediate neighbourhood more meaningfully and becomes a net provider of regional security.

The biggest challenge to Indian strategic interests comes from the rise of China in the region and beyond. India and China are two major powers in Asia with global aspirations and some significant conflicting interests. As a result, some friction in their bilateral relationship is inevitable. The geopolitical reality of Asia ensures that it will be extremely difficult, if not impos-sible, for *Hindi-Chini* to be *bhai-bhai* (brothers) in the foreseeable future.[1] If India and China continue to rise in the next few years, security competition between the two regional giants will be all but inevitable. If India is serious about its desire to emerge as a major global power, then it will have to confront the challenge of China's rise (Pant 2007, 54–71). China's defence modernization and the ambiguity surrounding its arms build-up is generating apprehension in New Delhi and has forced India to pursue its own defence modernization programme.

The nuclearization of India and Pakistan has forever changed the context in which wars will be fought in the region. It is part of the reason that elements within the Pakistani security establishment have become more adventurous. Realizing that India would be reluctant to escalate the conflict because of the threat of it reaching the nuclear level, sections of the Pakistani military and intelligence have pushed the envelope on the sub-conventional front, using various terror groups to launch assaults on India (Kapur 2008, 73–87). For India, this presents a structural conundrum: nuclear weapons have made a major conventional conflict with Pakistan unrealistic, yet it needs to find a way to launch limited military action against Pakistan without crossing the nuclear threshold. Nuclear weapons have allowed Pakistan to shield itself from full-scale Indian retaliation as well as to attract international attention to the disputes in the sub-continent. To overcome this constraint, India needs to preserve its conventional superiority vis-à-vis Pakistan and this implies increasing acquisition of conventional weaponry, especially after Pakistan's use of more than $10 billion-worth of US military aid to arm itself against India.

India's rising global economic profile has made the world take India more seriously as a major power and has made Indian elites more ambitious in defining their global role and aspirations. There is clearly an appreciation in the Indian policy-making circles of the country's rising capabilities. It is reflected in a gradual expansion of Indian foreign policy activity in recent years, in India's attempt to reshape its defence forces, and in its desire to seek greater global influence. India, the world's fourth-largest military power, had embarked on an ambitious plan to modernize its largely Soviet-era arms since the late 1990s as it started asserting its political and military profile in South Asia and the Indian Ocean region. India's armed forces had become increasingly ambitious, talking of their own revolution in military affairs. In line with India's broadening strategic horizons, its military acquisition is seeing a marked shift from conventional land-based systems to means of power projection such as airborne refuelling systems and long-range missiles. India is setting up bases abroad, patrolling the Indian Ocean to counter piracy and protecting the crucial sea-lanes of communication, and demonstrating a military assertiveness hitherto not associated with it (Giriharadas 2008). Yet, the lack of any credible military option against Pakistan has brought into sharp relief the fundamental weaknesses of Indian defence policy over the last several years.

India needs a defence policy that can actually take on all these challenges simultaneously. This is a difficult task to accomplish given the fact that the multiplicity and variety of challenges that India faces often require varied responses. Yet compared to any other time in its history, India faces an international environment that has so far allowed it to pursue a 'multi-vector' defence policy as its relations with all major global powers are on a stable footing.

India and its defence partners

India and Russia: the brewing discontent

Russia continues to be the country's most significant defence partner with defence contracts worth $14.2 billion currently underway with India (Shukla 2007). Not only is Russia the biggest supplier of defence products to India, but the India-Russia defence relationship also encompasses a wide range of activity that includes joint research, design, development and co-production (Shukla 1999, 130–34). India is now locally producing several Russian defence products, including the Brahmos supersonic missile, the T-90 tank and Sukhoi fighter aircrafts.

Russia has agreed to further expand defence supplies ties with India, both in content and range, and has also agreed to give its nod to co-operation in sophisticated spheres of technology about which the USA and other Western nations have seemed reticent. This includes technology related to the peaceful uses of space and atomic energy, the supply of the fifth generation of advance fighter aircraft and a whole range of other military equipment (*New York Times*, 23 November 2002). Indian and Russian defence companies are not only designing and developing, but will also be jointly marketing the anti-ship missile, Brahmos, in other countries. Russia has made a proposal to India to jointly develop a next-generation advanced jet trainer, with an eye on the global market. India and Russia have also signed a $450m. deal for the supply of the Smerch multiple-launch rocket system to India. This will be the largest supply of Russian weapons for the Indian army since the $800m. contract for the supply and licensed production of T-90 main battle tanks (*Press Trust of India*, 22 February 2005).

The Indo-Russian bilateral defence relationship has, though, come under strain in recent years as India adjusts to the changing nature of modern warfare and shifts its defence priorities to the purchase of smart weaponry, which Russia is ill-equipped to provide. Already, India's increasing defence ties with Israel and the gradual opening of the US arms market to India has made Russia relatively less exciting for India. The Indian military has been critical of an over-reliance on Russia for defence acquisition which was reflected in the Indian Naval Chief's view that there should be a rethink on India's ties with Russia in the light of the Russian demand of $1.2 billion more for the aircraft carrier, Admiral Gorshkov, purchased by India in 2004 (Unnithan 2007).

India is also sensitive to the fact that Russia enjoys an excellent defence relationship with China. It is the largest supplier of defence equipment to China, with the result that the modernization of the Chinese military owes a lot to Russia. Not only is this of direct strategic consequence to Indian security but it also creates a cascading effect whereby Russian military technology and know-how gets transferred to Pakistan via China. Therefore, the prospects of Indo-Russian defence and political co-operation will be assessed by India in the light of Russia's defence supplies and co-operation arrangements with China. Reports of Russia transferring special military technologies to China developed with Indian resources and exclusively for Indian armed forces are causing consternation in India. On the other hand, there are concerns in Russia about the growing Indian strategic alignment with the USA, just as Russia has been adopting an increasingly confrontational posture vis-à-vis the USA and the West.

India remains keen to diversify the stable of countries from which it buys arms and wants to reduce its dependence on Russia, especially after extended delays in Russian arms supplies and growing disenchantment in India regarding price escalations. Other states have been quick to entice India and the country's ties with Israel have been the most significant.

India and Israel: bond getting stronger

The ballast for Indo-Israeli bilateral ties is provided by the defence co-operation between the two states, with India emerging as Israel's largest arms market, displacing the USA, and with Israel becoming India's second-largest arms supplier (Kaura 2008). Israel was willing to continue and even step up its arms sales to India after other major states curbed their technological exports to the country following India's nuclear tests in May 1998. With Israel specializing in upgrading Russian equipment, it has emerged as an alternative source of high-tech defence procurement for India. The Indo-Israel defence partnership has reached a critical mass in recent years with the focus now being on moving from a buyer-seller relationship towards joint research and development projects, so that mutual synergies in defence can be better exploited (Watson 2003).

From anti-missile to high-tech radar systems, from sky drones to night-vision equipment, Indo-Israeli defence co-operation has known no bounds in recent times. According to some estimates, India has imported $5 billion-worth of defence equipment from Israel in the last five years alone (Dikshit 2007). The USA finally gave its approval to Israel's delivery of Phalcon Airborne Warning and Controlling Systems (AWACS) to India after initial reluctance about how this sale might affect the conventional weapons balance between India and Pakistan. India's AWACS project involves the integration of the Phalcon radar and communication system with the Russian Ilyushin-76 heavy transport military aircraft (Chazan and Solomon 2003). The project is now on schedule and is expected to be delivered by 2008–09.

India and Israel are also currently negotiating the possible sale of the Arrow-II antiballistic-missile defence system to India, which wants to strengthen its air defence capabilities. Though Israel is more than willing to sell the system, it needs US approval as the USA was a collaborator in the project. However, India has already acquired the advanced 'Green Pine' fire control radar systems from Israel. This is a transportable phased-array radar that forms a crucial component of the Arrow system and can detect and track incoming missiles from up to 500 km away.

The Indian navy plans to acquire about 10 more Israeli 'Barak' antimissile defence systems, in addition to the seven already procured for its major warships. Barak provides a close-in point defence system to India against Harpoon and Exocet missiles acquired by Pakistan. Israel and India have agreed to jointly develop and produce a long-range version of the Barak. India has also approved the purchase of a $97m. Israeli electronic warfare system for ships. India has decided to launch joint programmes with Israel in the field of electronics warfare. With Israel's strength in sensors and packaging, and India in fibre optic gyros and micro electro-mechanical systems, both Israel and India can neatly complement each other (*Indian Express*, 2 September 2004).

India's attempts to shore up its conventional defences to counter its nuclear-armed adversary, Pakistan, have been greatly supported by Israeli weaponry. This includes surface-to-air missiles, avionics, sophisticated sensors to monitor cross-border infiltration, remotely piloted drones, and artillery. It is instructive to note that Israel sent its laser-guided missiles to India during the Indo-Pak Kargil war of 1999, making it possible for the Indian Mirages to destroy Pakistani bunkers in the mountains. Also, when India was planning to undertake a limited military strike against Pakistan in June 2002 as part of 'Operation Parakram', Israel supplied hardware through special planes (Gupta 2004).

India's ties with Israel will be constrained by how far the USA wants this engagement to go. Though the USA has welcomed the growing ties between India and Israel, it has a significant veto over Israel's defence exports. It has generally approved high-tech military exports from Israel to India in recent years, yet it has been reluctant to give its nod to systems involving American technology or financial input. The USA has, for example, expressed its disapproval of the possible sale of Israel's Arrow anti-missile system to India, leading to the suspension of talks between India and Israel on this issue (Aneja 2003).

This is not to deny, though, that the growing security relationship between India and Israel has, to a large extent, been nurtured with the help of the USA. It is also a distinct possibility that once the US arms market becomes more fully open to India, the Israeli market would lose its relative attraction, especially with the USA lifting restrictions on high-tech trade with India, covering cutting-edge technology pertaining to civilian nuclear energy, space, missile defence and high-tech commerce.

India and the West: future beckons

India's ties with the USA have rapidly evolved in the last few years. After the conclusion of the nuclear pact, the USA is poised to emerge as India's main defence partner. The USA and India signed the 'New Framework for the US-India Defence Partnership' in 2005, which paves the way for stepped-up military ties, including joint weapons production and co-operation on missile defence. The agreement speaks of both sides working 'to conclude defense transactions, not solely as ends in and of themselves, but as a means to strengthen our countries' security, reinforce our strategic partnership, achieve greater interaction between our armed forces, and build greater understanding between our defense establishments'.[2] The Indian Navy acquired the 36-year-old warship, USS Trenton (renamed INS Jalashwa), from the USA for $50m. in its first major arms deal in 2007. The USA will also be delivering six C-130J Hercules transport aircraft for use by Indian Special Forces by 2011 for $962m. and negotiations are underway for a 12 heavy-lift Chinook helicopter deal worth around $600m. However, these pale in comparison with the biggest ever US-India defence deal – the sale of eight Boeing P-8 long-range maritime reconnaissance aircraft for $2.2 billion. India and the USA also plan to conclude the Logistics Support Agreement enabling the two to provide logistical support, refuelling and berthing facilities for each other's warships and aircraft (Pandit 2008). The US defence industry found it difficult to get a foothold in India mainly due to political reasons. Now with Indian-US ties on an upward trajectory, opportunities abound. The US companies seem ready to transfer technology and manufacturing capability to India, with Boeing even offering to co-produce its F/A-18 Super Hornet plane in India.

Though Israel has forced other Western states such as France and the United Kingdom (UK) lower down in the pecking order so far as defence exports to India are concerned, they remain engaged with India on a range of programmes. The Indian Air Force is buying 66 Hawk Advanced Jet Trainers, with 24 of these being built in the UK by BAE Systems, while the remaining 42 will be manufactured under 'licence build' in India by Hindustan Aeronautics Limited (HAL). The procurement of 57 additional Hawks is also in the pipeline, with the Air Force claiming 40 and the Navy getting 17 (Sharma 2008). The Indian Navy is upgrading its ageing fleet of Sea Harriers by installing more advanced avionics and weapons systems in the fighters. The UK will not only be supplying four Sea Harrier air frames to India to be cannibalized for spares, but also plans to locate a harrier post-design service station in India to overhaul and maintain the fighters (*Press Trust of India*, 17 February 2008).

India and France are also moving away from a traditional buyer-seller relationship to focus on joint research and development projects, transfer of technology and greater military exchanges. One of the largest Indo-French defence deals was signed in 2005 for the construction of six Scorpene submarines in India at the cost of $3.5 billion. The two countries are working on the joint development of quick-reaction short-range surface-to-air missiles (SRSAM). French-led European company European Aeronautic Defence and Space (EADS) will be jointly producing 1,000 SRSAM for the Indian Army in collaboration with India's DRDO to help develop the Kaveri aero-engine for India's indigenous Light Combat Aircraft (LCA). The French aviation major Dassualt will also be upgrading the Indian Air Force's fleet of Mirage 2000 fighters (Nair 2008).

Indian defence policy and its discontents

As India's defence ties with major global powers reveal, Indian defence policy has become more ambitious in recent years than it has ever been in the past. Yet some fundamental vulnerabilities continue to plague Indian defence policy. These include the marginalization of the military in the national security set-up; inability to think through the use of the military as an instrument of policy; and the lack of institutional capacity to give defence policy a long-term strategic orientation. These factors have led India to a sub-optimal defence policy, the most visible manifestation of which is India's ad hoc approach to defence acquisitions.

Marginalization of the military

After independence in 1947, Indian politicians viewed the Indian Army with suspicion as the last supporters of the British Raj. Accordingly, they did their best to isolate the military from policy and influence. This attitude was further reinforced by the views of two giants of the Indian nationalist movement, Mahatma Gandhi and Jawaharlal Nehru. Gandhi's ardent belief in non-violence left little room for the use of force in an independent India. It also shaped the views on military and defence of the first generation of post-independence political leaders in India. However, more important has been the legacy of Nehru, India's first Prime Minister, who laid the institutional foundations for civil-military relations in the country. His obsession with economic development was only matched by his disdain and distrust of the military, resulting in the sidelining of defence planning (Cohen 2001, 127–30).

Despite lacking military experience, Nehru and his Minister of Defence, V. K. Krishna Menon were actively involved in operational level planning before the outbreak of the Sino-Indian war of 1962. They 'directly supervised the placement of individual brigades, companies, and even platoons, as the Chinese and Indian forces engaged in mutual encirclement of isolated outposts' (Cohen 2001, 176). As a consequence, when China won the war decisively, Nehru and Menon were blamed. Menon resigned and Nehru's reputation suffered lasting damage. Civilians and the military recognized that purely operational matters were best left to the military. Since then the political leadership has laid down operational directives while leaving the actual planning of operations to the chiefs of staff (Chari 1977, 75).

Stephen Rosen, in his study of the impact of societal structures on the military effectiveness of a state, argues that while the separation of the Indian military from Indian society has preserved the coherence of the Indian army, it has also led to a reduction in the military effectiveness of the Indian state (Rosen 1996, 250–3). While India—unlike Pakistan—has successfully developed a sustained tradition of strict civilian control over the military since its independence, it has been unable to change institutions and procedures that would allow the military to substantially participate in the national security decision-making process. This has significantly reduced the effectiveness with which India can wield its military as an instrument of national power.

Inability to use force effectively

Ultimately, a state's vital interests can only be preserved and enhanced if the nation has sufficient power at its disposal. However, not only must a state possess such power, it must also possess the *will* to use it in pursuit of those interests. India's lack of an instinct for power is most palpable in the military realm where, unlike other major global powers throughout history, India has failed to master the creation, deployment and use of its military instruments in support of its national objectives (Tellis 2004). Nehru envisioned India's becoming a global leader without the use of armed forces, arguing that, 'the right approach to defence is to avoid having unfriendly relations with other countries – to put it differently, war today is, and ought to be, out of question' (Rao 1977, 5–6). However, the modern state system, in fact the very nature of the state itself, has been determined largely by the changing demands of war (Bobbitt 2003). A defining feature of any state is its ability to make war and keep peace, and yet over the years war has been systematically factored out of Indian foreign policy and national security matrix, calling into question India's ability to prevail in major wars of the future.

Few states face the kind of security challenges that confront India. Yet since independence, the military has never been seen as central to achieving Indian national priorities. India ignored the defence sector after independence and paid inadequate attention to its security needs. Indeed, it was not until the Sino-Indian War of 1962 that the Indian military was given a role in the formulation of defence policy (Subrahmanyam 1972, 126–33). Divorcing foreign policy from military power was a recipe for disaster, as India realized in 1962 when even Nehru was forced to concede that 'military weakness has been a temptation, and a little military strength may be a deterrent' (Kavic 1967, 192). This trend continues even today, as was exemplified by the policy paralysis in New Delhi after the Mumbai terrorist attacks when Indians, to their horror, found out that due to the blatant politicization of military acquisitions India no longer enjoyed conventional military superiority vis-à-vis Pakistan, throwing Indian military posture into complete disarray and resulting in a serious loss of credibility (Gupta 2009). A state's legitimacy is tied to its ability to monopolize the use of force and operate effectively in an international strategic environment and India had lacked clarity on this relationship between the use of force and its foreign policy priorities.

Lack of effective institutional capacity

In the realm of defence and national security, successive Indian governments have given short shrift to the building of institutional capacity. A major reason why a culture of long-term strategic thinking has failed to evolve in India is the lack of meaningful institutions that can effectively leverage a nation's resources in the service of clearly defined political goals. India's emergence as a major power is still a matter of potential. It is often assumed that India has the necessary institutional wherewithal to translate its growing economic and military capabilities into global influence, even though the Indian state continues to suffer from weak administrative capacity in most areas of policy-making. Indian defence policy continues to suffer from a lack of direction which can only be rectified if appropriate institutions are in place.

On national security issues, state institutions often do not work because the governments of the day do not want them to work. So, the onus falls on bureaucracy, which is not organized to think strategically. Moreover, it remains insular and disinterested in acquiring a broader perspective. Bureaucratic resistance was one of the main reasons why administrative reforms introduced by the present government at the beginning of its term were never taken to their logical conclusion. Declining professionalism, intellectual sloth, inability and unwillingness to acquire new knowledge and lack of dynamism have brought Indian bureaucracy to its ebb in the last few decades (Kaur 2001). Despite several committees recommending a variety of changes, bureaucratic inertia has prevented any of the important recommendations from getting implemented. Given the rapidity with which the international environment has been evolving, Indian bureaucracy often finds itself out of tune with the changing realities in the realm of foreign and security policy and, more often than not, tends to perpetuate the status quo by focusing exclusively on responding to events as and when they occur as opposed to conceptualizing at a strategic level.

In 1999 a serious crisis emerged between India and Pakistan when India discovered that Pakistani soldiers and militants had infiltrated the Indian side of the Line of Control (LoC) and had taken control of important strategic positions. The Indian intelligence failure was grave and it took Indian forces almost two months to reoccupy the territory under Pakistan's control, losing precious military and civilian lives in the process. This limited war under the nuclear umbrella threw Indian shortcomings in intelligence, inter-services co-ordination, equipment for armed forces and civil-military interface into sharp relief. The government appointed a committee to review this failure which made a number of recommendations on a range of issues, but the government did not follow through on most of the recommendations and little was done to remedy the fundamental weaknesses in the nation's nation-security set-up (Kargil Review Committee Report 1999).

It was hardly any surprise, then, that after the terrorist attacks in Mumbai in November 2008, which were as grave an intelligence failure as the Kargil fiasco, the Indian strategic elites returned to the same old debates about what kind of institutional reforms were needed to prevent such tragedies from recurring. Yet consensus continues to elude India though, as is the case after every crisis, some tinkering to the existing institutions and laws has been resorted to. Moreover, the temptation after every crisis is to have new structures, if only to demonstrate that 'action' is being taken, but the existing national security organizations remain under-funded and understaffed. It is not clear if the new ones will be any more effective.

Every government promises to make the National Security Council (NSC) a professional and effective institution, to make it work in an optimal manner whereby the NSC anticipates national security threats, co-ordinates the management of national security and engenders long-term planning by generating new and bold ideas. So far this has proved to be beyond the capacity of various governments. An effective institutional framework would not only identify the challenges, but it would also develop a coherent strategy to deal with it, organize and motivate the bureaucracy, and persuade and inform the public. The NSC, by itself, is not a panacea particularly in the light of the inability of the NSC in the USA to mediate successfully in the bureaucratic wars and effectively co-ordinate policy. However, the lack of an effective NSC in India is reflective of India's ad hoc decision-making process in the realm of foreign policy, with the result that not once in its more than six decade-long history has India produced a national security strategy document.

The higher defence organizational set-up in India continues to exhibit serious weaknesses with serious doubts emerging about its ability to prosecute wars in the contemporary strategic context. The institutional structures as they stand today are not effective enough to provide single-point military advice to the government or to facilitate the definition of defence objectives. Co-ordinated and synergized joint operations need integrated theatre commands, yet India has not found it necessary to appoint even a Chief of Defence Staff (Puri 2008).

Ad hoc defence acquisition

As a result of above-mentioned factors, India's defence acquisition continues to lack focus, with little strategic dimension. Indian bureaucracy and its archaic and ineffective procurement procedures remain a major hindrance. Decision-making remains slow as politicians and bureaucrats are wary of approving purchases due to a series of arms procurement scandals since the late 1980s. The armed forces have a dismal record in spending their capital acquisition funds and they have been returning large sums over the last several years primarily because of delays in decision-making on procurement. The Indian armed forces keep waiting for arms and equipment while the Finance Ministry is left with unspent budget year after year. Most large procurement programmes get delayed, resulting in cost escalation and the technological or strategic obsolescence of the budgeted items. Allowing the rollover of the unspent funds might save some of the problems by removing uncertainty over funding of the postponed programme and might even encourage long-term strategic thinking on defence policy.

It was the Kargil conflict of 1999 that exposed Indian vulnerabilities, as Pakistan realized that India did not have the capability to impose quick and effective retribution. The then-Indian Army Chief had famously commented that the forces would fight with whatever they had got, underlining the frustration in the armed forces regarding their inability to procure the arms they needed. Only because the conflict remained largely confined to the 150-km front of the Kargil sector did India manage to gain an upper hand by throwing the Pakistanis out of its side of the LoC (Joshi 2009). Then came the stand-off between the Indian and Pakistani armies across the LoC after the Indian Parliament was attacked in 2001 and, again, India lacked the ability to impose any significant cost on Pakistan quickly and decisively because of the unavailability of suitable weaponry and night-vision equipment needed to carry out swift surgical strikes against Pakistan-based terrorist groups (Bedi 2001; Sudarshan and Pillai 2002).

These crises forced the government to act and India saw a rise in its defence acquisitions for a while. However, soon the old mindset took over and political compulsions overshadowed the nation's defence requirements. When the new government came to power in 2004, it ordered investigations into several of the arms acquisition deals of the previous government. Meanwhile, India's defence expenditure as a percentage of GDP has been declining and a large part of the money is surrendered by the defence forces every year, given their inability to spend due to the labyrinthine bureaucratic procedures involved in the procurement process. Political vindictiveness and a risk-averse bureaucracy have ensured that while Pakistan has rapidly acquired US technology over the past eight years under the slogan of fighting the 'war on terror', the modernization of the Indian army has slipped behind a decade.

As a result, the situation in which India finds itself after the Mumbai attacks should come as no surprise: India no longer has the capability of imposing quick and decisive military costs on Pakistan and it does not enjoy the kind of conventional superiority vis-à-vis its regional adversary that it had enjoyed for the past five decades.

After Operation Parakram of 2001–02, the Indian Army did try to evolve a new doctrine to find an answer to Pakistan's perceived recklessness. This 'Cold Start' doctrine is basically an attempt to acquire the ability to fight limited wars under the nuclear umbrella (Ladwig 2007/08, 158–90). To resolve the dilemma confronting India post-1998, Indian strategists have focused on a military doctrine that might give them the ability to launch quick, decisive limited strikes against Pakistan to seize some territory before the international community could intervene, which can then be used as a post-conflict bargaining chip. This doctrine is still evolving and it is not clear how effective it would be in making sure that the conflict remains limited, as Pakistan might be forced to bring down its nuclear threshold to respond to this challenge. Moreover, the Army has found little support for this doctrine from the other two services and the civilian government has shown no interest in this venture. It is expected that this doctrine will once again come into the limelight as the Indian national security establishment desperately looks for policy options vis-à-vis Pakistan. Execution of this doctrine would, though, need the right kind of equipment, something India will have to acquire on a priority basis.

Facing criticism after the Mumbai attacks that its lethargic attitude towards defence acquisition has allowed India's conventional advantage vis-à-vis Pakistan to dissipate, the government has now decided to initiate fast-track acquisition procedures (Samanta 2009). For all its pretensions of undertaking a massive modernization programme, the three services lack even basic equipment. The Army is in desperate need of third-generation night-vision devices, assault rifles, and new generation bullet-proof jackets. The Navy needs UAVs for maritime reconnaissance and interceptor boats, while the Air Force needs low-level transportable radars and air defence missile systems.

The Indian desire to modernize and the West's desire to tap into the new market is leading to some gradual reforms. India remains notorious for its slow bureaucratic processes and some institutional interests are so entrenched in government policy that changes are difficult to accomplish. Yet external forces are propelling some alterations. These external forces include a backlash from Western industry over the slow and tedious contract process with the USA and Europe, making it clear that they want to sell to India, but the current structure of the procurement process makes it difficult. The US commitment to Indian defence procurement remains unquestionable and so the Indian polity seems eager to make the necessary changes in order to attract US industry. There is also huge potential for economic investment by the domestic defence industry if they can begin to grow themselves. At the moment, though, progress is slow and the Indian defence industry is small in comparison with many other countries.

As a result of this, India passed its new Defence Procurement Policy in 2006, which requires foreign countries with a contract of over $66m to invest 30% of the contract's value in the Indian defence and technology industries. This will help to build up local industry while Western companies are still being awarded huge defence contracts. The government is trying to get the private sector to invest in the domestic economy, but they are also trying to make sure they do not lose Indian industry and companies to international competition. It also allows India to conduct a balancing act between buying the latest high-tech defence equipment and appeasing the domestic industry. The challenge for the Indian government is to come up with a clear idea of what products they need and how to build up their own industry in the process by significantly reforming the domestic defence manufacturing sector, dominated by protected public-sector enterprises and ordinance factories.

Conclusion

India will continue to pursue its defence modernization programme and will remain a major buyer in the global arms market for the foreseeable future. Indian armed forces will continue to demand a greater share of governmental resources as they modernize and their role extends beyond protecting the borders: fighting insurgencies, tackling terrorism in urban areas and policing the South Asian region. Given India's role as a balancer in the international system, its ties with major global players such as the USA, Russia, the UK and France will remain strong and this will help it to diversify its defence purchases, though the role of the USA is set to increase substantially, with a relative decline in Russian influence. Yet for all the reasons outlined above arms acquisition will remain ad hoc in nature and will continue to inhibit India's potential to emerge as a significant global military power.

Indian defence expenditure as a percentage of GDP has been declining since 2004/05, with the last four years experiencing a more than 2 percentage point decline on this front. A mere increase in defence spending, though, would not be enough to make up for the deficiencies in the armed forces caused by years of inadequate funding and limited modernization. The debate on Indian defence policy tends not to go beyond increasing defence expenditure and big-ticket military acquisitions. What is needed is a restructuring of the Indian armed forces and the national defence set-up, which will allow them to operate with the utmost efficiency in a rapidly evolving domestic and global context.

Notes

1 'Hindi-Chini Bhai Bhai' (Indians and Chinese are brothers) was a popular slogan during the 1950s, the heyday of the Sino-Indian relationship, which became discredited after the 1962 Sino-Indian war.
2 For full text of the Agreement see www.indianembassy.org/press_release/2005/June/31.htm.

Bibliography

Aneja, Atul, 'U.S. Objects to Sale of Arrow Missiles to India', *The Hindu*, 8 September 2003
Bedi, Rahul, 'The Military Dynamics', *Frontline*, 21 June 2001
Behera, L. K., 'Rising Global Military Expenditure: Implications for India', *India Post*, 29 November 2007
——— 'India's Defense Budget 2008–09', *IDSA Strategic Comments*, 19 March, 2008, www.idsa.in/publications/stratcomments/LaxmanBehera190308Next.htm
Bobbitt, Philip, *The Shield of Achilles: War, Peace, and the Course of History*, New York, Anchor Books, 2003
Chari, P. R., 'Civil-Military Relations of India', *Link*, 15 August 1977
Chazan, Guy and Jay Solomon, 'Israel to Sell Radar to India', *Wall Street Journal*, 5 September 2003
Chengappa, Raj, 'The Real Boss', *India Today*, 11 December 2008
Cohen, Stephen P., *India: Emerging Power*, New Delhi, Oxford University Press, 2001
——— *The Indian Army: Its Contribution to the Development of a Nation*, New Delhi, Oxford University Press, 1990
Dikshit, Sandeep, 'Israeli Navy Chief on Maiden Visit', *The Hindu*, 7 August 2007
Economist Intelligence Unit, 'India's Future', *The Economist*, 29 September 2008
Giriharadas, Anand, 'Land of Gandhi Asserts Itself as Global Military Power', *New York Times*, 22 September 2008
Government of India, Ministry of Defence, *Annual Report*, 2007/08
Gupta, Shishir, 'Next Navy Chief Goes to Israel to Signal Smooth Bilateral Sailing', *Indian Express*, 11 July 2004
Gupta, Shekhar, 'No First Use Options', *Indian Express*, 17 January 2009
IISS, *The Military Balance 2008*, London, International Institute for Strategic Studies, 2008
——— *The Military Balance 2009*, London, International Institute for Strategic Studies, 2009
'India: Interest in Russian Weapons', *New York Times*, 23 November 2002
'Indian Navy may get four Sea Harriers from UK', *Press Trust of India*, 17 February 2008
AFP, 'India Plans to Spend More on Defense if Economy Grows', *Agence France-Presse*, 20 October 2005
'India, Russia to Sign $450 million Arms Deal', *Press Trust of India*, 22 February 2005
'India to Tie Up with Israel, U.S. for E-Warfare Systems', *Indian Express*, 2 September 2004
Joshi, Manoj, 'How Can Army Win Wars with Outdated Artillery?', *India Today*, 23 January 2009
Kapur, S. Paul, 'Ten Years of Instability in a Nuclear South Asia', *International Security*, Vol. 33 (2), Fall 2008.
Kargil Review Committee Report, *From Surprise to Reckoning*, New Delhi, Sage Publications, 1999
Kaura, G. S., 'India, Israel to Further Strengthen Defense Ties', *The Tribune*, 3 January, 2008
Kaur, N., 'To Stem the Decay', *Frontline*, 8–21 December 2001
Kavic, L., *India's Quest for Security: Defence Policies, 1947–1965*, Berkeley, University of California Press, 1967
Ladwig III, Walter C., 'A Cold Start for Hot Wars? An Assessment of the Indian Army's New Limited War Doctrine', *International Security*, Vol. 32 (3), Winter 2007/08
Nair, G. Sudhakar, 'India, France to Bolster Defence Ties, Build Missiles', *India Abroad*, 30 September 2008
Pandit, Rajat, 'India, US to Ramp Up Defence Ties under Obama Adm', *Times of India*, 13 December 2008
Pant, Harsh V., 'India in the Asia-Pacific: Rising Ambitions with an Eye on China', *Asia-Pacific Review*, Vol. 14 (1), May 2007
Puri, Raman, 'Armed Forces Command Structure', *Agni*, 2008
Rao, P. V. R., *India's Defence Policy and Organisation Since Independence*, New Delhi, The United Services Institution of India, 1977
Rosen, Stephen P., *Societies and Military Power: India and Its Armies*, Ithaca, Cornell University Press, 1996
Samanta, Pranab Dhal. 'Fast-forward on Security Purchases: 8 Months Maximum to Wrap Up Deal', *Indian Express*, 25 January 2009
Sharma, Ravi, 'IAF to get 40 more Hawk AJTs', *The Hindu*, 11 January 2008
Shukla, Saurabh, 'Russian Chill', *India Today*, 19 November 2007

Shukla, Vinay, 'Russia in South Asia: A View from India', in Gennady Chufrin, ed., *Russia and Asia: The Emerging Security Agenda*, Stockholm, SIPRI, 1999

Singh, Jasjit, *India's Defence Spending: Assessing Future Needs*, New Delhi, Knowledge World, 2001

Srinivas, V. N., 'Trends in Defence Expenditure', *Air Power Journal*, Vol. 3, No. 1, Spring 2006

Subrahmanyam, K., *Perspectives in Defence Planning*, New Delhi, Abhinav, 1972

Sudarshan, V. and Ajith Pillai, 'Game of Patience', *Outlook*, 27 May 2002

Tellis, Ashley J., *Future Fire: Challenges Facing Indian Defense Policy in the New Century*, paper presented at the India Today Conclave, New Delhi, 13 March 2004, www.ceip.org/files/pdf/futurefire.pdf

Unnithan, Sandeep, 'Battle over Gorshkov', *India Today*, 7 December 2007

Watson, Paul, 'Arms at the Heart of India-Israel Embrace', *Los Angeles Times*, 9 September 2003

6 Japan's arms procurement after the Cold War

Brad Williams

Introduction

Arms procurement in post-war Japan has been shaped primarily by two principles: indigenization (*kokusanka*) and anti-militarism. The former prioritizes the domestic development of defence equipment over licensed production and imports, while the latter, characterized as an aversion to the military establishment and the use of military force to resolve international disputes (see Berger 1993), has been manifested in a number of policies that have served to limit arms production. Japan has, then, not typically been a major importer and exporter of defence equipment. However, several international and domestic developments that have emerged following the end of the Cold War have created momentum for a revision of key elements of this restrictive policy, thereby raising expectations among some domestic actors who favour Japan assuming a more prominent role in the global arms market.

This chapter comprises four sections. The first provides an overview of the main public and private actors involved in arms procurement. This is followed by an examination of the anti-militaristic principles that have shaped domestic arms production, highlighting the challenges they have come under as Japan slowly treads the path towards normalcy in international security affairs. The subsequent need to modernize Japan's defence capabilities in the face of regional uncertainties has come at a time when there is mounting pressure to curb defence spending. Balancing these competing demands has seen quantitative reductions and qualitative improvements in the Japanese Self-Defence Force's (JSDF) capabilities – the subject of the next section of the chapter. Section four examines perhaps a greater threat to domestic arms procurement than declining defence budgets: systemic corruption. This not only adds significantly to the cost of defence acquisition programmes but also casts doubts on the integrity of the Ministry of Defence (MOD) and its ability to function as Japan's primary national security policy agency. The chapter then concludes with an analysis of how the current state of arms procurement in Japan impacts upon the global arms trade.

Arms procurement: the main actors

Ministry of defence

Before its change of status in early 2007, the Japan Defence Agency (JDA) was not an independent ministry. It was under the formal authority of the Cabinet Office and its head, the Prime Minister. The politician in charge of the JDA's administrative affairs was a Director-General who, while nominally a member of the cabinet, did not enjoy the full powers of a cabinet minister. In order to ensure civilian control over the JDA, its internal bureaux were often headed by officials seconded from other ministries. The JDA's lack of autonomy naturally extended to arms procurement, with transferred officials from the Ministry of Foreign Affairs (MOFA), the former Ministry of International Trade and Industry's (MITI) Aircraft and Ordnance Division and the Ministry of Finance's (MOF) Budget Bureau wielding significant influence over policy-making (Ikegami-Andersson 1992, 112–3; Samuels 1994, 323).

As a result of changes in Japan's security environment over the last 10–15 years, the JSDF's primary mission has expanded from defence of the home islands to incorporate domestic and international disaster relief activities and peace-keeping operations. This transformation has shifted the JDA's operational priorities from exclusively managing the JSDF to policy-making and planning, which, in turn, created a propitious environment for those within the defence establishment who have long sought to upgrade the JDA to the status of a full ministry (Japan Ministry of Defence 2007, 175). Japan's MOD was thus born on 9 January 2007. In accordance with this transition, the MOD is now headed by its own minister who is vested with supervisory and control powers. Unlike the JDA Director-General, the Minister of Defence is now empowered to, *inter alia*, ask the MOF directly for budget funding for the JSDF and call cabinet meetings to consider defence-related legislation and JSDF personnel affairs.

The new MOD has also undergone large-scale internal restructuring in recent years designed to enhance its policy-planning functions and crisis management capabilities. As will be discussed in greater detail below, MOD reforms have also been prompted by a number of defence procurement scandals, which have underscored the necessity of creating a more effective and transparent arms procurement system in Japan. As a part of the frequent restructuring of defence equipment and materials acquisition organizations, the JDA abolished the Central Procurement Office (*Chōtatsu Jisshi Honbu* or CPO, established in 1954) in 2001. The former CPO's contract and cost calculation functions were divided, with the former becoming the responsibility of the newly created Central Contract Office (*Keiyaku Honbu*), while the latter were transferred to an internal bureau. These two functions were reunited with the establishment, in July 2006, of an Equipment Procurement Office (*Sōbi Honbu* or EPO). A further reorganization was carried out in September 2007 when the Defense Facilities Administration Agency (*Bōei Shisetsuchō*) was abolished and its functions integrated into the MOD's Internal Bureau. At the same time, the EPO was renamed the Equipment Procurement and Construction Office (*Sōbi Shisetsu Honbu* or EPCO) and its responsibilities broadened to include creating estimation and technical standards, as well as examining implementation plans for defence construction projects. The EPCO has a staff of nearly 600, the vast majority of whom are non-uniform personnel. It comprises seven divisions, each headed by a Deputy Director, who is, in turn, under the authority of the Director (*honbuchō*). The eight Defence Facilities Administration Bureaux and five district offices of the former EPO across Japan were abolished and their tasks were incorporated into eight regional defence bureaux (located in Hokkaido, Tohoku, North and South Kanto, Kinki-Chubu, Chugoku-Shikoku, Kyushu and Okinawa (Bōeishō Sōbi Shisetsu Honbu).

Technical research and development institute

The Technical Research and Development Institute (*Gijitsu Kenkyū Honbu* or TRDI) is the primary research organization in Japan focusing on the advancement of defence-related technology. A defence R&D body was first established in 1952 and has undergone several processes of reorganization before assuming its current status as a special organ under the jurisdiction of the MOD. The TRDI is headed by a Director-General who is subordinate to the Minister of Defence. As of 2007, TRDI boasted a staff of 1,135, of whom 75% were civilians (47% research engineers and 28% administrative officials) and 25% uniform personnel from the three branches of the JSDF. The TRDI's budget in 2007 was approximately US $1.5 billion, which represented 3.8% of the total defence budget (Bōeishō Gijutsu Kenkyū Honbu). While the sums of Japanese government-funded defence R&D are comparable with those of its regional neighbours, they are quite low in relation to other advanced industrial countries. This may well reflect the Japanese emphasis on private rather than government-based production, which is also evident in the TRDI's role of co-ordinating private corporate participation in defence-related research projects, in addition to initiating and sponsoring defence R&D (Renwick 1995, 90). Japanese firms also benefit from the TRDI's heavy reliance on the private sector for R&D due to a practice in which 'researchers are routinely chosen as contractors when the projects proceed to production' (Samuels 1994, 192).

Arms manufacturers

The former JDA's relative lack of institutional autonomy opened the way for other actors to exert considerable influence in formulating defence policy. One such group has been Japan's major arms manufacturers. A prominent feature of arms production in Japan is that it is mostly carried out by major industrial conglomerates, which mainly produce civilian goods, and not by independent defence companies. The Japanese arms industry is oligopolistic; the top four defence manufacturers in 2006 – Mitsubishi Heavy Industries (MHI), Kawasaki Heavy Industries, Mitsubishi Electric and NEC, names familiar to many global consumers – accounted for just over 45% of JDA contracts, while the top 10 companies received over 60% (*Nihon Keizai Shimbun*, 25 August 2007, 13). Their location within these large *keiretsu* conglomerates has meant that Japan's major defence contractors do not rely significantly on military sales. For instance, MHI, which has consistently been Japan's largest arms manufacturer, earning it the label of the 'Japanese arsenal' (Ikegami-Andersson 1992, 81), earned just 9% of its total revenue from defence sales in 2006 (*Defense News* 2007). In contrast, the share of military sales out of total sales for the two largest US (and also global) defence contractors: Lockheed Martin and Boeing, was 90% and 50%, respectively (*Defense News* 2007). Many of Japan's arms manufacturers also specialize in the production of a narrow range of defence equipment and have mastered the development of dual-use civilian products and processes, which, in a process known as 'spin-on', can be employed for military purposes (Ikegami-Andersson 1992, 83; Samuels 1994, 26–7; Hughes 2005, 91). While most Japanese defence contactors differ from their US counterparts in terms of reliance on military sales, they are analogous in their dependence on subcontractors. As Richard Samuels (1994, 52, 185) observes, prime defence contractors in Japan are directly responsible for a fraction of nominal arms production and rely on the special high-level technologies possessed by subcontracting firms in most weapons sectors.

Another salient feature of many Japanese arms manufacturers is their close relationship with foreign, mainly US, defence contractors, which has enabled them to secure access to licensing agreements as a means of acquiring military technology. Relations between Japanese and US defence contractors have been institutionalized through the establishment of the USA-Japan Industry Forum for Security Co-operation (IFSEC). Created in 1997, IFSEC aims to promote bilateral defence industry dialogue and serve as an advisory mechanism for the US Department of Defense (DoD) and the MOD. In a Joint Declaration released in December 2002, it was further proposed that IFSEC: 1. create an environment for more open dialogue concerning future equipment and technological co-operation between both defence industries; 2. publish information on defence equipment procured by the USA and implement fast and efficient procedures for export licences; 3. flexibly manage Japanese Government arms export control policies; and 4. conclude an agreement on the protection of intellectual property rights for defence programmes and establish clear standards for protecting intellectual property rights for civilian dual-use technologies (Keidanren 2004, 13). At a time of declining defence budgets (at least in Japan) and rising weapons system development costs, pressure for closer bilateral defence industry co-operation, Japan's arms export restrictions notwithstanding, will continue to mount.

The Japanese defence industry is small by international standards: it had just three firms ranked in the top 50 defence companies in 2006 and contributed barely 0.5% to the nation's industrial production.[1] Declining defence budgets have adversely affected the arms industry, resulting in industrial restructuring in recent years. In two prominent cases of industrial withdrawal, Nissan Automobiles sold its aerospace business to Ishikawajima-Harima Heavy Industries (IHI) in July 2000, while Tōyō Communication Equipment sold its defence division to NEC in May 2004. In October 2002, IHI and Sumitomo Heavy Industries divested their shipbuilding and offshore businesses to create IHI Marine United. In the same month, NKK and Hitachi Shipbuilding also integrated their shipbuilding operations with the establishment of Universal Shipbuilding (Keidanren 2004, 8).

Industrial associations

Japanese firms engaged in defence production have established influential organizations to lobby on their behalf (Ikegami-Andersson 1992, 84). Two of the more prominent industry pressure groups are the Defence Production Committee (*Bōei Seisan Iinkai* or KDPC) of Keidanren (Japan Federation of Economic Organizations), the most important of Japan's business organizations, comprising the nation's largest corporations and industry-wide groups,[2] and the Japan Association of Defence Industry (*Nihon Bōei Sōbi Kōgyōkai* or JADI).[3]

The KDPC has been referred to as the 'private version of the Defense Agency' due to its role and influence on the former JDA (Yoshihara 1980, cited in Ikegami-Andersson 1992, 85). Among its activities, the KDPC issues reports and otherwise puts forward its views on aspects of armament policy. Perhaps unsurprisingly given its role and composition, the KDPC has been a key proponent of *kokusanka* of arms production over imports as a means of enhancing national security and improving military technology (Ikegami-Andersson 1992, 85; Koga 2000, 152–3).

JADI's original predecessor was first established in 1951 and was reorganized into the more familiar Japan Ordnance Association (*Nihon Heiki Kōgyōkai*) two years later, which represented the interests of Japan's defence manufacturers for more than three decades before becoming JADI in 1988. As a non-profit public corporation (*shadan hōjin*), JADI is under partial government supervision, with former MITI and JDA (now METI and MOD) officials on its board (Green 1995, 110). The majority (over 130) of Japan's corporations involved in the manufacture and repair of armaments are members of JADI, which, under the guidance of the METI and MOD, participates in a wide range of activities designed to promote defence-related R&D and production technologies. Some of these activities include conducting research on defence equipment, offering proposals on arms modernization and creating production bases, promoting co-operative links among defence manufacturers, establishing regulations and standards for defence equipment and co-operating with government arms export controls (Nihon Bōei Sōbi Kōgyōkai).[4]

Antimilitarism and arms production

Like other aspects of post-war Japanese defence policy, domestic arms production has been restricted by several anti-militaristic principles derived from the 1946 Constitution. While a strict interpretation of Article Nine prohibits Japan from maintaining a military establishment, Japanese governments since the 1950s have interpreted the so-called 'peace clause', in accordance with its status as a sovereign state under the UN Charter, as allowing Japan to exercise the right of national self-defence and to maintain the JSDF for this purpose (Hughes 2005, 32). Based on this constitutional interpretation, Japan has pursued an exclusively defence-oriented policy (*senshu bōei*), which has limited its military capacity to the minimum necessary for self-defence and effectively prohibited the possession of 'war potential' (*senryoku*). These are not entirely precise concepts, leaving open the possibility of future maintenance of powerful weapons, but in practical terms have meant that the JSDF do not possess power-projection capabilities (Hughes 2005, 33). Japan's military alliance with the USA, especially its position under the nuclear umbrella of its superpower patron, has also obviated the necessity of possessing such offensive capabilities. However, in response to regional uncertainties and a shift in the domestic political terrain, momentum for constitutional reform has slowly been gathering over the past decade, edging Japan incrementally (and fitfully) towards *de jure* recognition of the use of force as an instrument of statecraft.

Anti-militarism in Japan has also been manifested in a number of policy positions that have impacted upon arms production. The first of these is the restrictions on arms exports to communist states, countries under UN sanctions and parties to international disputes first enunciated by the administration of Prime Minister Satō Eisaku in 1967. There were loopholes in this policy, some of which were closed off in 1976 when the government of Prime Minister Miki Takeo, seeking to appeal to unaffiliated voters and a resurgent political opposition (Oros 2008, 109), ordered restraint on arms sales to all countries and also prohibited the export of military technology. In 1978 the MITI announced it would reinforce these regulations by placing restrictions on military technology based on the Foreign Exchange Law and Foreign Trade Control Law (Ikegami-Andersson 1992, 92). These restrictions, while mostly effective, have, though, been partially violated, firstly as a result of Prime Minister Nakasone's decision to sign the 1983 Exchange on Technology Agreement with the USA to facilitate bilateral technological co-operation on the contentious FS-X fighter project (now in service with the ASDF as the F-2) and, perhaps more significantly by exports of dual-use technologies with both civilian and military applications. There has been pressure in recent years to lift this ban in order to facilitate ballistic missile defence (BMD) co-operation, foster joint projects with the USA and other countries for developing interoperable defence equipment for multinational peace and security activities, and to ensure that domestic arms producers do not fall behind their overseas competitors (Hughes 2005, 90). Support for easing export restrictions has, though, been undermined by several incidents in which sensitive Japanese technology has been taken out of the country illegally. These cases have prompted the METI to seek a revision of the Foreign Exchange and Control Law by adding further items to the list of products subject to arms export controls (*The Japan Times*, 22 August 2008; *Shizuoka Shimbun*, 12 November 2008, 9).

During the same year that he announced a ban on arms exports, Prime Minister Satō introduced three non-nuclear principles, according to which Japan should not produce, possess nor introduce nuclear weapons. These three principles received widespread public support in a nation susceptible to the 'nuclear allergy' following the atomic bomb attacks on Hiroshima and Nagasaki, and also later earned Satō the Nobel Peace Prize. Some critics may point out the hypocrisy of the three non-nuclear principles given Japan's reliance on the US nuclear umbrella. Similarly, it is also important to note that the Japanese Government does not, in fact, consider the possession of nuclear weapons as necessarily unconstitutional if used for the purposes of self-defence (Hughes 2005, 33), although, until recently few have dared to publicly declare so for fear of violating a political taboo. Japan ratified the Non-Proliferation Treaty in 1976, reinforcing the first two principles, but has violated the third since revelations that nuclear weapons have periodically entered the country on US naval vessels.

The third of the anti-militaristic principles enunciated during the 1960s came in the form of a Diet (legislature) resolution in 1969 declaring Japan's commitment to the use of outer space exclusively for peaceful purposes. This resolution was interpreted as meaning Japan would limit its use of space to non-military activities. Japan's development of an indigenous satellite programme and participation in BMD since the 1990s, ostensibly to counter the threat of the Democratic People's Republic of Korea (North Korea), created pressure for a policy change from 'non-military' to 'non-aggression' in May 2008, which has paved the way for the government to 'station equipment in space compatible with a defence-oriented policy' (*The Japan Times*, 22 May 2008).

The final principle evincing the norm of anti-militarism in Japan emerged with Prime Minister Miki's announcement in 1976 that defence expenditure should be limited to 1% of gross national product (GNP). The Nakasone Government breached the 1% ceiling slightly in the late 1980s but since that time successive administrations have kept Japanese defence spending at around this limit. The analytical focus, in particular, on military expenditure as a percentage of GNP is misleading, though, as it underestimates Japanese military power. In absolute terms, Japan spends over $40 billion per year on defence, ranking it in the top five defence-spending countries, and possesses extremely powerful air and naval capabilities. Nevertheless, while the Japanese defence budget, as measured in nominal US dollar terms, continued to rise during the 1990s, it has remained fairly stagnant or even decreased slightly since then (Hughes 2005, 76–8; SIPRI). The defence budget's share of total government expenditure has been fairly stable at around 6% during the period 1975–2004 (Hughes 2005, 77). Procurement spending on arms and equipment, which accounts for about 18% of Japan's defence budget, has declined slightly over the last decade (Bōeishō 2008).

Quantitative reductions and qualitative improvements in JSDF capabilities

The principles for the defence of Japan and the troop and equipment levels needed to achieve these objectives are explicated in the National Defence Programme Outline (NDPO). Japan's first NDPO was formulated in 1976 during the period of détente between the two superpowers. The NDPO was revised in 1995 in order to make Japan's force structure better able to address the uncertainties of the post-Cold War period, as well as rising public expectations regarding international contributions. Since the revised NDPO was released in 1995, the fluidity and instability of the international environment has been accentuated further by the 'war on terror', which, combined with advances in military technology and the expansion and diversification of the JSDF's activities, has necessitated a shift in emphasis in Japan's basic defence force concept from deterrence to response capabilities. This shift in basic defence thinking was formalized with the cabinet's approval of new National Defence Programme Guidelines (NDPG) in December 2004. According to the NDPG, the desired role of Japan's JSDF in this altered security environment is to respond effectively to new threats and diverse situations, and to become proactively and aggressively involved in international peace co-operation activities. This flexible, effective and multifunctional defence force is to be supported by sophisticated intelligence capabilities and technology based on adequate military levels. It is also intended to be more productive with the limited resources available through enhanced efficiency and rationalization of personnel, equipment and management. This 'effective response oriented concept' is also driven by demographic (declining youth population) and financial pressures (budgetary allocations) in Japan (Bōeichō 2005, 93).

The NDPG calls for a general reduction in personnel and equipment levels across the three branches of the JSDF, which is to be carried out incrementally through the Mid-Term Defence Programme (MTDP, fiscal year—FY 2005/09). Specifically, the total number of JSDF personnel will be reduced from 160,000 to 155,000.[5] The GSDF's battle tanks and artillery will both be cut back from 900 to 600; the MSDF will decommission three destroyers and reduce combat aircraft from approximately 170 to 150, while the ASDF will cut around 50 combat aircraft.

For Japan's arms manufacturers, concerns arising from substantial cuts in Cold War-era conventional equipment have been tempered somewhat by procurement orders based on the continued modernization of Japan's defence capabilities. The current MTDP calls for the deployment of new transport planes (C-1), helicopters (CH-47JA/J) and aerial refuelling aircraft (KC-767) to help respond to an invasion of Japan's offshore islands. The deployment of the KC-767 is especially significant as it can be considered a power-projection capability, thus challenging the notion of a defence-oriented policy. Concerns that Japan is intent on developing such a capability were earlier aroused with the MSDF's procurement of Osumi-class transport ships. With flat-topped decks suited to the landing of helicopter transports, these vessels resemble small aircraft

Table 6.1 Comparison of equipment and personnel numbers under the 1995 NDPO and the 2004 NDPG

	1995 NDPO	*2004 NDPG*
SDF personnel	160,000	155,000
Regular personnel	145,000	148,000
Ready reserve personnel	15,000	7,000
GSDF		
Major units		
Regionally deployed units	8 divisions	8 divisions
	6 brigades	6 brigades
Mobile operation units	1 armoured division	1 armoured division
	1 airborne brigade	central readiness force
	1 helicopter brigade	
Ground-to-air missile units	8 anti-aircraft	8 anti-aircraft
	artillery groups	artillery groups
Main equipment		
Battle tanks	approx. 900	approx. 600
Artillery	approx. 900	approx. 600
MSDF		
Major units		
Destroyer units	4 escort flotillas	4 escort flotillas
(for mobile operations)		(8 divisions)
Destroyer units		
(regional district units)	7 divisions	5 divisions
Submarine units	6 divisions	4 divisions
Minesweeping units	1 flotilla	1 flotilla
Land-based patrol aircraft units	13 squadrons	9 squadrons
Main equipment		
Destroyers	approx. 50	approx. 47
Submarines	16	16
Combat aircraft	approx. 170	approx. 150
ASDF		
Major units		
Aircraft control and warning units	8 warning groups	8 warning groups
	20 warning squadrons	20 warning squadrons
	1 squadron	1 airborne early warning
		squadron (2 squadrons)
Fighter units	—	12 squadrons
Interceptor units	9 squadrons	
Support fighter units	3 squadrons	—
Air reconnaissance units	1 squadron	1 squadron
Air transport units	3 squadrons	3 squadrons
Aerial refuelling/transport units	—	1 squadron
Ground-to-air missile units	6 groups	6 groups
Main equipment		
Combat aircraft	approx. 400	approx. 350
(among which are) fighters	approx. 300	approx. 260

Source: Bōeichō 2005, p.105

carriers. While their thin decks are thought to make them unsuitable for vertical /short takeoff and landing operations, the Osumi-class transport ships, combined with MSDF plans to construct new helicopter-carrying destroyers, suggests 'that Japan is rehearsing carrier-building technology to reserve for itself this potential military option' (Hughes 2005, 82). Replacements for the P-3C fixed-wing patrol aircraft, improvements to E-2C early warning aircraft and E-767 early warning and control aircraft, introduction of the successor to the F-4 fighter and the modernization and upgrade of F-15 fighters are also expected to help the JSDF respond to new threats and diverse contingencies such as violations of Japanese airspace and intrusions from special operations vessels like those dispatched by North Korea in the past. Finally, the MTDP highlights the necessity of promoting R&D in, *inter alia*, mobile combat vehicles, command and control systems, and unmanned aerial vehicles (Bōeishō 2008, 322).

The most significant aspect of the NDPG is the procurement of a BMD system. The Japanese Government was initially somewhat reluctant to commit itself fully to BMD co-operation with the USA. Tokyo's position changed following North Korea's launch of a Taepo-dong missile that passed over Japan in August 1998. Japan began introducing the components of a BMD system in 2004. While BMD is designed to protect Japan from the threat of Pyongyang's medium- and long-range missiles in the short term, Japanese security planners are also clearly concerned by the People's Republic of China's missile capabilities over the long term, as well as Russia's regional missile forces (Hughes 2005, 111). BMD is a multi-layered defence system comprising land-based Patriot PAC-3 missile batteries, Aegis-equipped vessels, supporting sensors and a battle management (Japan Aerospace Defence Ground Environments, or JADGE) system. Under the BMD system, it is envisaged that incoming ballistic missiles would be intercepted by Aegis vessels in their mid-course phase and by Patriot batteries in their terminal phase. The NDPG calls for the acquisition of 16 PAC-3 fire units (FU)[6] and four Aegis BMD vessels. Four PAC-3 FUs were deployed in late 2007, while the remaining 12 will be introduced incrementally, which should be completed by late 2009. The first Aegis destroyer equipped with BMD capabilities became operational in December 2007, while the second underwent successful trials in September 2008. Two more Aegis vessels are scheduled to be upgraded and equipped with SM-3 BMD capabilities in 2009 and 2010. The introduction of and modifications to the sensors (FPS-5, FPS-3 radar) is expected to be completed by late 2011. JADGE, which will enable the BMD system to 'detect, track, weapon-assign and intercept ballistic missiles systematically by synchronizing weapons and sensors effectively' (Tanaka 2006, 6), should be fully operational by late 2011. The Japanese Government spent approximately ¥662 billion (approximately $670m.) on BMD between 2004 and 2008 and has requested an additional ¥128 billion for FY2009 (Japan Ministry of Defense 2008, 7–13).

As in many areas of national defence, Japan maintains a close relationship with the USA in BMD. Bilateral co-operation is evident in the recent deployment of US BMD assets to Japan such as FBX-T transportable radar, PAC-3 battalions and a guided-missile cruiser with BM mid-course interception capabilities, the USS Shiloh. USA-Japan co-operation has also been extended to research on Aegis BMD missiles (SM-3 BLK IIA). Research aims to improve the capabilities of future missiles rather than the current model and involves four key BMD interceptor missile technologies: the nosecone (protects the seeker and kinetic warhead during inner-space flight), seeker (discriminates and tracks targets by using infra-red radiation), kinetic warhead (attacks and destroys targets with kinetic energy) and the second-stage rocket motor.[7] Japan intends to develop independently the nosecone and second-stage rocket motor and co-operate with the USA on upgrading the seeker and kinetic warhead. The project has a nine-year schedule (FYs2006–14) and is estimated to cost the Japanese side around $1 billion–1.2 billion (roughly half of the total cost of the project), although reviews will be conducted as the project progresses (Japan Ministry of Defence 2008, 17–8).

Arms procurement corruption: the seemingly never-ending story

Since the early 1990s, the reputation of Japan's once-exalted bureaucrats has been tarnished considerably in the wake of a seemingly constant stream of corruption scandals. The former JDA has frequently come under the spotlight for improprieties in the procurement of defence equipment. In the most recent high-profile case former MOD Administrative Vice-Minister, Moriya Takemasa, was convicted in November 2008 for accepting bribes from a defence equipment trading company, Yamada Corp., in exchange for preferential treatment in the awarding of procurement contracts. The alarming regularity of defence procurement scandals (six major cases since 1994) might lead one to conclude that the MOD has been indifferent to the need for acquisition reform. This has not necessarily been the case. For instance, in response to a scandal in 1998 involving refund cuts for overcharged defence equipment, the JDA established a purportedly independent organization, the Defense Procurement Chamber (*Bōei Chōtatsu Shingikai*) in 2001, to examine whether procurement procedures are being properly conducted. However, considering the scale of annual MOD procurement, which amounts to thousands of items, and that the Defence Procurement Chamber only meets eight times per year, there are doubts concerning the comprehensiveness of the oversight process (*Mainichi.jp*, 16 July 2008). An attempt was also made to enhance the competitive aspect of the procurement process by seeking tenders from multiple contractors. Following a case in 1999 of collusion in the supply of jet fuel, an electronic tender system was introduced in September 2000 in order to detect improper bids at an early stage. Finally, in the aftermath of a bid-rigging scandal in 2006, the Defence Facilities Administrative Agency was disbanded and an Inspector-General's Office (*Bōei Kansatsu Honbu*) established (Okuyama 2007). These measures have clearly proven to be inadequate.

Causes

The prevalence of scandals involving the MOD can be largely attributed to the oligopolistic and monopsonistic nature of defence procurement and the pattern of politico-bureaucratic-industrial collusion in Japan. As noted above, defence production in Japan is concentrated in a small number of firms, specializing in the production of a narrow range of armaments. The defence establishment's preference, since the early 1980s for, first, domestic development, then licensed production before importation (Chinworth and Matthews 1996, 190), has had a dampening effect on Japan's foreign arms purchases. Indeed, approximately 90% of Japanese defence equipment is procured domestically (either by domestic or licensed production), while the remaining 10% is imported, mostly from the USA. Moreover, given government restrictions on arms exports, Japanese defence manufacturers are essentially only able to sell their products to one buyer: the MOD. The purchaser and sellers, then, have limited commercial options further tightening the bonds between the two.

This restrictive arrangement is reflected in the procurement contract system. Defence procurement in Japan is based on three types of contractual arrangements: 1. open tendering; 2. selective tendering, under which a small number of suppliers participate in the tendering process; and 3. limited tendering, a non-competitive procedure whereby the tendering process is restricted to a single firm, which is subsequently awarded a government contract. While competitive tenders are gradually increasing, the majority of defence contracts (in price terms) are based on limited tendering (*zuii keiyaku*).[8] The minimal impact of market mechanisms on arms procurement is the product of a predilection for considering defence-related issues as 'sacred ground' (*seiiki*). As Takano and Koseki (2007) note, as weapons are closely linked to national defence, their capabilities should remain secret, which would be undermined by open tendering procedures. While limited tendering might make the defence establishment feel secure that Japan's strategic competitors are unable to obtain important defence secrets, the process facilitates cosy ties between government and business, which, in turn, increases the likelihood of impropriety.

Industrial-bureaucratic collusion in defence procurement is also reinforced by a practice known in Japan as 'descending from heaven' (*amakudari*) (Ikegami-Andersson 1998, 168; Green 1995, 114). Under this practice, which is certainly not unique to Japan, retired government officials often find employment as advisers in companies that were under their former bureaucratic jurisdiction. Companies hope to benefit from the expertise and access to privileged information of former officials, while the bureaucracy seeks lucrative post-retirement employment for civil servants who have worked for many years at relatively low pay. While there are regulations governing *amakudari*, they have typically not been strictly enforced. In the context of defence procurement, the practice is driven by a system, under which most JSDF personnel must retire, depending on rank, between the ages of 53–56 (Takano and Koseki 2007). The problem of early retirement is compounded for those who cannot immediately access their benefits, leaving the retirees without an income for a period of time (*Sankei Shimbun*, 13 October 1999). Many retiring JSDF personnel are, then, forced to seek re-employment with companies in which they can utilize their knowledge and expertise: defence equipment manufacturers and trading companies. The practice of *amakudari* functions like a tradable commodity whereby defence personnel are able to exchange favours such as procurement contracts for the promise of post-retirement employment (Takano and Koseki 2007).

While industrial-bureaucratic collusion in defence procurement is not necessarily a unique feature of the Japanese political-economy, the prominent role of trading companies in the process sets Japan apart from many countries. As noted above, Japan imports approximately 10% of its defence equipment. Arms imports fall under two categories: general imports and Foreign Military Sales (FMS) procurement. Under FMS procurement, a foreign military does not deal directly with the US manufacturer. Instead, the US DoD acts as an intermediary in the procurement of defence equipment, services and training for the foreign buyer (in the case of Japan, the EPCO). In recent years, there has been a slight decline in domestic procurement and a concomitant rise in FMS due to the construction of new Aegis vessels and the introduction of the BMD system (Bōeishō 2007). An oversight deficit arises from utilizing Japanese trading companies as intermediaries for the importation of defence equipment from foreign manufacturers as the MOD is not a contracting party. This restricts the MOD's ability to ascertain cost validity and to confirm the authenticity of quality guarantees, etc., as it is reliant on the voluntary co-operation of foreign manufacturers, which is often not forthcoming (Takano and Koseki 2007; Bōeishō 2007). The MOD's inability to assess accurately contract prices heightens the opaqueness of the import procurement process, thereby creating a propitious environment for bill padding and other improper practices.

Given the propensity for impropriety, one wonders why the MOD uses trading companies as intermediaries for import procurement. Differences between Japan and many advanced industrialized countries in terms of language, business practices, laws, regulations and accountancy standards make commercial negotiations a difficult undertaking. Japanese trading companies possess vast, global networks and several decades of experience in conducting international business. There is a belief that not utilizing this knowledge and experience would constitute both a significant manpower and cost burden for the MOD (Takano and Koseki 2007). Moreover, there are many cases in which Japanese trading companies have exclusive selling rights and serve as agents for foreign defence manufacturers, obligating the MOD to use their services (Bōeishō 2007). The idea that knowledge and experience in import procurement negotiations resides more in Japan's trading companies than the MOD could be seen as a contradiction of Weber's concept of the rational bureaucracy. However, it must be pointed out that the MOD is a relatively small organization compared to its foreign counterparts. Moreover, in a country with traditionally strong anti-militarist sentiments (at least in the post-war era), it has suffered from a lack of prestige in the eyes of Japan's brightest aspiring civil servants who typically have been drawn to the more illustrious METI, MOF and MOFA. While the JDA's upgrade to full ministerial status has given it more influence in defence policy-making, which should improve its standing, its reputation (along with many government departments) has been sullied in recent years as a result of the seemingly unending procession of corruption scandals.

It would, of course, be unfair to apportion blame for these procurement scandals entirely to beleaguered bureaucrats and their corporate underlings; Japan's politicians also constitute an (albeit unclear) element of what has been referred to by some in Japan as the 'political-military-industrial-bureaucratic complex' (*sei gunsan kan fukugōtai*) (*Nikkan Berita*, 10 November 2007) and never seem to be far away when a scandal erupts. Lawmakers are given the opportunity to sit on parliamentary committees that deal with a broad range of defence matters and which also perform a general oversight function. As Neil Renwick (1995, 71) notes, Japan's 'political parties [also] have their own defence committees and members who specialise in procurement issues. The LDP ... ha[s] three groups with a particularly influential voice in defence and procurement matters: the Research Commission on Security, the National Defence Division, and the Special Committee on Military Bases'. While the 'Defence Tribe' (*Kokubō Zoku*) – mostly politicians from the ruling LDP specializing in defence issues – may not appear to be as enmeshed in clientelist networks to the extent of the other 'tribes' of policy specialists such as construction, transport and agriculture, their members do receive various forms of organizational support from Japanese defence contractors. According to some reports, the LDP receives 10m.–30m. yen ($100,000–$300,000) annually from Japanese defence contractors (*Nikkan Berita*, 10 November 2007; Nihon Kyōsantō Aichi-ken Iinkai 2003). Of course, political donations (*seiji kenkin* or 'political money') are not illegal, as long as they are within the limits prescribed by the Political Funds Control Law, although the issue of political fund-raising is extremely controversial in Japan due to the regular occurrence of money scandals involving mostly LDP politicians (see Hrebenar 2000, 59–83). Under suspicion that its members may have received illicit funding from an influential defence lobbyist and known 'fixer' in connection with the most recent corruption case involving Yamada Corp., the media spotlight was cast on the 'Defence Tribe'. When the investigation was concluded without uncovering any impropriety on the part of Japan's politicians, expectations of an impending transformation in the patronage-driven nature of the defence industry were subsequently dampened (Sawada 2008, 29).

Government countermeasures

Many of the measures outlined above have clearly failed to stem the tide of defence procurement corruption in Japan. In response to the 2007 Yamada Corp. corruption scandal, the Japanese Government announced a programme of comprehensive defence equipment acquisition reform. The MOD's reforms comprise seven measures:

- Direct consultation with overseas manufacturers to obtain estimates as a means of uncovering and eliminating bill padding.
- Increasing the number of import procurement specialists in EPCO from three to 10 people and enhancing local price survey functions in the USA.
- Facilitating the entry of overseas manufacturers into Japan through the publication of English-language materials relating to forthcoming procurement tenders.
- Budget requests for the establishment of a specialized import procurement department within EPCO.
- Employing chartered accountants and other personnel from outside the division who have experience with trading companies.
- Strengthening punitive measures against companies engaging in bill padding practices. These measures include forcing companies to refund the total amount paid in excess and doubling the penalty fees, which is currently equal to the amount charged in excess.
- Comparing trading companies' accounting records with estimates submitted to the MOD and conducting an import procurement survey that investigates companies' internal fraud prevention and legal compliance structures.

(Japan Ministry of Defence 2008, 15)

In connection with the first measure, the MOD has already begun to make use of the US webFLIS database. WebFLIS is the web version of the Federal Logistics Information System

(FLIS). Created in 1985, FLIS is an online repository of information relating to US military procurements such as equipment capabilities, manufacturer's details and costs. In one MOD investigation of suspected bill padding using webFLIS, it was revealed that three Japanese companies, Fuji Industries, Yamada Corp. and Kyokutō Bōeki Kaisha, had, on average, charged nearly eight times the standard cost set by the US DoD for 79 items contained in 31 contracts (Kaikei Kensain 2007, 1131). Measures designed to strengthen the system of checks on import procurements are effective in curbing corrupt practices such as bill padding. However, the measures outlined above are really band-aid solutions to what is a structural problem in Japan. Corporations around the world have demonstrated adeptness at conceiving new ways to circumvent a vast array of business laws and regulations. As the frequency of corruption scandals indicates, Japanese corporations have proved to be especially adroit in this regard. As long as the structure of collusive ties between the political, bureaucratic and industrial spheres in Japanese defence procurement remains intact, the next scandal seems inevitable.

Conclusion: implications for the global arms trade

Japan has not traditionally been a major player in the global arms market. This can partly be attributed to the emphasis on indigenizing arms production in order to enhance the nation's technological base, which has had a limiting effect on imports. Anti-militaristic principles played an especially important role, though, restricting Japan's military capacity to the minimum necessary for self-defence and effectively prohibited the possession of 'war potential'. These principles naturally also extended to arms exports with formal restrictions established in 1967, although they were breached by foreign sales of dual-use civilian products and bilateral technological co-operation agreements with the USA. This has influenced the structure of Japan's post-war arms industry, which mostly comprises production units located in large conglomerates that are non-reliant on military sales and are relatively small by international standards.

There are both opportunities and obstacles to Japan participating more actively in the global arms export market. In a time of declining defence procurement budgets and rising weapons system development costs, there is pressure from Japanese arms manufacturers, some of which have been forced to undergo painful restructuring, and their supporting industrial associations to ease export restrictions, which would potentially allow them to improve the corporate balance sheet through foreign arms sales. However, a series of scandals involving the defence establishment over the past decade threatens to undermine attempts to remove these constraints. A number of defence technology leaks in recent years would certainly make US arms manufacturers nervous about entering into technological co-operation agreements with Japanese companies, and make other foreign firms reluctant to bid for government defence contracts. The leaks have also led to a further tightening of arms export controls as the government attempts to keep sensitive technology out of the hands of unfriendly regimes. Similarly, arms procurement corruption – facilitated by collusive government-business ties, which are reinforced by oligopolistic and monopsonistic practices – damages the reputation of the MOD and Japanese arms manufacturers. This not only undermines the MOD's ability to function as Japan's primary national security policy agency, but also relieves mounting pressure for a relaxation of arms export restrictions. This, coupled with continued adherence to indigenization and residual anti-militarism, suggests Japan's emergence as a major player in the global arms trade is not imminent.

Notes

1 The small contribution of defence to Japanese industrial production can be a misleading indicator of its importance to the national economy as it glosses over the fact that at least one key industry, aircraft manufacturing, depends significantly on arms production (see Ikegami-Andersson 1992, 87).
2 Keidanren merged with Nikkeiren (Japan Federation of Employers' Associations) in 2002 to become Nippon Keidanren (Japan Business Federation).

3 The Society of Japanese Aerospace Companies (*Nihon Kōkū Uchū Kōgyōkai*) and the Shipbuilders' Association of Japan (*Nihon Zōsen Kōgyōkai*) are two additional industrial associations representing the interests of Japan's defence manufacturers.
4 JADI also comprises several subcommittees each focusing on a specific aspect of arms production.
5 However, regular personnel will be increased from 145,000 to 148,000 and ready reserve personnel cut from 15,000 to 7,000.
6 A fire unit comprises an engagement control station, radar set, antenna mask group, electric power plant and five launcher stations.
7 Research on the Aegis BMD missile aims for the following improvements: nosecone – increase the credibility of the separation of the kinetic warhead and improve the response performance; seeker – improve the capability to discriminate targets from decoys; kinetic warhead – improve the orbit collection capability and enlarge its interception area; and second-stage rocket motor – improve the flight speed and enlarge its interception area (Japan Ministry of Defence 2008, 17).
8 It should be noted that in terms of the number of contracts concluded, most are awarded on a competitive basis.

Bibliography

Berger, Thomas, 'From Sword to Chrysanthemum: Japan's Culture of Anti-militarism', *International Security*, Vol. 17, No.4, 1993
Bōeichō, *Nihon no Bōei 2005*, Tokyo, Zaimushō Insatsukyoku, 2005
——'Ippan Yunyū no Genjō to Mondaiten', www.mod.go.jp/j/info/sougousyutoku/pdf/siryou/02_02.pdf, November 2007
——*Nihon no Bōei 2008*, Tokyo, Zaimushō Insatsukyoku, 2008
Bōeishō Gijutsu Kenkyū Honbu, 'Soshiki Jōhō: Yosan', www.mod.go.jp/trdi/org/yosan.html
Bōeishō Sōbi Shisetsu Honbu (EPCO), 'Enkaku', www.epco.mod.go.jp/gaikyou/chapter1_1/chapter1_1.htm
Chinworth, Michael and Ron Matthews, 'Defense Industrialisation Through Offsets: The Case of Japan', in Stephen Martin, ed., *The Economics of Offsets: Defence Procurement and Countertrade*, Amsterdam, Harwood Academic Publishers, 1996
Defense News, 'Defense News Top 100', Defense News, 2007, www.defensenews.com/static/features/top100/charts/top100_08.php?c=FEA&s=T1C
Green, Michael, *Arming Japan: Defense Production, Alliance Politics, and the Postwar Search for Autonomy*, New York, Columbia University Press, 1995
Hrebenar, Ronald, *Japan's New Party System*, 3rd edition, Boulder, CO, Westview Press, 2000
Hughes, Christopher, *Japan's Re-emergence as a 'Normal' Military Power*, Adelphi Paper 368–9, London, International Institute for Strategic Studies, 2005
Ikegami-Andersson, Masako, *The Military-Industrial Complex: The Cases of Sweden and Japan*, Aldershot, Dartmouth Publishing Company, 1992
——'Japan', in Ravinder Pal Singh, ed., *Arms Procurement Decision Making, Volume 1: China, India, Israel, Japan, South Korea and Thailand*, Stockholm, Stockholm International Peace Research Institute (SIPRI), 1998
Japan Ministry of Defence, *Defense of Japan 2007*, Tokyo, Zaimushō Insatskyoko, 2007
——*Defense of Japan 2008*, Tokyo: Zaimushō Insatsukyoku, 2008
——'Japan's BMD', Japan Ministry of Defence, www.mod.go.jp/e/d_policy/pdf/bmd2008.pdf, September 2008
The Japan Times
Kaikei Kensain, 'Daisansetsu: Kokkai kara Kensa Yōsei Jikō ni kansuru Kensa Jōkyō', www.jbaudit.go.jp/report/all/pdf/0403_01.pdf, 2007
Keidanren, *Teigen: Kongo no Bōeiryoku Seibi no Arikata ni tsuite*, July 2004
Koga, Jun'ichirō, *Keidanren: Nihon o Ugokasu Zaikai Shinkutanku*, Tokyo, Shinchōsha, 2000
Mainichi.jp
Nihon Bōei Sōbi Kōgyōkai, 'Jigyō Katsudō', www.jadi.or.jp/katudou/index.htm
Nihon Keizai Shimbun
Nihon Kyōsantō Aichi-ken Iinkai, 'Bōei Kanren Kigyō no Juchugaku, Jimintō e no Seiji Kenkin Ichiran', www.jcp-aichi.jp/hiroko/backnumber/report/quotation/kuni030616_2.html, 16 June 2003
Nikkan Berita, www.nikkanberita.com
Okuyama, Tomomi, 'Fushōji Taisaku, Jikan wa Sōteigai', *Mainichi.jp*, via Factiva, global.factiva.com, 29 November 2007
Oros, Andrew, *Normalizing Japan: Politics, Identity, and the Evolution of Security Practice*, Stanford, Stanford University Press, 2008
Renwick, Neil, *Japan's Alliance Politics and Defence Production*, Basingstoke, Hampshire, Macmillan, 1995
Samuels, Richard, *'Rich Nation, Strong Army': National Security and the Technological Transformation of Japan*, New York, Cornell University Press, 1994
Sankei Shimbun
Sawada, Tadashi, 'Sekai e no Shikin: Riken no Yami Nokotta', *Tokyo Shimbun*, 30 August 2008
Shizuoka Shimbun
SIPRI, 'Military Expenditure of Japan', Stockholm International Peace Research Institute (SIPRI), www.sipri.org.contents/milap/milex/mex_database1.htm
Takano, Kōichirō and Tomohiro Koseki, 'Sōbi Chōtatsu: Ayaui Kankei', *Yomiuri Shimbun*, www.yomiuri.co.jp/feature/feature/fe8000/fe_071129_02.htm, 29 November 2007
Tanaka, Kota, 'Is the Enemy Strike Capability Necessary for Japan?', www.stimson.org/eastasia/pdf/strike_capability_tanaka.pdf, November 2006

7 Arming North Korea

Yong-sup Han

Introduction

The Democratic People's Republic of Korea (North Korea) is a unique country, which over the last five decades has always placed as the top priority the development of a defence industry, irrespective of economic conditions. Although the defence sector progressed to the extent that North Korea was able to provide the military with domestically manufactured weapons and equipment, and sometimes earn hard currency revenue from arms sales abroad, the economy has suffered from structural problems, with North Korea plunging towards the status of a failed nation.

Surprisingly, North Korea reinforced its policy orientation even after the end of the Cold War by institutionalizing a policy of 'military-first politics' in order to tighten the Kim family rule, rather than abandoning it in favour of economic development. More seriously, Kim Jong Il opted to confront the global non-proliferation regime by accelerating the nuclear weapons programme for the sake of its national security, while promoting the military in order to pre-empt any possible rebellion against his rule. Pyongyang exercised, with a nuclear card, dangerous sabre-rattling tactics vis-à-vis the USA and the rest of the world.

Nuclear brinkmanship served the purpose of promoting North Korea's domestic stability by consolidating the authority of Kim's leadership even in the midst of catastrophic natural disasters and economic chaos. However, this policy caused further isolation to North Korea and contributed to its continued backwardness, in contrast to the global trend of openness and co-operation.

The North Korean economy currently has few prospects, and neither does its defence sector. In order to develop its economy, North Korea may eventually remove the barrier between defence and the economy by allowing economic efficiency to allocate scarce resources. For economic efficiency to prevail, though, the leadership itself needs to face the reality of the situation and opt for openness and reform, which the People's Republic of China and Viet Nam have pursued successfully.

Moreover, developing asymmetric capabilities such as missiles and weapons of mass destruction (WMD) invoked US involvement in the deal with North Korea to no substantive avail. Pyongyang's twin policy of playing part of its nuclear card with the USA and four countries – China, the Republic of Korea (South Korea), Japan and Russia – in the six-party talks while keeping its nuclear weapon capabilities intact only prolonged and aggravated the dilemma that the country had to face earlier in order to save its economy and then its defence industry.

Against this backdrop, this chapter intends to analyse Pyongyang's strategic thinking and policy of 'military-first politics', the organizational structure of its industrial defence production, its military expenditure, the evolution of its defence industry, and its recent policy of developing missiles and WMD. In doing so, this chapter aims to identify the challenges and prospects for North Korea.

Pyongyang's strategic thinking and military-first politics

The doctrine of 'military-first politics' was instituted by Kim Jong Il, who has governed North Korea since the death of his father, Kim Il Sung, in 1994. The foremost objective of the policy of military-first politics is to preserve domestic stability and order in the midst of radical changes occurring as a result of both the demise of communism in the former Soviet Union and Eastern Europe, and Kim Il Sung's death after 50 years of one-man rule over North Korea. To maintain social order and the people's obedience to Kim family rule, Kim Jong Il needed to consolidate his control over the military and use it as an instrument for the political control of the population (*Rodong Shinmun*, 9 December 2003). For the military to supervise the workers' class inevitably meant the excessive politicization of the military, which had previously been under the control of the ostensibly workers' party during the Kim Il Sung era. Protecting Kim Jong Il's regime became a prime objective during the economic crisis in 1995–97, when the regime might have collapsed (Kim Duck-hong 2004, 16–7).

However, the policy of military-first politics further distorted North Korea's resource allocation mechanism. However necessary it was to divert resources from defence industry to the civilian economy, the policy of military-first politics prevented this from happening. Military-first politics were interpreted by Kim Jong Il's subordinates as placing the continuous build-up of military forces as the top priority in resource allocation. Indeed, spending on defence industry with the aim of ultimately become a state with nuclear power was seen as a shortcut to accomplishing Kim Jong Il's national goal of building a militarily strong and economically prosperous nation. The concept of a militarily strong nation required North Korea to expedite the process that would lead to nuclear power status, which in turn had the added benefit of deterring any possible attack by the USA, by threatening to use nuclear weapons whenever tensions rose on the Korean Peninsula. However, fighting a US-led war of hegemony on the Korean Peninsula was nothing but a political slogan that was constructed as part of the indoctrination of the population to obey the Supreme Commander at all times.

According to North Korean watchers in South Korea as well as in the rest of the world, the policy of military-first politics reflected Kim Jong Il's fear of isolation and of regime failure, which have been intertwined with paranoia about the USA and the rest of the world. Military-first politics reinforces its *Juche* ideology that is North Korea's version of socialism since the Kim Il Sung era. However, it goes one step further, idolizing Kim Jong Il as a semi-divine figure who can protect and provide for the entire North Korean population against all the challenges to the country.

Through military-first politics, Kim Jong Il's intention is to quell any potential resistance against the Kim family's rule, which might have been fatally affected through the inflow of external influence. The military has thus assumed the role and duty of building a shield against any possible attempt to undermine the Kim regime. The entire country has, thus, become more militarized than during the previous Kim Il Sung era, with resource allocation far more in favour of the defence industry.

The policy of military-first politics was consolidated by Kim Jong Il when he assumed the chairmanship of the National Defence Committee, instead of taking the presidency of North Korea. To empower the National Defence Committee, North Korea amended the Constitution in 1992 to make the Committee independent from the Central People's Committee and bestowed it with higher authority than this body. The National Defence Committee was described in the 1992 Constitution as the supreme military supervisory organization, which should command and control all armed forces and supervise all defence programmes. In accordance with the constitutional amendment, the highest authority over defence industry changed from the Party Central Military Committee to the National Defence Committee. Later, this organization change was strengthened by the introduction of the policy of military-first politics. In 1998 a constitutional amendment authorized Kim Jong Il and the National Defence Committee to oversee the implementation of the policy of military-first politics.

Since military-first politics is meant to uphold the North Korean military as a revolutionary force, it resulted in the reinforcement of the priority of strengthening the military, including the development of defence industry over the development of light industry and agriculture. The defence sector had been a major beneficiary in North Korea even before Kim Jong Il. Since 1966, Kim Il Sung had emphasized the defence build-up as a priority, although he also emphasized the importance of developing heavy industry. However, given the near-dictatorial rule that Kim Jong Il exercises as Chairman of the National Defence Committee, he has been able to dominate the decision-making process in North Korea in a way that has no precedent in other socialist countries. It became evident that those who were working in the economic sector could not overrule the military even when economic conditions worsened. Indeed, North Korean economic officials who have met their South Korean counterparts for inter-Korean economic co-operation have confessed that the military could overrule economic co-operation projects at any time.

A closer examination of North Korean tactical thinking reveals that North Korea has upgraded its long-established conventional deterrence policy to a more strategic level by developing a scheme of nuclear deterrence. As early as 1972, Kim Il Sung had asserted that his military strategy of *Juche* was based on combined warfare of simultaneous front and rear battlefields, reflecting modern warfare doctrine (Baek 2004, 209). North Korea's blitzkrieg doctrine is now accompanied by a nuclear deterrence strategy in order to deter the USA. In order to develop these strategic nuclear capabilities, Kim Jong Il accelerated the development of long-range missiles and nuclear weapons. In his view, North Korea could go on to develop its economy at full speed once its security problems have been resolved through the gaining of nuclear power status.

Organizational structure of military build-up and its resources

The role of the second economic council

As noted above, even under the Kim Il Sung era the defence sector had been the area of priority for North Korea. Within the government's decision-making process for budget allocation, the defence sector had not been affected by other sectors because budget allocation for defence was exclusively managed by the Second Economic Council, which is organized and authorized to function independently of the rest of the government.

It is not known when the Second Economic Council was first organized. One school of thought contends that it was in 1966, when Kim Il Sung launched the policy of building defence and the economy in parallel. Kim Il Sung directed the organization of the Council in order to implement his officially announced Four-Point Military Guidelines: equipping all the people with arms; transforming the whole country into an impregnable fortress; converting the armed forces into army cadres; and modernizing the military. At the time, Kim Il Sung reiterated that the ultimate goal of the simultaneous development of defence and the economy was to strengthen defence capabilities.

Another school of thought argues more convincingly that the Second Economic Council was created in 1972 (Hahm 2006, 254–8) when North Korea amended the Constitution to strengthen the Kim Il Sung regime in the midst of China's efforts at rapprochement with the USA. North Korea thus needed to implement Kim Il Sung's guidelines for strengthening defence capabilities more urgently than before. The year 1972 coincided with the time when North Korea began to hide the bulk of its military expenditure, which was officially announced two years in a row during the 1970–71 period, which amounted to over 30% of the government budget. From 1966 to 1971, there was a ministry of machinery and industry which was located within the administration. The Second Economic Council was allegedly created by merging the ministry of machinery and engineering with the Party Military

Committee. Changing from the open announcement of military expenditure to a policy of confidentiality implies the secret existence of the Second Economic Council, which began to allocate military expenditure for the production of weapons and military equipment independent of other government agencies. In 1992 this organizational structure was strengthened by Kim Jong Il's decision to bring the Second Economic Council under the supervision of the National Defence Committee.

Irrespective of when the Second Economic Council was organized, the Council took charge of research, development and manufacture of weapons and military equipment. The Council consists of eight bureaux, the Second Science Institute and external economic agency and resource companies (Lim 2006, 415–60). Each of its bureaux is responsible for manufacturing and developing its own weapons systems. Among the eight bureaux, the Comprehensive Planning Bureau is primarily in charge of developing a comprehensive plan by co-ordinating and finalizing all the strategies and programmes submitted by the seven other bureaux. The First Bureau handles the production of small weapons and munitions, and the operation of military facilities. The Second Bureau handles the production of tanks and armoured personnel carriers. The Third Bureau handles the production of artillery, self-propelled artillery and multiple rocket launcher systems. The Fourth Bureau is in charge of researching and developing various missiles, while the Fifth Bureau is in charge of developing biochemical and nuclear weapons. The Sixth Bureau produces naval ships, including submarines. The Seventh Bureau produces communication equipment and aircraft. The Ministry of the People's Armed Forces is only in charge of operating and maintaining the weapons and equipment that have been provided by the Second Economic Council.

Enigmas in North Korea's military expenditure

As North Korea achieved self-reliant defence industrial development that could provide conventional weapons and military equipment (except for large naval ships and fighter aircraft) in the 1980s, it not necessary to examine its military expenditure before then. More interesting and relevant is how North Korea's military expenditure has changed since the end of the Cold War and how it has provided the necessary resources to the defence sector.

An overall assessment of North Korea's military expenditure demonstrates that it has maintained a high level of military spending and also consistently kept military expenditure non-transparent. Table 7.1 shows that North Korea's officially announced military spending ranged between US$21.9 billion in 1994 to $17.7 billion in 2003. However, the announced military expenditure figures are as doubtful as the figures that had been officially released by the former Soviet Union and China during the Cold War era (Steinberg 1990, 675–99; Wallner 1997).

Today, it is no longer a secret that North Korea has hidden its military spending in various forms. Most North Korea experts claim that the official North Korean announcement of military spending only covers the operational costs for the North Korean armed forces. As noted above, the former Soviet Union set the precedent for disclosing less than one-third of the real defence budget (Steinberg 1990, 675–99). What has been hidden in North Korea's real defence budget can be explained by the existence of the Second Economic Council, which operates independently from the overall governmental budget process. What has been missing from official announcements on defence spending is military spending on weapons research and development, as well as acquisition and procurement by the Second Economic Council.

Chae-ki Sung has argued that North Korea's officially announced defence budget represents only the operational costs that are determined by the ministry of finance and the national planning board like other government budgets (Sung 2006, 315). On the other hand, the cost of weapons acquisition and research and development costs are not budgeted by the national planning board and the finance ministry, but instead by the Second Economic Council, as explained. Moreover, the cost of procuring foreign weapons systems and military equipment is

Table 7.1 North Korean GNP, government spending and military expenditure (unit: US$100m., current)

	GNP	Government spending	Estimated and (announced) defence spending
1991	229	171.7	51.3 (20.8)
1992	211	184.5	55.4 (21.0)
1993	205	187.2	56.2 (21.5)
1994	212	191.9	57.6 (21.9)
1995	223	208.2	63.0
1996	214	n.a.	57.8
1997	177	91.0	47.8
1998	126	91.0	47.8 (13.3)
1999	158	92.3	47.8 (13.5)
2000	168	95.7	50.0 (13.7)
2001	157	98.1	50.0 (14.1)
2002	170	101.0	50.0 (14.9)
2003	184	149.0	50.0 (17.7)
2004	208	25.1	17.9 (3.9)
2005	242	29.0	22.0 (4.6)

Source: ROK Ministry of National Defence 2006; for GNP and government spending see Bank of Korea 2006; 'ROK Unification Education School', Understanding North Korea, 2008, www.uniedu.go.kr. Figures in parentheses represent military expenditure officially announced by North Korea. Estimated military expenditure for 2004 and 2005 is derived from IISS 2007. The figures since 2002 have changed due to North Korea's new economic plan

also separately managed by Kim Jong Il and his loyal subordinates, which ensures additional direct funding to the armed forces. The overseas procurement fund is never officially announced. Thus, the official defence budget represents only part of true defence expenditure.

Since the North Korean economy recorded, with a few exceptions, consecutive negative growth rates during the 1990s, North Korea's defence spending needed to be scaled down to meet the challenges arising from the dire economic situation. This was particularly urgent during a three-year period between 1995 and 1997, when North Korea experienced catastrophic natural disasters and famine. For those years, no data were collected and no announcements on gross national product (GNP) and military expenditure were made. In 1996 North Korea did not officially announce its government budget. In addition, whatever defence spending figures the North Korean government officially announced could not be taken seriously by outside experts because the share of North Korea's military spending as a percentage of its GNP was well below most external estimates. It is estimated that although military spending has ranged between 25% and 30% of gross domestic product (GDP) since the early 1970s, North Korea has disclosed only one-third of its true defence spending (Sung 2004, 68).

However, it is striking that North Korea has not reduced its military expenditure despite economic hardship. Interestingly, in April 2006 the North Korean Supreme People's Assembly announced that military expenditure took up 15.9% of the government budget. Given the unique nature of the North Korean regime and its budget system, the actual defence budget is estimated to be around 30% of GNP (ROK Ministry of National Defence 2006, 19).

Evolution of North Korea's defence industry

This section will examine the evolution of North Korea's defence industrial development. In the 1950s, directly following the Korean War, the country focused on the recovery of its plants and constituted a defence industrial base by utilizing the fact that most heavy industry had been located in the northern part of the Korean Peninsula during the Japanese Colonial rule, and before and after the Korean War. By relying on Soviet and Chinese technological support for North Korea, Pyongyang built a defence industrial base by establishing 19 weapon-producing factories.

In the 1960s the North expanded its defence industrial base through reassembling basic Soviet and Chinese weapons systems. By 1962 Pyongyang could re-engineer Soviet type 7.62 mm RPD light weapons and by 1963 it could produce through re-assembly, the Soviet type 14.5 mm KPV heavy rifle. As explained earlier, North Korea then stepped-up efforts to modernize major ground weapons so as to implement the Four-Point Military Guidelines.

In the 1970s it entered the stage of the mass production of major weapons systems and equipment (Baek 2004, 200–3). It reached the stage of manufacturing tanks, self-propelled artillery and armoured vehicles for ground forces, and small submarines and high-speed vessels for the navy, mostly by copying Soviet and Chinese models. At the sixth Korean Workers' Party Congress in October 1980, Kim Il Sung announced that the principle of self-reliance in military defence had been accomplished, providing the country with formidable defence capabilities.

During the 1980s North Korea embarked on the qualitative upgrade of their existing weapons systems, and research and development for developing asymmetric capabilities such as missiles and WMD. Recognizing a numerical advantage in the conventional military balance, North Korea accelerated the development of weapons systems technology by strengthening technological co-operation with the former Soviet Union. In the latter half of the 1980s Pyongyang began to shift the focus of its weapons development programme from conventional weapons to strategic weapons. After fulfilling domestic needs for weapons systems and military equipment in terms of quantity, North Korea naturally then sought to achieve a technological leap. To upgrade the quality of weapons systems and military equipment, North Korea also sought military aid in the form of technology transfer from the former Soviet Union. During this decade, North Korea accomplished self-reliant production capacity in weapons systems and military equipment, as stressed by Kim Il Sung (Kim Il Sung 1990, 187–8). On the other hand, it also sought international arms sales to gain hard currency revenue, which had declined.

At the time, Kim Il Sung stressed (Kim Il Sung 1994, 81) that the quality of North Korea's other products did not match those of other advanced countries, though he claimed that weapons systems and military equipment were somewhat comparable with those of the world's advanced countries due to strict quality control and better management. Kim Il Sung's comment might have indirectly revealed the dilemma facing the North Korean leadership – whether it should continue to give priority to the defence industry or shift attention to economic development, in keeping with global trends. However, in the end, the North Korean leadership once again emphasized the need for accelerating the development of the defence industry instead of concentrating on economic growth (Kim Il Sung 1996, 284).

As the Cold War approached its end, the economic situation in the former Soviet Union and Eastern European countries worsened, which, in turn, heralded a worsening economic situation for North Korea. Yet, however stringent the overall economic conditions were, its defence industry had not been affected due to the full support of the North Korean leadership. Its objective of self-reliance in weapons systems production was reached when its defence industrial capacity could produce 90% or more of the required weapons systems. By the early 1990s, it was able to produce MiG-29 jetfighters through re-assembly, albeit with Russian technological support.

Barely escaping economic negative growth in 1999, North Korea endeavoured to redress the military imbalance vis-à-vis South Korea in air force capabilities by importing 40 MiG-21 fighters from Kazakhstan and Mi-8 helicopters from Russia, as well as developing its own fighters, though this was to no avail.

In the 1990s North Korea began to develop its own nuclear weapons programme after the former Soviet Union rescinded the Soviet Union-DPRK nuclear co-operation agreements in 1988. With the demise of the Cold War and the Soviet collapse, it became inevitable that North Korea would change its deterrence strategy at the tactical level. Conventional weapons and indigenous defence production capacities were not regarded as sufficient either to deter external threats or to underpin offensive attack. Accordingly, North Korea changed its strategic orientation of defence industry to manufacture and deploy WMD. This will be discussed in the next section.

Once such a choice has been made, it is difficult for change to take place without a change of leadership, accompanied by new thinking. Although the former Soviet Union changed its confrontational policy in favour of *glasnost* and *perestroika* in order to reduce the effects of the collapse of the Communist empire, North Korea missed the chance of changing its course. Despite realizing that continuous investment in defence would further drain resources available for economic development, North Korea stuck to the old thinking of developing defence industry in order to preserve the regime. Whereas Mikhail Gorbachev shifted the leadership's thinking from giving priority to defence to focusing on the economy by proposing the concept of reasonable defensive sufficiency in military security, North Korea tried to maintain its priority on military defence as a way of ensuring regime security. This has been consolidated by measures such as the role undertaken by the Chairman of the National Defence Committee.

Asymmetric strategy of military build-up: missiles and weapons of mass destruction

North Korea's missile development and foreign sales

North Korea first began to develop missiles in the 1970s. Pyongyang imported Soviet SCUD-Bs from Egypt and started to re-engineer missile technology with technological support from China. North Korea built missile plants soon after and succeeded in developing SCUD missiles, In 1984 Pyongyang successfully test-fired SCUD-B missiles with a range of up to 300 km. In 1986 North Korea test-fired SCUD-Cs after successfully upgrading the SCUD-B missile. Since 1987 North Korea has begun to earn hard currency by selling SCUD missiles to Iran, Syria, the United Arab Emirates (UAE) and other countries. The revenue earned from missile exports were estimated to reach $1 billion per annum. In 1988 the armed forces began to deploy SCUD missiles in North Korea. Soon after, North Korea launched the Rodong missile development programme and in 1991 test-fired the first missile, which initially ended in failure. In the same year North Korea constructed the test base for the Taepodong missile. In mid-1993 North Korea successfully test-fired the Rodong medium-range missile. News reports claimed that North Korea exported 150 Rodong missiles to Iran, after a North Korean military delegation visited Iran in March 1993. Thereafter, North Korea fielded Rodong missiles at its military bases, which astonished outside observers, as it had only conducted two tests, whereas Western states would normally deploy missiles only after extensive testing to establish their reliability.

The most alarming and surprising development was when North Korea test-fired the Taepodong I long-range missile in August 1998. The Taepodong missile is estimated to have a range of some 4,000 miles, as the US Department of Defense announced that debris from the third stage of the rocket fell in the northern Pacific (*Washington Times*, 16 September 1998).

North Korea's missile test-launches have been used not only to create a crisis situation to force the USA into direct negotiations with the country, in order for it to extract concessions, but also to demonstrate to potential buyers that North Korean missile products are reliable. It is known that North Korea exported Rodong missiles, their parts and technology to Pakistan and Iran and helped these two countries to develop their own medium-range missiles – Gauri missiles in the case of Pakistan and Shahab-III missiles in the case of Iran (Han 2004, 344–7).

There is little doubt that missile exports are a major source of revenue for North Korea. The principal buyers of North Korean missiles include Iran, Syria and the UAE. As shown in Table 7.2, North Korea earned a reasonable amount of hard currency from missile sales, as well as other defence products.

Table 7.2 North Korean arms sales (unit: US$ m., 1990 constant prices)

Year	Export	Import
1990	–	651
1991	138	30
1992	86	34
1993	423	15
1994	52	23
1995	52	72
1996	35	15
1997	14	6
1998	15	5
1999	11	175
2000	–	14
2001	64	24
2002	32	5
2003	–	5
2004	–	5

Source: SIPRI Yearbook 1994–2005

Pyongyang has indicated that it will stop missile exports to other countries if the USA compensated it with $1 billion annually for three years, on the grounds that the domestic production and deployment of missiles is an issue of sovereignty in which the USA should not interfere (Arms Control Association 2008). However, the USA has demanded that North Korea suspend not only its missile exports, but also domestic production and accede to the global missile technology control regime. In response, North Korea has demanded more inducements such as the normalization of relations with Washington and economic benefits in return for a moratorium on its missile test-launches. Pyongyang argues that domestic production cannot be suspended and that the economic sanctions card should not be played twice, because the USA promised to lift the economic sanctions after the Geneva Agreed Framework was signed between the DPRK and the USA in October 1994.

As a result of the 1999 missile talks between Washington and Pyongyang, North Korea agreed to set a moratorium on missile test-firing in return for the USA lifting economic sanctions. However, North Korea's exports of missiles and their parts continued throughout the 1990s, providing revenue of $560m. in the five-year period 1988–93. Interestingly, Kim Jong Il disclosed his own views to South Korean newspaper reporters who visited in August 2000, after the first-ever inter-Korean summit. He stated that North Korea could suspend missile test-firing if other countries such as the USA test-launched North Korean satellites twice or three times a year, as it also cost North Korea $200m.–$300m. to test-fire long-range missiles two or three times a year (*Joongang Ilbo*, 24 August 2000).

In 2002 missile negotiations between Pyongyang and Washington ended in stalemate after the North Korean nuclear issue again surfaced to draw the attention from Washington. North Korea's missile development met strong objections after its long-range missile test in August 1998. The USA raised the alert level in South Korea and pushed North Korea to the brink of war in order to force Kim Jong Il to choose either negotiations to give up long-range missiles, or to face a US-led demonstration of force to put pressure on the country.

Although North Korea did not resume missile testing until 4 July 2006, it continued to use the missile issue to counter the USA. Finally, North Korea used a missile test-fire in July 2006 to draw US attention again, in order to break the deadlock associated with the nuclear issue. At this critical juncture, North Korea conducted seven missile test-firings, which raised the level of tension on the Korean Peninsula.

Intelligence sources revealed that throughout the first half of 2003, North Korea continued to export significant ballistic missile-related equipment, components, materials and technical expertise to the Middle East, South Asia and North Africa (CIA 2003,10). Pyongyang attached high priority to the development and sale of ballistic missiles, equipment and related technology. Exports of ballistic missiles and related technology were one of the North's major sources of hard currency, which, in turn, supported ongoing missile development and production. In order to counter the development and deployment of the US-led missile defence system, North Korea appears ready to exercise its missile card whenever it deems necessary. Thus, ballistic missiles have become Pyongyang's political instrument, complementing its nuclear card.

Overall, North Korea has steadily expanded its ballistic missile programme, demonstrating the tight link between the missile programme, and the policy of military-first politics and the slogan of the militarily-strong nation. Kim Jong Il not only sees the benefit of the missile programme in ensuring international prestige and recognition, but also his country's deterrent power against the USA.

North Korea's nuclear development and biochemical capabilities

It is known that the North Korean nuclear development programme started as early as the mid-1950s, when it dispatched scientists and engineers to the former Soviet Union for training. It is also widely known that an actual nuclear weapons programme was put in place in the 1980s, after the nuclear complex was built in Yongbyon.

Unlike most other countries (except for India, Pakistan and Iran), which have conformed to the non-proliferation regime led by the USA after the end of the Cold War, North Korea has focused its defence policy on the research and manufacture of WMD. A compelling reason why the Kim regime pursued nuclear weapons development is that North Korea has little choice but to do so, as it does not want to lose the arms race vis-à-vis South Korea, given the North's dire economic conditions (*Korean Central News Agency—KCNA*, 9 June 2003).

This military-oriented thinking culminated in the North Korean head of delegation in the inter-Korean talks in 1993 threatening the South Korean counterpart to turn Seoul into a sea of fire once a war broke out. North Korea further accused the USA of posing an intolerable threat to, and putting pressure on North Korea. North Korea, thus, developed its own deterrence strategy according to which it should possess sufficient deterrent power to prevent the USA from launching a pre-emptive attack on the North. On the other hand, North Korea claimed that it won political and economic victory by engaging the USA at the Geneva talks. According to its calculations, North Korea earned valuable time for the further development and manufacture of nuclear weapons by relocating nuclear facilities and fissile materials at other facilities while gaining US support to replace its nuclear graphite reactors with light-water reactors. As the Geneva Agreed Framework stipulated a freeze on North Korea's current and future programme, it in fact left a loophole on North Korea's past nuclear programme.

North Korea's policy to develop nuclear weapons was most vividly demonstrated in its official announcement before its October 2006 nuclear test. North Korea stated that it needed to carry out a nuclear test as a prerequisite for securing a nuclear deterrent against the US threat. It stated that the capability to deter war had become necessary for the country's self defence and to protect the supreme interests of the state and the security of the Korean nation (KCNA, 4 October 2006). One North Korean supporter based in Japan argued that if North Korea develops formidable deterrent power and continues playing a strategy of brinkmanship with the USA, then the USA will withdraw from the Korean Peninsula permanently, leaving South Korea open to absorption by force or blackmail by North Korea (Kim Myung Chol, 4–8).

It is no longer a secret that North Korea has used its nuclear card both for negotiation purposes and at the same time to keep its nuclear weapons capabilities intact. Since 2003 Pyongyang has habitually used this tactic in order to create a window of opportunity favourable for North Korean negotiations. At times, when the George W. Bush Administration did not accept direct talks between Washington and Pyongyang, the North Koreans used the announcement of their possession of nuclear weapons, a nuclear test and the threat of military forces against South Korea, as blackmail. Though there has been some progress in bringing North Korea's nuclear programme in Yongbyon to the stage of disablement, it may take a long time to completely resolve the North Korean nuclear problem. Until the complete and verifiable elimination of North Korea's entire nuclear capabilities and programme is achieved, Pyongyang is expected to continue on its nuclear path.

As for chemical and biological weapon programmes, it is believed that North Korea has been producing poison gas and biological weapons since the 1980s. In December 1961 North Korea allegedly launched its chemical weapons development programme, including research and construction of production facilities in compliance with Kim Il Sung's 'Declaration of Chemicalization' (ROK Ministry of National Defence 2006). It is believed that approximately 2,500 to 5,000 tons of a variety of agents, including nerve agents, remain stored in a number of facilities scattered around the country, and that North Korea is capable of producing biological weapons involving the use of anthrax, smallpox and cholera. These chemical and biological weapons have never been brought to the negotiation table because the nuclear issue has been paramount for the USA and the rest of the world.

Prospects

As the world becomes more globalized through the revolution in information technology and knowledge-based networking, North Korea is getting left far behind owing to its isolation and reclusiveness. One major reason why North Korea has an underdeveloped economy is that it has consistently distorted its resource allocation in favour of the development of the defence sector. Domestically, the North Korean leadership has given preferential treatment to the defence industry by allocating military spending independent of the government budget through the Second Economic Council, which is independently organized and run by the National Defence Committee. In this context, the North Korean defence sector could thrive as long as it were able to fill the domestic demand for weapons systems and military equipment, and could generate some revenue from overseas arms sales.

However, defence industry output has begun to fall drastically, as domestic military demand is filled and given the worsening of the overall economic situation. Moreover, North Korea's overseas arms sales cannot be sustained because of the strict monitoring and sanctions on North Korea's arms deals with foreign countries, which have been initiated by the international community, led by the USA.

North Korea has lost much credibility and trust from the international community on account of its actions in trying to extract maximum benefits from its negotiations on nuclear and WMD issues, in return for Pyongyang's minimum concessions. Though partially successful in extracting some benefits from its nuclear negotiation with the USA and from the six-party talks, North Korea has, in fact, aggravated its security problems by forcing other countries to make more concerted efforts to denuclearize North Korea and by rendering the US alliance with South Korea and Japan stronger than ever.

Above all, North Korea's broken economic base can no longer sustain the defence industrial base because Kim Jong Il does not have enough funds for the military through the Second Economic Council. North Korea has already attained the status of a failing nation. Unless the inherent problems in its economy and defence sectors are rectified, there is certainly no way out of the vicious circle of a bad economy and an un-economical defence industry. It is also becoming increasingly difficult for North Korea to continue its arms sales to countries that used to purchase its weapons, not only because of sanctions on such arms transactions, but because several countries such as Iraq and Pakistan are no longer key buyers. According to the US

2006 Quadrennial Defense Review, the USA will reinforce proliferation security initiatives, thus presenting difficulties for North Korean arms exports (US Department of Defense 2006).

Unless North Korea makes a strategic decision to trade the entire nuclear weapons programme and capabilities for security and economic benefits, to be provided by other negotiation partners in future agreements in a complete, verifiable and irreversible manner, the country will be further isolated and suffer from chronic economic difficulties. It is, thus, time for North Korea to investigate the defence problem from a new angle, just as Gorbachev did before the end of the Cold War. Since global pressure on proliferators of missiles and WMD is expected to grow over time, North Korea will not be able to rely on its WMD alone to sustain and protect its regime.

The clock is ticking for North Korea, as the leadership is only concerned with reaping maximum utility from its nuclear card, while keeping nuclear capabilities intact. In the meantime, North Korea's defence industry for conventional weapons and military equipment is being degraded. North Korea's obsession with the arms race and with a deterrence strategy has to be overturned, so that it can best use other parties' willingness to negotiate. Without that radical change of strategic thinking, the policy of military-first politics is doomed to fail.

Bibliography

Arms Control Association, 'Chronology of U.S.-North Korean Nuclear and Missile Diplomacy', *Arms Control Today*, Vol. 38, June 2008, www.armscontrol.org/factsheets/dprkchron

Baek, Seung Joo, 'North Korea's Military Buildup and Strategic Outlook', in Jonathan D. Pollack, ed., *Korea: The East Asian Pivot*, Newport, Naval War College Press, 2004

Bank of Korea, 'Gross Domestic Product of North Korea in 2006', Press Release, Bank of Korea, 2006

Bennett, Bruce, 'The Emerging Ballistic Missile Threat: Global and Regional Ramification', paper presented at the Airpower Conference, Yonsei University, Seoul, June 1999

Central News Agency (KCNA)

CIA, 'The Acquisition of Technology Relating to Weapons of Mass Destruction and Advanced Conventional Munitions', unclassified report to Congress, US Central Intelligence Agency, July 2003, www.cia.gov/library/reports/archived-reports-1/jan_jun2003.htm

CNS, Special Report on North Korean Ballistic Missile Capabilities, Center for Nonproliferation Studies, Monterey Institute of International Studies, 22 March 2006, cns.miis.edu

DPRK People's Army, Pyongyang, KPA Military Press, 1987

Hahm, Taekyoung, ed., *The Military of North Korea: A New Look*, Seoul, Hanulbooks, 2006

Han, Yong-sup, *Peace and Arms Control of the Korean Peninsula*, Seoul, Pakyougsa, 2004

IISS, *The Military Balance 2004–2005*, London: International Institute for International Strategic Studies, 2004
——*The Military Balance 2007*, London: International Institute for International Strategic Studies, 2007
——*North Korea's Weapons Programmes: A Net Assessment*, London: International Institute for Strategic Studies, 2005

JoongAng Ilbo, joongangdaily.joins.com

Kang, Seok-seoung, 'DPRK Military Trend and ROK Security', *National Defense Journal*, November 2001

Kim, Duck-hong, 'Kim Jong Il is Korean Nation's Enemy', paper presented in the Seminar on North Korea's Reality and Arms Build-up Capacity, Research Institute for National Security Affairs, Korea National Defence University, 28 April 2004

Kim Il Sung, *Kim Il Sung Writings 36*, Pyongyang, Chosun Workers' Party Publishing, 1990
——*Kim Il Sung Writings 40*, Pyongyang, Chosun Workers' Party Publishing, 1994
——*Kim Il Sung Writings 44*, Pyongyang, Chosun Workers' Party Publishing, 1996

Kim Myung Chol, 'Marshal Kim Jong Il's War Plan', www.kimsoft.com/kim-war.htm

Kwak, Tae-hwan and Seung-ho Joo, eds, *North Korea's Second Nuclear Crisis and Northeast Asian Security*, Hamphshire and Burlington, Ashgate, 2007

Lim, Gang-taek, 'North Korea's Defense Industrial Policy', in *The ROK North Korea Research Association – North Korea's Military*, Seoul, Kyung-in Publishing, 2006

Ministry of National Defence, *Defense White Paper 2006*, Ministry of National Defence, Republic of Korea, 2006

Perry, William J., *The Perry Report*, US Department of State, 12 October 1999

Rodong Shinmun (North Korean Workers Party Press)

Rumsfeld, Donald H., 'Executive Summary of the Report to the Commission to Assess the Ballistic Missile Threat to the United States', 15 July 1998

SIPRI, *SIPRI Yearbook*, Stockholm, Stockholm International Peace Research Institute, various annual editions

Steinberg, Demitri, 'Trends in Soviet Military Expenditures', *Soviet Studies*, Vol. 42, No. 4, October 1990

Sung, Chae-ki, 'Economic Foundation of North Korean Military Power', in Taekyoung Hahm, ed., *The Military of North Korea: A New Look*, Seoul, Hanulbooks, 2006

—— 'North Korea's Economic Power and Military Economy', paper presented in the Seminar on North Korea's Reality and Arms Build-up Capacity, Research Institute for National Security Affairs, Korea National Defence University, 28 April 2004

US Congress North Korea Advisory Group Report to the Speaker of the U.S. House of Representatives, November 1999

US Department of Defense, *Quadrennial Defense Review 2006*, US Department of Defense, 3 February 2006

Wallner, D., 'Estimating Non-Transparent Military Expenditures: The Case of China (PRC)', *Defense and Peace Economics*, Vol. 8, 1997

Washington Times

8 Arms modernization in the Middle East

Riad A. Attar

The Middle East, a region that spans south-western Asia and north-eastern Africa, was coined in 1902 by naval officer Alfred Thayer Mahan and popularized in the United Kingdom (UK). Determining which states the Middle East includes is both subjective and objective. It is subjective in the sense that those member states would be included or excluded from the region following the rise of an international hegemony, a reaction to the regional imbalance of power, or a shift in public opinion in one or more Middle Eastern countries. For example, until the 1950s, few included Pakistan and Afghanistan as part of the Middle East; however, following the rise of the USA after the Second World War as the international hegemony and the adoption of the Baghdad Pact in 1955 in order to counter the threat to the regional balance of power, Pakistan has been included as part of the Middle East. Similarly, the Soviet invasion of Afghanistan in December 1979 helped incorporate Afghanistan into the region for practical reasons: among them recruiting Middle Eastern fighters against the Soviet invaders. On the other hand, Turkey has been considered a Middle Eastern country for the past century, but many Turks today, including the Islamic government, insist that they are Europeans and ought to be admitted to the European Union. The objective element of including or excluding a country from the region refers to how similar or different that country is from the regional core (the Arab countries). Thus, Arab culture, language, politics, physical features and economic structures may represent determining criteria to include or exclude a country from the region. An example: Iran is very much similar to the regional core in all dimensions. On the other hand, Israel is physically in the Middle East but differs from the regional core economically, politically and socially. In fact, Israel looks more like a European country than a Middle Eastern one (Anderson et al. 2009, 246–320; MacMillan 2002, 381–455; Fromkin 1989; Hudson 1977, 56–81; Microsoft Encarta 2007; Owen 2002, 239–50; Weatherby 2002, 1–4; Weatherby et al. 2009, 240–90).

In this study, Middle Eastern countries are divided into Arab Middle East and non-Arab Middle East. The Arab Middle East includes Algeria, Bahrain, Comoros, Djibouti, Egypt, Eritrea, Iraq, Jordan, Kuwait, Libya, Mauritania, Morocco, Oman, the Palestinian National Authority (PNA), Qatar, Saudi Arabia, Somalia, the Sudan, Tunisia, the United Arab Emirates (UAE), and Yemen. The non-Arab Middle East includes Afghanistan, Israel, Iran, Pakistan and Turkey. North Africa constitutes Algeria, Libya, Morocco, Mauritania and Tunisia. The Arab countries of Egypt, Jordan and Syria constituted the 'front line' against the State of Israel since its establishment in 1948 (see Abu-Qarn and Abu-Bader 2008). The coverage of the analysis will not include all the above-mentioned states; rather, it will include the major states that have significantly affected the regional military balance. This study explains the key trends in defence spending, arms procurement, arms modernization and military build-up in the Middle East. It will also evaluate the future prospects of the region in light of those trends and discuss policy implications.

Trends in defence spending in the Middle East

The Middle East consists of sub-regions located in Asia and Africa. Some of those sub-regions differ in language, culture, colonial background, political regime type and ideology. Correspondingly, the patterns of defence spending, arms trade and arms modernization reflect the political, ideological, cultural and level of conflict in each sub-region. This section explains the patterns in defence spending, arms trade, arms procurement and arms modernization in the sub-regions of North Africa, the 'confrontation' states (Egypt, Jordan and Syria), and the Gulf States. Dividing the Middle East into sub-regions is an approach that was initially introduced by Cordesman and al-Rodhan (2005).

Military expenditure data

Military expenditure data are collected from the *SIPRI Yearbook: World Armament and Disarmament* (1969, 1974, 1976, 1980, 1983, 1984, 1990, 1991, 1992, 1996, 1997, 2001, 2004, 2007 and 2008), published annually by the Stockholm International Peace Research Institute. SIPRI publishes long-term annual data of three different types: military expenditure in current prices (local currencies); military expenditure in constant US dollars; and military expenditure as a percentage share of gross domestic product (GDP). For the purposes of this chapter, it is not possible to use constant US dollar values of military expenditure from SIPRI 'as is'. However, it is possible to convert data to the same base year, as the base year changes several times over the period (1960–2006). All values of military expenditure in this study were converted to constant values using a 1985 base year, GDP deflator and exchange rates of local currencies to millions of US dollars.

Many scholars have criticized the quality of military expenditure data, suggesting that they may not be comparable across countries (see Brzoska 1981). All three major sources of military expenditure data (SIPRI, US Arms Control and Disarmament Agency—ACDA, and the International Institute of Strategic Studies—IISS) rely, at least in part, on definitions of military expenditure that are different for each country or group of countries. Thus, the comparability of data from countries using different definitions is highly questionable (Mintz and Stevenson 1995, 290; Lebovic and Ishaq 1987, 683). Therefore, this study uses SIPRI definitions for values across countries and across groups of countries. All the figures and tables in this study (Figures 8.1–8.7 and Tables 8.1–8.11) were developed based on data of military expenditure collected from numerous volumes of the SIPRI Yearbook over the period 1960–2008, at the 1985 price and exchange rate unless otherwise indicated.

Trends in defence spending and arms trade in North Africa

North Africa in this analysis includes Algeria, Morocco, Tunisia and Libya. Mauritania is not included in the analysis due to insufficient data on its military expenditure. North African countries differ from the rest of the Middle East in that they have not had any major interstate conflicts since their independence. Morocco treats the conflict of West Sahara as an internal conflict, in spite of Algerian support of the Polisario Front. Libya was the only North African country that had incursions beyond its borders.

Algeria and Morocco

Algeria, officially known as the Democratic and Popular Republic of Algeria, is the second largest country in the African continent after the Sudan. The military blocked radical Islamists from taking power after winning the election in 1991. As a result, the military has been involved in bloody fighting with Islamist armed groups ever since. The size of the National

Liberation Army (NLA) was 137,000 as of 2004. This is distributed between army, navy and air force, with 110,000, 7,500, and 10,000 personnel, respectively. The army has 1,000 main battle tanks (320 T-54/55, 330 T-62 and 350 T-72). The navy deploys two submarines, three frigates and 25 patrol boats. The air force has 175 combat aircraft (Su-24, MIG-23, MIG-25, MIG-29, MIG-21).

The NLA does not possess any nuclear weapons. It is equipped mainly with weapons from the former Soviet Union. In a February 2006 report, Defense Industrial Daily noted that a $4 billion arms sale was being considered between Algeria and Russia, involving fighter aircraft, tanks and air defence systems, with the possibility of additional equipment. According to the report, numerous sources had reported that a high-level Russian delegation in Algeria had closed $7.5 billion worth of arms contracts.

The Algerian package would be post-Soviet Russia's largest-ever single arms deal, when compared with Russia's weapons exports to all customers of $5–6 billion per year over the previous years. Figure 8.1 shows Algerian military expenditure from 1962 to 2006. Algerian military expenditure reflects the interaction between internal and external factors. Internal factors are determined by the type of political regime, while external factors are determined by external conflicts, especially with Morocco (see the CIA World Factbook; Cordesman 2002, 107–28; Microsoft Encarta 2007; World Disk Reference). During Houari Boumedien's regime, military power was linked to socialism and was best described as an 'army with a country, rather than a country with an army'. Thus, a strong army was seen as a necessary condition for the success of socialism and the economic development strategy of the regime. As Figure 8.1 shows, the rise in military expenditure from 1971 to 1976 coincided with the regime's first four-year plan (1971–74), and the border clashes with Morocco that culminated in 1976. The fact that the Algerian air and land forces did not perform well during the 1976 clashes with Morocco led Chadli Bendjedid's government to a military build-up that reached $1,492.36m. in 1980, compared with $1,294.45m. in 1979. In the following two years, in 1981 and 1982, though, military expenditure declined to $1,168.3m. and $797.47m., respectively.

On the other hand, Algeria was concerned with Libyan pressure on Tunisia. Thus, in 1983 it signed a treaty with Tunisia that obligated Algeria to protect Tunisia from Libyan military intervention. This treaty explains the increase in military expenditure from $797.42m. in 1982 to $1,168.8m. in 1983. There was a steady decline in military expenditure from 1988 to 1992, from

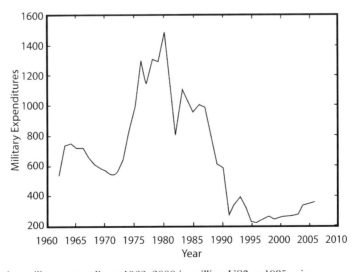

Figure 8.1 Algerian military expenditure 1962–2006 in million US$ at 1985 prices

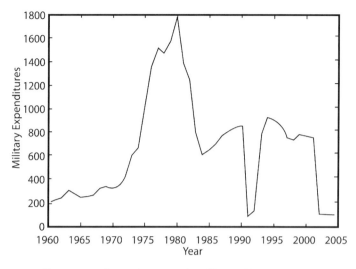

Figure 8.2 Moroccan military expenditure 1960–2005 in million US$ at 1985 prices

$997.4m. to $275.4m. This decline was due to three factors: the restoration of the relationship with Morocco, greater emphasis on economic development and the end of the Cold War.

The period that followed Bendjedid's rule (1992–99) was a period of instability. Three Algerian presidents came to power during that period: Mohamed Boudiaf, Ali Kafi and Liamine Zeroual. The first was assassinated and the other two were forced to resign under pressure from the generals. The common factor among the presidents of the post-Boumedien era was their attempt to balance the military's influence and the people's basic economic needs. The current president, Abdelaziz Bouteflica, seems to have been more successful than his predecessors because he has provided an element of regime stability and created a satisfactory balance between 'guns' and 'butter' (see Cordesman 2002, 107–28).

The size of the Moroccan armed forces was 196,300 as at 2002, distributed amongst army, navy and air force, with 175,000, 7,800 and 13,500 personnel, respectively. The Moroccan army has 744 main battle tanks (224 M-48A5, 420 M-60, 100 T-72). The navy deploys two frigates and 27 patrol boats. The Moroccan air force has 95 combat aircraft consisting of 39 F-5, 29 Mirage F-1, 4 0V10 and 23 Alpha jet. (see World Disk Reference). As Figure 8.2 shows, the pattern of Moroccan military expenditure is very similar to the Algerian pattern, as it is mostly a reaction to external pressure from Algeria. However, the Moroccan political system is more stable, as reflected by the endurance of its political regime measured on Gurr's (2007) Polity-IV Dataset.

Unlike Algeria, Morocco was not affected by the collapse of the Soviet Union, the impact being greater on socialist countries than non-socialist ones. Although the years that followed the disintegration of the Soviet Union saw a sharp decline in military expenditure, Morocco was able to allocate more resources for defence than Algeria from 1993 to 2001. Unlike Libya and Algeria, Morocco's pro-Western regime has allowed its armed forces access to alternative sources of sophisticated weapons systems from the USA and Western European countries, particularly France. Unlike Algeria, Morocco has also not suffered from conflicts in Morocco proper.

Tunisia and Libya

Habib Bourguiba, the leader of Tunisian independence and its ruler from 1956 to 1987, was a visionary and experienced leader who ruled his country with political skill. He pursued a policy of political nonalignment but maintained close relations with France and the USA. His position in support of the Arab-Israeli negotiations in the late 1960s caused problems for him in the Arab world. In November 1987 he was ousted by his newly appointed Prime Minister, Zine al-Abidine Ben Ali, who claimed Bourguiba was too ill and senile to govern. Bourguiba's legitimacy as the hero of independence, though, had allowed him to rule his country without any significant internal conflicts. This is one major reason why Tunisia has kept a relatively small army (CIA World Factbook, Leaders; Cordesman 2000, 225–54; Microsoft Encarta 2007).

The size of the Tunisian armed forces was 35,000 as of 2002. The army, navy and air force have 27,000, 4,500, and 3,500 personnel, respectively. The army has 84 main battle tanks (54 M-60A3, 30 M-60 A1). The navy deploys 19 patrol boats. The air force possesses 29 combat aircraft (12 F-5E/F, 12 L-59, 5 MB-326 K/L). Figure 8.3 displays Tunisian military expenditure from 1961 to 2005 in millions of dollars. Table 8.1 shows that the variations in military expenditure from 1961 to 1973 were very small, due to the lack of internal and external conflicts and the focus of Bourguiba on economic development (see World Disk Reference).

The pattern of military spending has changed as Tunisia's relations with Libya have been erratic since Tunisia annulled a brief agreement to form a union in 1974. The relationship deteriorated in 1980 when Libyan-trained rebels attempted to seize the town of Gafsa. Colonel Mu'ammar Muhammad al-Gaddafi, the Libyan head of state, made a similar, but less successful effort in 1982. In 1984 Libya had allegedly aided the sabotage of the pipeline between Algeria and Tunisia. In 1985 Gaddafi put pressure on Tunisia by expelling some 25,000–30,000 Tunisians working in Libya. He also provided funding to labour and radical Islamist groups that opposed Bourguiba (Cordesman 2002, 246).

The change in the pattern of Tunisian defence spending was a reaction to the external and internal conflicts caused by Libya. As Figure 8.3 shows, the increase began in 1974 ($20.3m.), and peaked in 1983 ($364m.) and 1985 ($357m.). President Ben Ali embarked on political reforms along secular lines when he came to power in November 1987. However, Tunisia's political reforms did not extend to its Islamist parties. The exclusion of Islamists triggered demonstrations that turned into violent clashes with police in December 1989 and February

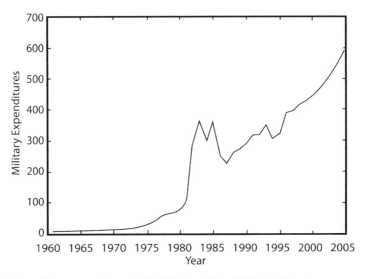

Figure 8.3 Tunisian military expenditure 1961–2005 in million US$ at 1985 prices

Table 8.1 Tunisian military expenditure 1962–74 in US$ m., at 1985 prices and exchange rates

Year	US$ m.	Year	US$ m.
1962	8.6	1969	10.5
1963	6.6	1970	10.5
1964	7.1	1971	11.8
1965	8.6	1972	10.5
1966	7.4	1973	13.8
1967	8.8	1974	16.1
1968	8.4		

Table 8.2 Libyan military expenditure 1997–2005 in US$ m., at 1985 prices and exchange rates

Year	US$ m.
1997	8.6
1998	6.6
1999	7.1
2000	8.6
2001	7.4
2002	8.8
2003	8.4
2004	10.5
2005	10.5

1990. The eruption of violence between the Islamist groups and Algerian authorities in early 1999 created deep concerns in Tunisia as well as in other North African countries. As shown in Figure 8.3, Tunisian military expenditure has increased significantly since 1991 in order to contain the surge of Islamist groups and to avoid a repeat of an internal conflict similar to the Algerian civil war. As of 2005, Tunisian military expenditure reached $604m., an increase of $317m. from 1990 (Cordesman 2002, 248; Waltz 1986).

The Great Socialist People's Libyan Arab Jamahiriya is the official name of Libya and perhaps this is part of its troubles. Colonel Gaddafi has always presented himself as a revolutionary and visionary leader. He used oil funds during the 1970s and 1980s to promote his ideology outside Libya, supporting subversive and terrorist organizations and activities to achieve his objectives. In 1973 he engaged in military operations in northern Chad's Aozou Strip, but was forced to abandon his last military stronghold in Chad at Faya Largeau in 1987. Gaddafi's adventure in Chad cost him heavily in terms of casualties and equipment. Table 8.2 shows Libyan military expenditure from 1997 to 2005 in millions of dollars; the pattern shows a small variation in Libyan defence spending during that period. It also suggests that UN sanctions imposed on Libya in 1992 have been effective (CIA World Factbook, Leaders; Cordesman 2002, 183; Gaddhafi 1977; Microsoft Encarta 2007).

Trends in defence spending and arms trade in the fertile crescent

The Fertile Crescent is a Middle Eastern region stretching across the northern part of the Syrian Desert and extending from the Nile Valley to the Tigris and Euphrates rivers. The name Fertile Crescent reflects the early development of irrigation and urban civilization in the region, especially in Mesopotamia. The region broadly corresponds to the present-day countries of Iraq, Syria, Lebanon, Israel, Palestinian Autonomous Areas and Jordan, and could be extended to Egypt and Turkey. This section explains the trends in defence spending in Egypt, Iraq,

Israel, Syria and Jordan. Individual countries in the Fertile Crescent could be better understood as dyadic units with Israel (Microsoft Encarta 2007; Weatherby 2002, 15–7).

Israel

In Hebrew and in Arabic the term *mamlakhah* means 'kingdom'. The adjective *mamlakhati* was an important feature of David Ben-Gurion's political vocabulary from the early part of his political career. He used it to emphasize the specifically political nature of the Zionist quest for Jewish self-determination. According to Cohen (1992, 201), 'at the fifth conference of Ahdut ha-Avodah in 1926, he defined Zionism's goal as "Hebrew *mamlakati* construction" [*banyan mamlkhti ivri*]'. Cohen provides an insightful chronicle to the formation of the Israeli army, guided and motivated by the *banyan mamlkhti ivri* ideology.

In defence policy, *mamlakhati* involved two principal manifestations that can be distinguished analytically, but which were inseparable. The first was tied directly to security needs and was a necessity: the unification of the Yishuv's (settlement) three undergrounds into a single army with a single command. The second was the political, cultural and educational role that Ben-Gurion assigned to the army in Israeli society. Simple survival strategy dictated the creation of a *tsava mamlakhati* (a *mamlakhati* army) by unifying the pre-state Zionist forces, all of which had distinct political orientations. The most important was the Haganah, which was the successor of the Hashomer (Guild of Watchman). By 1947 it had approximately 45,000 troops, 3,100 of whom belonged to its elite force, the Palmah. The Irgun paramilitary organization under the command of Mancheim Begin had some 2,000–2,500 troops. The smaller Stern organization had only a few hundred members (Cohen 1992, 228–31).

With the founding of Israel in 1947, the Haganah became the backbone of the Israeli Defence Forces (IDF). The fact that Israel was under threat from Arab forces made the unification of those groups an urgent priority. Thus, the Haganah, the Irgun and the Stern were unified into one state-controlled force on 26 May 1948, based on an ordinance issued by the Israeli Provisional Government. Accordingly, the IDF became the only legitimate Israeli military force; all other armed units were prohibited.

For most of its 60 years of existence, Israel has devoted a large share of its resources to defence, placing a high priority on the development of modern armed forces with sophisticated military technology and equipment, and on the ability to develop and supply these capabilities by its own means. Several reasons account for the technologically sophisticated weapons systems developed and used by the Israeli armed forces: the perceived need to maintain an independent supply of military hardware free from political restraints and potential embargo, the desire for 'military power multipliers' for weapons systems capable of producing quick and decisive results with few casualties, and the need to maintain a critical element of surprise which cannot be assured if the nation had to rely on imported systems (Merom 1999, 413–14, 417, 423–24; Peled 2001).

The size of Israel's armed forces as of 2002 was 167,600. This was distributed among army, navy and air force with 125,000, 7,600, and 35,000 personnel, respectively. The Israeli army has 3,950 main battle tanks (Centurion, M-60A1/3, Magach 7, Merkava). The navy deploys three submarines and 53 patrol boats. The Israeli air force has 688 combat aircraft (50 F-4E-2000, 62 F-15, 203 F-16). It is widely believed that Israel has nuclear capabilities with up to 100 warheads, deliverable via Jericho 1 and Jericho 2 missiles (Feldman and Shapir 2001, 63–71, 163–85; Peled 2001; World Disk Reference).

As Table 8.3 indicates, the pattern of Israeli military expenditure suggests a reaction to neighbouring countries, namely, Egypt, Jordan and Syria. The patterns in the dyads of Israel versus Egypt and Israel versus Jordan are clearer than Israel versus Syria, due to the availability of data from 1960 to 2006 in reference to Egypt and Jordan; in the case of Syria, the data cover only the period from 1986 to 2005. Table 8.3 reveals an increase in Israeli military spending following the Yom Kippur War (October War) in 1973. This increase was in

Table 8.3 Israeli military expenditure 1974–98 in US$ m. at 1985 prices and exchange rates

Year	US$ m.	Year	US$ m.
1974	6,948	1987	13,173
1975	94,795	1988	1,360
1976	133,963	1989	16,444
1977	174,783	1990	19,698
1978	194,151	1991	34,754
1979	357,632	1992	38,609
1980	82	1993	40,520
1981	185	1994	49,519
1982	351	1995	53,582
1983	894	1996	62,911
1984	4,487	1997	68,914
1985	4,487	1998	73,847
1986	13,079		

reaction to Egypt's relative success at the beginning of the war, particularly its ability to penetrate Israeli defence lines. As Table 8.3 shows, defence spending increased from $6,948m. in 1974 to $357,632m. in 1979, when measured in constant 1985 dollars.

Following the Camp David peace accord with Egypt in 1978, in 1980 Israeli military expenditure decreased sharply. However, the low level of defence spending changed after 1988 when Saddam Hussain, then President of Iraq, threatened to 'burn half of Israel'. In 1989 Israeli defence spending was $16,444.m., and it reached $73,847m. in 1998. The increase in defence spending from 1989 to 1998, as shown in Table 8.3 reflects a gradual pattern of increase. The close Israeli-American relationship made the USA the main supplier of the most advanced weapons to Israel. Israel, though, did not have to import any significant weapons systems from 1996 to 2000.

The IDF earned a high reputation in the region after it defeated Arab forces in 1948 and achieved a very swift victory in the Six Days War of 1967. Although the Yom Kippur War was the first shock to Israeli military strategists due to the initial success of the Egyptian forces, that shock was not enough to induce structural adjustments to their forces. It seems that Israeli military strategists had been inebriated with the Six Days War victories, especially their air campaign, which was able, at the start of the campaign, to destroy the backbone of Egyptian air forces within 190 minutes.

The success of the Israeli air campaign in 1967 has proved to have had some negative effects on the IDF. First, the IDF has become a lopsided army with greater dependence on air power than before; second, it perpetuated the simplistic 1967 war model, which led Israeli military strategists to underestimate the power of their enemies; third, it created a false notion of absolute superiority, which led to bureaucratic rigidity and a disregard of emerging conditions and powers in the region; and fourth, the overuse of the air campaign hurt Israel's reputation world-wide (see the Israeli Vinograd Report).

The Israeli Vinograd panel's final report on Israel's 2006 war in Lebanon stressed, in several places, that the IDF was not quite prepared for ground assault. Thus, in one way or another, the Vinograd report exposed an illusion that was strongly ingrained in the Israeli mentality, i.e. wars could be easily won by air strikes alone. It seems that part of the professional military failure in Lebanon had to do with the fact that Israel followed in the footsteps of the American model in Iraq and Afghanistan and the anachronistic Israeli model from 1967. It was astonishing to observe how the Israeli professionals had misread, analyzed and misinterpreted the strategic map of the region. More than updating their weapons and technology, the Israeli military establishment needed to update its doctrines, perceptions and evaluations of its enemies.

Egypt

The armed forces of Egypt are among the largest in the region, consisting of an army, navy and air force. The army is the largest within the military establishment of Egypt; it is estimated to number around 320,000. The navy has a total of 20,000 personnel as well as 375,000 reservists. The paramilitary force numbers around 330,000, which consists of the Central Security Forces, the National Guard, the Border Guard Forces and the Coast Guard (Attar 2007, 225–40).

Egyptian President Colonel Gamal Abd an-Nasir (Nasser)'s regime perceived Israel as a threat to Pan-Arabism, and he constantly called for the destruction of Israel. The Egyptian military build-up, which began during the Nasser regime, continued until 1974 as shown in Figure 8.4. At the beginning of his reign in 1970, Colonel Anwar Sadat introduced himself as a continuation of Nasser's regime; the military build-up thus exhibited the same pattern. Figure 8.4 shows Egyptian military expenditure from 1970 to 2006 in millions of dollars. Egyptian military expenditure went from $1,457m. in 1960 to $12,260m. and $15,154m. in 1973 and 1974, respectively. The peak in defence spending as shown in Figure 8.4 followed the October War in 1973 (Attar 2007, 235; Roskin and Coyle 2008, 96).

The pattern of Egyptian military spending in the late 1970s reflects the spirit of the Camp David accord signed between Egypt and Israel on 11 September 1978. There was a sharp decline in military spending from $13,399m. in 1977 to $ 2,873m. in 1981. In 1981 President

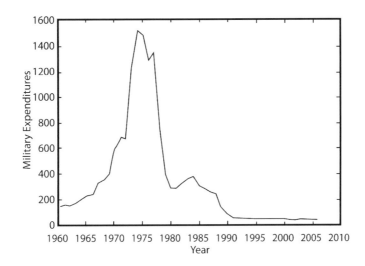

Figure 8.4 Egyptian military expenditure 1960 2006 in million US$ at 1985 prices

Table 8.4 Egyptian military expenditure 1989 2006 in US$ m. at 1985 prices and exchange rates

Year	US$ m.	Year	US$ m.
1989	1,468	1998	437
1990	780	1999	430
1991	471	2000	442
1992	469	2001	368
1993	484	2002	386
1994	484	2003	449
1995	448	2004	425
1996	442	2005	443
1997	446	2006	449

Sadat was assassinated and succeeded by Hosni Mubarak, who continued his commitment to the Camp David accord and the peaceful policies of Sadat. As Table 8.4 shows, there was a significant decline in Egyptian military spending from 1989 to 2006, which indicated that the peace process that began during Sadat's regime provided Egypt and Israel with the opportunity to redirect their resources to other sectors of their economies (Quandt 1986, 364).

After the middle of the 1970s, most Egyptian weapons systems were imported from France and the UK. French weapons included Dassault Mirage F-1 fighters, Dassault Mirage III fighter-bombers, Dassault Falcon-20 transport aircraft and Marta R55 Magic air-to-air missiles. UK weapons included Hawk fighters, Westland Sea King anti-submarine warfare helicopters, assault helicopters, fast patrol boats and Jaguar strike fighters. After 1980 Egypt broadened its sources of weapons imports to include Brazil, the People's Republic of China, France, Italy, Spain, Romania and the USA. However, after the 1990s, Egypt leaned heavily on the USA as the main supplier of its weapons. Egyptian weapons imports from the USA included air-to-air missiles, F-16 fighters, submarines, anti-tank missiles, main battle tanks, helicopters, air-to-surface missiles, towed guns and trainer aircraft (SIPRI 1976; 1991).

Jordan

In 2004 the Jordanian armed forces totalled 100,500 personnel. The number is distributed between the army, the navy and the air force with 85,000, 500 and 15,000 personnel, respectively. The Jordanian armed forces are loyal to the monarch. They have a reputation for thorough training and professionalism. The forces are dependent on Western support for credit for purchasing advanced arms and equipment (Feldman and Shapir 2001, 185–95; World Disk Reference).

The pattern of Jordanian military expenditure according to Figure 8.5 reflects the Jordanian reaction to the conflicts in the region and its search for regime survival in a turbulent political environment; Jordan has thus evolved in the 'eye of the storm'. From 1968 to 1970, the Jordanian Government was paralyzed by the armed presence of the Palestine Liberation Organization (PLO). In September 1970 the Jordanian army and the PLO clashed in a bloody fight that resulted in the ousting of the PLO from Jordan. Thereafter, King Hussein of Jordan consolidated his authority by widening his popular power base, strengthening the army, and

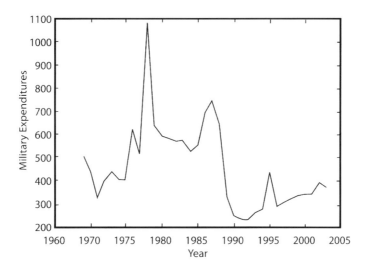

Figure 8.5 Jordanian military expenditure 1969–2003 in million US$ at 1985 prices

Table 8.5 Jordanian military expenditure 1980–88 in US$ m. at 1985 prices and exchange rates

Year	US$ m.
1980	593
1981	585
1982	571
1983	577
1984	258
1985	556
1986	695
1987	748
1988	648

Table 8.6 Jordanian military expenditure 1995–2003 in US$ m. at 1985 prices and exchange rates

Year	US$ m.
1995	437
1996	289
1997	299
1998	320
1999	332
2000	342
2001	339
2002	391
2003	368

advocating developmental and social welfare programmes (Anderson et al. 2009, 76–83; Ashton 2008; CIA World Factbook, World Leaders; Shlaim 2008).

As Figure 8.5 shows, there was a $45m. increase in military expenditure in 1973, which was the year of the Yom Kippur War. However, there was no significant increase or decrease up to 1977. A significant increase of Jordan's military expenditure began in 1978, with a value of $1,098m. when the Iranian revolution emerged as a credible threat to most Arab countries. Table 8.5 shows the Jordanian military expenditure during the Iran–Iraq War of 1980–88. The peace process that began in Madrid, Spain between most Arab countries and Israel in October 1991 slowed down the arms build-up in the region. More importantly, shortly after the signing of the Declaration Principles, Israel and Jordan entered into separate negotiations that led to the signing of the Wadi Araba Peace Treaty (WAPT) in October 1994. The WAPT addressed security, boundary demarcations and border crossing, control of water resources, police operation, environmental issues and the establishment of normalized relations. Both parties agreed not to join, aid or co-operate with any party intending to attack the other side and to prohibit military forces or equipment that could harm the other side from entering their territories. Thus, the relatively low military expenditure from 1995 to 2003 according to Table 8.6 reflects the spirit of peace and co-operation between the two countries. The Jordanian average defence spending during the period 1980–88 was $687.8m., compared with the average of $339.2m. during the period 1994–2003, which followed the peace treaty (Feldman and Shapir 2001, 17–19).

Saudi Arabia

The traditional Saudi security doctrine concerns threats from radical Arab regimes. These concerns emanate from the Kingdom's bitter experience with Egypt's Nasser in the 1960s,

Libya's Gaddafi since 1969, South Yemen's communists (1967–90), and Iraq's Saddam Hussain until 2003. The radical Arab threat to Saudi Arabia is perceived as part of a communist plan to destroy the citadel of Islam and spread atheism in the Arab World.

The Saudis countered the Soviet-Arab radical threat by supporting Islamist movements in the Arab and Muslim worlds. The Saudis not only offered financial and material support to those movements, but also introduced *Wahhabism* to them (a fundamentalist version of Islam). Since the late 1970s, growing *Wahhabi* movements have been seen in the Arab-Islamic World, which have expanded to Muslim communities in Europe and the USA. The Soviet invasion of Afghanistan in 1978 raised Saudi Arabia to the position of the great defender of Dar al-Islam (the abode of Islam). Saudi Arabia was the financial and spiritual supporter of the 'mujahidin' in Afghanistan until the defeat of the Soviet Union in 1989.

The pattern of Saudi military expenditure is best understood by examining four phases: first, the period of Egyptian-Saudi reconciliation (1968–77); second, the Soviet invasion of Afghanistan (1978–89) concurrently with the Iranian revolution in 1979 and the Iran–Iraq War (1980–88); third, the Iraqi invasion of Kuwait in August 1990, which resulted in the first Gulf War involving a coalition led by the USA on 17 January 1991; and fourth, 11 September 2001, which marked the attack on the World Trade Center and the Pentagon in the USA, and up to the present.

Following the Egyptian defeat in the 1967 Six Days War and the death of Nasser in 1970, Saudi King Faisal ibn Abd al-Aziz (1903–75) drew closer to Egypt's new President Sadat. The significant growth in Saudi military expenditure from 1973 ($2,876.92m.) to 1975 ($14,168.50m.) could be explained by Saudi financial assistance to Egypt in preparation for the 1973 Yom Kippur War, and its assistance in rebuilding the Egyptian army during the post-war years. The Egyptian-Saudi connection froze after President Sadat visited Israel on 19 November 1977 and in the wake of his signing the Camp David peace accord with Israel on 17 September 1978.

Three monumental events have deeply impacted Saudi Arabia and led to changes in its national security arrangements: the Soviet invasion of Afghanistan in 1978, the Iranian revolution in 1979 and the Soviet defeat and withdrawal from Afghanistan in 1989. The trend in Saudi defence spending reflects the impact of these events, as shown in Figure 8.6. Saudi military expenditure sharply increased from 1977 ($11,613.98m.) to 1986 ($20,604.40m.).

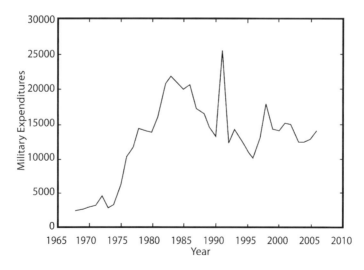

Figure 8.6 Saudi Arabian military expenditure 1968–2006 in million US$ at 1985 prices

Saudi military purchases, as displayed in Table 8.7 reflect Saudi Arabia's urgent strategy in reference to facing the rapidly emerging conditions in Afghanistan and Iran in the late 1970s. Traditionally, Saudi Arabia has been the guardian of the Arab Gulf States. Thus, after the Iraqi invasion of Kuwait, the Kingdom utilized its influence to liberate Kuwait.

As Figure 8.6 and Table 8.8 show, there was a tremendous increase in Saudi military expenditure, from \$13,274.54m. in 1990 to \$25,518.78m. in 1991, following the invasion of Kuwait. According to World Disk Reference, Saudi Arabia's contribution to the 1991 Gulf War reached \$55 billion. Military equipment was purchased from the USA, the UK, France and Canada. Weapons systems were augmented, including the deployment of Patriot missiles and AWACS early warning radar aircraft.

The presence of American forces in Saudi Arabia was perceived by al-Qa'ida as an occupation of the Holy Land, and they held the Saudi ruling family responsible for that presence. As a result, the dynamics of the threat to Saudi Arabia were changed from external to internal threats. Several attacks were launched on 29 May 2004 by al-Qa'ida on Saudi and American targets inside the Kingdom. Earlier, the 11 September 2001 attacks, which involved 11 Saudi nationals, placed Saudi Arabia in the forefront of the 'war on terror', which required maintaining a high level of military spending from 2001 to 2006, as can be seen in Figure 8.6 and Table 8.8.

Table 8.7 Saudi Arabia registered arms trade with industrialized and Third World countries

Recipient	Supplier	No. ordered	Weapon designation	Weapon description	Year of order
Saudi Arabia	France	250	AML-90	AC	1978
		900	AMX-10	AC	1978
		300	AMX-30S	MBT	1975
		–	MM-40-Exocet	ShShM	1978
		8	P-32 Type	PB	1976
		–	R-440 Crotale	Landmob SAM	1979
		–	Shahine	Landmob SAM	1979
	Indonesia	40	C-212 Aviator	Transport	1978
	USA	916	AGM-65A	ASM	(1979)
		240	AIM-7F Sparraw	AAM	1978
		240	AIM	AAM	1978
		660	AIM-9P	AAM	(1979)
		9	–	Coverette	1977
		4,292	Dragon-FGM-77A	ATM	(1979)
		45	F-15 Eagle	Fighter/interc	1978
		15	F-15B Eagle	Fighter/Trainer	1978
		12	M-106-A1	Mortar/Carrier	1979
		26	M-113-A1	ICV	1979
		–	M-163 Vulcan	AAV	(1977)
		6	M-557-A1	Cargo	(1979)
		170	M-60-A1	MBT	1976
		118	M-60-A1	MBT	1979
		6	M-88-A1	ARV	1979
		–	MIM-23B-Hawk	Landmob SAM	1976
		–	MIM-43A Redeye	Port SAM	1977
		200	Model 209 AH-IS	Hel	1976
		117	Rgm-84a Harpon	ShSh	1977
		100	RGM-84A Harpon	ShSh	(1979)
		4	–	FPB	1974
		15	TF-15A Eagle	Trainer	1978
		94	V-150 Commando	APC	1978

Source: SIPRI 1980

Table 8.8 Saudi Arabian military expenditure 1973–89 in US$ m. at 1985 prices and exchange rates

Year	US$ m.	Year	US$ m.
1973	2,876.92	1990	13,274.54
1974	3,205.38	1991	25,518.78
1975	6,137.95	1992	12,266.03
1976	10,191.01	1993	14,348.54
1977	11,613.98	1994	12,327.06
1978	14,168.50	1995	10,795.12
1979	13,822.84	1996	9,990.16
1980	13,660.72	1997	12,930.18
1981	16,013.13	1998	17,760.68
1982	20,637.57	1999	14,114.27
1983	21,950.18	2000	13,741.44
1984	20,562.52	2001	14,985.35
1985	19,875.54	2002	14,748.08
1986	20,604.40	2003	12,244.79
1987	17,181.07	2004	12,322.79
1988	16,487.20	2005	12,599.77
1989	14,466.46	2006	13,844.77

The size of the Saudi armed forces was 106,500 active personnel as at 2002. This number is distributed between the army, navy and air force, with 75,000, 15,500 and 16,000 personnel, respectively. The Saudi army has 1,055 main battle tanks (315 M-1A2 Abrams, 290 AMX-30 and 450 M60A3). The navy deploys four frigates, four corvettes and 26 patrol boats. The air force has 294 combat aircraft consisting of 29 F-5, 158 F-15, 85 Tornado IDS and 22 Tornado ADVs (see World Disk Reference). As Table 8.9 shows, Saudi Arabia ranked eighth among the 15 countries with the highest military expenditure in 2007, at $33.8 billion, which constitutes 3% of the world's military expenditure.

Syria

As of 2002 the Syrian armed forces comprised army, navy and air force, with 215,000, 4,000, and 40,000 personnel, respectively. The army had 4,500 battle tanks (T-55/MV, T-62M/K and T-72/72M); the navy possessed two frigates and 18 patrol boats; and the air force deployed 548 combat aircraft such as Su-22/24 and MIG-21/23/25/29 jetfighters (CSIS, Israel and Syria Conventional Military Balance; Feldman and Shapir 2001, 289–300; World Disk Reference).

Data on Syrian military expenditure are available only for the period from 1980 to 2005. The pattern during that period can be divided into three phases, based on the Syrian-Soviet and, later, the Syrian-Russian relationship: the pre-Mikhail Gorbachev era, during the Gorbachev era, and the post-Gorbachev era, as shown in Table 8.9.

Before the Gorbachev era (1985–91), the Soviet Union used to sell weapons systems to some countries in the Middle East, such as Algeria, South Yemen (no longer a state) and Syria, under favourable conditions as they belonged to the Soviet bloc. The growing economic problems and the policy shift towards the end of the Cold War during Gorbachev's rule led Moscow to lose interest in its former clients. Consequently, the Soviet Union required cash when selling their weapons systems (Feldman and Shapir 2001, 17; Golan 1992, 220–2).

The declining trend in Syrian defence spending as shown in Table 8.9 reflects the change in the Syrian-Soviet relationship during Gorbachev's rule. Syrian defence spending decreased from $5,731m. in 1980 to $494m. The decline in Syrian military spending continued until 1998, picked up in 1999 (to $635m.) and reached $783m. in 2005.

Table 8.9 Countries with the highest military expenditure in 2007 in US$, at 2005 prices and exchange rates

Rank	Country	Spending ($bn)	World share (%)
1	USA	547	45
2	United Kingdom	59.7	5
3	China, People's Repub.	58.3	(5)
4	France	53.6	4
5	Japan	43.6	4
Sub-total top 5		*762*	*63*
6	Germany	36.9	3
7	Russia	(35.4)	(3)
8	Saudi Arabia	33.8	3
9	Italy	33.1	3
10	India	24.2	2
Sub-total top 10		*925*	*76*
11	South Korea	22.6	2
12	Brazil	15.3	1
13	Canada	15.2	1
14	Australia	15.1	1
15	Spain	14.6	1
Sub-total 15		*1,008*	*83*
World		*1,214*	*100*

Source: SIPRI 2008

Table 8.10 Syrian military expenditure 1980–2005 in US$ m. at 1985 prices and exchange rates

Year	US$ m.	Year	US$ m.
1980	5,731	1993	174
1981	5,289	1994	157
1982	4,389	1995	141
1983	4,434	1996	104
1984	4,084	1997	96
1985	4,255	1998	95
1986	3,146	1999	635
1987	2,316	2000	732
1988	494	2001	681
1989	918	2002	696
1990	n.a.	2003	825
1991	279	2004	925
1992	230	2005	783

Trends of arms procurement in the Gulf region

The Persian Arab Gulf (PAG) consists of Bahrain, Kuwait, Qatar, the UAE, Iran, Iraq, Oman and Saudi Arabia. This section focuses on Iran, Iraq, the Arab states in general and Israel.

Iran and Iraq

Conflicts between Iran and Iraq are deeply rooted in the history of the two countries. Predation – the desire to completely eliminate another state as a sovereign entity (in this case Iraq as the targeted state) – has characterized the Iranian-Iraqi relationship. Similarly, the predatory trend has characterized the relationship between Iran and other small states in the PAG, particularly Bahrain. What made the Iranian threats credible was the power and influence that Iran retains. Iran's ideological, religious and cultural influence has given it great influence, especially when these soft powers are backed up by assertive military power. Iran has more than 500,000 men under arms, including the 120,000-strong Revolutionary Guard Corps, as of 2002. The testing of medium-range cruise and ballistic missiles has heightened concern over Iran's possible military objectives, as it can now theoretically strike as far as Israel. Iran has also announced plans to launch its own satellite system.

The long war with Iraq from 1980 to 1988 diminished Iran's military power; however, the country has rebounded and its political regime has proved resilient. It defied the whole world, rebuilt and developed its army, and aggressively pursued an active nuclear programme. Contrary to the claims of the Iranian leadership, the fact that Iran keeps threatening other nations indicates that the objectives of its nuclear programme are not limited to civilian purposes; the military purposes of the nuclear programme seem to be part of Iranian military doctrine (Anderson et al. 2009, 81–7; CIA World Factbook, World Leaders; Cleveland 2000, 454–6; Feldman and Shapir 2001, 129–47; Microsoft Encarta 2007, Iran; Pierre 1997, 264–71).

The Iranian armed forces consist of an army of 350,000, an air force of 18,000 and a navy of 52,000 personnel. The Iranian army possesses 1,565 main battle tanks (M-47/48/60A1, Chieftain MK3/5, T-54/55/62/72); the navy has three submarines, three frigates and 56 patrol boats; and the air force deploys 306 combat aircraft (F-4D/E-F-SE/F, Su-24, F-14, F-7, MIG-29, Mirage F-1E). Iran has an ambitious nuclear programme, which potentially makes it a very dangerous country when considering the fact that its leadership has not refrained from constantly announcing to the whole world Iran's intentions of wiping some countries off the world map. Nuclear weapons in the hands of the Iranian 'clergy' have, then, been seen by some as a doomsday scenario (Crook 2006, 953–7; World Disk Reference; CSIS, Iran/Iranian Nuclear Weapons; globalsecurity.org, Iran).

Figure 8.7 shows the pattern of Iranian military expenditure during two political eras: the era of Shah Muhammad Reza Pahlavi (1941–79), and the era of Ayatollah Ruhollah Khomeini's revolution (1979–). During the Shah's era, the Iranian armed forces were the most powerful army in the region. Iranian military expenditure from 1960 to the fall of the Shah in

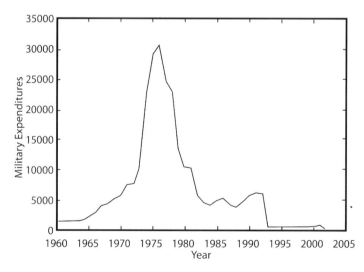

Figure 8.7 Iranian military expenditure 1987–2004 in million US$ at 1985 prices

Table 8.11 Iran, Kuwait and Bahrain military expenditure 1980–94 in US$ m. at 1985 prices and exchange rates

Year	US$ m. Iran	US$ m. Kuwait	US$ m. Bahrain
1980	10,623	1,352	154
1981	10,404	1,473	196
1982	5,738	1,227	259
1983	4,625	1,502	281
1984	4,209	1,573	309
1985	4,997	1,560	151
1986	5,210	1,992	194
1987	4,218	1,657	193
1988	3,753	2,030	224
1989	4,698	2,494	226
1990	5,755	n.a.	221
1991	6,054	n.a.	265
1992	947	7,392	293
1993	386	3,765	300
1994	380	4,418	285

1979 showed a consistent pattern of increase, as shown in Figure 8.7. The short period from 1977 to 1978 was one of political instability, which preceded the Islamic revolution in 1979. Although Iran engaged in a bloody war with Iraq from 1980 to 1988, its military spending declined sharply from $10,653m. in 1980 to $3,753m. in 1988. This can be attributed to the utilization of the Shah's military arsenal during the war.

Iran has developed its own national technologies and achieved a great deal of progress in the area of arms R&D, thus it has been able to spend much less on importing technologies and material, compared with other Gulf states. In this respect, the comparison of military spending between Iran and other PAG states, as seen in Table 8.11, does not reflect the military power differential among them. Iran can develop more weapons systems at a much lower cost by relying on its own scientific and technological capabilities, compared with the Gulf states, which purchase ready-made weapons at very high prices, as well as expensive operational and maintenance costs.

During the Shah's regime, Iran's weapons suppliers included France, Italy, the UK and the USA. Imports included air-to-surface missiles, ship-to-ship missiles, submarines, helicopters, towed surface-to-air missiles, tracked surface-to-air missiles, tanks and airborne warning and control planes. After the revolution, Iran imported weapons from Russia, China, the Democratic People's Republic of Korea (North Korea), Argentina and Ukraine.

Arms modernization

The war between Iraq and Iran (1980–88) and the first Gulf War between Iraq and an American-led coalition force from 34 nations (August 1990–February 1991) led to a reassessment of military capabilities and triggered an arms race in the Middle East region. This has manifested in the continuing attempts of major Middle Eastern states in pursuing missile, nuclear, biological and chemical weapon programmes.

The Arab world

Between 1976 and 1985, the Arab world spent more than $380 billion, or about eight times Israeli military expenditure, to modernize their armed forces. Egypt, Qatar, Saudi Arabia and the UAE established the Arab Organization for Industrialization (AOI) in 1975. The AOI was part of the Arab strategy to make a great leap forward in assimilating new technologies. The approach was tried first in research and scientific institutions in Egypt, the idea being to utilize existing scientific and research and development capability in nuclear, space, electronics, information and energy technologies to update military capabilities (Pierre 1997, 259–60).

Some Arab states such as Iraq and Egypt substituted arms imports with local production. For example, Iraq developed the al-Hussain, al-Abbas and al-Faw-1 missiles. The Arab countries sought to build advanced technological bases such as the Condor II missile project. Beginning in 1984, Iraq started a co-operative effort with Egypt and Argentina to develop a high-technology, two-stage missile system designed for a range of around 1,000 km, called BADR 2000 by Iraq and Egypt, and the Condor II by Argentina. This missile was to be built first as a two-stage rocket using solid fuel technology. The programme was intended to be realized in close co-operation with the Arab League Industrial Development Organization (ALIDO), with its headquarters in Baghdad. Egypt, Iraq and Libya were also among Arab countries that pursued nuclear, biological and chemical weapons programmes (globalsecurity. org, Global Security Project, and Weapons of Mass Destruction around the World/Egypt).

The suppliers of weapons to Iraq until 1976 included the former Czechoslovakia, France, the UK and the former Soviet Union. During Saddam Hussain's regime (1979–2003), Russia was a key supplier of Iraq's weapons systems, but other suppliers also included Brazil, China, Egypt, France, Italy, Jordan, Libya, Spain, the UK, the USA, Chile, the former Czechoslovakia, Germany and Italy. Iraq had significant research and development programmes in missile technology, as well as chemical and biological weapons. For instance, Iraq developed rockets with ranges from 50 km to 1,200 km, and payloads of 400kg–4,500kg, respectively.

Iran's state-run industry has expanded considerably and the country has been exporting military equipment to the Middle East and elsewhere. Substantial investment has been made in new facilities for research, development and production. Some weapons systems have been based on foreign designs, mainly from China or Russia, while others have been developed entirely in Iran (Alhomayed 2008; Iranian Military Procurement 2009; Pierre 1997, 265; globalsecurity.org, Weapons of Mass Destruction around the World/Iran).

Israel

Israel has sought to employ new weapons technologies to ensure its security and survival, especially after it was hit by Iraqi missiles during the first Gulf War. It has done so by concentrating on civil and military R&D to achieve a degree of self-reliance. It has also entered into R&D agreements with other countries, especially the USA. By using its own scientific and technological capabilities and its good relationship with a number of developed countries, Israel has been able to produce a wide range of advanced weapons systems. As a result, Israel developed its own advanced fighter, Lavi, its own modern battle tank, the Merkava, and a host of advanced missiles, including the Barak anti-missile missile and the Arrow anti-Ballistic missile (ABM) system. Israel co-operates with several leading US companies, including Martin Marietta, General Dynamic and Raytheon (Pierre 1997, 260–1; Sholam 1998; Peled 2002; Zrahiy 2008).

Conclusion

The patterns of arms trade in the Middle East can be described as follows: 1. The volume of arms imports is influenced by the involvement of the nations in conflict; the cases of Algeria, Morocco and Tunisia in the Arab Maghreb, and Egypt, Israel, Jordan and Syria in the Arab Mashreq, attest to that pattern. 2. Military expenditure in the Middle East follows an action-reaction pattern: Algeria versus Morocco, Tunisia versus Libya and Egypt, Jordan and Syria versus Israel. 3. The purchasing of arms is constrained by the economic ability of the importers to finance military spending; as an example, the ability of Algeria and Syria to purchase arms diminished after Gorbachev advocated the policy of *perestroika*, which changed the favourable conditions under which arms were purchased. 4. It is not feasible to analyse conflicts in the Middle East in isolation from the global arms trade involving major powers. The findings of this study confirm earlier conclusions reported in Mintz (1986), which reveal that the Middle Eastern nations clearly react to the armament behaviour of their rivals. The study suggests that peace talks among former enemies such as Egypt, Jordan and Israel have brought down military spending, providing them with opportunities to reallocate those resources to societal welfare programmes.

Bibliography

Abu-Qarn, A. S. and S. Abu-Bader, 'Structural Break in Military Expenditures: Evidence for Egypt, Israel, Jordan and Syria', *Peace Economics, Peace Science and Public Policy*, 14(1), 2008

Alhomayed, Tariq, 'The Iranian Catapult', *Asharq Alawat*, 31 December 2008, asharq-e.com/news.asp?section=2&id=13375

Anderson, Lisa, *The State and Social Transformation in Tunisia and Libya, 1830–1980*, Princeton (New Jersey), Princeton University Press, 1996

Anderson, Roy R., Robert F. Seibert and Jon G. Wagner, *Politics and Change in the Middle East*, London, Longman, 9th edition, 2009

Ashton, Nigel, *King Hussein of Jordan: A Political Life*, New Haven, CT, Yale University Press, 2008

Attar, Riad A., 'Egypt', in Karl DeRouen and Paul Bellamy (eds), *International Security and the United States: An Encyclopedia*, Westport, CT, Praeger Security International, 2007

Brzoska, Michael, 'The Reporting of Military Expenditures', *Journal of Peace Research* Vol. 18, No. 3, 1981

Carnegie Endowment for International Peace, *Chemical and Biological Weapons in the Middle East*, www.carnegieendowment.org/publications/index.cfm?fa=view&id=11745&prog=zgp&proj=zme,znpp

Center for Strategic and International Studies (CSIS), *Research Focus: Defense and Security Policy*, www.csis.org/about/researchfocus

——*Israel and Syria: Conventional Military Balance*, www.csis.org/component/option,com_csis_pubs/task,view/id,5142

——*Iran/Iranian Nuclear Weapons*, www.csis.org/%20id=?cx=006046696219301290917%3A23rjzx7mdwy&cof=FORID%3A11&q=iran&sa=Search&option=search#915

CIA, *The CIA World Factbook*, www.cia.gov/library/publications/the-world-factbook

——*World Leaders*, Central Intelligence Agency, www.cia.gov/library/publications/world-leaders-1/index.html

Cleveland, William L., *A History of Modern Middle East*, 2nd edition, Oxford, Westview, 2000

Cohen, Mitchell, *Zion and State: Nation, Class and the Shaping of Modern Israel*, New York, Columbia University Press, 1992

Cordesman, Anthony H., *The Arab-Israeli Military Balance in 2000*, Washington, Center for Strategic and International Studies, 2000

——*A Tragedy of Arms: Military and Security Developments in the Maghreb*, Westport, CT, Praeger, 2002

Cordesman, Anthony H. and K. al-Rodhan, 'The Middle East Military Balance: Definition, Regional Developments and Trends', 2005, www.csis.org

Crook, John R., 'Continuing Efforts to Curtail Iranian Nuclear Program', *The American Journal of International Law*, Vol. 100, No. 4, October 2006

Engdahl, F. William, *A Century of War: Anglo American Oil Politics and the New World Order*, London, Pluto Press, 2004

Federation of American Scientists, *Egypt: Chemical Weapons Program*, Federation of American Scientists, www.fas.org/nuke/guide/egypt/cw

Feldman, Shai and Yiftah Shapir, eds, *The Middle East Military Balance 2000–2001*, Israel, Jaffee Center for Strategic Studies, 2001

Fromkin, David, *A Peace to End All Peace: The Fall of the Ottoman Empire and the Creation of the Modern Middle East*, New York, Henry Holt and Company, 1989

Gaddafi, Mu'ammar al-, *The Green Book*, 1977, www.geocities.com/Athens/8744/readgb.htm

globalsecurity.org, *Weapons of Mass Destruction (WMD): Badr-2000/ Project 395/ Condor II*, GlobalSecurity.org, www.globalsecurity.org/wmd/world/iraq/badr-2000.htm

——*Weapons of Mass Destruction (WMD): Technical Corps for Special Projects*, GlobalSecurity.org, www.globalsecurity.org/wmd/world/iraq/techcorp.htm

Golan, Galia, 'Gorbachev's Difficult Time in the Gulf', *Political Science Quarterly*, 107(2), Summer 1992

Gurr, Ted Robert, 'Polity IV Project: Political Regime Characteristics and Transitions, 1800–2007', 2007, www.systemicpeace.org/polity/polity4.htm

Hudson, Michael C., *Arab Politics: The Search for Legitimacy*, New Haven, CT, Yale University Press, 1977

Intelligence Resource Program: Egypt, Federation of American Scientists, www.fas.org/irp/threat/missile/egypt.htm

International Crisis Behavior Project, www.icbnet.org

International Financial Statistics, www.imfstatistics.org/imf/logon.aspx

International Monetary Fund, *International Financial Statistics YEARBOOK (Vol. LII)*, Washington, IMF, 1999

Iran: Missiles, Federation of American Scientists, www.fas.org/nuke/guide/iran/missile

'Iranian Military Procurements', www.irandefence.net/showthread.php?t=3110 (accessed 4 January 2009)

'Israel Defense Forces', Wikipedia, en.wikipedia.org/wiki/Israel_Defense_Forces

Lebovic, James and Ahmad Ishaq, 'Military Burden, Security Needs, and Economic Growth in the Middle East', *Journal of Conflict Resolution*, *31*, 1987

MacMillan, Margrate, *Paris 1919: Six Months that Changed the World*, New York, Random House, 2002

Merom, Gil, 'Israel's National Security and the Myth of Exceptionalism', *Political Science Quarterly*, 114(3), Autumn 1999

Microsoft Encarta, 2007

Mintz, Alex, 'Imports as an Action-Reaction Process: An Empirical Test of Six Pairs of Developing Nations', *International Interaction*, 1986

Mintz, Alex and Huang Chi, 'Guns versus Butter: The Indirect Link', *American Journal of Political Science*, 35 (3), August 1991

Mintz, Alex and Randolph Stevenson, 'Defense Expenditures, Economic Growth, and the Peace Dividend: A Longitudinal Analysis of 103 countries', *Journal of Conflict Resolution*, 39 (2), 1995

'Missiles of Illusion', *Newstin*, www.newstin.co.uk/tag/uk/72944362

Owen, Roger, 'The Dog That Neither Barked Nor Bit: The Fear of Oil Shortages', in William Roger Louis and Roger Owen, eds, A Revolutionary Year: The Middle East in 1958, Washington, Woodrow Wilson Center Press, 2002

Peled, Dan, 'Defense R&D and Economic Growth in Israel: A Research Agenda', Samuel Neaman Institute for Advanced Studies in Science and Technology, 2001, econ.haifa.ac.il/~dpeled/papers/ste-wp4.pdf

Peled, Yoav and Gershon Shafir, *Being Israeli: The Dynamics of Multiple Citizenship*, Cambridge, Cambridge University Press, 2002

Pierre, Andrew J., ed., *Cascade of Arms: Controlling Conventional Weapons Proliferation in the 1990s*, Washington, Brooking Institution, 1997

Quandt, William. B., 'Camp David and Peacemaking in the Middle East', *Political Science Quarterly*, 101(3), 1986

Roskin, Michael G. and James J. Coyle, Politics of the Middle East: Cultures and Conflicts, Upper Saddle River, NJ, Prentice Hall, 2008

Seale, Patrick, *Asad: The Struggle for the Middle East. Berkeley*, California, University of California Press, 1990

Shlaim, Avi, *Lion of Jordan: The Life of King Hussein in War and Peace*, New York, Knopf, 2008

Sholam, Danny, 'Chemical and Biological Weapons in Egypt', *The Non Proliferation Review*, Spring 1998, cns.miis.edu/pubs/npr/vol05/53/shoham53.pdf

SIPRI, *SIPRI Yearbook*, Stockholm, Stockholm International Peace Research Institute, various editions (1974, 1976, 1980, 1983, 1990, 1991, 1992, 1996, 1997, 2001, 2004, 2007, 2008)

'Syrian-Soviet Relations', April 1987, www.country-data.com/cgi-bin/query/r-13564.html

Waltz, Susan, 'Islamist Appeal in Tunisia', *The Middle East Journal*, 40(4), 1986

Weatherby, Joseph, *The Middle East and North Africa: A Political Primer*, New York, Longman, 2002

Weatherby, Joseph, et al., *The Other World: Issues and Politics of the Developing Word* (6th edition), New York, Pearson Longman, 2009

World Disk Reference: A Country List, dev.prenhall.com/divisions/hss/worldreference

Zrahiy, Zivi, 'Another Record Year for Defense Spending in 2008', Haartz.com, 2008, www.haaretz.com/hasen/spages/939217.html

9 Iran's defence spending and arms procurement

Ephraim Kam

Iran's military build-up following the Islamic revolution, and especially since the 1990s, is the outcome of several factors: the changes that have taken place in Iran's threat perception and strategic environment, as well as the security concept that has been developed by the revolutionary regime; the state of the military infrastructure and the armed forces left by the Shah regime; the changes that took place in the Iranian military system during the eight years of the war with Iraq, 1980–88, and especially the severe losses and damage caused by the traumatic war; the Western arms embargo imposed on Iran since the war; the difficulties in acquiring qualitative arms from non-Western sources; and the economic crisis that affected Iran's military expenditure during the 1980s and the 1990s, and which still affects its military build-up.

Due to all these factors, the Iranian regime had to make difficult decisions regarding its order of priorities – between military and civilian needs; regarding the various components of the military build-up; as well as between conventional and non-conventional military capabilities.

The changes in Iran's threat perception

Traditionally, Iran has perceived itself as located within a circle of instability, violence, threats and crises. For centuries, Iran has had to cope with two historical threats: the Russian threat in the north and the Iraqi threat in the west. During the last generation, three major wars took place in the Gulf area, in one of which Iran itself was involved, namely the Iran–Iraq War. The USA, a major threat to Iran, has deployed and used large military forces close to Iran's borders, in Iraq and Afghanistan. Iran's western and eastern neighbours, Pakistan and especially Iraq and Afghanistan, are unstable states, and the Iranians are concerned that this instability might spread into their territory.

Since the early 1980s, dramatic changes have taken place in Iran's threat perception. For generations, Russia and the Soviet Union were perceived by Iran as a historical threat: the Iranians were always concerned that the Russian giant would penetrate into Iran and occupy parts of its territory. The Shah was also afraid that the Soviet Union might try to undermine his regime and replace it with a Communist one. Yet, as of the late 1980s the Soviet Union collapsed, Russia and Iran have no longer a common border, and both countries co-operate extensively in military, technological and economic fields.

Secondly, in Iranian eyes, Iraq has been a historical threat as well. Iran and Iraq have been rivals for centuries. From the viewpoint of Iran, Iraq has represented the spearhead of a hostile Sunni Muslim world (though Iraq is today dominated by Shi'a). Most importantly, the Iraqi invasion of Iran in 1980 led to an eight-year war between the two states, in which Iran was eventually defeated. Yet Iraq was significantly weakened during the 1990–91 first Gulf War, and lost all its military capabilities following the American military operation in Iraq in 2003. In fact, as of 2003, Iraq has disappeared as a military player in the Middle East arena and no longer poses a military threat to Iran for the foreseeable future.

On the other hand, since the late 1980s the USA has emerged as the most significant threat to Iran. The USA is making a major effort to weaken Iran militarily and economically, isolate it politically and undermine its Islamic regime. For the Iranian fundamentalist leadership, the USA represents the evil of the corrupt Western world. Most importantly, the American administration is explicitly threatening to attack the nuclear sites, and perhaps other strategic targets, in Iran. The Iranians are particularly concerned about the deployment of large American forces in the neighbourhood of Iran – in Iraq, Afghanistan and the Gulf area – and about its encirclement by regimes linked to the USA.

To these concerns one should add the Israeli threat, which has emerged since the early 1990s. From the Iranian viewpoint, the severity of the Israeli threat is more limited than the three former ones. Yet, Iran is concerned about a possible Israeli attack against its nuclear installations, especially as Israel is explicitly threatening, and making military preparations, to carry out such an operation.

In Iran's view, the bottom line of these concerns is that it needs a strategic answer in order to cope with these threats. Indeed, while the threats from Russia and Iraq have declined, they have not disappeared altogether, and the Iranians take into account the possibility that they might re-emerge in the future. Furthermore, Iran's number one enemy is a superpower, which proved twice during the current decade that it would not hesitate to attack Iran's neighbours in order to bring down their regimes whenever they crossed the line, according to American judgement. These concerns have led the Iranian regime to several conclusions (Shamkhani 1998):

- The main threat to Iran is the distant threat – the American threat and, to some extent, the Israeli one. The close threats – the Russian and Iraqi ones – are limited for the time being.
- The main component of Iran's security concept should be deterrence. Hence, Iran needs strategic military capabilities to deter its enemies and defend its country if attacked.
- Iran has to achieve hegemony in the Gulf area, in order to affect the main developments in its neighbourhood and to become a Middle East power. This desire was shared by the Shah regime as well, but it now has a different meaning: the objective is not only to maintain Iran's superiority over its neighbours, but also to limit American presence and influence in the region.
- Iran has to develop self-reliance in military affairs. In the meantime, it has no other choice but to acquire weapons and military equipment from external sources, yet gradually it should build a large and comprehensive independent defence industry in order to meet its military needs.

With this background, the following analysis will examine Iran's military build-up, as well as its arms procurement and defence expenditure.

The military build-up during the Shah regime

The basis for the Iranian military build-up was created during the Shah regime. As an outcome of his strategic concept, the Shah built, especially during the 1970s, the largest, strongest and most modern armed forces in the Gulf area, and one of the largest armed forces in the entire Middle East. Using his strategic alliance with the USA and the United Kingdom (UK), as well as his vast oil revenues, the Shah acquired large amounts of qualitative weapons systems and military equipment mostly from the West. At the same time, the Shah regime started to develop local defence industry, with an eye to producing ammunition, spare parts and auxiliary systems at the first stage, and major weapons systems for his armed forces at a later stage (Chubin 1997, 229).

The Shah had access to the best arms sources. Most of the weapons systems purchased by Iran came from American industry, with some from the UK. Thus, between 1972 and 1976 Iran purchased American arms to the value of US$10.4 billion. Moreover, within the framework of the 1977–81 five-year plan, Iran was expected to acquire additional arms at the value of $10 billion–$15 billion, but the supply of arms was stopped in 1979 following the Islamic revolution. In addition to its reliance on the American market, the Shah regime developed other arms sources – mostly the UK, which as of 1972 supplied Iran with arms to the value of $3.5 billion – as well as France, West Germany, Italy and even the Soviet Union. This massive arms procurement was accompanied by a process of unprecedented increase in the size of Iran's armed forces, which were expanded from 200,000 troops in 1972 to 350,000 troops in 1977. This huge increase, together with the large arms deliveries, translated into substantial defence expenditure. In 1976 defence expenditure was 17.4% of Iran's gross domestic product (GDP) – more than in any of the years of the war with Iraq (Iran: A Country Study 1978: 398, 408, 414–6).

In developing military power, the Iranian air force received the highest priority, in terms of the allocation of money and manpower, as it was perceived by the Shah as the most important element of deterrence, and as a vehicle for using Iranian power against long-range targets. The air force was based on American armaments and its arsenal of aircraft included almost 200 Phantom F-4 strike aircraft, about 80 Tomcat F-14 interceptors equipped with Phoenix air-to-air missiles and about 165 F-5 older strike aircraft. In addition, in 1978 the Shah ordered 160 F-16 fighting Falcon, seven AWACS airborne radar systems and heavy transport helicopters, but this deal was cancelled by the new Islamic regime. By the end of this stage of the build-up, the air force had planned to deploy more than 600 fighters, most of them state-of-the-art (Iran: A Country Study 1978, 406; Hashim 1994, 4–5).

During the Shah regime, the Iranian ground forces had the strongest armoured and mechanized power in the Gulf area. They included qualitative tanks: almost 900 British Chieftains and about 450 American M-60A1s, in addition to 400 older American M-47 and M-48 tanks. Moreover, towards the end of the Shah era, Iran ordered an additional 1,220 Chieftains from the UK, but the revolutionary regime cancelled this deal as well. By the time the Shah regime collapsed, the army aviation had the largest helicopter force in the Middle East – almost 800 helicopters, most of them made in the USA (Iran: A Country Study 1978, 453).

The Iranian navy was the largest and most modern navy in the Gulf during the Shah regime. Originally, most of its combat vessels came from the UK, but they were gradually replaced by American ones. By the end of the Shah era, the navy included three missile destroyers, four missile frigates, four missile corvettes, six missile boats and about 50 smaller boats. The build-up programme planned for the late 1970s and early 1980s was even more impressive. Iran ordered from the USA four modern Spruance class destroyers and three Tang class submarines; six IKL-209 class submarines from Germany; six Lupo class frigates from Italy; and four landing craft from the UK. All these deals were cancelled by the Islamic regime (Iran: A Country Study 1978, 405, 436; Jordan 1992).

This brief review of the Iranian military build-up under the Shah is aimed at understanding the military build-up during the Islamic regime from a wider perspective. The build-up during the Shah regime, at the conventional level, had been much more intensive than that under the Islamic regime, in terms of quantity and especially qualitatively. The defence expenditure, the volume of the arms deals and deliveries, as well as the efforts to upgrade and modernize weapons systems had been much more impressive under the Shah than during the subsequent years, even during the years of the war with Iraq.

The Islamic revolution and the war with Iraq

During the first decade of the revolutionary regime, most of the qualitative components of the Iranian armed forces were lost. The fundamentalist regime had paid a very heavy price for its extreme ideological approach. Immediately after coming to power, the new regime cancelled all arms deals, valued at billions of dollars, with the USA and with other Western governments.

In the meantime, an American-European arms embargo was imposed on Iran. This was, to a large extent, due to the radical nature of its regime, which in turn increased the damage caused to its military capabilities. The US-made qualitative weapons systems delivered under the Shah started to erode following the cessation of American technical support and the supply of spare parts and ammunition, upon which the Iranians were dependent.

Yet there is no doubt that the main factor in Iran's military build-up under the Islamic regime has been the impact of the war with Iraq and the lessons that the Iranians have learned from it. During the later stages of the war, Iran found itself in a state of strategic inferiority vis-à-vis Iraq in almost every aspect. This inferiority made it impossible for the Iranians to continue the war and, by the summer of 1988, it was forced to agree to a ceasefire with Iraq under conditions that they had previously rejected. The main problem was the disruption of the arms supply to the Iranian armed forces. Due to the American-European embargo, Iran did not succeed in developing alternative arms sources, while Iraq enjoyed a vast supply of weapons systems from the Soviet Union and Western Europe. As a result, Iran had to content itself with the supply of inferior weapons, delivered by Third World countries, especially the People's Republic of China and the Democratic People's Republic of Korea (North Korea), and others which it sometimes acquired from arms dealers.

Towards the end of the war, Iran's armed forces were in a severely degraded condition. About half of its arms arsenal had been destroyed during the fighting and Iran was unable to replace the losses. Most of the qualitative weapons systems did not survive the war. Out of the 875 Chieftain tanks that had started the war only 200 were left; out of the 460 M-60A1 tanks, only 150 remained. Only about 100 operational aircraft were left: 15 Tomcat F-14 out of 80, 40–50 Phantom F-4 out of 190, and 45 F-5 out of 165 aircraft at the beginning of the war. The weapons systems left in the Iranian arsenal gradually became obsolete, since the Iranians were unable to get suitable spare parts or replace them with new modern arms due to the embargo. The low technical quality of the Iranian logistical system brought about constant losses of military equipment, due to amortization, obsolescence, erosion and lack of spare parts (Middle East Strategic Balance 1988–89, 170; 1990–91, 238–41; 1994–95, 215–6; Cordesman and Hashim 1997, 183–5).

Beyond the outcome of the war and the state of the Iranian armed forces, other considerations have affected the trends in their military build-up after the war. Arms sources remained a major problem. The American-European embargo, which still exists now, has prevented Iran from acquiring qualitative Western weapons systems and upgrading its arms arsenal. The Soviet Union had supplied limited amounts of arms to Iran, but only during the first part of the war. Due to these constraints and since Iran had no better alternative, China became the main arms supplier to Iran during the 1980s. Some of the weapons supplied by China were obsolescent: T-59/69 tanks, F-7 interceptors and HQ-2J air defence systems. However, the supply also included more advanced systems, such as Silkworm, C-801 and C-802 naval cruise missiles, Houdong missile boats as well as missile and nuclear technology. During 1981–89, China supplied Iran with arms estimated at $2.7 billion and at $2.4 billion during 1989–92. China remained an important arms supplier to Iran during the 1990s as well (Eisenstadt 1997, 7; Einhorn 1997, 11).

Following the war, an important change took place in Iran's relations with Russia. Since the late 1980s Russia has agreed, as a result of economic and regional considerations, to supply major weapons systems to Iran. At the same time Iran, which during the first decade of the revolution refused to develop significant relations with the Soviet Union, changed its approach toward Russia due to its urgent need of advanced weapons and technology.

Arms transfers to Iran since the 1990s

In order to cope with the severe decline of its military power following the war, the Iranian supreme command prepared in the late 1980s a comprehensive build-up plan. According to various reports, the plan aimed at building a large ground force which would include at least 1,500–2,000 tanks, thousands of armoured vehicles and hundreds of artillery pieces; a modern air force, which would rely on 300 qualitative combat aircraft; an advanced air defence system; and a modern navy which would include three submarines and missile boats equipped with naval cruise missiles. Most of the weapons systems were expected to be acquired from Russia and partly from China (Eisenstadt 1996, 36–7).

Within the framework of this plan, Iran concluded four arms deals with Russia between 1989 and 1991, to the value of $5.1 billion dollars. The main items included in these deals were 1,000 T-72 tanks, 1,500 BMP-2 Infantry Fighting Vehicles (IFV), 24 Mig-29 interceptors, 12 Sukhoi-24 ground attack aircraft, two SA-5 air defence systems and three submarines (Kortenko 2001).

Yet, the Russian arms market has been problematic as well. Following the collapse of the Soviet Union, Moscow was no longer ready to supply its clients with weapons at discount prices. Instead, the Russians demanded full payment in hard currency for the delivery of military equipment. Moreover, the Russian Government has been under American pressures not to supply qualitative arms to Iran and, in several cases, agreed to refrain from supplying certain kinds of weapons systems to the Iranians. In September 1994, during the summit meeting between American President Bill Clinton and Russian President Boris Yeltsin, the Russian President agreed that his government would not conclude new arms deals with Iran, and would complete the supply of arms under existing contracts until the end of 1999 (US Congress Hearings 1998). This secret understanding significantly reduced the supply of Russian arms to Iran.

The American administration has not limited its pressures to the Russian government. Since the 1990s American pressures have been exerted also on the Eastern European and Chinese governments to refrain from supplying not only nuclear technology but also conventional arms to Iran. This policy has been partly effective. By the mid-1990s, the Czech Republic, Poland and Hungary had promised the American administration that they would not conclude new arms deals with Iran, after completing the supply of military equipment under existing contracts (SIPRI 1997, 348). Since the build-up plan relied on acquiring Russian-made weapons systems – from Russia or from Eastern European countries – or on Chinese and North Korean versions of Russian models, the difficulty in acquiring sufficient amounts of weapons systems has affected the entire build-up programme.

Iran has faced another major problem: financial difficulties. Since the revolution Iran has had to cope with a significant economic crisis. The crisis, which was worsened by the war with Iraq, negatively affected Iran's build-up plans during the war. During that time, Iran could still cope with the burden of its external debt. However, once the war was over, the external debt grew to an unprecedented size, severely eroding Iran's foreign currency reserves and weakening its ability to obtain credit.

The political difficulties in importing weapons systems and the financial problems have not enabled Iran to meet its arms acquisition plans as well as its build-up programmes, and Iran was, then, forced to cancel or postpone many of them during the 1990s. The outcome was a significant reduction in the volume of arms transfers to Iran since the early 1990s.

Iran's decision to significantly cut its arms imports was affected by three considerations. First, as long as Iran had to cope with the economic distress and the enormous external debt, it had no chance to carry out an intensive build-up programme – including the upgrading of its weapons systems as well as replacing the losses of the war – within a short period of time. Second, the time factor was not urgent. Under the circumstances that had developed by the early 1990s, when Iraq and the Gulf states could not really threaten Iran, and since Iran could not cope anyway with the American threat, there was no need to give priority to a conventional military build-up. Third, as a temporary alternative to a conventional build-up, Iran decided to concentrate on developing those components of strategic power that could give an

Table 9.1 Arms transfers to Iran 1986–99, in US$ bn at 1999 prices

1986	1987	1988	1989	1990	1991	1992	1993	1994	1995	1996	1997	1998	1999
3.1	2.2	3.3	2.4	2.3	1.9	1.0	1.6	0.4	0.4	0.4	0.9	0.4	0.1

Source: ACDA, World Military Expenditures and Arms Transfers, 1997, table 2; US Department of State, Bureau of Verification and Compliance, World Military Expenditures and Arms Transfers, 1999–2000, table 2

effective and quick defensive-deterrent answer to Iran's strategic interests and security needs. These components were the programmes to develop weapons of mass destruction (WMD) – especially nuclear weapons – and long-range ballistic missiles, and to build capabilities to defend Iran's interests in the Gulf area.

The reality is that since the first Gulf War, Iran is facing, in its view, a window of opportunity – while Iraq is weak, the Russian threat has almost disappeared, the danger of a confrontation with the USA or with Israel cannot be ignored but does not seem imminent, and the other threats are rather limited. Under these circumstances, Iran has had to choose between focusing on a conventional build-up and giving priority to building non-conventional power, since its resources were insufficient to fully develop both capabilities. Iran's rational decision was to concentrate at that stage on non-conventional capabilities, at the expense of conventional ones, since the development of WMD would give a faster and more direct answer to the threats emanating from the USA, Israel and, in the longer run, Iraq as well.

The outcome of these considerations was a significant reduction in the deliveries of most of the conventional weapons systems, especially Russian-made systems. Between 1993 and 1996 Russia supplied Iran with weapons estimated to the value of $1.3 billion, mostly in the framework of the contracts concluded before 1991. However, during the same three years both governments concluded new arms deals to the estimated value of only $200m. and between 1997 and 2000 they signed further deals to the estimated value of only $300m. At the same time, the estimated value of arms transfers from China to Iran was reduced from $2.4 billion during 1989–92, to $900m. during 1993–96, to $400m. during 1997–2000, and to $200m. during 2003–06 (Grimmett 1994–2008).

Among the weapons systems that Iran had wanted to acquire from Russia, but eventually was forced to abandon, were some of the most advanced weapons: almost 600 T-72 tanks, more than 1,000 IFVs, Sukhoi-27 air superiority fighters, Sukhoi-25 close-support aircraft, Mig-31 long-range interceptors, Tu-22M bombers and S-300 surface-to-air missiles. According to one report, the value of the deals that were cancelled or not signed with Russia amounted to more than $5 billion. In this framework, Iran did not carry out arms deals that had been already concluded with Russia between 1989 and 1991 to the value of $1.5 billion.

Thus, the grand plan to build a large armoured and mechanized corps and a modern air force have brought only limited results. The arms transfers in these fields have, until now, included about 520 T-72 tanks – 420 from Russia and 100 from Poland – and several hundred T-55/59/69 tanks delivered by China and former communist countries; about 400 BMP-2 IFVs from Russia; 24 Mig-29 interceptors and 12 ground attack aircraft from Russia; several air defence systems from Russia and China; three K class submarines from Russia; 10 Houdong missile boats and C-801/802 naval cruise missiles from China. Most of these weapons were delivered to Iran during the first half of the 1990s. Since then, Iran has received only a small number of new weapons systems – mostly air defence systems and military helicopters from Russia (Middle East Strategic Balance 1997, 195–203; Eisenstadt 1996, 36–7; Cordesman and Hashim 1997, 180).

By the late 1990s, two important developments had affected Iran's efforts to upgrade its arsenal of weapons systems. First, the Russian Government was ready to resume talks with Iran regarding a large arms deal. Secondly, Iran's oil revenues had significantly increased following the rise in oil prices. Since 1997, especially under the presidency of Vladimir Putin, negotiations between the Russian and Iranian governments focused on the supply of advanced arms to Iran. During these negotiations, Iran presented its long-range build-up programme and expressed interest in basing it on advanced Russian weapons. According to Russian sources, the Iranian requests pertained to a wide range of arms, especially advanced combat aircraft and military helicopters, T-80U and T-90S modern tanks, BMP-3 modern IFVs, S-300 sophisticated long-range air defence systems, tactical surface-to-surface missiles, naval cruise missiles and fast missile boats. The estimated value of the Iranian requests, according to Russian and Iranian sources, was $7 billion–$10 billion (Pronina 2001; Petrovich 2001; Mukhin 2000; Fulghum 2001).

The negotiations between the two governments lasted several years. In November 2000, the Russian Government cancelled the 1994 secret understanding with the USA in which it promised not to sign any new arms deals with Iran. The Russian announcement led to the conclusion, in October 2001, of a framework agreement for military-technical co-operation between Russia and Iran. It was understood between the governments that the agreement would be the basis for further negotiations regarding a large-scale arms deal.

So far, the intensive negotiations as well as the framework agreement have produced limited results. Between 1999 and 2001 three agreements were signed for supplying 56 Mi-171 transport helicopters (Novichkov 2001). Since 2000 two agreements have been signed regarding the supply of air defence systems. In 2000–01 Russia delivered to Iran SA-16 man-portable anti-aircraft missile systems, and in 2005 Russia provided Iran with 29 Thor-M1 middle-range air defence systems. Yet, the most important Iranian request is the S-300 air defence system, one of world's most effective all-altitude regional air defence systems. Iran is interested in the system, at least since 2001, mostly in order to defend its strategic sites, especially its nuclear facilities. However, although Iran has indicated several times that Russia has agreed to sell the system, the Russian Government announced only in early 2009 that the deal had been signed in 2007, but that the system has not yet been delivered to Iran.

It should be added that between 1993 and 1996, Iran negotiated with China, as well as with several Eastern European governments, for large-scale arms deals. Iran was interested in combat aircraft, tanks, infantry fighting vehicles, fast missile boats and other weapons systems. It is not clear whether these deals were not concluded, or whether they were concluded but not implemented. In any case, it is clear that the large amounts of weapons in which the Iranians were interested have not been delivered.

Table 9.2 summarizes the arms transfers to Iran since 1981 and demonstrates the significant decline in arms deliveries to Iran since the mid-1990s, following the end of the war with Iraq and the first stage of the military build-up. Yet, the table also emphasizes two interesting facts. First, although Russia has replaced China as the top arms supplier to Iran, China has

Table 9.2 Arms deliveries to Iran, by supplier, 1981–2007, in US$ m., current prices

	Soviet Union / Russia	*China*	*West Europe*	*Others*	*Total*
1981–84	370	540	1,670	3,350	5,930
1985–88	0	2,210	2,500	3,170	7,880
1989–92	2,000	2,400	900	1,000	6,300
1993–96	1,300	900	200	200	2,600
1997–2000	800	400	400	100	1,700
2000–03	300	0	0	500	800
2004–07	400	200	0	200	800

Source: Grimmett 1989, 1997, 2001, 2008

remained the most important supplier during the entire period since the Islamic revolution. Secondly, although European governments have imposed arms embargos on Iran since the early 1980s, Western Europe was an important supplier of arms especially during the Iran–Iraq War, and to a lesser extent until the late 1990s. Since there is no information about the supply of major weapons systems by European governments to Iran – with the exception of small naval units and light anti-aircraft missiles delivered by Sweden – it can be assumed that European companies sold Iran military equipment such as secondary systems and military technology.

Economic distress and defence expenditure

Although Iran is one of the world's largest oil producers and exporters, it has faced severe economic distress since the Islamic revolution, mostly due to the decline of oil prices during the 1980s and 1990s, the costs and damage of the long war with Iraq, and ineffective economic policy. The need to rebuild the armed forces and to reconstruct the civilian infrastructure after the war, and at the same time to feed a poor nation of more than 60m. people, has forced Iran's leaders to make hard decisions regarding defence expenditure.

There are no reliable data regarding Iranian defence expenditure. The Iranian Government provides some data regarding its defence budget, but as in many other cases, they seem to be partial and misleading. No wonder that Western research institutes give very different estimates regarding Iranian defence expenditure. It should be assumed, then, that at least some of these estimates are significantly inaccurate. Nonetheless, it is still possible to uncover some general trends in Iranian defence expenditure.

In 1989 the Iranian parliament allocated almost $10 billion for defence expenditure during 1990–95. Iran claimed that even this budget was not fully used and only $6.4 billion was actually spent; it later presented higher numbers. In 1996 the secretary of the Iranian National Security Council stated that the annual defence budget since 1989 had been $2.7 billion on average. Since the mid-1990s, the Iranian Government has significantly increased, in Iranian currency terms, the defence budget. This increase was between 8% and 50% per year during the period between 1996 and 2003. The reasons given for these increases were the need to face the growing American presence in the Gulf and rising oil revenues (Eisenstadt 1996, 2; Eisenstadt 2001; Cordesman 1999, 50; Moore 1994, 373). Yet, since the increases were in local currency, it is not clear whether they reflected a real and significant increase. In any case, according to the estimate of the US Department of Defense, the Iranian defence budget for 2000–01 was $6 billion, and was expected to stay at that level during the coming years (Proliferation: Threat and Response 2001, 34).

It is clear that since the late 1980s, Iran's defence expenditure has declined, following the end of the war with Iraq. According to a US Government estimate, Iran's defence expenditure between 1985 and 1988 was $12 billion–$15 billion per year. After the end of the war, between 1989 and 1991, expenditure declined to the level of $9 billion–$10 billion per year, and to the level of $5 billion–$7 billion per year between 1992 and 1999 (Cordesman 1999, 41, 45; Eisenstadt 1996, 2). This decline is explained by several reasons: the economic distress and the need to cut the heavy external debt; the regime's decision to allocate substantial budgets for civilian needs after eight years of a traumatic war; Iraq's weakness, which enabled Iran to postpone part of its military build-up; and the political difficulties in acquiring qualitative weapons systems, which forced Iran to limit its arms deals.

Conclusion

The build-up of the Iranian armed forces during the last two decades is a unique case. On the one hand, Iran has the largest armed forces in the Middle East, in terms of manpower and order of battle, yet they lost most of their weapons systems during the war with Iraq, and most of the remaining weapons are obsolete and need replacement and upgrading. Iran planned comprehensive build-up programmes to replace and upgrade its equipment, yet they produced limited results. Iran negotiated large arms deals with Russia and China, yet they have led to the delivery of only small amounts of weapons. In fact, since the mid-1990s, Iran has received only air defence systems – which so far do not include the S-300 system preferred by Iran – and several dozen transport helicopters from Russia.

The reasons for this phenomenon are two-fold. First, Iran faces severe difficulties in developing arms sources. The American and European markets are closed to them since the Islamic revolution, and the Russian and Chinese markets are problematic. Even after the Russian Government cancelled the 1994 secret understanding with the American administration to avoid selling additional arms to Iran, Washington is still exerting pressure on Moscow not to sell strategic weapons to Iran, and the Russian reluctance, so far, to sell the S-300 air defence system to Iran is probably the outcome of this pressure. Secondly, Iran faces economic problems and financial difficulties, which limit its capability to conclude large arms deals. Indeed, since the late 1990s its economic condition has improved due to the rise of oil prices. Yet the Iranian regime is under heavy pressure to address domestic socio-economic distress and, thus, needs to give priority to civilian needs rather than military ones.

At the same time, Iran is developing two alternative solutions to the weakness of its conventional capabilities. The first is self-reliance. Since the late 1980s Iran has significantly developed its defence industry. This industry is now producing a wide range of weapons and military equipment: ballistic missiles and rockets, combat aircraft, unmanned aerial vehicles, tanks, infantry fighting vehicles, artillery guns, mini-submarines and many other weapons. Some of these weapons have been absorbed by the Iranian armed forces. The quality of most of these weapons is still not high, and many of the projects initiated by the military industry have failed. Yet, Iran has gained important experience in producing weapons and it has gradually managed to improve the quality of its weapons systems.

The second solution is much more significant. Iran is developing WMDs. It already possesses operational, self-produced ballistic missiles and it is constantly upgrading the range and accuracy of those missiles. Iran also has chemical and biological warfare capabilities. Most importantly, Iran is on its way to acquiring nuclear weapons and, if not stopped, will almost certainly obtain nuclear bombs in a very short time, probably within the next few years. The acquisition of these capabilities allows Iran to lag behind in its plans for a conventional military build-up.

Bibliography

Armaments Control and Disarmament Agency (ACDA), World Military Expenditures and Arms Transfers, 1997, Washington, Armaments Control and Disarmament Agency, 1997

Chubin, Shahram, 'Arms Procurement in Iran: ad hoc Decision Making and Ambivalent Decision Makers', in Eric Arnett, ed., *Military Capacity and the Risk of War: China, India, Pakistan and Iran*, New York: Oxford University Press/SIPRI, 1997

Cordesman, Anthony, *Iran's Military Forces in Transition: Conventional Threats and Weapons of Mass Destruction*, Westport, CT, Praeger, 1999

Cordesman, Anthony and Ahmed Hashim, *Iran: Dilemmas of Dual Containment*, Boulder, Westview, 1997

Department of State, World Military Expenditures and Arms Transfers, 1999–2000, Washington, Bureau of Verification and Compliance, US Department of State, 2001

Einhorn, Robert, 'Engaging China on Nonproliferation', testimony before the Subcommittee on International Security, Proliferation and Federal Services of the Senate Committee on Government Affairs, in *Chinese Arms and Technology Transfers to Iran*, Asia and Pacific Rim Institute, Washington, 10 April 1997

Eisenstadt, Michael, *Iranian Military Power: Capabilities and Intentions*, Policy Paper No. 42, The Washington Institute for Near East Policy, Washington, 1996

——'Chinese Military Assistance to Iran: Trends and Implications', in *Chinese Arms and Technology Transfers to Iran: Implications for the U.S., Israel and the Middle East*, Asia and Pacific Rim Institute, Washington, 1997

——'Russian Arms and Technology Transfers to Iran: Policies Challenges for the United States', *Arms Control Today*, Vol. 31, No. 2, March 2001

Fulghum, David, 'Iran Specifies New Weapons Mix', *Aviation Week and Space Technology*, 26 March 2001

Grimmett, Richard F., *Conventional Arms Transfers to Developing Nations, 1989–1996*, CRS (Congressional Research Service) Report, US Library of Congress, 1989

——*Conventional Arms Transfers to Developing Nations, 1994–2008*, Congressional Research Service (CRS) Report, US Library of Congress, 1994–2008

Hashim, Ahmed, *Iranian National Security Policies under the Islamic Republic: New Defense Thinking and Growing Military Capabilities*, Occasional Paper No. 2, The Henry L. Stimson Center, 1994

Hearings before the Subcommittee on Near Eastern and South Asian Affairs of the Committee on Foreign Relations, US Senate, 105th Congress, 1st Session, 17 April and 6 May 1997, Washington, 1998

Iran: A Country Study, 3rd edition, Washington, The American University, Washington, 1978

Jordan, John, 'The Iranian Navy', *Jane's Intelligence Review*, 1 May 1992

Kortenko, Igor, 'Renewal of Russian-Iranian Cooperation Suggests Iran May Become Third Largest Importer of Russian Military Equipment', *Nezavisimoye Voyennoye Obozreniye*, Moscow (in Russian), 1 January 2001

Middle East Strategic Balance, Tel-Aviv, The Jaffee Center for Strategic Studies, Tel-Aviv University, various editions

Moore, James, 'An Assessment of the Iranian Military Rearmament Program', *Comparative Strategy*, Vol. 13, No. 4, 1994

Mukhin, Vladimir, 'From Visit Set to Fire Up Low Russian Arms Sales', *Nezavisimaya Gazeta (The Russian Journal)*, 23 December 2000

Novichkov, Nikolai, 'Iran to Buy More Russian Transport Helicopters', *Jane's Defence Weekly*, 13 July 2001

Petrovich, Boris, 'Russia Said Being Circumspect in Arms Sales to Iran', *Moscow Novyye Izvestiya* (in Russian) 2 October 2001

Proliferation: Threat and Response, Washington, US Department of Defense, January 2001

Pronina, Lyobov, 'Tehran Turns to Moscow to Fulfill Weapon Needs', *Defense News*, 22–28 October 2001

Shamkhani, Admiral Ali, 'Interview on Channel 2', Iranian TV, FBIS-NES-98-217, 5 August 1998

SIPRI, *SIPRI Yearbook 1997*, Stockholm, Stockholm International Peace Research Institute, 1997

10 Post-Cold War defence procurement in Europe

Andrew D. James and Thomas Teichler

Introduction

European states, not least the United Kingdom (UK), France and Germany, spend more on defence procurement than any other countries in the world, except the USA, the People's Republic of China and Japan. In this chapter, we will discuss how defence procurement in Europe has changed since the end of the Cold War.

The concept of defence procurement is usually tied to the purchasing and investment activity of the Ministry of Defence (MoD) of a country. We are aware of the fact that a government acquires arms also for other forces like border control or the police. However, these are mostly financed from other budgets such as the Ministry of the Interior. For the sake of clarity and comparability we will stick to the more limited understanding outlined above. Also in this case, it has to be borne in mind that the procurement of the MoD comprises a variety of items such as arms and weapons systems, services to support these systems, but also dual-use products such as computers and communication devices and purely civil products and services like food or fuel. Indeed, as we shall go on to note, the definition of what constitutes defence procurement is more than an academic point but has been at the heart of the debate over the appropriate balance between national and European regulation of procurement by ministries of defence.

If we take 'European defence procurement' to mean the sum total of procurement budgets spent by European ministries of defence, this in turn raises the question of how we define 'Europe'. During the Cold War, 'Europe' was normally considered to be the European members of NATO. This NATO Europe definition included Norway and Turkey (who were not members of the European Union—EU), but excluded members of the EU, including Sweden (a neutral country with one of the largest defence procurement budgets in the EU).[1] Since the end of the Cold War, the membership of both NATO and the EU has changed with an eastward expansion to include countries such as Poland, the Czech Republic, Slovakia and so forth. The EU has also become an important security actor with a military dimension raising debates and tensions about the respective roles of NATO and the EU and the future of the transatlantic alliance. This changing notion of what constitutes 'Europe' is an important element of our story.

Within NATO, and increasingly within the framework of the EU, European governments have faced growing pressures to spend more on defence, spend more effectively and spend more collectively. This chapter makes three main points. Firstly, we chart changing spending patterns at the national level and note that, after its dramatic post-Cold War decline, procurement spending is rising again, but with significantly changed priorities for new capabilities. Secondly, we discuss how procurement practices have been altered to use private finance and expertise. Thirdly, we emphasize the significant changes that are occurring at the European level. We argue that, although European defence procurement remains diverse and fragmented, there is an increasing number of activities taking place at the European level that give influence over national procurement decisions. We conclude by pointing to potential future developments in European defence procurement.

The historical context

Western Europe and NATO

During the Cold War, Western Europe's demand for defence equipment was driven primarily by the perceived threat from the Soviet Union and Warsaw Pact and its alliance commitments to NATO. Western European defence procurement spending was considerable and represented a significant economic and technological burden for Europe.[2] NATO commitments influenced not only the level of defence procurement spending but also the type of equipment procured. Western European members of NATO were mainly focused on the territorial defence of the European mainland and the protection of the North Atlantic sea lanes. This had consequences for military doctrine, structure and equipment. Only the UK and France had significant requirements for expeditionary war fighting equipment as a consequence of their post-colonial legacy of overseas territories and commitments.

Western European defence spending, although high, was dwarfed by that of the Soviet Union and the USA. US spending was consistently two-to-three times higher than that of Western Europe combined. This transatlantic spending gap presented Western European countries with a profound dilemma, namely how to retain a degree of doctrinal and technological autonomy from the USA while working alongside it in NATO. In the immediate post-War period, European governments faced intense pressure from American policy-makers to adopt American ideas about military production, force structure and training, as well as to procure American weapons (Geiger and Sebasta 1998; Geiger 2008). Throughout the Cold War, there were repeated calls from the USA for the standardization of military equipment within NATO (implicitly or explicitly based on US armaments) and US calls for 'burden sharing' between Europe and the USA. At the same time, Europeans expressed anxieties about a growing US-European 'technology gap' and pressured for a more balanced 'two-way street' in the transatlantic arms trade in which the US purchased more European military equipment (Kirby 1979).

Within the NATO framework, there were some efforts to promote co-operation in European procurement. In 1968 the Eurogroup was formed with the objective of making a more effective European contribution to NATO. Eurogroup co-ordinated some European investment initiatives as well as European procurement of some US equipment (Sandler and Hartley 1999). In 1976 the defence ministers of the European NATO nations (except Iceland) established the Independent European Programme Group (IEPG) with the aims of improving Europe's ability to collectively produce high technology weapons systems and expanding arms sales to the USA. Such initiatives were characterized by tensions between national, European and Atlantic interests and had only a modest impact on the main procurement challenges (Kirby 1979).

The national character of the European defence market

Europe's bloody history meant that it was inevitable that defence played an important part in the beginning of the European integration process after the Second World War. In the early 1950s there were attempts to create a supranational European Defence Community (EDC) to integrate the defence activities of the six Member States of the European Coal and Steel Community (ECSC). The EDC envisaged the creation of a European army, a common defence budget and permanent military structures and centralized military procurement (Trybus 2006).

The failure of the EDC in 1954 led to two important developments for European defence procurement. The six members of the ECSC plus the UK established in 1954 the Western European Union (WEU). Three years later, the six Member States of the ECSC founded the supranational European Economic Community (EEC) as the focus for the less controversial issue of economic integration.

In recognition of the political sensitivity of defence, the 1957 Treaty of Rome founding the EEC provided, through Article 223, the possibility for a Member State to exclude certain activities from the provisions of the Treaty on the grounds of 'essential interests of its security'. Article 223 of the Treaty of Rome has been incorporated into subsequent European treaties as Article 296 and states:

1 The provisions of this Treaty shall not preclude the application of the following rules:
   (a) No Member State shall be obliged to supply information the disclosure of which it considers contrary to the essential interests of its security;
   (b) Any Member State may take such measures as it considers necessary for the protection of the essential interests of its security which are connected with the production of or trade in arms, munitions and war material; such measures shall not adversely affect the conditions of competition in the common market regarding products which are not intended for specifically military purposes.
2 The Council may, acting unanimously on a proposal from the Commission, make changes to the list, which it drew up on 15 April 1958, of the products to which the provisions of paragraph 1.(b) apply.[3]

Article 223/296 has had profound consequences for the character of the European defence market. As Martin Trybus notes: 'The result was that from the mid-1950s defence and security were clearly separated from the supranational mainstream of European integration' (Trybus 2006, 670). Article 223/296 was subsequently interpreted by Member States as representing an automatic or categorical exclusion of all armaments on the list from the provisions of the EC Treaty. As Trybus observes: 'For decades there was no unanimous understanding and no ruling of the European Court of Justice to clarify the interpretation of the exemption. This allowed the interpretation of the Member States to prevail, thereby leading to separate national markets for armaments in practice' (Trybus 2006, 673).

The consequence of the armaments market being *de facto* left out of the European economic integration project was that separate national armaments markets persisted in Europe. These armaments markets remained largely unaffected by the emergence of European legislation on competition, state aid, merger control and public procurement, which increasingly regulated private enterprises, services and the public sector. A Single European Market gradually emerged in civilian sectors, services and public procurement of non-defence goods. In contrast, national defence markets remained closed, lacked transparency and were often highly discriminatory towards national suppliers. Concerns about 'security of supply' also acted as a source of fragmentation and, in the case of imports, governments often sought off-set arrangements obliging arms sellers to reinvest ('off-set') arms sales proceeds in the purchasing country. The use of off-sets was, of course, in common with arms trade practice around the world, despite growing questions about their legality under international trade and European common market rules (Kuechle 2006; Heuninckx 2008).

The economic consequences of national fragmentation

The 1970s and 1980s saw the publication of a series of reports identifying the costs of these national defence markets and proposing common transatlantic or European defence procurement.[4] The 1975 Callaghan Report *US-European Economic Cooperation in Military and Civil Technology* argued that NATO was characterized by massive and wasteful duplication of R&D, short production runs failing to exploit economies of scale and duplication of logistics support. Callaghan proposed a North Atlantic common defence market and open government procurement of defence equipment. The 1978 European Parliament Klepsch Report on European Armaments Procurement Cooperation identified similar sources of waste through R&D

duplication, unco-ordinated purchasing leading to short, inefficient production runs and duplication of logistics associated with non-standardized equipment. The Report recommended the creation of a European Armaments Procurement Agency based on the IEPG with the aim of creating a single European Community market in defence equipment. The 1979 Greenwood Report submitted to the European Community on European Technological Cooperation and Defence Procurement considered the opportunities and obstacles for the rationalization of procurement and the structuring of the West European defence market. Again, a European Defence Procurement Agency was advocated whilst the practical political difficulties were acknowledged. A 1992 study for the European Commission, The Costs of Non-Europe in Defence Procurement, estimated cost savings of at least 10%–15% from a liberalized competitive market (Hartley and Cox 1992).

In summary, defence procurement in Western European countries during the Cold War, though substantial, was dwarfed by that of the USA and this presented European governments with a profound military and technological dilemma. The failure of the European Defence Community meant that defence remained apart from the process of growing European economic integration. Defence markets remained national and protected and this had important implications for the economics of European defence as well as interoperability within the NATO alliance.

Changing procurement patterns at the national level

European defence procurement relative to other countries

In comparison to the Cold War period, defence procurement in Western Europe has changed in some important respects since 1990: governments spend less, they spend more on new military capabilities and they increasingly employ new methods for their procurement activities. Two things, though, have remained unchanged, namely the high levels of absolute defence spending of some European governments compared to the rest of the world and the spending gap between Europe and the USA. Table 10.1 shows that, in absolute terms, four European countries are ranked among the 10 largest defence spenders in the world: the UK, France, Germany and Italy. The UK spends more than any other country in the world except the USA. The defence budgets of France and Germany are larger than that of Russia or India.[5] As a bloc, the EU Member States spend over US$300 billion on defence or about 20%

Table 10.1 The 10 countries with the highest military expenditure in 2007, in market exchange rates terms at constant 2005 prices

Rank	Country	Spending in US$ bn	% of GDP, 2006
1	USA	547	4.0
2	United Kingdom	59.7	2.6
3	China, People's Repub.	(58.3)	2.1
4	France	53.6	2.4
5	Japan	43.6	1.0
6	Germany	36.9	1.3
7	Russia	(35.4)	3.6
8	Saudi Arabia	33.8	8.5
9	Italy	33.1	1.8
10	India	24.2	2.7

Source: SIPRI 2008, p.178

Notes: Parentheses indicate an estimated figure

of the world total. Given that these are figures for overall defence budgets and that governments spend at least 15% of it on equipment, some European governments (and thereby the EU as a whole) are among the largest arms procurers in the world (SIPRI 2008).[6]

In global terms, European governments may spend a great deal on arms procurement, but it is almost exclusively the comparison to the USA that has been the focus of European attention. The USA spends three times as much on defence equipment as the whole of the EU combined (EDA 2008). Significantly, when their defence budgets are measured as a share of their gross domestic product (GDP), it should be noted that the Europeans spend less than those countries (with the exception of Japan). Indeed, we must emphasize that there has been little political appetite for a substantial increase in defence budgets in Europe. European citizens have shown that they are more inclined to favour 'security' over 'defence' spending and this has had a direct impact on the level of investment in defence procurement by European governments.

There have always been voices that have argued that Europe should spend more on its defence, but whilst these have found favour with the defence policy community they remain in stark contrast to the broader political context. Soon after the end of the Cold War, European governments were called to close the 'spending gap' if they indeed wanted to share in the leadership of the transatlantic Alliance (Cornish 1996; Lansford 2005). By the late 1990s, the relative performance of US and European forces in the first Gulf War and in the NATO air campaign in the Balkans prompted growing concerns about a transatlantic capability gap. At the same time, some Europeans expressed anxieties about the gap for European industrial and technological competitiveness (James 2006).

Equally, there was a growing awareness of the gap between Europe's growing political aspiration to become an independent defence and security actor and the limitations of its own military capabilities. Accordingly, it is argued, if the EU is indeed serious about becoming an independent actor on the world scene then European governments need to increase their spending on defence (Keohane 2001; Lindley-French and Algieri 2004). In this context, the EU High Representative for Foreign and Security Policy, who is also the Head of the European Defence Agency (EDA) concluded a decade and a half after the end of the Cold War that 'we should spend more, spend better and spend more together' (Solana 2006).

This points to the emergence of a European frame of reference for defence procurement, which we will argue is the most significant innovation since the end of the Cold War and which will be analysed in greater detail below. However, before this we will briefly assess how much European governments spend on defence procurement, on what they spend it, and the methods they employ for their procurement.

Changing levels of procurement spending

Almost all of the current research on Europe's defence spending provides macro-level data on Europe as a whole (Coonen 2006). We will equally start our analysis with a naïve notion of 'European procurement' as an aggregate of the procurement of all EU NATO members and only later turn to a disaggregate analysis.[7] It will reveal three things: European procurement spending declined until the mid-1990s and it rose again only after 2001; the pattern of change varies significantly from country to country and, finally, the bulk of defence procurement is concentrated in six countries.[8] Important for our argument is not so much the exact amount of money spent but rather the trends in that spending.

Alteration in spending levels

European spending on armaments had begun to fall in the late 1980s but, as Figure 10.1 shows, that fall accelerated with the end of the Cold War. The successful agreement on disarmament treaties and the retreat of Soviet forces from Central and Eastern Europe added to

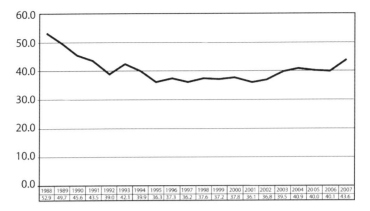

Figure 10.1 Equipment expenditure of Western EU NATO countries 1988–2007, in billion US$ in constant (2005) prices (excluding Norway and Turkey)
Source: SIPRI 2008, NATO 2008

the expectation that security in Europe could be provided at lower levels of armaments; calls for significant cuts in defence spending and for a fair distribution of the peace dividend were voiced (*The Economist* 1995).

By 1995 European defence procurement spending had fallen by almost one-third. For seven years thereafter it remained by and large constant and started rising again after 2001. Although the growth trend continued until 2007 (the latest year for which, at the time of writing, figures were available), European governments still spent as an aggregate one-quarter less on defence equipment than at the end of the Cold War.

National differences in spending

Figures 10.2 and 10.3 highlight that the pattern of change in equipment spending varied between different Western European countries and that spending patterns were not synchronized over time. On the one hand, not all countries reduced their expenditure right at the beginning of the 1990s, the exceptions being the UK, France, Greece and Denmark. On the other hand, in some countries, namely Germany, the UK, the Netherlands, Italy and Spain, reductions have been more dramatic than in other states.

Since 2001 European governments have increased their equipment expenditure again. The global 'war on terror' and the resulting commitments of many European countries in the operations in Iraq and Afghanistan, but also the naval missions in the Mediterranean and the Gulf, have led to an enlargement of most procurement budgets. There are some important exceptions to this upward trend in European defence procurement spending, not least in the case of Germany and Italy. In contrast to the UK and France, German defence procurement spending has remained more or less flat for the last decade and remains a small share of national GDP, even by European standards. Given the importance of German defence procurement within overall European spending, the political constraints on increased German spending have had consequences for European military capability as a whole.

Another issue of considerable importance to European military capability development is the share of the total defence budget available for defence procurement. There is significant variation across countries in the ratio of equipment expenditure to total defence spending: four countries spend more than 20% of their defence budget on equipment: the UK, France, Spain and Romania. While the majority of countries use between 10% and 20% for procuring armaments, Belgium, Portugal and Luxemburg shares account for less than 10% (NATO 2008).

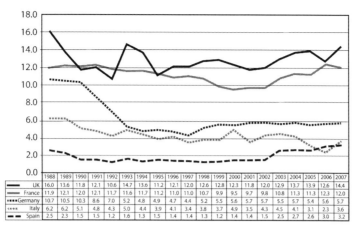

Figure 10.2 Equipment expenditure of selected EU NATO countries 1988–2007, in billion US$ in constant (2005) prices
Source: SIPRI 2008, NATO 2008

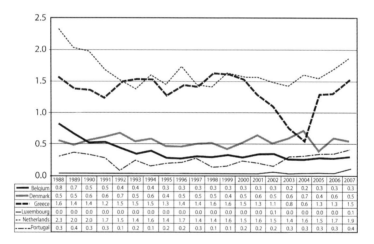

Figure 10.3 Equipment expenditure of selected EU NATO countries 1988–2007, in billion US$ in constant (2005) prices
Source: SIPRI 2008, NATO 2008

Concentration of procurement spending

One of the reasons why German procurement spending is so important to Europe as a whole is because of the highly concentrated character of European defence procurement. Thus, six countries account for the overwhelming share of European defence procurement spending. The UK, France, Germany, Italy, Sweden and Spain[9] accounted in 2007 for 86% of the aggregated procurement budget and 97% of R&T budget of EU Member States.[10] The UK and France are by far the biggest spenders with equipment expenditure of more than $12 billion a year, much greater than Germany, which spends half that figure, and Italy and Spain which spend about one-quarter of this amount. The Netherlands, Poland and Greece form a third group of countries, as they use with more then $1.5 billion per year more resources than the remaining countries, which all spend $1 billion or less on defence equipment.

Thus, the UK and France together account for about two-thirds of the procurement and three-quarters of the R&T expenditure of all EU governments. The leading role of both countries will become even more prevalent when the issue of military modernization or transformation is taken into account.

Procurement for military modernization

The demands on European defence budgets stem firstly from the continuing need of most European countries to pursue transformation of their militaries from a Cold War posture focused on territorial defence, to one that provides a substantial ability to conduct force projection operations. National defence reviews, NATO efforts to enhance European capabilities and the European Capability Action Plan (ECAP) process have placed an emphasis on investments in mobility and network-centric capabilities. The USA (under the George W. Bush Administration at least) pursued a vision of wholesale transformation of its forces and pushed the rest of NATO to do likewise. Instead, European governments have pursued a more incremental and selective development of new capabilities such as strategic airlift, C4ISR (command, control, communications, computers, intelligence, surveillance and reconnaissance), precision weapons and more mobile armoured vehicles, where they believe they are most likely to improve the effectiveness of their armed forces. The new security environment has placed an emphasis on acquiring the capabilities of command and control, mobility, reconnaissance and surveillance, strike, and aiming at a better co-operation between different services ('jointness') and together with services from other countries ('combinedness') (Bundesministerium der Verteidigung 2006).

Modernization as a priority

European governments have since the end of the Cold War only slowly embraced the need for a modernization of their armed forces. Though the need to adapt doctrine and mission was recognized immediately, the drive for military reform was slow throughout the 1990s. 'Downsizing'

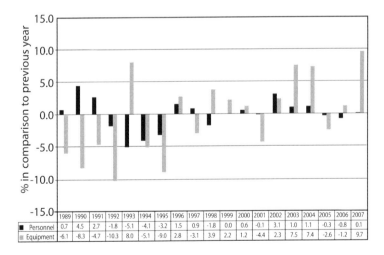

	1989	1990	1991	1992	1993	1994	1995	1996	1997	1998	1999	2000	2001	2002	2003	2004	2005	2006	2007
Personnel	0.7	4.5	2.7	-1.8	-5.1	-4.1	-3.2	1.5	0.9	-1.8	0.0	0.6	-0.1	3.1	1.0	1.1	-0.3	-0.8	0.1
Equipment	-6.1	-8.3	-4.7	-10.3	8.0	-5.1	-9.0	2.8	-3.1	3.9	2.2	1.2	-4.4	2.3	7.5	7.4	-2.6	-1.2	9.7

Figure 10.4 Changes in expenditure on equipment and personnel in comparison with previous year of EU NATO countries 1989–2007, in billion US$ in constant (2005) prices
Source: SIPRI 2008, NATO 2008

was top on the agenda, which mainly meant coping with reduced budgets rather than overhauling concepts, organization and equipment in general. Thus, as Figure 10.4 illustrates, funding for equipment was reduced at a much more dramatic pace than budgets for personnel, as this was politically less controversial and administratively easier to implement.

It was not until the beginning of the new millennium that European governments embarked on the modernization of their militaries. Figure 10.4 indicates significant increases in aggregate European equipment spending after 2001, which in part reflects, in our view, a move towards modernization of the armed forces. The drive for modernization originated from a comparison of the EU with the USA. The stark reality of the wars in the Balkans demonstrated the limited ability of European countries to ensure stability and peace even in their most immediate neighbourhood. These wars deepened an impression already gained during the first Gulf War that the US military had embraced new concepts and technologies that made it far more effective than any European force and made it increasingly difficult for allies to operate together (Spillmann and Krause 2000; Ribnikar 2002; Nickening and Petrovic 2008). The experience is seen as the origin for the European Security and Defence Policy (ESDP), which has from its outset emphasized the need for military capability improvement (Howorth 2000). European participation in military operations in Iraq and Afghanistan gave an added urgency to the need for modernization of military equipment and – through Urgent Operational Requirements – it short-circuited the traditionally long and drawn out defence procurement process.

The role of NATO and the EU

Both NATO and the EU have been instrumental in driving the agenda of military modernization of European countries. NATO's New Strategic Concept of 1991 spoke of a new security environment characterized by multidirectional risks rather than a global threat and requiring an adaptation of military doctrine (NATO 1991). The development of a European Security and Defence Identity was envisioned to allow for greater European participation in the leadership of the Alliance in exchange for increased contributions to the joint defence effort, but it failed (Cogan 2001). The USA agreed to European defence policy outside NATO, but kept pressing European countries 'to project power ... rapidly deploy forces over long distances, sustain operations for extended periods of time, and operate jointly with the United States in high intensity conflict' (United States Congress 1998). The 'Prague Capabilities Commitment', the NATO Response Force and Allied Command Transformation, all agreed upon in 2002, are but some expressions of this policy, albeit with limited success (NATO 2005; Archick and Gallis 2008).

In the EU, governments had agreed already in 1992 on the so-called Petersberg Tasks, but it was only from 1999 onwards that the EU became involved in the issue of military modernization. In that year the governments set the Helsinki Headline Goal 2003: to 'be able to deploy ... and then sustain forces capable of the full range of Petersberg tasks ... in operations up to ... 50,000–60,000 persons' (Rutten 2001). While the Military Capabilities Commitment and Improvement Conferences, held in November 2000 and 2001, respectively, identified gaps between available and required forces and formulated a European Capabilities Action Plan (ECAP) to make good on the recognized shortfalls, they did not link these results in any way to armaments procurement, something that was to be done only after the creation of the EDA in 2004 (Schmitt 2003).

The role of the UK has been pivotal for the focus of co-operative efforts in both organizations on the improvement of military capabilities (UK Ministry of Defence 2003). The hope that the EU would be more successful than NATO in forging a European contribution to the Transatlantic Alliance and to lead in Europe was at the root the UK's reversal of its long-held opposition to a more independent European defence effort in 1998. While the UK and France put the emphasis of ESDP from the beginning on the improvement or creation of capabilities for expeditionary warfare, other countries, like Germany, Sweden and Finland, stressed the more civil aspects of the new policy (Howorth 2000). These more general differences point to the large diverse patterns in which European countries go about the modernization of their armed forces.

This evidence for increased spending on new military capabilities should not hide the fact that actually only a small amount of money is indeed free for new projects catering to the modernization of the military. A few large programmes take the lion's share of existing equipment spending. Thus, the Eurofighter programme is expected to consume over half the modernization budgets of Germany, Italy and Spain in coming years. In addition, equipment budgets are squeezed by the cost of operations in Afghanistan, Iraq and elsewhere.

Trying to spend better: new models and practices in European defence procurement

The political constraints on increased defence spending faced by European governments have caused them to seek new ways to spend what money they have more effectively. We have already noted that European governments have been exhorted to 'spend more, spend better and spend more together' and one way to 'spend better' has consisted in the application of new procurement concepts and models. Procurement policies, practices and cultures differ considerably between the ministries of defence in Europe (Mawdsley 2000). These have influenced the rate and character of adoption of new procurement practices.

Outsourcing

There has been a significant trend for European defence procurement spending to shift from equipment to services, and services now represent a growing share of defence procurement budgets. In the UK, which has moved furthest along the road of outsourcing and privatization, support contracts with industry covering logistics, maintenance, repair and upgrade, IT and facilities management account for £9 billion of its £16 billion procurement budget (UK Ministry of Defence 2005).

This has grown as European ministries of defence place an increasing emphasis on through-life management of equipment and increasingly seek to outsource non-operational activities that have previously been undertaken by the military, such as training, repair and maintenance, and logistics. This growth in outsourcing and services is being driven by military over-stretch and efforts to reduce personnel costs. Continuing pressures on defence budgets have increased ministry of defence requirements for solutions that reduce directly employed manpower numbers and costs whilst providing for 'boots on the ground'.

Outsourcing of maintenance and logistics has been explored by many European governments. In 2006–07 the Swedish government engaged in intensive efforts to outsource engineering and maintenance services for its armoured vehicle fleet, with emphasis on through-life support. In 2008 Finland's Ministry of Defence announced that it would outsource the Army's Equipment Maintenance Unit (EMU) in a bid to reduce military spending and operating costs (O'Dwyer 2008).

Public-private partnerships

In some instances, outsourcing has been linked to new service-oriented models of provision, including forms of public-private partnership. In these procurement models, governments pay private companies for equipment and services on the basis of availability and usage and the through-life risks of ownership lie with industry. The trend towards through-life management of defence equipment has encouraged such developments. At the same time, pressures on defence budgets have increased government efforts to use government finance more efficiently. This has included the use of private finance instruments especially to enhance the affordability of projects involving significant capital expenditure (RUSI 2004).

In the UK, public-private partnerships have been used as part of broader efforts by the Labour Party governments since 1997 to introduce more private finance and management into the financing and operation of public infrastructure. The 1998 Strategic Defence Review emphasized the importance of public-private partnerships as a means of generating the efficiency savings necessary to fund the MoD's defence equipment programme. Parker and Hartley (2003) note how public-private partnerships comprise partial asset sales, concessions, joint ventures and partnerships that seek to integrate the private and public sector. The MoD has explained its use of public-private partnerships and private finance initiatives (PFI) in terms of value for money, improved efficiency and the potential to transfer risk to the private sector (UK Ministry of Defence 2001). Public-private partnerships have been applied to the provision of training, equipment, property and accommodation, support services, utilities and information technology, and by 2004 the MoD had signed 52 PFI contracts with a capital value of £4.3 billion, which is more by far than any other European country (RUSI 2004).

Although Germany and France have been more cautious with the use of this procurement method, they have equally shifted risks to private companies. In Germany only three major projects within the MoD and a number of smaller programmes with the services, especially the air force, had been in place by 2004 (Bundesverband Public Private Partnership – Arbeitskreis Verteidigung und Sicherheit 2005). More recently, the German Government has placed flagship projects like the supply, operation and maintenance of the Bundeswehr's IT and communication system Herkules and the through-life maintenance of the A400M with private investors (Defense Industry Daily 2008). HIL GmbH (Heeresinstandsetzungslogistik GmbH) is responsible for planning, direction and execution of maintenance and logistics support for all land systems of the German Armed Forces.

The French procurement agency DGA launched its first public-private partnership only in January 2008. The contract did not only include the replacement of 54 Gazelle helicopters with 36 rotorcrafts EC 120 but also their operation, service and repair (Sotty 2008). Spain has involved the private sector in its satellite communication system, which is operated by Hispasat to the Xtar-Eur and Spainsat satellites providing bandwidth for the Spanish and Danish armed forces. Hispasat is possessed by private and government-owned companies (Mulholland 2007).

Shifting risks to private actors clearly has its limits, as the current financial crisis has aptly demonstrated. The advantages of private finance are challenged, at least in the UK. While the MoD points to cost savings of 5%–40% through the use of private finance, scholars doubt these figures (Parker and Hartley 2003). In the case of defence procurement, it remains to be seen for what kind of activity private management models are appropriate. Given that the current credit crisis is regarded to be at least in part caused by loose regulation and oversight of private (financial) institutions, it can be assumed that the public climate for new procurement solutions will not remain as favourable as it has been in the past. Instead of trying to 'spend better' through new modes of procurement, European governments might, then, try to 'spend more together' and engage in higher levels of co-operation.

Pooling of assets

There have long been calls for the pooling of military assets between European governments and the development of jointly-owned capabilities. Within NATO, the NATO airborne warning and control (AWAC) is a long-standing example, but efforts to promote pooling at the European level through the EDA have made very little progress. Maulny and Liberti (2008) identify three factors that they believe may work in favour of pooling in the future: budgetary pressures that can compel governments to seek procurement savings; the fact that the cost of maintaining pooling capabilities would be much lower than when acting independently; and the prospect that a pooling of resources would offer the benefits of interoperability on the battlefield, and thereby help foster harmonization.

They note that there are four types of pooling: (i) sharing of capabilities, whereby member states create common capabilities through the provision of national capabilities, and there is no structure to organize their use; (ii) pooling of capabilities, which involves an integrated structure to organize the use of national capabilities: the most concrete example being the European Airlift Centre (EAC); (iii) pooling through acquisition, where national capabilities do not exist and are substituted by multilateral capabilities, and the multilateral organization owns the assets (as is the case with NATO AWAC); and (iv) role sharing, whereby certain capabilities are relinquished on the assumption that another country will make it available when necessary.

The emergence of a European dimension

Institutional initiatives during the 1990s

One notable development since the end of the Cold War has been the emergence of an institutional and regulatory framework for defence procurement within the EU. The 1990s saw a number of institutional initiatives aimed at enhancing European armaments co-operation, making more efficient use of European resources through requirements harmonization and opening up national defence markets to cross-border co-operation. Accompanying the 1991 Maastricht Treaty, was a declaration from the WEU ministers calling for further examination of the possibilities for enhanced co-operation in the field of armaments, with the aim of creating a European Armaments Agency. In 1992 the functions of the IEPG were transferred to the WEU and the Western European Armaments Group (WEAG) was formed. In 1996 the WEAG countries agreed to establish the Western European Armaments Organization (WEAO). Originally only tasked to tender research and development contracts, governments reserved the possibility to develop the WEAO into a fully-fledged (Western) European Armaments Agency, although political differences between European governments meant that this did not make progress. In the same year, France, Germany, Italy and the UK established the Organisation Conjointe de Coopération en Matière d'Armement (OCCAR). Though focused on the management of collaborative projects, the founding countries explicitly mentioned the option for OCCAR to administer further tasks and also to evolve into a European Armaments Agency. In 1998 these governments, together with Spain and Sweden, signed a Letter of Intent, leading to a Framework Agreement two years later. It was aimed at facilitating the restructuring of their defence industries at a European level.

However, progress on developing an institutional and regulatory framework that would open up the European market to cross-border trade was slow. In 1988 the IEPG approved an action plan for the creation of an open European defence equipment market and in its Coherent Policy Document (CPD), the WEAG laid down a set of general aims and principles for a European defence equipment market. The CPD was first drafted in 1990 and revised in 1999, and foresaw cross-border competition and non-discrimination of suppliers on the grounds of nationality as basic principles of defence procurement. It also included a number of specific measures to enhance transparency and competition, such as the publication of contract bulletins and monitoring of intra-WEAG trade. The CPD constituted a commitment by member states to change their procurement practices, but it was not legally binding and failed to lead to harmonization of rules. Writing in 2005, Schmitt noted: 'Overall, its record is rather poor, its principles have hardly been implemented, and its impact on cross-border competition has been – at best – limited' (Schmitt 2005, 13).

The 1990s also saw an effort by the European Commission to enter the debate about the creation of a European defence equipment market. The Commission published two

Communications in 1996 and 1997. In its 1997 Communication, the Commission outlined measures in 14 areas of strategic importance including public procurement. The Commission suggested that a regime based on a distinction between three different types of defence goods be drawn up. It thereby anticipated the complex solution that was established in the 2000s by the Commission and the EDA (European Commission 1997). The proposals were rejected by the Member States, which saw them as an undesirable extension of Commission competence and a threat to national sovereignty.

European Defence Agency

We have already noted how the idea of a European defence procurement agency can be traced back to the 1950s and the EDC, and it came back onto the European political agenda during the debates over the draft European Constitution. In 2004 the EU Member States established an agency in the field of defence capabilities development, research, acquisition and armaments within the scope of the Common Foreign and Security Policy (CFSP) of the EU Treaty (European Council 2004). There are 26 participating Member States in the EDA.[11] The EDA is supposed to complement rather than replace the defence procurement agencies of the Member States. The EDA approach towards defence procurement matters has been to develop a voluntary intergovernmental regime based on monitoring and peer pressure.

In the field of defence procurement, the participating Member States have adopted a voluntary and non-binding intergovernmental regime that aims at enhancing transparency for defence procurement contracts which are exempted from Community rules on the basis of Article 296. This regime includes a Code of Conduct on Defence Procurement agreed in 2005. The Code of Conduct establishes a set of principles that may be applied to all defence procurement opportunities of over €1m. All relevant new defence procurement opportunities in Europe will be published on a single online portal operated by the EDA, the Electronic Bulletin Board on Government Contract Opportunities. Fair and equal treatment of all companies will be assured through evaluation of the offers on the basis of transparent and objective standards. The fundamental criterion for the selection of the contractor will be the most economically advantageous solution for a particular requirement, taking into account, among other things, considerations such as costs (both acquisition and life cycle), compliance, quality and security of supply and offsets. The EDA monitors the implementation of the Code and also manages the Electronic Bulletin Board.

The Code of Conduct relates to government contracts, and to ensure open market access for small and medium-sized enterprises and also for suppliers from the newer Member States the EDA was also tasked by the participating Member States to develop a Code of Best Practices in the Supply Chain. This aims to promote openness, transparency and fair competition at the contract and sub-contract level and includes, for the selection of suppliers and sub-contractors, principles similar to those of the Code of Conduct. This is complemented by the EDA's Electronic Bulletin Board on Defence Contract Opportunities, which provides details of industry-to-industry contracting opportunities.

The participating Member States have also addressed other impediments to an open European defence equipment market. A Framework Agreement for Security of Supply was agreed in 2006 under which subscribing Member States agreed to assist and expedite others' defence requirements, especially in situations of urgent operational requirements. Security of Information regulations have been agreed for the protection of classified and commercially sensitive information released during the procurement process. A Code of Conduct on Offsets was agreed in 2008 which sets out guidelines for progress towards closer convergence of offset policies and practices and to gradually reduce the use of offsets, and under which Member States committed themselves to increase transparency by reporting on their offset rules and practices on a consistent basis.

Heuninckx (2008) observes that the EDA's Code of Conduct is very similar to the WEAG Coherent Policy Document. The non-binding nature of the CPD and the Code of Conduct is seen as a major weakness by some (Schmitt 2005; Kuechle 2006). However, Heuninckx (2008) argues that the Code of Conduct probably has a better chance of succeeding because of its institutional context, timing and the use of peer pressure and reciprocity.

The European Commission

We noted how Article 223 of the Treaty of Rome (Article 296 of the Treaty of Amsterdam) has been used by Member States to exempt almost all defence procurement from European Internal Market rules. However, beginning in the late 1990s, the European Court of Justice ruled in a series of cases that the use of these exemptions must be limited to clearly defined and exceptional cases and does not create a general or automatic exemption (Trybus 2006; Heuninckx 2008).

In September 2004 the European Commission issued a Green Paper on Defence Procurement, proposing various options to improve transparency and openness of defence markets between EU Member States (Commission of the European Communities 2004). The Green Paper was followed by an Interpretative Communication on the application of Article 296 of the Treaty, which was adopted in December 2006 (Commission of the European Communities 2006). This Communication clarified the conditions for the use of Article 296 and gave guidance to awarding authorities for their assessment of whether defence contracts can be exempted from Community rules or not.

However, the Commission went further when, in December 1997, it published its draft Directive on Defence Procurement (Commission of the European Communities 2007). The Commission's proposal was largely based on the design and rationale of the existing 2004 Public Procurement Directive, but the Commission argued that as the rules of that Directive had been developed for non-military and non-sensitive procurement, they did not sufficiently take into account the particular needs of such procurements. The draft Directive, the Commission argued, had specific features tailored to the characteristics of sensitive public defence and security contracts. In particular, the draft Directive provided for more flexibility in the procedures of defence procurement authorities in the awarding of contracts and for the safeguards required to guarantee the security of information and supply. Member States will still be able to use Article 296 to exempt defence and security procurement contracts which are so sensitive that even the new rules do not satisfy their security needs. In most cases, though, the Commission argued that Member States should be able to use the new Directive without any risk to their security.

The new procurement rules were adopted by the European Parliament in January 2009 and mark a potentially important development for the European defence market. The Commission argues that the new rules will mean that the use of Article 296 will be limited to truly exceptional cases, in line with the intention of Article 296 and European Court of Justice rulings; national procurement rules will follow common standards; and the principles of the Treaty, in particular transparency, non-discrimination and openness will be implemented in defence and security markets.

The procurement directive was part of the Commission's 'defence package', which also contained a proposal for a Directive on intra-community defence transfers. In all Member States, the export of defence-related products (including comprehensive military equipment as well as sub-systems, components, spare parts and technologies) is subject to national licensing schemes. The Commission argued that this national system of licensing schemes not only imposes a significant administrative burden on companies, but also induces significant lead times – up to several months. Furthermore, defence industries and EU governments cannot fully rely on their supply chains because of the legal uncertainty resulting from the need for individual authorization of transfers. These divergences constitute a major impediment to industrial competitiveness and a considerable obstacle to the emergence of a European Defence Equipment Market (EDEM), as well as the functioning of the Internal Market. The Commission argued that this system is out of proportion with actual control needs, noting that licence applications for intra-community transfers are indeed hardly ever rejected.

The Commission's intra-community transfer directive proposed to simplify and harmonize licensing conditions and procedures by replacing national licences with a streamlined system of general or global licences. This built on the work of the Letter of Intent Framework Agreement, which included efforts to simplify export and transfer procedures. Equally, the EDA Code of Conduct encourages subscribing Member States to simplify intra-community transfers and transits of defence goods and technologies.

Conclusion

In summary, following the end of the Cold War arms procurement of European governments was significantly reduced, but has recently regained in terms of volume, without reaching the high levels of spending of the mid-1980s; especially since the beginning of the new millennium it has focused on the development of new military capabilities. Procurement is characterized by an increasing involvement of private enterprise regarding financial contribution, risk sharing and management. Finally, European governments have extended their co-operation on arms procurement and embedded it into a much wider joint effort of security and military collaboration. These are quite remarkable developments for the short time span of 15 years.

These developments can be explained in light of the interaction of three factors. First, the changed security environment after the end of the Cold War required European militaries to prepare for new types of missions that ultimately also called for different kinds of equipment. The advance of technology facilitated not only their development, but also inspired an entirely new way of thinking about arms and military operations in terms of effects and capabilities. It also required the consideration of industries formerly not part of the military industrial complex (MIC) and opened up new possibilities for co-operation with private actors as well as other European governments. Both factors were framed by the decision of European governments to develop the EU as an international actor, as formulated and institutionalized in the European Security and Defence Policy.

For the future Europe faces considerable challenges in the area of defence procurement. The USA continues to be the most important reference point for European governments and is by far the largest procurement spender and leads in many ways the conceptual development regarding modernization, weapons systems and procurement practices. American strategic influence is buttressed by US leadership in NATO and by the fact that the country remains the most significant source of military equipment for most European states. European governments have raised their profile vis-à-vis the USA through the EU, by developing an independent notion of security and of security policy. The ongoing search to be 'a different kind of security actor' is also reflected in the continued turf battles between the EU and NATO, which need to be resolved.

The second challenge concerns the role of EU institutions for defence procurement. On the one hand, the EDA is still carving out a role for itself in relation to the Commission, which has, due to its supranational character, much greater room for initiating new activities or legislation than the EDA. On the other hand, both organizations will need to find ways to shape a policy area, which will largely remain under national responsibility. In this context the treatment of the Defence Procurement Directive will be indicative. It could open up those markets in Europe that remain protected, but its impact will depend on its proper and fair implementation by all Member States.

Thirdly, it remains to be seen to what extent EU Member States will indeed procure more together than previously, and on what conditions. The exchange of information and the development of common concepts in the EDA and by the Commission still need to lead to major new collaboration projects. The fact remains that six countries are spending significantly more than the remaining countries, raising the issue of burden sharing for the purposes of EU security and defence policy. These countries have a specific interest in maintaining a defence industrial base, with others demanding offsets for their participation in joint programmes, which in turn collides with the rules emerging from the directive of the Commission.

This leads us to a final challenge: the issue of increasing interdependence but lacking mutual defence commitments in the EU. For the time being, mutual defence is not part of the EU Treaty and most countries are content with it being catered for by NATO. However, increased procurement (and defence industrial) co-operation will, over time, lead to a situation in which an EU without a mutual defence clause will be regarded as an oddity. As we can see, defence procurement has not only found a place in the European integration project but significant implications for its success. It is this fact that has, in our view, been the most significant change in European defence procurement after the end of the Cold War.

Notes

1 There are now 24 European members of NATO, 21 of which are also Member States of the EU. There are six countries that are members of the EU, but are not part of NATO (NATO 2008).
2 The defence burden of European NATO members, measured as the share of military expenditure of the GDP in percent, was as high as 3.9% for the period from 1970 to 1974. It fell to an average of 3.3% for the last five years before the end of the Cold War. The share of equipment expenditure rose in the same period from an average of 13% of the total defence budget to more than 15% (NATO 1995).
3 The list to which Article 296 refers covers 15 categories of arms, munitions and war materials and had never been officially published until 2001.
4 Sandler and Hartley (1995) provide a useful summary of the key reports and the following passages utilize that summary.
5 The order changes if expenditure is measured in terms of purchasing power parity (PPP). In this case the estimated budgets of China and Russia and India's expenditure are higher than those of the UK, France and Germany. Still, there are four European countries among the 10 largest military spenders. On the problems involved in comparing military expenditure see SIPRI 2008.
6 This estimate seems justified in light of the fact that NATO countries spend an average of 16% of their defence budgets on defence equipment, with most of the larger spenders paying clearly more than that, in some cases up to 25% (NATO 2008).
7 We base our examination on combined data provided by SIPRI and NATO. Only SIPRI provides defence expenditure data in constant prices and only NATO reports the share of equipment expenditure as part of the overall defence expenditure of its members. We exclude Norway and Turkey from the aggregate numbers and focus on EU NATO countries.
8 'Defence procurement' is equalled with NATO's 'equipment expenditure', including all money spent during the fiscal year on the procurement of new equipment for the armed forces, as well as research and development. It differs from national and EU definitions and, then, figures quoted here may vary from those provided by national and European authorities. While most countries report according to this standard, France, Italy and Luxembourg do not (NATO 2008).
9 Sweden has not been considered so far, as there is no consistent data over time and in line with the NATO definitions used here.
10 Strictly speaking, only of the 26 participating Member States, i.e. all EU members except Denmark. All calculations are based on EDA 2007.
11 All the Member States of the EU except Denmark participate in the Agency (under Article 6 of the Protocol on the position of Denmark annexed to the Treaty on European Union and to the Treaty establishing the European Community, Denmark does not participate in the formulation and implementation of EU decisions and actions which have defence implications).

Bibliography

Aben, J., *Économie politique de la défense*, Paris, Éditions Cujas, 1992
Anthony, Ian, 'Review Article: Arms Procurement after the Cold War: How Much is Enough to do What (and How Will We Know?)', *International Affairs*, Vol. 74, 1998
Archick, Kristin and Paul Gallis, *NATO and the European Union*, CRS (Congressional Research Service) Report, US Library of Congress, RS32342, January 2008
Boyer, Y., 'Technologies, défense et relations transatlantiques', *Politique Etrangère*, Vol. 4, 1994

Bundesministerium der Verteidigung, White Paper 2006 on German Security Policy and the Future of the Bundeswehr, 2006, www.bmvg.de/portal/PA_1_0_LT/PortalFiles/C1256EF40036B05B/W26UWAMT995INFODE/W+2006 +eng+DS.pdf?yw_repository=youatweb

Bundesverband Public Private Partnership – Arbeitskreis Verteidigung Und Sicherheit, Positionspapier des Arbeitskreises 'Verteidigung und Sicherheit', August 2005, www.bppp.de/media/file/71.Positionspapier_AK_Vtdg-Sicherheit_2005.pdf

Cogan, Charles G., *The Third Option: The Emancipation of European Defence 1989–2000*, Westport, CT and London, Praeger, 2001

Commission of the European Communities, Commission Green Paper of 23 September 2004 on defence procurement, 2004

——— Interpretative Communication from the Commission of 7 December 2006 on the application of Article 296 of the Treaty in the field of defence procurement, 2006

——— Proposal for a Directive of the European Parliament and of the Council on simplifying terms and conditions of transfers of defence-related products within the Community, COM(2007) 765 final, Brussels, 2007

Coonen, Stephen J., 'The Widening Military Capabilities Gap Between the United States and Europe: Does it Matter?', *Parameters*, Autumn 2006

Cornish, Paul, 'European Security: The End of the Architecture and New NATO', *International Affairs*, Vol. 72, 1996

Council of the European Union, 'Council Joint Action 2004/551/CFSP of 12 July 2004 on the establishment of the European Defence Agency', 2004, eur-lex.europa.eu/LexUriServ/site/en/oj/2004/l_245/l_24520040717en001700 28.pdf

De Vestel, P., *L'industrie européenne de l'armement*, Brussels, GRIP, 1993

Defense Industry Daily, 'IBM and Siemens in Germany Take Up the Labours of HERKULES', *Defense Industry Daily*, 7 April 2008, www.defenseindustrydaily.com/ibm-siemens-in-germany-take-up-the-labours-of-herkules-02925

EDA, 'Defence Facts', European Defence Agency, various years, www.eda.europa.eu/facts.aspx

——— 'European–United States Defence Expenditure in 2006', European Defence Agency, 2006, www.eda.europa.eu/facts.aspx

European Commission, *Implementing European Union Strategy on Defence-Related Industries*, European Commission Com(97) 583 of 04/12/1997, Annex II), Brussels, 1997

European Council, 'Council Joint Action 2004/551/CFSP of 12 July 2004 on the establishment of the European Defence Agency', 2004

Geiger, Till, 'The British Warfare State and the Challenge of Americanisation of Western Defence', *European Review of History*, 15 (4) August 2008

Geiger, Till and Lorenza Sebesta, 'A Self-Defeating Policy: American Offshore Procurement and Integration of Western European Defence Production, 1952–56', *Journal of European Integration History*, Vol. 4, No. 1, 1998

Geopowers, METEOR: Sprengversuch, www.geopowers.com/Machte/Deutschland/Rustung/Rustung_2005/rustung_ 2005.html, 2005

Grant, Robert P., 'The RMA – Europe Can Keep in Step', Occasional Papers 15, June 2000, Western European Union Institute for Security Studies, Paris, 2000

Guay, Terrence, *At Arm's Length*, London, Macmillan, 1998

Hamel, A., *L'européanisation de la politique aeronautique française de defense: entre civilianisation de l'industrie et recomposition de l'etat (1944–2004)*, Paris, L'Institut d'Etudes Politique de Paris, mention science politique, 2004

Hamilton, Daniel S., ed., *Transatlantic Transformations: Equipping NATO for the 21st Century*, Washington, John Hopkins University, 2004

Harrison, Michael, 'City Backs BAE in Stand-off with Hoon Over Arms Contracts', *The Independent*, 24 April 2004

Hartley, Keith and Andrew Cox, *The Cost of Non-Europe in Defence Procurement*, study carried out for the Commission of the European Communities, DG III. Brussels, European Commission, 1992

Heuninckx, Baudouin, 'Towards a Coherent European Defence Procurement Regime? European Defence Agency and European Commission Initiatives', *Public Procurement Law Review*, 17 (1) 2008

Howorth, J., 'Britain, France and the European Defence Initiative', *Survival*, Vol. 42, 2000

James, Andrew D., 'The Transatlantic Defence R&D Gap: Causes, Consequences and Controversies', *Defence and Peace Economics*, Vol. 17, No. 3, June 2006

Keohane, Daniel, 'More Bang for Our Bucks', *New Statesman*, Vol. 30, November 2001

Kirby, Stephen, 'The Independent European Programme Group: The Failure of Low-Profile High-Politics', *Journal of Common Market Studies*, 18 (2), 1979

Kosovo: Lessons from the Crisis, report presented to Parliament by the Secretary of State for Defence, June 2000 (CM 4724), www.mod.uk/NR/rdonlyres/31AA374E-C3CB-40CC-BFC6-C8D6A73330F5/0/kosovo_lessons.pdf

Kuechle, Hartmut, *The Costs of Non-Europe in Defence*, study requested by the European Parliament Subcommittee on Security and Defence, Brussels, European Parliament, 2006

Lansford, Tom, 'Introduction: US Security Policy and the New Europe', in Tom Lansford and Blagovest Tashev, eds, *Old Europe, New Europe and the US: Renegotiating Transatlantic Security in the Post 9/11 Era*, Hampshire, Ashgate, 2005

Lindley-French, J. and F. Algieri, *A European Defence Strategy*, Gütersloh, Bertelsmann Foundation, 2004

Maulny, Jean Pierre and Fabio Liberti, *Pooling of EU Member States Assets in the Implementation of ESDP*, study requested by the European Parliament Subcommittee on Security and Defence, Brussels, European Parliament, 2008

Mawdsley, Jocelyn, *The Changing Face of European Armaments Co-operation: Continuity and Change in British, French and German Armament Policy 1990–2000*, unpublished PhD thesis, Department of Politics, University of Newcastle upon Tyne, 2000

Ministry of Defence, 'Defence Acquisition', Ministry of Defence Policy Papers, No. 4, Ministry of Defence, UK, December 2001, www.mod.uk/NR/rdonlyres/1B07C74B-F841 4E78 9A13-F4A0E0796061/0/polpaper4_def_acquisition.pdf

———'Delivering Security in a Changing World', Defence White Paper, Ministry of Defence, UK, December 2003, merln.ndu.edu/whitepapers/UnitedKingdom-2003.pdf

———'Defence Industrial Strategy', Ministry of Defence, UK, 2005, www.mod.uk/NR/rdonlyres/F530ED6C-F80C-4F24-8438-0B587CC4BF4D/0/def_industrial_strategy_wp_cm6697.pdf

Mulholland, David, 'The European Dilemma', *MilsatMagazine*, October 2007 Edition, www.milsatmagazine.com/cgi-bin/display_article.cgi?number=1755629244&method=print

NATO, The Alliance's New Strategic Concept, NATO, 1991, www.nato.int/docu/comm/49 95/c911107a.htm

———*NATO Handbook 2001*, 2001, www.nato.int/docu/handbook/2001/index.htm

———'NATO Prague Capabilities Commitment: What Does This Mean in Practice?', www.nato.int/issues/prague_capabilities_commitment/in_practice.htm, 2005

———'NATO Defence Expenditure', various years, www.nato.int/issues/defence_expenditures/index.html

Nickening, P. and D. Petrovic, 'Das neue Auftragsbuch des Heeres — Interview mit dem Befehlshaber des Heeresführungskommando, Generalleutnant Otto', *Internationales Magazin fuer Sicherheit*, Vol. 05, 2008

O'Dwyer, Gerard, 'Finnish Firm Seeks Work From Nordic Neighbors', *Defense News*, 17 August 2008, www.defensenews.com

Ortiz-Dominguez, Carlos, 'The New Public Management of Security: The Contracting and Managerial State and the Private Military Industry', *Public Money and Management*, forthcoming, 2009

Parker, David and Keith Hartley, 'Transaction Costs, Relational Contracting and Public-Private Partnerships: A Case Study of UK Defence', *Journal of Purchasing and Supply Management*, Vol. 9, 2003

Ribnikar, D., *Les leçons de la campagne du Kosovo*, IRIS/PUF, 2002

RUSI, 'Private Sector Involvement in the Public Sector', *Whitehall Papers* (Royal United Services Institute), Vol. 63, 2004

Rutten, Maartje, *From St-Malo to Nice. European Defence: Core Documents*, Paris, Institute for Security Studies of WEU, 2001

Sandler, Todd and Keith Hartley, *The Economics of Defense*, Cambridge: Cambridge University Press, 1995

———*The Political Economy of NATO*, New York, Cambridge University Press, 1999

Schmitt, B., *European Capabilities Action Plan (ECAP)*, Paris, EU Institute for Security Studies, 2003

———*Defence Procurement in the European Union: The Current Debate*, report of an EUISS Task Force, Paris, European Union Institute for Security Studies, 2005

SIPRI, *SIPRI Yearbook 2008*, Oxford, Oxford University Press, 2008

Solana, Javier, 'Research and Technology: An Imperative for European Defence', speech at the EDA Research and Technology Conference in Brussels, 9 February 2006, Times Higher Education, 10 February 2006, www.timeshigher education.co.uk/story.asp?storyCode=201333&sectioncode=26

Sotty, Tania, 'First Public-Private Partnership for Defence', 2008, www.defense.gouv.fr/defense_uk/breves/premier_partenariat_public_prive_pour_la_defense

Spillmann, Kurt R. and Joachim Krause, *Kosovo: Lessons Learned for International Cooperative Security*, Bern and New York, Peter Lang, 2000

Struck, P., *30.03.2004 Rede auf der Pressekonferenz*, Bundesministerium der Verteidigung, 2003

Taylor, Claire, *UK Defence Procurement Policy*, London, House of Commons, 2003

Taylor, Trevor, *Defence, Technology and International Integration*, London, Frances Pinter, 1982

The Economist, 'The Price of Staying Secure', *The Economist*, Vol. 334, 14 January 1995

Treaty Establishing the European Community, eur-lex.europa.eu/en/treaties/index.htm

Trybus, M. 'The new European Defence Agency: a contribution to a common European security and defence policy or a challenge to the Community acquis?', 43 Common Market Law Review 667 703, 2006

United States Congress, *Executive Amendment no. 2310, Congressional Record, April 27, p. S3657*, 1998

11 Defence spending and procurement in post-Communist Russia

Alexander A. Pikayev

Introduction

The Russian Federation is one of the world's largest arms exporters. According to official figures, this amounted to between US$5 billion–$7 billion a year in 2000s. Unlike the majority of other arms exporters, Russia imports very little and relies almost entirely on domestic production to supply its armed forces.

The Russian military and defence industry experienced extreme difficulties after the collapse of the Soviet Union. This was caused by three factors: 1. the deep recession of the economy in the 1990s; 2. the sudden and dramatic demilitarization without sound conversion plans; and 3. the disintegration of the Soviet Union. Between 1991 (the year of the Soviet collapse) and 1998 (when the economy was at its lowest point), the Russian Federation reduced by about half its gross domestic product (GDP). The government failed to collect sufficient revenue needed, among other things, for maintaining the armed forces and weapons procurement at adequate levels. For several years, Russia's defence budget fell to below $10 billion – minuscule compared with the size of the armed forces, which totalled 1.5m. personnel, as well as thousands of nuclear weapons.

As a result of the demilitarization, the defence sector contracted much more than the economy in general. In 1992, the first year of the post-Communist era, national defence procurement decreased by 10 times compared with the previous year. The collapse of the Soviet Union further exacerbated the situation for, as a result, important elements of the national defence industry remained outside Russian jurisdiction, which significantly complicated co-operation between industrial enterprises in producing weapons systems.

This led to a situation in the 1990s when the Russian Armed Forces failed to procure any meaningful amount of weaponry in all major weapons categories, such as missiles, aircraft, naval ships, helicopters and armoured vehicles. For example, in the Soviet era, the missile industry annually produced approximately 100 strategic ballistic missiles a year, while in the post-Communist era, the rate has never exceeded 10 missiles. During the 1990s, the situation was the same for other major categories of conventional weapons, including aircraft, helicopters and tanks.

The collapse of domestic procurement made Russia's defence industry almost completely dependent on foreign contracts, and its very survival became linked with arms exports. For more than a decade, the national defence enterprises worked to supply foreign nations and not the Russian Armed Forces as they used to do. There were two major markets for the Russian arms industry: the People's Republic of China and India.

The situation improved only after 2000. The rapid economic growth that the country experienced in 1999–2008 increased governmental revenue and permitted it to substantially increase defence budgets. Thus, in 2008 the defence budget exceeded $30 billion. However, this has not been immediately translated into increased procurement. Military expenditure still remains low for a country the size of Russia. Despite considerable growth, Russia's defence budget is still lower than that of medium-sized nations such as France and the United Kingdom, with their much smaller militaries and more stable neighbourhoods.

Much of the increased defence expenditure has been spent on improving social conditions and living standards for the military servicemen. In the 1990s officers failed to receive proper housing from the government, to which they were entitled under Russian law. Their salaries were also much lower than in the civilian private sector and young people were reluctant to enter a professional military career, while those who were already in the military wanted to leave. The conditions in barracks deteriorated and food for conscripts was sub-standard. Thus, much of the initially increased funds went into rectifying these matters, rather than for buying military hardware.

Insufficient funding also prevented adequate combat training. Military manoeuvres were rare and conducted only periodically in the 1990s. Due to fuel shortages, military aircraft rarely flew and naval vessels did not leave port. Air and naval patrols became the exception, rather than the rule. Decreasing combat efficiency, though, could not be tolerated for long, as the country was involved in several low-intensity conflicts. Moreover, the military capabilities of neighbouring states were being modernized. This made the training of the military and increasing of their combat preparedness a top priority next to improving living standards for soldiers. However, this meant that defence procurement was not given priority. Under these circumstances, arms exports have remained important in maintaining Russia's defence industry.

General priorities of Russia's federal budget, 2007–11

Before examining defence spending, it is important to analyse its role in the Russian budgetary process. According to Russian Presidential directives,[1] there are five major strategic budgetary priorities: 1. developing national innovation by promoting fundamental and applied research and advanced technologies; 2. investing in human resources, including education and health systems; 3. developing infrastructure, particularly in transport, communications and energy; 4. improving national governance and law enforcement institutions; and 5. maintaining national defence preparedness and the security of citizens.

A key fiscal priority (until the 2008 economic crisis) was maintaining a balanced federal budget. Reducing significant inflation, which was around 10% annually after 2000, was a major goal. In order to achieve this, the authorities artificially removed monetary flows from the national economy by investing the budgetary surplus not into state-supported industrial or infrastructure programmes or into reducing the tax burden, but into reserve funds kept abroad in international financial instruments. Interestingly, in early 2008 Russian Government investments in such US institutions as the now-bankrupt FreddyMac and FannieMay housing mortgage agencies exceeded national defence expenditure by several times. At its peak, in mid-2008, the overall amount of financial assets controlled by the Russian Government – Central Bank hard currency reserves together with two reserve funds of the Ministry of Finance – exceeded $700 billion. This was more than 20 times larger than Russia's defence expenditure for that year.

Defence spending was, thus, last on the list of Russia's budgetary and fiscal priorities. Nevertheless, the government recognized that the country needed to spend significantly in order to support its military and defence industry. In the long-term budgetary strategy to 2023, the Ministry of Finance stated that such expenses were necessary for national development. According to the Ministry, one priority of the Russian budget was to support sovereignty as well as one of the strongest armed forces in the world, including the maintenance of its nuclear weapons. The document outlined six priorities for defence spending: 1. maintaining high combat preparedness of the armed forces; 2. the re-equipment of the armed forces; 3. developing a mobile army; 4. countering terrorism; 5. preventing local conflicts; and 6. meeting national emergencies, including natural disasters, and post-emergency recovery.[2]

The major indicators of the Russian federal budget can be seen in Table 11.1.

Table 11.1 Main indicators of the Russian federal budget, 2007–11

No.	Main characteristics	2007 (by law)	2008 (by law)	2009 (projection)	2010 (projection)	2011 (projection)
	m.rubles					
1	Gross domestic product	31,225,000.0	42,240,000.0	51,475,000.0	59,146,000.0	67,610,000.0
	Increase from 2007, %		35.3	64.9	89.4	116.5
	Increase from previous year, %		35.3	21.9	14.9	14.3
2	Gross income	6,965,300.0	8,965,700.0	10,927,137.7	11,733,612.3	12,838,964.1
	Increase from 2007, %		28.7	56.9	68.5	84.3
	Increase from previous year, %		28.7	21.9	7.4	9.4
	Including oil and gas revenues		4,249,000.0	4,692,509.6	4,526,198.4	4,637,479.8
	Share from gross income, %		47.4	42.9	38.6	36.1
3	Expenditure	5,463,500.0	7,021,900.0	9,024,655.0	10,320,314.6	11,317,684.8
	Increase from 2007, %		28.5	65.2	88.9	107.2
	Increase from previous year, %		28.5	28.5	14.4	9.7
	Including provisionally approved expenditure				258,000.0 (2.5% of gross expenditure)	565,900.0 (5.0% of gross expenditure)
4	Gross oil and gas transfer		2,135,000.0	2,531,125.0	2,661,570.0	2,501,570.0
5	Reserve fund		3,500,000.0	5,147,500.0	5,914,600.0	6,761,000.0
6	Upper limit of state domestic debt		1,804,200.0	2,119,739.2	2,836,689.3	3,703,224.7
7	Upper limit of state foreign debt		$43.3 bn or €32.1bn	$41.4 bn or €27.8 bn	$41.7 bn or €29.2 bn	$40.9 bn or €29.2 bn
	Inflation rate, %	8.0–8.5	7.0	8.5	7.0	6.8
9	Proficit	1,501,800.0	1,943,800.0	1,902,482.7	1,413,297.7	1,521,279.3

No.	Main characteristics	2007 (law)	2008 (law)	2009 (projection)	2010 (projection)	2011 (projection)
	% of GDP					
1	Gross income	22.3	21.2	21.2	19.8	19.0
	Including oil and gas revenues		10.1	9.1	7.7	6.9
2	Gross expenditure	17.5	16.6	17.5	17.4	16.7
	Including provisionally approved expenditure				0.4	0.8
3	Gross oil and gas transfer		5.1	4.9	4.5	3.7
4	Reserve fund		8.3	10	10	10
5	Upper limit of state domestic debt		4.3	4.1	4.8	5.5
6	Proficit	4.8	4.6	3.7	2.4	2.2

Since 2007 the Russian federal budget has been approved three years at a time. The last plan, adopted in 2008, indicated that the government expected significant GDP growth through 2008–11. In 2011 this indicator would increase by 116.5% (including inflation), compared with 2007. The government also aimed to reduce the share of GDP redistributed through the federal budget. It wanted to decrease inflation and dependence on oil and gas revenues. In 2008 it was expected that almost half of budgetary income would consist of such revenue, but the authorities aimed to reduce this dependence to 36% by 2011.

However, Table 11.1 also shows that the forecast has been based on optimistic expectations of revenue from oil and gas exports in 2009 and beyond. It was calculated based on the assumption that the price for a barrel of Urals crude oil in 2009 would be $95, $90 in 2010 and $88 in 2011. However, in reality the price for a barrel of Urals crude at the beginning of 2009 hardly exceeded $40, and prospects for the recovery of oil prices remained uncertain. Moreover, growth forecasts for 2008 were not fulfilled, given the dramatic fall in the oil prices during the second half of the year and the corresponding contraction in Russia's economic growth during the same period (less than 6% instead of the expected 8% on a year-on-year basis).

The draft budget was based on the expectation that non-oil and gas budgetary incomes would not increase in terms of the percentage of GDP. The lower rate of economic growth might make the absolute year-on-year fall of such income quite possible. Oil and gas revenues, though, will almost certainly drop dramatically. On the contrary, expenditure will likely increase due to the significant economic stimulus package approved in autumn 2008. This is likely to lead to a situation in 2009 where the budget is in deficit and the government has to reduce spending.

Defence spending in the Russian federal budget

Table 11.2 shows the structure of federal expenditure for 2007–11. There are 11 major categories for such spending: 1. national defence; 2. national security and law enforcement; 3. national economy; 4. housing and utilities; 5. environmental protection; 6. education; 7. culture, cinema and mass media; 8. health care and sport; 9. social policy; 10. transfers between budgets; and 11. general matters. This classification is provided in Article 1 of the Federal Law 'On the 2009 budget and for the planned period of 2010 and 2011'. More detailed classifications can be found in Appendix 12 to the Federal Law.

Of those 11 major items, national defence has the second highest budget, after an item called 'transfers between budgets'. The latter covers subsidies from the federal budget to two social funds – the Pension Fund and the Fund for Medical Insurance. Although they receive their share of taxes, very often this is insufficient to cover necessary expenses. Also, the 'transfers' finance the budgets of poor regions, thus representing an important tool of federal regional policy. In 2007, the last year of real expenditure reported, 58% of gross expenditure of the federal budget went on items that were in one way or another associated with social and economic development. Among them: transfers between budgets, social policy, health care and sport, culture, cinema and mass media, education, environmental protection, housing and utilities, and national economy. The latter covers expenses for developing infrastructure and support of strategic branches of the economy.

At the same time, in 2007 only 15% of the federal budget was spent on national defence. This constituted slightly more than 2.6% of GDP and reflects the general trend since 2000. In any given year since 2000, the share of defence spending has fluctuated between 2.5% and 3% of GDP. This suggests that the rapid increase in defence spending since 2000 was not due to a policy of remilitarization, as reflected in the federal budget, but simply correlated with economic growth. Indeed, the figures for the increase in the defence budget have not exceeded the indicator for general economic growth.

The expected trend in general federal expenditure to 2011 also shows that priority has been given to social and economic objectives. In 2008 the share of the above-mentioned items

Table 11.2 Structure of federal expenditure, 2007–11

Line Items	2007 (law) bn rubles	2008 (law) bn rubles	% of gross expenditure	Increase from 2007, %	2009 (projection) bn rubles	% of gross expenditure	Increase from 2008, %	% of GDP	2010 (projection) bn rubles	Increase from 2009, %	% of GDP	2011 (projection) bn rubles	Increase from 2010, %	% of GDP
Gross expenditure	5,463.5	7,021.9	100.0	29	9,024.7	100.0	29	17.5	10,320.3	14	17.4	11,317.7	10	16.7
Including open part		5,781.0	82.3		8,010.5	88.7	39	15.6	8,890.1	11	15.0	9,546.6	7	14.1
General state matters	808.2	870.3	12.4	8	1,317.4	14.6	51	2.6	1,236.8	−6	2.1	1,203.9	−3	1.8
National defence	822.0	1,016.7	15.1	29	1,277.5	14.2	26	2.5	1,390.7	9	2.4	1,480.5	6	2.2
Including open part	446.7	509.1	7.3	14	712.6	7.9	40	1.4	735.0	3	1.2	806.9	10	1.2
National security and law enforcement	662.9	827.2	11.8	25	1,085.9	12.0	31	2.1	1,198.3	10	2.0	1,266.1	6	1.9
Including open part		521.8	7.4		756.9	8.4	45	1.5	833.6	10	1.4	888.7	7	1.3
National economy	497.2	771.3	11.0	55	1,039.4	11.5	35	2.0	1,181.2	14	2.0	1,384.8	17	2.0
Housing and utilities	53.0	64.0	0.9	2.1	107.7	1.2	68	0.2	118.3	10	0.2	110.3	−7	0.2
Environmental protection	8.1	9.9	0.1	22	13.8	0.2	40	0.03	14.7	7	0.03	15.1	3	0.02
Education	277.9	336.1	4.8	21	423.1	4.7	26	0.8	468.8	11	0.8	484.9	3	0.7
Culture, cinema and mass media	67.8	93.7	1.3	38	113.9	1.3	22	0.2	114.4	0.4	0.2	114.4	0	0.2
Health and sport	206.4	230.0	3.3	11	365.8	4.1	59	0.7	379.4	4	0.7	382.2	1	0.6
Social policy	215.6	275.6	3.9	28	297.7	3.3	8	0.6	338.6	14	0.6	307.9	−9	0.5
Transfers between budgets	1,844.3	2,523.3	35.9	37	2,982.0	33.0	18	5.8	3,621.1	21	5.8	4,001.7	11	5.9

increased to 61.2% of budgetary gross expenditure. In 2011 they would constitute 60.1%, still higher than their share in 2007. Among them, the fastest growing items in the period 2007–11 are national economy, transfers between budgets, and housing and utilities. The rise of those items will be faster than the increase in budgetary gross expenditure in general. The fourth and fifth fastest-growing items are environmental protection, and health care and sport.

For the period 2007–11, national defence is the sixth-fastest growing. It will increase from 822.0 billion rubles in 2007 to 1,016.7 billion in 2008, and to 1,480.5 billion in 2011. While the ruble has been significantly devalued against the dollar since September 2008 (by more than 40% between September 2008 and late January 2009), defence spending could still increase from more than $32.0 billion in 2007 to $36.5 billion in 2009, if the average ruble-to-dollar rate does not exceed the estimated average annual exchange rate of 35 rubles to the US dollar for 2009.

However, in relative terms the role of national defence in federal expenditure will decrease, from 15.0% of gross expenditure in 2007 to 14.2% in 2009, and to 13.1% in 2011. In terms of its share of GDP, the downturn could be even faster, falling from 2.6% in 2007 to 2.4% in 2010, and to 2.2% in 2011. If that happened, the indicator would go below 2.5%, the lowest ever since 2000.

According to the Ministry of Finance 2023 Budget Strategy, defence expenditure should be kept at a level of 2.5% of GDP during the whole period. This means that the annual increase should not exceed average expected economic growth of 6%. However, the relative drop of the share below 2.5% planned for 2010 and 2011 would have to be compensated by an increase in later years. The Strategy pointed at four major items that could be decreased after 2011 as a possible compensation. Amongst them are general state matters, national security and law enforcement, national economy, and housing and utilities.[3]

However, the 2023 Budget Strategy still plans that after 2011, defence spending as a percentage of GDP will be lower than in the period 2000–08. During this period, the indicator has never dropped below 2.5%, and was close to it only for three years: 2004, 2006 and 2007. For five years the indicator was higher than 2.5% and in 2002 it reached almost 3.0%. However, even relatively higher figures after 2000 were below the benchmark established by the National Security Council in 2000. It had planned that until 2020, the share of defence expenditure should constitute not less than 3.2% of GDP.

Another problem is linked to the fact that the budget's national defence priority does not cover all expenses related to defence. Official Russian budgetary documents contain budgets of individual federal ministries and agencies, including the Ministry of Defence. Only three of 11 of the major budgetary items do not have any relation with the Ministry of Defence (national security and law enforcement, national economy and environmental protection). The Ministry's expenditure is covered not only by the national defence item, but also by seven other major items of the federal budget (see Table 11.3). Among them are: general state matters (sub-item international relations and international co-operation); housing and utilities (sub-item housing); education; culture, cinema and mass media; health care and sport; social policy; and transfers between budgets.

Beyond the national defence item in the budget, the Ministry of Defence expected to receive 194.2 billion rubles, or 2.8% of gross expenditure in 2008. If this was added to the funds in the national defence item, the total would be 1,210.9 billion rubles. Together, national defence in the budget and the expenses of the Ministry of Defence from other budgetary items total 17.2% of gross expenditure, or almost 2.9% of GDP.

In 2009 it was planned to increase substantially the Ministry of Defence funding from items other than national defence. This is expected to be 247.1 billion rubles, which represents an increase of 52.9 billion rubles, or more than 27%. It would be even more than the rise in national defence budgetary allocation expected in 2009. However, it was planned that both parts of the expenses would increase slower than the gross expenditure and, thus, even relatively faster spending from non-national defence items could not divert a relative downward trend in the share of military-related spending in the federal budget. Together, in 2009 the national defence spending

Table 11.3 Expenditure of the Ministry of Defence (m. rubles)

No. in budgetary classification	Item	2008 (by law)	2009 (projection)	2010 (projection)	2011 (projection)
187	*Ministry of Defence of the Russian Federation*	*659,445.3*	*898,410.8*	*823,870.6*	*914,148.4*
187 01	General state matters	4.3	3.7	3.9	4.1
187 01 *08*	*International relations and international co-operation*	*4.3*	*3.7*	*3.9*	*4.1*
187 02	National defence	465,878.5	651,261.0	690,007.5	766,779.2
187 05	Housing and utilities	31,157.6	44,436.0	42,286.1	49,138.1
187 05 *01*	*Housing*	*31,157.6*	*44,436.0*	*42,286.1*	*49,138.1*
187 07	Education	32,561.3	43,733.7	45,879.8	48,844.1
187 08	Culture, cinema, mass media	1,728.8	3,615.8	3,827.0	4,593.5
187 09	Health care and sport	23,126.1	32,687.1	37,372.1	39,996.4
187 10	Social policy, including:	102,658.2	120,591.9	2,226.4	2,377.8
187 10 *01* 4900101	*Pensions for servicemen and members of their families*	*94,892.8*	*110,424.8*		
187 11	Transfers between budgets	1,504.0	2,081.6	2,267.7	2,415.1

plus Ministry of Defence funding from other budgetary items could total 1,524.6 billion rubles, but this would constitute 16.9% of gross expenditure, which would be less than in 2008.

However, in terms of the share of GDP, it was planned that 2009 gross expenditure would constitute a higher share of GDP – 17.5% compared with 16.6% in 2008. Therefore, in 2009 a significant increase of expected Ministry of Defence funding from both national defence and other items might allow a rise in the share of defence-related spending by 0.1 percentage point, to almost 3%.

The trend of expenses for the Ministry of Defence from the non-national defence items beyond 2009 cannot continue. The biggest sub-item – military pensions – disappeared from the Ministry of Defence budget plans for 2010 and 2011. This statistical correction would trigger an absolute decrease of the Ministry 2010 budget, to 823.9 billion rubles, down from the 898.4 billion planned for 2009.

In 2008 the majority of funds covered by non-national defence items were represented by military pensions (almost 95 billion rubles), education (32.6 billion), housing (31.2 billion), and health care and sport (23.1 billion). In other words, social-related expenses for the military are calculated outside the framework of national defence spending, though it could be argued that such expenses represent a part of defence expenditure. In 2009 these items will rise. Spending on pensions will increase to 110.4 billion rubles (16.3%), 44.4 billion (42.6%) for housing, 43.7 billion (34.3%) for education, and 32.7 billion (41.3%) for health care and sports. Interestingly, much more significant increases have been planned for the Ministry of Defence expenses coming from items in culture, cinema and mass media. This can be explained by a desire by the authorities to improve the image of the Russian military, which was seriously damaged by reports of abuse of conscripts in barracks, poor living standards in the military and other misdemeanours. The Ministry of Defence thus plays a significant role in federal expenditure due to non-national defence items. Among them are: housing and utilities (almost half of overall expenditure at 48.7% in 2008), social policy (36.3%), education, health care and sport (approximately one-10th).

However, these plans were elaborated upon and approved in mid-2008, when a considerable increase in oil and gas revenues was expected. Since the start of the global economic crisis in autumn 2008, and the corresponding drop of energy prices, it seems highly unlikely that the Russian Government will be able to maintain the expected increase in budgetary expenditure, especially for 2009. The basic budgetary figures would thus have to be reconsidered some time in the first half of 2009.

Structure and dynamics of national defence expenditure

Several Russian ministries and agencies operate national defence items. Among them, the Ministry of Defence plays the leading role. In 2008 it controlled 465.9 billion rubles (or 45.8%) of all national defence expenditure, planned at 1,016.7 billion rubles. In 2011 it is expected that the Ministry will spend 766.8 billion from a total of 1,480.5 billion rubles (51.8%). This suggests that by 2011, the Ministry of Defence will play an even larger role in operating this item.

National defence expenditure covers the expenditure of other ministries and agencies beyond that of Defence. They include: the Ministry for Industry and Energy, Federal Agency for Atomic Energy, Federal Agency for Industry, Federal Service for Defence Order, Federal Agency for Supplies of Arms, Military and Special Equipment, and Material Deliveries and the Federal Space Agency, amongst others.

The national defence item is divided into eight sub-items (see Tables 11.4 and 11.5). They are: 1. the armed forces; 2. mobilization and preparedness of reserve forces; 3. mobilization preparedness of the economy; 4. preparedness to participate in collective security and peacekeeping; 5. maintaining the nuclear weapons complex; 6. implementation of international obligations in the area of military and technical co-operation; 7. applied defence research; and 8. other expenses related to national defence.

Table 11.4 Structure of national defence expenditure, 2007–11 (%)

Items	2008 (law)	Draft budget		
		2009	2010	2011
Russian Armed Forces	72.1	71.5	75.2	74.8
Mobilization and preparedness of reserve forces	0.6	0.5	0.4	0.4
Mobilization preparedness of the economy	0.3	0.3	0.3	0.4
Preparedness to and participation in providing collective security and peacekeeping	0.1	0.0	0.0	0.0
Nuclear weapons complex	1.7	1.8	2.0	2.0
Implementation of international obligations in the area of military and technical co-operation	0.4	0.2	0.2	0.2
Applied defence research	13.1	12.9	11.4	10.4
Other	11.7	12.8	10.6	11.8
Total	*100.0*	*100.0*	*100.0*	*100.0*

Sub-item 02.01: the armed forces[4]

The sub-item includes expenses for supporting the servicemen (salaries, food and material supply, combat training, fuel, transportation, utilities and communications), as well as federal task programmes in the interests of national defence.

The greatest funding was provided for the following articles:

- Federal task programmes (FTPs): 11,225.9m. rubles in 2009, 12,785.0m. in 2010 and 9,389.5m. in 2011, which was significantly reduced compared with the previous 2008–10 budget;
- Combat training: 32,185.2m. rubles in 2009, 33,258.4m. in 2010 and 35,435.0m. in 2011. The main expense here is fuel. The expenses would be significantly higher than funding approved a year before;
- Material supply: 111,977.6m. rubles in 2009, 132,883.3m. in 2010 and 135,575.8m. in 2011. These funds would be used primarily for supporting the armed forces;
- Military units: 382,088.8m. rubles in 2009, 413,940.3m. in 2010 and 448,158.0m. in 2011. This figure represents a significant increase compared with the previous budget for 2008–10;
- Mortgages for servicemen: 18,216.6m. rubles in 2009, 18,865.5m. in 2010 and 14,228.7m. in 2011. This represents an increase of 1.5–2 times compared with the previous budget for 2008–10.

Sub-item 02.03: mobilization and preparedness of reserve forces

The sub-item includes expenses such as military commissions for medical checks for conscripts, as well as spending on the training of reservists, including conducting reservist field training courses.

Sub-item 02.05: preparedness to participate in collective security and peace-keeping

The sub-item includes expenditure on peace-keeping activities, which are planned at 119.0m. rubles in 2009, 126.6m. in 2010 and 132.8m. in 2011. This constitutes a significant increase compared with the previous budget for 2008–10.

Sub-item 02.08: applied defence research

This includes expenditure on implementing international agreements and co-operation within the Commonwealth of Independent States, applied research and development in the areas of

Table 11.5 Structure of expenditure under national defence item, 2007–11

Items	No. in budgetary classification	2007 (law) bn rubles	2008 (law) bn rubles	2008 (law) Increase to 2007, %	2009 (projection) bn rubles	2009 (projection) Increase to 2008, %	2010 (projection) bn rubles	2010 (projection) Increase to 2009, %	2011 (projection) bn rubles	2011 (projection) Increase to 2010, %
National defence	02	822.0	1,016.7	23.7	1,277.5	25.7	1,390.7	8.9	1,480.5	6.5
Including open expenses[1]		446.7	509.1	14.0	712.6	40.0	735.0	3.1	806.9	9.8
Armed Forces	02.01	370.8	733.1	97.7	913.4	24.6	1,045.6	14.5	1,107.3	5.9
Including open expenses			420.0		569.4	35.6	620.0	8.9	670.4	8.1
Mobilization and preparedness of reserve forces	02.03	5.9	6.2	5.1	6.7	8.1	6.1	-9.0	6.11	0.0
Including open expenses			5.2		6.7	28.8	6.1	-9.0	6.1	
Mobilization preparedness of the economy			3.5		3.5	0.0	3.7	5.7	6.3	70.3
Preparedness to and participation in providing collective security and peacekeeping	02.05	0.8	0.6	-25.0	0.1	-83.3	0.1	0.0	0.1	0.0
Including open expenses			0.6		0.1	-83.3	0.1	0.0	0.1	0.0
Nuclear weapons complex			17.1		22.4	31.0	27.5	22.8	29.1	5.8
Implementation of international obligations in the area of military and technical co-operation			3.9		2.9	-25.6	2.9	0.0	3.0	3.4
Applied defence research	02.08	120.5	133.3	10.6	164.8	23.6	157.9	-4.2	153.7	-2.7
Including open expenses			9.1		13.6	49.5	13.8	1.5	11.7	-15.2
Other national defence	02.09	79.1	119.0	50.4	163.6	37.5	146.7	-10.3	174.8	19.2
Including open expenses			74.8		122.8	64.2	95.0	-22.6	118.6	24.8

Notes:
1 Appendix 12 to the Federal Law

implementing international agreements on arms reductions and military confidence-building measures. It also includes several federal task programmes and investments in construction. Beyond these, the sub-item covers research on developing armaments, military and special equipment and other production tools. Major expenditure under this sub-item consists of:

- Federal task programmes: 5,072.7m. rubles in 2009, 4,979.3m. in 2010 and 3,625.7m. in 2011. This exceeds the levels planned in the previous three-year budget for 2008–10;
- Research in developing armaments, military and special equipment and other production tools as a part of state order not included in the state armament programme: 6,254.0m. rubles annually, which is equal to that planned in the previous three-year budget for 2008–10.

Sub-item 02.09: other defence expenditure

This sub-item includes the following: 1. federal task programmes; 2. budgetary investments in construction, not included in federal task programmes; 3. military units and bodies; 4. dismantling and elimination of armaments under arms control agreements; 5. implementation of state activities related to national defence; 6. implementation of national agreements and other obligations on limiting and reducing arms, and military confidence building; 7. organizational and educational activity with youth. This sub-item was increased by 1.5 times compared with the budget for 2008–10. Major expenditure is in the following areas:

- Federal task programmes: 73,703.5m. rubles in 2009, 54,695.1m. in 2010 and 52,242.9m. in 2011;
- Budgetary investments in construction projects not included in the federal task programmes: 8,362.5m. rubles in 2009, 27,854.7m. in 2010 and 53,646.5m. in 2011;
- Military units and bodies: 11,411.3m. rubles in 2009, 1,525.7m. in 2010 and 1,656.0m. in 2011. In 2009 the planned expenditure increased by eight times compared with the previous 2008–10 budget.

A review of national defence expenditure shows that there is insufficient transparency and the figures provided do not lend to detailed analysis. In particular, the published figures do not provide any details on the modernization of the armed forces. They also do not cover expenditure on the maintenance and operational use of weapons systems and other equipment. The open budget does not provide any detailed information on combat training and major field manoeuvres. The available information also shows that the national defence budget for 2009–11 contained significant increases for servicemen's salaries, pensions, housing and other social benefits. Beyond this, the rise in expenditure on combat training, contained in sub-item 02.01 reflects the desire of the authorities to make the armed forces more proficient.

One of the stated goals of the budgetary policy is a transition to an all-volunteer armed forces. Since 2008 the period of compulsory military service has been reduced from two years to one year. To pave the way for a transition to an all-volunteer force, the government decided to increase salaries, with a plan to allocate 9.5 billion rubles in 2008 and 9.8 billion in 2009. In addition, the Minister of Defence established the Fund of the Ministry of Defence through Minister of Defence Order N400, which was signed on 2 August 2008.[5] The Fund would be financed from the national defence budget (sub-item 02.01). This order permits the further increase of salaries to 30,000 professional military officers. The Fund would be allocated 25 billion rubles in 2009, 33 billion in 2010 and 44 billion in 2011. This means that in 2009, an average awarded officer eligible for this bonus might receive almost 70,000 rubles extra per month (approximately $2,000 based on the expected ruble-to-US dollar exchange rate in 2009). This is almost six times more than the salary of a lieutenant. In 2011 the average monthly pay for an officer could reach more than 122,000 rubles. The bonuses would be paid to commanders of regiments and divisions and to highly-qualified specialists. This would cover units that maintain permanent combat readiness in the Ground Forces, strategic aviation, submarine fleet, Strategic Rocket Forces and Space Forces. In 2009–11 the average regular salary of officers will also be adjusted according to inflation.

Procurement

The Russian budget does not provide any figures on procurement expenditure, which is hidden in secret items. It is also likely that some procurement items have been included in federal task programmes. The amount of financing for procurement is partially available and is summarized in Table 11.6. However, it provides few details on future procurement plans.

From open sources, it is known that procurement funding has increased significantly from 2000, along with the general rise in the national defence budget. However, that increase does not match the general rise of the defence budget, due to the urgent need to fund troops' training and officers' salaries, pensions and housing. The increase in procurement funding also did not bring about the expected growth in actual numbers of weapons systems. This is due to the fact that prices for new armaments and military equipment have surged on account of the high rate of general inflation, which has been around 10% annually over the last decade. Also, problems of financing in the 1990s have reportedly affected Russia's defence industry, which has in turn affected the development of new weapons systems and military equipment.

In 2006 Russia adopted the State Armaments Programme for 2007–15. According to this plan, within a period of nine years, about 110 silo-based and mobile Topol-M (SS-27) intercontinental ballistic missiles, 50 new strategic bombers and more than 30 major surface ships and strategic and attack nuclear-powered submarines would be commissioned. In 2007–08 Russia also tested several new strategic weapons systems. They include the new multiple-warhead RS-24 intercontinental ballistic missile and Bulava submarine-launched ballistic missile. Provided test trials are successful, it would be logical to expect their procurement in the foreseeable future.

The State Armaments Programme planned to modernize conventional forces, which have been particularly affected by insufficient funding in the past. By 2015, 40 tank, 97 motor rifle and 50 airborne battalions would be modernized. The modernization includes the acquisition of some very modern weapons systems. For instance, five brigades will be armed with Iskander short-range nuclear-capable surface-to-surface missiles, and two regiments with the new Uragan M1 rocket systems. The national air defence system would also be improved by 2016 through the commissioning of the new Voronezh missile attack warning radars, Konteiner over-the-horizon radars, and the Nebo, Podlet and Rezonans radar systems.

However, although production will be stepped up, Russia's defence industry will still be operating at a relatively modest scale during the period 2007–15. The annual production of new strategic missiles might be in the low 10s. Strategic bombers would be produced at a rate of fewer than 10 a year. Several surface ships and nuclear-powered submarines would be produced every year. The annual production of armoured vehicles might reach several 10s. These figures remain far below the industrial capacities of the former Soviet Union, which annually produced many thousands of units of major categories of armaments and military equipment, such as missiles, airplanes and armoured vehicles.

Forces modernization and procurement is one of the top priorities of the Russian authorities. On 28 June 2005, the National Security Council adopted a decision to change the proportion of funds spent on supporting the military and its modernization. At the time, the ratio was 7:3 in favour of supporting the military. By 2011 the proportion would change to 5:5, and by 2015 to 7:3 in favour of modernization. However, considerable funds were diverted to increasing salaries, pensions and improving housing for the military in 2009–11, which means that this objective is unlikely to be met. As a result, Moscow has in fact failed to

Table 11.6 Expenditure from the national defence item on federal task and presidential programmes (m. rubles)

No.	Name of programme / sub-programme	2008 (law)	2009 (projection)	2010 (projection)	2011 (projection)
1	FTP 'World Ocean'	66.6	72.4	81.0	125.0
1.2	Sub-programme 'Military and strategic Russian interests in the World Ocean'	66.6	72.4	81.0	125.0
2	FTP 'State border of the Russian Federation (2003 10)'	102.5	102.5	122.9	
3	FTP 'Restructuring missiles, ammunition and explosives stockpiles, making safe storage system against fire and explosions for 2005 10'	7,131.0	6,489.6	7,162.4	
4	FTP 'Complex measures against wrong use of narcotics and illegal narcotrafficking for 2005 09'	46.8	48.2		
5	Presidential programme 'Elimination of the chemical weapons stockpiles in the Russian Federation'	22,937.1	27,041.3	19,982.9	21,129.0
6	FTP 'Global navigation system'	4,368.6	9,538.0	11,171.4	7,271.3
6.1	Sub-programme 'Operation and development of the GLONASS system'	4,015.2	8,895.6	9,923.0	6,418.1
6.2	Sub-programme 'Modernization and development of advanced navigation equipment for special consumers'	353.4	642.4	1,249.3	853.2
7	FTP 'Industrial dismantlement of armaments and military equipment (2005 10)'	4,671.9	6,702.0	5,175.3	
7.1	Sub-programme 'Industrial dismantlement of the nuclear submarines, surface ships with nuclear energy units, ships of the nuclear technical support and rehabilitation of coastal support bases (2005 10)'	2,394.7	3,118.2	2,652.5	
8	FTP 'Development of Russian space launch facilities for 2006 15'	4,414.3	58.6	110.8	91.8
9	FTP 'National system for chemical and biological security of the Russian Federation (2009 13)'		927.0	1,007.7	1,095.3
10	FTP 'Economic and social development of the far East and Trans-Baikal regions until 2013'		2,000.0		
11	FTP 'Developing basing for the Black Sea Fleet on the territory of the Russian Federation in 2005 20'	2,834.0	3,721.0	3,734.0	8,261.4
12	FTP 'Improving federal system of intelligence and control of the airspace of the Russian Federation (2007 10)'	1,069.5	1,170.0	1,222.0	
13	FTP 'Social and economic development of the Chechen Republic for 2008 11'		202.2	116.3	
14	FTP 'Improving fulfilment of positions of sergeants and soldiers by the volunteers, and transition to fulfilling positions of sergeants of the Armed Forces, other troops, military units and bodies, as well as sailors of the navy by the volunteers (2009 15)'		26,009.6	16,683.3	21,983.3
Total open expenses		47,641.7	96,810.4	80,473.8	67,353.4
Including additional expenses			39,975.5	29,215.6	

implement its own modernization priorities and has remained stuck in the policy of previous years, which focused on improving the terms and conditions provided to military personnel at the expense of the re-armament and modernization of the armed forces in general.

Under 14 open federal programmes (see Table 11.6), the federal authorities planned to spend 292.3 billion rubles in 2008–11. The open federal programmes could be divided into four groups: 1. the safe dismantling of weapons; 2. military infrastructure development; 3. military reform; and 4. procuring and deploying new weapons systems.

Four programmes involve the safe dismantling of weapons. They consist of: 1. restructuring and developing safe storage sites for missiles and ammunition; 2. eliminating the chemical weapons stockpile; 3. developing chemical and biological safety and security; and 4. dismantling of armaments and military equipment including nuclear submarines. This is the most expensive part of open federal defence programmes. Some 131.5 billion rubles or 45% of all open defence programmes would be allocated to the programmes from 2008–11. The expenditure on the presidential programme for eliminating chemical weapons, at 91.1 billion in 2008–11, represents the lion's share. This category also includes two other significant programmes: restructuring missile and ammunition storage sites (20.8 billion, the fourth-largest open defence programme), and the dismantling of weapons (16.5 billion, the sixth-largest). The latter includes a sub-programme for dismantling old nuclear-powered submarines, which will cost 8.2 billion rubles in 2008–10.

A single but significant programme deals with military reform. This involves the training of professional non-commissioned officers, which is an important component for the transition to all-volunteer forces. In 2009–11 the government planned to spend 64.7 billion rubles on the programme, or 22.1% of all expenditure on open defence programmes. This makes it the second-largest programme after the elimination of chemical weapons.

Five programmes involve the procurement and deployment of new weapons systems. The largest is the development of the GLONASS system. This dual-use global positioning system would enhance various civil capabilities, as well as improve military capabilities, including the accuracy of missiles. The government will spend 32.3 billion rubles on the programme in 2008–11, which makes it the third-largest open defence programme. Another significant programme in this group is aimed at rebuilding Russian air defence capabilities, for which 3.4 billion rubles was allocated in 2008–10.

Finally, there are four programmes revolving around military infrastructure development. In 2008–11 total expenditure for these is expected to be 25.5 billion rubles. The largest of the programmes, involving 18.6 billion rubles, aims to build up the Russian infrastructure for the Black Sea fleet, ahead of the expiry of the lease at the Ukrainian port of Sebastopolis in 2017. This is the fifth-largest open defence programme.

Conclusions

Providing a reliable forecast for Russian budgetary defence policy in the foreseeable future is difficult for two reasons. Firstly, the country's defence budget remains insufficiently transparent. A considerable part is officially declared secret and other defence-related expenditure is presumably hidden under civilian items. Secondly, the sharp decrease in oil prices during the last five months of 2008 and consecutive decrease of Russia's budgetary revenues would inevitably force the Russian Government to recalculate its basic budgetary parameters, including defence expenditure.

However, available budgetary data permit a few conclusions. Moscow seems strongly committed to keeping its defence expenditure modest, within a 3% share of GDP, despite evident problems in defence funding. For the period 2008–11, it planned to further decrease the share of defence spending, despite a huge expected budgetary surplus. Within the defence budget, the stated priority has been to increase the proportion of funding for military modernization and re-armament programmes, as well as on measures aimed at raising the quality of military personnel and its combat proficiency. However, the more pressing need to increase the terms and conditions of military personnel has made this objective difficult to fulfil. Given the severe budgetary constraints expected in the immediate future, achieving this change will be much more problematic.

Despite the expected fall in revenue, Russia's budgetary situation will remain better than in the 1990s. This could allow some modest procurement of weapons systems and military equipment to modernize the armed forces. However, given known trends in defence spending and procurement, Russia's defence industry, which inherited enormous capabilities from the former Soviet Union, will remain interested in foreign markets for its weapons systems and other military equipment. However, the Russian defence industry could face a different and more serious challenge. Almost two decades of insufficient investment in the modernization of facilities and technology, and the lack of domestic demand, could combine to undermine its performance on the international market. It may also face growing competition from other producers, while potential buyers could decide to reduce their procurement as a result of the global economic crisis from late 2008.

Notes

1 Draft Law on the Budget of the Russian Federation, Presidential submission to the Federal Assembly of the Russian Federation, 23 June 2008 (in Russian), www.kremlin.ru/text/appears/2008/06/202940.shtml.
2 Budget strategy of the Russian Federation until 2023, Russian Ministry of Finance, 2008 (in Russian), www.minfin.ru/ru.
3 Budget Strategy of the Russian Federation until 2023, Russian Ministry of Finance, 2008 (in Russian): www.minfin.ru/ru.
4 Appendix 12 to the Federal Law.
5 'On Rewarding Officers of the Russian Armed Forces Using Money', Order of the Russian Federation Minister of Defence on 2 August 2008, N400 (registered by the Ministry of Justice on 15 August 2008, N12127), Rossiyskaya Gazeta, N 178, 22 August 2008 (in Russian).

Bibliography

Arbatov, Alexei, *Russian Military Policy Adrift*, Carnegie Briefing Paper, Vol. 8, Issue 6, Carnegie Moscow Center, Moscow, November 2006, www.carnegie.ru/en/pubs/briefings/brifing%2011_06%20E.pdf
Arbatov, Alexei and Pyotr Romashkin, 'The 2007 Russian Defense Budget and Trends in Military Policy', in *Russia, Arms Control, Disarmament and International Security*, Moscow, IMEMO, 2007
Blair, David, 'Russia Defence Spending Soars', *Daily Telegraph*, 27 January 2009, www.telegraph.co.uk/news/worldnews/europe/russia/4361792/Russia-defence-spending-soars.html
Romashkin, Pyotr, 'Russian Projected Defense Outlays for 2008–2010. Synopsis of Federal Law No. FZ 198 (2007)', in *Russia, Arms Control, Disarmament and International Security*, Moscow, IMEMO, 2008
—— 'Defense Outlays in the 2006 Federal Budget', in *Russia, Arms Control, Disarmament and International Security*, Moscow, IMEMO, 2006
Russia's Military Budget 2004–2008, warfare.ru/?catid=239&linkid=2279
'Russian Defense Budget May Rise 25% in 2009', *USA Today*, 18 September 2008, www.usatoday.com/news/world/2008-09-19-Russia-defense_N.htm
'Russian Defense Spending Increased 25 percent', *Pravda.ru*, 19 September 2008, english.pravda.ru/news/russia/19-09-2008/106406-russia_defense_budget-0
Russian Military Budget, globalsecurity.org, www.globalsecurity.org/military/world/russia/mo-budget.htm
Russian Military Budget Expenditures, globalsecurity.org, www.globalsecurity.org/military/world/russia/mo-budget-expenditures.htm
Stallenheim, Petter, Catalina Perdomo and Elisabeth Sköns, 'Military Expenditure', in *SIPRI Yearbook 2008*, Stockholm: Stockholm International Peace Research Institute, 2008

12 Arms modernization in Latin America

Mark Bromley and Iñigo Guevara

Introduction

Since the end of the Cold War, Latin America has enjoyed a prolonged period of limited regional tension. With the exception of the 1995 Alto-Cenepa War between Ecuador and Peru there have been no interstate conflicts and the region has seen the development of several initiatives aimed at economic and security co-operation and integration. Most of the interstate disputes over border demarcation that have led to conflict in previous years were resolved (Arévalo de León 2002, 14). Following prolonged periods of extensive militarization during the many military dictatorships of the 1970s and 1980s, defence spending remained low and activity in the global arms market was limited as new civilian governments sought to assert control over defence policies.

Despite this period of prolonged calm, Latin America remained a region where one country's arms acquisitions had the potential to impact negatively on regional security. The purchases of other states were still watched for signs of changes to the regional military balance and states sought to prevent or respond to perceived inequalities in military capabilities. For example, in 2005 tensions developed between Peru and Chile regarding Chile's acquisition of F-16 fighter aircraft from the USA.

Although the 'old' threats of interstate conflict rescinded, parts of the region remained beset by an array of 'new' security threats, including criminal violence, drugs-trafficking, social marginalization and guerrilla insurgencies. In certain cases, tackling these threats has led to an increased role for the military in internal security issues, as has recently occurred in Brazil and Mexico. In other cases this has led to improved forms of co-operation between states, including the development of an innovative array of confidence- and security-building measures. In others, unilateral action by one state has strained relations with neighbours and increased regional tension, as was the case with Colombia's attack on a FARC (Revolutionary Armed Forces of Colombia) camp in Ecuador in March 2008.

In recent years Latin America has seen a significant increase in both military spending and arms imports. The volume of arms transferred to Latin America during 2003–07 was 47% higher than in 1998–2002 (*Miami Herald*, 17 September 2007, 16A). This jump in arms transfers has led some to warn of a serious deterioration in the security and stability of Latin America. In September 2006 Óscar Arias, President of Costa Rica, citing recent purchases by Chile, Venezuela and others, declared that the region 'has begun a new arms race'.

The recent rise in military spending and arms acquisitions does show some elements of competitive behaviour by states in the region. For example, Brazil's apparent desire to keep pace with Venezuela's modernizations seems to be driving certain of its acquisition decisions. Some of Peru and Colombia's purchases seem to be in response to recent buys on the part of Chile and Venezuela, respectively. None the less, the majority of acquisitions have been primarily motivated by efforts to replace or upgrade military inventories in order to maintain existing capabilities; respond to predominantly domestic security threats; strengthen ties with supplier governments; boost domestic arms industries; participate in peace-keeping missions; or bolster the country's regional or international profile.

Indeed, as this chapter demonstrates, the overwhelming impression presented by the region is one of continuity rather than change, with several states enacting long-delayed acquisition programmes due to improved economic situations and ageing equipment, rather than launching completely new programmes in response to the actions of neighbouring states.

In terms of suppliers, many commentators have noted the emergence of Russia as a significant exporter to Latin America as one of the most interesting developments in recent years (*LASSR*, December 2004, 11). While Russia's recent success in Venezuela has gained headlines, the true picture is again one of continuity rather than change. Russia has long been an important supplier to several countries in the region. Seven countries have purchased military hardware from Russia in the past decade: Argentina, Brazil, Cuba, Colombia, Ecuador, Peru and Mexico. Military helicopters have proven particularly successful, a pattern that has been continued with Brazil's purchase of 12 MI-35M combat helicopters at the end of 2008.

Latin America has never been under the exclusive thrall of any one supplier. The USA has provided the majority of supplies to certain countries during certain periods, but has never enjoyed a monopoly. Along with Russia, European and Israeli companies have long had a strong presence in Latin America, often deriving opportunities from the USA's unwillingness to supply certain advanced military technology. This pattern dates back to the 1960s when the USA refused to sell advanced combat aircraft to Latin America, and Peru responded by acquiring Mirage 5 fighters from France in 1967, becoming the first country in the region to acquire supersonic fighter aircraft.

This chapter analyses key trends in defence spending and arms procurement in Latin America between 1990 and the end of 2008. With the exception of Brazil, the largest country in Latin America, states have been grouped together based on geographic or political links. In each case a brief overview is provided of significant arms imports and acquisitions along with an analysis of the sources of the equipment and motivations for different purchases. Where relevant, information is also provided on developments in each country's domestic defence industry as well as any notable arms exports. The conclusions provide a brief overview of developments in the region as well as their overall relevance for the global arms trade.

Mexico and Central America

Mexico's military spending is relatively low as a percentage of gross domestic product (GDP), when compared with other countries in Latin America. Recent operational needs have seen a rise and an increase of 20% is being considered for 2009, but this would still leave spending at below 1% of GDP (*JDW*, 23 December 2008). Mexican procurement has also been limited by regional standards but it has drawn on a diverse array of suppliers. From 1990 to 2008, Mexico acquired military hardware from Belgium, Brazil, the People's Republic of China, Canada, the Czech Republic, Denmark, Germany, Israel, Finland, France, Italy, Qatar, Russia, South Africa, Spain, Sweden, Switzerland, Ukraine, the United Kingdom (UK) and the USA.

During the 1990s army procurement focused on a fleet of 504 armoured personnel carriers (APC) from second-hand sources including AMX-VCI infantry and Timoney Mk.V/BDX wheeled APCs from Belgium and France. An attempt to provide the Mexican army with an airmobile capability through the transfer of 73 UH-1H from US Army stocks failed and the helicopters were returned to the USA after they were found to be ill-suited for operations in Mexico's high central altitude (*Air Forces Monthly*, December 1999, 14).

During the 1990s, the navy renovated its major surface combatant fleet, acquiring six frigates, two amphibious warfare vessels and two auxiliary ships from the US Navy at reduced prices. Local production of ocean patrol vessels (OPVs) began during the 1990s, with eight

Holzinger 2000 class vessels delivered from local shipyards (SHCP 2001). Six locally produced Oaxaca-class OPVs are planned, with two already delivered and two in production.

Prior to the mid-1990s, Mexican air force and navy helicopter procurement was dominated by Western aircraft. Since then, Russian and ex-Soviet equipment has taken their place, with 12 Mi-8T, 40 Mi-17 and two Mi-26s transferred between 1994 and 2001. Some 10 Antonov An-32 transports were also acquired for the navy and air force. The navy and the air force also took delivery of US$130m.-worth of surplus Israeli equipment during the early 2000s. Sales included two C-130E Hercules and four IAI Arava transports and four CH-53 Yasur helicopters for the air force, and two Aliya-class missile craft equipped with Gabrile SSM and three E-2C Hawkeye airborne early-warning aircraft for the navy.

In 2001 the air force acquired its first airborne early-warning capability with the $250m. purchase of one EMB-145SA and two EMB-145RS surveillance platforms from Brazil. This deal marked a shift in the country's defence procurement policy from purchases of surplus kit to newly-built equipment. Another example is the $14m. deal with China for new NORINCO M-90 howitzers, chosen in preference to surplus 105-mm Light Gun howitzers from the UK (SHCP 2004). However, it remains uncertain whether budget constraints will allow this change in acquisition policy to continue.

Since 2006 acquisitions have been redirected towards anti-drugs operations, with purchases of intelligence and surveillance force multipliers such as the Hermes 450 and Skylark I UAVs acquired through a $25m. deal with Israel in 2008 (*JDW*, 10 September 2008, 10). Also in 2008, the navy announced a $252m. deal for six CN-235MPA Persuader maritime patrol aircraft, as well as deals for three AS-565MB Panther embarked helicopters, to be delivered from 2010 (SHCP 2009). These purchases follow the acquisition of 39 CB90H (Polaris) fast assault craft from Sweden in 2000 for the Mexican Navy, which were also slated for anti-drugs operations (Dockstavarvet 2008).

Mexico's anti-drugs capabilities are also being supplemented by US military aid under the Merida initiative, aimed at improving the ability of Mexico and the countries of Central America to combat the threats associated with drugs-trafficking, transnational crime and terrorism (US Department of State 2007). In January 2009 the USA allocated $99m. for two Cessna 208 Caravan surveillance planes and an undisclosed number of Bell 412EP helicopters (*El Universal* online, 8 January 2009). A total of $205m. has been allocated for military acquisitions during fiscal year (FY) 2008, falling to $120m. for FY 2009, and $9m. for FY 2010 (US Congress 2008).

Central America is a relatively small defence market, with only four of the region's six Spanish-speaking countries fielding full-scale armed forces. Panama and Costa Rica rely on internal and public security forces for defence, while Guatemala, El Salvador, Honduras and Nicaragua still have relatively large stocks of weapons from the violent civil wars that peaked during the 1980s. Equipment is mostly ageing and largely inoperable in much of the region. In recent years, several impounded aircraft have been put into operational service.

In 2008 Guatemala, the largest country in the region, announced plans to modernize its armed forces and acquire six EMB-314 Super Tucano and 10 fast patrol boats from Brazil. Its only other significant acquisition since 1990 was of five T-35 Pillan trainers in 1998. El Salvador's large military shrank during the 1990s from 60,000 troops to about 15,000. Equipment acquisitions during this period were limited to five T-35 Pillan trainers and five Bell 412EP helicopters in the late 1990s and 2000s, and three second-hand IAI Arava STOL transports from Israel in 2007 (AFM, December 2007, 41; AFM, June 2008, 20). Outgoing President Saca announced in early 2009 that the government would seek $150m. for a military modernization programme (*elsalvador.com*, 8 January 2009).

The Honduran Air force received four Maule MXT-7-180 Super Rocket light aircraft in 2008, but this has been the only significant addition to its armed forces since 1990 (Fuerza Aérea de Honduras 2008). Its manpower and budget has also suffered a considerable decline. Finally, Nicaragua exported a significant amount of its inventory to Costa Rica, Ecuador and

Peru during the early 1990s, including 18 Mi-17 Hip, seven Mi-25 Hind radars and several hundred SA-16 SAMs, but did not make any significant acquisitions itself.

Venezuela and Colombia

Venezuela's military spending remained relatively stagnant during the 1990s and early 2000s and arms acquisitions were limited. Prior to 2006, the most significant transfers of major conventional weapons were in 1990–91 when France delivered 18 Mirage-50 combat aircraft, in 2000–02 when Italy delivered 12 SF-260M trainer aircraft and Poland delivered 18 M-28 transport aircraft. Until 2005 the primary sources of military equipment were the USA and Western Europe, which together accounted for 79% of Venezuela's imports for 1990–2005.

Since 2005 this picture has changed dramatically. Backed by rising oil prices, Venezuela boosted its military budget to $2.57 billion in 2007, an increase of 78% on 2003. Military spending is slated to rise further, to $3.1 billion in 2008 and $4.14 billion in 2009 (*JDW*, 12 November 2008, 7). This jump in spending has supported a raft of major arms acquisitions, the majority of which have been sourced in Russia. Between 2005 and 2007, Russia and Venezuela signed 12 contracts for arms supplies worth over $4.4 billion (*Kommersant* online, 25 September 2008). These deals covered the acquisition of 10 Mi-35 combat helicopters, three Mi-26 heavy transport helicopters, 40 Mi-17 multi-role helicopters, 100,000 AK-103 rifles and 24 Su-30MK combat aircraft. Contracts have also been signed for the construction of two factories in Venezuela, which will produce AK-103 rifles and related ammunition (*El Nacional* online, 1 June 2006). Since 2005 Venezuela has also signed deals for four Littoral Patrol Vessels and four frigate-size vessels from Spain, and 12 K-8 trainer aircraft and up to 10 JYL-1 radars from China. Venezuela has also signed a $1 billion military agreement with Belarus covering the installation of surface-to-air missile (SAM) systems (AP, 23 July 2007).

During 2007 and 2008 there were also reports of ongoing discussions on a raft of additional purchases by Venezuela, including Su-35 and Su-39 combat aircraft, An-74 and Il-76 transport aircraft, Il-78 tankers, Mi-28 combat helicopters, TOR-M1 and S-300 SAM systems, BMP-3 armoured vehicles, T-72 tanks and Kilo Class submarines, all from Russia. However, as of January 2009, no contracts had been signed for any of these deals.

Venezuela's arms purchases are geared towards a number of different goals. Many of Venezuela's acquisitions are replacements for outdated or obsolete weapons systems and, even with the signed deals, Venezuela still has limited capabilities in certain areas, including air transport. Since his election in 1999, President Hugo Chavez has sought to build stronger economic and political ties with non-Western states, particularly Russia, China, Belarus and Iran, and weapons purchases have been a means of cementing these links. President Chavez has also claimed that the USA may one day invade Venezuela to depose his government and, along with other Venezuelan officials, has highlighted deterring such an attack as a key rationale for many purchases (*JIR*, January 2007, 66).

In October 2006 the USA imposed an arms embargo on Venezuela, depriving it of spare parts for its existing US-supplied stocks. US re-export restrictions have also blocked Venezuela's attempts to purchase military equipment from the Czech Republic, Brazil, Israel, Spain and Sweden.

Colombia has steadily increased its military spending since the end of the Cold War, rising from $1,150m. in 1990 to $5,329m. in 2007. Meanwhile, a special tax levied in 2006 is set to finance about $4 billion-worth of equipment before President Alvaro Uribe leaves office in 2010 (*Defence Industry Daily*, 3 February 2009). When measured as a percentage of GDP, Colombia has had the highest level of military spending in Latin America since 2003. Colombia's main source of military equipment is the USA, which accounted for 71% of its arms imports between 1990 and 2007, much of which was funded by US aid. Since 1996, the USA has provided $5,800m. in military and police aid to Colombia.

Funds were initially focused on police counter-drugs operations, but the remit of the assistance has expanded, including military counter-drugs operations since 2000, and military counter-insurgency operations since 2002 (Center for International Policy et al. 2007, 16). Acquisitions funded by US aid since 1990 include five C-130B Hercules Transport aircraft, 33 OV-10 Bronco ground attack aircraft and over 100 Bell-205, Bell-212 and Blackhawk helicopters. However, US policy on military and police aid to Colombia has shifted since the Democratic Party gained a majority in the US Senate at the start of 2007, with a greater emphasis being placed on the human rights record of the Colombian security forces and the freezing or reduction of funds (*Reuters*, 19 April 2007).

Significant non-US purchases since 1990 include 14 EMB-312 and 25 EMB-314s from Brazil, delivered in 1992–93 and 2006–07, Griffin guided bombs and Python-3 air-to-air missiles from Israel, delivered in 2002–03 and 2005, and transport aircraft and 155mm howitzers from Spain. Despite its close ties with the USA, Colombia has also purchased military equipment from Russia in recent years. Colombia took delivery of 10 Mi-17 transport helicopters in 1997 and six more units were transferred in 2002. The initial purchase was reportedly prompted by US refusal to supply Blackhawks. In 2005 Colombia signed a deal for the local assembly of Russian-built BTR-80 APCs.

Since 1990 Colombian acquisitions have been driven by its four-decade-long war against left-wing insurgent groups and the fight against the drugs trade. However, since 2005 Colombian officials and commentators have also paid close attention to Venezuela's arms acquisitions (*Miami Herald* online, 27 April 2005). Colombia has diverted some of its investment towards attaining a credible conventional defence capability, leading some to claim a reversal of the government's previous emphasis on counter-insurgency equipment (*Semana*, 28 October 2006). Evidence includes the acquisition of 155 mm howitzers and C-295M transport aircraft from Spain, and 24 Kfir C.10 multi-role fighters and a B-767 converted to tanker configuration from Israel. However most attention continues to be focused on combating domestic threats.

The Andean republics (Ecuador and Peru)

Between 1990 and the 1995 Alto-Cenepa War between Ecuador and Peru, both countries took advantage of the end of the Cold War and the availability of large quantities of surplus equipment from both sides of the Iron Curtain. However, while Ecuador traditionally sourced its equipment from France, the UK and the USA, Peru favoured weapons from Russia and the former-Soviet Union. Indeed, Peru was the first non-socialist Latin American country to acquire weapons from the Soviet Union in 1973.

Ecuador's main acquisitions during these years were of a pair of Leander-class frigates decommissioned from the UK Royal Navy and two C-130B Hercules transports and A-37B Dragonfly COIN aircraft from US Air Force stocks. Peru's main acquisitions consisted of a $25m. contract with the newly elected government of Nicaragua, covering 7 Mi-25 Hind gunships, 15 Mi-17 helicopters and over 200 Igla SAMs, plus radars and logistic equipment. The army also acquired 18 Mi-17 helicopters from Russia, as well as several An-32 Cline transport aircraft from different sources.

After the Alto-Cenepa War, the modernization of both countries' armed forces took very different directions. While Peru sought to acquire a number of systems from second-hand sources in order to bolster and increase its capabilities, Ecuador sought to rationalize and enhance what it already had, upgrading eight of its Kfir C.2 fighter-bombers to the CE standard. The only significant purchase consisted of 222 SA-16 Gimlet MANPADS from Russia, this being the most notable time that Ecuador strayed from its traditional sources.

The Peruvian approach saw a $654m. deal with Belarus for the acquisition of 16 MiG-29 fighters and 18 Su-25 fighter-bombers, plus a large stockpile of missiles. This was the first major arms deal between a Latin American country and a former Soviet republic. The deal was plagued with corruption and severe after-sales support problems (El Comercio online, 5 June 2007). Belarus, which inherited a large number of former Soviet equipment, lacked the industrial capacity to adequately support the hardware it sold and the only companies that could provide an adequate overhaul and maintenance service were unwilling to do so. Peru agreed to acquire three brand new MiG-29SEs for $126m. from RAC-MiG before the Russian company agreed to provide an adequate service support for the ex-Belarus MiG-29s (Congreso de Peru 2002).

After signing a peace treaty in 1998, both countries disengaged from their long-standing competition with each other. However, their defence acquisitions continue to be heavily influenced by their respective neighbours' capabilities (Colombia's in the case of Ecuador and Chile's in the case of Peru).

Ecuador's threat perceptions are now mainly directed towards securing the northern border with Colombia (AFM, May 2006, 80). On 1 March 2008 Colombia attacked a FARC camp inside Ecuador. Ecuador had protested previous Colombian incursions into its airspace, most of which were carried out in hot pursuit of FARC forces (IISS 2007, 51). However, the March attack drew attention to Ecuador's ageing equipment and failing capacity to respond to threats inside and outside its borders. This accelerated and enhanced an armed forces modernization programme that began life in 2006. Originally focused on providing a stand-off surveillance capability to detect oil smugglers, the programme expanded to include providing surveillance on the border with Colombia. Relations with Colombia look set to be the main driver of Ecuadorian arms acquisitions during the next few years.

Total announced procurement spending since 2006 has reached $500m.; the air force has selected 24 EMB-314 Super Tucano attack aircraft, seven HAL ALH Dhruv tactical helicopters from India and new Chinese radars (*JDW*, 21 January 2009, 11). The Chinese purchase follows an October 2008 military co-operation agreement between China and Ecuador covering the exchange of military hardware for oil (*JDW*, 17 October 2008).

The army is to upgrade its existing five Super Puma helicopters and acquire new electronic surveillance systems, as well as replace its existing fleet of tanks with surplus Chilean Leopard 1V MBTs (*JDW*, 30 April 2008, 12; *JDW*, 9 January 2009, 11). The navy took delivery of a pair of Leander frigates surplus to the Chilean Navy and it ordered the IAI Heron and Searcher UAVs to be used in maritime surveillance activities (AFM, December 2008, 22).

Since 2000, Peru has focused on the Nucleo Básico Eficaz (NBE—Basic Efficient Nucleus) programme aimed at putting large amounts of stored or unserviceable equipment back into service. The 2002 Quiñonez Plan, implemented in 2007, centred on repairing helicopters, trainers and transport aircraft. It included the return to service of most of the MB-339AP, EMB-312 Tucano, Zlin Z-242, most of the larger transports from a variety of sources, and the Mi-17 fleet. The next phase of the programme will comprise the upgrade of the combat fleet: the Mirage 2000 fleet will be upgraded through a $120m. package with France, followed by a $60m. contract for the Su-25 Frogfoots and a $106m. for the upgrade of the MiG-29 fleet to a near SMT standard (El Comercio online, 24 Jul 2007; AFM, October 2008, 21).

The Peruvian Army's only significant acquisition in recent years has been a purchase of Spike and Kornet anti-tank missiles in early January 2009 – an apparent response to Chile's acquisition of Leopard 2 tanks (*peru.com*, 7 January 2009). This underlines the fact that although there are undoubtedly closer and friendlier relations with Chile, the modernization or expansion of its capabilities is still a matter for concern to Peru.

The central republics (Bolivia, Uruguay and Paraguay)

Bolivia, Uruguay and Paraguay are very different countries with distinct procurement policies, yet upon closer examination they display a number of common threads. All three have been relatively minor importers of military equipment during the 1990s, accounting for only 2% of total transfers to Latin America. They are also very interesting players in the global arms trade, acquiring equipment more often found in the museums of other states in the region. At the same time, Bolivia and Paraguay are heavily influenced by several regional and external powers (Argentina, Brazil and Taiwan in the case of Paraguay, and Venezuela, Spain and China in the case of Bolivia) and have relied on their generosity for many of the equipment needs. In contrast, Uruguay has shown greater independence in its procurement policies. Uruguay's substantial international peace-keeping commitments have been the main drivers in this area; a motivation which has often enabled it to obtain surplus equipment at lower than market prices, mainly from NATO countries.

With the end of the Cold War, Uruguay gained access to the lucrative surplus opportunities in both Eastern and Western Europe. The disbandment of the UK presence in Hong Kong saw Uruguay become the last recipient and operator of the Westland Wessex helicopter. From 1991 to 2002, the Uruguayan Navy and Air Force acquired 16 units. The navy acquired five surplus East German vessels as well as two Commandant Rivière-class frigates from France in 1991. The end of the Cold War also saw a shift towards the former Warsaw Pact countries as Uruguay sought to take advantage of the low prices on offer. Contact with the Czech Republic saw the acquisition of 60 OT-64 APCs in 1995, followed by a second batch of equipment that included 30 OT-64 APCs, 15 BMP-1 infantry fighting vehicles (IFV), six 2S1 (M1974) 122 mm SP howitzers and three MT-LB logistics vehicles. A 1997 deal with Israel saw the acquisition of 15 Ti-67 (modernized T-55) tanks and nine TCM-20 AA systems (Guevara 2005, FAM 57–62).

In a limited number of cases, Uruguay has acquired new hardware, such as 13 SF-260M basic trainers in 1999, an Indra Lanza 3D radar system in 2006 or 16 Boston Whaler patrol boats, but most of what it has received since 2000 has been obtained on the second-hand market. Examples include two Bell 212s obtained on the Dutch civilian market, three IA-58 Pucara attack aircraft from the Colombian Air Force, six former German Army Bo-105s, two Joao Belo (Commandant Rivière) class frigates from Portugal, four UH-1H helicopters from the Spanish Army and 40 General Dynamics Cougar 6x6 APC from Canada. The first 16 Cougars are to deploy to Congo (MONUC), while a second batch will be sent to Haiti's MINUSTAH (*JIDR*, January 2009, 21). The new patrol boats will also be deployed to Haiti.

Bolivia continued receiving limited amounts of aid from the USA in the immediate post-Cold War period, mainly as support for anti-drugs operations. This comprised six UH-1H Iroquois helicopters and a single C-130B Hercules transport. From the early 1990s, though, China became a new source for inexpensive equipment, with artillery holdings bolstered by the arrival of 36 Type 54-1 122-mm howitzers and 18 Type 67 AA guns in 1994. This was followed by some 10,000 AK-47 assault rifles and 28 HN-5A MANPADs during 1996. From 2001 the army also acquired HJ-8A Red Arrow anti-tank missiles from China. The arrival of an indigenous, left-wing government headed by President Evo Morales in 2006 has placed renewed attention on the armed forces' equipment and roles. The immediate priority for the Morales government has been restoring air mobility and this led to the acquisition of a mix of transport aircraft from the second-hand civilian sector during 2006–07. Bolivia has acquired a Fokker F.27, two BAE 146s, a Beech 1900D, a Convair CV-580 and a DC-10, all of which will be operated by the military-run TAM airline (*SAORBATS* online, 4 March 2008).

Venezuelan aid is not new to Bolivia and included a squadron of F-86 Sabre jet fighters in 1973 and eight VT-34 Mentor basic trainers in 2004 (AFM, August 2006, 24). Since 2006 Venezuela has loaned two AS-532 Cougar medium-lift helicopters under the SICOFAA (Air Forces of the Americas Co-operation System) and transferred two SA-316 Alouette III light helicopters. The loss of one of the Cougars and one of the Alouettes (in separate accidents) as well as the floods in 2007 highlighted the need for further helicopter acquisitions. In February 2008 Morales announced the pending acquisition of up to seven helicopters, including two for civil defence roles (*EFE*, 14 February 2008). Attention has since shifted to securing the country's airspace. In December 2008 Morales announced that he had authorized the acquisition of six L-159 ALCA jet fighters from the Czech Republic for $57.8m. (*JDW*, 7 January 2009, 11). Morales also announced that these would be the country's first purpose-bought anti-drugs fighter aircraft.

One of the poorest countries in Latin America, Paraguay's recent acquisitions have been donations from Taiwan and, more recently, Brazil and Argentina. In 1990 Taiwan provided the air force with six AT-33 armed jet trainers and in 1995 offered to donate 12 F-5E/F Tiger II tactical fighters. As these would have been a drain on already scarce operational resources, Taiwan instead provided six UH-1H Iroquois helicopters, which arrived in 2001. In 2005 Brazil donated six T-25C Universal basic trainers and offered to provide a complete overhaul to the fleet of 40 ENGESA EE-9 and EE-11 armoured cars that Paraguay acquired from Brazil in 1984. Argentina is increasingly becoming the country's main source of military aid, with six Bofors L/60 AA guns delivered in 2007 and a commitment to deliver up to 20 WW2 M9 track APCs and M-1935 75-mm field howitzer (*SAORBATS* online, 22 July 2008). Paraguay's only significant acquisition during the past few years was a single CASA C-212-400 Aviocar transport aircraft delivered in 2003.

Brazil

Between 2003 and 2007 Brazil accounted for 46% of total military spending in Latin America. Significant post-1990 arms transfers to Brazil include the transfer of four second-hand Type-22 frigates from the UK and a second-hand aircraft carrier from France. During the late 1990s and early 2000s a number of major weapons purchases were either cancelled, delayed or replaced with less ambitious purchases. Plans to purchase new fighter aircraft to replace the Mirage IIIs and F-5s in service – the 'F-X' programme – were originally outlined in 2000 but delayed and then down-sized in favour of second-hand Mirage 2000s, F-5s and upgrades to the existing fleet. Overall, Brazil fell from being the 21st-largest recipient of military equipment in the world for the period 1998–2002, to the 32nd-largest for 2003–07.

Collectively, France, Germany, the UK and the USA accounted for 79% of arms transfers to Brazil between 1990 and 2007, with the UK accounting for 27%, followed by France with 22%. Post-2006 deliveries have included 12 second-hand Mirage-2000C combat aircraft from France; 11 second-hand F-5E/F combat aircraft from Jordan; 12 C-295M transport aircraft from Spain; and six S-70 Blackhawk helicopters from the USA. Brazil is also modernizing its fleet of F-5E combat aircraft, equipping them with Derby air-to-air missiles from Israel.

Since mid-2007, Brazil has made a series of announcements on a set of long-planned, though frequently delayed, weapons acquisitions, signalling a renewed willingness to improve and upgrade its military forces. In July 2007 the government revived a long-standing project to build a nuclear-powered submarine. First discussed in 1979, though subject to numerous delays, the latest version of the plan will involve Brazil investing 1 billion reais ($560m.) over eight years to purchase technology to build the submarine and to develop a nuclear reactor with Argentina to power the boat (*Reuters* online, 11 July 2007). Brazil is also moving ahead with plans to build 50 EC-725 Super Cougar helicopters and four conventional submarines. In addition, Brazil has re-launched the 'F-X' combat aircraft programme, allocating $2.2 billion for an initial procurement of 20–36 aircraft, although the final number purchased may be up to 120 (*Flight International* online, 12 November 2007). Acquisitions will be backed up by an increase in Brazil's military budget, which rose from 6.5 billion reais ($3.64 billion) in 2007 to 10 billion reais ($5.6 billion) in 2008 (*Xinhua* online, 31 October 2007).

Other Brazilian arms purchases continue to be hampered by the lack of a centralized procurement system. As a result, different branches of the armed forces continue to pursue parallel programmes for the acquisition of similar weapons systems, as with the army's and marines' efforts to purchase amphibious armoured personnel carriers. While the army has launched and re-launched competitions for a new family of vehicles to be developed and built locally based on a foreign design – the VBTP-MR, which is based on the IVECO Puma – the marines have opted for an off-the-shelf purchase of General Dynamics Land Systems Piranha III. To date, the Marines have 12 Piranhas in service and 18 more on order, while development of the VBTP-MR is yet to reach fruition (*JDW*, 21 November 2008, 12).

Brazil's post-Cold War acquisitions have been motivated by a number of priorities. First and foremost, Brazil has focused on the acquisition of capabilities that will help it to better police the country's vast coastline and remote border areas, particularly in the Amazon region (*Mercopress* online, 6 November 2007). There has also been speculation that certain of Brazil's purchases, particularly the revived and expanded FX2 programme, may be a response to Venezuelan arms acquisitions. Brazil's 2007 procurement announcements came in the wake of a string of commentaries by Brazilian analysts and former government officials raising questions about Venezuela's arms purchases (*LASSR*, November 2007, 11).

Brazil has also long sought use of its foreign arms acquisitions as a means of boosting its domestic arms industry by insisting on significant levels of technology transfer and this remains the case today. During the 1980s Brazil had the most successful military industry in Latin America with well-developed production capabilities in the fields of tanks, infantry fighting vehicles, troop carriers, heavy trucks, aircraft and rocket launchers (AP online, 4 September 2008). It was a significant exporter of military equipment and the 11th-largest supplier in the world for the period 1984–88. However, much of this success was based upon transfers to Iraq during the Iran–Iraq War and the industry suffered greatly after the conflict ended in 1988. Today, Brazil is able meet most of its procurement needs within certain fields of the aerospace sector and light armoured vehicles through local production, but has not regained the level of exports it had in the mid-1980s.

To strengthen Brazil's defence industry, the government has stated that the arms procurement deals announced since mid-2007 will include production in Brazil and significant levels of technology transfer (*Mercopress* online, 6 November 2007). France's Eurocopter and DCNS have emerged as the key winners in the latest round of contract awards, largely due to their greater willingness to meet Brazilian demands on these issues. If Brazil is to achieve a long-term increase in the size of its defence industry it will need to boost its level of arms exports. In this regard, Brazil may be helped by the latest round of defence modernization plans among Latin American states. During 2008 there were reports of advanced negotiations on the sale of EMB-314s to Bolivia, Chile, the Dominican Republic, Ecuador and Guatemala. Prior to 2008 the only foreign buyer for the EMB-314 had been Colombia.

Southern cone (Argentina and Chile)

Chile and Argentina began the 1990s with recent memories of the right-wing military dictatorships that ruled both countries during much of the 1970s and 1980s (up till 1983 in the case of Argentina and 1990 in the case of Chile). One of the legacies of the long years of military rule in Chile is a constitutionally guaranteed appropriation for defence spending via the so-called 'copper law', in which the armed forces receive 10% of revenue for defence procurement from copper sales from the state-controlled CODELCO. In contrast, one of the legacies in Argentina has been strained relations between the civilian governments and military forces, and frequent accusations of under-funding by the latter.

Despite the Copper Law, Chile's military spending remained relatively stable during the 1990s and early 2000s. Indeed, Chile's military spending fell from 4.3% of GDP in 1990 to 3.2% in 1997. Major acquisitions during these years included 25 second-hand Mirage fighter aircraft from Belgium, delivered in 1995–96. Chilean defence budgets increased significantly in the 2000s, partly fuelled by an increase in world copper prices, nearly doubling in size between 1997 and 2007. This increase has funded a wave of major arms acquisitions under an ambitious force modernization programme.

Since 2005 Chile has taken delivery of 10 newly built F-16C/D combat aircraft from the USA; 18 second-hand F-16AM/BM combat aircraft, two second-hand Doorman frigates and two second-hand Van Heemskerck frigates from the Netherlands; three second-hand Type-23 frigates from the UK; 24 second-hand M-109 155-mm self-propelled guns from Switzerland; the first 112 of 140 second-hand Leopard 2A4 tanks from Germany; two Scorpene submarines built by France and Spain; and Derby and Python-4 air-to-air missiles from Israel. In 2008 Chile also placed an order for 12 EMB-314 Super Tucano aircraft from Brazil. Increased arms transfers have seen Chile rise from the 38th-largest recipient of military equipment for the period 1998–2002, to the 12th-largest recipient for the period 2003–07 and the largest in Latin America. Despite this rise, Chile accounted for just 2% of global transfers of major conventional weapons for the period 2003–07.

Chile's acquisitions replace mostly ageing or decommissioned systems and most purchases are of second-hand equipment. However, the purchases of F-16 aircraft, Scorpene submarines, Type-23 frigates and Leopard 2A4 tanks also indicate a significant qualitative advance, particularly in comparison with the armed forces of other countries in the region. Indeed, Chile has emerged with the most advanced military force in Latin America. These acquisitions, particularly the 2002 purchase of F-16s, sparked some concerns in Bolivia and Peru, both of which have long-standing border disputes with Chile (*JDW*, 6 July 2005, 8). At the same time, Chile has also been involved in the development of a range of Confidence Building Measures (CBMs) with its neighbours on defence and security issues (Bromley and Perdomo 2005).

Chile has also been a supplier of military equipment to other states in Latin America. Between 1991 and 2002 Chile supplied 37 of its indigenously produced T-35 Pilan aircraft to the Dominican Republic, El Salvador, Guatemala, Panama and Paraguay. More recently, Chilean sales have been boosted by the increased procurement activity of other states in the region, particularly in Ecuador. In 2008 Chile delivered two second-hand Leander frigates to Ecuador and is also upgrading two of its Type 209 submarines. Reports in early 2009 indicate that Chile and Ecuador have reached an agreement on the sale of 30 second-hand Leopard-1Vs which Chile acquired in 1999–2000, but is retiring to make way for the Leopard 2A4s from Germany (*JDW*, 14 January 2009, 11).

Argentina's military spending remained largely static during the 1990s. However, in contrast to Chile there has been no subsequent upswing in spending during the 2000s. Indeed, in constant (2005) dollars Argentina's military spending actually fell from $2,074 billion in 1997 to $1,752 billion in 2007. Much of this drop is attributable to the 2002 financial crisis, which saw the Argentine economy contract by 10.9%, leading the government to default on a number of international loans, while making it harder for the government to obtain new credit for weapons purchases. Indeed, the financial crisis led to the shelving of a number of air force modernization projects (Perlo-Freeman 2003).

Compared with Chile, Argentina has not been a major player in the global arms trade in recent years. Several major acquisitions were made in 1998–2000 but subsequent purchases have been limited. Since 1990, 35% of Argentina's arms acquisitions have come from Germany and 55% from the USA.

Argentina's position in the world arms market is affected by its strong defence industry, which allows the military to fulfill many of its equipment needs domestically. The Argentine defence industry has managed to produce or design a range of systems under licence, including main battle tanks, submarines, ground attack aircraft and howitzers. Argentina was the first Latin American country to design and fly an indigenous jet fighter, and is also the first in the region to establish a programme for the development of an indigenous UAV (*Unmanned Vehicles*, May 2008, 24).

In October 2007 Argentina announced the launch of a multi-year funding programme designed to restore and enhance the operational capabilities of the armed forces. The plan may result in $200m. a year of additional funding for the period 2008–13 (*JDW*, 31 October

2007, 32). Argentina is also advancing long-standing plans to purchase new fighter aircraft and was understood to be considering offers of second-hand Mirage-2000 aircraft from France and second-hand F-16s from the USA. However, as with the rest of Argentina's modernization plans, the fighter aircraft plan has yet to bear fruit in terms of concrete orders (*Mercopress* online, 22 December 2007). It remains to be seen whether the current financial crisis will affect Argentina's force modernization plans in the same way that plans were affected by the downturn in the early 2000s.

Conclusions

The overall picture that emerges from this survey of recent developments with regard to arms modernization in Latin America is one of continuity rather than change. Several countries in the region have embarked on ambitious arms modernization programmes, fuelled either by rising commodity prices, as in Chile or Venezuela, or increased national prosperity, as in Brazil. However, despite the warnings of a regional arms race, most of the purchases that have taken place in recent years are the culmination of long-discussed acquisition plans, most of which are aimed at replacing or updating obsolete systems. While defence spending and imports have increased in recent years, this also comes off the back of a prolonged period of falling or stagnating budgets and often vocal criticism from the military concerning underfunding.

That said, questions can still be asked with regards to the wisdom and suitability of many of the purchases. In particular, Venezuela's Su-30 acquisition was criticised by many as a waste of resources and out of proportion with the actual defence needs of the country. Brazil's renewed interest in a nuclear-powered submarine has also drawn attention for similar reasons. In addition, there are clear signs of competitive behaviour in certain purchases that states have made recently, with Peru keeping a close eye on Chile's acquisitions and Colombia and Brazil both eyeing Venezuela.

As noted, many commentators have recently drawn attention to the emergence of Russia as a key supplier to Latin America. However, perhaps the more interesting development identified in this chapter is the growing role of other emerging suppliers, such as China and, to a lesser extent, India. These countries look set to join the long list of suppliers competing for Latin American business, possibly driving down prices and undermining any attempts on the part of the USA to limit the introduction of certain weapons systems into the region.

Also noteworthy is Brazil's rediscovered insistence on high levels of technology transfer in its latest round of arms acquisitions, and the extent to which this is favouring French suppliers at the expense of both the USA and Russia. Other countries also appear to be seeking to strengthen their defence industrial base through the licensed production of foreign-designed equipment. However, the extent to which states will succeed in this regard remains an open question. Overall, the level of capability in the region's defence industries is lower now than it was in the 1980s, when Argentina and Brazil were able to produce an array of different technologies from scratch.

Brazil's long-term goal is to re-energize its own domestic defence industry and regain the level of exports it achieved in the 1980s. The extent to which it manages to achieve this goal may depend on the extent to which it is able to capitalize on the latest round of regional modernization programmes among other countries in the region. Chile's defence industry is also benefitting from the latest round of acquisitions, particularly those being made by Ecuador. Both countries will provide interesting indicators of the extent to which defence industries in the region are becoming truly revitalized.

Still unclear is how the latest financial crisis will affect the continent's arms-acquisition programmes. During 2001–02 many acquisition programmes were cancelled as governments battled with the fallout from the Argentine financial crisis. If, as many predict, the global financial crisis that started in 2008 is more severe than in the early 2000s, it could have a serious impact on state defence plans. Upcoming fighter-aircraft purchases by Brazil and the extent to which Venezuela follows through on its set of follow-on purchases from Russia, will provide a clearer bell-weather in this regard.

Bibliography

Note: Unless otherwise stated, all information relating to arms transfers mentioned in this chapter is based on the information provided by the SIPRI Arms Transfers Database, www.sipri.org/contents/armstrad/at_db.html (accessed November 2008 January 2009).

Air Forces Monthly (AFM)

Arévalo de León, Bernado, 'Good Governance In Security Sector As Confidence Building Measures In The Americas: Towards Pax Democratica', DCAF, Geneva, 2002

Associated Press (AP)

Bromley, Mark and Catalina Perdomo, *CBMs in Latin America and the Effect of Arms Acquisitions by Venezuela*, Real Instituto Elcano Working Paper No. 41, September 2005

Center for International Policy et al., 'Below the Radar: U.S. military programs with Latin America, 1997–2007', a joint publication from the Center for International Policy, the Latin America Working Group Education Fund, and the Washington Office on Latin America, March 2007

———'Just the Facts: A Civilian's Guide to U.S. defense and security assistance to Latin America and the Caribbean', a joint publication from the Center for International Policy, the Latin America Working Group Education Fund, and the Washington Office on Latin America, justf.org

Congreso de Peru (Congress of Peru), *Hechos del Conflicto Fronterizo con el Ecuador*, 2002, www.congreso.gob.pe/comisiones/2002/CIDEF/denuncias/c_compara.pdf

Defence Industry Daily

Dockstavarvet, 'The IC 16 M Success Continues', press release, 14 August 2008

EFE

El Clarín (online)

El Nacional (online)

El Universal (online)

elsalvador.com

Flight International

Fuerza Aérea de Honduras, 'Llegada de las Maule', July 2008

Grimmett, Richard F., *Conventional Arms Transfers to Latin America: US Policy*, CRS (Congressional Research Service) Report, US Library of Congress, 97–512 F, 5 August 1997

Guevara, Iñigo, 'Ejército Nacional Uruguayo (Uruguayan National Army)', in *Fuerzas Militares del Mundo*, Madrid, Ikonos Press SL, 2005

IISS, *The Military Balance 2007*, London: International Institute for Strategic Studies, 2007

Jane's Defense Weekly (JDW)

Jane's Intelligence Review (JIR)

Jane's International Defense Review (JIDR)

Kommersant (online)

Latin American Security & Strategic Review (LASSR)

Mercopress (online)

Miami Herald

Perlo-Freeman, Sam, 'Survey of military expenditure in South America', A background paper to the SIPRI Yearbook chapter on military expenditure, June 2003

peru.com

Reuters

SAORBATS (online)

Secretaría de Hacienda y Crédito Público (SHCP) [Ministry of Finance and Public Credit], Causan Baja del Servicio Activo de la Armada de México 19 Buques, press release, 19 July 2001

———Cartera de programas y Proyectos de Inversión, SEDENA, Adquisición de obsueros, August 2004

———Presupuesto de Egresos de la Federación (PEF) 2009 [Federation 2009 Expenditure Budget], Secretaría de Marina (SEMAR) [Ministry of the Navy], Programas y Proyectos de Inversión, 2009, www.apartados.hacienda.gob.mx/presupuesto/temas/pef/2009/temas/tomos/13/r13_pir.pdf

Semana (Bogotá)

Unmanned Vehicles

US Congress, *Merida Initiative to Combat Illicit Narcotics and Reduce Organized Crime Authorization Act of 2008*, 11 June 2008

US Department of State, *Joint Statement on the Merida Initiative: A New Paradigm for Security Cooperation*, 22 October 2007

Xinhua (online)

13 The global arms trade

Challenges for Africa?

Martin Rupiya

Introduction

In the realm of global arms trading, does Africa matter? There are huge contrasts between the continent and other regions, most of which do not depict Africa as of any consequence. Global arms trading is serious business, reaching US$60 billion in 2007, confined to only five industrialized countries: the USA, Russia, France, the United Kingdom (UK) and Germany, with Spain and Italy not far behind (Grimmett 2008, 1–4; Holtom et al. 2008). These countries account for over 80% of arms sold over a seven-year period, 2000–07 (Shah 2008). Curiously, the arms trade is also limited to a handful of recipients, only one of which is African: Egypt. Table 13.1 shows the top 10 in the period 1999–2006.

Furthermore, the People's Republic of China and Ukraine must also be considered significant players. In the case of China, whilst the country is a major recipient of arms from the industrialized countries, it also features as a major source supply for quantities of conventional weapons to several African states. Meanwhile, the African continent, especially the 47 sub-Saharan states, has the majority of its members, 28, firmly lodged in the World Bank and International Monetary Fund (IMF) category of Highly Indebted Poor Countries (HIPC). This means that the majority of African states cannot afford to pay the vast sums involved in the global arms trade. Yet, the reality has been and continues to be that Africa remains at the very heart of global arms trading with serious implications for much-needed social improvement and development. Why this phenomenon continues to hold true is the purpose of this chapter, which is structured to provide an analysis of the rationale, causes and implications of the global arms trade against Africa's quest for stability and development. This chapter argues three main reasons: the foreign policy interests of weapons manufacturers; the fragility of African states, forced to survive on marshalling superior military power; and, finally, that traditional trade relations inherited over time, combined, represent the motivations for placing

Table 13.1 Arms sales by agreements to developing nations, 1999–2006 (US$)

Country	Sales (in bn)	Percentage
India	31.9	13
Saudi Arabia	26.4	11
China, People's Repub.	16.0	7
United Arab Emirates	14.3	6
Pakistan	13.7	6
Egypt	12.3	5
Israel	9.5	4
South Korea	8.9	4
Syria	6.1	3

Source: Grimmett 2007

Africa at the heart of this dynamic now and in the future. Any efforts to reverse this trend will have to come from a policy convergence of the three constituencies. Holtom et al. provide a more elaborate menu of motivations when they argue that:

> Acquisitions have been primarily motivated by efforts to replace or upgrade military inventories ... ; to respond to predominantly domestic security threats; to strengthen ties with supplier governments; to enhance domestic arms industry capability; or to bolster regional or international profile.
>
> (Holtom et al. 2008)

Part of the explanation for the continued involvement of even new states with global arms trade is what Robin Luckham asserts in his analysis of 'Africa: Arming the State', in which he argued that:

> Military muscle: the arms business is booming south of the Sahara. So is the power and prestige of Africa's men in uniform. Weapons are indeed evocative symbols of state power and national independence ... as the military's fire power has grown so has its political power.
>
> (Luckham 1984)

Luckham, then, sees a mendacious relationship between weapons acquisition and political influence viewed as a precondition for the consolidation of most post-colonial states. Furthermore, this quest by the political elite has found resonance with the foreign policy interests of the major global arms manufacturers, prepared to deliver weapons not for commercial reasons, but for other national interests. Based on an understanding of industrialized world readiness to feed this ready and waiting dimension of the political elite on the African continent, this chapter argues that rather than address the more fundamental issues of poverty reduction, food and human security interests of the common citizen, there is an intersection between the foreign policy intentions of the five or six leading global arms leaders and the African political elite, which will keep the dark, poor continent in the global arms trade for a long time to come. Therefore, we must first define our understanding of the global arms trade in Africa that informs this discussion.

Secondly, it is also useful to paint a brief picture of the common political trend that characterizes the Africa that has emerged since the significant changes in global international relations following the end of the Cold War in 1991. The continent is emerging from the politically stultifying grip of the strong-man and one-party state systems that were a common feature following widespread decolonization in the 1960s. This is an Africa in transition, characterized by fragile and even collapsed states, led by an insecure and generally frightened political elite, precariously dominating the state capitals and little else. Most of the regimes have not had the inclination or the opportunity to embark upon nation building and consolidation of the state (Clapham 2001).

Even where it appears that this has happened, the fragility of African states has still to be fully appreciated. For instance, the speed and extent of signs of state collapse and ethnic differences in the stalled Kenyan election at the end of 2007 demonstrates the point. Furthermore, some of the largest African states are still without stable central governments and fall into what can be termed 'treaty states'. These include the Democratic Republic of Congo (DRC), Algeria, Sudan, Kenya, Angola, Burundi, Mozambique and Zimbabwe, where state control is contested and shared under some legal arrangement before a nationally legitimate entity can emerge. Consequently, these treaty states represent something of an interim measure, unable to turn their attention to the weighty matters of state consolidation. Within the countryside their authority is openly challenged by a variety of rebel groups, as has been or continues to be the case in Angola, Uganda, Sudan, Chad, Mozambique, Cote d'Ivoire, Somalia, Burundi, Rwanda, DRC, Central African Republic (CAR), Guinea Bissau, Eritrea and Ethiopia amongst others.

The continent fell under the international rivalry of the Cold War, with leaders forced to choose between East and West and, by implication, continue to be propped up within undemocratic environments under the sphere of influence dynamic. The clearest illustrations of this would be the USA support of President Mobutu Sese Seko in the then Zaire (now DRC), and the equally unqualified Russian support for President Mengistu Haile Mariam in Ethiopia. The contemporary Africa we are now dealing with is that emerging from these periods of nuanced international relationships, which had direct influence on global arms trade with the continent.

Samuel Huntington in his seminal work, *The Third Wave: Democratisation in the Late Twentieth Century*, provides the most useful theoretical framework of the external/international forces pushing for democratic transition and the context of local responses that we see on the ground in African states (Huntington 1993; London 1993). Furthermore, Huntington in his theory also warned us of possible reverses that may occur in the democratization process and, significantly, how some of the states actually could serve as catalyst for a broader regional reversal. The effects of Somalia in the Horn of Africa, Kenya in eastern Africa, the DRC in Central Africa, Zimbabwe in southern Africa and Cote d'Ivoire in western Africa fall into this category: where debilitating circumstances have a contagious regional effect. As a result, Huntington warned us to be wary and prepare to respond quickly to potential reverses, which may than precipitate a wider influence.

An interesting observation by Huntington showed the percentage of reverses that are part of each wave, from the first in 1828–1926, followed by the second in 1943–62 and the current one, which began in the 1970s.

International modalities of trade with a continent of states that are unable to pay

Despite the African continent's inability to pay for major weapons systems from the industrialized countries, African states have continued to receive arms. So what are the major reasons for this seemingly odd relationship? First, arms trade is not a generalized business but something that is closely tied to decisions by states to address core security concerns in terms of domestic major weapons supply. The economic capacity to do this is relative, for only a handful of countries have been able to do so, including the USA, Russia, Germany, France, the UK, Italy, China, Portugal and Spain. In each weapons-manufacturing state, developing nations protect and support the national military industrial base from foreign intrusion, while recouping some costs on research and development from limited sales outside. This means that the industry is not intended for profit, but is heavily subsidized and imbued in the ethos of national security.

In order to cover the seemingly unsustainable cost, with the only significant cost recovery occurring from weapons sales to the Near East and Asia, in the case of Africa, only the military appears to be going through modernization, leaving other sectors gasping for resources. In this environment, major powers have resorted to 'creative selling', including counter-trade, debt relief and offering almost unrestricted credit for clients to purchase arms from them (Grimmett 2008, 6). For example, Russian sales to Latin America have been structured around what is referred to as flexible debt forgiveness, for purposes of encouraging them to acquire new arms. A similar arrangement has been seen in the UK and France during 1999–2008, when clients were treated to special weapons systems as part of maintaining traditional links and solidarity. In some instances, this relationship has been carefully managed, as seen in the Mark Abrams tanks production plants located in Egypt by the USA, which not only provides opportunities for local jobs, but is a strong foreign-policy statement of military co-operation and allied interests. In the case of the French, the Reinforcement Capacities of African Militaries peace-keeping notion (RECAMP) has witnessed the positioning of military equipment in former Francophone countries, a clear link with a desire to perpetuate and strengthen former colonial ties through military association. More recently, the European Union approach to arms sales in the former Eastern European states is instructive:

> There are inherent limitations on … European sales due to the smaller defense budgets of many of the purchasing countries. Yet creative seller financing options, as well as the use of co-assembly, co-production, and counter-trade agreements to offset costs to the buyers continue to facilitate new arms agreements.
>
> (Grimmett 2008, 5)

This assertion was made in the light of fierce competition between the European and US arms manufacturers, in which the former sought to protect the regional market (Grimmett 2008, 5).

What this signifies is that states that desire to acquire weapons do not necessarily have to have the financial wherewithal, as this can be bridged by mutual foreign-policy interests of the major suppliers, to result in deliveries based on some future commitment.

Definition of arms trade: Africa and the global community

Engagement in the global arms trade, which has seen China, India and Pakistan receiving nuclear weapons assistance from the industrialized world differs greatly from the norm on the African continent. In Africa, the greatest threat is in fact the AK47 rifle, which has become the weapon of choice for both governments and rebel groups (Tutu 2009). The two African countries with nuclear capability, Egypt and South Africa, both decided for different reasons (in 1965 for Egypt and in 1993 for South Africa) to voluntarily abandon pursuing 'offensive' nuclear weapons (Rupiya 2004). This should be distinguished from their use of nuclear technology for peaceful purposes, such as generating electricity. This apart, the reality of arms trade between Africa and the major suppliers is conventional weapons, including ships, submarines, aircraft-fighters, helicopters, transporters, tanks, armoured cars, heavy artillery and mortars. Using this definition, then, what is the evidence of weapons in Africa? Below we reflect on some of the weapons delivered during 2000–07 (Grimmett 2008, 61).

From Table 13.2 we can see that Africa has sufficient tanks and self-propelled guns, artillery, armoured personnel carriers, combat aircraft, helicopters, ships and submarines to engage in several small wars for a long time to come. Certainly from the ongoing agreements and foreign policy positions of states, this is likely to continue.

Defining the global arms trade in relation to arms transfers to Africa

When quantifying weapons deliveries to Africa, one has to examine two components: agreements signed between governments, which is not true of those weapons going to rebel movements; and secondly, actual deliveries of items supplied. Significantly, this recommended measurement does not take into account those weapons supplied to rebel movements or even those intended to be received by states which then fall into rebel hands, given the deniability clauses around the arms trade as well as the dubious end-user certificates. The latter is an international instrument designed to determine the end user of weapons delivered by any supplier, a system that has been abused to the point that it now lacks integrity or relevance. To further reinforce this point, recently a Ukrainian ship plying the waters off Somalia fell victim to the increasing piracy. On board were 33 tanks, complete with large quantities of ammunition, destined for an African country off the East African coast. It has never been made clear whether these were arms ordered by Kenya or the Sudan, a country under

Table 13.2 Weapons delivered to African countries, 2000 07

Weapons category	USA	Russia	China, People's Repub.	Major European states	Other European	All others
2000 03						
Tanks and self-propelled guns	0	10	60	0	180	60
Artillery	0	430	160	20	470	480
APCs and armoured cars	0	150	0	50	550	360
Major surface combatants	0	0	0	1	0	0
Minor surface combatants	0	2	9	10	20	27
Guided missile boats	0	0	0	0	0	0
Submarines	0	0	0	0	0	0
Supersonic combat aircraft	0	10	10	0	40	30
Subsonic combat aircraft	0	10	0	0	10	0
Other aircraft	0	0	20	10	20	10
Helicopters	0	70	10	10	40	20
Surface-to-air missiles	0	70	0	0	70	20
Surface-to-surface missiles	0	40	0	0	0	0
Anti-ship missiles	0	0	0	0	0	0
2004 07						
Tanks and self-propelled guns	0	0	0	0	280	10
Artillery	0	0	240	0	1,120	650
APCs and armoured cars	0	0	370	50	160	130
Major surface combatants	0	0	29	3	0	1
Minor surface combatants	0	0	0	9	20	7
Guided missile boats	0	0	0	0	0	1
Submarines	0	0	0	2	0	0
Supersonic combat aircraft	0	20	10	0	0	0
Subsonic combat aircraft	0	0	0	10	0	0
Other aircraft	0	0	40	0	10	10
Helicopters	0	30	0	30	20	10
Surface-to-air missiles	0	100	0	10	0	0
Surface-to-surface missiles	0	0	0	0	0	0
Anti-ship missiles	0	0	0	10	0	0

Source: Arms Deliveries to the World by Major Suppliers, 1999 2006, http://www.photius.com/ranking/ arms_sales_major_suppliers_1999_2006html accessed 30 January 2009. Data compiled by the Federation of American Scientists, Washington DC, USA

Note: All data are for calendar years given. Major West European data includes France, United Kingdom, Germany, and Italy totals as an aggregate figure. Data relating to surface-to-surface and anti-ship missiles by foreign suppliers are estimates based on a variety of sources having a wide range of accuracy. As such, individual data entries in these two weapons delivery categories are not necessarily definitive

sanctions and, therefore, unable to openly procure arms, but the reality is that an African rebel group then had well-equipped tanks in its hands. In conventional terms, you need a tank to fight a tank and much more importantly, you need a higher ratio. Hence, for the 33 tanks known to have been taken, a counter force deployed would have to have, as a minimum, over 100 tanks before mounting an offensive.

The requirement of tanks by leaders precariously holding onto power in many new and emerging states is something that has continued to have resonance. This is true of both civilian and military leaders. For example, in both successful and unsuccessful military coup attempts, the tank or its alternatives – such as the open-backed Toyota Land Cruiser, in which a couple of drums of fuel are loaded and normally a 14.5 double barrelled machine gun with an anti-air capability is mounted alongside – have continued to feature. This trend was witnessed in Ghana with Lieutenant Jerry Rawlins marching on the castle; Staff Sergeant Samuel Doe in Liberia and Captain Thomas Sankara in Upper Volta. In late December 2008, a military coup followed the reported death of President Lasana Conte, who left behind no obvious successor (ABC News, 2008). Led by 44-year old Captain Moussa Dadis Camara, the first sight of the new leader was of him perched on a smoke-belching tank, careering around the city with him wrapped in the Guinean flag.

During February 2008, Chad's former military coup leader in 1990, President Idris Derby, faced the arrival of several cruisers, commanded by the rebel Union of Forces for Democracy and Development, elements of a splinter group, UFDD-F, led by Mahamat Nouri, as well as the Rally of Democratic Forces, deep inside the capital, N'Djamena. The State House was pounded until the rebels were overcome by a French intervention force. Soon afterwards, cruisers from the Darfur rebel movement, Justice for Equality Movement appeared in Khartoum, Sudan, succeeding in causing consternation amongst the local population, demonstrating that Sudanese government forces had not succeeded in putting down this group and its supporters. Further evidence of the fragility of these states is the existence of long-running protracted battles between ethnic and regional groups, such as those in Sudan between north and south; the conflict in northern Uganda that started in 1986 between the Lords's Resistance Army and the Uganda People's Defence Forces. There are also similar examples in Cote d'Ivoire, Burundi, Chad, Rwanda, Eritrea and Ethiopia. In each instance, the central government has failed to stamp out the internal challenge and survive only as a result of showing the impenetrable defences of the nation.

However, each of the protracted conflicts has generated other dimensions, such as refugees, millions of internally displaced people, as well as turning fertile food-producing areas into theatres of war resulting in acute food insecurity. With governments already weakened by efforts for simple self-preservation, these new manifestations of conflict have met with little or no capacity to respond.

The second cause fuelling arms procurement by the African political elite is the sharp religious and cultural divide within communities. This has become more marked since the 'war on terror' launched by the USA following the events of 11 September 2001. In an already-volatile area such as the Horn of Africa, this has emerged as one of the most divisive issues, even pitting the African Union against the neighbouring Arab League, to which countries such as Sudan and Egypt enjoy dual membership.

Another factor in arms procurement by African countries is the regional instability over territorial disputes, a common feature of the colonially drawn borders. In May 1963, when the then Organization of African Unity (OAU) was established, the issue was seen as a flash point and recommendations were made to 'accept the inherited' borders and only later, when the whole continent had been decolonized, return to the issue. In reality, though, the issue has refused to disappear and continues to undermine national and regional security. Former colonial powers acting in support of particular regimes in the different countries has exacerbated an already trying situation. The response by African states has been to invest in arms and newer weapons systems. The most graphic example of this is the difficulty in harmonizing regional security interests amongst former colonial countries in West Africa, where Nigeria and Ghana, former British colonies, have found themselves pitted against the eight former French colonies. While the latter enjoy a common currency, greater access to French weaponry and a common language, regional security co-ordination has not come naturally.

Taking this into account, Robin Luckham is correct when he asserts that heavy weapons represent the evocative symbol of state power, but also the effective instrument for state survival (Luckham 1984, 1). He further points out that, 'several countries now have quite powerful armoured corps including tanks and modern artillery' (Ibid).

Africa and a (restrictive) arms treaty?

Given the dynamics of global arms trade and the negative implications of the process and impact of arms acquisition on the African continent, it continues to exist without restrictive instruments (Lamb 2007, 1–4; Ryu 2008). Numerous attempts have been made but, to date, all have failed to create restrictive instruments to curb arms trade with mostly poor African states. There have been episodic events associated with the United Nations, European Union and African regional structures, imposing arms embargoes against particular regimes. Because of the selective nature of these mechanisms, though, most have been ineffective. In a short policy paper seeking to provide the German Government with options over a trade treaty aimed at developing a mechanism for regulating the trade of conventional arms, a process that had been given impetus by the United Nations General Assembly Resolution 61/89 passed in 2006, it was acknowledged that the arms trade had proven immune to attempts by multilateral intervention. The reason for this conspicuous resistance was stated as emanating from the fact that conventional weapons had traditionally been accepted as providing a positive and legitimate function in the states' responsibility towards maintaining national security (Erickson 2007, 1). Furthermore, Holtom et al. have noted, after surveying events in both Afghanistan and the Sudan, that:

> UN arms embargoes imposed on armed non-state actors have thus far failed to stop their arms acquisitions. Second, major arms suppliers have been willing to show their support for the government in a conflict zone by directly supplying it with arms.
>
> (Holtom et al. 2008)

What this means is that for either armed non-state actors or governments wishing to acquire arms, existing international restrictive treaties, including UN embargoes, have had their provisions set aside for purposes of gaining political and economic influence with the actors during, and much more importantly after, conflict. Furthermore, the demand for weapons either during conflict situations or simply as a considered measure by a sitting government or armed group has created sufficient opportunity for arms suppliers, making the sum impact of restrictive treaties almost meaningless.

What are the salient causes fuelling the global arms trade with Africa?

The first cause argued to have fuelled the arms trade on the continent is the interests of the weapons manufacturers and suppliers. Consequently, participation in global arms trade is a manifestation of a) domestic requirements of arms production, and b) foreign policy interests in which the state seeks to register its influence in the competitive international relations arena. Furthermore, on this note, arms trade by producing nations may be conducted between multiple states, organized as a regional security entity and not necessary in a bilateral manner. In the case of the USA, as stated before Congress, the country's policy on arms trade is based on the conviction to:

> … assist friendly and allied nations in developing nations to maintain the ability to deal with domestic and regional security threats as part of its foreign and national security policy.
>
> (Hartung and Berrigan 2005)

The same could be said of both Russia and France, two countries cited in the conventional arms transfers as avoiding established sanctions and embargoes to supply arms and equipment to preferred clients. Finally, a similar charge has been laid at the door of Eastern European states, such as Ukraine, which has managed to offload Soviet-style weaponry to willing African states. According to the Congressional Research Service findings, even the North Atlantic Treaty Organization (NATO) has facilitated arms sales to new members whilst allowing them to dispose of old weapons to other less-developed states (Grimmett 2008, 6).

> Africa has become an attractive and profitable dumping ground for nations and arms manufacturers eager to get rid of weapons stocks made superfluous by the end of the Cold War or by technological developments.
>
> (Elbadawi and Sambanis 2000:11)

In the case of China, a key source of small arms, aircraft, artillery and mortars to most African states, its trade terms have been highlighted as not commercially based, but:

> ... a means to enhance [China's] status within the international political arena and increase its ability to obtain access to significant natural resources, especially oil.
>
> (Copson et al. 2008)

What areas would justify major arms procurement on the African continent?

While the global arms trade can be criticized as serving the narrow mutual interests of foreign powers and the political elite on the African continent, there are at least two areas in which such an engagement would be welcome. Ultimately, participation in these two areas would result in improved military capacity, which would transform the current insecurity of the states' citizens and, therefore, constitute justifiable expenditure or debt. The first of these areas is the level of maritime insecurity associated with the coastal countries of the continent. According to an assessment by the then US Acting Secretary of State for African Affairs, Charles Snyder, speaking at the American Enterprise Institute in 2004:

> ... there are really no African coastal navies, in the sense of having large capacities.
>
> (Sorbara 2007, 56)

For now, South Africa is the only country in sub-Saharan Africa that has been able to re-equip its navy since independence in 1994, with submarines and battleships from Germany as well as new combat and air-transport aircraft from Sweden. Meanwhile, in North Africa, Egypt continues to be in the lead, receiving significant military assistance, including assets and co-production facilities from the USA in the context of the Middle Eastern Arab–Israeli conflict. The rest of the continent has remained without significant modern assets to police the coastal zones.

As if to demonstrate the lack of military response capacity, piracy in the last few years has increased and dominated the two regions of the Bight of Benin within the Gulf of Guinea in West Africa, as well as off the East African Coast of Sudan, Somalia, Djibouti and Kenya. In the first zone in West Africa, the region is rich in mineral deposits, including hydrocarbon exploration and production oil. Current estimates suggest that deep, offshore reserves of as much as 75% hydrocarbons lie between the Gulf of Mexico and West Africa, capable of providing something like 181 billion barrels of oil (Sorbara 2007, 56).

The same source points towards very limited capacity against the well-armed rebel groups equipped with fast boats and able to move with ease within the Atlantic and further inland in the Niger Delta, threatening oil refinery plants, production rigs and supply lines. Sorbara quotes the Nigerian Naval Commander, admitting that owing to a lack of investment, his force could only muster 60%–65% capacity to respond, leaving the citizens and the major source of Nigerian economic activity at the mercy of rebel groups. On the African continent, only a country such as Nigeria would be able to find the resources required to establish the necessary military capacity; if they cannot, then there is even less wherewithal and capacity among the other countries.

Recognizing the African maritime insecurity, the USA hosted a maritime conference in West Africa, aimed at developing appropriate regional security policy in harmony with external players. The motivation for the USA was to seek to reduce its reliance for oil on the volatile Middle Eastern region and increase its uptake from the more stable regions of Africa, such as Nigeria and Angola amongst others. In percentage terms, the USA seeks to increase its oil from these sources by about 12%–25% in the next 10 years and it is, therefore, very interested in stamping out the growing piracy. So here we have a mutual area of interest, not necessarily now confined to the survival of the fragile African state, but much more broadly aiming for security that is likely to impact positively to stabilize African economies and bring general security and wellbeing to the common citizen. At the conference, when an assessment was made of existing maritime capacity of neighbouring states of Nigeria, some interesting features became noticeable, including an inventory of existing maritime capacity.

The conference noted that Angola has limited capacity based on a naval contingent of 1,000 men equipped with a limited number of patrol boats, most of which are not seaworthy; Ghana's 1,000-strong navy relies upon four ex-German patrol boats to cover the vast maritime territory; Ghana had received several surplus US naval transporters under the Excess Defence Article programme in 2005. Cameroon's 1,300-strong navy was in a slightly better shape, equipped with 17 ex-French coastal patrol boats and two 30-foot amphibious craft. Gabon's 500 naval personnel had between them three patrol boats and two amphibious craft, while Sao Tome, an island in the middle of the Atlantic, had a very small navy of little consequence to constitute meaningful defence. Equatorial Guinea's navy has 10 patrol boats purchased from Israel in 2004. This should be compared with increasing attacks by the Ijaw-led Movement for the Emancipation of the Niger Delta, which had the capacity to attack any nation's offshore rigs, including those of the oil company, Shell, kidnapping crew of the floating production, storage and offloading vessels, as well as other passing ships (Sorbara, 2007, 56–8).

The preliminary conclusions we can draw from the above inventory include that: a) there are limited resources to establish credible naval forces, with no country demonstrating a real capacity to dominate its own or contiguous maritime threats. To this end, except for Nigeria, most appear to have the obligatory 1,000 or fewer naval personnel, but with minimal assets; b) most assets appear to be hand-me-downs: second-hand or surplus equipment from the USA, France, Germany and Israel, with no state-of-the-art or regionally-specific boats or craft designed for the treacherous African coastal region and the inland Niger Delta operations; c) because the maritime insecurity does not necessarily threaten the survival of the state in the capital cities, there has been no attention to or significant resources allocated towards eliminating this problem and improving the economic conditions as well as the general plight of the citizens.

The situation in West Africa could still be contained if early corrective action were taken. However, by comparison, this is not the case when we consider piracy in the Horn, off the coast of Somalia. In the Indian Ocean maritime security has broken down, characterized by elements of Islamic contest, collapsed states, a lack of military capacity amongst coastal states and finally, the inability to intervene by the regional body, the Inter-Governmental Authority on Development (IGAD). The IGAD region is the only one in which it has members fighting one-another, in Ethiopia and Eritrea, while ethnic differences have also threatened to break apart neighbouring states. More recently, the deployment of Ethiopian troops in Somalia under the African Union peace-keeping mission caused reaction by the Somalis until the Ethiopian troops were forced to withdraw. Key differences include a historical dispute over territorial rights by Greater Somalia and Ogaden territory, resulting from annexation after the 1977 war. Secondly, there is a faith-based dimension to the dispute, emanating from the Islamic Courts Unions, which have taken over at the grassroots level, forcing out the Transitional Federal Government that had been cobbled together in Nairobi, supported by the UN as an alternative to the chaos reigning in Somalia since the collapse of General Siad Barre's regime during the 1990s.

Operating from a country without any recognizable government, the rebel/piracy groups have dominated, bringing into sharp focus the continent's maritime insecurity.

Left to their own devices, the political differences in Somalia have spawned the age-old craft, piracy, now threatening the lives of a large number of refugees and internally displaced people. Piracy in Somalia has spread to rebellion both on land and off the coastline, where global food relief supplies meant for the most vulnerable are commandeered, as well as normal international and regional trade. Owing to the lack of local military capacity, there has been an international response, with foreign ships now gathered to combat the menace as well as assist in the passage of vessels plying the sea route. Naval assets come from the USA, NATO, the UK, Germany, Ukraine, Russia, China and India. Significantly, though, the presence of these naval assets is not necessarily co-ordinated with the mainland African countries, nor with the continental African Peace and Security Architecture organized by the African Union. As it is currently constructed, the African Peace and Security Architecture is organized around the Peace and Security Council, mirroring the UN Security Council structure and under this, complemented by a Military Affairs Committee, is a strategic think tank for the African Union. Under this is the African Standby Force, organized around the geographic pillars of north, south, east, central and west Africa, in which each region is supposed to muster a brigade to be placed at the disposal of the African Union. Within this structure there is little mention of maritime security components, demonstrating the weakness and general vulnerability of the continent towards providing security for this dimension.

Piracy off the coast of Somalia has, then, confirmed several elements related to African security. In the first instance, it confirms the phenomenon of weak and collapsed states, a development since the 1990s. This has drawn the interest of outside powers, including the USA, which see this as 'ungoverned' space in which international terrorism may thrive. Secondly, it confirms the inability of regional states to respond to problems in neighbouring states and impose law and order. Where Ethiopian forces attempted to do so as part of the African Union peace-keeping mission, it opened up old wounds based on ethnic differences, threatening to bring the whole region into conflict. Finally, piracy has resulted in the presence of many foreign naval assets, usurping the foundations of sovereignty and nationhood of African states while serving as a platform for new international struggles for domination. Off the Somali coast, only NATO naval assets are co-ordinating their actions with those of the USA, leaving Russia, Ukraine, China and India participating outside the 'Western Alliance'. While this may curb local piracy, it will not bring with it an enduring African naval capacity to undertake the maritime policing of the region in the future.

Hence the strong recommendation in this chapter for structured engagement in the global arms trade in the maritime arena. This could revolve around the areas of policy development, asset provision and training. In all cases, the levels envisaged are such that no country, including the oil-producing states such as Nigeria, now under pressure from the collapsed global oil prices, can afford to fund this initial infrastructural requirement, nor sustain it. Africa needs targeted support towards enhancing its maritime security.

The second vital area of the global arms trade that could be beneficial to human security and development in Africa is attention to the continent's air space. Security in African air space has little to recommend it, with references that we can cite reflecting on the defence and security dimension in the region episodic at best. Yet, in many countries there is an infrastructure in place, left over from colonial periods, which could be easily harnessed to create an effective and secure continental air-space network. For the time being, in the absence of such a mechanism, African states and even commercial entities continue to be blind to external actors exploiting the security gaps to maximize profits.

Regarding the African Standby Force, both in west and southern Africa some co-ordination has been noted, in the case of regional intervention by the Economic Community of West

African States Monitoring Group (ECOMOG) in Liberia (1990), Sierra Leone (1990), Guinea (2008) and more recently in Cote d'Ivoire (2005–08). The same can be said of South African Development Community (SADC) forces, which operated as a regional entity in Mozambique (1980s–92), Lesotho (1999) and more recently in the DRC (1999–2007).

The strengthening of Africa's air space security could be achieved through close co-operation, the acquisition of land-based surveillance systems, and shared air transport and combat-type assets organized at a regional level (akin to what we have seen with the Scandinavian hybrid brigade). This latter method emphasizes particular country capabilities, which combine in practice to alleviate the recognized insecurity.

Conclusion

The international arms trade is dominated by the five largest exporters: the USA, Russia, France, the UK and Germany, with Spain and Italy not far behind. The main reasons for engaging in global arms trading are: a) the need to maintain strong domestic defence industries, and b) employing arms as a tool of generating influence within the international security arena (Erickson 2007:1; Holtom et al. 2008). Recipients in the developing nations include a handful of countries including India and China, with only one African country in the group: Egypt. However, despite this, the continent has remained and looks set to continue at the heart of the global arms trade as the result of a number of factors. Prominent amongst these is the nature of the African state in which acquisition and possession of conventional arms has become a pre-requisite for survival. Africa's non-state actors have demonstrated their ability to marshal sufficient fire power to overwhelm the standard defence material of African states. The resulting meeting of minds between industrialized states' arms exporters and African state recipients has resulted in the removal of essential attention and resources from much-needed poverty reduction and food security.

Until an answer is found to the post-colonial challenge of building a strong African state imbued with democratic notions in which institutions are established to replace the benign, strong-man syndrome, regimes in power will remain wedded to the idea of gaining and retaining power through the barrel of a gun. This is translated into the acquisition of armoured personnel carriers, tanks, artillery pieces and heavy mortar bombs, complemented by a limited number of transport and combat aircraft, complete with helicopters as the basis of symbolic trappings of power. Against this is the typical African rebel group, armed with cruisers and AK47s and, in some instances, as recently witnessed in Somalia, fully-equipped with tanks, threatening capital cities such as N'Djamena in Chad, Khartoum in Sudan, or larger areas such as northern Uganda by the Lord's Resistance Army.

Meanwhile, the industrialized states – for reasons of foreign policy, support for the domestic defence production industry and, sometimes, simply to dispose of surplus or obsolete equipment – will continue to see the African market as a viable arms market, this regardless, as argued above, of whether or not the countries can afford to buy arms. The earlier discussion on the forms of payment clearly showed the creative financing, debt forgiveness and counter-trading practices that have become the norm in securing these arms contracts. Stated clearly: when purchases are made, no money need pass between the contract partners or, where it does, the amounts do not reflect the actual costs, making affordability a minor consideration in the exchange.

In terms of acquiring arms for the purpose of political survival, no attention has been paid to at least two areas that we think offer much broader national security and could justify the levels of military expenditure normally associated with large-scale weapons and arms trade. The first is the strengthening of Africa's maritime security, based on actions taken by each coastal state as well as the regional security groupings. As circumstances stand, within the African Peace and Security Architecture, in which the African Standby Force is prominent, there is no continental plan for addressing maritime insecurity. The second area would be to remedy the lack of co-ordination within the aviation arena, which leaves African air space open to abuse. In both these instances, targeted expenditure is lacking and, if approached from a regional perspective, would result in significant benefits for military expenditure in poor and resource-challenged African states. These changes are unlikely to come from policies pursued by the arms manufacturers, but would instead emerge from a paradigm shift within the sub-Saharan African political context.

Bibliography

Arms Deliveries to the World by Major Suppliers, 1999–2006, www.photius.com/ranking/arms_sales_major_suppliers_1999_2006html (accessed 30 January 2009), data compiled by the Federation of American Scientists, Washington, DC

Clapham, Christopher, 'Rethinking African States', *African Security Review*, Vol.10 (3), 2001, www.iss.co.za/Pubs/ASR/10N03/Clapham.html

Copson, Raymond W., Kerry Dumbaugh and Michelle Lan, *China and Sub-Saharan Africa*, Congressional Research Service (CRS) Report RL133055, 2008, www.fas.org/sgp/crs/row/index.html

Elbadawi, Ibrahim and Nicholas Sambanis, 'Why Are There So Many Civil Wars in Africa? Understanding and Preventing Violent Conflict', *Journal of African Economics*, December 2000, siteresources.worldbank.org/DEC/Resources/warsinAfrica.pdf

Erickson, Jennifer L., *The Arms Trade Treaty: The Politics Behind the UN Process*, Working Paper, Research Unit, European and Atlantic Security, German Institute for International and Security Affairs, FG3-WP 09, Berlin, July 2007

Grimmett, Richard F., *Military Technology and Conventional Weapons Expenditure Countries: The Wassenaar Arrangement*, CRS (Congressional Research Service) Report, US Library of Congress, RS20517, 29 September 2006

——*Conventional Arms Trade and Developing Nations, 1999 – 2006*, CRS (Congressional Research Service) Report, US Library of Congress, RL34187, 26 September 2007

——*Conventional Arms Transfers to Developing Nations, 2000 – 2007*, CRS (Congressional Research Service) Report, US Library of Congress, RL34723, 23 October 2008

Hartung, William D. and Frida Berrigan, *Militarization of U.S. Africa Policy, 2000 to 2005: A Fact Sheet*, Arms Trade Resource Centre, Axis of Influence-World Policy Institute – Research Project, 2005, www.worldpolicy.org/projects/arms/reports/AfricaMarch2005.html

Holtom, Paul, Mark Bromley and Pieter D. Wezeman, 'International Arms Transfers', in *SIPRI Yearbook 2008*, Stockholm, Stockholm International Peace Research Institute, 2008

Huntington, Samuel, *The Third Wave: Democratization in the Late Twentieth Century*, Norman, University of Oklahoma Press, 1993

Lamb, Guy, *Beyond 'Shadow Boxing' and 'Lip Service'*, Occasional Paper 135, Institute for Security Studies, April 2007, www.iss.co.za

London, Scott, *Book Review: Samuel Huntington*, The Third Wave: Democratization in the Late Twentieth Century, 1993, www.scottlondon.com/reviews/huntington.html

Luckham, Robin, 'Africa: Arming the State', *New Internationalist*, Vol. 139, September 1984, www.newint.org/issue139/military.htm

Rupiya, Martin, 'Book Review: Steyn Hannes, Richard van de Walt and Jan van Loggernberg, Armament and Disarmament South Africa's Nuclear Experience', *African Security Review*, Vol.13 (1), 2004, www.iss.co.za/pubs/ASR/13No1/Books.pdf

Ryu, Alisha, 'Treaty Conference Seeks to Regulate Global Arms Trade', *Voice of America*, 3 September 2008, www.voanews.com/archive/2008-09/2008-09-03

Shah, Arup, *Arms Trade A Major Cause of Suffering: The Arms Trade Is Big Business*, 9 November 2008, worldbank/research/org

Sorbara, Mark J., 'Oil Security: The United States and Maritime Security in the Gulf of Guinea', *Petroleum Africa*, July 2007

Steyn, Hannes, Richard van de Walt and Jan van Loggernberg, *Armament and Disarmament South Africa's Nuclear Experience*, Pretoria, Network Publications, 2003

Tutu, Desmond, 'Governing Global Arms Trade', *The Australian*, 20 January 2009

Part III

The arms industry after the Cold War

14 The global arms trade after the Cold War

Siemon T. Wezeman

Introduction

After rapid growth in the 1970s, the volume of arms transfers reached its highest level since the Second World War in the early 1980s. This was the period of major East–West tensions, culminating in the early-Reagan years where the USA under President Ronald Reagan decided to out-compete the communist bloc, resulting in thriving US trade with European North Atlantic Treaty Organization (NATO) allies as well as other allies (e.g. Japan and Australia), trade between European NATO allies, supplies from the Soviet Union to Warsaw Pact allies and imports by neutral European countries. East and West clashed militarily by proxy in different regions (e.g. Angola, Ethiopia-Somalia and Afghanistan), resulting in other extensive flows of arms. Also, other conflicts and tensions, particularly the Iran–Iraq War, which had a wider impact on Middle Eastern levels of armament, as well as the continuing Arab–Israeli and India–Pakistan conflicts, pushed up the demand for arms (SIPRI database; SIPRI Yearbook). In the late-1980s, that is before the Cold War had officially ended, the level started to decrease, but the most pronounced dip can be seen in the period from 1989 to 1995. A few subsequent years of growth were largely related to the People's Republic of China emerging as an arms market and the military modernization of other states in Asia, as well as ongoing modernization in the Middle East, where Iraq and Iran were perceived as threats by rich oil-exporting Gulf countries. The 1997 financial crisis that mainly hit Asia and the slump in oil prices saw another downward trend. New economic growth, higher oil prices and realignment of the defence policies of European countries were the main reasons for increased arms trade after 2000.

The arms trade changed in many respects after the Cold War, and it may even seem to have changed radically. Certainly there have been some profound changes in, for example, the level of technology traded, in relations between supplier and recipient, and the lists of suppliers and recipients. There have also been some significant changes in the volume of trade and in discussions on the normative aspects of the arms trade. Notwithstanding these, there has been more continuity in the arms trade than change. Technology is continuously developing and it follows that arms trading, like any other goods being traded, will also over time incorporate the new technological levels, as has been the case in the past. Supplier-recipient relations have altered and will continue to do so. The arms market during the post-Cold War period is probably more of a buyers' market then before, with buyers being able to shop around more than during the Cold War, but many buyer-recipient relations have never been stagnant – competition between suppliers was then as murderous and politically loaded for many of the major and minor markets as it is now. A more radical development is the decrease in the volume of transfers – to about half of what it was just a few years before the Cold War ended. A potentially radical development is also the change in the international environment, which has provided opportunities to discuss normative aspects of the arms trade and agree on some limited level of multilateral controls. However, it still remains to be seen

Table 14.1 Volume of transfers of major conventional weapons after the end of the Cold War. Index based on 1989 = 100

Year	Index value
1982	128
1983	121
1984	115
1985	107
1986	112
1987	115
1988	106
1989	100
1990	86
1991	80
1992	69
1993	75
1994	64
1995	65
1996	68
1997	80
1998	78
1999	69
2000	53
2001	55
2002	49
2003	54
2004	60
2005	60
2006	70
2007	72

Source: SIPRI Arms Transfers Database, 15 February 2009

how much further the agreed principles on responsible arms trade can and will be translated into broad and effective control of the arms trade.

This chapter explains why the proliferation of conventional arms continued after the end of the Cold War, examining broadly the determinants of suppliers to allow or refuse arms transfers and of recipients to decide on arms acquisitions in general and arms imports in particular. It will look at some of the trends among the suppliers and recipients, among the weapons being traded and the types of trade. The chapter will provide the reader with an idea of the changes that occurred in the two decades since the end of the Cold War, but will also underline the continuity of the arms trade during that period. While predicting the future is near impossible – who could have predicted in 1986 that within three years the Cold War would end – the chapter provides pointers to possible trends in the coming years. However, the general pattern is almost inescapable: states will continue to acquire weapons and will be able to do so from states that produce weapons without much legal or moral restriction.

Limitations on arms transfers after the Cold War

The arms trade has long been a hot topic of debate amongst decision makers and in society in general. Ethical as well as practical arguments to control and reduce as much as possible armaments in the world have been heard for a long time. During the Cold War, much of the debate focused on weapons of mass destruction (WMD) and some of it was overridden by what seemed to be a desperate struggle between the East and the West, in which high levels of armaments were the only guarantee of survival and where limitations on arms transfers did not fit.

The end of the Cold War gave rise to hopes of a world where most if not all countries could work together to achieve peace and security. This included a perceived opportunity to reduce armaments significantly, to stop the proliferation of conventional weapons and prevent excesses, such as the destabilizing build-ups of weapons in regions of tension, the fuelling of armed conflicts, the supply of weapons to countries with little means to pay for the weapons or operate them without burdening their economies too much, or to provide authoritarian regimes with the tools for repression. Such high ideals were evident in the very first years of the 1990s and were enshrined in policy statements adopted by different international organizations and forums. These ultimately took the form of different sets of criteria that were to act as guidelines for a controlled and responsible arms trade. These sets include:

- P5 Guidelines for Conventional Arms Transfers (1991)
- EU Criteria (1991 and 1992; in 1998 adopted as the EU Code of Conduct on Arms Export)
- OSCE Principles Governing Conventional Arms Transfers (1993)
- UN General Assembly criteria
- Wassenaar Arrangement on export control for conventional arms and dual-use goods and technologies (1995)

The basic ideas underlying these criteria had already been embedded in General Assembly documents and resolutions that led to the establishment of the United Nations Register of Conventional Arms in 1991 (UN 1991). All these sets of criteria are worded slightly differently, but they address roughly similar potential risks resulting from arms transfers in more or less the same ways. The risks identified were:

- Increasing international tensions through arms transfers leading to potentially destabilizing build-ups of arms
- Prolongation and intensification of ongoing armed conflict, including internal conflicts
- Provision of means for human rights abuse
- Diversion of scarce resources from economic development
- Endangering the security of allies
- Diversion of legally transferred weapons to the illegal circuit

While these criteria established some basic principles and implied certain norms for responsible arms transfers, they were political statements, not legally binding treaties. Therefore, they did not prohibit any transfers. Furthermore, the language of all the criteria is vague enough for governments to give any interpretation on what could still be considered as responsible. Arms trade remained legal. The UN Charter and in particular Article 51 on the right of states for self-defence, also provided an almost blanket excuse for arms transfers.

The only internationally accepted legal limitations on arms transfers are UN arms embargoes established by the UN Security Council. The option of such Security Council embargoes existed during the Cold War, but was used only on two occasions (against Rhodesian and South African white minority regimes). However, UN arms embargoes, together with other sanctions, were rediscovered as an instrument to put pressure on states, non-state armed groups engaged in a conflict, or states not behaving according to internationally agreed rules or norms. Since the end of the Cold War 27 UN arms embargoes have been established for shorter or longer periods (SIPRI/SPITS 2007). While most states or non-state actors targeted by a UN arms embargo are very small importers of weapons, the effect of Security Council arms embargoes on the volume of global arms transfers has been significant because Libya and Iraq, two major markets during the Cold War, were among them. More importantly, though, is that the embargoes have begun to establish some norms for responsible arms transfers.

In addition to the UN embargoes, a few international treaties banning certain types of weapons (e.g. the Convention on Certain Conventional Weapons, Anti Personnel Mines Treaty, Cluster Munitions Treaty) legally limit transfers from and to countries that are party to the treaties. Also, these treaties, while not having any major impact on the volume of weapons transferred, have been instrumental in sparking discussions on tighter norms for responsible arms transfers.

These attempts to establish norms led to an initiative in 2006 at the UN level to agree globally on a tighter set of criteria for responsible arms transfers and to enshrine these in a legally binding Arms Trade Treaty (ATT). This ATT was suggested by different non-governmental organizations (NGOs) in 2003 and while it is currently difficult to imagine how it will change much in the short or even medium term, it may finally lead to fulfilling some of the hopes of the immediate post-Cold War period.

The continuing arms trade

There is little doubt that the arms trade has changed with the end of the Cold War. The volume of trade has been significantly lower than during the hottest periods of the Cold War. However, the change was less radical than might be expected. By and large, the arms trade has remained legal business as usual, with decisions on exports and imports made at a national level mainly based on national considerations. The general determinants for the import and export of weapons remained largely those of the Cold War and earlier periods. The specific grounds for individual countries to sell or buy weapons, or for each specific deal, will often be a mix of demand and supply side factors.

Demand side factors

Determinants for the demand for weapons by states were identified in the literature long before the Cold War ended. While not always expressed in the same words, they can be listed as six factors:

- Continuing threats and perceived threats to national security
- Internal security
- International status
- Access to technology
- Economic reasons
- Status of the military in internal politics

Continuing threats and perceived threats to international security

Real and perceived threats to international security, both from states and non-state actors, remain the strongest reason for states to acquire weapons. Because military forces are in general maintained mainly to defend a country against existing, potential or perceived 'enemies', arms acquisitions by one country are linked often directly to acquisitions by other countries. This can be observed in almost all countries, but has particularly been the case in the Middle East and Asia. In these two regions, major international tensions between states existed in the Cold War period, and after 1989 the international security situation in these regions did not improve. In Asia, the main arms importing region, Chinese military modernization linked to Chinese policies of unification and ambitions in, for example, the South China Sea, the Korean peninsula stalemate and the India-Pakistan conflict (which in 1999 almost led to full-scale war)

Chinese expansion in Asia

gave strong impetus to major arms procurement. In the Middle East, the Arab-Israeli conflict remained a reason for several countries to keep importing large volumes of weapons. The threat perceived by the Arab Gulf countries as emanating from revolutionary Iran gave a similar impetus for Saudi Arabia, the United Arab Emirates (UAE) and the smaller Arab Gulf states to acquire more and better weapons. These two regions, both during the Cold War period and also in the post-Cold War era, together with Europe, were the main arms importing regions.

In Europe, the security situation improved dramatically when the Warsaw Pact disintegrated and most European countries became integrated into the European Union (EU) and NATO. However, while the size of European armed forces saw major reductions, in some cases by over 75% in manpower, and correspondingly the need for weapons became less, Europe remained a major arms importing region. Here arms acquisitions were also driven mainly by real and perceived threats to international security, but many of these were seen not to come from neighbouring countries, but from regions outside Europe. These distant threats deman-ded a whole new force structure with significant investment in new types of weapons and military equipment.

It is normal that countries react and counter-react in their arms acquisitions. Often this leads at one point to some level of equilibrium. However, if antagonists have foreign policies perceived as 'aggressive', the action-reaction process may speed up, resulting in an arms race – antagonists keep reacting to arms acquisitions by the other party, resulting in a spiral of more and more weapons being added to inventories. The action-reaction dynamic is often not localized. Other states will start to feel threatened by the build-up of the original antagonists and will react in turn with arms acquisitions, setting in motion new action-reaction patterns and increasing the danger of conflict.

There are signs that such arms races exist in the post-Cold War period. While China has reduced the size of its armed forces, its rapid military modernization has led to reactions from other countries in East and South-East Asia, as well as the USA. More recently, India has started to react to China's rise. In turn, China seems to be reacting to arms acquisitions by its neighbours. A similar regional pattern is visible in the Middle East, where many states react against Iranian modernization, particularly its acquisition of ballistic missiles and its potential acquisition of nuclear weapons.

Because stopping such patterns of armament depends very much on trust, such arms races are difficult to stop once they start, and the action-reaction pattern will be a major driving force for the arms trade. The results can be economic devastation (e.g. the USSR in the late 1980s), or pressure by the one 'on top' to use the temporary military advantage.

Internal security

Protecting the government from armed non-state actors trying to overthrow it through armed rebellion, or protecting the integrity of the state territory from rebels fighting for independence, is in many countries an important task for military or well-armed para-military forces and an important determinant for arms acquisitions. In some regions, such as sub-Saharan Africa or parts of South-East Asia, it is more important than protection against other states. In addition, military or para-military forces have in many countries police tasks – mainly protecting civilians from organized, large criminal gangs. However, whilst the provision of internal security is important, it does not result in large volumes of arms trading. Only a small percentage of the total global arms trade can be linked directly to internal security.

International status

Most countries striving to become a 'power', either on a regional or a global level, see significant-sized armed forces equipped with advanced weapons as an important symbol and instrument of being a power. In these cases, the weapons are not acquired to counter any threat, but because they 'fit' with power status. Brazilian acquisitions of an aircraft carrier and a nuclear submarine in recent years are clearly more power symbols than anything else.

As supplying weapons is often seen as a high level of acceptance by the supplier of the state or its government to whom it delivers the weapons, recipients may try to get foreign governments to sell them symbolic amounts of weapons. Such supplies will enhance the status of the recipient. Libyan orders of small amounts of weapons from several European countries after the UN and EU embargoes on Libya were lifted had probably more to do with enhancing Libya's status as a responsible actor, than any real need for the weapons ordered.

Access to technology

Countries may decide to acquire certain weapons not because they are absolutely needed, but because the import of the weapons gives access to specific weapons technology that can be used in the local arms industry. This can come in two forms. A country may import smaller or larger volumes of weapons to learn and basically steal the technology for use in indigenously designed products. China is the most obvious example of this. China has imported large volumes of weapons from Russia since the end of the Cold War. Most of these helped directly to modernize Chinese forces, but almost all Russian weapons and technology seem to have been partly copied illegally and integrated into Chinese indigenous designs. Much smaller volumes of European and Israeli weapons have also been imported and either copied or used in the development of similar Chinese weapons. On the other hand, the Republic of Korea (South Korea), India and Brazil follow a pattern of import, local assembly and licensed production of advanced weapons to learn from the process and in a fully legal manner, either co-operating with the original suppliers to further develop weapons or to partly achieve a local high-tech arms industry with indigenous designs.

Economic reasons

Arms imports may have economically positive effects through the spin-off of imported technology into civilian industry. The idea to kick-start a high-tech industry by importing advanced weaponry and starting assembly and licensed production is not new. This spin-off effect may result in general high-tech industry development (e.g. electronics or composite materials), or in a local high-tech arms industry that may be able to compete on world markets. For example South Korea, India and Brazil import, assemble and engage in licensed production of advanced weapons partly to achieve local high-tech industry development. However, as the spin-off effect on civilian industry is limited, these countries mainly seek to establish an arms industry suitable for export.

Arms imports have a negative effect on the trade balance, employment and government income through taxation. For some countries, this has been a reason in the past to establish indigenous arms industries that would keep funds and employment at home. However, maintaining such industries and developing new weapons has become more and more costly. Arms imports can, then, be cheaper than national development and production: by tying into an existing large production run giving cheaper units, by not having to build up an arms industry, or to divert skilled and educated human resources for the local design and production of weapons. Again, this is not new for the post-Cold War period. Switzerland and Canada gave up on their indigenous designs for combat aircraft in the 1950s partly because these would cost much more than imported aircraft. India and Japan have in the last few years came to the same conclusion. In the case of Japan, imports will now substitute for an indigenously designed combat aircraft; in the case of India, the issue is still undecided.

Status of the military

Lastly, the status of armed forces in internal politics and society, or the status of specific parts or services within the armed forces can be a determinant for arms acquisitions. In states with a history of recent military interventions in politics or with military governments, it is not uncommon that arms be acquired in order to enhance the status of the military or as a means to keep the military happy with 'toys for boys'. Acquisitions in, for example Chile and Brazil seem partly the result of this.

Supply side factors

The determinants for the supply of weapons by states were also identified in the literature long before the Cold War ended. These consist basically of two factors:

- Political – gaining allies or leverage
- Economic – profits, market access and raw materials

Political determinants

During the Cold War the USA saw gaining allies around the world as an important part of the East–West struggle, as did the Soviet Union. Arms supplies were seen as an 'incentive' or 'carrot' to get countries to align themselves or at least to remain neutral. Arms supplies were, of course, also the logical follow-on to alliance agreements as the necessary means or 'stick' needed by allies to fight off external or internal enemies ideologically allied to the other bloc. Smaller, non-aligned suppliers used arms supplies in similar ways, with, for example China providing weapons to several African countries to counter Soviet influences or gain recognition as the only China. In the post-Cold War period, there seemed at first sight no need to use arms transfers as a tool of foreign politics. However, the need for allies did not disappear with the end of the Cold War, and gaining political influence remained an important reason for arms supplies. The USA has continued to provide arms supplies as aid or on preferential conditions, or supplies of advanced weapons as a reward for US-friendly policies. Important allies such as Egypt and Turkey received significant military aid during the 1990s, worth several billions of US dollars annually. The global 'war on terror' increased from 2001 the importance of the political factors in US arms supplies. Countries such as Pakistan, the Philippines and Afghanistan received most of their US weapons as aid in return for action against US-designated 'terrorist' groups. To cement a partnership with India mainly to balance China, the USA agreed to supply high-tech weapons only shortly after strongly criticizing India for its nuclear programme in 1998.

Arms supplies for political reasons may not always lead to the desired results of gaining faithful and reliable allies. Once a relationship is established, both sides are open to blackmail. The supplier may refuse to supply certain equipment or certain volumes of equipment unless the recipient behaves in a certain way, but recipients may just as well refuse to take certain action unless more or better weapons are delivered.

Stopping transfers as punishment may be less common and recent cases indicate that embargoes by single suppliers are not very effective in modifying a recipient's behaviour. The United Kingdom (UK) and US embargoes on India and Pakistan in reaction to their nuclear tests in 1998 could only be seen as a symbol of dissatisfaction. While they had a temporary effect on the readiness of Indian and Pakistani forces, there was no sign of influence on Indian and Pakistani efforts to build up nuclear forces, and only a negative impact on Pakistan's willingness to act against the Taliban. A similar US embargo on Venezuela only deepened the rift between the two countries. In all three cases the embargoed country did suffer temporarily, but was able to find quickly other suppliers to fill the gap. In the case of India and Pakistan, one can even argue that the embargo may have been counter-productive and led to a stronger emphasis in both countries on nuclear weapons.

In a few cases, weapons have been supplied for unselfish political reasons – reasons not directly linked to the national political agenda of the suppliers, but more for a broader objective, such as to support actions by the recipient that are providing security for third parties. The best examples of this are gifts of weapons to UN and African Union peace-keeping forces and of military equipment for maritime patrol and disaster relief to developing countries.

Economic motives

Economic motives are probably the most important reason for suppliers to allow arms exports. These may be purely profit motivated. Arms exports have a direct impact on employment, the balance of trade, and government income through direct or indirect taxation. Arms exports also enable a larger production run of weapons already planned for national consumption, making the price per unit lower (mainly by spreading research, development and industrial tooling costs over more units, and recovering some of these costs from exports). The choice to export for economic reasons is an easy one. Which government does not want to be seen as promoting jobs or improving the trade balance?

However, probably more often, economic motives go deeper than simple profit or jobs and can be linked to the political-strategic issue of maintaining an arms industrial base. This is particularly true for the largest exporters. The USA, Russia and France all underline the importance of a broad arms industrial base to remain as independent as possible from foreign suppliers, in order to be able to maintain an independent foreign policy. However, it is a well-documented fact that the development and operation of weapons is becoming more and more expensive with each new generation of weapons and that maintaining the ability to design and produce a wide range of weapons is extremely costly. There are four solutions to this problem: get allies and divide up military tasks; forgo the acquisition of a whole spectrum of weapons but concentrate on last-resort weapons (WMD) or alternative military doctrines (so-called asymmetric warfare); co-operate with other countries in development to spread the costs; or recoup costs by selling weapons to foreign customers.

For some suppliers the choice to export is an absolute necessity. Without exports some countries would have to close down significant parts of their arms industry. This would not only impact on employment, but also directly on national security. Russia, for instance, was in a position soon after the Cold War ended where it was unable to support the arms industry or the development of new weapons from the national defence budget. To keep the defence industry alive, and to be able to afford at least the minimum of research and development, Russia had no other option than to export as many weapons as possible.

Aside from the economic benefits directly related to specific arms sales, deeper economic motives may be linked to the arms trade. These are mainly related to either gaining access to markets for non-military products by supplying weapons as a show of friendliness or acceptance, or by gaining access to raw materials. This is, though, also not new to the post-Cold War period. US supplies of military equipment to various oil-producing states was in the 1970s linked to efforts to access or even control energy resources. More recent sales by the USA, UK, France, Russia and China to resource-rich countries in the Middle East and Africa are suspected to at least partly have been given a green light for the same reason.

Changes and continuities among suppliers and recipients

Trends among suppliers

The list of suppliers has not significantly changed with the end of the Cold War. To a large extent the countries that were on that list around 1980 (or for that matter around 1970) are

Table 14.2 Top 10 suppliers since 1978

Rank	1978–83	1984–89	1990–95	1996–2001	2002–07
1	USSR	USSR	USA	USA	USA
2	USA	USA	USSR/Russia	Russia	Russia
3	France	United Kingdom	Germany	France	Germany
4	United Kingdom	France	United Kingdom	United Kingdom	France
5	Germany	China, People's Repub.	China, People's Repub.	Germany	United Kingdom
6	Italy	Germany	France	Ukraine	Netherlands
7	China, People's Repub.	Czechoslovakia	Netherlands	China, People's Repub.	Italy
8	Czechoslovakia	Italy	Italy	Netherlands	China, People's Repub.
9	Netherlands	Netherlands	Czechoslovakia	Sweden	Ukraine
10	Israel	Sweden	Sweden	Italy	Israel

Source: SIPRI Arms Transfers Database, 15 February 2009

more or less the same as in 1995 or 2005. What is more, the relative positions on that list have not changed dramatically. The Soviet Union and the USA were during the Cold War by far the largest suppliers. Both are large countries that built up extensive arms industries during the Cold War capable of producing the broadest range of military equipment. After 1989, the USA and Russia (which on the break-up of the Soviet Union inherited the bulk of the Soviet arms industry) remained the unthreatened leading suppliers, accounting for over 50% of all deliveries of major weapons annually.

Among the next tier of suppliers some changes did take place. France, Germany and the UK remained a class apart, but exports from the medium European suppliers in Eastern Europe (primarily Poland and the Czech Republic – a successor state of Czechoslovakia) fell dramatically. A large part of their exports was to the Soviet Union or its allies, or dependent on inter-COMECON (Council for Mutual Economic Assistance) arrangements for production. As soon as the Soviet block fell apart, the Eastern European countries lost most of their market and access to components from the Soviet Union and today only Poland has a sizeable arms industry left.

In the 1960s, 1970s and 1980s many countries, including most of the larger or richer developing countries tried to establish an arms industry capable of producing weapons for local use and for export. Often these countries' high hopes were soon dashed, either because the local weapons did not live up to expectations or because more developed competitors carried the largest markets. The post-Cold War period saw several countries finally becoming consistent suppliers. Israel and, more recently, South Korea have established themselves as exporters of some importance. Israel has been especially successful in the growth areas of electronics, unmanned systems and guided weapons. However, underlining the difficulty of really breaking through, South Africa, which had developed an advanced arms industry in the 1970s and 1980s, did not to reap much benefit, and Brazil, which had done well with simple weapons in the 1980s, did not manage to break through into the lucrative high-tech weapons market and virtually disappeared as an exporter in the 1990s.

Trends among recipients

The list of recipients has always fluctuated more than that of suppliers, particularly over short periods. A relatively large acquisition may push a recipient high up the list, even into the top 10, to drop quickly when all weapons are delivered. As can be seen from the table of

Table 14.3 Top 10 recipients since 1978

Rank	1978–83	1984–89	1990–95	1996–2001	2001–07
1	Libya	India	Japan	Taiwan	China, People's Repub.
2	Iraq	Iraq	Turkey	China, People's Repub.	India
3	India	Japan	India	Turkey	UAE
4	Syria	Saudi Arabia	Saudi Arabia	Saudi Arabia	Greece
5	Saudi Arabia	Syria	Egypt	South Korea	South Korea
6	Algeria	USSR	Greece	India	Israel
7	Egypt	USA	South Korea	Japan	Egypt
8	East Germany	Egypt	Taiwan	Greece	Australia
9	Japan	South Korea	United Kingdom	Egypt	Turkey
10	Israel	Czechoslovakia	Israel	United Kingdom	USA

Source: SIPRI Arms Transfers Database, 15 February 2009

the top 10 recipients, only two countries – India and Egypt – have been consistently included since 1978. However, almost all listed countries are consistently among the top 20% of recipients.

The most important changes were:

- A number of major recipients disappeared for long periods after being put under a UN arms embargo
- Soviet clients lost their supplier
- China became a major importer

As mentioned, the number of UN arms embargoes increased dramatically after 1989, and targeted among others were two of the largest Cold War buyers of arms – Iraq and Libya – for almost the entire post-Cold War period.

With the demise of the Warsaw Pact and the Soviet Union, Eastern European recipients significantly reduced their arms acquisitions and several Soviet clients that depended heavily on Soviet willingness to supply weapons for free, on credit or as part of special barter arrangements, such as Syria, the Democratic People's Republic of Korea (North Korea) and Cuba, virtually disappeared from the field. While Eastern European countries, after their integration in NATO and the demands that have been put on their military contribution to the alliance, have returned to some extent as recipients, the non-European former Soviet clients have not.

The end of the Cold War came at a time when China was once more engaging in a thorough modernization of its armed forces. Flush with financial means resulting from China's rapid economic growth and exports, but with an arms industry that was decades behind in technology, China went shopping and became almost overnight the largest importer of weapons globally. However, in the last few years, China's indigenous arms industry has turned out more advanced weapons and China's imports have decreased significantly. The Chinese modernization resulted in growing perceptions of threat in several other Asian countries, which maintained or increased their arms acquisitions. Asia actually saw little decrease in absolute terms since the early-1980s – imports of major weapons in that period are practically the same as in the last few years. In relative terms, Asian countries became more important as recipients: in the early 1980s, Asia accounted for some 20%–25% of all imports, while in the last five years, the average has been over 40% of all imports.

Trends in technology

Technical developments have always had an impact on arms trade. New weapon technologies will lead to modernization and increased demand, especially if the technologies are revolutionizing warfare. During the Cold War, the development of guided air-defence weapons and supersonic combat aircraft changed warfare rapidly and saw a large demand amongst more developed countries for these new technologies.

The 1990s was a period with some rapid technological progress, most obviously in the field of computers and communication. This also had an impact on the way war was waged. The so-called revolution in military affairs (RMA) emphasized precision, intelligence and communication as a war-winning concept. The Gulf War of 1990–91 seemed to prove the concept and to have brought about a revolutionary change in how wars are won. It took only a few weeks of actual fighting for the Coalition to defeat the Iraqi armed forces. There seemed obvious lessons to be learnt: chiefly that air power could determine the outcome of war. Other lessons included the fact that precision-guided munitions (PGMs) had come a long way since first used on a larger scale in the Viet Nam War; that Soviet weapons were qualitatively inferior; and that reconnaissance, electronic warfare, and command and communications were significant force multipliers. These views were reinforced by the experience of the 1999 NATO actions in Kosovo and the 2003 invasion of Iraq. Such interpretations gave impetus to two reactions. For those states that wanted to be a power that counted in the world and that could afford the investment, the reaction was to modernize armed forces and pursue high-tech solutions. For those that could not afford to do so and were willing to face the wrath of a large part of the global community (e.g. Iran, North Korea), the solution was to concentrate on developing WMD.

One possibly significant issue with an impact on the future arms trade is that with the most complicated weapons, mainly combat aircraft, becoming so expensive to develop that very few countries can afford to do so, the number of producers and, thus, suppliers will soon be limited to no more than a handful or possibly even just one. This would give significant options for controlling the proliferation of conventional weapons. Currently the USA is the only country with a fifth-generation combat aircraft programme that has yielded a product: the F-22 and, soon, the F-35. Being in this monopoly position has given the USA the option to refuse to sell the F-22 to even its closest allies.

Of course, for many smaller developing countries, acquiring or developing high-tech weapons or WMD is not an option, as they are costly to develop and, moreover, the countries' adversaries are often internal and would not possess high-tech weapons or large forces that needed to be countered with high-tech solutions. For these countries, the trends are more or less what they have always been: imports of relatively small volumes of simple weapons such as small arms and light weapons (SALW), and small handfuls of simple larger weapons. It is in these countries that most conflicts are fought and the killing is generally done with simple weapons. More people have been killed since the end of the Cold War by small numbers of simple, sometimes almost outdated weapons, than by high-tech weapons.

Mobility

The end of the Cold War had a significant impact on the role of most NATO and World Trade Organization (WTO) members' armed forces. During the Cold War these armies were mainly geared to fighting a full-scale war on the European mainland and the northern Atlantic Ocean. For this they were equipped with large numbers of heavy weapons.

In the post-Cold War era, the threat of a large-scale war in Europe evaporated and European countries started to focus on perceived threats further afield. The large and heavy European armies were replaced by smaller, more professional armies meant mainly for rapid deployment on smaller operations outside Europe. This had an impact on equipment, which not only became less in number, but changed from heavy to lighter weapons that could be easily transported over long distances by air. In addition, a new emphasis was placed on 'strategic mobility' – capabilities to transport and support forces over several thousand kilometres. For European countries this meant a strong emphasis on light combat systems and transport capabilities.

In other parts of the world this change from heavy to light was less profound or non-existent. Armies in the Middle East and South Asia remain large and equipped with large numbers of heavy weapons. For example, tanks used to be the mainstay of land forces in Europe in the 1980s, but currently only a fraction of the number of tanks then in service has survived and demand for new tanks is minimal. In the Middle East or South Asia, though, there is little change in the demand for tanks and other heavy equipment.

Small arms and light weapons

Most deaths from armed conflict occur in conflicts fought by forces equipped with very few and simple major weapons. SALW play a relatively important role in these conflicts, being responsible for most conflict deaths. However, even the volume of SALW used in the conflicts is extremely limited. Under all the trade in advanced and expensive weapons hides the much more limited trade in SALW. This trade remains less transparent then the trade in major weapons and has been more difficult to quantify. Its value is estimated at some US$1 billion per year, up to 10% of the total trade in weapons (Small Arms Survey). While SALW technology is also changing, the trade in simple SALW like the Kalashnikov will remain a small but important and deadly part of the arms trade.

Type of trade

Arms transfers can come in two different categories:

- sales
- aid (free gifts)

Sales

Arms sales form the bulk of all arms transfers. Probably over 90% of all transfers today are in the form of sales. Arms sales can take different forms of payment, with cash, credit or barter being the most common. This is not different from the Cold War period. However, it is not known what percentage of all sales are made on a cash, credit or barter basis, and if there have been significant changes in the relative importance of each type of payment.

Arms sales differentiate also in their structure. Many sales agreements are not for simple direct deliveries of weapons in return for payments, but include direct or indirect offsets. Offsets are not new to the post-Cold War period, but they remain significant. Some countries believe direct offsets will help them to acquire the technology and know-how to develop an arms industry with indigenous products. Others just use offsets to open a market for what is already produced by their industry. Licensed production was used for economical or arms-industrial reasons in a similar way as offsets.

Co-operative development and production is mainly the result of the increasing costs to develop new advanced weapons and guaranteeing large production runs. Such co-operation did exist in the Cold War period for a number of mainly inter-European aircraft projects (Jaguar, C-160, Alpha Jet, Tornado), but saw expansion after 1989 in combat and transport aircraft, helicopters, combat ships and air-defence systems. This consists of not only bi- and multi-lateral co-operation with the EU, but also limited co-operation between the USA and close allies (e.g. the F-35 JSF).

Pressure to export

One of the consequences of the major changes in defence policies in Europe and North America after 1989 was significant cuts in the size of armed forces. Manpower was reduced in many states by over 50% and inventories were slashed accordingly. This left the existing arms industry in a situation where a large part of their secure local market disappeared. The downsized forces did, after a few years, find the need for new weapons for new out-of-area tasks, but for the arms industry, downsizing or developing other markets became a reality. As in all businesses, downsizing is not seen as the best option by the industry. Because downsizing meant job losses, it also carried penalties at the political level. Therefore, the arms industry found a ready ear with governments for increased exports. This was strengthened by the desire by some of the most important producing countries to keep a 'strategic' industry capable of producing much of the equipment needed locally, and at minimal costs, which meant that production runs needed to be as large as possible. In turn, lower local demand meant resorting to a policy of arms exports.

For several Eastern European countries and former Soviet states, the break-down of the local economy and the financial inability to acquire more than the smallest volumes of weapons meant strong pressure to export. This pressure became extreme because arms were often the only industrial products these countries could compete with on the world market. Russia, in particular, was forced to export as many weapons as possible to keep the arms industry alive, and chose, then, to allow large deliveries of advanced equipment to China, despite the fact that China was believed to have few scruples about copying technology and despite some strong fears about arming a potential adversary. However, without these exports in the 1990s, the Russian arms industry would not have survived – orders from the Russian armed forces were minimal, often just a small percentage of what they were in the Cold War period.

Aid

Arms transfers as military aid, mainly linked to efforts to gain political influence through arms transfers, are not uncommon. Aid was used by both blocs during the Cold War to provide reliable, but poor allies with weapons in the 'fight' against the other bloc, or to gain political influence. This practice did not disappear after 1989. There is no evidence that arms transfers as aid, that is for free, have diminished strongly since the end of the Cold War. The only obvious change has been a diminished level of such aid from the most advanced NATO countries to Greece, Turkey and Portugal. These three received during the Cold War extensive amounts of older weapons from other NATO countries, in particular the USA and Germany. As part of the 'Cascade' in the early 1990s they received substantial amounts for a few years. After that, the aid flow dried up to a very low level. However, this was partly as a result of the three countries developing economically and thus being able to buy new weapons instead of accepting old ones as aid.

The level of military aid to gain political influence during the Cold War has probably been overrated. Certainly the USA provided substantial aid, but aid flows from the Soviet Union appear to have been rather limited – in most cases important clients in the developing world, such as Angola, Syria and Cuba, actually paid for their Soviet weapons either in goods (oil or sugar), cash or with credit.

Currently the USA is still providing substantial military aid, at several billion US dollars per year, to Israel and Egypt through the Foreign Military Financing programme, and also to many states as part of the 'war on terror'. Other countries provide limited military aid, e.g. Turkey to Georgia, Azerbaijan and several states in Central Asia as part of a foreign policy aimed at becoming a regional power and leader of 'Turkish' states. Less 'selfish' aid has been given as well, for example UK supplies to Sierra Leone to rebuild the army, or German gifts of weapons to the UN for equipping peace-keeping forces in the former Yugoslavia.

Illegal trade

Illegal (or illicit as it is often called today) trade has become a hot topic in the 1990s and became a focal point of international discussion and action. There are good reasons to assume that the illegal arms trade has grown in volume and importance since the Cold War. Illicit trade also rightly became emphasized due to the more extensive attention paid to the small but deadly conflicts in developing countries. Generally one of the warring parties would be a rebel group that could only buy weapons in an illegal manner. However, such conflicts and the resulting illegal trade with rebels were common in the Cold War period as well. For instance, deliveries by the USA and other countries to the Afghan mujahidin in the 1980s, while considered legal from the US point of view, were of course illegal. However, with the many more UN embargoes established after 1989, it is likely that the illegal trade in arms has increased. The main reason for the international focus on illegal trade most likely lies in the fact that it is easy for all countries to agree on initiatives to combat this issue. While such initiatives are important, they should not be overestimated. The bulk of arms transfers remains legal, but may give more problems than the illicit trade – problems that have been recognized (see 'limitations' above) but are difficult to address without agreement on legitimacy issues.

Arms trade can be illegal for three reasons:

- The weapons traded or the manner of trading is illegal by virtue of an international treaty.
- The manner or destination of trading is against the national laws of the country from which territory they are supplied, through which territory they are transported or to which territory they are delivered.
- The recipient or the supplier is under UN sanctions.

All three grounds existed during the Cold War. Several international treaties banned certain weapons (e.g. 'dum-dum' bullets), or materials. Many countries did have laws or regulations on the supply, transport or acquisition of weapons in the form of national export laws, transport safety laws or laws on procurement procedures. UN Security Council arms embargoes had been used. At the same time all three types of illegal transfers did occur during the Cold War. However, the post-Cold War period saw much more development in the control of illicit arms than in the whole 40 years of the Cold War. Several new treaties banning specific weapons or certain trade practices were agreed upon. The Ottawa Treaty banned nearly all anti-personnel mines, including the trade in them, while the Oslo Treaty did the same for most cluster munitions. Many states established new national export legislation. A UN treaty on corruption also established clear rules to prevent bribes and other corrupt practices of officials, including in arms sales. The UN established more than 24 arms embargoes. However, this means that it is likely that more trade is illegal in one way or another – old habits of using bribes or transporting weapons without the proper documentation die slowly. With many more places under UN embargo, but with clear demand for weapons from the targets of the embargoes and with weak monitoring and enforcing mechanisms, it is only natural that illegal transfers should increase. Reports by UN sanctions monitoring groups as well as by NGOs clearly show that such transfers are taking place.

Bibliography

Center for Defense Information (CDI), www.cdi.org

Federation of American Scientists (FAS), Arms Sales Monitoring Project, www.fas.org/programs/ssp/asmp/index.html

Gallick, Daniel, ed., *World Military Expenditure and Arms Transfers*, US Department of State, Bureau of Verification and Compliance (previously by ACDA; near annual; last published 2002)

Grimmett, Richard F., *Conventional Arms Transfers to Developing Nations*, Congressional Research Service (CRS), annual editions

Laurance, Edward J., *The International Arms Trade*, New York, Lexington, 1992

National reports on arms exports and *European Union Annual Report according to Operative Provision 9 of the European Union Code of Conduct on Arms Exports*, www.sipri.org/contents/armstrad/atlinks_gov.html

Pearson, Frederic S. and John Sislin, *Arms and Ethnic Conflict*, Lanham, MD, Rowman and Littlefield, 2001

Pierre, Andrew J., ed., *Cascade of Arms: Controlling Conventional Weapons Proliferation in the 1990s*, Washington, The World Peace Foundation/Brookings Institution Press, 1997

SIPRI, Arms Transfers Database (data on transfers of major conventional arms since 1950), Stockholm, Stockholm International Peace Research Institute, www.sipri.org/contents/armstrad/at_db.html

——*SIPRI Yearbook*, Stockholm, Stockholm International Peace Research Institute (SIPRI), annual editions, www.sipri.org

SIPRI/SPITS, *United Nations Arms Embargoes: Their Impact on Arms Flows and Target Behaviour*, Stockholm International Peace Research Institute (SIPRI) and Uppsala University Special Program on the Implementation of Targeted Sanctions (SPITS), 2007, www.sipri.org/contents/armstrad/embargoes.html

Small Arms Survey (SAS), annual editions, www.smallarmssurvey.org

UN, United Nations Register of Conventional Arms (UN Register), disarmament.un.org/cab/register.html

15 Globalization revisited

Internationalizing armaments production

Richard A. Bitzinger

Approximately 15 years ago, the author wrote:

> The globalization of the arms industry entails a significant shift away from traditional, single-country patterns of weapons production toward internationalization of the development, production, and marketing of arms. While wholly indigenous armaments production may be on the decline, multinational arms production – through collaboration on individual weapons systems and increasingly via inter-firm linkages across the international arms industry – appears actually to be expanding. In several instances, in fact, multinational armaments production is increasingly supplementing or even supplanting indigenous or autonomous weapons production or arms imports. The emergence of an increasingly transnational defense technology and industrial base is fundamentally affecting the shape and content of much of the global arms trade.
>
> (Bitzinger 1994, 170)

At the time, immediately following the collapse of Communism and the end of the Cold War, it appeared that the world's defence industry was undergoing a major reformation and restructuring, along the lines of a more globally open and integrated process of developing, manufacturing, and marketing arms. Major cuts in defence spending (the so-called 'peace dividend') during the 1990s left the world with considerably more capacity and capability to develop and produce arms than it either needed or could reasonably afford. This state of affairs, in turn, forced a major retrenchment and consolidation among leading arms producers. Hundreds of thousands of defence workers around the world were made redundant, as factories cut back production or even closed down. Additionally, armaments production became increasingly concentrated in the hands of fewer but larger defence firms, as these companies either merged or acquired the military assets of other corporations exiting the defence business altogether. Consequently, the 1990s saw the emergence of several mega-defence firms: Lockheed Martin, Northrop Grumman and Boeing in the USA, for example, and BAE Systems, Thales and DASA in Europe.

As domestic arms markets shrank, the overseas market grew in importance. European defence firms are highly dependent upon foreign markets. By the start of the 21st century, companies such as BAE Systems (United Kingdom), Thales (France), Dassault (France) and Finmeccanica (Italy) were earning up to 75% of their revenues from foreign sales. In the USA several major weapons systems, such as the F-15 and F-16 fighters and the M-1A1 main battle tank, were being produced solely for export. For many firms, foreign sales were no longer a supplemental form of income, they were increasingly critical to the health of the defence industrial base.

At the same time, the global arms market became more complex and competitive. The large numbers of motivated sellers in the West created a 'buyer's market' in arms in which nearly every conceivable kind of conventional weapon system was on the table. Additionally, the end of the Cold War division of the world into communist and capitalist camps greatly opened up the global defence market, and arms sales were, for the most part, no longer restricted for ideological reasons. Consequently, arms exporters had to be ready to deal, and offering potential buyers incentives such as industrial participation ('offsets'), technology transfers and foreign direct investment, increasingly became part of the cost of doing business.

Finally, as the costs of new-generation military programmes grew, cross-border co-operation made increasing economic sense. Through *ad hoc* partnerships, strategic alliances, joint ventures and even transnational mergers and acquisitions (M&A), arms manufacturers hoped to share the costs and risks of researching, developing and manufacturing new weapons systems, leverage their comparative advantages in certain arms-manufacturing niches, improve access to innovative foreign technologies, increase economies of scale in production, and reduce wasteful duplication of effort in armaments production.

Smaller and emerging arms-manufacturing states – such as Australia, Brazil, Canada, Israel, Singapore, South Africa and the Republic of Korea (South Korea) – especially felt the pinch. For them, the post-Cold War dilemma was not simply one of dealing with reduced domestic demand and excess defence industrial capacity – increasingly, it was a matter of sheer survival. Since they were typically both consumers and producers of arms, they had both advantages and challenges: as arms buyers, they could 'hold hostage' access to their national arms markets in exchange for receiving lucrative offsets from foreign arms suppliers; as manufacturers, they needed to find international partnerships to provide them with new markets for their products, as well as new technologies and new sources of funding in order to advance their defence industrial bases.

Against this backdrop, the globalization of the defence industry seemed inevitable. As the global arms industry became smaller and more concentrated, as defence firms, with their governments' approval, increasingly went abroad in search of markets, risk-sharing partners and new business opportunities, it appeared likely that the defence industry would become more integrated globally, as more armaments production – from research and development (R&D) to manufacturing and marketing – was carried out transnationally. To an extent, this did occur. Certainly, the arms industry today is much more internationalized than it was 30, 20, or even 10 years ago. The question is, has it fundamentally altered the global arms industry as a whole?

In fact, while there has certainly occurred considerable change within some of the global arms industry – particularly in Western Europe, where much of the defence sector has become regionalized in terms of production or ownership – the bulk of the world's arms-producing infrastructure remains remarkably unaltered. The US defence industrial base is pretty much the same as it was immediately after the Cold War: a highly insulated sector that dominates the world's arms market through the force of massive US defence spending and an export juggernaut. What is even more remarkable is that much of the world's defence industry outside Europe and America – the 'second-tier' of smaller and emerging arms-producing states – have continued to emphasize autarky in defence manufacturing, despite the enormous costs. In general, the globalization process has not unfolded nearly as deterministically as one might have supposed 15 years ago. That said, the defence industrial landscape has certainly evolved greatly over the past decade and a half, and the process is unending.

Western Europe: limits to regionalization

Perhaps no other element of the world's arms industry has experienced more globalization than in Western Europe. Since the end of the Cold War, the European defence industry has increasingly engaged in pan-European solutions to pan-European problems of economic and technological competitiveness, particularly when it comes to critical, next-generation technologies and military systems. As a result, armaments production in Europe is increasingly being carried out on a regional, rather than national, basis. Current major European co-operative arms programmes include the Eurofighter Typhoon (Germany, Italy, Spain and the UK); the Tiger attack helicopter (France and Germany); the NH-90 military transport helicopter (France, Germany, Italy, the Netherlands and Portugal); the EH-101 military transport helicopter (Italy and the UK); the Boxer multi-role armoured vehicle (Germany and the Netherlands); and the FREMM multi-mission frigate (France and Italy). In particular, the past decade or so has seen the European defence industry expand – again, on a regional, co-operative basis – into programme areas that were previously ceded to the US industry, such as:

- Strategic Airlift: A400M transport aircraft (Belgium, France, Germany, Luxembourg, Portugal, Spain, Turkey, UK)
- Advanced air-to-air missiles: Meteor (France, Germany, Italy, Spain, Sweden, UK); IRIS-T (Germany, Greece, Italy, Norway, Sweden)
- Space systems: Galileo satellite navigation system (France, Germany, Italy, Spain, UK); Helios II surveillance satellite (France, Germany); Skynet 5 satellite communications system (UK, France, Germany)
- Unmanned combat systems: Neuron UCAV (France, Sweden, Greece, Spain, Switzerland, Sweden)
- Standoff precision-guided weapons: Storm Shadow/Scalp (France, UK); Taurus (Germany, Sweden)
- Missile defences: FSAF/PAAMS surface-to-air missile (France, Italy, UK)

Accordingly, Europe's leading defence firms have greatly expanded their regional operations through different types of pan-European teaming arrangements, strategic alliances, joint venture companies, and even mergers and acquisitions. In many areas of European armaments production, then, multinational collaborative efforts have become the norm and are rooted in transnational enterprises. Important pan-European arms manufacturing operations include:

- Airbus Military Company, a consortium operated by Airbus Industries to design and manufacture the A400M transport aircraft; member countries include Belgium, France, Germany, Luxembourg, Portugal, Spain, Turkey, UK.
- Astrium, a Franco-German-Spanish satellite joint-venture company, which in addition owns and operates satellite production facilities in the UK.
- Eurocopter, a Franco-German joint-venture company which produces, among other things, the Tiger attack helicopter.
- MBDA, an Anglo-French-Italian joint-venture missile company, which is the lead contractor for the Meteor missile, and which additionally owns minority stakes in two German missile firms, BGT (20%) and LFK (30%), as well as a 40% share in Empresas de Missiles Española, Spain's leading guided weapons company.
- NH Industries, a Franco-German-Italian-Dutch consortium building the NH-90 heavy-lift military helicopter.

At the same time, Europe's leading arms industries increasingly pursued M&A activities beyond their borders, acquiring or making substantial investments in defence firms in other European countries. As such, in the case of Europe, the regionalization of arms production can be viewed as a transnational extension of the overall consolidation process taking place within the defence industry. For example:

- BAE Systems is a partner in MBDA and Airbus Industries, and it owns defence subsidiaries in Sweden (Bofors Defense and Hägglunds); it also holds a 20% stake in the Swedish military aircraft manufacturer Saab.

- Thales, a self-described 'multi-domestic' company, has acquired wholly owned subsidiaries in both the Netherlands and the UK, as well as sizable investments in other defence concerns in Germany, Italy, Portugal and Spain. Currently, approximately 33% of Thales's European workforce is based outside France.
- ThyssenKrupp Marine Systems of Germany owns and operates shipyards in Greece and Sweden.
- The European Aeronautic Defence and Space Company (EADS) is perhaps the ultimate result of pan-European defence consolidation. It was created in 2000 through the merger of DaimlerChrysler Aerospace (DASA) of Germany, France's Aerospatiale Matra, and CASA (Construcciones Aeronauticas SA) of Spain. EADS is a truly transnational defence firm: the company is headquartered in a 'neutral' country (the Netherlands), and it has two chief executive officers, one French and one German. In addition to controlling 80% of Airbus Industries and 47% of Dassault, the French combat aircraft manufacturer, EADS owns or has substantial shareholdings in several pan-European joint ventures, including Eurocopter, MBDA, Astrium, Taurus systems, Inmize (a Spanish missile company), and ATR (a Franco-Italian joint venture building regional transport aircraft). Outside of its three home countries, EADS also has a large industrial footprint in the UK, with over 12,000 employees, and it also owns a 27% stake in Patria Industries, Finland's leading defence firm.

In addition to regionalizing operations on a pan-European scale, Europe's leading defence firms greatly expanded beyond Europe and the transatlantic relationship in order to create a truly global network of ownership arrangements, international joint ventures and other co-operative approaches. As a result, European arms manufacturers are much more globalized than their opposite numbers in the USA, particularly when it comes to the so-called second-tier arms-producing states in Africa, Asia and Latin America:

- BAE Systems operates several subsidiary or joint-venture operations in Australia, Canada, Singapore and South Africa. For example, BAE Systems acquired a 20% stake in South Africa's Advanced Technologies and Engineering (ATE), and it recently gained that country's Land Systems OMC armoured vehicle manufacturing firm when it bought Alvis.
- Thales has operations or holdings in several non-European countries, including Australia, Brazil, South Korea and South Africa. It owns 100% of Australian Defence Industries (now Thales Australia), the country's leading producer of naval vessels, military vehicles and ordnance. Thales owns subsidiaries in Singapore (Avimo) and South Africa (African Defence Systems), and it operates joint ventures with South Korea's Samsung Electronics and with Malaysia's Sapura. Altogether, nearly 15% of the company's workforce is located outside Europe (Thales corporate website).
- EADS has industrial operations and joint ventures in several regions around the world, mainly through the ongoing activities of its national corporate groupings. CASA of Spain, for example, has had a longstanding arrangement with Indonesian Aerospace to jointly manufacture the CN-235 transport aircraft. DaimlerChrysler Aerospace (DASA), meanwhile, already had a sizable industrial presence in South Africa's arms industry prior to the EADS merger. Eurocopter controls Australian Aerospace Pty, and it is currently producing the EC-120 light helicopter in co-operation with Singapore Technologies Aerospace and CATIC of the People's Republic of China. Finally, Airbus (which is 80% owned by EADS) recently signed up South Africa as a partner on the A400M transport aircraft project – the programme's first non-European industrial participant.
- Finally, several smaller European defence firms have increasingly globalized their operations. Saab recently acquired Grintek Ltd, a South African defence electronics firm, while the French jet engine manufacturer Snecma recently acquired Denel Airmotive of South Africa, a maker of small aero-engines. Dassault owns a 5.7% share in the Brazil aircraft manufacturer Embraer.

Despite the prevailing currents driving European defence firms to seek supranational solutions to the challenges of technological and economic competitiveness, the globalization of the European arms industry – indeed, even the regionalization of the arms industry – is by no means a predetermined or clear-cut process. In the first place, protectionist and parochial interests still exert very powerful influences on national decision-making when it comes to arms procurement and production. Governments continue to give considerable thought to national requirements when it comes to economic benefits (jobs, industrial participation, export potential, keeping public monies from flowing out of the country), security of supply (self-sufficiency, reducing a country's vulnerability to foreign sanctions or embargoes), and technology (maintaining the national defence technology base). Consequently, even in the UK – perhaps the most open defence procurement market in Europe – there is still a lot of political pressure to protect home industries and home markets first, and to look for international co-operative avenues when economic and technological considerations force them (Chuter 2004; Ministry of Defence (UK) 2002; Bitzinger 2005). Even then, most European governments continue to insist on a fair return (*juste retour*) on their investment in collaborative programmes, in terms of workshares and technology-sharing.

Even within an ostensibly transnational corporation such as EADS, most armaments production is still conducted on a more or less national basis, and firewalls still exist to protect national proprietary technologies. Germany and Spain, for example, still zealously guard their workshares on the Eurofighter, as do the German and French divisions of Eurocopter when it comes to building the Franco-German Tiger attack helicopter. International collaborative programmes undertaken under the auspices of EADS – such as the A400M transport aircraft or the Skynet 5 communications satellite – are still run more as *ad hoc* consortia than as truly transnational programmes based on comparative economic and technological advantage.

For its part, EADS has so far failed to create a truly transnational corporate culture, and considerable tensions remain between the various French, German and Spanish agents. There is growing concern that EADS is becoming essentially a 'French' company – a belief that was only strengthened by rumours in 2004–05 that EADS was planning on acquiring a large piece of Thales, which would have marginalized the German role in the company. This concern was further highlighted by the row within EADS a few years ago over the selection of new German and French co-CEOs, when the then-head of Airbus, Frenchman Noel Forgeard, was widely perceived as trying to consolidate control of the company under a single, French chief executive (Lewis 2004; Mulholland 2005; Bitzinger 2005).

In fact, there is already very little that is 'German' in EADS in terms of programmes. The French dominate many corporate business areas, including Airbus, missiles (MBDA), Eurocopter and Space (the Ariane launcher). Most German activity is concentrated in defence work (such as Eurofighter), but this business segment constitutes only around one-quarter of all EADS revenue (EADS corporate website; Bitzinger 2005).

The Spanish element within EADS has voiced similar complaints about the French ascendancy within the company. For example, CASA was supposed to take the lead in the design and manufacture of the pan-European A400M transport aircraft, but the Airbus leadership subsequently decided to shift A400M development to its headquarters in Toulouse, France, leaving CASA with only final assembly. Consequently, some Spanish officials have called for Spain to increase its stake in EADS from its current 5.5%, in order to give Madrid a larger say in how the company is run (Agüera 2005).

At the same time, European defence firms tend to mirror the protectionist sentiments of their governments. Most defence companies in Europe still see their countries as captive markets and they are not above playing the protectionist card when it comes to securing contracts. Germany, for example, recently approved acquisition of the German submarine builder HDW by ThyssenKrupp from its US owners, One Equity Partners, and it furthermore passed legislation greatly curtailing foreign ownership of national strategic industries (Mulholland 2005).

In addition, the UK has sought ways to keep BAE Systems's Hawk trainer jet programme alive, France acquired Nexter's (formerly GIAT) new CAESAR artillery system, Spain bought additional frigates from its Navantia shipyards, and Sweden purchased additional Gripen fighter jets to keep Saab's production lines open. According to the European Defence Agency (EDA), in 2007 less than 20% of all European Union (EU) defence procurement was procured through European collaboration (EDA 2008, 10, 33).

In the case of BAE Systems, the company appears to be shifting its emphasis away from Europe in favour of the USA, both reducing its involvement in continental defence programmes while increasing its activities in North America (see below). BAE Systems has concluded that trying to break into other European countries' highly protected national arms markets, or working with other European firms on third-party sales, is no longer worth the effort (Bitzinger 2005). In recent years, then, the company has sold off its stakes in Airbus and Astrium (a pan-European satellite company), reduced its stake in Saab from 35% to 20% (and returned its 50% share in Gripen International, a Swedish-British company to globally market the JAS-39 Gripen fighter jet), divested itself of the German small-arms manufacturer Heckler & Koch, and broken up its joint-ownership arrangement with Siemens of the German electronics firm STN Atlas and sold its remaining assets in the company. It has also dissolved AMS, its avionics and communications joint venture with Finmeccanica and sold off its share of the business to its former Italian partner. BAE Systems plans to remain in Europe mainly where it expects to extract long-term profitability or find large enough markets to support a company of its size, such as in the missile, fighter aircraft and commercial jetliner sectors; hence, it is preserving its stakes in MBDA, Airbus and the Eurofighter programme. (In a related incident, in 2004, British helicopter producer GKN sold off its share in AgustaWestland helicopters – which produces the EH-101 military helicopter, among other products – to Finmeccanica; the Italian company now owns and operates all helicopter production facilities in the UK.)

It also remains to be seen how much influence pan-European defence institutions such as the EDA and OCCAR (Europe's supranational defence procurement agency) will ultimately have promoting a pan-European arms market and defence industry. A critical weakness of the EDA is that it does not have its own research or procurement budget, nor does it have a large enough staff to actually manage joint weapons programmes. The EDA can only propose and encourage collaborative projects among the EU Member States; it cannot purchase systems or administer these projects (Keohane 2004, 2; Tigner 2005). In fact, the EDA's first Chief Executive, Nick Whitney openly stated that the Agency's 'preferred approach' was to 'win the intellectual battle', by persuading EU Member States to open up their national defence markets and increase joint procurement (Chapman 2005, 6). For its part, OCCAR has responsibility for only a handful of collaborative programmes, many of which were initiated several years ago and handed off in retrospect to this authority.

Transatlantic arms co-operation: continuing disappointment

If pan-European defence industrial integration has apparently reached a plateau, transatlantic arms co-operation has cooled off even more. Interestingly, the barriers to collaboration seem to stem more from the American, rather than the European side. Despite strong pressures from France (and perhaps Germany) for a 'European preference' in procurement and production, most European arms producers – companies and countries alike – have largely remained keen on building bridges to the US defence industry. The reasons are simple to see. The USA is easily the world's single largest arms buyer, with a procurement budget at least four times greater than all of Europe combined. Therefore, few European firms are prepared to write off the US market completely. For many European defence companies, capturing even a small fraction of the US defence business could translate into sizable revenue. In this regard, then, these firms are pursuing both pan-European and transatlantic linkages, depending on where they perceive maximum profitability.

Consequently, many of Europe's arms manufacturers have laboured hard in recent years to enter the US arms market or to partner with US firms on export-oriented products.

As already noted, BAE Systems has particularly expanded its North American activities in recent years, and since the late 1990s the company has acquired more than 12 US defence firms. Most recently, BAE Systems bought United Defense Ltd (UDL), which builds the Bradley infantry fighting vehicle and the Paladin self-propelled howitzer, and Armor Holdings, which manufactures military, law enforcement and personnel safety equipment, on the expectation that it will earn significant revenue servicing, maintaining and upgrading armoured and mine-resistant ambush-protected (MRAP) vehicles for the US military. Finally, BAE Systems is the only Level One partner in the US-led F-35 Joint Strike Fighter (JSF) programme, which promises considerable long-term revenue – perhaps even more than the Eurofighter Typhoon (particularly when it comes to third-party exports). Consequently, BAE Systems does more business in North America (£6.4 billion worth of sales in 2007) than in the rest of Europe (£2.6 billion), or, indeed, even the UK (£3.4 billion)! North America, in fact, has become the company's single largest market, accounting for 41% of all corporate income in 2007 and making BAE Systems the sixth-largest contractor to the US Department of Defense (DoD) (BAE Systems corporate website).

Other British firms are also increasingly active in the US defence industry, to the detriment of Europe, including Rolls Royce, Smiths Industries, Meggitt and QinetiQ. Overall, Washington appears to have a much higher 'comfort level' with British acquisitions of the US defence businesses than with other potential European investors, and this is reflected in the fact that British firms outnumber their European counterparts in FDI in the US defence sector by a wide margin (Mulholland 2004; Carson 2002).

Defence industries in Italy, Spain and Sweden have been equally comfortable having a foot in both the European and transatlantic camps. Due to their much smaller sizes, companies such as Saab, Finmeccanica and Navantia have had to be much more flexible and nimble players in the global defence business than their larger European cousins, such as Thales or EADS. Consequently, these companies have increasingly pressed their comparative advantages and core competencies – for example, shipbuilding in Spain, helicopters in Italy, aerospace and C4ISR in Sweden – to excel at being niche players in the global arms industry. This has often entailed partnering with US firms. Finmeccanica, for instance, is a member of the JSF team, as well as being a partner with the USA on the C-27 transport aircraft. Navantia is collaborating with Lockheed Martin on the Advanced Frigate Consortium (AFCON), which integrates a smaller version of the Aegis SPY-1 air defence combat system into a frigate-sized naval vessel (which, in turn, has been sold to Norway and Australia). Sweden, meanwhile, is currently co-operating with the US Army on the Excalibur precision-guided artillery round, and it has contracted to several US firms, such as Boeing and IBM, on its nascent network-based defence concept.

Even French companies are not prepared to abandon the potential of the US defence market. Thales operates a joint venture with Raytheon to develop and market radars and command and control systems around the world. The company was the 46th-largest contractor to the US DoD in fiscal year (FY) 2006 (Department of Defense (USA) 2007), and it intends to double its sales to the USA over the next decade.

EADS is also eager to expand into the US defence market. North America is EADS's largest market outside Europe and it is nearly as big as the rest of the world combined. The company already has more employees in the USA than it has outside Europe. The company recently opened a factory in Mississippi to produce helicopters for the US Border Patrol and a facility in Alabama to manufacture the CN-235 transport aircraft for the US Coast Guard. EADS also set up an Airbus design centre in Kansas and is prepared to establish a production plant in the USA to build tanker aircraft for the US Air Force, should it win that contract. In late 2004 EADS made its first US acquisition, buying Racal Instruments Inc., a manufacturer of testing devices, for US$105m. (Mulholland 2004).

Considering how much the European defence industry has regionalized and even internationalized its way of doing business, the US defence industry, in contrast, has remained surprisingly aloof from the globalization process. The US defence industry – a few exceptions notwithstanding – appears to have lost much of its earlier enthusiasm for globalizing its operations. Part of the reason for this waning interest can be attributed to structural or bureaucratic impediments: it is often difficult for US firms to penetrate a highly protected European arms industry and to reconcile differing national/corporate cultures, such as the European reluctance to engage in workforce downsizing and other radical consolidation efforts. More importantly, though, it has simply been much easier – and increasingly more profitable – for these firms to content themselves with dominating the world's largest and most captive defence market: the USA. US defence firms easily capture more than 90% of all defence contracting in its home market, which in turn comprises nearly 50% of all global spending on arms (including R&D) (Skoens and Weidacher 1999, 410). Moreover, this has been a rapidly growing arms market, as US spending on procurement and R&D more than doubled between 2000 and 2008, from $116 billion to $255 billion (Kosiak 2008, table 4). Not surprisingly, then, the major US defence companies garner only a small percentage of their revenues – typically around 10%–15% – from non-US markets. Ironically, the US defence industry nevertheless dominates the global trade in off-the-shelf arms sales, capturing roughly 40% of a market worth nearly $60 billion in 2007 (Lorell et al. 2002, 25–6; Grimmett 2008, 28).

All told, then, the US arms industry is simply under much less pressure than its European counterparts to aggressively look beyond its borders for business, or to engage in innovative collaborative efforts to capture foreign market share. This corporate indifference to the defence industry globalization process in general, and to transatlantic arms collaboration in particular, has been matched by a general lack of responsiveness and commitment on the part of the US government (CSIS 2003, 25–6). This is not a criticism of just the recently departed George W. Bush Administration – no US administration has ever strongly and consistently pushed transatlantic arms collaboration as a key North Atlantic Treaty Organization (NATO) action plan. The George Bush Sr Administration launched no new initiatives in this regard, while Clinton's Administration efforts tended to revolve around a handful of showcase projects, such as the Medium Extended Air Defense System (MEADS), only to lose interest if they ran into major technological or political problems. In fact, one has to go back to the mid-1980s and the so-called Nunn Amendment programmes to find any 'golden age' in NATO armaments co-operation; as a result of this initiative the USA and its European allies launched more than 25 collaborative arms projects. Even then, most of these programmes failed within a few years, as seed funding ran out and the US DoD chose to pursue US-only programmes (Bitzinger 1993, 20–1, 25–7). Only the JSF – which grew out of the joint US-UK Advanced Short Take-Off and Vertical Landing (ASTOVL) programme and which was transformed by the Clinton Administration into a truly multinational development programme – appears to have succeeded.

For its part, the George W. Bush Administration more or less ignored the issue of pan-NATO arms co-operation. Given its preoccupation with fighting the global 'war on terror' and on the conflicts in Afghanistan and Iraq, transatlantic arms co-operation was simply never at the top of its national security agenda – it was not even a critical aspect of its defence industrial policy. In addition, increased US defence spending has undermined any sense of budget-driven urgency to engage in cost-sharing co-operative programmes, with the sole exceptions of the JSF and missile defence (Mulholland 2003). Even then, the US DoD does not appear to be interested in most foreign technologies – witness its general indifference to European industrial participation in missile defence (Kington 2003; Kington and Ratnam 2003). As one high-level study, completed in early 2003, noted, the DoD mostly views foreign participation to be a nuisance at best, and, therefore, largely operates along a bureaucratic default mode that 'favors national programs and often kills cooperative projects' (CSIS 2003, 25–6). If anything, it appears content to cherry-pick foreign innovations on an *ad hoc* basis or to pursue foreign participation as much for political cover as for any technological or financial benefits.

Consequently, transatlantic armaments collaboration is at its lowest point in decades, and the USA must bear the lion's share of the blame for this state of affairs. Admittedly, Europe has its problems with committing to transatlantic arms co-operation. It has often been lukewarm to collaborative projects that place it in a decidedly junior role, even though it may lack the funding or the technology to participate at a higher level. It has not been above bowing to parochial interests, such as in the recent selection of a European engine over its less expensive Canadian competitor to power the A400M transport aircraft. However, if the USA were seriously committed to expanding transatlantic arms co-operation, creating an active transatlantic defence market and building a transatlantic defence industry, it would have the power to make it happen.

The one current success – the Joint Strike Fighter – could show the way forward for future collaborative efforts, at least at the level of project-specific teaming. The JSF project proves that international co-operative arms programmes can succeed at both the economic and technological levels, as long as there is long-term commitment and resolve on the part of the most senior executives in the US military and civilian leadership. This means crafting a truly co-operative programme that values and actively seeks out foreign capital and expertise. The JSF model does *not* mean US leadership and European subordination – in fact, any attempt to relegate the European arms industry to permanent junior status is almost certain to fail. Rather, the critical lessons of this programme are the need for risk- and benefits-sharing, noble work, an end to unwieldy offsets and workshare arrangements, and early agreement as to technology-sharing and third-party exports. The concern here is that the JSF may be the exception that proves the rule. Without follow-on projects, the JSF model could be a one-off deal. So far, the US leadership has not applied the JSF model to other international programmes.

The defence industry outside Europe and America: continuing emphasis on autarky

Finally, it is surprising how little the rest of the world's arms producers have globalized their operations, particularly in the Asia-Pacific, which comprises the highest concentration of arms-producing nations outside of North America and Europe, and is also a region of considerable growth in arms manufacturing, in terms of value, types of systems and increasing technological sophistication. Given the enormous economic and technological challenges facing these so-called 'second-tier' arms producers – i.e. smaller arms-producing states such as Australia, Brazil, Japan and South Africa, or aspiring great-power states, such as China, India and perhaps even South Korea – one would have thought that these countries would be prime candidates for embedding themselves in the globalization process (Bitzinger 2003, 6–7). Armaments production is an immensely capital- and technology-intensive industry, requiring significant investment in R&D, production facilities and skilled personnel. Consequently, small-scale arms manufacturing of the type generally found in countries outside Europe and America is rarely cost-effective. In fact, by the late 1990s, it was obvious that most of these second-tier arms-producing states had failed to gain much in the way of an independent, self-sustaining defence technology and industrial base. Most tended to suffer from shortages of skilled personnel and sufficient scientific and technical infrastructures to pursue breakthroughs and applied research in many critical defence technologies and, consequently, were often deficient when it came to indigenous capacities for weapons design, engineering and manufacture (Bitzinger 2003, 24–38). As a result, they still tended to rely heavily upon foreign suppliers when it came to design, R&D and arcane, sophisticated technologies (such as propulsion, sensors, guidance systems, aerodynamics, information technologies and microelectronics).

Yet, overall there appears to have been little inclination among the smaller arms-producing nations to abandon autarky in exchange for playing a subordinate role in a globalized division of labour (i.e. a 'core-periphery' approach to globalized armaments production) (Bitzinger 2003, 69–76). If anything, the commitment of many of these countries to preserving – and in some cases, even expanding – local defence industrial bases has never been stronger. Despite technological hurdles and high entry costs, other factors – particularly perceived national security imperatives, projected technology spin-offs and even national pride – continue to be very strong impulses acting on most second-tier arms-producing states.

To be sure, some smaller arms-producing states have embraced globalization. In particular, Australia and South Africa have accepted very high degrees of foreign investment and ownership in their national defence industrial bases. Some of Australia's largest arms firms, including ADI and Australian Aerospace, are now wholly owned subsidiaries of foreign corporations. South Africa's defence industry is also heavily foreign-owned. BAE Systems, for example, has acquired Land Systems OMC, as well as a 51% stake in Paradigm System Technologies and 20% of ATE, a local defence electronics firm. Other recent foreign investments in the South African defence industry include the purchase of Denel Airmotive (which makes small aeroengines) by Turbomeca of France, the acquisition of Altech Defence Systems (renamed African Defence Systems) by Thales, and Saab's purchase of Grintek's Avitronics and Communications division, as well as buying 20% of Denel Aerostructures. In addition, South African arms firms have established a number of joint ventures and strategic alliances with foreign companies. Overall, South Africa's arms industry is struggling to recast itself, both structurally and strategically, as a 'natural partner' in future international collaborative arms activities. In general, much of the indigenous defence industry views co-operation and link-ups with leading arms-producing states as critical to its survival, and many local firms see their future in playing an important, if niche, role as a supplier and systems integrator of subsystems and components of foreign weapons systems.

Other second-tier arms-producing states have also accepted some globalization of their defence industrial bases (in the case of Malaysia, it is actually government policy to work toward integrating local defence firms into the global production chain as preferred subcontractors and second-tier suppliers) (Balakrishnan 2008, 135–55). Brazil's Embraer has established manufacturing subsidiaries in the USA and China. In South Korea, Samsung has created a joint venture with Thales to produce and market defence electronics systems. Singapore Technologies Engineering (STEngg) owns a 25% stake in the Irish company Timoney, which produces suspension systems for armoured vehicles, and it has also acquired the US shipbuilder Halter Marine as a wholly owned subsidiary; altogether, STEngg has more than 2,500 workers – nearly a quarter of its labour force – employed outside Singapore (Karniol 2003). India has revised its laws to permit foreign companies to invest in local defence firms, allowing them to buy shares in these companies worth up to 26%; in 2009 New Delhi approved a joint venture between BAE Systems and local company Mahindra & Mahindra to develop and produce land combat systems, such as MRAPs, for both the domestic Indian and international defence markets (Grevatt 2009). Even China has said that it will privatize and list some of its assets of its large defence industrial enterprises (admittedly only non-military factories) (Dickie and Mitchell 2009). At the same time, unlike Europe there appears to be no desire or drive to regionalize armaments production, particularly in the Asia-Pacific region, as a means of rationalizing production or pooling technological strengths or financial resources.

Some second-tier arms-producing countries – such as Israel, Singapore and South Africa – appear to have adopted a niche production approach to local arms manufacturing, choosing to manufacture and market products where they may find lucrative overseas sales (Israel's defence industry, for example, typically exports more than three-quarters of its output), or where they might find good fits within the global supply chain. These countries may still be reliant upon foreign sources for major weapons systems, but they avoid total dependency by leveraging their core competencies to give them comparative advantages in internationalized production programmes.

Yet, all these efforts and initiatives appear to be the exceptions that prove the rule: that autarky is still the singular, prevailing tendency among the second-tier arms-producing states. What stands out among these countries is their continued emphasis on pursuing techno-nationalist goals of self-sufficiency when it comes to weapons development and manufacturing. Among these nations, there is an almost obsessive preference for self-reliance in arms procurement and production, and hence, they are investing considerable resources into their defence technological and industrial bases. Japan, for example, has never permitted any foreign investment in its defence industry; additionally, it is currently ploughing billions of dollars into two new programmes to develop a maritime patrol aircraft and a cargo plane. Both China and India have never given any indication that they will ever privatize their huge state-owned defence behemoths; rather, they will continue to protect and nurture these industries as strategic assets (as does Indonesia with its failing aircraft-manufacturing venture). Even in the highly globalized South African defence sector, the process seems to have reached saturation point and, in 2003, Pretoria refused BAE Systems's bid to buy minority stakes in Denel's Aviation and Ordnance groups.

Interestingly, South Korea has particularly committed itself to a strategy of 'cooperative self-reliant defense' (Noh 2005, 5), which includes the goal of 'acquiring the ability to independently develop primary weapons systems for core force capability' (Ministry of National Defence 2000, 145). At the same time, the South Korean government sees the indigenous defence industry as an important symbol of the country's 'coming of age', both as a high-technology powerhouse and as a regional power. Consequently, Seoul has put a strong emphasis on a 'domestic weapons first' policy, which includes the indigenous development of fighter aircraft, large surface combatants, missile systems and perhaps even nuclear-powered submarines. It has particularly promoted its aerospace sector as a key strategic industry, pumping billions of dollars into building a supersonic jet trainer (the T-50), which it plans to use as a starting point for eventually developing a state-of-the-art fighter jet. Seoul also expects to greatly expand its defence exports, a market where it has traditionally been a bit player. South Korea has sold artillery and tank technology to Turkey, infantry fighting vehicles to Malaysia and light trainer planes to Indonesia. It also expects to sell hundreds of its T-50s around the world, in trainer, light-attack and fighter variants (Jung 2009, 34).

Rightly or wrongly, such techno-nationalist sentiments are critical to understanding defence industrialization strategies throughout much of the second-tier arms-producing world. Many of these countries – particularly in the Asia-Pacific – appear willing to pay the premium for achieving high levels of autarky in arms acquisition. The challenge for them is whether such a go-it-alone strategy will actually result in sustainable and technologically advanced domestic defence industries.

Conclusions

Looking back over the past 15 years or so, it is apparent that 'the globalization of armaments production' has not been nearly as transformative as predicted – at least, not across the board. Certainly the European defence industry has experienced a major, perhaps even fundamental, makeover. Increasingly, defence equipment is being procured and produced collaboratively and more and more defence production is in the hands of international joint ventures (e.g. Eurocopter), multinational corporations (e.g. BAE Systems, Thales), or transnational firms (e.g. EADS). Nevertheless, even after more than 15 years of defence industrial consolidation, the European arms market remains highly fragmented and domestic arms-manufacturing capabilities zealously sheltered. In 2007 only 21% of British, 19% of German and 18% of French procurement spending was dedicated to European collaborative programmes (EDA 2008, 34).

Clearly, protectionism – or 'economic patriotism', to use a French term to describe national preferences when it comes to defence procurement – is still alive and well within the EU. Most procurement and military R&D spending within the EU is still concentrated in redundant and often competing national programmes, further eroding the overall buying power of European equipment budgets. The European arms market is beset with a number of duplicative and competing programmes, such as three fighter aircraft (Rafale, Eurofighter and Gripen), two heavy-lift utility helicopters (the EH-101 and the NH-90), at least three air-defence surface combatants (the Franco-Italian Horizon, the Spanish F-100 frigates and the British Type-45 destroyer), and countless armoured vehicle projects. Where there is collaboration, there is too much emphasis on *ad hoc* co-operative programmes that do little to make the outlay of scarce defence dollars (or euros) more cost-effective.

Outside Europe, the globalization process has advanced even less. Transatlantic armaments collaboration has largely stagnated. The US defence industry, the beneficiary of several years of rising military spending by Washington, has had little incentive to 'go global' in the manner of multinational joint ventures and overseas acquisitions, and many earlier initiatives to push for expanded international (and especially transatlantic) armaments co-operation have withered; the US defence industry's idea of internationalization is simply to sell its wares off-the-shelf (or through licensing arrangements) to foreign customers. The British have made some inroads into investing in the US defence industrial base, but they appear to be the exception that proves the rule.

Globalization involving second-tier arms-producing countries has also flattened. While some countries, such as Australia and South Africa, appear comfortable with the idea that much of their domestic industrial bases can be foreign-owned, most others have flatly rejected this idea. Rather, these countries continue to emphasize autarky in armaments production, or at least continue to shield their defence sectors from foreign penetration. Some, such as China, India and South Korea, are actually expanding their defence sectors, pumping considerable new resources into these industries, while others, such Israel and Singapore, are seeking niche areas where they can find lucrative export earnings.

So, have we reached a saturation point when it comes to the globalization of the defence industry? It is possible, but it is equally likely that the global defence industry is simply in a period of strategic pause and that it is still digesting the often traumatic experiences of the past 15 or 20 years of consolidation and rationalization. Certainly if defence spending world-wide falls again, pressures on governments and defence firms to consider radical solutions, such as additional globalization efforts, could increase. Perhaps the globalization process has not turned out to be as paradigm-shattering as one would have predicted 15 years ago, but at the same time the global defence industry is certainly a far different thing today – more integrated and interconnected globally – than it was then. Moreover, the process of reform, readjustment and restructuring within the global arms industry is a dynamic one, and the globalization process may yet take on renewed momentum in the future. In 15 years hence, the defence industry could look as different from today as it was 15 years past.

Bibliography

Agüera, Martin, 'Why Spain Wants More of EADS', *Defense News*, 11 April, 2005

BAE Systems, *Annual Report 2007*, 2008, www.baesystems.com

Balakrishnan, Kogila, 'Defense Industrialization in Malaysia: Development Challenges and the Revolution in Military Affairs', *Security Challenges*, Summer 2008

Bitzinger, Richard A., *The Globalization of Arms Production: Defense Markets in Transition*, Washington, Defense Budget Project, 1993

——'The Globalization of the Arms Industry: The Next Proliferation Challenge', *International Security*, Fall 1994

——*Towards a Brave New Arms Industry?* Adelphi Paper No. 356, International Institute for Strategic Studies, London, 2003

——author's interviews in Europe with defence industry representatives, March 2005

Carson, Iain, 'Transformed? A Survey of the Defense Industry', *The Economist*, 20 July 2002

Chapman, John, *Will the EU Get Tough on Opening Up National Defense Procurements?*, Brussels, The New Defense Agenda, 18 April 2005

Chuter, Andrew, 'U.K. To Set Industry Strategy in 2005', *Defense News*, 11 November 2004

CSIS, *The Future of the Transatlantic Defense Community: Final Report of the CSIS Commission on Transatlantic Security and Industrial Cooperation in the Twenty-first Century*, Washington, Center for Strategic and International Studies (CSIS), January 2003

Department of Defense, *100 Companies Receiving the Largest Dollar Volume of Prime Contract Awards, Fiscal Year 2006*, Washington, US Department of Defense, 2007

Dickie, Mure and Tom Mitchell, 'Beijing Seeks to Encourage Enterprise in Defense', *Financial Times*, 5 January 2009

EADS website, www.eads-nv.com

EDA, *Defense Data of EDA Participating Member States in 2007*, Brussels, European Defense Agency, 12 December 2008

Grevatt, Jon, 'India Approves JV Between BAE Systems and Mahindra', *Jane's Defense Weekly*, 9 January 2009

Grimmett, Richard F., *Conventional Arms Transfers to Developing Nations, 2000 – 2007*, CRS (Congressional Research Service) Report, US Library of Congress, RL34723, 23 October 2008

Jung, Sung-ki, 'S. Korea's Defense Exports Top $1B in '08', *Defense News*, 6 January 2009

Karniol, Robert, 'Singapore's Defense Industry: Eyes on Expansion', *Jane's Defense Weekly*, 30 April 2003

Keohane, Daniel, *Europe's New Defense Agency*, London, Center for European Reform, June 2004

Kington, Tom, 'Hurdles Slow U.S.-Europe Missile Defense', *Defense News*, 7 October 2003

Kington, Tom and Gopal Ratnam, 'Europe Wary of U.S. Missile Defense Promises', *Defense News*, 13 October 2003

Korea Institute for Defence Analyses, *Defense White Paper 1999: Republic of Korea*, Seoul, Korea Institute for Defence Analyses, 1999

Kosiak, Steven M., *Analysis of the FY 2009 Defense Budget Request*, Washington, DC, Center for Strategic and Budgetary Assessments, 2008

Lewis, J. A. C., 'Germany Fears France is Pushing to Dominate EADS', *Jane's Defense Weekly*, 24 November 2004

Lorell, Mark A. et al., *Going Global? U.S. Government Policy and the Defense Aerospace Industry*, Santa Monica, RAND, 2002

Ministry of Defence, *Defense Industrial Policy, MoD Policy Paper No. 5*, London, Ministry of Defence (UK), October 2002

Ministry of National Defence, *Defence White Paper 1999*, Seoul, Ministry of National Defence (ROK), 2000

Mulholland, David, 'Drive for a Transatlantic Market Stall in the U.S.', *Jane's Defense Weekly*, 29 October 2003

——— 'European Invaders Snap Up U.S. Companies', *Jane's Defense Weekly*, 3 November 2004

——— 'German Industry – Feeling the Squeeze', *Jane's Defense Weekly*, 30 March 2005

Noh, Hoon, *South Korea's 'Cooperative Self-Reliant Defense': Goals and Directions*, KIDA Paper No. 10, Seoul, Korea Institute for Defense Analyses, April 2005

Sköns, Elisabeth and Reinhilde Weidacher, 'Arms Production', in *SIPRI Yearbook 1999*, Oxford, Oxford University Press / Stockholm International Peace Research Institute, 1999

Thales website, www.thalesgroup.com

Tigner, Brooks, 'European Defense Agency May Buy UAVs', *Defense News*, 25 April 2005

16 Defence industry restructuring and consolidation in Europe

Michael Brzoska

Introduction

The defence industry in Europe – here limited to the Member States of the European Union (EU) and the European Free Trade Association (EFTA) – has undergone major structural change since the mid-1980s. It has become more European. However, in contrast to most other economic sectors that fall under community governance, it remains legally, and to a large extent also politically, under national control. This has led to a growing divergence between the economic realities of growing transnational interdependence among defence-related companies and continuing national political control over the sector. This partial Europeanization of arms production has major implications for arms exports. A mixed structure of governance has emerged, legally under full control by national governments but *de facto* also shaped by decision-making in company boards and European institutions. Governments remain reluctant to cede sovereignty over defence production to European institutions, even though a good part of it is not under the control of a single European government any more. One important reason for this structure of governance over arms production and exports in Europe are differences among Member States about the preferred structure of a European defence industry.

This chapter first gives a brief overview of the framework of arms production in Europe after the end of the Second World War. It than recounts the period of major change between the mid-1980s and the early 2000s. The major factors driving restructuring and consolidation – shrinking markets after the end of the Cold War, company policy, competition with the USA, economic integration in Europe and the development of a European security and defence policy – are briefly noted. The following section analyses attempts and approaches to institutionalize a European defence industry, and why these have largely failed. In the final section the consequences of the incomplete Europeanization of defence production for arms exports from Europe are addressed.

Historic background

After the end of the Second World War, a historic process was set in motion, starting in Western Europe and successively encompassing a greater part of the continent: the creation of a community of states. The prime motive was to prevent the next war among Europeans. Starting with six Member States – Belgium, France, Germany, Luxembourg, the Netherlands and Italy – in 1952, as the European Community of Coal and Steel (ECSC), the community has grown to 27 states, now called the EU, with another three in the associated EFTA. The approach to war prevention chosen was to improve economic welfare in Member States through trade and economic interdependence. True, the ECSC introduced an arms control instrument by putting the production of steel, traditionally a major input to arms production, under supranational control. However, this was secondary to the creation of a common market first for coal and steel and later for a wide variety of commodities and services (Cooper 2004).

In parallel to the process of Western European integration, the Cold War gripped Europe. Already in 1948, the Western European Union (WEU) had been founded, a defence alliance of Belgium, France, Luxembourg, the Netherlands and the United Kingdom (UK). It was originally aimed as much against Germany as against the emerging Eastern European bloc dominated by the Soviet Union. The WEU never had much political or military importance, as it was quickly superseded by the much larger North Atlantic Treaty Organization (NATO), which was clearly directed against the Soviet Union. Germany became a member of the WEU in 1954 and NATO in 1955. In Eastern Europe, a similar military organization was built with the Warsaw Treaty Organization.

In Western Europe, the parallel existence of a European economic community and a transatlantic defence alliance led to a strict separation between economic and military affairs. All matters related to armed forces, including defence production, were outside the realm of the institutions of the European Community. While in theory a framework for defence industrial integration among its Member States could – and should, given the problems of multiple types of weapons systems produced among its members – have been provided by NATO, the alliance never mustered the political will to do so, despite various attempts. The USA, with by far the largest defence industry, was as unwilling to open up its market to European competitors as were the Europeans. Within NATO, defence production remained the prerogative of Member States,[1] with collaborative projects among members as the highest form of co-operation (Brzoska and Lock 1992).

As a result of this institutional setup, Western European states established their own domestic defence industries. While supranational bodies of the European Community increasingly were entrusted with the regulatory control of economic activity in Europe, defence production remained fully under national control. Faced with the decision to procure weapons from the outside or produce them domestically, practically all opted for indigenous production, though often with foreign input of technology. The structure that emerged largely reflected industrial capabilities and geopolitical ambitions: The UK and France developed the largest and most technologically advanced industries, followed by Germany, Sweden, Italy and Spain. In each of these countries, the full range of major weapons systems – tanks, fighter aircraft, warships, missiles – was produced, albeit often with technological support from the USA or in collaboration with other European countries (Brzoska and Lock 1992). Several smaller Western European states, such as the Netherlands and Switzerland, also had sizeable defence production (see Table 16.1), though generally limited to a few sectors. The defence companies in Europe producing arms were mostly in public ownership and highly protected by governments through procurement decisions and subsidies. In economic terms, producing many types of weapons systems in small numbers with high subsidies led to high weapon prices and procurement costs to European taxpayers. This was only partly offset by an increasingly diverse and transnational base of suppliers of components for arms production. In general, Western European governments encouraged the development of a second and third tier of mostly private-owned and transnationally oriented producers of components, but insisted on tight national control over the first tier of major arms producers.

The defence industrial situation was markedly different in Eastern Europe. Defence industry was not exempted from the process of economic integration, which the Soviet Union directed. While there was hardly any organized division of labour among arms-producing countries in Western Europe, defence producers in Eastern Europe had to specialize according to plans drawn in the Soviet Union. Some countries, for instance Poland and Czechoslovakia, were entrusted with the production of tanks, while others, such as East Germany and Hungary, were to specialize on electrical and electronic equipment. The overarching priority, though, was to preserve the dominance and viability of the Soviet arms industry (Kiss 1998).

Table 16.1 Estimated employment in arms production in Europe (numbers of direct and indirect employees, in 000s)

	1988	1993	1998	2003	Percentage reduction 1988–2003
United Kingdom	460	380	280	200	57%
France	405	345	267	240	41%
Germany	240	160	95	80	67%
Poland	220	120	70	50	77%
Czechoslovakia	140	105	53	26	81%
Spain	100	50	25	20	80%
Estonia	100	60	25	15	85%
Romania	90	60	20	12	87%
Italy	80	50	35	26	68%
Sweden	45	34	26	25	44%
Belgium	30	15	8	6	80%
Bulgaria	30	10	5	5	83%
Hungary	30	6	2	2	93%
Others	100	70	40	20	80%
Total Europe, in m.	2.1	1.5	1.0	0.8	62%

Source: BICC, Conversion Survey 1996, Oxford: Oxford University Press; BICC, Conversion Survey 2005, Baden-Baden: Nomos

Defence industry restructuring in the 1980s and 1990s

The national-oriented setup of defence production in Western Europe survived into the 1980s, even though its costs to taxpayers, problems with the standardization of equipment within NATO and anomaly in the process of European economic integration had been obvious for years (Klepsch 1978; Hartley and Cox 1992). One major reason was the arms export boom of the 1970s and early 1980s, from which many European arms producers greatly benefited. The high levels of income of exports, particularly to Arab states, could be used to reduce the financial burden of national defence industries on European governments.

Defence industry consolidation in Western Europe only picked up speed in the second half of the 1980s. It went, in general, through three phases, though not necessarily in this order: national consolidation, privatization and Europeanization. A final, fourth phase, namely that of globalization, has only been reached by one European company, BAE Systems.[2]

Table 16.2 lists the 12 largest arms producers in 1988 and what had happened to them by 2006. It indicates the high degree of change, but also continuity particularly among the largest companies. The six largest arms producers in 2006 all had been among the 12 largest in 1988, although only some of them, such as DCN, the state-owned French naval shipyard, and Rolls Royce had already existed with this name in 1988.

During the first phase of consolidation of the European arms industry, 'national champions' were created by governments or with strong government support, in each sector of defence production, sometimes also encompassing more than one sector. Examples include Daimler-Benz Aerospace (DASA) and the shipbuilder Thyssen Industries in Germany, Aérospatiale in aerospace and Thomson-CSF in electronics in France, British Aerospace and GEC Marconi in electronics in the UK, and Finmeccanica covering all sectors in Italy. These companies were given preferred status in national procurement as well as other forms of government support (DeVestel, 1995; Serfati 2000).

Either prior to becoming 'national champions' (DASA, British Aerospace) or afterwards (Aérospatiale, Thomson-CSF, Finmeccanica), companies were privatized. While in the early 1980s

Table 16.2 The largest arms-producing companies in Europe, 1988 and 2006 (turnover in US$ bn, 2006 prices). Global ranking excludes Soviet Union (1988) and People's Republic of China (1988, 2006)

Rank in Europe	1988				Rank in Europe	2006		
			Global rank	Turnover			Global rank	Turnover
1	British Aerospace	United Kingdom	7	8.8	1	BAE Systems	3	24.1
2	Thomson SA	France	12	7.6	4	Thales	10	8.2
3	GEC Marconi	United Kingdom	14	6.6		BAE Systems		
4	Daimler Benz	Germany	15	5.8	2	EADS	7	12.6
5	Aérospatiale	France	22	3.9		EADS		
6	DCN	France	24	3.8	6	DCN	18	3.4
7	IRI	Italy	26	3.6	3	Finmeccanica	9	9.0
8	Dassault-Breguet	France	28	3.6				
9	EFIM	Italy	33	2.6		Finmeccanica		
10	Fiat	Italy	34	2.6		Finmeccanica		
11	Philips	Netherlands	35	2.6		Exited defence		
12	Rolls Royce	United Kingdom	39	2.4	5	Rolls Royce	16	4.0

Source: SIPRI Yearbook 1990, 2008, www.sipri.org/contents/milap

over 70% of arms production in Western Europe occurred in state-owned enterprises, public majority ownership of defence companies had become very limited by the end of the 1990s, focused on some sectors, such as shipbuilding and nuclear weapons (Serfati 2000).

The third stage, of Europeanization of arms production, remains incomplete. Many first-tier defence companies in Europe continue to be firmly rooted in their home country, with production sites in only one country and most of their sales to their domestic procurement agencies. While for many exports are important, few have similar sales in other European countries as they have to their domestic procurement agencies. In fact, there is only one 'true' European defence company, European Aeronautic Defence and Space (EADS). EADS came about as the result of a merger between DASA, Aérospatiale and CASA (Construcciones Aeronauticas SA) of Spain. It has major production facilities in all three countries, but its official headquarters is in the Netherlands, for tax reasons. Other large defence companies in Europe, such as Thales (earlier called Thomson-CSF) and Finmeccanica, remain primarily national, with headquarters in their home countries, but with shareholders, sister companies, subsidiaries and employees in several European countries. In the case of Thales, for instance, about 34,500 of its total 68,000 employees at end-2008 were employed in France, about 23,500 were in the rest of Europe and 10,000 were elsewhere in the world.[3]

Only BAE Systems has gone a step further and become a global company with only a small share of total sales to UK procurement authorities. Its sales in the USA are higher than those in the UK. Of its 97,500 employees at end-2007, 34,000 were located in the UK, 1,700 in other EU countries and 44,000 in the USA.[4]

By the end of the 1990s, the creation of BAE Systems, EADS and Thompson-CSF/Thales provided three industrial poles around which most of the major companies in aerospace and defence electronics in Western Europe – with some exceptions such as Finmeccanica – were grouped. Europeanization was much slower in other sectors of defence production, particularly ordnance and shipbuilding, but national borders were also permeated here, for instance through the transnational acquisitions of the German company Rheinmetall and US company General Dynamics in the ordnance sector, and the merger of German company HDW (now part of Thyssen Industry) with Swedish shipyard Kockums in shipbuilding.

Defence companies in Eastern Europe generally had very difficult times during the late 1980s and 1990s. Employment dropped drastically in all Eastern European countries and, with the exception of Poland where labour unions successfully lobbied for the maintenance of some facilities, more so than in any of the Western European countries (see Table 16.1). A few companies were bought up by larger companies from Western Europe or the USA, but most either vanished completely or converted to civilian production. None of the former Eastern European arms producers has become a major competitor for arms sales on the European level (Kiss 1998).

Factors driving defence industry restructuring in the 1980s and 1990s

Shrinking markets and the end of the Cold War

Procurement budgets in Europe and other markets served by European defence companies shrank substantially beginning in the mid-1980s, prior to the end of the Cold War. The early 1990s were a time of major cuts. Although exact figures are hard to come by, it is safe to estimate that procurement decreased by more than 30% in Western Europe and almost 90% in Eastern Europe between the mid-1980s and the mid-1990s. In addition, the arms export boom of the 1970s and early 1980s came to a halt (Serfati et al. 2000).

Shrinking markets increased the problems of small markets for the still largely national arms industry in Europe in the late 1980s. Small markets imply that production runs are low, thus limiting economics of scale. This is particularly problematic for products with high fixed initial costs, as is the case for most weapons systems. Furthermore, the divided European markets led to much duplication of research and development expenditure, further raising the costs of arms production in Europe.

The pressure on European governments to cut procurement costs grew with the end of the Cold War. The earlier justification of needing defence industries to be able to supply even in times of war, when supply from far-away allies was not guaranteed, did not carry much weight any more. European governments were forced to lower levels of support for domestic defence industries out of financial considerations, even more so in Eastern than in Western Europe (Serfati et al. 2000).

Company policies

Lower subsidies and demands for lower prices in turn put pressure on privileged national producers. These had to attempt to become more productive and increase their markets if they wanted to stay in arms production. Many did not find this is a promising option and exited the defence market, either through conversion of facilities to the production of civilian goods or by sale to competitors (Costigan and Markusen 1999). A rough estimate is that about one-quarter of all major defence companies in Western Europe in the late-1980s saw their future in defence markets, which generally required great enhancement of their business outside their national market through acquisitions of facilities in other countries (Serfati et al. 2000).

US competition

Western European arms producers were actually beset by two problems of size: the size of their domestic markets in Europe and the much larger market of the USA, which allowed US companies larger production runs and thus lower unit costs.

Even though the USA also reduced its procurement, the difference in size became particularly acute for European defence companies in the late 1980s and early 1990s. They feared that cost-consciousness customers, include their home governments, might buy from US companies, which benefited, in addition to the much larger production runs, from the US Government's policy to continue to support research and development expenditure for new weapons systems, even in times of lower procurement. Furthermore, the Pentagon urged US companies to become more competitive, for instance by subsidizing mergers among major companies (Costigan and Markusen 1999).

The increased US competition and fear of greater willingness of Western European governments to consider US products supported a fundamental change in the behaviour of many defence companies in Western Europe, which had earlier preferred safe and protected national markets over a general policy of openness including their domestic markets. While much of the restructuring and consolidation in the late 1980s had been driven by national governments, company boards primarily took the initiative in the 1990s, often pushed by financial investors (Mampaey and Serfati 2004). One case in point is the merger between British Aerospace and GEC Marconi in 1998. The governments of France, Germany and the UK had talked about a merger between Aérospatiale, British Aerospace and DASA to form a large European aerospace and defence company. However, the majority of financial investors in the City of London preferred a more globally oriented solution and disliked the strong influence the French Government would have in the proposed company. Finally, British Aerospace dropped out of the merger talks and instead consolidated its British and US prospects by buying GEC Marconi (and becoming BAE Systems), while Aérospatiale and DASA went ahead without British Aerospace.

Economic integration in Europe

European economic integration has seemingly proceeded in jumps. One such jump occurred in 1992, with the creation of the single market. Other noticeable events in European economic integration were the introduction of the European Monetary Union in 1996 and the adoption of the legal procedures for the establishment of European companies in 2001.

A sole focus on political decisions on further integration hides, though, the underlying economic forces of market expansion and company strategies. As a result, Europe has in many sectors of industry become one market. This includes sectors such as production of materials and electronics, which are of great importance to arms production. The lower tiers of the defence industrial base in Europe have slowly become, and now are to a large extent, European (James 2001).

The growing interdependence of industrial production in Europe increased the anomaly of national defence industries. First-tier defence companies partly coped by sourcing transnationally, but particularly the large industrial companies, which had internationalized and for which arms production was only a minor activity in their portfolio, found it cumbersome to apply different rules to defence production. Many of these, including Philips, Siemens and Renault-Peugeot, left the defence market by selling their subsidiaries or defence units to other companies intending to increase their defence business.

Development of a European security and defence policy

The 1990s also brought a change in the outlook of the EU. Step-by-step it added issues of foreign, security and defence policy to its political agenda, the Common Foreign and Security Policy (CFSP) in 1992 and the European Defence and Security Policy (ESDP) in 1999. While foreign, security and defence policy remain under the control of national governments in the European Council, and did not become 'communitized' policies under the European Commission, the impression gained weight in the 1990s that the EU was on the way to co-ordination, harmonization and, ultimately, integration of these policies. For the defence industrial sector this implied major changes both in supply and demand. On the supply side, integrated defence policies would mean that all producers would operate under the same conditions in all of Europe, with no national protection or subsidy. On the demand side, European defence policy integration would, so it was widely expected, result in greater co-ordination, if not in the end joint procurement of weapons (Becher et al. 2003).

As will be discussed in the next section, European defence industrial integration has not proceeded very far on the demand side and only a little on the supply side. Still, the impression that the process would speed up was widespread in the 1990s, including among defence industrial companies, not least because of their own lobbying efforts in Brussels and national capitals to achieve this effect (Lovering 2000).

Frameworks for European defence production

Much of the Europeanization of defence production that occurred in the 1980s was driven by the companies, which struggled to compete, make profits and grow. There has been no lack of proposals, as well as offices and agencies, to support and guide the restructuring of the defence industry in Europe. Examples include the WEU Armaments Agency,[5] OCCAR (Organisation Conjointe de Coopération en matière d'Armement),[6] the Framework Agreement[7] and the European Defence Agency (EDA),[8] as well as several initiatives by the European Commission.[9] The basic idea of these initiatives was to provide the foundations for a European defence market, with common rules and tenders open to all European competitors. However, the multitude of efforts at institutionalization is not a sign of success, but rather one of failure.

Co-ordination and harmonization of procurement among European countries remains the exception rather than the rule. There is still no level playing field for European companies on all European markets, despite some progress, for instance through the introduction of a 'Code of Conduct on Defence Procurement' by the EDA.[10] The main cause for the resilience of national privileges has been the lack of agreement on the future of defence production in Europe. The effectiveness of institutions has generally been limited by internal divisions among participating states about their roles and power, and the unwillingness of national governments to yield sovereignty over a sector when its future course is not clear.

A European defence industry

One vision for the future of the defence industry is that of a strongly competitive internal European defence market with no protection against other European producers, but with, at least initially, high levels of protection against outside competitors, especially those from the USA. The idea of a European defence industry has several variants. One, which might be identified as the originally French approach, is that of a highly regulated European defence industry. Regulation could aim at identifying 'European champions' in the major fields of arms production (fighter aircraft, transport aircraft, tanks, missiles, artillery, large warships, small warships, etc.), or at balancing national participation in production, or a combination of both. In effect, the co-development projects that were established among Western European arms producers starting in the 1960s illustrate this approach. However, only some such co-developments led to long-term co-operation, for instance those between Aérospatiale and DASA in the fields of anti-tank missiles and helicopters (Brzoska and Lock 1992). Another variant of the European defence industry, promoted in the past by some of the smaller European countries, suggests a more market-oriented consolidation of defence producers in Europe into one or two companies, either in each of the major defence fields, or even in several of them. The proposal, then, remains firmly within the realm of a traditional political-strategic approach to arms production. It also reflects more or less the current structure of defence production in Europe (Serfati et al. 2000).

However, such a truly European arms industry requires major revision of current national arms industrial and procurement policies. National procurement would need to be fully opened up for European competition, or better still, be co-ordinated at the European level so that companies could deal with one single, European, buyer. Current national policy instruments, such as national arms export policies and priorities in research and technology, would need to be abandoned, or at least reduced in importance in favour of co-ordination or co-operation. National decision-making would need to be superseded by European decision-making. The Framework Agreement, if one were used, would address many of the relevant supply-side issues, by regulating, for instance, common security requirements and security-of-supply problems. Other institutions, such as OCCAR and EDA could deal with the demand side. Until now, though, these organizations have not been able to achieve the degree of cohesion and comprehensiveness necessary for a European defence market. Quite a few observers have thus concluded that a common European arms industry requires a true common European Foreign and Security Policy as a precondition, instead of a CFSP run by nation states (Serfati et al. 2000).

A transatlantic market

One alternative, unsuccessfully aired during the Cold War and currently pushed for by the largest European defence companies, as well as the UK Government, is that of an Atlantic defence industry. Europe and the USA would open their markets fully to competitors from the other side of the Atlantic. Given the current levels of protection both in the USA and Europe, this would probably have to occur in steps. A first step would be to promote partnerships between companies in the USA and Europe to compete in both markets, for instance through 'teaming'. Supposedly, this would, in the longer run, foster the already existing collaborations and capital-related links, including cross-capital participation. European companies could, thus, gain access to the US arms procurement market, while US companies could be given a prime contractor responsibility in European countries. Depending on the balance of this expansion of transatlantic liberalization, more open competition by US and European companies could follow.

European governments have increasingly accepted the economic integration logic in civilian markets and supported the World Trade Organization's efforts to implement it; however, several, led by France, have refused it for the defence production sector (Serfati et al. 2000). They argue that European companies would generally not be competitive and Europe would lose its independent defence production capabilities. They argue that there can be no level playing field for companies from the USA and Europe, given the current imbalance in procurement as well as research and development spending. At least during the George W. Bush Administration, they could also point to the general unwillingness of the USA to open its procurement market to competition.

Muddling through

Neither a European nor a transatlantic approach to arms production in Europe has, so far, been politically acceptable to a sufficient majority of Member States. Under current legal rule, enshrined in Article 296 of the Amsterdam Treaty, all Member States would have to agree to make defence industrial production legally a European issue. If the Constitution Treaty, ratification pending in early 2009, were adopted, a group of Member States could come together and cease national control over defence industrial policy to a supranational institution.

However, for the time being, this does not look likely. Recent debate in the EDA as well as on initiatives by the European Commission in the field of procurement and inter-industry trade have demonstrated that most EU Member States are currently unwilling to give up sovereignty over defence production (Aalto et al. 2008). They are keen to continue to be able to prefer national producers and also to be able to shape national arms export policies. Without a major political push for a common European defence policy, or a change of rules in NATO, the current situation, which is marked by increasing integration of defence production in Europe, both in terms of supply of components and cross-border ownership but national governance over the industry on the one hand, and strong national control over the fate of the industry on the other hand, is likely to continue.

This practice has obvious costs compared with the opening up of the national defence market to wider competition from other countries from Europe, or even more suppliers, including the USA (Hartley 2006). Some arms producers also suffer economically as markets remain smaller than they could be. Muddling through is also in contradiction to the promotion of globalization by European states in other industrial sectors, as well as the political, economic, technological and military ambitions of the EU. However, it has benefits and advantages, which so far outweighed these costs. One obvious benefit is that it allows national governments to use defence production for policy aims, whether they are domestic – for instance to support a certain region or sector economically – or concern foreign relations to specific governments that are keen on a close arms-transfer relationship. Another advantage is that muddling through keeps Europe politically together – presented with the stark choice of either going European or transatlantic, France and the UK would most likely not agree on the same option and go separate ways. Allowing governments to legally stay in control, and involving European institutions where there is sufficient consensus, is politically convenient. Finally, reducing procurement costs by widening the market also has economic disadvantages – for those producers and countries that are less competitive. Compared with the industrial structures a common European defence market would likely support, Europe's defence industry is oversized. While the large European defence producers, such as BAE Systems, EADS and Thales, would probably gain from opening defence markets further, many smaller producers, often located in economically disadvantaged regions, would likely lose.

Consequences for export policies

Article 296 of the Amsterdam Treaty, as well as identical provisions in earlier EU treaties, provides the legal justification for continuing national control over arms exports for EU Member States. This stands in contrast to external trade in general, which has been a community issue since the establishment of the European Economic Community in the late 1950s, as well as internal market policy, which has come under EU control with the introduction of the single market in 1992. After 1992, foreign trade was in principle a community matter, except for explicitly exempted areas, such as the arms trade.

In the past, arms-export policies by Member States in Europe differed widely. Exports from Eastern Europe largely went to Soviet allies, while exports from Western European states went to Western allies. However, there were substantial differences among Western European producers. Some, such as the UK, France and, at least in the 1960s, Germany, at least partially used arms exports as an instrument of diplomacy in addition to making money from it. Others, such as Norway, were reluctant suppliers, basically not selling arms outside Europe. Still others, such as Spain and Italy during the 1980s, basically sold to any customer that could pay and was not openly allied to the Soviet Union (Brzoska and Ohlson 1987).

These differences in export policies first created problems in co-production agreements among Western European producers. Starting in the 1960s, several arrangements were established that necessitated agreements among governments on which country's arms-export controls would apply. Examples include the British-French Gazelle helicopter or the French-German Milan anti-tank missile. In general, governments agreed to cede decisions over exports to the state where final assembly of the weapon system occurred. In some cases, such as the MRCA Tornado combat aircraft, this led to different export policies applied to one product, in this case aircraft assembled in the UK, Italy and Germany. Companies in countries with stricter export regulations, in this case Germany, obviously were not happy with this outcome and lobbied for similar rules for all partners. Governments that used to be more restrictive than others partly gave in to these demands at various times, but export policies among European states continued to differ.

However, loss of control by national governments over exports of relevant technologies and commodities grew with the Europeanization of markets in general. They generally decided to go with the trend of increasing integration of components from many countries into weapons systems, even if that meant that they could not influence where these components would finally end up. At the same time, though, the interest in some form of joint decision-making or at least information-sharing grew among EU Member States, particularly after the introduction of the single market in 1992. After some intense negotiations, regulations on dual-use goods was adopted in 1995. These regulations in principle allow the free transfer of dual-use goods, without licensing procedure, inside the European market. It leaves decision-making over dual-use goods exports outside EU territory with national governments. However, a consultation mechanism is instituted for those cases where applications for exports are sought in a state different from the one in which the goods were manufactured. The regulations include a list of goods covered by them, which excludes arms and other military goods.[11]

Another attempt to align export policies among European countries extended from the efforts to harmonize the foreign policies of EU Member States, leading to the adoption of the rules and regulations of the CFSP. While the CFSP has no explicit mechanisms for arms exports, it provides a number of instruments for harmonizing decision-making by Member States. One is political decisions by the European Council, the highest decision-making body of the EU. The European Council has on various occasions adopted statements on arms export policy. In 1991, for instance, prior to the legal establishment of the CFSP, the Council called on Member States to observe seven criteria when making decisions on arms exports. An eighth criterion was added in 1992. Another important body is the General Affairs and External Relations Council (GAERC), essentially the meeting of foreign ministers of Member States. The GAERC, in addition to agreeing on political positions – such as on the Arms Trade Treaty – and making political statements, can decide upon Common Positions. These are binding for Member States. In this way, the GAERC has authorized a number of arms embargoes to be implemented by Member States, as well as deciding on special initiatives, for instance in the area of small arms.[12]

The most important initiative within the CFSP was the EU Code of Conduct on Arms Exports adopted in May 1998. Member States agreed to exercise 'high common standards' for control. Notable among the criteria was a commitment not to sell arms when there was a 'clear risk' that the weapons would be used for internal repression or aggressively against another country. They also agreed to take eight criteria into account when making their export decisions.

EU states pledged not to approve arms exports in cases where:

- The sale would violate the exporting state's commitments under the UN Charter or specific arms control agreements;
- there is a 'clear risk' that the weapons will be used for internal repression;
- the arms could provoke or prolong armed conflict;
- there is a 'clear risk' that the arms would be used aggressively against another country.

In addition, EU members agreed to take into account when making their export decisions:

- The risk of use of weapons against allies;
- the risk of unintended diversion of technology, the importing state's record on terrorism, implementation of humanitarian law (non-use of force against civilians), and arms control agreements;
- the effectiveness of the importing state's export control laws and mechanisms;
- the economic situation in the importing state, including relative levels of military and social spending.

The EU Code of Conduct has had substantial impact on arms-export policies of Member States. All Member States, including those joining after 1998, include the Code's eight criteria in their national regulations on arms exports. A group of national representatives, the EU Council Working Group COARM, exchanges information among Member States on their arms exports and discusses contentious cases. It also developed a User's Guide to help national licensing authorities in the interpretation of the Code's criteria. An annual report on EU arms transfers has been published since 1999, giving non-governmental organizations (NGOs) much material to compare export policies of Member States.[13] Empirical investigations confirm that the differences between arms exports by Member States have narrowed, though not necessarily in the direction of the highest of standards among members (Bromley et al. 2007; Tinchieri 2008; Bromley and Brzoska 2007).

Efforts to provide a legal foundation for the EU Code succeeded in December 2008, when the EU Council adopted Common Position 2008/944/CFSP.[14] Member States are now required to apply the Code of Conduct in their licensing procedures. The Common Position

Table 16.3 The importance of arms sales to other EU Member States in relation to total sales, 2007

	(1) Arms exports to EU member states	(2) Arms exports to all destinations	(1)/(2) in percentage
Austria	1,100	1,379	80%
Belgium	237	900	26%
Bulgaria	12	378	3%
Czech Republic	122	478	26%
Denmark	97	196	49%
France	3,144	9,849	32%
Germany	1,297	3,668	35%
Italy	3,261	4,744	69%
Netherlands	397	874	45%
Poland	3	287	1%
Spain	184	1,962	9%
Sweden	396	717	55%
United Kingdom	241	1,312	18%
All EU members	*10,661*	*27,100*	*39%*

Source: 10th Annual Report According to Operative Provision 8 of the European Union Code of Conduct on Arms Exports, Official Journal of the European Union, C 300/1, 22 November 2008, eur-lex. europa.eu/LexUriServ/LexUriServ.do?uri=OJ:C:2008:300:0001:0374:EN:PDF

Note: Value of licences; for some countries data are incompletely reported to the European Union

also widens the scope of the Code to include controls of arms brokering, transit transactions and intangible transfers of technology.

In a parallel effort, the European Commission has been trying to move arms-export policies towards harmonization. Their primary goal during 2005–08 was to lift controls for the trade of military goods within the EU. Allowing arms producers to shift arms to the EU member country of their choice would, though, reduce the possibility of Member States shaping their national export policies. At the end of a long negotiation process, Member States were only willing to agree to a partial lifting of intra-community transfer controls. The arrangement that was reached in late 2008 is similar to the one for dual-use goods, albeit only for goods that Member States agreed to place under it. The 'Directive of the European Parliament and of the Council on Simplifying Terms and Conditions of Transfers of Defence-Related Products within the Community' allows certain defence goods, excluding most major weapons systems, to be traded without prior licensing within the EU. If exports outside the EU are foreseen, however, a licence from the producing country needs to be obtained. Governments can also exceptionally revoke the provisions for licence-free intra-community trade for specific types of military goods if they deem this necessary.[15]

The various initiatives of European policy on arms and dual-use goods reflect the reality of an increasingly transnational European defence production base. Table 16.3 illustrates the importance of intra-EU trade in military goods. The definition of 'military goods' falling under the EU Code also includes a long list of components specifically designed and destined for use in weapons systems.[16] As a result, much of the trade recorded in Table 16.3 is trade in technology and commodities other than complete weapons systems. Table 16.3 also indicates that the importance of intra-EU trade differs among EU Member States. Germany, France, the Netherlands and Italy, as well as some of the smaller Western European producers sent a large share of their exports of goods on the military list to other EU Member States, while the shares are smaller for Spain and some of the arms-producing countries in Eastern Europe. The data contained in Table 16.3 needs to be treated with caution, though, as there are differences from year to year. Also, some countries, such as the UK, do not report complete data on the value of licences.

Conclusions

National control over arms exports in Europe has lost a good part of its power when companies can 'licence shop' for a good part of their business by choosing suppliers of components and locations of final assembly of weapons systems. A number of decisions have been made at the EU level, which aim to harmonize military exports from the EU. However, despite the existing legal provisions and joint institutions, decision-making over arms exports continues to legally rest with Member States. France and the UK, in particular, have been unwilling to cede control over their arms-export policies. The result of the divergence of economic, political and legal realities of arms production and arms exports in Europe is a complex system of multi-level governance. Legal prerogatives and specific policy priorities of member governments mix with business interests by arms producers, bureaucratic interests of EU institutions and the will of Member States to harmonize policies across the EU. While this arrangement carries costs, both financial and political, it has a number of advantages, which make its continuation likely. It allows national governments to continue to influence defence industries, while giving them a high degree of commercial flexibility. It avoids a showdown in the EU over which model for the European defence market is to be preferred. Finally, it corresponds, in a particular way, to the general trend in the EU of preferring governance, of joint decision-making of stakeholders, over old-fashioned forms of government. For arms exports from Europe this means that they are less and less exports from one of the Member States, but are increasingly becoming European arms exports. With increasingly dense relations among arms producers in Europe, as well as the liberation of markets for dual-use goods, *de facto* decision-making is divided informally between national governments, company boards and EU institutions.

Notes

1 Germany was an exception until the early 1980s. An increasingly small part of its defence production was under WEU control until that time (see Brzoska 1986).
2 The evolution of select major European defence companies over time in diagram form can be found at www.sipri. org/contents/milap/milex/aprod/m_and_a/YB_06_Company_Distribution.pdf
3 www.thalesgroup.com/About-us/Key-Figures.html
4 www.investis.com/investors/downloads/annualreport2007.pdf
5 www.weu.int/weag/ahsgeaa.htm
6 www.occar-ea.org
7 www.fco.gov.uk/resources/en/pdf/pdf11/fco_ref_sl_europeandefence
8 www.eda.europa.eu
9 ec.europa.eu/internal_market/publicprocurement/dpp_en.htm
10 www.eda.europa.eu/genericitem.aspx?area=Organisation&id=198
11 For details see ec.europa.eu/trade/issues/sectoral/industry/dualuse/index_en.htm
12 ec.europa.eu/external_relations/cfsp/intro/index.htm
13 Links to the annual reports can be found at consilium.europa.eu/cms3_fo/showPage.asp?id=1484&lang=en
14 *Official Journal of the European Union* L 335/99 of 8 December 2008, eur-lex.europa.eu/LexUriServ/LexUriServ.do?uri=OJ:L:2008:335:0099:0103:EN:PDF
15 ec.europa.eu/enterprise/regulation/inst_sp/defense_en.htm
16 The list is printed in the *Official Journal of the European Union*, L 88/58 of 29 March 2007, eur-lex.europa.eu/LexUriServ/site/en/oj/2007/l_088/l_08820070329en00580089.pdf

Bibliography

Aalto, Erkki, Daniel Keohane, Christian Mölling and Sophie de Vaucorbeil, *Towards a European Defence Market*, Chaillot Paper 113, Paris: European Union Institute for Security Studies, 2008
Becher, Klaus, Gordon Adams and Burkard Schmitt, *European and Transatlantic Defence-Industrial Strategies*, ESF Working Paper No. 10, January 2003
Bromley, Mark, 'The Europeanisation of Arms Export Policy in the Czech Republic, Slovakia, and Poland', *European Security*, Vol. 2, No. 16, 1997
Bromley, Mark and Michael Brzoska, 'Towards a Common, Restrictive EU Arms Export Policy? The Impact of the EU Code of Conduct on Major Conventional Arms Exports', *European Foreign Affairs Review*, Vol. 13, No. 3, 2007

Brzoska, Michael, *Arms Export Policy: Control, Direction and Restriction of West German Arms Exports to the Third World*, Frankfurt, Haag and Herchen, 1986

Brzoska, Michael and Peter Lock (eds), *Restructuring of Arms Production in Western Europe*, Oxford, Oxford University Press, 1992

Brzoska, Michael and Thomas Ohlson, *Arms Transfers to the Third World 1971–85*, Oxford, Oxford University Press, 1987

Cooper, Robert, *The Breaking of Nations*, New York, Atlantic Books, 2004

Costigan, Sean S. and Ann R. Markusen (eds), *Arming the Future: A Defense Industry for the 21st Century*, New York, Council on Foreign Relations Press, 1999

De Vestel, Pierre, *Defence Markets and Industries in Europe: Time for Political Decisions?*, Chaillot Paper 21, Western European Union, Paris, November 1995

Hartley, Keith, 'Defence Industrial Policy in a Military Alliance'. *Journal of Peace Research*, Vol. 43, No. 4, 2006

Hartley, Keith and Andrew Cox, *The Costs of Non-Europe in Defence Procurement*, Executive Summary, Study carried out for The Commission of the European Communities DG III, Brussels, 1992

James, Andrew, *The Defence Industry and Globalisation – Challenging Traditional Structures*, Stockholm, Defence Research Establishment, 2001

Kiss, Yudit, *The Defence Industry in East-Central Europe: Restructuring and Conversion*, Oxford, Oxford University Press, 1998

Klepsch, Egon (rapporteur), Report drawn on Behalf of the Political Affairs Committee on European Cooperation in Arms Procurement, Doc. No. 83/78, European Communities, European Parliament, Strasburg, 8 May 1978

Lovering, John, *Global Arms Economy*, London, Pluto, 2000

Mampaey, Luc and Claude Serfati, 'Les groupes de l'armement et les marchés financiers: vers une convention guerre sans limites?', in Francois Chesnais, ed., *La Finance Mondialisée: Racines Sociales et Politiques, Configuration, Consequences*, Paris, La Découverte, 2004

Serfati, Claude, ed., *Government-Companies Relations in the Arms Industry: Between Change and Stability?*, Brussels, Office for Official Publications of the European Communities, 2000

Serfati, Claude, Michael Brzoska, Björn Hagelin, Elisabeth Sköns and Wim Smit, eds, *The Restructuring of the European Defence Industry: Dynamics of Change*, Luxembourg, Office for Official Publications of the European Communities, 2000

SIPRI, *SIPRI Yearbook*, Stockholm, Stockholm International Peace Research Institute, various annual editions

Tinchieri, Lucca, 'Is the 1998 Code of Conduct on Arms Exports Adequate to Support the EU's Promotion of Human Rights?', *Hamburger Beiträge*, No. 149, Hamburg, Institut für Friedensforschung und Sicherheitspolitik, 2008

17 The US defence industry after the Cold War

Elisabeth Sköns

Introduction

During the 20 years since the end of the Cold War, the US defence industry has undergone profound changes. While these changes are multifaceted and have varied over time, it is possible to identify two major types of development, linked to changes in the defence demand. First, during the period 1989–98, when defence demand was falling, defence companies developed strategies to adjust to the contraction of the market. Second, during the period since 2001, when there has been a massive increase in US military spending as a result of the policies of the George W. Bush Administration, in particular due to the Iraq war, there has been a strong expansion of the US defence industry, in individual company arms sales, and a strong increase in the private military services industry. With the incoming Barack Obama Administration in January 2009, a new period may be in the making.

While domestic defence demand and government policies are important factors determining the size and shape of the defence industry, there are also more long-term technological and economic drivers, which developed during the Cold War and continue to have an impact on the post-Cold War defence industry. This chapter analyses the developments in the US defence industry during the two periods of contraction and expansion. It begins with an account of the post-Cold War trend in US defence demand and of the more long-term drivers affecting the defence market.

US defence demand and long-term changes in the defence market

During the first post-Cold War decade, 1989–98, there was a virtually continuous decline in US military expenditure, interrupted only in fiscal year (FY) 1992, when there was a one-year surge linked to the 1991 Gulf War. US outlays on national defence fell by 29% in real terms between FY1989 and FY1998, the year when US post-Cold War military spending was at its lowest level (OMB 2008, table 6.1). Over this 10-year period, there was a decline even in nominal terms, from US$304 billion in FY1989 to $268 billion in FY1998. Procurement expenditure dropped from $81.6 billion to $48.9 billion (by 41% in nominal terms), while expenditure on military research, development, test and evaluation (RDT&E) stayed roughly flat (OMB 2008, table 3.2 and figure 1). In FY1998 US defence outlays began to grow again, but initially only at a modest rate. Overall, the US defence industry faced a substantial fall in domestic defence demand during the 1990s.

Since FY1998 US defence outlays have increased continuously and since 2001 the increase has been rapid. During the period FY2001–08 they increased from $305 billion to $607 billion (corresponding to a nominal increase of 99% and a real increase of 56%). The strongest increases took place in FY2002 and FY2003, with real increases of almost 11% in each year (OMB 2008, table 6.1). Procurement spending increased from $48.2 billion in FY1998 to $131 billion in FY2008 and $142 billion in FY2009. These trends in US military expenditure have had an important impact on the US defence industry during the post-Cold War period.

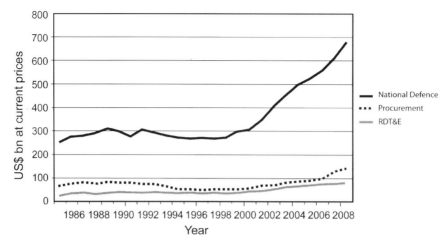

Figure 17.1 US outlays on national defence, procurement and RDT&E, fiscal years 1985–2008, at current prices
Source: US Office of Management and Budget 2008, table 3.2

In addition, a number of qualitative and more long-term factors, which were reinforced or emerged during the Cold War, have continued to have an impact on the defence industry after the end of the Cold War. These long-term drivers include developments in the technological requirements and costs for advanced weapons systems; changes in military doctrines and warfare; and a changing relationship between military technologies and technologies developed for commercial markets.

First, the rapid development towards more complex and expensive weapons systems during the Cold War, to stay in the forefront of technology and maintain military capabilities, has resulted in a strong increase in the unit cost of weapons systems, which in turn has exerted a pressure on defence budgets, in particular in periods of reduced military expenditure.

Second, developments in information and communication technologies have been exploited for changes in warfare, as referred to by concepts such as the revolution in military affairs (RMA), information-based warfare, and network-centric warfare. This involves an adaptation in warfare and by military organizations to absorb the latest changes in technologies and is expected to result in a major shift in demand from traditional defence industry sectors producing weapon platforms (such as aircraft, vehicles and ships) towards sectors producing a range of technologies and systems required for advanced command, control, communications, computers, intelligence, surveillance and reconnaissance (C4ISR) capabilities and towards companies able to integrate these into broader interconnected and inter-communicative systems.

Third, the long-term shift in technological innovation and technological lead from the military sector to the civilian sector has resulted in or reinforced the potential to exploit commercially developed technology for military applications, often referred to as 'spin-ins' or 'spin-ons' (in contrast to 'spin-offs' from the military to the commercial sector).

These qualitative factors constitute an important background to an understanding of the post-Cold War restructuring of the US defence industry as well as of the challenges of the government in maintaining a defence industrial base.

The period of declining demand: the 1990s

Defence companies faced with declining domestic demand have three main strategic options of adjustment: (i) to reduce their dependency on defence sales, either by full or partial exiting from defence production, or by diversification into civil products; (ii) to strengthen their position on the domestic arms market, by military diversification or military specialization; and (iii) to specialize on the international arms market, through local presence or direct exports (Dunne and Surry 2006).

At the end of the Cold War there were great expectations of a fundamental downsizing of the defence industry and a diversification, or even conversion, into non-defence sectors, which would lead to the realization of a 'peace dividend', not only in the USA but in all major arms-producing countries that had been actively engaged in the Cold War.

In the USA defence analysts predicted cuts in defence contracts by up to 50% and that defence companies would reinvest their earnings, skilled workforce and technologies in new non-defence products and markets. Advocates for civil-military integration and dual-use technology development argued that this would enhance the quality of military equipment and increase the pace of technological spin-offs (Mowery and Rosenberg 1989; Alic et al. 1992). Advocates for peace and economic development pushed for active conversion policies that would support companies, workers and communities to adjust to downsizing (Bischak 1991; Dumas and Thee 1989; Melman 1988).

The actual developments turned out to be rather different. The reasons for this were analysed at the end of the 1990s by a study group on defence demobilization and its implications for the US economy and world arms trade, under the auspices of the US Council on Foreign Relations, chaired by Ann Markusen. They identified two main factors behind the actual developments in the US defence industry during the 1990s: contradictory US Government policies towards the defence industry and the role played by the financial sector in the restructuring of the US defence industry (Markusen and Costigan 1999).

In the early 1990s, the Bill Clinton Administration pursued both a policy to encourage diversification of the defence industry into civilian production and a policy to promote mergers and acquisitions (M&As) and arms exports, which encouraged companies to consolidate and focus on defence markets.

The diversification policy was part of a policy for civil-military integration, which included a dual-use strategy and a programme to encourage spin-offs from military to civilian production. This policy was based on a realization of the changed relationship between military and commercial technology, which had forced the Department of Defense (DoD) to contract commercial companies for some critical technologies, and made it conclude that it could no longer rely exclusively on defence companies. This policy required a major procurement reform, aiming to buy commercial off-the-shelf (COTS) components (i.e. ready-made products that are available for sale on the commercial markets) and to encourage firms to become integrated civil-military producers (Gansler 1995). The main policy measure to encourage diversification into commercial production was the Technology Reinvestment Programme (TRP) initiated in early 1993, which was designed to support spin-offs of defence technology to civilian production in order to reduce the cost of commercial technology to the DoD (Markusen and Costigan 1999, 17).

The TRP provided competitively allocated grants to defence companies partnering with commercial firms and universities to acquire knowledge about marketing and low-cost production, and to transfer dual-use technologies into the civilian sector. This, in turn, would contribute to economic recovery and help displaced defence workers transit to new employment. The TRP was terminated already in 1994, as a result of a shift in the majority in the US Congress. However, even without this political change, it would probably not have survived for long, since it lacked strong support from other actors also. The competitive process meant that there were many losers, which undermined support from the defence industry. The largest and best-positioned companies were hostile to the programme's potential for creating competitors and new technologies that might undermine their own market positions. Finally, trade unions were disappointed at the weak links between the TRP and demonstrable job creation (Stowsky 1999, 152–4).

The policy to introduce financial incentives for defence companies to engage in M&As was also initiated in 1993. It was announced by Deputy Secretary of Defense William Perry at a dinner, later referred to as 'the last supper', sponsored by the DoD for some 20 defence industry executives. It was based on the realization that the post-Cold War reductions in the US defence budget would require a significant consolidation of the US defence industry in order to avoid costly duplication. The content of this merger policy was that the DoD could permit companies to add their costs of business combinations – such as costs for closing facilities and elimination of jobs – to existing cost-plus weapon contracts with the DoD, if a senior DoD official certified that projected savings from the restructuring would result in overall net savings (because of reduced unit costs) to the DoD in the future (Sköns and Cooper 1997, 242). This was a major reversal of traditional DoD policy to oppose full-scale M&As among large defence firms in order to maintain a plurality of contractors in each major sector for the sake of competition.

The M&A process in the US defence industry was reinforced and assumed its specific shape due to the major role played by the financial sector in this process. Markusen (1997) has described how a group of US investment bankers and business consultants targeted the defence industry, motivated by short-term economic gain, saw the potential in the great cash reserves and opportunities for real estate liquidation and labour force rationalization in the defence industry. US defence companies had generated large profits and cash reserves during the Cold War arms build-up in the 1980s and operated at inefficient levels. Many of the large defence contractors operated on attractive urban real estate and the salary levels in many of these companies were considerably higher than in the civilian sector. Thus, there was money to gain from buying and selling defence companies, instituting rationalization schemes, liquidating real estate and then selling them off with profits. Through the activities of the financial sector, the restructuring process took the shape of creating 'pure play' defence (military-specialized) companies by undertaking M&As of defence operations, divesting non-defence operations, exiting higher-cost urban locations and cutting employment.

In 1997 the merger policy was reversed. By that time, it had become evident that the mergers did not produce the anticipated savings and that few defence production lines were closed down. Furthermore, the rate of concentration had been fast, challenging competition in some areas. To ensure some degree of maintained competition, the government decided to prevent a proposed merger in 1997 between Northrop Grumman and Lockheed Martin, and a proposed acquisition by General Dynamics of United Defense. While this put an end, at least temporarily, to mega-mergers among the top defence companies, it was soon resumed again.

The third element in US Government policies during the early 1990s was a new policy on arms exports to support the defence industry. The industry had argued that they needed to increase exports of existing weapons systems to compensate for shrinking US orders and that, then, the US arms export policy should explicitly take defence industrial base issues into account. In 1995 the government issued two policy briefs: one stating that industrial base concerns would, henceforth, be weighed in the arms export licensing process; and the other introducing policies to increase subsidies for arms exports and eliminate fees on arms exports (Gold 1999, 254–5 and 261). This was the first time that economic considerations were explicitly acknowledged in US reviews of arms-export permits (Gold 1999, 254).

The actual development in the US defence industry during the 1990s was dominated by two main processes: an initial process of downsizing, in terms of a reduction of company arms sales, and efforts towards diversification into civilian production; and a subsequent process of M&As during which several companies exited the defence industry, while others grew in size.

Between 1990 and 1993, the combined arms sales of the 45 largest US defence companies in 1990 (those on the SIPRI list of Top 100 arms-producing companies in the world apart from the People's Republic of China) decreased from $112 billion to $97.3 billion (SIPRI Arms Industry Database). The decline was fairly general. Out of the 45 companies, 36 experienced reduced arms sales and 11 of these a reduction of 25% or more. A few companies also downsized through divestitures of their defence operations already during this period. The most extreme examples are General Dynamics and General Electric, with arms sales reductions of 64% and 63%, respectively, primarily as a result of divestitures. General Dynamics sold its Missiles Systems, Military Aircraft and Cessna, and General Electric divested its Aerospace division.

During this early period, few companies increased their arms sales (nine out of the 45). Increases were most often not due to organic growth, but to acquisitions of other defence companies or of defence units of other companies. For example, Lockheed acquired the military aircraft activities of General Dynamics in 1992; Martin Marietta acquired the aerospace activities of General Electric in 1993; and Loral acquired the missiles unit from LTV in 1992 and the defence units from IBM in 1993.

Some companies were successful in diversifying into civilian production, i.e. in shifting people and technologies into new product lines for civilian markets. This was true in particular for those that could build on conglomerate strengths. Examples of this in the early 1990s were General Motors (in particular its subsidiary, Hughes), Rockwell, Texas Instruments and TRW (Markusen and Costigan 1999, 16). A study by Oden (1999) shows that up until the end of 1994, diversifying defence firms reinvested more of their earnings in R&D, achieved lower defence dependency ratios, and did as well or better in terms of profitability than those that sought to consolidate or expand their defence specialization.

As a result of this development, several companies reduced their dependence on arms sales during the early 1990s. Out of the top 45 US defence companies, 14 reduced the share of arms sales in their overall sales between 1990 and 1993, and eight companies reduced this share by more than five percentage points: EG&G, General Electric, Martin Marietta, Raytheon, Sequa, Texas Instruments, Textron and Thiokol. In most of these cases, the reduced shares were a sign of successful diversification, rather than merely of lost arms sales. Among the eight companies with highly reduced arms sales shares, all but one (Sequa) increased their civilian sales. Three companies – Martin Marietta, Texas Instruments and Textron – increased the share of civilian sales in their total sales by more than 15%.

The merger policy introduced in 1993 set off a series of very large M&A deals, including several mega-deals with a value of $1 billion (see Table 17.1). While this process had begun earlier, the number and size of M&A deals increased vastly after 1993.

The M&A process resulted in a profound concentration of the US defence industry during the rest of the 1990s – and beyond. The scope of the concentration is indicated by the number of companies that disappeared from the SIPRI Top 100 List, either because they had been acquired in full by other defence companies or because they had divested their defence operations. Among the top 50 US defence companies in 1993, at least 18 companies had disappeared as independent defence companies by 1999, either because they had been acquired in full by other defence companies or because they had divested their defence operations. Another indication of the extent of concentration is that what had been 50 major defence firms at the beginning of the 1990s had been merged into only six large defence firms by the end of the 1990s (Gansler 2007, 1). These were (in order of arms sales in 1999) Lockheed Martin, Boeing, Raytheon, Northrop Grumman, General Dynamics and Litton, with 1999 arms sales in the range of $3.9 billion–$18.7 billion. The merger process also resulted in greatly increased arms sales of the largest defence companies. Between 1990 and 1999, six companies more than doubled their arms sales and three of these tripled their arms sales.

US arms exports fluctuated between $22 billion and $26 billion during the period 1990–96 and then increased to $33 billion in 1999, according to data from the US Department of State, while DoD data on Foreign Military Sales – which do not include commercial arms sales – show an increase from $10 billion to $17 billion between 1994 and 1999 (see Table 17.2).

Increased arms exports served to support the US defence industry during the period of declining domestic demand in the 1990s. However, in spite of the liberalization of US arms

Table 17.1 Major mergers and acquisitions within the US defence industry, 1990 99

Year	Buyer company	Acquired company/unit	Seller	Deal value (US$m.)
1990	Loral	Ford Aerospace	Ford Motor Corp.	715
1990	Carlyle	BDM International	Loral	130
1991	Textron	GD-Cessna	General Dynamics	
1992	Carlyle and Northrop	Vought Aircraft	LTV	260
1992	GM-Hughes Aircraft	GD Missile Systems	General Dynamics	
1992	Loral	LTV Missiles Division	LTV	
1993	Carlyle	Magnavox Electronics	Philips, Netherlands	
1993	Lockheed	GD Military Aircraft	General Dynamics	1,525
1993	Loral	IBM Federal Systems	IBM	
1993	Martin Marietta	GE Aerospace	General Electrics	3,000
1994	Martin Marietta	GD Space Launch Systems	General Dynamics	
1994	Northrop	Grumman	(Merger)	2,100
1994	Northrop Grumman	Vought Aircraft (remaining 51%)	Carlyle	
1995	Alliant Tech Systems	Aerospace business	Hercules	
1995	Allied Signal	Defence division	Northrop Grumman	
1995	Boeing	Defence unit	Litton	
1995	General Dynamics	Bath Iron Works	Shareholders	
1995	Litton	Defence division	IMO Industries	
1995	Litton	Teledyne-Electronics	Teledyne	
1995	Lockheed	Martin Marietta	(Merger)	
1995	Lockheed Martin	GE Aircraft Engines	General Electric	
1995	Loral	Unisys Federal Systems	Unisys	860
1995	Raytheon	E-systems	Shareholders	2,300
1996	Boeing	Defence business	Rockwell International	3,200
1996	General Dynamics	Vehicle Systems	Teledyne	
1996	Hughes Electronics	Magnavox Electronic Systems	Carlyle	
1996	L-3 Communications	Ocean Systems	Allied Signal	
1996	Litton	Defence unit	Hughes Electronics	
1996	Lockheed Martin	Loral-defence and aerospace	Loral	9,100
1996	Northrop Grumman	Defence electronics	Westinghouse	3,600
1996	Raytheon	Electrospace and airborne technologies	Chrysler	475
1997	Alliant Tech Systems	Defence systems	Motorola	
1997	Boeing	McDonnell Douglas	(Merger)	13,300
1997	Carlyle	United Defense	FMC and Harsco	850
1997	General Dynamics	Advanced Technology Systems	Lucent	
1997	General Dynamics	Computing Devices International	Ceridian	600
1997	General Dynamics	Defence and armaments units	Lockheed Martin	450
1997	Hughes Electronics	Marine Systems division	AlliantTechsystems	
1997	ITT Industries	Kaman Science Corpn	Kaman	
1997	Northrop Grumman	Logicon	Shareholders	740
1997	Raytheon	Defense Systems and Electronics	Texas Instruments	2,900
1997	Raytheon	Defence division	GM Hughes Electronics	9,500
1997	TRW	BDM International	Shareholders	1,000
1998	DRS Technologies	Electro-optical systems unit	Raytheon	45
1998	General Dynamics	NASSCO		415
1998	L-3 Communications	Ocean Systems	Allied Signal	67
1998	L-3 Communications	SPD Technologies		230
1998	Raytheon	Communications Systems	Allied Signal	63
1999	Allied Signal	Honeywell	(Merger)	14,000
1999	BF Goodrich	Rohr Industries		1,300
1999	Computer Sciences	Nichols Research		391

Table continued on next page.

Table 17.1 (continued)

Year	Buyer company	Acquired company / unit	Seller	Deal value (US$m.)
1999	General Dynamics	Communication and electronic systems	GTE	1,050
1999	ITT	Space & Defense Communications	Stanford Telecommunications	190
1999	Litton	Avondale		529
1999	Northrop Grumman	Ryan Aeronautical	Teledyne	140
1999	United Technologies	Sundstrand		4,300

Source: SIPRI files

Table 17.2 US arms exports, 1989–99 (figures are in US$ bn, in fiscal years)

Definition	1989	1990	1991	1992	1993	1994	1995	1996	1997	1998	1999
Arms export deliveries	17.3	21.9	26.2	25.1	25.4	22.2	22.9	22.8	31.7	27.0	33.0
Arms export agreements	30.2	50.5	58.2	29.9	58.3	39.2	28.5	38.3	34.4	35.6	59.2
FMS deliveries						9.8	12.1	11.7	15.7	13.9	16.7

Source: Arms exports: US Department of State (WMEAT) 2003; FMS: US DSCA 2005 and 2007

Note: FMS is Foreign Military Sales, i.e. US Government sales of defence articles and defence services to a foreign government or international organization

exports and the increased subsidies for them, arms exports did not by far compensate for the fall in domestic demand. While US arms exports increased by $11 billion between 1990 and 1999, the fall in domestic procurement was $32 billion over the same period. The main reasons for this were the simultaneous decline in the international defence market and the relatively small export share of the US defence industry.

The concentration process in the US defence industry during the 1990s undermined defence conversion and civil-military integration, produced fewer, more politically powerful defence-specialized firms, and diminished competition in some weapons lines (Markusen 1998). Towards the end of the 1990s there had been a marked reduction of suppliers. A study by the US Government Accounting Office concluded that there had been a dramatic reduction in the number of prime contractors in 10 of 12 markets that the DoD had identified as important to national security (GAO 1998). The most severe reduction in competition was in the tactical missile, fixed-wing aircraft and launch vehicle markets. The role played by the financial sector in the restructuring of the US defence industry also had a negative impact on the adjustment of US procurement programmes to post-Cold War requirements. For example, the financial sector was able through its DoD connection to prevent the termination of some Cold War-type weapons systems produced by firms in which they had a major stake (Markusen 1998).

Around the turn of the century, there were strong pressures to increase the US defence budget. Throughout the 1990s, the DoD had maintained a high level of R&D activities and kept all major procurement programmes alive on the drawing board, while squeezing personnel and operations and maintenance budgets. However, defence budget planning was dominated by the fundamental conflict between weapons costs and readiness costs within the strict budget ceilings. By the end of the Clinton Administration in January 2001, there was a growing mismatch between stated force requirements and budgetary resources, and expectations that substantial additional resources would be needed for new technologies (Gold 2002, 313–4).

The expansion period (since 2001)

The policies of the Bush Administration following the terrorist events on 11 September 2001 (9/11) changed the environment for the US defence industry dramatically. The two wars – in Afghanistan from 2001 and in Iraq from 2003 – launched as the global 'war on terror' involved a massive increase in US military spending, as well as a rapid increase in the outsourcing of formerly military function to private industry. DoD contracts to private industry for military goods and services experienced a virtual boom. Between FY2000 and FY2006, overall DoD contracts to private companies increased from $133 billion to $295 billion, while contracts to the top 100 defence prime contractors increased from $83 billion to $180 billion (see Table 17.3).

The defence contracts awarded during this period have had a profound impact on the US defence industry. They generated an increase in the arms sales of the largest companies even greater than during the 1990s, and resulted in a change in the sectoral composition of defence industry arms sales. They also attracted non-US defence companies, wanting to access the US defence market through acquisitions of defence companies located in the USA.

The DoD contracts were heavily concentrated to the larger US defence companies. The value of the combined DoD contract awards to the top 25 defence companies more than doubled between 2001 and 2006, from $57 billion to $123 billion (see Table 17.4) and accounted for over two-thirds of total DoD contract awards to the top 100 defence contractors. The size of individual contract awards increased to immense proportions. For example, the 2006 contract awards to Lockheed Martin, of $26.6 billion, is roughly equal in size to the entire gross domestic product of countries like Bulgaria, Lebanon and Syria, and of any country in Africa except Nigeria and South Africa.

These contracts resulted in greatly increased arms sales of the top 25 US defence companies, which more than doubled between 2001 and 2007 (see Table 17.4). The companies with the strongest growth in arms sales were providers of military services and suppliers of military electronics, military vehicles and mine-resistant armour. Over the period 2001–07, seven companies among the top 25 in 2007 had more than tripled their arms sales, four of which were main providers of military services (L-3 Communications, EDS, CACI International and ManTech International), two were main suppliers of military vehicles (AM General and Oshkosh Truck), while one was a supplier of military electronics (DRS Technologies).

Other companies outside the top 25 have become major defence companies as a result of the wars. For example, two companies that provide mine-resistant ambush protected (MRAP) vehicles – Force Protection and Navistar – had arms sales of $890m. and $620m. in 2007. These companies have benefited greatly from the Iraq war, for which the demand for services and vehicles has expanded greatly.

The private military services industry has also been a main beneficiary of the wars. However, privatization and outsourcing of military functions is a longer-term trend beginning in earnest at the end of the Cold War. This was the result of two main trends: first, the large

Table 17.3 US Department of Defense prime contract awards, 1998 2006 (figures are in US$ bn, in fiscal years)

	1998	1999	2000	2001	2002	2003	2004	2005	2006
Total DoD prime contract awards	118.1	125.0	133.2	144.6	170.8	209.0	230.7	269.2	295.0
Awards to top 100 DoD contractors	71.0	75.5	82.5		107.2	133.8	146.8	163.2	180.1

Source: US DTIC, for FY1996, FY2004, FY2005 and FY2006

Note: Contract awards include RDT&E, supplies and services of all types, i.e. both military and civil

Table 17.4 The top 25 US defence companies 2007, in arms sales and DoD contracts

Rank	Company	DoD contract awards (US$ m.)		Arms sales (US$ m.)		
		2001	2006	2001	2007	Change (%)
1	Boeing	13,341	20,293	20,650	30,480	+48
2	Lockheed Martin	14,687	26,620	17,860	29,400	+65
3	Northrop Grumman	5,153	16,627	8,970	24,600	+174
4	General Dynamics	4,907	10,526	7,790	21,520	+176
5	Raytheon	5,576	10,069	11,160	19,540	+7
6	L-3 Communications	495	5,198	1,720	11,240	+554
7	United Technologies	3,373	4,453	5,580	8,760	+57
8	Science Applications	1,748	3,211	2,530	6,250	+147
9	Computer Sciences	819	2,884	1,810	5,420	+199
10	Honeywell	902	1,679	3,280	5,020	+53
Sub-total	*10 companies*	*51,001*	*101,560*	*81,350*	*162,230*	*+ 99*
11	KBR[1]	427	5,603	930	5,000	+ 438
12	ITT	808	2,522	1,300	3,850	+196
13	General Electric	1,747	2,328	1,900	3,460	+82
14	DRS Technologies	—	478	510	3,230	+533
15	AM General	147	1,944	330	2,670	+709
16	EDS	223	2,008	530	2,540	+379
17	Textron	572	814	1,230	2,510	+104
18	Alliant Techsystems	494	1,128	1,060	2,460	+132
19	URS Corporation[1]	165	1,369	1,200	2,290	+ 91
20	Rockwell Collins	362	824	1,070	2,230	+108
21	Harris	381	1,339	860	1,720	+100
22	Goodrich	—	344	840	1,600	+91
23	Oshkosh Truck	558	941	420	1,570	+274
24	CACI International	249	681	330	1,390	+321
25	ManTech International	166	321	370	1,350	+265
Total	*25 companies*	*57,300*	*123,382*	*94,230*	*200,100*	*+ 112*

Source: DoD contract awards: US DTIC for FY2001 and FY2006; arms sales: SIPRI Arms Industry Database

Note:
1 The data in the column for 2001 is for the year 2002 for KBR and URS

supply of laid-off military personnel as a result of the cuts in military spending after the end of the Cold War, combined with the widespread demand for such personnel from weak states facing internal conflict; and second, the increased privatization and outsourcing by governments in advanced market economies of a wide range of functions that were previously carried out by the armed forces or defence ministries. Furthermore, to some extent private industry had provided military services also during the Cold War, in that companies that produced advanced military equipment had provided some types of services, such as maintenance and technical services for the equipment delivered by them, and which required their technological competence and knowledge about the systems they had produced (Singer 2003; Wulf 2005).

While the trend for privatization and outsourcing of military services has older roots, it has been greatly reinforced during the war in Iraq. The expansion of the military services industry is reflected in the composition of the SIPRI Top 100 defence companies. The number of companies specializing in provision of military services has increased from 10 companies in the top 100 in 1996, to 18 companies in the Top 100 in 2006 (Perlo-Freeman and Sköns 2008). In addition to the service-specialized companies, which have emerged and grown rapidly during the post-9/11 period, a number of more traditional defence companies also provide an increasing number of military services. The services provided by private industry range from research and analysis to technical services, operational support (such as the provision of management of military bases, logistics and training) and outright armed security (such as protection of diplomats, company sites and civilian convoys in conflict zones) (Perlo-Freeman and Sköns 2008, 6).

The traditional defence companies, including those producing weapon platforms, have also increased their arms sales in this period. For example, the US Aerospace Industries Association reports that US aerospace industry sales of military aircraft increased from $35.2 billion in 2001 to $54.2 billion in 2007, while the sales of missiles increased from $10.4 billion to $12.4 billion in 2007 (AIA 2008). The largest sales were in fighter aircraft, followed by helicopters and military transport aircraft. Within the military aircraft segment there was a rise in R&D, aftermarket sales and unmanned aerial vehicle (UAV) sales. The US aerospace industry was reported to experience the strongest and broadest upturn, begun in 2004, since the Second World War, as a result of a simultaneous expansion in the commercial and military segments, an almost unprecedented occurrence (AIA 2008).

The lucrative defence market during the post-9/11 period has also resulted in increased specialization towards the defence market. Of the top 25 US companies in 2007, 17 increased the share of arms sales in their total sales between 2001 and 2007, and nine of these increased this share by more than 10 percentage points (see Table 17.5).

One of the most spectacular developments in the US defence industry during the post-9/11 period is the surge in profits. During the period 2001–07, defence company profits have reached record heights. Profit ratios (net profit as a share of total sales) increased for all but three of the top 25 US defence companies in 2007. For six companies the profit ratio increased by more than five percentage points. Overall, for the 22 companies in Table 17.5 with profit data and an arms sales share greater than 10%, their profit ratio (their combined net profits as a share of their combined total sales) increased by 3.6 percentage points between 2001 and 2007. The top 10 companies in Table 17.5 increased their combined profits from $4,745m. in 2001 to $20,848m. in 2007 and the combined profits of the 22 companies in Table 17.5 with profit data and an arms sales share greater than 10% increased from $7,229m. to $25,716m. (Table 17.5; SIPRI Arms Industry Database).

Jacques Gansler, a former US Under-Secretary of Defense for Acquisition, Technology and Logistics in the Clinton Administration in the 1990s, notes how in this environment of vastly increased defence company arms sales and profits, 'there was growing concern, on the part of the government, that this money was not used to invest in capital equipment or research and development, but rather to continue to buy-up the smaller firms … and to reward the corporate executives with huge annual bonuses', and how 'there was increasing concern as to whether or not there was adequate competition taking place within this consolidated defence industrial structure' (Gansler 2007, 2).

While the reasons for this enormous increase in the profits of the US defence industry remain to be investigated in more detail, it is clear that the wars have contributed to this in at least two ways. First the increased demand in itself has most likely had an impact through its upward effect on the prices of military systems and services. Second, the fact that the wars were financed primarily through emergency supplementary budgets probably had a major impact, since this meant that DoD purchases under this type of funding were not subject to the regular budgetary process and reduced congressional oversight (GAO 2008). In addition, it is not clear how much funding for weapons procurement through emergency supplemental funding was required for the wars and how much is more appropriately attributed to long-term modernization requirements, in particular during the last years of the Bush Administration, when a progressively broader definition of what constituted the 'war on terror' was adopted (Kosiak 2008).

Table 17.5 The top 25 US defence companies 2007, in profit ratios and defence dependency

Rank		Arms sales share			Profit ratio			
		(%)		Change (ppt)	(%)		Change (ppt)	Profits ($ m.)
2007	Company	2001	2007	2001–07	2001	2007	2001–07	2007
1	Boeing	35	46	11	4.9	6.1	1.3	4,074
2	Lockheed Martin	74	70	-4	-4.4	7.2	11.6	3,033
3	Northrop Grumman	69	77	8	3.5	5.6	2.1	1,803
4	General Dynamics	64	79	15	7.8	7.6	-0.2	2,080
5	Raytheon	70	92	22	-4.7	6.9	11.6	1,474
6	L-3 Communications	73	81	8	4.9	5.4	0.5	756
7	United Technologies	20	16	-4	6.9	7.7	0.8	4,224
8	Science Applications	42	70	28	0.3	4.6	4.3	415
9	Computer Sciences.	16	33	17	3.0	3.3	0.3	545
10	Honeywell	14	15	1	-0.4	7.1	7.5	2,444
Total Top 10		*42*	*51*	*9*	*2.4*	*6.6*	*4.1*	*20,848*
11	KBR[1]	16	57	41	–	3.5	–	302
12	ITT	28	43	15	5.9	8.2	2.3	742
13	General Electric	2	2	0	10.9	12.9	1.9	22,208
14	DRS Technologies	89	98	9	3.5	5.0	1.5	166
15	AM General	60			1.8			
16	EDS	3	11	8	6.4	3.3	-3.1	729
17	Textron	10	19	9	1.3	6.9	5.6	915
18	Alliant Techsystems	59	59	0	3.8	5.3	1.5	222
19	URS Corporation[1]	38	25	-13	1.5	1.5	-0.1	132
20	Rockwell Collins	38	51	13	4.9	13.3	8.3	585
21	Harris	44	41	-3	1.1	11.3	10.2	480
22	Goodrich	20	25	5	7.3	7.6	0.3	483
23	Oshkosh Truck	29	25	-4	3.5	4.2	0.7	268
24	CACI International	58	72	14	3.9	4.1	0.2	79
25	ManTech International	85	93	8	0.2	4.6	4.4	67
Total for 22 companies[2]		*36*	*47*	*10*	*2.9*	*6.4*	*3.5*	*25,716*

Source: SIPRI Arms Industry Database

Notes: ppt is percentage points;
1 Data in the column for 2001 are for 2002 for KBR and URS;
2 The 22 companies include all but KBR and AM General (for which profit data are lacking), and General Electric (which is excluded because of its low arms sales share and large total sales and profits, which would distort the average for companies focused on defence)

The wars have also served to postpone recommended or planned changes in the US defence industry. Throughout the post-Cold War period several DoD reports have recommended a major transformation of the US procurement process and in the US defence industrial base. In 1999 a study by the Defense Science Board recommended changes to adjust to an increasingly globalized industry (Department of Defense 1999). In 2001 Defense Secretary Donald Rumsfeld announced the need for a major 'transformation' of DoD procurement processes (*New York Times*, 18 August 2001). In 2003 the DoD issued a report on 'Transforming the Defense Industrial Base: A Roadmap' (Department of Defense 2003), the basic idea of which was to begin thinking of DoD acquisitions and the defence industrial base in terms of capabilities (such as combat support, power projection, integrated battle-space, etc.) rather than in terms of traditional programmes and weapon platforms (such as aircraft, ships and vehicles).

However, such changes have not been implemented. According to Gansler, the most obvious reason for this is the war in Iraq and the almost exclusive focus by the DoD on this war. He

Table 17.6 US arms exports, 2000–07 (figures are in US$ bn, in fiscal years)

	2000	2001	2002	2003	2004	2005	2006	2007
Arms export deliveries	12.9	9.2	10.1	11.1	11.7	12.1	12.6	12.8
Arms export agreements	17.5	11.4	13.0	14.5	12.6	12.9	16.3	24.9
Procurement and RDT&E	89.3	95.5	106.9	121.0	137.0	148.0	158.4	172.7
Export % of proc. +RDT&E	*14.4*	*9.6*	*9.4*	*9.2*	*8.5*	*8.2*	*8.0*	*7.4*

Source: Arms exports: Grimmett 2008; government expenditure: OMB 2008, table 3.2

notes that 'with enormous political pressure to not change, and with adequate resources, there was no recognition of any urgency to begin the process of transformation', and that instead there has been 'a consolidation of the 20th century defence industry' (Gansler 2007, 5).

US arms exports have increased only slightly in real terms during the period 2001–07, while the value of arms export agreements has fluctuated and ended with a strong increase in 2007 (see Table 17.6). The importance of arms exports for the US defence industry tends to have decreased rather than increased, as indicated by the reduction in the ratio of arms exports to domestic spending on arms procurement and RDT&E over this period (see Table 17.6). Contrary to this, foreign sales of aerospace products (military and civil) have become increasingly important to the US aerospace industry and have become more geographically balanced in recent years to reduce the reliance on any one market (AIA 2008). US exports of military aerospace products increased from $9 billion in 2004 to $13.2 billion in 2007. Exports of military aircraft, primarily fighter aircraft and fighter bombers, increased from $2.3 billion in 2004 to $4.2 billion in 2007 (AIA 2008).

While there has been no major change in the level of US arms exports, there has been a significant change in US arms-export policy and in recipients of US arms exports. Arms exports and military assistance to allies in the 'war on terror' was an integral part of the Bush Administration's policy. Critics have pointed out how this was contrary to US traditional arms-export policy, according to which arms exports should not undermine long-term security and stability, weaken democratic movements, support military coups, escalate arms races, exacerbate ongoing conflicts, cause arms build-ups in unstable regions, or be used to commit human rights abuses. However, during the post-9/11 period, decisions on arms exports often gave precedence to other considerations, such as support for the USA in its efforts to combat international terrorist networks, or for its military operations in Iraq and Afghanistan. Studies by the US Center for Defense Information show how weapons and military assistance were provided to weak and failing states and countries that have been repeatedly criticized by the Department of State for human rights violations, lack of democracy and support for terrorism (CDI 2007). During the period 2001–05 total US arms sales (Foreign Military Sales and Direct Commercial Sales) to 25 countries that provided strategic services to the USA in its anti-terrorism operations were four-times higher than in the five years prior to 2001. These countries also received 18-times more US military assistance (Foreign Military Financing and International Military Education and Training) during the period 2001–05 than during the previous five-year period (CDI 2007). Such increases in arms sales were partly due to the lifting of sanctions and restrictions to certain countries immediately after 9/11, for example India, Pakistan, Armenia, Azerbaijan and Tajikistan.

Summary and conclusions

The post-Cold War period has seen a profound growth, concentration and compositional change in the US defence industry. There has been strong growth in the arms sales of the major traditional defence companies, both through M&As and through organic growth during the post-9/11 period. At the same time a number of new companies have entered the group of major

US defence companies, partly through the emergence and growth of a large military services industry and partly due to the growing demand for military equipment for the Iraq war. There has also been significant concentration into a few major defence companies.

Over the entire post-Cold War period, the combined arms sales of the top 25 defence companies have increased from $97 billion in 1990 to $200 billion by 2007 (see Table 17.7). The arms sales of the largest US defence companies have increased immensely: five-fold for Boeing, three-fold for Lockheed Martin and four-fold for Northrop Grumman.

A measure of the changing composition of the US defence industry is the fact that out of the top 45 US defence companies in 1990, only 14 remained as independent defence companies by 2007. Instead, a number of new companies entered the defence industry throughout the 1990s and up to the present in an ongoing process. Many of the new entrants specialize in military services of different types, primarily IT and technical services, manifesting the strong trend in US DoD outsourcing of previously military functions to private industry.

During the first decade of the post-Cold War period domestic demand for the US defence industry declined even in nominal terms. Initially this resulted in a reduction in the arms sales of most major defence companies, and in efforts to diversify into civilian production. This process was overtaken by a rapid process of M&As from 1993 onwards, promoted by the merger policy of the US Government and reinforced by the role played by the financial sector. This resulted in a strong concentration of the defence industry, a vast increase in company size of the leading defence companies and a reduction in competition.

The Clinton Administration sought to support arms exports to facilitate the adjustment process of the defence industry, manifested in its policy initiated in 1995 to relax arms exports by including defence industrial concerns as a criteria to consider in the licensing process and to increase subsidies for arms exports. However, the defence industry was not able to compensate for the reduction in domestic demand by increased arms exports, as arms exports constituted a limited share of US defence industry arms sales, and as the demand on the international arms market had also dropped to a lower level during the 1990s than during the Cold War.

By the end of the 1990s, a mismatch between stated force requirements and planned budgetary resources had emerged. This was generated by the neglect to make major cuts in weapons acquisition programmes in spite of the cuts in spending on arms procurement, and by maintaining R&D spending at high levels. It was clear that this mismatch would have to be

Table 17.7 The top 10 US defence companies in 1990 and 2007, in arms sales and defence dependency

Company	Arms sales (US$ m.)	Arms sales share (%)	Company	Arms sales (US$ m.)	Arms sales share (%)
McDonnell Douglas	9,890	61	Boeing	30,480	46
General Dynamics	8,300	82	Lockheed Martin	29,400	70
Lockheed	7,500	75	Northrop Grumman	24,600	77
General Motors	7,380	6	General Dynamics	21,520	79
General Electric	6,450	11	Raytheon	19,540	92
Raytheon	5,500	57	L-3 Communications	11,240	81
Boeing	5,100	18	United Technologies	8,760	16
Northrop	4,930	90	Science Applications	6,250	70
Martin Marietta	4,600	75	Computer Sciences.	5,420	33
Rockwell International	4,100	33	Honeywell	5,020	15
Total 10[1]	*59,650*	*36*	*Top 10*[1]	*162,230*	*51*
Top 25[1]	*97,430*	*38*	*Top 25*[1]	*200,100*	*47*

Source: SIPRI Arms Industry Database

Note:
1 The totals exclude companies with an arms sales share <10%

resolved, either by crash cuts in procurement programmes or by a substantial increase in military spending.

The policy developed by the Bush Administration in response to the terrorist attacks on US cities on 11 September 2001 solved the mismatch between planned requirements and planned spending through the massive increase in US military spending to finance the wars in Afghanistan and Iraq. The increase in company arms sales during the post-9/11 period as a result of increased DoD defence contracts by far outpaced the increase during the 1990s as a result of the M&As. In addition, the arms exports generated by the 'war on terror' policy also contributed to increased arms sales.

Simultaneously, there has been a shift in the sectoral composition of the US defence industry due to the rapid expansion of the private industry for military services as a result of outsourcing of military functions. The post-Cold War period has also seen an increase in defence dependence of the major defence companies, as well as a strong increase in profits.

In spite of this profound increase in size of the industry and of individual companies, as well as a dramatic restructuring and concentration, there has been little change in the functioning and the dynamic of the industry. While at the end of the Cold War and throughout the 1990s it was recognized that long-term trends in technology and warfare would require a significant restructuring of the US defence industry, and a transformation of the DoD and the US weapons acquisition process, to adjust to the new environment, the US Government policy responses to the end of the Cold War in the 1990s and to the 9/11 attacks have meant that such changes have not been implemented. Instead, there has been a consolidation of the 20th-century defence industry. In this sense, there is a great element of continuity in the US post-Cold War defence industry.

Bibliography

Aerospace Industries Association (AIA), *2008 Year End Review and 2009 Forecast: An Analysis*, AIA Research Center, Washington, 10 December 2008, www.aia-aerospace.org/industry_information/economics/year_end_review_and_forecast

Alic, John et al., *Beyond Spin-off: Military and Commercial Technology in a Changing World*, Cambridge, MA, Harvard Business School Press, 1992

Bischak, Greg, ed., *Towards a Peace Economy in the United States: Essays on Military Industry, Disarmament and Economic Conversion*, New York, St Martin Press, 1991

CDI, *U.S. Arms Exports and Military Assistance in the 'Global War on Terror'*, Center for Defense Information (CDI), Washington, 6 September 2007, www.cdi.org/program/document.cfm?DocumentID=4080&from_page=./index.cfm

Department of Defense, *Defense Science Board Report on Globalization and Security*, US Department of Defense, Defense Science Board (DSB), Washington, 1999

——— *Transforming the Defense Industrial Base: A Roadmap*, US Department of Defense, Office of the Deputy Under Secretary of Defense (Industrial Policy), Washington, February 2003, www.acq.osd.mil/ip

Department of State, *World Military Expenditures and Arms Transfers 1999 2000*, Washington, US Department of State, Bureau of Verification and Compliance, 6 February 2003, www.state.gov/t/vci/rls/rpt/wmeat/1999_2000/index.htm

DSCA, *Foreign Military Sales, Foreign Military Construction Sales and Military Assistance Facts as of September 30, 2004*, US Department of Defense Security Cooperation Agency (DSCA), Washington DC, 2005

——— *Historical Facts Book 2007, as of September 30, 2007*, US Department of Defense Security Cooperation Agency (DSCA), Washington, 2007, www.dsca.mil/data_stats.htm; www.fas.org/programs/ssp/asmp/externalresources/governmentdocuments_index.html

Dumas, Lloyd and Marek Thee, eds, *Making Peace Possible: The Promise of Economic Conversion*, Oxford, Pergamon Press, 1989

Dunne, Paul and Eamon Surry, 'Arms Production', in *SIPRI Yearbook 2006*, Oxford, Oxford University Press, 2006

Gansler, Jacques, *Defense Conversion: Transforming the Arsenal of Democracy*, Cambridge, MA: The MIT Press, 1995

——— 'US Defence Industrial Policy', *Security Challenges*, Vol. 3, No. 2, June 2007

GAO, *Defense Industry Consolidation and Options for Preserving Competition*, US General Accounting Office (GAO), Report to Congressional Committees, GAO/NSIAD-98-141, Washington, April 1998

——— *Global War on Terrorism: Reported Obligations for the Department of Defense*, US Government Accountability Office (GAO), GAO-08-1128R, Washington, 15 September 2008

Gold, David, 'The Changing Economics of the Arms Trade', in Markusen, Ann and Sean Costigan, eds, *Arming the Future*, New York, Council on Foreign Relations Press, 1999

——— 'US Military Expenditure and the 2001 Quadrennial Defense Review', in *SIPRI Yearbook 2002*, Oxford, Oxford University Press, 2002

Grimmett, Richard F., *Conventional Arms Transfers to Developing Nations, 2000 – 2007*, CRS (Congressional Research Service) Report, US Library of Congress, RL34723, 23 October 2008

Kosiak, Steven, 'Cost of Wars in Iraq and Afghanistan, and Other Military Operations Through 2008 and Beyond', Center for Strategic and Budgetary Assessments, Washington, 15 December 2008, www.csbaonline.org

Markusen, Ann, 'The Economics of Defence Industry Mergers and Divestiture', *Economic Affairs*, Vol. 17, No. 4, December 1997

——'The Post-Cold War Persistence of Defense Specialized Firms', in Gerald Susman and Sean O'Keefe, eds, *The Defense Industry in the Post-Cold War Era: Corporate Strategies and Public Policy Perspectives*, Oxford, Elsevier, 1998

Markusen, Ann and Sean Costigan, eds, *Arming the Future: A Defense Industry for the Twenty-First Century*, New York, Council on Foreign Relations Press, 1999

Melman, Seymour, *The Demilitarized Society: Disarmament and Conversion*, Montreal, Harvest House, 1988

Mowery, David and Nathan Rosenberg, *Technology and the Pursuit of Economic Growth*, Cambridge, Cambridge University Press, 1989

Oden, Michael, 'Cashing-in, Cashing-out and Converting: Restructuring of the Defense Industrial Base in the 1990s', in Ann Markusen and Sean Costigan (eds), *Arming the Future: A Defense Industry for the 21st Century*, New York, Council on Foreign Relations Press, 1999

OMB, *Budget of the United States Government FY2009: Historical Tables*, US Office of Management and Budget (OMB), Washington, DC, White House, March 2008

Perlo-Freeman, Sam and Elisabeth Sköns, *The Private Military Services Industry*, SIPRI Insights on Peace and Security, No. 1, September 2008

'Rumsfeld Says Plans for Military Transformation are Limited', *New York Times*, 18 August 2001

Singer, Peter W., *Corporate Warriors: The Rise of the Privatized Military Industry*, Cornell Studies in Security Affairs, Ithaca, NY, Cornell University Press, 2003

SIPRI, SIPRI Arms Industry Database, www.sipri.org

Sköns, Elisabeth and Julian Cooper, 'Arms Production', *SIPRI Yearbook 1997*, Oxford, Oxford University Press, 1997

Sköns, Elisabeth and Reinhilde Weidacher, 'Arms Production', *SIPRI Yearbook 2000*, Oxford, Oxford University Press, 2000

Stowsky, Jay, 'The History and Politics of the Pentagon's Dual-Use Strategy', in Ann Markusen and Sean Costigan, eds, *Arming the Future*, New York, Council on Foreign Relations Press, 1999

US DTIC, *DoD Top 100 Companies and Category of Procurement*, US Defense Technical Information Center (DTIC), US Department of Defense, Washington, annual editions, www.dtic.mil

Wulf, Herbert, *Internationalizing and Privatizing War and Peace*, Houndmills, Palgrave Macmillan, 2005

18 The United Kingdom arms industry in a globalized world

Sam Perlo-Freeman

Introduction

The United Kingdom (UK) is the world's third-largest military spender (after the USA and the People's Republic of China), has what is probably the second-largest arms industry,[1] and is – depending on one's choice of measure – somewhere between the second- and fifth-largest arms exporter. Certainly, after the USA, the UK arms industry is one of the largest and most technologically advanced in the world, forming part of the 'second tier' of arms producers (Krause 1995), along with France, Russia, Italy, Germany and Japan.

As in other countries, the UK arms industry faced a significant drop in demand following the end of the Cold War. As well as causing major job losses, the new environment forced companies to seek new strategies, resulting in some fundamental changes in the industrial and corporate landscape. While some observers hoped for a process of 'conversion' of military to civil production following the end of the superpower confrontation, this was not a significant feature of the changes that took place – even before the upturn in UK and global (especially US) military spending that began in the late 1990s. While some UK firms flirted with diversification into civil production, most of these efforts were unsuccessful (Dunne and Surry 2006). Among the most important trends that have taken place in the UK arms industry since the end of the Cold War are: consolidation and concentration, with a series of major mergers and acquisitions amongst arms-producing companies, leading in particular to the emergence of BAE Systems (the former British Aerospace) as an overwhelmingly dominant player in the UK industry; specialization, whereby, after some initial flirting with diversification into civil markets, companies that remained in the arms industry have tended to focus more narrowly on arms production and services, or closely related fields; government policy-driven expansion of the industry to encompass the service sector, through the outsourcing to private industry activities formerly performed by the military establishment; and internationalization – a two-way process, with US and continental European companies acquiring ownership of significant sections if the UK arms industry and, even more so, UK companies acquiring ownership of arms companies in the USA and elsewhere.

This chapter reviews the development of the UK arms industry since the end of the Cold War, expanding on the trends described above, and discussing the implications for the UK's role in the global arms trade. The second section discusses some of the main overall trends in the industry, presenting available quantitative data. The third section looks at the main corporate changes in the industry since 1989, and the resulting corporate landscape at the time of writing, the end of 2008. The fourth section considers the UK Government's policy with respect to the arms industry and trade, the nature of the political relationship between government and industry, and the implications for the UK's role in the global arms trade. The final section concludes.

Major trends

The UK arms industry, in common with those in most of the rest of the industrialized world, faced a significant drop in demand following the end of the Cold War. The primary source of demand for the industry – British military spending – fell steadily, although not particularly rapidly, over the late 1980s and most of the 1990s, by a total of 24% in real terms between 1988 and 1998. Since then spending has increased, especially since 2001 due to the wars in Iraq and Afghanistan, but still remained in 2007 around 11% below its 1988 level (see Table 18.1).

One trend that is much clearer is the fall in employment in the arms industry (Table 18.1), as rising productivity has combined with steady or falling demand. Direct employment in the arms industry[2] fell sharply through the early and mid-1990s, reaching just over half its Cold War level by the turn of the century, before recovering very slightly. The number of jobs supported by exports has fallen proportionately more than that supported by MoD spending, despite the fact that export sales have held relatively steady.

Estimating the overall level of arms production in the UK (or other countries) is surprisingly difficult. An attempt to do so involves two main problems: one of definition and one of measurement. The problem of definition is of deciding just when goods or services supplied to the military should be considered products of the 'arms industry', or when they should be considered merely civilian goods and services supplied to the military. One may choose a suitable definition, but applying it consistently is problematic, and the absence of any generally agreed definition aggravates the measurement problem.

Even given an accepted definition of the arms industry, the essential problem of measurement is that this 'industry' in fact consists of elements from numerous industrial classifications (such as aerospace, electronics, shipbuilding, etc.). There is no single Standard Industrial Classification (SIC) code or group of SIC codes that encapsulates any reasonable definition of the arms industry.

Attempts to measure the arms industry might be approached from the demand side (the volume of military goods and services procured by the national military from domestic industry,

Table 18.1 UK military spending and arms industry employment, 1988/89–2006/07

Year	UK Military spending (£m., current)	UK military spending (£m. constant 2000)	MOD spending direct employment ('000)	Exports direct employment ('000)	Total direct employment ('000)
88/89	19,290	30,724	230	65	295
89/90	20,868	30,838	225	75	300
90/91	22,287	30,084	220	75	295
91/92	24,380	31,089	215	60	275
92/93	22,850	28,090	180	50	230
93/94	22,686	27,459	170	40	210
94/95	22,490	26,564	145	45	190
95/96	21,439	24,487	135	70	205
96/97	22,330	24,895	120	90	210
97/98	21,612	23,363	115	45	160
98/99	22,477	23,495	125	50	175
99/00	22,548	23,208	120	35	150
00/01	23,552	23,552	125	30	155
01/02	24,874	24,429	125	30	155
02/03	26,991	26,082	135	30	165
03/04	29,338	27,547	140	30	170
04/05	29,524	26,924	135	35	170
05/06	30,603	27,140	145	25	165
06/07	21,454	27,031	135	25	160

Source: Military spending data from SIPRI, based on figures from NATO and the UK Defence Statistics. Milex data is presented on a fiscal year basis, from April to March. Constant UK£ spending is calculated using the Consumer Price Index (CPI) as a deflator, treating each fiscal year's expenditure as if it fell within the calendar year in which it began. Employment data is from UK Defence Statistics

plus exports), or from the supply side (the revenue of arms companies). Supply side measurement presents numerous obstacles: identifying all companies involved in the arms industry, distinguishing military from civil revenues, avoiding double-counting (counting the revenues of both subcontractors and the prime contractors they supply), and separating arms sales revenues into those originating from UK operations and those from overseas subsidiaries.

The demand side is more promising. The MoD provides statistics on total spending by the MoD with UK industry, broken down by SIC classifications, shown in Table 18.2 (column 2). Not all of this spending, of course, consists of military goods and services (for example it includes food, electricity, public transportation, etc.), and especially in the services categories it is not always possible to separate out which classifications are military-specific. Furthermore, the classifications used have changed over the period considered. MoD spending on construction has been omitted from the total in Table 18.2 to obtain a consistent series, as this was not included in the total until 1991/92.

None the less, the total figure at least measures the demand generated within UK industry as a whole by MoD spending. This figure fell significantly in real terms over the 1990s, but has recovered substantially since its low point of 1996/97, and by 2006/07 was almost equal to its Cold War level. The fall in UK military expenditure has been somewhat mitigated by the fact

Table 18.2 MoD expenditure with UK industry and arms exports, 1988/89–2006/07 (figures in £m. Real figures are constant 2000 prices)

1. Year	2. MoD spend with UK industry[1]	3. Of which identifiable arms spending[2]	4. UK arms exports[3]	5. Real MoD spend + exports[4]	6. Real MoD arms + exports[4]	7. Real arms exports[4]
1988/89	8,241	6,748	2,775	17,546	15,168	4,420
1989/90	8,582	6,864	3,125	17,300	14,761	4,618
1990/91	8,870	7,040	4,467	18,003	15,533	6,030
1991/92	10,032	7,508	3,488	17,241	14,022	4,448
1992/93	9,062	6,685	3,118	14,973	12,051	3,833
1993/94	9,134	6,523	2,969	14,649	11,489	3,594
1994/95	8,522	5,932	2,946	13,545	10,486	3,480
1995/96	8,750	5,950	4,723	15,388	12,190	5,394
1996/97	9,005	6,192	6,177	16,926	13,790	6,887
1997/98	10,140	6,130	6,684	18,187	13,852	7,225
1998/99	11,100	6,770	6,030	17,906	13,380	6,303
1999/00	10,440	5,990	4,250	15,120	10,540	4,374
2000/01	10,990	6,000	4,406	15,396	10,406	4,406
2001/02	11,660	6,320	4,216	15,592	10,348	4,141
2002/03	12,820	6,160	4,120	16,370	9,934	3,981
2003/04	13,450	5,840	4,548	16,900	9,754	4,270
2004/05	13,260	5,770	5,162	16,800	9,969	4,707
2005/06	14,720	6,350	4,527	17,069	9,646	4,015
2006/07	15,110	6,340	4,697	17,022	9,485	4,037

Source: UK Defence Statistics

Notes:
1 Excluding construction;
2 See note 3 in the chapter for categories covered;
3 Includes 'identified arms exports' and 'estimate of other aerospace equipment'. Data are presented by calendar year and are listed here according to the closest overlapping fiscal year, i.e. the figure for 1988 is listed under 1988/89;
4 Figures deflated using CPI. Fiscal year figures are assigned to the calendar year in which they begin before being added to exports and deflated

that an increasing portion of the MoD's expenditure has been open to the commercial arms industry due to the outsourcing of functions formerly performed by military personnel or MoD civil servants. This includes a greater proportion of the equipment budget through the increasing outsourcing of maintenance, repair and overhaul (MRO); of the research and development (R&D) budget, in particular due to the privatization of the MoD's Defence Evaluation and Research Agency (DERA) in 2001, creating the company QinetiQ; and the operations budget, due to the outsourced management of military bases, which has become a systematic policy across military installations.

Moreover, while it is not possible to completely separate out the categories of spending that can be considered part of the 'arms industry' from the rest, there are a number of categories, which are fairly consistent across the period, that relate fairly clearly to military equipment, including maintenance. The total value, in nominal terms, of these categories, is shown in Table 18.2 (column 3).[3] These categories have fallen rather more sharply than the total MoD spend.

The second source of demand for the UK arms industry is arms exports. The MoD presents estimates for the volume of exports from the UK industry (including non-UK-owned companies)[4] (see Table 18.2, columns 4 and 7). These have had a more mixed performance since the end of the Cold War, depending as much on success in winning contracts with particular major customers such as Saudi Arabia and India as on secular trends in military expenditure. As Table 18.2 shows, UK arms exports fell in real terms during the early 1990s before rising sharply in the mid- to late 1990s as a result of major deliveries to Saudi Arabia and others, and subsequently falling back again. Overall, exports are not far off their end of Cold War levels.

Adding together the total MoD spend with industry (less construction) plus exports, this total had by 2006/07 almost exactly regained its real-terms Cold War levels from 1988/89 (Table 18.2, column 5). However, the total of MoD military equipment categories plus exports has clearly fallen, by nearly 40% in real terms since 1988/89 (Table 18.2, column 6).

What cannot be measured from this table is the growth of the military services industry, as this falls within aggregated categories which cannot be separated into military and civilian services. It is clear from the available data that MoD spending in all services has increased substantially. However it is also possible to see that a number of definitely civilian categories – such a food, electricity, etc. – have increased in real terms. This would imply that the total value of the 'arms industry' – including MoD and exports – has fallen somewhat over the period in question.

The overall conclusion of this is that the arms industry as a whole has probably shrunk somewhat since the end of the Cold War, falling particularly rapidly in the early-to-mid 1990s before recovering. The fall in expenditure on military equipment by the UK MoD has fallen substantially, but this has been mostly – though probably not completely – made up for by the growth in the military services industry. The volume of arms exports has been rather variable, but in recent years has not been much less than at the end of the Cold War, in real terms. Considering the overall demand generated by military customers – domestic and foreign – for UK-based industry, including civil industry, this total is now virtually back to its Cold War levels.

Restructuring of the UK arms industry

An indication of the extent of the changes in the structure of the UK arms industry can be seen from a casual glance at the list of UK companies in the SIPRI tables of the 'Top 100' arms-producing companies for 1989 and for 2007 (Tables 18.3 and 18.4) (Anthony et al. 1991, Perlo-Freeman 2009). Only two companies from the 1989 list – British Aerospace and Rolls Royce – remain in the 2007 list, and even BAE have changed their name to BAE Systems. A third company, Vosper Thorneycroft, which was just below the Top 100 in 1989 still exists as VT Group. The other companies in the list have either been acquired by other

Table 18.3 UK arms-producing companies in the SIPRI Top 100, 1989

Company	Top 100 Rank 1989	Arms sales 1989 (£m.)	Arms business now with
British Aerospace	4	4,050	BAE Systems
GEC	18	1,759	BAE Systems
Lucas Industries	29	298	Goodrich (USA)
Rolls Royce	42	741	Rolls Royce
VSEL	54	530	BAE Systems
Hunting Associated Industries	61	396	Babcock, others
Smiths Industries	66	360	General Electric (USA), Smiths Group
Thorn EMI	70	330	Thales (France)
Racal	78	296	Thales (France)
Ferranti-International Signal	80	288	BAE Systems
Devonport Management	87	248	Babcock
Dowty Group	88	241	BAE Systems, SAFRAN (France), Ultra Electronics, General Electric (USA)
Westland Group	90	240	Finmeccanica (Italy)
Siemens-Plessey Electronic Systems (Siemens)	n.a.	(subsidiary) 240	
BAE Systems Hawker Siddeley	95	215	Some with Meggitt

Source: SIPRI Arms Industry Database. Final column based on SIPRI Yearbooks, company annual reports and websites

companies, domestic and foreign, exited the arms industry by closing or selling their military business, or been broken up.

The story in between these 'before and after' tables relates to how industry – and government – have responded to the fall in demand for military equipment from the UK industry chronicled in the previous section, as they tried to maintain profitability in the changed environment. All major weapons systems producers shed jobs, as can be seen from the employment figures above. Beyond this, the industry has gone through four main processes: concentration, specialization, expansion into services, and internationalization.

Concentration

The UK arms industry is more concentrated today than at the end of the Cold War. Much of that concentration can be expressed in terms of one company, BAE Systems. Their share of the total arms sales of UK companies in the SIPRI Top 100 was 40% in 1989; in 2007 it was 65%. This rather overstates the case: BAE probably has a rather higher proportion of its revenues originating from outside the UK than the average, while the 2007 list excludes foreign-owned companies operating in the UK, which are far more significant than was the case in 1989. None the less, the extent of BAE's dominance of the industry has undoubtedly increased.

The armoured vehicle sector within the UK is now entirely within the hands of BAE Systems. This was completed when BAE acquired armoured vehicle-maker Alvis (just below the Top 100 in 1989) in 2004 (Surrey 2005), which had previously acquired Vickers Defence, makers of the Challenger Tank, from Rolls Royce in 2002 (Sköns & Baumann 2003, 408), and the armoured vehicle activities of GKN in 1998.[5] BAE are now the manufacturer of 95% of the UK's armoured vehicle fleet (Ministry of Defence 2005).

BAE also acquired a substantial stake in the UK's military shipbuilding industry with the acquisition of Marconi Electronic Systems from GEC in 1999 – GEC having previously acquired

Table 18.4 UK companies in the SIPRI Top 100, 2007

Company	Top 100 rank 1989	Arms sales 1989 (£m.)	Background
BAE Systems	2	14,924	Formerly British Aerospace
Rolls Royce	17	2,292	Identity unchanged
QinetiQ	33	1,082	Formed from the part-privatization of the UK Defence Evaluation & Research Agency (DERA) 2003
Babcock International	35	960	Engineering and services group, manages naval dockyards. Grown rapidly since mid-1990s.
VT Group	37	935	Formerly shipbuilder Vosper Thorneycroft. Moved into services, expanded rapidly from mid-1990s.
Serco	46	721	Corporate and government services group. Rapid increase in military business from late 1990s.
Cobham	51	610	Military electronics and aerospace. Formerly FR Group. Rapid expansion from mid-1990s.
GKN	57	476	Engineering group, arms sales are aerospace subsystems. Acquired Westland Helicopters in 1994, but subsequently sold Westland and armoured vehicle business.
Meggitt	70	334	Aerospace subsystems. Rapid expansion from 2001.
Ultra Electronics	76	310	Military electronics. Spun-off from Dowty Group in 1993. Rapid expansion from late 1990s.

Source: SIPRI Arms Industry Database. Background information based on SIPRI Arms Industry Database, company websites and Annual Reports, SIPRI Yearbooks (various years)

VSEL in 1995,[6] which manufactured the UK's nuclear submarines, including the Defiant-class that carry the UK's Trident nuclear weapons system. The other major UK shipbuilder is VT Group, the former Vosper Thorneycroft; however, in 2008 BAE and VT Group merged their surface shipbuilding and support activities into a single joint venture company, BVT Surface Fleet, in a move linked to the order of two new 65,000-tonne aircraft carriers by the UK Government. BAE have a 55% stake in the joint venture, and VT Group have an option to sell their 45% stake to BAE after a year (Perlo-Freeman and Sköns 2008, 270). At the time of writing, it has recently been reported (late January 2009) that VT Group have decided to exercise that option and sell their stake to BAE in July 2009, for £380m., to concentrate on their service business.[7] The other UK shipbuilder is Babcock International, although their business is much more oriented towards naval and other services. Their position in the naval services industry was consolidated in 2007 with the acquisition of Devonport Management, which runs the Devonport naval dockyard, from American firm KBR. Both the Devonport acquisition and the BVT joint venture were strongly supported by the UK Government, which wanted further consolidation of the shipbuilding industry before approving the carrier purchase.[8]

BAE were already the only UK manufacturer of fixed-wing military aircraft by 1989. In fact, the only complete aircraft they manufacture on their own is the Hawk trainer; in terms of major combat aircraft they are involved in the Eurofighter Typhoon along with Franco-German European Aeronautic Defence and Space (EADS) and Finmeccanica of Italy, and the US Joint Strike Fighter programme as a junior partner to Lockheed Martin. BAE also have a stake in the UK missile sector through their Matra BAE Dynamics Alenia (MBDA) joint venture with EADS and Finmeccanica, in which BAE hold 37.5%.

The only areas of major weapons systems in which BAE now do not have a dominant (or indeed any) position in the UK are helicopters and engines. The UK's helicopter manufacturer, Westland Helicopters, is now part of the AgustaWestland subsidiary of Italy's Finmeccanica. Westland had been acquired by engineering conglomerate GKN in 1994. They formed the

AgustaWestland joint venture with Finmeccanica in 2001, but then sold their 50% stake to the Italian company in 2004.[9] Rolls Royce remain the UK's dominant manufacturer of marine and aircraft engines, military and civil.

BAE made their major move into the military electronics field with their acquisition of Marconi Electronic Systems from GEC in 1999. This was the single biggest arms industry merger in UK history, at £6.5 billion.[10] BAE had previously acquired a number of other military electronics businesses, including Siemens Plessey Electronic Systems in 1998.[11]

The military electronics sector, though, presents a far more diverse landscape than those of major weapons systems and platforms. Other major companies in the field include Thales of France (formerly Thomson-CSF), which acquired parts of Thorn EMI in 1995, then Racal and Pilkington Optronics (which had acquired the rest of Thorn EMI) in 1999; General Electric of the USA, which acquired Smiths Aerospace in 2007; Cobham and Meggitt, which were already in existence as UK companies in 1989 but have grown exponentially since then; General Dynamics UK, which have established a UK presence organically rather than through acquisitions; and Ultra Electronics, a spin-off from Dowty Group in 1993, which have likewise grown rapidly.

Consolidation in the industry resulted from the difficulty for smaller companies to maintain profitability in the face of reduced demand, or even to maintain productive capability given the naturally 'lumpy' patterns of demand for major weapons systems. This in part explains the differing pattern of consolidation in different sectors of the arms industry. While demand for major weapons systems and platforms from the UK industry has decreased significantly, military electronics has been a growing sector as the revolution in military affairs (RMA) has placed an increasing premium on high-tech electronics and communications – C4ISTAR[12] – linked to the network-centric warfare concept, while the services sector has also greatly expanded as a result of the government policy of outsourcing. Thus, these sectors have continued to generate sufficient demand to support a wide variety of players.

Specialization

UK arms-producing companies are today more specialized than those in 1989. As a crude measure, the total arms sales of the 10 UK companies in the SIPRI Top 100 for 2007 represent 62% of those companies' total sales; while in 1989, the ratio of arms sales to total sales for these companies stood at just 17%. In particular, a number of companies such as GEC and Thorn EMI, which formerly had a relatively small share of arms sales in their overall business, have exited the arms industry, while BAE have divested civil interests, such as the Rover car company, a stake in telecoms firm Orange, as well as all their civil aerospace production (which ended with the sale of their 20% stake in Airbus to majority owners EADS in 2006).[13] The company now estimates that 95% of its revenue is from military activities, according to information supplied to SIPRI.

The process of specialization, both in the UK and the USA, has been the product of investor pressure for companies to focus on 'core competencies', as well as a reflection of the fact that arms companies have developed specialized knowledge in dealing and winning contracts with a single governmental customer, rather than at competing in the commercial marketplace (Dunne and Surry 2006).

The characterization of UK arms companies as specialized must come with a qualification; they are specialized not necessarily as pure arms producers, but in arms and closely related civilian technologies. For example, 'defence and aerospace' companies such as Cobham, Meggitt and Rolls Royce, 'defence and security' firms such as Thales and QinetiQ, or military and civil electronics firms such as Ultra. In the field of electronics and communications, in particular, military technology is increasingly based on 'spinning-in' commercially developed technologies, so that the civil and military sides offer considerable synergies (Dunne and Surry

2006). Service companies such as Babcock and VT Group likewise provide civil government outsourcing services, as well as their core military services businesses.

Expansion of the services sector

While UK military equipment spending has fallen significantly since the end of the Cold War, opportunities for private industry to benefit from military activity have expanded through the increasing outsourcing of a range of activities formerly carried out by the armed forces or the Ministry of Defence. Along with the USA, the UK has been one of the pioneers of this process, although other countries are following suit to varying degrees. This has allowed the rapid expansion of a private military services industry, providing a range of services to the military including IT services, R&D, equipment maintenance, repair and overhaul, facilities management, training, logistics support to deployed forces, and armed security in conflict zones.

The reasons for this trend are both ideological and practical (see, for example Perlo-Freeman and Sköns 2008, Wulf 2005). Both Labour and Conservative governments in the UK have adopted strongly pro-free market, neo-liberal ideologies and policies, stressing the superiority of the private sector over the public, and thus seeking to bring both private-sector finance, management and values into the public sector. This has not by any means been confined to the military sector, encompassing health, education and many other key government activities. The Private Finance Initiative (PFI) has sought to bring private capital and management into major public investment projects, such as schools, hospitals and military bases.

In the military sector, this ideological preference for private involvement has been supplemented by the practical problems created by the major reduction in military manpower since the end of the Cold War, combined with the increasing focus of the armed forces on expeditionary missions, which has generated severe problems of military 'overstretch'. Thus the government has sought to outsource 'non-core' activities to allow military personnel to concentrate on 'core' missions. (Although some tasks, such as training, that would once have been thought of as core military tasks have also been outsourced to a significant degree.)

Four of the top 10 UK arms companies are now predominantly military services providers, as opposed to equipment producers: QinetiQ, the company formed from the part-privatization of the MoD Defence Evaluation & Research Agency in 2001; VT Group, formerly shipbuilder Vosper Thorneycroft, which specialize in naval management support services, MRO, training and through-life support for a variety of military equipment, but which also manage a variety of US military bases through their VT Services Inc. subsidiary; Babcock, which operate a number of UK naval bases and provide engineering, training and support services for the UK armed forces; and Serco, which also engage in military facilities management, including a one-third stake in the UK Atomic Weapons Establishment (AWE) at Aldermaston (although their military business is a fairly small share of their total sales).[14] Other companies active in providing services to the UK MoD include the US company EDS (now owned by Hewlett Packard) which manage large parts of the MoD's IT infrastructure, and KBR (formerly a subsidiary of Halliburton), which have been most prominent in providing logistics to the US military in Iraq, but which also have a global logistics supply contract with the MoD.

A further development worth noting is the creation of the privatized Defence Technical Academy in St Athan's, South Wales, a £12 billion, 25-year PFI venture that will provide training to all branches of the UK (and some overseas) armed forces, training up to 4,500 students at any one time. The DTA will be provided by the Metrix Consortium, which was given preferred bidder status in 2007. The consortium includes QinetiQ, EDS, Raytheon, AgustaWestland, Serco, Sodexho (a French services company that provides domestic (non-military) services to the UK MoD), and the Open University.[15]

The services sector has provided a highly valuable cushion for arms companies in the face of declining military equipment expenditure. Much military services activity, such as the management of naval dockyards, relates to very long-term activities that are not subject to the vagaries of major equipment plans.

Internationalization

At the time of the last years of the Cold War, the UK arms industry, like most national arms industries, was overwhelmingly owned by UK-owned companies, the operations of which were also based almost entirely in the UK. While some collaborative projects existed, for the most part arms production was still a national affair.

The global arms industry today is much more internationalized, reflecting the difficulties of maintaining a purely national 'defence industrial base' (DIB) for any country other than the USA, given the scale required for economic production of complex modern weapons systems. Internationalization has taken the form of both increased international collaboration in armaments projects (in particular within Western Europe), and in increased patterns of cross-border ownership within the arms industry. This section focuses on the latter trend, which has been a particularly strong feature of the UK industry. Significant sections of the UK industry are now foreign-owned, while UK companies have acquired substantial overseas operations, such that in many cases only a minority of their operations remain in the UK. The US industry, which serves the overwhelmingly largest customer for military equipment and services, has been a particular target for acquisitions by UK companies.

Foreign ownership of UK arms companies

The willingness of the UK Government to allow foreign companies to acquire ownership of parts of the UK DIB reflects both a general attitude to industrial policy that has strongly encouraged inward investment in UK manufacturing; and in the military sector, the increasing realization that complete self-sufficiency in arms production is impossible in the modern world, given the complexity of modern weapons systems and technology. While the government still places great stress on maintaining what it sees as key capabilities within the UK DIB, it defines the UK DIB as consisting of the assets, technologies and skills that operate within the UK – regardless of ownership (Ministry of Defence 2005).

Some of the main foreign companies with operations in the UK are:[16]

- Finmeccanica, with 9,137 UK employees in 2007. Their UK businesses include Westland Helicopters (4,000 employees) and the UK branches of Selex Communications, Selex Galileo and Selex Sistemi Integrati, as well as various other military electronics operations and a 37.5% stake in MBDA.
- Thales, with 8,141 UK employees and UK-originated revenue of €1,836m. in 2007. Their military electronics business in the UK gained its first major foothold with the acquisition of Racal and Pilkington Optronics in 2000. Thales UK are involved in the UK's CVF aircraft carrier programme and are the lead contractor in the Watchkeeper Unmanned Aerial Vehicle (UAV) programme.
- EADS, with around 15,000 UK employees; the great majority of these, though, are with Airbus, most of the business of which is civil. However, they also have several other military electronics, missile (MBDA), military space and services businesses. They are also the lead contractor in the Air Tanker consortium providing the UK's £13 billion 27-year Future Strategic Tanker Aircraft PFI agreement, whereby the MoD will lease air-to-air refuelling aircraft from the consortium.
- General Electric acquired Smiths Aerospace, the main arms-producing division of Smiths Group in 2007. The division became General Electric Aviation Systems. The number of

UK employees is not known, but Smiths Aerospace employed 11,000 people in total in the USA and UK.

- EDS Defence, a division of IT services company EDS, with around 3,500 employees in the UK. EDS Defence provides IT services to the UK MoD, including as the lead contractor in the ATLAS Consortium, which won the £4 billion 10-year Defence Information Infrastructure contract with the MoD in 2005.
- General Dynamics UK, with 1,700 employees involved in a range of C4ISTAR and services businesses, most notably the contract for the UK Army's Bowman communications system.
- Lockheed Martin, with 1,500 employees, as well as a one-third stake in AWE at Aldermaston.
- Raytheon, with around 1,700 employees, although many of these are engaged in civil electronics and security.

Overall, the UK Department of Trade & Industry (DTI) estimates that around 25% of the UK arms industry is foreign-owned, based on the number of employees in companies engaged in arms production (Ministry of Defence 2005). Foreign-owned companies represent, then, a significant, though far from dominant, portion of the UK DIB.

UK ownership of foreign arms companies

British companies' ownership of overseas arms industries is considerably larger than the reverse. For example, BAE Systems employ around as many people in the USA alone (44,000 in 2007[17]) as all the companies listed above employ in the UK combined. In particular, since the mid-1990s almost all UK arms companies (except Babcock) have made major US acquisitions, so that many now have more of their operations in the USA than in the UK. Table 18.5 shows the US 'footprint' of the UK companies in the SIPRI Top 100 for 2007.

The desire to make US acquisitions on the part of UK arms companies is not hard to explain: the US Government represents overwhelmingly the largest military customer in the world and since the late 1990s this source of demand has been rapidly growing, in contrast to Western European demand, which has been essentially level since the big falls of the early-to-mid 1990s. While some export markets, such as India and Saudi Arabia, have been profitable arenas for UK companies, the USA offers by far the greatest potential for expansion.[18]

Table 18.5 The US footprint of UK-owned arms companies

Company	Value of US acquisitions 2003 08 ($m.)	% of sales to USA, 2007	% of assets in USA, end 2007	% of employees in USA, end 2007
BAE Systems	9,683.0	41[1]	67	45[1]
Rolls Royce	0.0	30	13	14
QinetiQ	1,114.0	41[1]	43[1]	41
Babcock	0.0	<1	<1	<1
VT Group	138.5	24	19	33
Serco	638.0	11[1]	14	14[1]
Cobham	1,703.0	47	39	41
GKN	366.0	65[2]	n.a.	n.a.
Meggitt	2,258.0	49[1]	68[1]	53[1]
Ultra Electronics	245.0	37	48[1]	n.a.

Sources: SIPRI Yearbooks, company websites and annual reports.

Notes:
1 Figures for US & Canada
2 Figures for GKN Aerospace only

Furthermore, sales to the US military tend to require a US presence. The USA, despite its overwhelming lead position in military spending, is not, relatively speaking, a major arms importer (see SIPRI Arms Transfer Database, for example). A list of the top 100 US Department of Defense (DoD) contractors for 2007 includes only three overseas arms producers – BAE Systems, Rolls Royce and EADS[19] – and the bulk of these contracts are likely from these companies' US operations.

UK arms companies have in this regard enjoyed, up till now, a uniquely privileged position in their ability to secure US Government consent for US acquisitions, largely on account of the close strategic relationship between the UK and the USA. Until Finmeccanica's US$5.2 billion acquisition of DRS Technologies in 2008,[20] there had been no really major acquisitions of US companies by continental European companies. Furthermore, for certain UK companies, including BAE and Rolls Royce, the US Government has relaxed the requirement for a 'proxy board' for foreign-owned US subsidiaries; this requires the US company to be run by a separate board composed mostly of US citizens, allowing the foreign owner only very limited strategic control over the acquired company. In place of this, more privileged foreign companies now operate under 'Special Security Agreements' (SSA) designed to protect sensitive US technology, but which allow the parent more control.[21]

BAE Systems's US acquisitions dwarf those of all other UK companies. They first established a major presence in the USA with the acquisition of GEC's Marconi Electronic Systems in 1999, by which they acquired the US company Tracor, acquired by GEC the year before. Several smaller-scale purchases from 2000–03 expanded this significantly, but the major leap in their US operations came in 2005 with the acquisition of land systems company United Defense for $4.2 billion, followed by military vehicles company Armor Holdings in 2007, also for $4.2 billion. These have put BAE in the ranks of the top 10 contractors to the US DoD.[22]

BAE describe the UK, USA, Australia, Sweden, South Africa and Saudi Arabia as their 'home markets'. With their acquisition of Tenix Defence in 2008 they are now the largest arms-producing company in Australia,[23] while their acquisition of Hägglunds (as part of Alvis) in 2004 and Bofors (as part of United Defense) in 2005 makes them the second largest in Sweden.[24]

The share of BAE's revenues resulting from UK operations is quite hard to ascertain, as it is not specified in the company's annual reports or other publicly supplied information. However, a reasonable estimate can be made based on the divisional breakdown of their revenues and other available information. If one treats their revenues from Saudi Arabia as being essentially dependent on their UK operations (in that the equipment they provide and support comes from a government-to-government deal between the UK and Saudi Arabia, with BAE's share of it coming from their UK operations), I estimate that a little under half of BAE's revenues in 2007 resulted from their UK activities.[25]

British arms companies thus stand, for the most part, with one foot on either side of the Atlantic – and with the strongest growth possibilities lying on the US side. It would be wrong to conclude, though, that the UK market is unimportant to these companies, or could be easily dispensed with if circumstances were less favourable. In the UK, companies like BAE, QinetiQ, Rolls Royce and VT Group enjoy long-established relationships with the UK Government and are seen as key partners for long-term projects. In the USA they are relative newcomers competing amongst a far larger number of big players.

Industrial policy

According to Krause (1995), countries develop arms industries and arms trade for three primary motivations: wealth, power and victory in war. Military industrial development may be seen as a means of spurring general industrial development and arms exports may be seen as a good way of earning foreign currency. The ability to produce and export advanced weapons technology may be seen as giving a country status and influence; it confers both the ability to maintain and expand the capabilities of the country's armed forces, and to use the power to transfer (or withhold) that technology to other countries to further strategic goals.

Economic motivations are often used in defence of arms exports, but in fact the proportion of UK industry and trade dependent on arms production of any sort is small; in any case, the UK Government has shown little enthusiasm in other spheres for maintaining or developing manufacturing industry, preferring to leave this to the market.

Thus the government's primary interest in its relations with the arms industry may be seen as the desire, common to all countries that aspire to great or even intermediate power status, to sustain as advanced and autonomous a military industrial base as may be possible given the economic and technological constraints that country faces. Tied up with this, though, may be seen the political influence wielded by the major corporate actors (especially, in the UK case, BAE) in this same military industrial complex (MIC) that the government creates and maintains.

The lobbying power of arms companies within governments with which they maintain a deep, long-term set of relationships has been frequently documented (e.g. Higgs 1990, Dunne 1993). A 'revolving door' between the two sees government ministers and senior civil servants – such as former Minister of Defence under the current Labour Government, George Robertson – taking up senior positions within the arms industry, and conversely senior industry executives being awarded with positions in government. A network of policy committees in the defence field includes a high proportion of voices from the arms industry, but few from more independent, critical perspectives, institutionalizing the industry's influence in policy-formation (Campaign Against Arms Trade 2005). The National Defence Industries Council is perhaps the most significant of these, which is a prime forum for the discussion of defence industrial policy between industry and government, and which has a key role in the monitoring of the Defence Industrial Strategy (Ministry of Defence 2005, 2).

The consequences for the arms trade are not hard to see in terms of the government's willingness to permit exports to highly repressive regimes and regions of conflict. Stavriankakis (2008) documents how, despite what is on paper a strong set of export-control criteria, in practice the export licensing decision-making process has an institutional bias towards a permissive interpretation of these criteria, with pro-control voices within government having only a weak influence on the outcome. Successive UK governments have also at best turned a blind eye to, at worst actively engaged in, bribery as a means of securing export orders for UK companies (e.g. Gilby 2008). Perhaps most notoriously, in December 2006 the government compelled the Serious Fraud Office to terminate an investigation into alleged corruption in BAE's sales to Saudi Arabia, an investigation that threatened the agreement of a new £40 billion-contract by BAE with Saudi Arabia for Eurofighter Typhoon aircraft. The government also provides economic support to arms exports in a variety of ways, most notably through the Export Credit Guarantee Department (ECGD). These subsidies for the arms trade have been extensively discussed by academics and non-governmental organizations (NGOs) (e.g. Ingram and Isbister 2004).

Such enthusiastic support for arms exports is neither new nor peculiar to the UK. It is worth asking, though, how the changing structure of the industry has affected and is likely to affect in future the government's relationship with the arms industry, and the consequences of this for the UK's role in the arms trade.

The changes that have taken place in the UK and global arms industries since the end of the Cold War have certainly changed the parameters of the government's relationship with industry, and the nature of the economic and technological constraints faced, but have not removed the underlying motivation to retain and develop what the government sees as key military industrial capabilities within the UK. The government expresses this motivation very clearly in its 2005 Defence Industrial Strategy (Ministry of Defence 2005), where it sets out fully how it sees this underlying goal as operating within the changed national and global industrial landscape.

One of the biggest questions raised by the internationalization of the UK arms industry is as to what is meant by the 'UK DIB', or even whether such a specifically national base can be said to exist. The DIS, following the earlier 2002 Defence Industrial Policy paper,[26] defines the UK 'defence industry' as consisting of 'all defence suppliers that create value, employment, technology or intellectual assets in the UK. This includes both UK and foreign-owned companies'. Conversely, foreign subsidiaries of UK-owned companies are not treated as part of the UK industry, although they are seen in a positive light if they result in skills and technologies flowing back to the UK industry.

The DIS recognizes that no country other than the USA is able to maintain a complete, 'cradle-to-grave' capability in all types of weapons systems, but seeks to identify those capabilities the government regards as crucial to keep onshore for reasons of fundamental security, or for strategic reasons – in particular, the desire to retain 'operational independence' in the use of military technology, including that acquired from overseas. One aspect of this criterion is an emphasis on systems integration and through-life support capabilities for all major weapons systems, so as to be able to continuously support and upgrade systems, and integrate new technologies into existing weapons platforms, which are expected to have very long service lives. At present a wide range of new major platforms are planned or under construction, including the two new 65,000-tonne CVF aircraft carriers, Astute class submarines, Type 45 destroyers, the US Joint Strike Fighter (JSF), the EADS A400M transport aircraft, and the Future Rapid Effects System (FRES) family of land vehicles; but after these, there are no plans to begin development of a further generation.

A major policy shift in the DIS is a move away from open competition as the normal mode of acquisition, towards a system of long-term 'partnering agreements' with single companies or consortia for the support of different classes of equipment. This is both a reflection of the emphasis on through-life support and an acceptance of the virtual monopoly position of certain companies – especially BAE Systems, but also, for example, AgustaWestland for helicopters – in particular sectors. This aspect of the DIS has raised considerable controversy amongst some commentators,[27] due to the dangers in terms of cost in handing such a strong monopolistic position to BAE in particular. Within the first year of publication of the DIS, partnering agreements had been reached by the MoD with AgustaWestland for helicopters and BAE Systems for the army's land vehicles fleet. A further 15-year partnering agreement was reached in 2007 with a newly formed surface vessels joint venture between BAE Systems and VT Group: BVT Surface Fleet. BAE has also signed a number of agreements for long-term support of the UK's fixed-wing aircraft.[28]

While the effects of the DIS are yet to be fully seen, it suggests no diminution in the government's support for arms exports. Indeed, the DIS is perhaps likely to entrench the arms companies, BAE Systems in particular, even more deeply in the workings of government. The focus on long-term partnerships with effective monopoly suppliers, which the DIS describes as a move away from a 'transactional' mode of dealing with industry towards ongoing collaboration, the increasing trend towards PFIs where companies are engaged in the daily business of military operations, and the 'contracting for availability' approach, where companies have an ongoing responsibility for making equipment available to the MoD,[29] all suggest an even closer intertwining of government and industry than has already developed. Instead of simply making a once-and-for-all delivery of equipment to the military, private companies become responsible for the day-to-day provision of military capability. The DIS is also widely seen as reinforcing BAE's dominant role in the UK industry (e.g. Hartley 2008), establishing them as an inseparable partner to the government in the provision of the UK's military capability. The inclination of the government to promote the interests of BAE and other chosen partners, in export control policy and elsewhere, is at the very least unlikely to weaken.

Paradoxically, the internationalization of the arms industry, far from loosening the government's attachment to a no longer clearly defined 'domestic' industry, may even have sharpened their concern to maintain the UK DIB; as the DIS points out, arms companies – whether UK- or foreign-owned – now have a choice of where to direct their investments in order to maximize their profits. The UK Government is, then, in a position of competing to make the UK market more attractive for this investment to maintain capabilities within the UK-based industry. The US market, in particular, is explicitly recognized by the government as offering by far the strongest growth potential for UK arms companies. While the government in no way wishes to discourage UK companies from making US acquisitions, it wants to ensure that this is not at the expense of maintaining and developing UK capabilities and technologies. The concern is probably not so much that companies like BAE would simply shut up shop in the UK – the virtually guaranteed revenue stream they enjoy from the UK Government would make that a self-defeating move – but rather that they might allow their UK base to stagnate as investments are directed towards the USA.

To encourage both UK- and foreign-owned arms companies to continue to invest in the UK, then, requires that such investments offer these companies sufficient profit potential – something that UK domestic acquisition on its own is unlikely to be able to do, especially as the DIS envisages a tailing off in demand for new major platforms after the completion of the current swathe of projects. Exports offer, then, a means of providing companies with an expanded market with greater profit potential, as the fixed costs of production have already been paid. The government's incentive to maintain a permissive export control regime is thus strong.

Conclusions

The UK arms industry has undergone radical changes since the end of the Cold War. It employs far fewer people and has significantly reduced its output of military equipment – but it has filled the majority of that gap with revenue from military services outsourced by the UK Government. The production of major weapons systems has become highly concentrated, with BAE Systems dominating in land systems, fixed-wing aircraft and naval vessels, while Agusta-Westland monopolize helicopter production and MBDA missiles. However, the UK industry supports a much more diverse range of suppliers in the military electronics, aviation sub-systems and military services segments. None the less, BAE stand in a category of their own in their central, dominant role within the UK industry.

Internationalization has seen both large-scale investment by foreign arms companies in the UK industry and, even more so, an ever-growing US footprint on the part of most major UK-owned companies, some of which now do more business in the USA than the UK. One implication of this internationalization is that both UK- and foreign-owned arms companies have a choice of where to direct their investments in order to achieve the highest returns, a factor that helped spur the UK Government into producing its 2005 DIS, in an effort to spell out to industry which capabilities it sought to retain within the UK. The DIS signals a move away from open competition in arms procurement towards long-term partnering agreements with industry, with an emphasis on through-life support and continual upgrade of weapons systems. The dominant position of BAE Systems as a key partner in many sectors is reinforced by the DIS.

The relationship between the government and BAE (and to a lesser extent other UK arms companies) is, thus, becoming ever-more symbiotic. For the government, BAE represents a large and crucial portion of the UK DIB, including many of the key capabilities the government seeks to maintain to preserve the UK's position as a major military power. Such a strategy does not allow the government to risk BAE taking their investment elsewhere, in particular to the USA. Conversely, while the UK no longer represents the majority of BAE's revenue, the UK Government offers a secure, continuous revenue stream through various partnering agreements, as well as a permissive environment for large and highly lucrative export contracts such as the Saudi deal, in which the government itself often invests significant political capital.

The trends in the UK industry and in industrial policy, then, point towards both a strengthened institutional voice for the arms industry within government, and perhaps also a strengthened strategic motivation for the government to favour the interests of the arms industry. Therefore, despite growing public concern over arms transfers, the prospects for a more restrictive – and ethical – arms-trade policy in the UK are not encouraging.

Notes

1 The term 'arms industry' throughout this chapter refers to the activities of commercial businesses (including those in the public sector) providing military-specific goods and services to military customers.
2 That is, by 'defence contactors' – indirect employment, which includes suppliers to arms companies who may or may not be part of the arms industry themselves, has followed a similar trend.
3 The categories included are: Weapons and Ammunition, Aircraft and Spacecraft, Shipbuilding & Repairing, Electronics, Precision Instruments, Data Processing Equipment (although some of this may be regular civil computers), Other Electrical Engineering, Motor Vehicles and Parts (which is separate from the   presumably civil retail and wholesale of motor vehicles), and Other Mechanical and Marine Engineering. It excludes food, fuels, electricity, telecommunications, postage, metals, chemicals, textiles, leather goods and clothing, office furniture, stationery, construction and various categories of 'Other' manufacturing and services.
4 These data consist of official National Statistics data for 'identified defence exports', plus an estimate for 'other aerospace equipment' that does not easily match SIC codes.
5 Guerrera, F. 'Jobs axed in £78 million Alvis and GKN Defence merger', *The Independent*, 16 September 1998, www.independent.co.uk/news/business/jobs-axed-in-pounds-78m-alvis-and-gkn-defence-merger-1198483.htmlA.
6 BAE Systems corporate website, 'Heritage – 1995 Marconi Marine', production.investis.com/heritage/nonflash/lineage/sea/1995_marconi_marine_vsel (retrieved 21 March 2009).
7 Chuter, A. 'VT Group selling BVT Surface Fleet stake to BAE', *Defense News*, 28 January 2009, www.defensenews.com/story.php?i=3921836.
8 Perlo-Freeman, S. and Sköns, E. (2008).
9 GKN corporate website, 'History', www.gknplc.com/Groupoverview/History.asp (retrieved 21 March 2009).
10 BAE Systems, *Annual Report*, 1999, p.25.
11 'BAE and DASA buy Siemens division', *Flight International*, 5 November 1997, available at www.flightglobal.com/articles/1997/11/05/28881/bae-and-dasa-buy-siemens-division.html. See also SIPRI website, 'The evolution of BAE Systems', www.sipri.org/contents/milap/milex/aprod/m_and_a/baesystems.pdf/download.
12 Computers, Command, Control, Communications, Intelligence, Surveillance, Target Acquisition and Reconnaissance.
13 'BAE confirms possible Airbus sale', *BBC News*, 7 April 2006, news.bbc.co.uk/2/4886154.stm.
14 Information from company websites and annual reports.
15 QinetiQ company website, 'About Metrix', www.qinetiq.com/home_metrix_review/about_metrix.html.
16 Information from company websites and annual reports.
17 BAE Systems, *Annual Report*, 2007, p.30.
18 For example, Wagstaff-Smith, K. 'QinetiQ CEO sees opportunities in US, tougher prospects in UK', *Jane's Defence Weekly*, 3 December 2008, p.19.
19 Information from US Federal Procurement Data System (FPDS), www.fpds.gov.
20 'Finmeccanica completes acquisition of DRS Technologies for 5.2 billion U.S. dollars', Finmeccanica corporate press release, 22 October 2008.
21 Examples of proxy board agreements and SSAs are available from US Defense Security Service, 'Foreign ownership, control or influence: types of FOCI mitigation instruments', www.dss.mil/GW/ShowBinary/DSS/isp/foci/foci_mitagation.html. See also Ashbourne, A., *Opening the US Defence Market*, Centre for European Reform (CER) Working Paper, CER: London, October 2000.
22 *SIPRI Yearbook*, various years.
23 Ferguson, G. 'BAE Systems buys Tenix', *Defense News*, 18 January 2008, www.defensenews.com/story.php?F=3316705&C=asia.
24 Based on figures from the Swedish Defence and Security Industry Association, www.soff.se/home.html#.
25 BAE Systems Inc., incorporating BAE's Land Systems & Armaments and Electronics, Information and Support divisions, had revenue of US$14,908m. in 2007 (converted from UK£ at the rate of £1 = $2, the average for 2007). However, some of these divisions' employees are outside the USA. BAE had 44,000 employees in the USA, and the two divisions had total employees of 51,300. If we assume proportionate revenue, we get $12,787 revenue from the USA as an approximation. BAE Systems Australia had revenue of $468m. in 2007, according to *Australia Defence Magazine*. The Swedish Defence and Security Industry Association gives revenue for BAE's Swedish subsidiaries totalling $598m. BAE also accounts for its 20% share in Saab on an equity basis, giving implied revenue of $698m. BAE Land Systems South Africa had revenue of $177m. in 2006 – allowing for some growth we might estimate around $200m. for 2008. Finally, we must account for BAE's most significant equity investment, their 37.5% stake in MBDA, with 2007 revenue of $4,105m. in 2007, giving BAE revenue of $1,539m. However, some of MBDA's revenue derives from the UK. SIPRI has figures for MBDA revenue from France and Italy, and revenues from Germany are also provided by EADS. The company also has some limited operations in the USA,

but making some small allowance for this gives an estimate of at least $800m. for MBDA UK, giving $320m. for BAE. Adding up all the above overseas-origin revenues (excluding Saudi Arabia) gives a total of $16 billion, out of total BAE revenues of $31.4 billion, leaving just under half coming from UK-dependent revenues (including those from Saudi Arabia).

26 'Defence Industrial Policy', UK Ministry of Defence Policy Papers No. 5, October 2002, www.mod.uk/NR/rdonlyres/25726BCE-8DD6-4273-BE8D-6960738BEE0A/0/polpaper5_defence_industrial.pdf.

27 For example, Hartley (2008); former head of UK Defence Procurement Peter Levene also criticized this move: Jameson, A. 'Levene attacks defence strategy', *The Times*, 14 February 2006, business.timesonline.co.uk/article/0,9069-2038881,00.html.

28 MoD, 'Defence Industrial Strategy, 6 months on', speech by Defence Procurement Minister Lord Drayson, 8 July 2006, www.mod.uk/DefenceInternet/AboutDefence/People/Speeches/MinDP/DefenceIndustrialStrategySixMonths On.htm; and Chuter, A. 'BAE to maintain UK Typhoons', *Defense News*, 4 March 2009, www.defensenews.com/story.php?i=3974078.

29 For example the Future Strategic Tanker Aircraft (FSTA) agreement with EADS, where the company own the fleet of planes and lease their use to the MoD, who pay according to usage, see MoD Fact Sheet on FSTA, www.mod.uk/DefenceInternet/FactSheets/ProjectFactsheets/FutureStrategicTankerAircraftfsta.htm; examples of 'contracting for availability' include the UK's Eurofighter Typhoon fleet and the Watchkeeper UAVs. See 'Britain's Future Contracting for Availability Approach', *Defense Industry Daily*, 2 December 2007, www.defenseindustrydaily.com/britains-future-contracting-for-availability-approach-04333; 'UK fighters fly to availability based contracting', *Defense Industry Daily*, 4 March 2009, www.defenseindustrydaily.com/uks-eurofighters-fly-to-availability-based-contracting-04337; and Chuter, A. 'U.K. to extend UAV-by-the-hour deal', *Defense News*, 12 March 2009, www.defensenews.com/story.php?i=3986998.

Bibliography

Anthony, Ian, Agnès Courades Allebeck, Gerd Hagmeyer-Gaverus, Paolo Miggioano and Herbert Wulf, 'The 100 Largest Arms-Producing Companies, 1989', Appendix 8A in *SIPRI Yearbook 1991*, Oxford, Oxford University Press, 1991

Campaign Against Arms Trade, 'Who Calls the Shots: How Government-Corporate Collusion Drives Arms Exports', February 2005, www.caat.org.uk/publications/government/who-calls-the-shots-0205.pdf

Dunne, J. Paul, 'The Changing Military Industrial Complex in the UK', *Defence Economics*, Vol. 4, No. 2, March 1993

Dunne, J. Paul and Eamon Surry, 'Developments in the Arms Industry Since the End of the Cold War', Section III in 'Arms Production', Chaper 9 in *SIPRI Yearbook 2006*, Oxford, Oxford University Press, 2006

Gilby, Nicholas, 'Corruption and the Arms Trade: The U.K. Ministry of Defence and the Bribe Culture', *Economics of Peace and Security Journal*, Vol. 3 No. 1, 2008

Hartley, Keith, 'European Defense Industrial Policy and the United Kingdom's Defence Industrial Base', *Economics of Peace and Security Journal*, Vol. 3 No. 1, 2008

Higgs, Robert, ed., *Arms Politics and the Economy: Historical and Contemporary Perspectives*, New York, Holmes and Meier, 1990

Ingram, P. and R. Isbister, 'Escaping the Subsidy Trap: Why Arms Exports are Bad for Britain', British American Security Information Council, Oxford Research Group and Saferworld, September 2004

Krause, Keith, *Arms and the State: Patterns of Military Production and Trade*, Cambridge, Cambridge University Press, 1995

Ministry of Defence (MoD), *Defence Industrial Strategy Defence White Paper*, CM6697, UK Ministry of Defence, December 2005, www.mod.uk/nr/rdonlyres/f530ed6c-f80c-4f24-8438-0b587cc4bf4d/0/def_industrial_strategy_wp_cm6697.pdf

Perlo-Freeman, Sam, 'The SIPRI Top 100 Arms-Producing Companies, 2007', Appendix 6A in *SIPRI Yearbook 2009*, Oxford, Oxford University Press, 2009

Perlo-Freeman, Sam and Elisabeth Sköns, 'The Private Military Services Industry', *SIPRI Insights*, No. 1, Stockholm International Peace Research Institute, September 2008

—— 'Arms Production', Chapter 6 in *SIPRI Yearbook 2008*, Oxford, Oxford University Press, 2008

SIPRI, SIPRI Arms Industry Database, www.sipri.org

SIPRI, *SIPRI Yearbook*, Stockholm, Stockholm International Peace Research Institute, various annual editions

Sköns, Elisabeth and H. Baumann, 'Arms Production', Chapter 11 in *SIPRI Yearbook 2003*, Oxford, Oxford University Press, 2003

Stavriankakis, Anna, 'Licensed to Kill: The United Kingdom's Arms Export Licensing Process', *Economics of Peace and Security Journal*, Vol. 3 No. 1, 2008

Surry, Eamon, 'Table of Acquisitions, 2004', Appendix 9B in *SIPRI Yearbook 2005*, Oxford, Oxford University Press, 2005

UK Defence Statistics, National Statistics Online, various annual reports, www.statistics.gov.uk/statbase/Product.asp?vlnk=1123&More=N

Wulf, Herbert, *Internationalizing and Privatizing War and Peace*, Basingstoke, Palgrave Macmillan, 2005

19 Defence industries in Israel

Yaacov Lifshitz

Establishing an advanced defence industry was one route whereby Israel was seeking to achieve a qualitative edge to compensate for its inherent quantitative inferiority. In 2007 sales of Israel's defence companies amounted to US$8,150m., of which 24% were designated for domestic use of the Israel Defence Forces (IDF) (*The Marker*, 2 September 2008), the balance being export sales and sales of subsidiaries operating outside of Israel. Local defence production accounted for some 2%–3% of gross domestic product (GDP), considerably less than 20–30 years ago, thereby also having less influence than before on the economy. Meanwhile, the Israeli defence industry became a major player in the global arms market, ranking fifth-largest among arms exporters in 2006 (SIPRI 2008, 296).

The first part of this chapter traces notable milestones in the evolution of the Israeli defence industrial sector. The second part elaborates on defence exports, explaining their rapid and continuous expansion over several decades. The third part discusses the direct and indirect ways in which the development of defence industries affected overall economic performance, and comments on some micro-economic implications. The concluding part suggests some lessons from Israel's experience.

Main developments

From strategic self-sufficiency to technological force multipliers

Arms production started in British-mandate Palestine during the 1930s, to provide means of self-defence to the Jewish community confronting at the time a hostile, much larger Arab population. For more than a decade, it remained primarily an underground activity but, nevertheless, accomplished remarkable capabilities. Indeed, during the War of Independence in 1948–49, existing workshops were already capable of producing items that significantly contributed to the military effort.

In the early 1950s, under circumstances of ceasefire agreements that failed to bring peace to the Middle East, Israel was in need of arms and military equipment to protect itself, but encountered severe political barriers in attempting to acquire them abroad. Particularly frustrating was the Tripartite Declaration of 1950, by which the UK, France and the USA undertook to limit arms supplies to the belligerents in the region. It was an intolerable situation for the newly born state, and serious concerns evoked as to whether the needs of self-defence could be met based on imports alone. The government thereby adopted a dual strategy that became a fundamental feature of Israeli defence policy for many years: no effort was spared to exploit opportunities for foreign purchases and, at the same time, substantial resources were invested in expanding indigenous production capabilities. The domestic defence industry was thus perceived primarily as a release from absolute dependence on foreign supply sources.

Towards the end of 1953, the embargo was relaxed. Most significant were the emerging supply relations with France and from the mid-1950s to 1967 France became the primary source – and often the sole source – for defence imports, providing Israel with up-to-date weapons. However, Israel remained faithful to its dual strategy and was determined to develop a defence-industrial base of its own. At that stage, local production under licence commenced, nourished by fruitful co-operation with French companies. In addition, for the first time, locally designed changes and adaptations were implemented in obsolescent weapons systems, converting and upgrading them in response to new regional threats. Soon locally developed electronic packages were added also to more advanced, recently acquired weapons, making them suitable for special missions.

Yet as long as supplies from France continued, domestic defence production remained relatively limited in scope. The defence industry developed mainly within the government sector and its relative weight in the economy was still low. The great leap forward occurred when during the Six-Day War, France ceased supplies and imposed an embargo on arms transfers to Israel. Industrial goals broadened, the defence industry was called upon to provide strategic self-sufficiency for Israel and, in particular, to release the country from absolute dependence on foreign suppliers, even for major weapons systems. The first steps towards this aim included the assembly of the Nesher, an Israeli version of the Mirage 5, and the upgrading of the British Centurion tank, both projects involving locally developed and produced subsystems. However, before long Israel began to develop and produce a fighter aircraft of its own (the 'Kfir'), a main battle tank (the 'Chariot'), missile boats and varied types of missiles. The defence industrial base was largely expanded at this stage, extending beyond the government sector through newly established privately owned companies (some of which involved foreign partners), and its relative weight in the economy rose. The self-sufficiency doctrine thus established dominated defence industrial policy for 15–20 years, and only in the late 1980s, due to stable, ongoing supplies from the USA, doubts about the import option began to dissipate and its priority gradually declined.

Opportunities for procurement abroad were an important, perhaps the most important, factor, but not the only one that determined the approach to the role of domestic defence industry. Even before the French embargo trauma, two opinions were in debate (Klieman and Pedatzur 1991, 73–4). One asserted that it was unrealistic to expect that Israel could produce all the armaments the IDF required, there would always be a need for imports, and thus the domestic defence industry should concentrate primarily on improving imported systems and adapting them to the special theatre conditions and to the IDF warfare doctrine. The other view held that even in optimistic political scenarios there are no grounds to assume that foreign acquisitions could meet all requirements for military equipment and, then, as large a proportion as possible of the necessary equipment should be produced locally. The first view, held mainly by military people, reflected concerns that vast investments in domestic industry, bearing fruit only in the course of time, would impede force build-up and war preparedness of the army in the short term. It was rooted, too, in doubts about the technological capabilities of the domestic industry, and warned that with local products the IDF would be using inferior equipment, technologically backward compared with what was obtainable elsewhere. The other opinion, held mainly by civilian officials who were particularly active in developing procurement ties with France and in continually seeking out other sources abroad, seemed more aware of problems created by dependence on foreign suppliers and more confident of the abilities of Israel's scientific and engineering community. Economic considerations also influenced both groups. While the first one stressed the limitations of a small economy, the second emphasized that developing an advanced, technology-intensive defence industry fitted in with the country's general economic goals and with its comparative advantages. Events of the late 1960s, namely the French embargo followed by British unwillingness to sell Israel advanced tanks, made a formal decision between the two views superfluous.

Throughout the years in which the self-sufficiency concept was dominant, it clearly did not mean absolute independence, and no strategic or economic justification was claimed for complete autarky in arms production. In the early 1980s, though, several reasons combined to justify a reassessment of the self-sufficiency policy even in its less-binding form. Available procurement sources and American grants were, as noted earlier, very important. Yet, even more important were economic constraints. The race for superior performance raised the cost of developing and producing novel armaments to the point where it was doubtful whether a small economy could afford the economic price demanded by a self-sufficiency-oriented defence-production policy. Some maintained that adherence to the self-sufficiency policy in defence could lead to economic dependence with severe political, eventually military, implications (Peri and Neubach 1984, 34–7). Specific claims were raised as well. First, despite large investments, only partial independence was attained: in the mid 1980s, the Israeli content of overall military capital, including the value of local improvements in foreign systems, was estimated at only 25%–30% (Halperin 1987, 1,003). Second, in a small country, the relatively large resources tied up in development and production programmes of major weapons systems imply great macro-economic risks; even if absolute costs are lower than in large countries, in percentages of gross national product (GNP) they are far higher (Halperin, 1987, 1,001). Third, dependence on foreign supplies has been replaced by dependence of the defence industry itself, particularly on critical imported components and, in some cases, on foreign technologies. Finally, critics suspected that developing the defence industry retarded economic growth in other sectors.

Signs of a gradual change in domestic defence production policy became evident in the early 1980s, reaching a turning point with the decision to cancel the Lavie programme for developing a new fighter aircraft. The emerging new perception focused on the idea that the industry has to supply the IDF with force multipliers by means of original, unique technological solutions, while self-sufficiency was relegated to second place. The importance of technological force multipliers grew at that time due to the accelerated technological advance of the battlefield, and original solutions became imperative because of ever-more open international arms markets and the resulting unprecedented proliferation of new military technologies. The new conditions reinforced the idea that only indigenous unique development, unobtainable in the market and concealed until used in battle, could assure Israel of qualitative advantages and the ability to surprise.

The change in priorities had important implications for the defence industry. First, it reduced overall demand for local production in monetary terms. Second, it implied a fundamental restructuring of the industry. If self-sufficiency is not a principal goal, domestic products and imports are complementary rather than substitutes, and it is possible to acquire expensive platforms abroad and then add on to them original, surprising features developed and produced locally. Such an approach reduces the need for plants to produce and assemble platforms, and increases demand for industrial entities specializing in systems development and production instead. Eventually, it renders large parts of existing facilities and machinery unnecessary, and may dictate overall downsizing and substantial change in manpower composition. Besides, emphasis on original and unique technological solutions requires increased research and development (R&D) expenditure, and justifies government support in maintaining several parallel know-how centres in every principal technological area; competition among them is more likely than any other means to stimulate originality and innovation. Finally, while self-sufficiency does not run contrary to an aggressive defence export policy, prioritizing force multipliers imposes severe restrictions on exports because of secrecy concerns.

From supplying the local customer to a major player in the global market

The move towards local development and production of major weapons systems in the late 1960s marked the beginning of unprecedented rapid growth for Israeli defence industry, which continued for nearly 20 years. However, there were two distinctive sub-periods: until about 1976, the driving force was domestic defence demand, while later, it was rapidly increasing exports.

In 1975 Israel's defence expenditure reached an all-time high. Following the Yom Kippur War (October War) in 1973, there were urgent needs to rehabilitate the army, make equipment functional again and replace depleted inventories, and domestic expenses soared, accounting for 16% of GDP. It became evident that the economy could not cope with such an exceptionally high level of domestic defence demand any longer and, in the coming years, local currency budgets decreased, or grew at a moderate rate only. In addition, during the 1970s, defence imports from the USA expanded and the massive supplies of US arms made it necessary to allocate increasing budgets for absorbing and maintaining them, so reducing further the amounts left for domestic development and production of military equipment. Meanwhile, vast investments undertaken during the years of high demand in the early 1970s became fully ready for utilization. The defence industries thus confronted diminishing domestic demand on one hand, while having at their disposal larger capacity than ever before on the other hand, and had to look for alternative markets.

Sporadic defence export transactions took place already in the 1950s, including outdated weapons systems withdrawn from the IDF, along with relatively simple small arms and ammunition produced locally. However, by 1975 defence exports amounted to no more than $170m., constituting at the time some 15%–20% of total sales of the defence industry. From the mid-1970s to the late 1980s, exports increased approximately 10-fold in current US dollar prices, and their share in defence industry activities grew substantially. In effect, the industry came to depend on export sales: in the second half of the 1980s, these ranged from 60% to 80% of the larger companies' sales. For several years thereafter, the annual level continued at approximately $1,500m., but in the second half of the 1990s, growth resumed. At the turn of the century, defence exports exceeded $2,000m., and by 2006 reached the level of $3,000m.

The main factors that contributed to the success of defence exports are discussed in detail later. Here, though, it is worthwhile noting four main developments that characterized its course. First, starting from relatively simple small arms and ammunition, defence exports later expanded to more sophisticated systems and equipment, some of which incorporated the most advanced technologies available. Second, in their early phases defence exports targeted the sub-market of developing nations, but then successfully penetrated advanced industrial countries, with a constantly growing proportion of goods sold to these countries. Third, in many instances export activity involved industrial co-operation with domestic companies in target countries, and particularly in the post-Cold War era took advantage of growing demand for upgrading customers' military equipment through such collaborative frameworks. Fourth, in line with the general trend of globalization, and to improve their positioning in overseas markets, Israeli defence companies did not make do with temporary collaborative arrangements, typically dedicated to a specific project, but acquired also full ownership of local companies in both developed and developing countries. For similar reasons, sometimes they established permanent joint ventures with foreign defence companies to serve the requirements of the latter home market, as well as to enhance sales to third parties' markets world-wide. These developments became more frequent in the 2000s.

Initially, the perception was that defence exports primarily serve as a measure to counterbalance local demand fluctuations, thereby saving the companies high adjustment costs in labour and production facilities. Indeed, Israel provides a clear illustration of the role that exports may have in balancing out local demand fluctuations. The defence industry continued to expand until the mid 1980s, despite the levelling off in domestic sales, due to growing defence exports. The further growth of exports was even more crucial in the later 1980s. Following years of high inflation, the government adhered to a restrained fiscal policy, and Defence Ministry orders from domestic industries decreased sharply. Yet export sales compensated for this, so that only a moderate reduction took place in overall defence industry activity. The stabilizing effect of the defence exports made it possible, then, to avoid expensive adjustment processes of shutdowns, workforce turnover and the like for almost 20 years.

However, things changed for the worse in the early 1990s. The effectiveness of defence exports in balancing out local demand fluctuations depends not only on their overall volume, but also on at least two main conditions: the composition of export sales and the structural and organizational flexibilities of the industry. The more export composition deviates from that of local sales, the more specific development and production infrastructure it requires, and over time labour and production equipment surpluses may emerge in particular lines and factories. Indeed, these kinds of structural imbalances were discernible at the beginning of the 1990s in the Israeli defence industry. The defence exports did not necessarily replace the domestic sales of the same plants, and while some parts of the industry maintained full employment, in other companies, or even in certain plants of the same company, production capacity surpluses developed.

In these circumstances, structural and organizational flexibilities are critical, i.e. companies should have the competence to adjust production capacity to changing demand patterns as quickly and smoothly as possible. However, defence industries are often slow to respond to demand changes. Structural rigidities are sometimes a result of a company's size and organizational complexity, or of the relatively high capital intensity, but in the main, they arise from the high degree of specialization of labour and capital employed by defence industry. Restructuring barriers are even more prominent in government-owned companies, where political considerations often interfere with managerial decisions, particularly with those related to labour adjustments. The Israeli defence industry was not immune to these difficulties and the imbalances thereby created adversely affected its performance.

The situation further deteriorated in the post-Cold War era, when exports stopped growing and the world arms market turned into a buyers' market, with keen competition that eroded producer profits. In fact, the high dependency on export backfired and almost all of the companies suffered large losses and severe cash flow problems. The worst financial situation developed within the three large government-owned defence companies: Israel Aerospace Industries (IAI), Israel Military Industry (IMI) and Rafael. None the less, it should be emphasized that even there, were it not for defence exports, the severity of the crisis and the adjustment costs needed would have been considerably greater.

Accelerated growth through restructuring and consolidation

The core of Israel's defence industrial base consists of four large companies that rank among the largest industrial enterprises in the country. In 2007 two of the 10 largest industrial companies in Israel were, by volume of sales, defence companies (see Table 19.1). The small number of large-sized companies resulted in a high degree of concentration: of more than 200 companies defining themselves as engaged in defence production (Ministry of Defence 2007), the big four accounted for 88% of the sales. Notably, in the last decade the combined sales of the four largest companies more than doubled in current dollar prices: from $3,026m. in 1997 to $7,143m. in 2007 (Dun & Bradstreet 1998; 2008).

Over the years, there were changes in ownership of defence companies, but in most cases in the opposite direction to that typical of other countries. In the 1950s, the industry developed principally through government bodies. Later on the circle widened, the number of non-governmental defence companies grew, and the government even sold its share in companies it helped to establish. Conspicuous in the 1960s and 1970s was the proliferation of companies owned jointly by Israelis and foreign partners. In the 1980s, though, most of the latter withdrew and the companies went over to total Israeli ownership. Foreign investors had individual reasons to sell their holdings and no common denominator could be found. Yet the trend, as it developed, was the reverse of the internationalization prevailing in recent decades in the defence industry of other countries. At present, except for minority holdings in Elbit Systems, the shares of which are traded on the Nasdaq National Market, there are almost no foreign investors in the Israeli defence industry.

Table 19.1 Israel's largest defence companies, 2007

	Rank	Total sales (US$m.)	Exports / overseas sales as % of total sales	Number of employees
Israel Aerospace Industries	5	3,310	82	15,570
Elbit Systems	8	1,982	80	7,600
Rafael	14	1,286	58	5,460
Israel Military Industries	26	575	56	3,150
Plasan	53	303	98	720
TAT Technologies	150	90	92	500
Magal	178	73	78	300
Soltam Systems	188	67	79	330

Source: Dun & Bradstreet, 2008

A still more significant issue was the role played by government ownership. Three of the four largest defence companies – IAI, Rafael and IMI – are government-owned and their sales in 2007 made up some 63% of all sales of the entire Israeli defence industry. Government ownership had a clear influence on corporate culture and management patterns. For one, formal limitations in several areas deprive government-owned companies of the managerial flexibility necessary for operating in a businesslike fashion (Lifshitz, 2003, 232–3). Besides this, the need arises on occasion to consider government political and public sensitivity and restrict or postpone unpopular steps (e.g. closing unprofitable plants). Sometimes government-owned company executives assumed, not without grounds, that the government would not let them down and would bail out companies in distress. Over the years, such a morally hazardous approach in effect led government defence companies to demonstrate clear preference for rapid growth over profitability and, even when demand conditions deteriorated, they strove to preserve their size. Finally, the three companies started as Ministry of Defence departments, and only at a later stage – IAI in 1968, IMI in 1990 and Rafael in 2001 – became genuine businesses. The transition required setting up accounting and costing systems hitherto non-existent, as well as other organizational adjustments, but government ownership hardly encouraged such processes and they moved forward only in the 1990s, under crisis conditions.

The details of the crisis and the various recovery measures undertaken have been discussed elsewhere (Lifshitz 2003, 238–41). Here, though, at least three of their main outcomes should be noted. First, recovery involved a comprehensive restructuring, including closing plants and laying off thousands of workers. By 1997, the workforce of government-owned defence companies accounted for no more than 52% of their size in the mid 1980s, decreasing from 43,700 to about 23,000 employees (Sadeh 2001). The companies thus became lean and more efficient, better prepared to compete in the global arms market, and could achieve, as they did, rapid growth in subsequent years. Second, management greatly improved, adopting ways of thinking that were more businesslike and attributing higher priority to profitability and cash flow considerations. Consequently, in the course of time their financial situation became more solid, in its turn allowing expansion into new areas and product families, and investment in an increasing number of business partnerships with foreign defence companies. These favourable developments also contributed to the rapid growth obtained thereafter. Third, the crisis and the way it was handled provided a clear illustration of government ownership disadvantages for both the companies and the government itself, inevitably leading to the conclusion that the government should seek to privatize the greater part of the companies as soon as possible. However, not all parties concerned agreed with this course of action. Particularly reluctant to any change in ownership were the powerful labour unions, and the government, exposed as it was to political pressures from interested parties, was slow and hesitant in enhancing privatization initiatives. Indeed, in the passing decade the progress made in this direction was small.

While government-owned companies paved their way back to accelerated growth mainly through internal restructuring and sometimes by setting up joint ventures with foreign partners, the privately owned part of the defence industrial sector adopted a course of local consolidation. Elbit Systems led the process and through a series of mergers and acquisitions became the second-largest group, including El-Op Electro-Optic Systems, Tadiran Communications, Elisra, Cyclon Aviation Products and a few other smaller companies. In 2007 Elbit Systems's share amounted to 66% of all sales of the privately owned defence companies in the country. However, Elbit Systems was not alone in the mergers and acquisitions (M&A) campaign. Although on a more modest scale, the Mikal group, too, was very active and acquired more than 20 small companies within a relatively short period, including Soltam Systems, ITL Optronics and Saymar. In 2007 the group's sales totalled $170m. and they might have reached $250m. by 2008 (*The Marker*, 18 September 2007).

Actually, the sales of privately owned companies did not grow through acquisitions alone. The consolidation process generated synergetic effects that strengthened industrial capabilities and expanded marketing opportunities, thus allowing for rapid internal growth as well. With that, realization of economics of scale and other advantages is still incomplete. Most likely then, privately owned companies' volume of activities, and its corresponding share in overall sales of Israel's defence industry, will continue to increase in the coming years. In fact, it is not without grounds to assume that as the trend develops, the dominance of government ownership will give way to a more common structure, making Israel's defence industry in this respect more similar to other advanced industrial countries. This will definitely be the case if the government simultaneously enhances its privatization efforts.

Success factors of defence exports

Israel's defence exports grew at an exceptionally rapid pace, almost continuously for three decades, certainly an unusual performance that deserves some further explanation. In the beginning, as argued above, defence companies needed to turn their production capacity to exports to ensure employment of available facilities and labour. Yet, were it not for some specific factors that justified defence exports in their own right, the developments that followed would have been hardly as successful as they were.

In line with common economics, a country's success in exporting goods and services depends on its industries' competitive advantage in the relevant international markets. Several measures may indicate such industries' competitive advantages: their share in the country's export, their market share in world trade (Porter 1990, 744), and the direction and rate of change of their exports compared with global changes in the relevant markets. Although in varying degrees at times, all these measures indicated that Israel's defence industries had competitive advantages in the world arms market (Lifshitz 2003, 302–3). While all of Israel's exports amounted to only a few 1,000ths of total world trade over the years, its defence exports were about 2% of the peak of world arms trade in 1987, their share increased in the 1990s and reached almost 7% in 2006 (SIPRI 2008, 296). Moreover, in certain relevant market segments, after excluding types of major weapons systems not produced in Israel, Israel's share was much higher.

The classical factor proportion theory of international trade further teaches that competitive advantages of countries reflect their different factor endowments. This notion may well serve as a starting point in explaining Israel's success in defence exports. Israel is relatively abundant in high-quality human capital, particularly in scientists, engineers and other technologically oriented workers extensively employed in defence industries, usually in higher proportions than in other industries. In addition, Israel is endowed with an abundance of knowledgeable and experienced manpower in the military domain. The knowledge and experience accumulated during military service are later translated into specific expertise in development, production and marketing of military systems when former service personnel join the civilian labour force. The economic explanation assumes, then, that high-quality human capital and military knowledge and expertise have endowed Israel's defence industry with competitive advantages, and have enabled it to succeed in the world arms market.

An interesting study, based on defence exports data for 1969–91, examined this assumption empirically (Tishler & Rotem, 1995). Besides measures of the relative abundance of high-quality human capital and military expertise, the study considered the size of the domestic defence market, world-wide demand for arms and the effect of wars. The study also attempted to find out whether the scope of Israel's civilian and defence exports were mutually associated in any manner. In all the estimated equations, the relative abundance of high-quality human capital was the most important factor, and its influence on the scope of defence exports was positive and statistically significant. The effect of military knowledge and expertise was also positive, but not statistically significant (the problem may possibly lie in choosing suitable variables). The empirical findings, then, supported the factor-endowments explanation for trade. Other results were mostly as expected, including a positive and statistically significant relation between civilian and defence exports.

The market characteristics and the business nature of arms transfers suggest some more success factors, or at least explain why apparent limitations did not in effect undermine Israel's efforts to expand its defence exports. First, the oligopolistic circumstances typical of the international arms market make it possible to set prices above production costs, so that dis-economies of scale are less significant and do not necessarily imply low profitability (Berglas 1983, 34). Besides which, the secrecy enveloping the arms trade often reduces price sensitivity, too. Particularly in selling to Third World countries, where prices were not presumably the main factor considered in choosing supply sources, it was possible to set up compensating prices for whatever dis-economies might arise. Having said that, though, it should be noted that production series of military equipment of other arms producers tend to be small, too, and in many items, Israel's production series were large enough to achieve economies of scale.

Second, delivery time is usually an important factor in choosing arms suppliers. In this respect, the Israeli defence industry demonstrated clear advantage owing to considerably faster development processes. Short development periods were an outcome of the close teamwork and effective communication between engineers and technicians in the industry and end users in the IDF. Evidently, a common background of military service and of studying at the same engineering schools made for particularly fruitful interaction. Moreover, direct contacts and continuous communication between users, developers and producers made it possible to offer innovative operational solutions. These advantages primarily benefited the IDF, but in no few instances also contributed to the Israeli defence industry's competitiveness in the world arms market. In a similar manner, the Israeli defence industry often gained competitive edge by offering military equipment with proven performance on the battlefield.

Third, with time, potential customers frequently considered arms purchases not as transfers of finished products only, but wished to use them as a lever for establishing their own defence industrial base. Israel could offer know-how and was often ready to co-operate with these countries, so their demands for offset arrangements of various sorts thus found pragmatic open-mindedness on the Israeli side. At the same time, interested countries considered Israel to be a source of advanced technology and to have up-to-date and proven experience. Moreover, Third World countries perceived Israel as closer to their own economic and social problems, and often preferred the Israeli source and interaction with Israeli experts over co-operation with Western industrial countries. Since the 1980s, with the expanded demand for upgrading weapons systems, the rich experience of Israel's defence industries in this area also came to the fore. A notable example in the 2000s is the Turkish project for upgrading 170 American M-60 main battle tanks, involving a group of Israeli defence companies headed by IMI and Elbit Systems (*Jane's Defense Weekly*, 6 June 2007).

In a more general sense, the last argument points at the technological qualities of the Israeli defence exports as another possible success factor. The technological over-sophistication of Western weapons systems was often a deterrent in transferring them to the less-advanced industrial countries. Customers in these countries were reluctant to acquire them, preferring less technologically intensive equipment that was simpler to operate and maintain, and sometimes better fitting their theatre and warfare doctrines. On the other hand, most developing countries that established their own defence industries were unable to penetrate markets in advanced industrial countries, because their technological level remained low. Israel, on its part, occupied a middle position in the world's arms market. Inasmuch as technological sophistication mattered, the country's defence exports ranked between traditional major suppliers in advanced industrial countries and new, smaller suppliers in developing countries, capable of offering a variety of systems that met the needs of both developing and developed countries.

Technological qualities were an important factor in penetrating the more advanced segment of the arms market, but to no less an extent arrangements relating to Israel's defence imports from the USA, too, were instrumental in achieving this goal (Klieman 1992, 261–71). Israel attempted over the years to make its special relationship with the USA, and its defence imports from there in particular, into a lever for enhancing defence exports. These efforts were on various levels, but most substantial results were obtained firstly through buybacks by American arms manufacturers selling military equipment to Israel and later by joint ventures of Israeli and American defence companies. On the buybacks route, commitments to this effect were explicitly included in import contracts and although no valid data are available about actual realization, partial information suggests that sales within this framework reached sizable levels. Moreover, over the years, sales of subsystems and components extended beyond the weapons systems intended for Israel alone, and trade relations that began as a forced commitment for reciprocal acquisition later turned into voluntary transactions, out of pure economic-technological considerations no longer connected to Israel's arms purchase transactions *per se*.

The close acquaintance that developed between the defence industries of the USA and Israel gave rise, especially since the late 1980s, to joint ventures of companies from both countries for the development, production and marketing of novel weapons systems. There were various models of co-operation: division of labour in development and production; co-opting US firms into the production of military systems developed in Israel, as a way of penetrating the US market; joint marketing to third parties; and others. The extent to which Israel's defence industries have penetrated the US market and attained co-operation with US counterparts is another example of the special status achieved by Israel, the 'young' arms producer, on the world market.

Finally, since arms transfers are not simply part of the regular circulation of goods among countries, but rather involve political motives and attitudes of both suppliers and recipients, it is important to note their influence as well. In essence, Israel as a supplier adopted a pragmatic political approach that did not take exception to its involvement in world arms trade *per se*, and decided about military sales on the merit of each case. In the early stages, this approach was a result of Israel's enforced diplomatic isolation. Defence exports were justified as an instrument in competing for international influence, gaining political support and cementing bilateral relations (Klieman 1992, 61–84). In fact, defence exports paved communication routes where no other relations existed: in the 1960s with African states, in the 1970s with the Shah's Iran, and later with the People's Republic of China and others (Sadeh, 2001). Political interests gained and they, in turn, contributed to the growth of defence exports.

On the recipients' side, changes occurred from time to time and while some markets closed for political reasons, others, previously closed, opened up. Developments in the aftermath of the Cold War provide a good example: countries that were formerly in the Soviet sphere of influence and had refrained from any commerce with Israel, found a suitable partner in the Israeli defence industries for upgrading and adjusting Soviet arms systems to Western standards. Even more significant was the opening of the Indian market in the 2000s: practically non-existent on Israel's defence export map in previous years, India presumably accounts for about one-third of Israel's annual defence exports in the later 2000s (*Business Week*, 28 August 2008).

Macro- and micro-economic consequences

Until the latter half of the 1960s, and again since the early 1990s, the defence industry exerted no real macro-economic influence. In the interim, though, for 20 years the defence industry became a very important factor, affecting macro-economic and structural processes in the entire economy. In the mid 1960s, the Israeli economy experienced a recession and the expanded domestic production for defence that followed the Six-Day War in 1967 and the French embargo imposed then, was a crucial factor in resuming economic activity. In particular, it created vast employment opportunities and offered attractive jobs for recent scientific and engineering immigrants. It also led to an extraordinary expansion in investment and, as defence demand was concentrated in technology-intensive industries, industrial growth as a whole took that direction. Between 1968 and 1984, the share of industries such as electronics, aerospace and optical instruments rose from 6% to 24% of total industrial output (Berman & Halperin, 1990, 150). The accelerated development had qualitative facets, not just quantitative ones. The level of mechanization rose, factories introduced advanced quality-control systems and so forth, and these improvements did not remain in the domain of the defence industry alone, but spread through subcontracting into many other plants, which then had to comply with the higher standards. Defence industry was thus an important agent of modernization, contributing to productivity growth in the entire economy. Finally, most of the time defence industry grew through increased exports, thus contributing to the balance of payments. In effect, defence exports favourably affected the balance of payments not only directly, i.e. through the increasing volume, but also indirectly, by paving the way for civilian goods. Military equipment penetrated overseas markets previously unknown to Israeli industry, and products made in Israel gained a reputation that helped broaden customer circles, at first for plants producing civilian goods within the defence industry itself, and later for other industries, too.

The rapid growth of defence industry raised criticism from time to time, though, pointing to at least two apparent undesirable macro-economic effects. First, critics asserted that defence industry is by nature an unstable economic activity, subject to unpredictable demand fluctuations and, given its size, may induce instability in the entire industrial sector, even in the economy as a whole. Second, possible crowding-out effects were noted, supposedly retarding growth in the civilian sector. In particular, it was argued that competition over a limited quantity of scientists and engineers caused steep wage increases, making it hard for civilian companies, which sell their products in competitive markets, to recruit and employ skilled employees, thus eventually hindering their growth. It was further argued that the negative crowding-out effect was more significant than the positive spill-over effects of technology transfers from defence to civilian industries (Halperin 1987, 1,002–3).

Both arguments appear to be in doubt. Concerns about instability did not materialize and, indeed, no other economic sector in Israel enjoyed continuous growth or maintained a stable aggregate level of activity for so long as did the defence industry. When defence production eventually declined in the 1990s, its weight in the economy was already relatively low and the macro-economic effect was not great. As to arguments about the crowding-out effect, they may have been valid for a short time. Civilian high-tech industry grew rapidly from the late 1970s and within only five years its accumulated growth was similar to what the defence industry achieved in about 15 years (Berman & Halperin, 1990, 156). Such development could hardly have taken place if civilian industry had not followed the path already opened for it by a sophisticated defence industry and, most importantly, without defence industry's outstanding contribution to the supply of skilled labour. In other words, even if defence industry did cause some delay in the development of certain industries, the technological and human infra-structure it put in place enabled those industries to close the gap rapidly with subsequent impressive achievements.

Regarding spill-over effects, there were a few remarkable direct applications of military technologies in civilian use, but by far more important were the indirect effects. Most sig-nificantly, former defence industry employees set up companies, or served as their technolo-gical backbone, addressing civilian market needs by making use of knowledge and experience acquired in defence development and production. In the 1990s such companies numbered in the thousands. Most of them were still immature at the turn of the century and the high-tech crisis world-wide negatively influenced their prospects. Some, though, won international recognition as technological leaders and, not less importantly, were highly valued by the international investor community. Notably, in the years 2001–07 foreign investment in Israeli hi-tech companies, directly and through the capital markets, amounted to no less than $28,400m. (Bank of Israel 2008, table G.14).

Turning to micro-economic consequences, the main question was whether the cost of dollars saved through domestic defence production favourably compared with the cost of obtaining foreign currency in other ways, i.e. with the prevailing effective exchange rate. In Israel's special circumstances, where targeted US aid grants financed most defence imports, some argued that domestic defence production, by definition, was not economical. Set against dol-lars saved by domestic production, there are dollars the apparent opportunity cost of which is zero, and however efficient domestic production may be and however low the cost of the dollar it saves, that cost can never be less than zero. Admittedly, this is a flawed argument inasmuch as aid grants are limited and fully utilized. Domestic production of some items releases grant funds for the procurement of others and, therefore, aid dollars also have an opportunity cost greater than zero.

Observers challenged the micro-economic rationale of defence production on other grounds as well. Most serious was the argument pointing at the apparent impossibility of realizing economies of scale due to relatively small production runs and frequent quantity fluctuations over time for budgetary reasons. Yet, on the other side of the equation there were certain factors that made defence production in Israel cheaper than abroad. First, having relatively abundant skilled labour, its cost in Israel was lower than among producers of arms and mili-tary equipment in the major industrial states. Second, battlefield experience gave Israeli users a unique ability to define and specify operational requirements, and close contact between users and developers made it possible to translate requirements accurately and effectively into development and production programmes. Such conditions led to economies in R&D resour-ces and shortened processes of malfunction detection and correction. Finally, differing from major arms manufacturers that tend to develop military equipment that can be used anywhere in the world, domestic Israeli production was free to focus on a narrower range of perfor-mance capabilities, more suitable to the local climate and the size of the arena, and more compatible with the IDF warfare doctrines. This, too, brought cost economies and improved the cost-effectiveness of indigenously produced military equipment.

In this context, an interesting question arises as to whether by enlarging production series, export sales reduced unit production costs, thereby reducing procurement expenditure of the IDF as well. This reasoning often supported the efforts invested in expanding defence exports and in many instances, export prospects factored into economic calculations provided a con-vincing argument for launching development programmes for new weapons systems. Indeed, some advanced arms currently at the disposal of the IDF would not have been developed in the first place, were it not for the prospects of exporting them. However, the expectations for cost savings were not always realized. For secrecy considerations, and especially consistent with the emphasis on force multipliers in supplying the IDF, the export of certain types of military equipment was forbidden, or was permitted only after they were exposed in operational campaigns, and in degraded versions. Therefore, when export became possible, the IDF was already acquiring generations of equipment that were more advanced and the extended production for export had little effect on the costs of the new items, if any. Additionally, Israel could not export some of the more expensive military equipment indigenously developed and produced, as they contained components acquired from the USA and selling them to third parties required US prior consent, which was extremely hard to obtain. Israel's experience, like that of larger arms suppliers in industrial countries, also demonstrated that competition on the world arms market often compelled producers to sell at marginal pricing, i.e. at prices covering variable production costs only, without any contribution to lowering prices for the domestic customer. In fact, domestic sales sometimes subsidized exports rather than the other way around. Finally, cost savings due to economies of scale through exports diminished over time, as an increasing part of the domestic defence industry's activities became completely unrelated to local sales.

Lessons and prospects

Establishing an advanced defence industry was one route whereby Israel was seeking to achieve a qualitative edge to counterbalance its quantitative inferiority. In the early stages, painful experiences when relying on foreign sources overshadowed this primary goal and signalled out the more ambitious goal of strategic self-sufficiency. However, Israel's experience clearly teaches that obtaining strategic self-sufficiency through developing an indigenous defence industrial base is an unrealistic goal for a small economy. Moreover, it is also an unnecessary course of action. Since the mid-1980s, the defence industry could greatly contribute to Israel's national security efforts by following the concept that it should avoid investments in major platforms and concentrate instead on innovative applications, mostly based on proven technologies.

Israel's experience also reveals that a defence industrial base initially established to meet local demand, may soon find it necessary to search for additional markets. Indeed, export is essential for Israel's defence industry to keep its critical mass because the local market is too small to support it. With that, Israel's success in the global arms market does not reflect necessity only, but takes advantage of various factors rendering competitive edges. In essence, Israel's defence exports gained advantage from occupying a middle position in the world's arms market between traditional major suppliers in advanced industrial countries and new, smaller suppliers in developing countries.

Other lessons refer to economic consequences. On the one hand, contrary to early concerns, domestic defence production did not become a source of macro-economic instability. On the other hand, though, contrary to early expectations, certain micro-economic advantages did not materialize either, or at least their impact was relatively small. Positive spill-over effects were extremely important, but most of them were indirect and sometimes hard to identify. Indeed, if not for defence R&D heritage, the wave of thousands of new high-tech companies and start-ups that spread over the country in the 1990s and 2000s would have been much smaller and eventually less successful.

Regarding the role of government ownership in developing a defence industrial base, Israel's experience does not provide a clear lesson. Admittedly, most of the time government ownership favourably contributed to the evolution of the defence industry. This changed in the aftermath of the Cold War, though, when the rules of the game in the world arms market changed and managerial flexibilities, including prompt response to business opportunities of mergers and acquisitions domestically and abroad, became crucial factors for success. In this respect, the recently observed trend whereby privately owned defence companies are increasing their share in the industry, may indicate steps in the right direction, thus improving prospects for further accelerated growth in the coming years.

Bibliography

Bank of Israel, *Annual Report 2007 — Statistical Appendix and Complementary Data*, Jerusalem, 2008

Berglas, Eithan, *Defence and the Economy: The Israeli Experience*, Jerusalem, The Maurice Falk Institute for Economic Research in Israel, Discussion Paper 83.01, 1983

Berman, Eli and Ariel Halperin, 'Skilled Labor Force, Security and Growth', in David Brodet, Moshe Yustman and Maurice Teubal, (Eds), *Industrial-Technological Policy for Israel*, Jerusalem, Jerusalem Institute for Israeli Studies, 1990

Business Week

Dun & Bradstreet, *Israel's Leading Enterprises 1997*, Israel, Dun & Bradstreet, 1998

—— *Israel's Leading Enterprises 2007*, Israel, Dun & Bradstreet, 2008

Halperin, Ariel, 'Force Buildup and Economic Growth', *Economic Quarterly*, Vol. 131, 1987

Jane's Defense Weekly

Klieman, Aharon, *Double-Edged Sword: Israel Defence Exports as an Instrument of Foreign Policy*, Tel-Aviv, Am Oved, 1992

Klieman, Aharon and Reuven Pedatzur, *Rearming Israel: Defense Procurement through the 1990s*, Tel-Aviv, Jaffee Center for Strategic Studies, 1991

Lifshitz, Yaacov, *The Economics of Producing Defense*, Boston, Kluwer Academic Publishers, 2003

Ministry of Defence, *Israel Defense Sales Directory 2007/8*, Tel-Aviv, Ministry of Defence (Israel), 2007

Peri, Joram and Amnon Neubach, *The Military-Industrial Complex in Israel*, Tel-Aviv, International Center for Peace in the Middle East, 1984

Porter, Michael E., *The Competitive Advantage of Nations*, New York, The Free Press, 1990

Sadeh, Sharon, 'Israel's Beleaguered Defense Industry', *Middle East Review of International Affairs*, Vol. 5, No. 1, 2001

SIPRI, *SIPRI Yearbook 2008*, Stockholm, Stockholm International Peace Research Institute, 2008

The Marker

Tishler, Asher and Ze'ev Rotem, 'Factors Explaining the International Success of the Israeli Defence Industry', *Economic Quarterly*, No. 3, 1995

Part IV

Key issues in the global arms trade

20 The military industrial complex

J. Paul Dunne and Elisabeth Sköns[1]

Introduction

When the size of the military sector in a country and its importance to the economy, or indeed its cost to the economy, come under scrutiny the existence of a 'Military Industrial Complex' (MIC) is often alluded to. In general it is meant to represent the groups within society that benefit from military spending and its growth, but what is meant by it is often vague and sometimes inconsistent (Fine 1993). Despite being most used in critical analyses, the source of the term is more conservative. It was introduced by Dwight Eisenhower, an ex-military Republican President of the USA, who was concerned about the combined power of the large military establishment and the arms industry, which he called the military industrial complex (Albertson 1963).

This was later developed by social scientists framing it as coalitions of vested interests within the state and industry, which could lead to decisions being made which were in the interest of the coalition members and not necessarily in the interests of national security. These coalitions could include some members of the armed services, of the civilian defence bureaucracy, of the legislature, of the arms manufacturers and of their workers.

Much of the work on the MIC sees it as a fairly clear and constant feature of the Cold War, when in the absence of a 'hot war' between the two superpowers to test the strength of the adversary, it was possible to overemphasize and exaggerate threats to justify high levels of military spending. Since the end of the Cold War, there have been profound changes in the international security environment. World military expenditure began to fall in the late 1980s, at first gradually for a couple of years with improving East-West relations, then sharply in 1992 after the disintegration of the Soviet Union in 1991. At the same time, the fixed costs of research and development (R&D) for major systems continued to grow, both for platforms and for the infrastructure (e.g. satellites, strategic air assets) and the information-based systems needed to support network-centred warfare. These trends in military expenditure and technology have led to considerable changes in the Defence Industrial Base (DIB) and in the relations between it, the state and the military. This does mean that the MIC has changed, but it does not mean it has disappeared or even become less powerful.

The next section considers the origin and theoretical foundation of the concept MIC. It is followed by a review of the actual features of what is generally understood as the MIC, as it developed during the Cold War. The chapter then considers what a number of major developments in the post-Cold War period imply for the MIC, with particular emphasis on the arms industry, its structure and effects. Finally, it assesses the degree to which the end of the Cold War has resulted in a fundamental change of the MIC and its implications.

Theorizing the military industrial complex

The idea of an MIC in the USA was introduced by President Dwight Eisenhower who in his 1961 farewell address warned against the potentially strong influence and power generated by the 'conjunction of an immense military establishment and a large arms industry', which had been created through the massive military mobilization during the Second World War, which led him to plead that 'we must guard against the acquisition of unwarranted influence, whether sought or unsought, by the military-industrial complex. The potential for the disastrous rise or misplaced power exists and will persist' (Eisenhower 1961).

While constituting a potentially important set of economic actors, there have been limited attempts by economists to analyse the MIC. As for mainstream economists, the existence of an MIC is seen as something of an anomaly. The neoclassical economics approach is based upon the notion of a state with a well-defined social welfare function, reflecting some form of consensus, recognizing some well-defined national interests, and threatened by some potential enemy/ies. Governments allocate military budgets to deal with perceived threats and there is a trade-off between 'guns' and 'butter' (Dunne and Coulomb 2009). This implies that national governments make decisions about the need for defensive and offensive capabilities, decide the best way to achieve these in terms of force structures and weapons procurement, and then decide on the form of DIB required. Thus, for input budgeting and for programme or output planning, the problem is seen as finding the most efficient means of producing aspects of national security. Ideally, the DIB should then be the most efficient way of supporting the production of the optimal level of security (Hartley and Sandler 1995).

One problem with this perspective is that it ignores the political and social dynamics of the arms production and procurement systems. The size and importance of the DIB within many countries has inevitably led to it linking into other parts of society and the economy. Once we move beyond seeing the DIB as a passive capability to provide weapons systems and recognize the fact that it may have proactive tendencies (rent seeking and efforts to capture the customers/regulators), these linkages become important. More recent neoclassical literature has addressed these issues and attempted to integrate political factors, such as bargaining and interest groups, which determine sources of weapons and levels of protection. However, this still represents a partial analysis focusing on particular aspects of the process. It does not address the complex dialectical interaction between the demand side and the supply side, in which both will influence each other and set the parameters for decision making, which can be a complex dynamic process that can be both contradictory and conflicting (Dunne 1995).

More general analyses locate the DIB firmly within the context of the wider MIC and relate it to the functioning of the capitalist economic system. The MIC represents a set of interests that might diverge from the interests of capitalism, what Smith (1977) characterizes as the liberal or institutional perspective. This view hinges on the nature of an MIC as composed of conflicting interest groups and institutional linkages. The MIC becomes a self-generating structure (agency) which embodies the interests of various groups in society. The strength of these vested interests and their competition for resources leads to internal pressures for military spending, with external threats providing the justification. The MIC imposes a burden on the rest of society and has adverse effects on the civilian sector. It crowds out civilian resources, and the companies involved develop a culture which leads to inefficiency and waste and an increasing reliance on defence contracts as they become less able to compete in the civilian market (Dumas 1986; Melman 1985). The theoretical underpinnings of this approach were originally based on C. Wright Mills's analysis of the power elite (Mills 1956), but there are also variants, which follow a Weberian focus on the role of bureaucracy and the work of John Kenneth Galbraith on coalitions (Slater and Nardin 1973) and, in the US context, the work of Veblen on the importance of the military 'waste' to the ideological and institutional structure of the US economy (Cypher 2008).

There is also a considerable amount of work undertaken from a Marxist perspective. While this approach is often typified as focusing on a ruling class concept of the MIC (Brunton 1988), it is more varied than this suggests. The role of military expenditure in the development of capitalism is seen as wider and more pervasive than in the institutional approach, but with the

MIC constrained by the laws of motion of the capitalist system. Within the Marxist approach there are a number of strands which tend to differ in their treatment of crisis and in the extent to which they see military expenditure as necessary for capital accumulation (Dunne 1990).

The underconsumptionist approach developed from the work of Baran and Sweezy (1966) sees military spending as important in preventing realization crises (crises caused by difficulties in selling products due to deficient demand, which means that profits cannot be realized). Unlike other forms of government spending, it allows the absorption of surplus without increasing wages and so maintains profits. In this way the MIC provides a valuable service to maintaining capitalism. A similar perspective focuses on the tendency for capitalist economies to overproduce. In this theory, military expenditure is wasteful and the allocation of resources into it prevents overheating. Thus the inefficiencies of the MIC and the DIB play a positive role in capitalist development creating the 'permanent arms economy' (Howard and King 1992). Empirical work, starting with Smith (1977), has, though, failed to find support for the underconsumptionist approach and its prediction of a positive economic effect of military spending (Smith and Dunne 1994).

This overview shows that there is no clear theoretical conceptualization of the MIC. Indeed, the concept appears to be of most value as a descriptive rather than an analytical concept (Fine 1993). This has led some researchers to focus on the dynamics of the MIC at an empirical level. Smith and Smith (1983) argue that the MIC should be seen as a coalition of interests and that the focus should be on the structural pairings that have developed between particular sections of private industry and particular parts of the military, which have inevitably led to mutual interests. In contrast, Brunton (1988) argues that the MIC should be seen as an evolving system of institutions rather than focusing on individual components. While the MIC is not a clear theoretical concept, it is apparent that there is an MIC that can influence policy on military spending. There are some similarities with other 'industrial complexes' in areas such as health and education, but there are important differences in detail, in particular the fact that the arms industry produces the means of violence.

The Cold War military-industrial complex

When Eisenhower referred to the unwarranted influence of the MIC, he was focusing on something historically specific. In the past there had been large US and international defence companies but their size and their relations with the state differed markedly. During the First World War, arms production was largely dealt with by government arsenals and until the beginning of the Second World War there was no real national planning for defence and so no dependence of major US companies on military spending. The coming of the New Deal in the 1930s had led to the federal government taking on more roles and responsibility and to the use of national economic planning for economic and military security (Schwarz 1990). The start of the Second World War spurred unprecedented technological innovations and created huge demand for industry. Industry, universities and the military were linked and huge government-funded R&D efforts led to patents which were then given to companies, with aircraft and electronics production given special status. This represented a fundamental change in attitudes and at the end of the war procurement cuts led to this new defence industry lobbying for arms procurement to maintain its size. The fall of the 'iron curtain' answered their calls, with the Soviet Union threat requiring the maintenance of a permanent army and a permanent defence industry to protect US interests. The Soviet nuclear explosion of 1949, the Communist takeover in China in the same year, and the Korean War (1951–53) contributed to halting the downward trend of US military spending and set the scene for the development of a mature MIC (Chapman and Yudken 1992, 2).

A number of developments assisted the new defence industry. A new Department of Defense (DoD) in the USA in 1947 introduced civilians into the defence bureaucracy, particularly in the aftermath of the New Deal, and changed the focus of concern from purely military ones to the attendant economic impacts of changes in the defence budget, the standing army and the defence industry (Schwarz 1990). The management of the DoD was no longer only in the hands of military personnel, but also corporate executives, who provided what was seen as important expertise, by moving from their companies through a 'revolving door' that would see them work in the Pentagon before going back to their companies. In 1961 McNamara left the presidency of the Ford Motor Company to become Secretary of Defense, to bring modern corporate techniques to the conduct of military affairs. In addition, the Cold War saw the continued development of links between universities and the military, with the Pentagon becoming an important source of funds for research (Chapman and Yudken 1992, 3; Giroux 2007).

Within the military there had been a number of important changes in the Second World War. The increasing importance of advanced technology, particularly in the new aerospace industry, saw the need for the military to engage with industry. The professionalization of the forces, moving to volunteer armies, with a standing army in peacetime led to unforeseen problems. In wartime, military officers' status and rank are generally gained through military achievement, but in peacetime it is more likely to be by pleasing superiors and advancing weapons systems and programmes. There are numerous examples of how such careerism in the military services led to continued support for unsuccessful systems, tied in with the interests of particular officers involved in procurement with particular contractors and even government officials (Chapman and Yudken 1992). Examples also abound of troops being provided with expensive and poor equipment, when better alternatives existed, as Page (2006) illustrates for the United Kingdom (UK). In addition, inter-service rivalry led to some less than sensible decisions on procurement of weapons systems (Chapman and Yudken 1992, 5–10). A technological arms race erupted from the standoff with the Soviet Union and the DoD's increasing budgets were justified by alleged capability 'gaps' in missiles, bombers, warheads and a general over-representation of Soviet military prowess – all of which are now known to have been illusory (Chapman and Yudken 1992).

Within this Cold War context, the national governments were clearly the main customers of the defence companies and this meant that the arms market evolved into a monopsonistic structure, a market with one dominant customer and a number of suppliers. This was bound to influence the behaviour of the firms as they moved from being more general manufacturers to become defence specialists, because of the high potential returns, and they started to become experts at getting money out of the government rather than competing in the market. They had to deal with the elaborate rules and regulations on contracts, which were needed to compensate for the absence of any form of competitive market and to assure public accountability. The 'revolving door' facilitated linkages, with military personnel and civil servants moving to defence contractors with which they had had dealings, and staff from defence contractors moving into the bureaucracy (Adams 1981; Higgs 1990).

Companies sought involvement in the development programmes for technologically advanced weapons systems as the best means of obtaining the subsequent production contracts. This led to 'buy ins', where firms understated risk or cost to win initial contracts, with a view to making up the losses later. They could rely on risk being borne by government, which often financed R&D and in some cases provided investment in capital and infrastructure. This led to an emphasis on performance rather than on cost of high-technology military systems, with more concern with how good it sounded than whether it worked. Early versions of cruise missiles are a case in point. In addition, programmes saw 'gold plating', where the military continually requested extras or continuous technological improvements over the contract period, so allowing renegotiation of contracts or additional payments, usually to the advantage of the contractor (Dunne 1995).

Operating within a market with these peculiar characteristics was bound to influence the nature of the companies and this led to both barriers to entry and to exit. Market, technological and procedural barriers meant that not only was it difficult for companies to enter into the defence sector to produce weapons systems, or to upgrade from subcontractor status, but also that it was difficult for the defence companies to leave the industry. Thus the Cold War DIB showed remarkable stability in terms of its composition of main contractors. In most countries the main contractors had a monopoly or near-monopoly position and in many cases were state owned. Such market structures, combined with high military spending, lobbying, regional dependence, limited transparency and oversight, created incentive structures which led to high weapons costs, corruption and inefficiencies within the arms producers that were argued to have externality effects on civil industry (Dumas 1986; Melman 1985).

These conditions and processes make up what is commonly referred to as the MIC – a powerful set of actors with vested interests in high military spending, which in the specific ideology of the Cold War could marshal resources to pursue their particular interests.

Much of the discussion about the constitution, mechanisms, processes and behaviour of the MIC refers to the particular US situation. In Europe things were rather different, with state ownership, more direct state involvement in the arms industry and much smaller domestic defence markets. Some have argued, though, that the basis for a form of MIC with similar dynamics could be identified in the UK and other countries (Dunne 1995; Lovering 1990).

Post Cold War developments

Since the end of the Cold War, there have been a number of developments that have had implications for the nature of the MIC. Certainly, the end of the Cold War saw profound changes in the international security environment. World military expenditure peaked in the late 1980s, fell gradually between 1989 and 1990 with improving East-West relations, then dropped sharply in 1992 after the disintegration of the Soviet Union in 1991. The international arms trade dropped by a half between the 1982 all-time high and the 1995 trough, then fluctuated somewhat until it began to increase consistently in 2003 (SIPRI Arms Transfers Database). Procurement of weapons also fell sharply, with SIPRI (Sköns and Weidacher 2000) estimating that arms production (domestic demand plus exports minus imports) in 1997 was 56% of its 1987 level in the USA, 78% in France and 90% in the UK. These changes had a direct impact on the demand for the products of the MIC and the environment in which they operate, calling into question the ability of even the major countries to maintain a comprehensive domestic defence industrial base. Governments found it harder to justify previous levels of support for the industry and 'competitive procurement policies aimed at value for money were introduced in a number of countries' (Dunne and Macdonald 2002).

In the USA, though, there have been developments that went against this trend and had important impacts on the US military establishment and arms industry. Most importantly, while there was an initial period of military expenditure cuts and arms industry downsizing, military spending began to grow again in 1999 and has increased rapidly since 2001, due to the massive spending made possible under the global 'war on terror' label (see the Elisabeth Sköns chapter in this volume) and justified primarily with the wars in Afghanistan and Iraq. Contrary to previous US funding practice, these wars were funded through supplemental appropriations outside the regular annual defence budget requests. This was not only for the initial period, when it might be justified by the fact that war costs are difficult to predict, but continuously for five-to-six years, with some correction only after repeated critical reviews by the US Government Accountability Office (GAO 2008) and requests from Congress. This practice had two important implications: it produced an overly optimistic picture of the funding requirement for the war and reduced the level of legislative oversight, as requests for supplemental appropriations go through a less comprehensive process than regular defence budget requests (Kosiak 2008, 48–9). In addition, the scope of what could be included in the supplemental was successively increased by the George W. Bush Administration not only to cover incremental costs directly related to operations, as traditionally would have been the case, but also to cover the cost of other programmes and activities that were, at best, only indirectly related to the wars. In 2006, new DoD guidance for war appropriation requests made it possible for the armed services to include virtually anything in their requests for war-related appropriations (Kosiak 2008, 53). This is likely to have reinforced linkages between the military and the arms industry, as it provided scope for adding on non-war-related items in a rapidly expanding defence budget (Sköns chapter in this volume). In addition, Congress was criticized for becoming a spectator rather than a check on Presidential power, with some members supporting crucial decisions to direct war funding to their home districts. In 2002 Congress abandoned its duty to deliberate a declaration of war on Iraq and handed the administration a blank cheque (Wheeler 2004).

In addition to the changes in the levels of demand for arms, new technologies have enabled new types of warfare and changed the nature of the demand. Communication and control technologies have become increasingly important in the theatre of military operations. Network-centred warfare, the use of satellites, communications equipment and multi-node networks changed the nature-of-demand part of the revolution in military affairs (RMA), a term used to emphasize the way that improvements in information technology, precision targeting and smart munitions created the possibility of a new form of warfare, network-centred warfare. The internet came to play an important role in the development of communications, but it also provides a further area of potential security threats. While it is unlikely that the USA and Europe (the North Atlantic Treaty Organization—NATO) will face an enemy that can provide a symmetric response, this is unlikely to stop arguments that other countries, such as the People's Republic of China, may well do so in future. For now, the most likely strategic concerns will be with more informal guerrilla-type conflicts, with different implications for weapons systems required (Dunne et al. 2006). This uncertainty about the enemy and the growth of 'homeland security' are also adding on new types of demand. In particular they are making communications and surveillance technologies increasingly important (Smith 2009).

NATO and European Union (EU) troops are also increasingly involved in peace-keeping roles around the world. Apart from changing the nature and structure of the forces, and possibly creating somewhat different military systems requirements (although some successful lobbying to maintain the use of systems already in production has taken place), it will require interoperability between armed forces from different countries and, therefore, greater harmonization in military systems, in particular for information and communication. NATO enlargement has also required countries joining the alliance to replace old and Warsaw Pact systems with new US and European ones and has, consequently, increased demand.

On the supply side there were a number of important developments including increased concentration, technological change, subcontracting and internationalization. The end of the Cold War did not bring about the expected diversification of the defence industry. Instead there was a rapid process of ownership concentration through mergers and acquisitions. In the USA there was a striking change in industrial policy. During the Cold War industrial planning was undertaken through the Pentagon, but this was only implicit industrial planning (Markusen and Yudken 1992, 51–5). In 1993 a merger wave was stimulated by the 'last supper' when Pentagon Deputy Secretary, William Perry, told a dinner of defence industry executives that they were expected to start merging. It ended when the Pentagon decided it had gone far enough and blocked the merger of Lockheed Martin with Northrop Grumman in early 1997 (Page 1999, 213–4). This left four major contractors and the only major change since then has been the takeover by Northrop Grumman of the aerospace and information technology company TRW, making them the third-largest US arms producer after Lockheed Martin and Boeing (SIPRI 2002). This led to a massive increase in the size of the major defence companies, which is also likely to lead to an increase in their power. To the extent that it also resulted in an increased specialization in defence, as argued by Markusen and Costigan (1999), it is also led to increased interest in lobbying for major defence contracts. In an environment of growing budgets this could mean further growth in the size of the industry, as well as its dependence on the domestic arms market, more efforts to influence government decisions, including more pork barrelling.

The increased fixed costs in production that assisted industrial restructuring also led to arms producers resorting to commercially available civilian technologies and products. This was a marked change, as from the end of the Second World War to the 1980s military technology had tended to be in advance of civilian technology, but by the 1990s in many areas, particularly electronics, military technology lagged behind the civilian sector. This was largely because the long lead-times involved in military procurement meant that much of the technology was obsolete before the system came into service (Smith 2009). Whereas in the past the spin-off of military technology to the civilian sector was an important argument for the value of military production, now there is more spin-in of civilian technology to the military. Many areas of technology that were once the preserve of the military and security services, such as cryptography, are now dominated by commercial applications. Increased numbers of components that go into the major weapons systems are commercial 'off-the-shelf' (COTS) products, produced by manufacturers who would not see themselves as part of the arms industry (Dunne 1995). This has also meant that subcontracting has become increasingly important for arms producers as they can generally get components that are not defence specific at cheaper prices from the specialist producers. This means they outsource work to other companies, increasing the links with the civil sector and bringing new types of company, particularly from the electronics and IT sectors, into the defence industrial base (Dunne et al. 2007a, 2007b). This means it has become less clear which companies benefit from defence contracts, reducing the visibility of the defence industrial base. Subcontracting has also reduced the degree of in-house manufacturing for the main arms producers, changing the nature of the companies. They have tended to lose some of their direct manufacturing capacity, retaining mainly design, R&D and integration skills–in addition to the skills required to gain and negotiate contacts with government (Markusen and Costigan, 1999).

Another important factor has been the internationalization of arms production in the post-cold war period. This has taken two forms, the internationalization of ownership and the internationalization of supply chains. Although defence companies still rely on domestic support through procurement and support for exports, governments have been increasingly willing to recognize that the costs of high-technology R&D when combined with smaller national production runs have made it more necessary to make economies of scale through international collaboration and industrial restructuring. This has led to marked increases in cross-border mergers and acquisitions and cross-ownership in the arms industry, with considerable internationalization of the content of advanced weapons systems (Dunne and Surry, 2006). As early as 1985 the Congressional Defence Joint Oversight Committee on Foreign Dependency found that the guidance system of an air-to-air missile had 16 foreign-produced parts. Contractors have continued to identify preferred suppliers and to use a wider range of them (Dunne, 2006a; Hayward 2001).

Despite the degree of internationalization it is not clear how much it has changed the dynamics within the MIC. Companies appear to remain significantly dependent on the government of the country in which they are located, regardless of ownership relations. International supply chains provide flexibility and potential cost reductions for firms, but could make them more vulnerable if they become dependent on international subcontractors. They also reduce the visibility of the defence industrial base and could lead to governments and workers from other countries being involved in lobbying for orders

A major reason for the relative stability of the cold war DIB was the existence of barriers to entry and exit. The industry has gone through changes, but barriers to entry are likely to remain considerable as the marketing of military products differs from commercial products, and personal contacts and networking are likely to remain more important than general advertising. Market demand for arms is also limited by government and is likely to be inelastic. This means that entrants cannot rely on an expansion of the market to accommodate them as prices are reduced, but are likely to have to fight against and replace incumbents. There is also likely to be considerable brand loyalty given the nature of the products. Customers may require compatibility with previously purchased weapons systems, or may provide follow-on orders from previous contracts. Barriers to exit are also likely to remain as price competition makes the civil market place very different to the world of defence companies. Defence contracts can be safe and profitable and often involve long-term commitments. The market is cyclical and even in lean spells it may be worth staying in the market in the expectation of better times, particularly as government is still likely to bail out major contractors in trouble. Furthermore, when there are cuts in domestic sales, governments are likely to provide assistance for foreign sales (Dunne and Surry 2006). This suggests that the industrial component of the concept of an MIC may still see a relative stability in the core actors – with changes on the periphery.

One major development that has introduced some new faces is the significant expansion of the military services industry since the end of the Cold War. This has been the result of the outsourcing of functions that once were provided by military forces or defence ministries to private companies and was expanded greatly during the war in Iraq (Singer 2003; Wulf 2005). The military services provided by private industry include not only the provision of armed security, the most publicized activity of this industry, but a wide range of other services. These include research and analysis, various types of technical services – such as information technology, system support, and maintenance, repair and overhaul of military equipment – and operational support, including logistics and intelligence services. While some of these services, such as equipment maintenance have been an integral part of the arms industry for a longer time, the expansion has seen a growth in the number of companies specializing in military services. This has been a significant change in both the structure of the DIB, with new companies such as KBR, previously owned by Halliburton, becoming a major DoD contractor for its provision of construction in conflict zones (Briody 2004), and in the nature of the MIC, as companies providing military services are often engaged directly in conflict zones giving them a direct vested interest in the continuation of armed conflict. In this way, their interests are different and more problematic than the vested interests of military goods-producing companies, the products of which are also in high demand during peacetime (Perlo-Freeman and Sköns 2008, 13).

Military production has developed a very specific geographical distribution in most countries, as the location of factories and facilities has historically reflected security concerns rather than just economic ones. This has led to large defence-dependent communities in various locations within any country with a large defence industry. The changing nature of the industry and of security has had implications for the geographical pattern of production and closures cause considerable problems for communities, as often the jobs lost are rather different to those available. While evidence suggests that defence workers, given their high skills, find new jobs relatively easily, it is usually lower-paid work and there is considerable disruption. The increased internationalization of the supply chain also has implications for the geographical distribution of production and employment, reducing the major contractors' impact on their traditional local economies. This can also impact upon local politicians' interests in the defence budget (Dunne, 1995).

European dimensions

The concept of an MIC was developed in the USA and is most readily applied there. In the post-Cold War world the process of restructuring in Europe was more complicated, as restructuring necessarily involved cross-border mergers, which raised political issues. The major players in Europe also had quite different ownership structures, including a substantial degree of state ownership in France. Both factors made a financially-driven merger boom of the US type more difficult. None the less, there was an increase in concentration and by 2005 the Western European restructuring process had resulted in a web of cross-border ownership and collaboration relationships in aerospace and electronics. Concentration in the defence industry is still not as high as in comparable high-tech industries, though, suggesting that market forces have not been allowed to work freely in the procurement, production and sales of weapons systems. This could also be the result of a segmentation of the arms industry with strong concentration in aerospace and electronics and less in other defence industrial sectors. At the systems level in aerospace and electronics oligopolistic tendencies are emerging at the international level, while in other sectors industry remains nationally fragmented (Dunne 2006b; Sköns 2005).

In addition, the privatization of previously state-owned companies impacted on the integration of the Western European defence industry as previously state-controlled companies were forced to operate according to corporate business principles. The true impact on government influence and control is less clear, though, and differs across countries depending on their government's policy towards their private defence industry. What may turn out to be more important in the long run is the emergence of a security industry outside the traditional defence industry: the privatized military industry engaged in outsourced military services that have previously been provided within the military establishment, and the security industry engaged in the provision of goods and services for personal safety, primarily to the private sector but increasingly also to the government sector (Sköns 2005).

In the UK most of the defence industry has been privatized, while in the rest of Europe the state still owns much of the industry, but has been changing. Privatization is taking place and the UK Government's Public Private Partnerships (PPP) policy, launched in 2000, is having considerable influence. One part of this is the Private Finance Initiative (PFI), where the public sector contracts to purchase quality services on a long-term basis, in order to take advantage of private-sector management skills, which are stimulated and focused by having private finance at risk. PFI can include concessions and franchises, where a private-sector partner takes on the responsibility for providing a public service, including maintaining, enhancing or constructing the necessary infrastructure. This initiative is having an important impact on relations between state and industry in the UK and is influencing government policy abroad (Dunne 2006b).

In Europe, efforts were made to create both harmonization of requirements (demand side) and a more open defence market (a 'level playing field') (supply side). The European Defence Agency (EDA) was created to help EU Member States develop their defence capabilities for crisis-management operations under the European Security and Defence Policy. It was intended to encourage EU governments to spend defence budgets on meeting future challenges, rather than past (Cold War) threats and to help identify common needs and promote collaboration. Article 296 of the EC Treaty restricts cross-border competition by allowing Member States to claim an exemption on national security grounds from normal EU public procurement rules. The EDA Code of Conduct on Defence Procurement launched in 2006 deals with cases where exemptions are invoked, which has been the case for more than 50% of defence equipment purchases. It is intended to ensure that there is transparent and fair competition. In 2009 the European Parliament adopted a Directive to complement this, which recognizes the specific features of the defence and security markets and which might lead to a weakening of competition (Dunne 2006b; EDA website).

All of these developments have led to a set of state-industry relations that look rather different to those of the old Cold War MIC, but they still suggest a dominant role for national governments and continuing close links between government, industry and the military. In Europe privatization has reduced direct state links, but indirect ones remain powerful, though in some ways less visible, as in the USA. The structure of the MIC has changed and expanded, but its component parts would still seem to remain powerful lobbying groups in all countries (Dunne 2006b).

Conclusions: continuity and change

The concept of a Military Industrial Complex was a useful vehicle for understanding the success of the military establishment in receiving unprecedented government budget allocations in the USA and other advanced economies during the Cold War. It is a problematic concept theoretically, but retains some useful descriptive value, in particular in assisting in an evaluation of the changes that have taken place since the end of the Cold War.

What Eisenhower referred to as the MIC developed into a powerful and idiosyncratic structure, with strong linkages between elements within the military, government, legislature, capital and labour, and the dynamics of the Cold War provided justification for the unprecedented growth of military spending without any obvious change in threat. The Cold War defence industry was a very specific industry: its size, structure, trade are all determined by government policy with an emphasis on performance rather than cost, risk borne by government, elaborate rules and regulations on contracts, and close relations between contractors, procurement executive and military. As a result there were strong barriers to entry and barriers to exit, which led to the Cold War DIB showing remarkably stability in terms of its composition of main contractors.

With the end of the Cold War there were a number of important developments that impacted upon the MIC. There were significant cuts in demand for arms, with the reductions in military spending and trade. Coupled with the introduction of competitive practices the power of the MIC in many countries was reduced. In the USA, though, there were developments that went against the trend, with military spending starting to grow again in 1999 and increasing rapidly in 2001, with the 'war on terror'. In addition, there were changes in the manner in which wars were funded, which introduced flexibility to arms procurement and reduced Congressional oversight. The result of this was to strengthen linkages between the military and the arms industry in the USA.

There were also changes in the nature of the demand in the arms market, with the RMA making communication and control technologies increasingly important in the theatre of military operations. Strategic concerns shifted to asymmetric warfare, with different implications for weapons systems required, while the growth of 'homeland security' also added new types of demand. In addition, the increasing involvement of NATO troops in peace-keeping roles has implications for force structures, arms and military systems requirements. The implications of these developments for the industry can be overstated. There is still lobbying for the maintenance of Cold War legacy systems – e.g. arguing that peacekeepers need the systems being developed and that NATO may face new superpowers, such as China, in future – and it has had some success.

The end of the Cold War did not bring about the expected diversification of the defence industry. Instead there was a rapid process of ownership concentration in the USA through mergers and acquisitions. This led to an increase in the size and power of the major defence companies. Increased fixed costs in production led to arms producers resorting to commercially available civilian technologies and products, spin-in replaced spin-off and many areas of technology that were once the preserve of the military are now dominated by commercial applications. Subcontracting has become increasingly important, bringing new types of company, particularly in the electronics and IT sectors. This means it has become less clear which companies benefit from defence contracts, reducing the visibility of the defence industrial base.

Within all major producing countries internationalization of ownership and supply chains took place. European producers sought US defence companies to try to break into the growing market, though only the UK was successful, and major producers sought component producers world-wide. Companies remained dependent on their home government, regardless of ownership relations, but these developments did further reduce the visibility of the defence industrial base and in some cases led to governments and workers from other countries being involved in lobbying for orders.

A major reason for the relative stability of the Cold War DIB was the existence of barriers to entry and exit. The industry has gone through changes, but barriers to entry are likely to remain considerable and this suggests that the industrial component of the concept of an MIC may still see a relative stability in the core actors, with changes on the periphery. One major source of new companies was the significant expansion of the military services industry since the end of the Cold War. Companies have been providing military services directly in conflict zones giving them a direct vested interest in the continuation of armed conflicts.

Marked changes have taken place in Europe, with privatization and EU-level legislation changing the state industry relations, but their impact can be overstated. Certainly change is likely, but whether that is in the direction of a European-wide MIC is unclear. At present the transatlantic links would seem to be USA–UK and while privatization of European companies is changing the state-industry relations closer to that of the USA, it is not clear that it will reduce their influence.

Overall, it is clear that there has been considerable change in the nature and extent of the MIC, but it is unclear exactly what the implications of this are. The Defence Industrial Base has certainly seen some considerable restructuring and concentration world-wide, with increasing US dominance and US-European links developing. Old arms contractors have changed, becoming systems integrators, outsourcing nationally and internationally, spinning in civil technologies and components, rather than spinning off innovations for the civil sector. However, despite some new players, the old specialist military companies remain dominant and are engaged in takeovers to acquire expertise in new areas. There is little evidence to suggest that the links between the industry, the military, government and the legislator have weakened and it would still seem that it is a political rather than economic logic that controls the international arms market. Probably the best way to describe the changes that have taken place is that there has been change, but also a remarkable degree of continuity within the MIC. The concerns of Eisenhower are certainly still relevant as the post-war restructuring may well have left an MIC that is just as pervasive and powerful, more varied, more internationally linked and less visible.

Note

1 The authors are grateful to Jürgen Brauer for comments.

Bibliography

Adams, Gordon, *The Iron Triangle: The Politics of Defense Contracting*, New York, Council on Economic Priorities, 1981

Albertson, Dean, ed., *Eisenhower as President*, New York, Hill and Wang, 1963

Baran, Paul and Paul Sweezy, *Monopoly Capital*, London, Monthly Review Press, 1966

Briody, Dan, *The Halliburton Agenda*, New Jersey, John Wiley, 2004

Brunton, Bruce G., 'Institutional Origins of the Military Industrial Complex', *Journal of Economic Issues*, Vol. 22, June 1988

Brzoska, Michael and Peter Lock, eds, *Restructuring of Arms Production in Western Europe*, Oxford, Oxford University Press, 1992

Chapman, Gary and Joel Yudken, *Briefing Book on the Military-Industrial Complex*, Washington, Council for a Livable World Education Fund, December 1992

Cypher, James M., 'Economic Consequences of Armaments Production: Institutional Perspectives of J. K. Galbraith and T. B. Veblen', *Journal of Economic Issues*, Vol. XLII, No. 1, March 2008

Dumas, Lloyd, *The Overburdened Economy*, University of California Press, 1986

Dunne, Paul, 'The Political Economy of Military Expenditure: An Introduction', *Cambridge Journal of Economics*, Vol. 14, No. 4, December 1990

——— 'The Defence Industrial Base', in Keith Hartley and Todd Sandler, eds, *Handbook in Defense Economics*, Elsevier, 1995

——— 'The Making of Arms in South Africa', *Economics of Peace and Security Journal*, Vol. 1, No. 1, January 2006a, www.epsjournal.org.uk/pdfs/eps_v1n1_dunne.pdf

——— 'Sector Futures: Defence', Report for Cambridge Econometrics, European Monitoring Centre on Change website, a project of the European Foundation for the Improvement of Living and Working Conditions, 2006b, www.emcc.eurofound.eu.int/sector_futures.htm

Dunne, J. Paul and Fanny Coulomb, 'Peace, War and International Security: Economic Theories', in Jacques Fontanel and Manas Chatterji, eds, *War, Peace and Security*, Bingley, Emerald, 2009

Dunne, J. Paul, Maria Garcia-Alonso, Paul Levine and Ron Smith, 'Determining the Defence Industrial Base', *Defence and Peace Economics*, Vol. 18, No. 3, 2007a

——— 'The Evolution of the International Arms Industries', in Wolfram Elsner, ed., *Arms, War, and Terrorism in the Global Economy Today-Economic Analyses and Civilian Alternatives*, New Brunswick, NJ, Transaction Publishers and Zürich, LIT, 2007b

——— 'Managing Asymmetric Conflict', *Oxford Economic Papers*, Vol. 58, 2006

Dunne, J. Paul and Gordon Macdonald, 'Procurement in the Post Cold War World: A Case Study of the UK', in Claude Serfati, ed., *The Future of European Arms Production*, Cost A10 Action, Brussels, European Community Office for Official Publications, 2002

Dunne, J. Paul and Eamon Surry, 'Arms Production', in *SIPRI Yearbook 2006: Armaments, Disarmament and International Security*, Oxford, Oxford University Press, 2006

Eisenhower, Dwight D., 'Farewell Radio and Television Address to the American People, January 17, 1961', *Public Papers of the President of the United States, Dwight D. Eisenhower, 1960 61*, Washington, 1961 (reproduced in Pursell, Carroll W., ed., *The Military-Industrial Complex in Theory and Fact*, New York, Harper and Row, 1972)

Fine, Ben, 'The Military Industrial Complex: An Analytical Assessment', *Cyprus Journal of Economics*, Vol. 6, No. 1, June 1993

Gansler, Jaques S., 'US Defence Industrial Policy', *Security Challenges*, Vol. 3, No. 2, 2007

——— 'Transforming the US Defence Industrial Base', *Survival*, Vol. 35, No. 4, Winter 1993

Giroux, Henry, *The University in Chains: Confronting the Military Industrial Academic Complex*, Boulder, Paradigm, 2007

Government Accountability Office (GAO), *Global War in Terrorism: Reported Obligations for the Department of Defense*, GAO-08 1128R, Washington, 15 September 2008

Hartley, Keith and Todd Sandler, eds, *Handbook of Defense Economics*, Vol. 1, Amsterdam, Elsevier, 1995

Hayward, Keith, 'The Globalisation of Defence Industries', *Survival*, Vol. 43, No. 2, Summer 2001

Higgs, Robert, ed., *Arms Politics and the Economy: Historical and Contemporary Perspectives*, New York, Holmes and Meier, 1990

Howard, Michael and John King, *A History of Marxian Economics: Volume 2, 1929 90*, London, Macmillan, 1992

Kosiak, Steven M., *Cost of the Wars in Iraq and Afghanistan, and Other Military Operations through 2008 and Beyond*, Washington, Center for Strategic and Budgetary Assessments, 2008

Lovering, John, 'Military Expenditure and the Restructuring of Capitalism: The Military Industry in Britain', *Cambridge Journal of Economics*, Vol. 14, No. 4, December 1990

Markusen, Ann and Sean Costigan, eds, *Arming the Future: A Defense Industry for the 21st Century*, New York, Council on Foreign Relations Press, 1999

Markusen, Ann, Peter Hall, Scott Campbell and Sabina Dietrick, *The Rise of the Gunbelt*, Oxford, Oxford University Press, 1991

Markusen, Ann and Joel Yudken, *Dismantling the Cold War Economy*, Basic Books, 1992

Melman, Seymour, *The Permanent War Economy: American Capitalism in Decline*, New York, Simon and Schuster, 1985

Mills, C. Wright, *The Power Elite*, Oxford, Oxford University Press, 1956

Page, Erik, 'Defense Mergers: Weapons Cost, Innovation, and International Arms Industry Cooperation', in Ann Markusen and Sean Costigan, eds, *Arming the Future: A Defense Industry for the Twenty-First Century*, New York, Council on Foreign Relations Press, 1999

Page, Lewis, *Lions Donkeys and Dinosaurs*, London, William Heinemann, 2006

Perlo-Freeman, Sam and Elizabeth Sköns, *The Private Military Services Industry*, SIPRI Insights on Peace and Security, No. 1, September 2008

Schwarz, Jordan A., 'Baruch, the New Deal and the Origins of the Military Industrial Complex', in Robert Higgs, ed., *Arms, Politics and the Economy: Historical and Contemporary Perspectives*, New York, Holmes and Meier, 1990

Singer, Peter W., *Corporate Warriors: The Rise of the Privatized Military Industry*, Cornell Studies in Security Affairs, Ithaca, NY, Cornell University Press, 2003

SIPRI, *SIPRI Yearbook: Armaments, Disarmament and International Security*, Stockholm International Peace Research Institute, Oxford, Oxford University Press, various annual editions

——— SIPRI Arms Transfers Database, www.sipri.org/contents/armstrad

Sköns, Elisabeth, 'Omstruktureringen av vesteuropeisk forsvarsindustri: markedskrafternas logikk' [Restructuring of the West European Defence Industry: The Logic of Market Forces], in Janne Haaland Matlary and Oyvind Osterud, eds, *Mot et avnasjonalisert forsvar?* [*Towards a Denationalized Defence?*], Oslo, Abstrakt Forlag, 2005

Sköns, Elisabeth and Reinhilde Weidacher, 'Arms Production', in *SIPRI Yearbook 2000*, Oxford, Oxford University Press, 2000

Slater, J. and T. Nardin, 'The Concept of the Military Industrial Complex', in Steven Rosen, ed., *Testing the Theory of the Military Industrial Complex*, Lexington, MA, Lexington Books, 1973

Smith, Ron, 'Military Expenditure and Capitalism', *Cambridge Journal of Economics*, Vol. 1, 1977

——— *Military Economics: The Interaction of Power and Money*, Basingstoke, Palgrave Macmillan, 2009

Smith, Ron and Paul Dunne, 'Is Military Spending a Burden? A Marxo-Marginalist Response to Pivetti', *Cambridge Journal of Economics*, Vol. 18, 1994

Smith, Ron and Dan Smith, *The Economics of Militarism*, London, Pluto Press, 1983

Wheeler, Winslow, *Wastrels of Defense: How Congress Sabotages U.S. Security*, Annapolis, MD, Naval Institute Press, 2004

Wulf, Herbert, *Internationalizing and Privatizing War and Peace*, Houndmills, Palgrave Macmillan, 2005

21 Defence spending and development

J. Paul Dunne and Mehmet Uye[1]

Introduction

Military spending is an important issue for the international economy. It is an expenditure by governments that has influence beyond the resources it takes up, especially when it leads to or facilitates conflicts. At the same time most countries need some level of security to deal with internal and external threats, but these can certainly have opportunity costs as they can prevent money being used for other purposes that might improve the pace of development. Such issues are particularly important for developing countries, as in the post-Cold War world most wars have been internal and have involved the poorest countries, and this is unlikely to change.

When governments undertake military spending, they provide wages and salaries and cover other expenses for the armed forces, and procure arms for them. Unfortunately the only reliable data available are on military spending and so in reviewing the literature we simply have to recognize that arms transfers are an important component of military spending. In developing countries it is very likely that the arms will be imported, particularly any advanced weapons systems, and hence will become a drain on precious reserves of foreign exchange. This suggests that the opportunity cost of military spending is likely to be higher than simply the expenditure, once arms transfers are taken into account.

With the end of the Cold War there were considerable reductions in military expenditure, although not consistently across all regions. However, as the SIPRI Yearbooks show, in more recent years the declining trend has bottomed out and military expenditure is increasing. While there have been conflicts, with internal conflict being a major concern for the developing world and a few major international conflicts, the major pressure to increase military spending has not been the result of obvious strategic needs, but of internal pressures by vested interests.

General trends do, of course, always hide more complex patterns. Some countries have increased military spending because of local insecurity, while others have done so due to encouragement from arms-producing companies pushing for arms exports. There has also been continued use of economic arguments to justify security expenditure, or to argue against reductions. Even within the developing country group there is a real heterogeneity of countries, in terms of their stage of development, nature of development, the state of their neighbours, their military burden and the degree of military involvement in the state.

Review of research issues

Research in this area has to deal with a number of important data availability, measurement, methodology and theoretical issues:

Data availability and measurement problems

It is important to treat the published military expenditure data with care, especially when looking at developing countries. There are numerous problems with the data, definitions, coverage, accuracy, etc., which make it particularly difficult to use figures for comparison across countries or to aggregate to larger groups. There is also growing evidence that important amounts of security expenditure do not enter the accounts or budgets of developing countries.[2] Such problems are also reflected in the fact that different data sources, such as SIPRI, the Arms Control and Disarmament Agency (ACDA), IISS, IMF and World Bank, can give markedly different numbers.[3]

Such differences are particularly important for cross-section analyses of countries, but not so much for time-series data. If looking over time, the concern is with the changes rather than the absolute or relative values of variables and as long as the definitions do not change significantly and systematically one can be relatively confident of the analysis. In most cases researchers are left with only the published sources to use and these are, at least, the products of attempts to achieve consistency.[4] There can be large differences in the reliability of data across countries and not all arms transfers necessarily show up in the defence statistics.

Developing countries may also differ in the way in which they treat or define military-related aid, the fungibility of aid, and the way in which arms sales are financed (Brzoska 1994).

In an ideal world, we would be able to use military procurement budgets, as this clearly reflects spending on arms transfers; however, such data are generally not available for developing countries, or if so, they are of questionable reliability. In fact, there is some evidence that arms imports may not even be included in military spending figures in many countries (Omitoogun and Hutchful 2006).

Theoretical considerations

Applied work is usually restricted to economic growth rather than development because of the problems of defining and measuring development.[5] A theoretical model is important for any empirical study but much of economic theory does not have an explicit role for military spending as a distinctive economic activity. However, this has not prevented the development of theoretical analyses as discussed in Dunne and Coulomb (2008). The dominant neoclassical approach sees the state as a rational actor that balances the opportunity costs and security benefits of military spending in order to maximize a well-defined national interest reflected in a societal social welfare function. Arms spending can then be seen as a public good and the economic effects on military expenditure will be determined by its opportunity cost, the trade off between it and other spending. Early models of economic growth, which assume exogenous technical change, have been extended, to allow for the effects of changes in education and technology that produce endogenous growth.

The Keynesian and Institutionalist approach sees a proactive state that uses military spending as one aspect of state spending to increase output through multiplier effects in the presence of ineffective aggregate demand. In this way, increased military spending can lead to increased capacity utilization, increased profits and hence increased investment and growth. The Institutionalist approach combines a Keynesian perspective with a focus on the way in which high military spending can lead to industrial inefficiencies and to the development of a powerful interest group composed of individuals, firms and organizations that benefit from defence spending, usually referred to as the military industrial complex (MIC). The MIC increases military expenditure through internal pressure within the state, even when there is no threat to justify such expenditure.

Finally, the Marxist approach sees the role of military spending in capitalist development as important, though contradictory. There are a number of strands to the approach which differ in their treatment of crisis, the extent to which they see military expenditure as necessary to capitalist development, and the role of the MIC in class struggle. One offshoot of this approach has provided the only theory in which military spending is both important in itself and an integral component of the theoretical analysis, the underconsumptionist approach.

This sees military spending as necessary to maintain capitalism and prevent stagnation. Monopolistic companies produce goods and control labour costs leading to inadequate consumption. Military spending is a wasteful way – in the sense of not creating any further output – of creating demand to allow companies to sell their goods and realize their profits.

How arms transfers and military spending influence economic growth

In empirical work the fact that there is no agreed theory of growth among economists means that there is no standard framework into which military spending can be fitted. Clearly, in developing countries military spending, conflict and economic capacity (education, governance, institutions, natural resources) all interact to influence growth.[6] The theoretical work has allowed the identification of a number of channels through which military spending can impact on the economy. The relative importance and sign of these effects and the overall impact on growth can only be ascertained by empirical analysis.

- Labour: An important problem in developing countries is creating adequate skilled and educated labour as the economy develops. Military spending can have both positive and negative effects. The military can train soldiers and conscripts with valuable technical and administrative skills which they take into civilian life. It can also have a modernizing effect, with organizational skills and modern attitudes tending to break up social rigidities. On the other hand, these effects may be insignificant and the military may attract scarce skilled labour and valuable resources away from the civilian industrial sector and place a fetter on growth. The transferability of skills may be limited and the military may be no more, or less, modern than civil institutions. Military spending might also be at the expense of education and training expenditure (Deger 1985; Nabe 1983).
- Capital: Military spending can have positive or negative effects on both savings and investment. It is argued that if increases in military expenditure are funded by taxation, then if this expenditure is reduced in the future savings propensities may increase. In developing countries, though, raising new revenue from taxation can be difficult, thus military expenditure may be funded by increased money supply, which may lead to inflation, which can reduce savings. A direct impact can result from military expenditure being directly at the expense of education and health, requiring increased private provision and lowering private savings. Again, the impact of military expenditure on investment is an empirical question. On the one hand it is hypothesized that it can crowd out investment. On the other hand it can boost demand, output and profits and lead to increased investment (other forms of government expenditure could also have the same impact). It is possible, though, that bottlenecks could prevent any significant positive effect. In addition, the effects of infrastructural investment by the military can be either to benefit industry, or be purely of military value remote from and irrelevant to the civilian sector (Smith and Smith 1980; Deger 1986).
- Technology: Imports of arms can introduce advanced product and process technology to local industry, particularly if offset deals mean that local production takes place through licensing, and this could have positive externalities for the rest of industry particularly. This will obviously depend on the degree of development and the existence of an advanced sector, with trained and educated workforce and support industry. On the other hand, poor countries may not have the skilled workers and technicians and the offset-based companies may use mainly expatriates, having little impact on the local economy and being unsustainable once the order is fulfilled. Alternatively, it could create an advanced production sector with little linkage to the rest of the country and dependent on government for support (Brauer and Dunne 2006).
- External relations: The impact of military expenditure on the balance of payments will depend upon whether or not a country produces arms and whether or not it receives

military-related aid. In most developing countries imports of weapons will place a huge burden on the economy, through the use of scarce foreign exchange, and will make trade deficits difficult to avoid. This may be offset by military-related aid, exports of arms and import substitution, but in general military spending is likely to be a burden on the trade balance. In addition, evidence suggests that military-related debt in developing countries is substantial and that the financial burden of earlier arms imports via debt service has grown over time. On the other hand, the military may provide security from threats, encourage foreign investment, and have links with foreign powers with an interest in the region that can be beneficial to trade, investment and aid. However, this must be weighed against the possibility of involvement in conflict and the damaging effects multinational investment and aid can have on weak client economies (Brauer & Dunne 2002, Brzoska 1983).

- Socio-political: Military expenditure may provide the conditions under which development can take place. The military may provide control and discipline of labour, reduce internal conflict and be a modernizing influence. As discussed above, they can impart discipline on conscripts, making them more suited to industrial labour when they leave the forces, and can provide skills that can be of value in the civil sector. It is possible, though, that the military sector and its technology are capital intensive and so far removed from the rest of the economy as to impart little of value in terms of spin-offs. It may also take skilled labour away from the civil sector and military regimes may be conservative, corrupt, inefficient and a fetter on economic development (Scheetz 2002; Smith and Smith 1980).

- Debt: Military expenditure has been considered an important variable in explaining the rise of foreign debt in a number of developing countries, suggesting that this has led to reduced economic growth. The relationship between military expenditure and external debt can be in one of two forms. In general, as a budget item, military expenditure creates the need for funding. If a rise in military expenditure, say, cannot be financed through taxation, it will create a deficit. This may be financed in four different ways: printing money, using foreign exchange reserves, borrowing abroad and borrowing domestically. Each of these methods has some limits and implications, which are widely discussed in the literature.[7] Although there are links between the implications of methods used, as a first approximation, the methods of deficit financing are associated with different macroeconomic imbalances: money printing with inflation; foreign reserve use with the onset of an exchange crisis; foreign borrowing with an external debt crisis. Debt can also influence the interest rate, which may feed back on investment (Dunne and Lamb 2004; Brzoska, 1994).

- Conflicts: An interesting literature has developed that looks at the natures of conflicts and the extent to which they are encouraged by military expenditure. Clearly the costs of conflict are high and can be made higher through increased military expenditure (IANSA, Oxfam and Saferworld 2007); however, it is not that straightforward, as military spending and arms races do not inevitably lead to conflict and it might be that it is the underlying causes of conflict that are driving the observed expenditure. In addition, some of the most damaging and bloody wars have been achieved with relatively little in the way of funds or arms transfers (e.g. Rwanda) (Collier 2007; Murdoch and Sandler 2002).

- Demand: Clearly, military spending in common with any form of government expenditure will have effects on aggregate demand and in situations of less than full employment will lead to increased output, with income multiplier and accelerator effects through investment. Developing countries are unlikely to be resource constrained, but given their supply constraints, in terms of physical and human capital, the impact of increased expenditure may be relatively small. It is also open to debate whether military expenditure is the best form of government expenditure to use for expansionary growth (Dunne and Perlo-Freeman 2003).

- Arms races: An arms race is normally considered as a dyadic action-reaction – two countries each increasing their arms as a result of the other. The existence of arms races will mean that military spending will have a more marked effect on neighbours and other countries. Even if increases in military expenditure were to have a positive effect to start with, this is unlikely to continue as the expenditure ratchets up. Some literature has emphasized a wider form of arms races in cross-section and panel –Rosh security web – and alliance effect and regional externalities[8] (Dunne and Smith 2007).

- Identification: An important issue in empirical work is the identification problem that results from the fact that we observe military spending and growth changing, and both are influenced by security threats. If the economic determinants of growth are constant, but there are variations in the security threat, a negative relationship between military expenditure and output will be observed. On the other hand, if the threat is constant but the economic variables are changing, a positive relationship between military expenditure and output will be observed. This can be used to explain some countries' experiences with different combinations of growth and military expenditure. It also suggests caution in interpreting the results of empirical studies (Smith 2000).

Clearly, all of these channels will interact and their influence will vary depending on the countries involved. For example, a relatively advanced developing country, such as one of the Asian 'tigers', will have concerns over the industrial impact of their involvement in arms production, the technology and foreign direct investment benefits versus the opportunity cost, while a poorer African economy may be more concerned with the conflict trap in which they find themselves.

Summarizing the debate: empirical results

Once we move beyond a broad-stroke theoretical understanding towards an empirical analysis it becomes necessary to be more specific about the questions to be addressed and the way in which they are to be analysed. There are choices to be made, many of which will be conditioned on the theoretical perspective adopted and the data availability. There has been some confusion within the literature as a result of not recognizing such differences in the nature of studies and that the empirical results are likely to be very sensitive to the measurement and definition of the variables, to the specification of the estimated equations (especially the other variables included), the type of data used and the estimation method. In addition, the theoretical positions discussed above have generally been developed in the analysis of developed countries and applied to developing countries with some adjustments to the empirical model to take account of some of their particular features. This is hardly the best way to undertake such an analysis. The resulting variety of studies does make comparisons rather difficult and explain some of the seemingly contradictory findings. Whether or not the overall impact of military spending on development is positive or negative depends upon the relative magnitudes and signs of these channels and in the absence of any theoretical consensus, this can only be determined empirically.

The debate in the empirical literature on the economic effects of military spending started with the contribution of Benoit (1973, 1978), which purported to show that military expenditure and development went hand in hand. This led to considerable research activity using econometric analysis to overcome the deficiencies, most of which has tended not to support Benoit, but there is still no consensus view. There were two responses to this: one to criticize the approach that Benoit took in looking at a number of countries and arguing that the complexities and specificities of the processes call for more detailed individual country case studies, introducing qualitative information (Ball 1983; Kaldor 1991). The second was to argue that Benoit's empirical work was flawed and this led to a plethora of econometric studies.

Some of the earlier contributions employed models that had both Keynesian and neoclassical features, within simultaneous equation systems. This approach emphasized the importance of the interdependence between military spending, growth and the other variables, with the majority of the studies tending to confirm the existence of negative impact of military expenditure on economic development. The studies did vary in their use of data. Some dealt with cross-section averages, others with time-series estimates for individual countries, while others were more comprehensive (Dunne 1996). Attempts have been made to investigate sample stratifications. More recently, these types of modelling approaches have become rarer, but have not contradicted the earlier findings, with Galvin (2003), in a cross-section study of 64 developing countries, using simultaneous equation models, finding defence has a negative effect on growth and the savings–income ratio, this being greater for middle-income countries.

Another response was with empirical studies that used neoclassical single equation growth models, introducing military spending (burden, per capita or absolute value) as the, or one of the, independent variables. Frederiksen and Looney's (1983) re-examination of Benoit's data in this manner divided the countries into resource constrained and resource unconstrained and found the significant relation for military expenditure on growth only held for the resource unconstrained group; it was negative for the resource constrained. Other studies tended to find a positive or insignificant effect of military expenditure on growth, though there were studies that found negative effects (Dunne 1996). More recently, studies have tried to deal with some limitations of the earlier studies, some using extended growth models, including Knight et al. (1996), who found that high levels of military spending detract from growth by reducing productive capital formation and distorting resource allocation. More recently Ram (2003), using a large panel of countries, found no evidence of crowding out, but clear differences across groups of countries, while for a smaller number Yakovlev (2007) found military expenditure negatively related to economic growth. Given such heterogeneity, he argued that care was needed in interpretation.

An important concern with the single equation approach was that it explicitly assumed that military expenditure is exogenously determined and that the causality goes from military expenditure to growth, both of which were brought into question by Joerding (1986). Other studies then investigated the causal links (using statistical definitions of causality referred to as 'Granger causality' to distinguish the concept from theoretical causality) between military expenditure and economic growth, with, in general, the studies finding no dominant result. Some recent contributions have also tried to deal with the possibility that the milex/growth nexus may be more complicated that has been assumed with non-linear relationships and different effects at different levels of expenditure. Given the complexity of such models, the studies tend to focus on a small number of countries. Cuaresma and Reitschuler (2003) estimate that threshold regressions show that there is a level-dependent effect of military spending on growth, i.e. positive externality effect for low levels of military spending, but negative for high, while Pieroni (2008) finds a clear negative effect.

Another concern of researchers was to allow for the opportunity cost of military spending, or the trade-off between military spending and other forms of welfare expenditure. While this approach is somewhat problematic, as it suggests that if money was not spent on military spending it would be spent elsewhere and it often does not allow for the fact that it is possible to have more of both with economic growth, there have been some interesting studies, but no consensus. Some early studies found weak evidence of military spending crowding out spending on education and health in developing countries, but others found no evidence of trade-offs. More recently, Aslam (2007) considered 59 developing countries and found little evidence of trade-offs overall, but with some regional variation.

An alternative to these types of studies was provided by the existence of large country macroeconometric models and other forms of world models, developed for other purposes but able to be used to look at the impact of changes in military spending. The advantage of such models is that the impact of using military spending for other purposes can be analysed. A pioneering study by Leontief and Duchin (1983) used a world model to consider the effects of disarmament in the major powers and transference of the resources to low-income countries, finding it to be positive, though not particularly significant. Cappelen et al. (1982) made similar findings and Gleditsch et al. (1996) provided a collection of studies, linked into the use of a world model to illustrate the clear benefits of the 'peace dividend'. There are few individual country studies for developing countries using relatively large macromodels for obvious reasons. Such analyses do differ from the usual studies of growth, as they are no longer searching for the long-run determinants of growth, but considering the short-run 'peace dividend' impact, while at the same time allowing for government policy to adjust in a manner that deals with problems of economic adjustment.

While developing countries have limited arms production capabilities, they do have some, and many have aspirations to become important arms exporters. At the same time the trade in weapons is hugely important in providing foreign exchange for a limited number of countries, providing a drain on foreign exchange and debt burdens for a lot more, and providing the possibility of developing weapons production for others through offset deals. Brauer (2002) found that a number of formerly developing nations have 'graduated' from relatively low levels and sophistication of arms production to a relatively high level, coinciding with the continued development of their civilian industrial capabilities. Among the remaining developing nations, between 25 and 35 were engaged in some form of arms production and arms (re)exports by the 1990s. Brauer argues that if anything, the development of indigenous arms industries in developing nations depends crucially on already established civilian capacities and that no one has ever presented a convincing case that arms exports provide net foreign exchange. Brauer and Dunne (2004) is an edited collection that provides a range of studies on the role of offsets in development. They find virtually no case where offset arrangements have yielded unambiguous net benefits for a country's economic development. As a general rule, arms-trade offset deals are seen to be more costly than 'off-the-shelf' arms purchases and create little by way of new or sustainable employment. They do not appear to contribute in any substantive way to general economic development and, with very few exceptions, do not result in significant technology transfers, even within the military sector.

As mentioned, for many countries arms procurement will need foreign exchange and this may well require borrowing. This has led to a number of studies on the effect of military spending upon debt, clearly an empirical question. Early work followed Brzoska (1983) in suggesting that the impact of high external borrowing due to defence on a country's overall growth performance and resource allocation depends on the country's capacity for international borrowing. More recently Brzoska (2004) found that indebtedness due to arms imports had not increased as much during the 1990s as it did during the 1970s, increased commercialization meant that countries had to pay for weapons (they could no longer rely on military aid) and poor countries were less important as customers. Dunne and Lamb (2004) find military burden to have a positive effect on the share of external debt in gross domestic product (GDP) for a panel of 11 small industrialized economies.

The post-Cold war era led to important changes in the nature of conflicts. The end of proxy wars and superpower involvement did not reduce conflict, but did reduce their intensity, and saw a dominance of civil or intra-state wars. The nature of wars clearly changed, with a blurred distinction between war and organized crime and, while local, the wars tended to have a transnational connection (Kaldor 2006). There were fewer real military battles than in the past, but instead skirmishes and attacks on civilians. Collier and Hoffler produced a series of careful and detail empirical studies which looked at the cause of conflict and explanations for their continuation/duration. The results suggested that it was greed (often represented by the proportion of primary commodities in GDP and other such indicators) rather than grievance that explains civil wars. This work led to a lively debate, the result of which was the acceptance that grievance may be involved in starting conflicts, but that they are likely to be captured by more economic concerns over time (Collier 2007).

Another issue of concern has been to understand what determines military spending in developing countries. Whether it is strategic or economic factors – because they feel they need to or because they can afford to. One possibility is that they respond to other countries and engage in arms races. There are a number of studies on arms races, but it is difficult to find compelling empirical evidence of arms races of the Richardsonian action-reaction type between pairs of countries, though there is evidence of some interrelation. This is rather surprising, but linked to the problems of using empirical data to operationalize the models. They are clearly more suited to analyse situations in which countries are in conflict, such as India–Pakistan and are, therefore, of limited applicability. More importantly, though, they have failed to perform well empirically (Dunne and Smith 2007). Dunne and Smith (2007) moved beyond dyadic arms races to develop the Rosh (1988) idea of a security web, the aggregate military spending of enemies, allies and potential enemies, finding them to be important. More recent literature has recognized that whereas the arms races of the Cold War opposed comparable actors, the new conflicts are asymmetrical, between countries with high-tech weapons and those without (Dunne and Smith 2007).

Previous surveys of the military spending growth literature include Chan (1987), who found a lack of consistency in the results, Ram (1995) who reviewed 29 studies, concluding little evidence of a positive effect of defence outlays on growth, but that it was also difficult to say the evidence supported a negative effect. Dunne (1996) covered 54 studies and concluded that military spending had at best no effect on growth and was likely to have a negative effect, certainly that there was no evidence of positive effects, while Smith (2000) suggested the large literature did not indicate any robust empirical regularity, positive or negative, though he thinks there is a small negative effect in the long run, but one that requires considerably more sophistication to find. Smaldone (2006), in his review of Africa, considers military spending relationships to be heterogeneous, elusive and complex, but feels that variations can be explained by intervening variables. They can be both positive and negative, but are not usually pronounced, although the negative effects tend to be wider and deeper in Africa and most severe in countries experiencing legitimacy/security crises and economic/budgetary constraints.

Overall, while there is no consensus on the economic effects of military spending, the most common finding is that military burden has either no significant effect, or a negative effect on economic growth for developing countries. Summarizing the result of our survey of 103 studies on the economic effects of military spending, where case studies refer to single or small groups of countries and the unclear category, implies mixed or insignificant results.

Almost 39% of the cross-country studies and 35% of the case studies find a negative effect of military spending on growth, with only around 20% finding positive for both types of studies. As Hartley and Sandler (1995) pointed out, if we distinguish between the supply side models and those which have a demand side, there is more consistency in the results. Models allowing for a demand side and hence the possibility of crowding out investment tend to find negative effects, unless there is some reallocation to other forms of government spending, while those with only a supply side find positive, or positive but insignificant, effects. That the supply side models find a positive effect is not a surprise, as the model is inherently structured to find such as result (Brauer 2002a). Given this, the fact that over 40% find unclear results could be interpreted as providing further evidence against there being a positive impact of military spending on the economy.

Table 21.1 The economic effects of military spending

Type	Total No.	% Positive	% Negative	% Unclear
Cross-country	63	19	38	43
Case studies	40	20	35	45
Total	103	20	37	43

It is also worth noting that the military burden, or share of military spending of GDP, is relatively low in most developing countries (less than 2% for low-income countries) relative to other components of GDP, such as health and education. As a result, one might not expect to find a statistically significant effect on the path of national income, when there are so many other influences. Aside from when countries are engaged in conflict, one might not expect to find significant impacts of arms transfers and military spending, which makes it interesting that so many do.

This means that there is the potential for developing countries to cut military spending with, at worst, no harm to economic performance and, at best, higher economic growth. The macroeconometric modelling literature that allows evaluations of military spending to other forms of government spending does suggest that there are likely to be economic benefits. These benefits could depend upon sensible economic policies and support of the international community, particularly if they occur after a conflict, as discussed in the next section.

Conclusions

Military spending is an expenditure by governments that has influence beyond the resources it takes up, especially when it leads to or facilitates conflicts. While countries need some level of security to deal with internal and external threats, these have opportunity costs, as they prevent resources from being used for other purposes, which might improve the pace of development. Such issues are clearly important for the poorest economies.

While there are problems with data on military expenditure, especially when attempting to make comparisons, all of the available data suggest that the clear trend for reduction in military spending after the end of the Cold War has ended. Military spending, aside from some important regional differences, is on the increase and this raises important issues for the developing world. To consider what these issues are likely to be this paper has provided a review of research on the military expenditure-development nexus. As a starting point for a comparison of the empirical studies, a survey of the methodological and theoretical issues was undertaken. There are a number of schools of thought but no consensus in these general theories on the impact of military spending on economic growth. Much of the empirical work has focused on Keynesian and neoclassical models and considers a number of channels by which military spending can effect growth. Whether or not it is positive is seen to be an empirical one.

It is important to recognize the interdependence of the demand and supply side and to consider the determinants of military spending. The results of the empirical studies are mixed but do tend to suggest that in developing countries economic conditions are not the most important determinant of military burden.

The empirical analyses of the economic effects of military spending, including arms transfers, suggests that there is little or no evidence for a positive effect on economic growth and that it is more likely to have a negative effect, or at best no significant impact at all. A range of approaches are used, with the studies finding positive effects (often insignificant ones) generally adopting a single equation estimation approach. Studies that have attempted to develop simultaneous models to allow for a variety of indirect effects have tended to find that military spending has a negative impact on growth. Some studies have investigated the statistical causality of military spending and economic growth, but with no dominant result.

Overall, these results suggest that reducing arms and military spending need not be costly and can contribute to, or at the very least provide the opportunity for, improved economic performance in developing countries. There are still problems, though, in countries moving to lower levels of military spending. Support is likely to be required at a national and international level, including assistance from the developed world.

In addition, there is not necessarily an automatic improvement in development as a result of arms and military spending reductions; it something that requires good governance, management and support (Brauer 1990). An early influential study by Smith and Smith (1980) suggested

Table 21.2 Developing nations' arms producers/exporters, c.1985–95

ACDA		Brzoska	Rana
Arms exporters			Producers of 'small arms'
Afghanistan	1994	Algeria	*Argentina*
Argentina	all years	*Argentina*	Bangladesh
Brazil	all years	Bangladesh	*Brazil*
Cape Verde	1985	Bolivia	*Chile*
Chile	all years	*Brazil*	*China, People's Repub.*
China, People's Repub.	all years	Burkina-Faso	Cuba
Cuba	1985, 1988, 1989	Myanmar	Dominican Republic
Egypt	all except 1991, 1995	Cameroon	*Egypt*
Ethiopia	1990	*Chile*	*India*
Greece	all years	*China, People's Repub.*	*Iran*
India	all except 1988, 1989, 1992	Colombia	*Iraq*
Indonesia	all except 1986, 1987	Dominican Republic	*Libya*
Iran	1985–90	*Egypt*	*Malaysia*
Iraq	1991–95	*India*	*Mexico*
Jordan	1986–89, 1994	Indonesia	Namibia
North Korea	all years	*Iran*	*Nigeria*
Kuwait	1988, 1992	*Iraq*	*North Korea*
Libya	1985–92	Côte d'Ivoire	*Pakistan*
Malaysia	1994, 1995	*Libya*	Peru
Mali	1989	*Malaysia*	*Philippines*
Mexico	all years	*Mexico*	*South Africa*
Nicaragua	1992, 1995	Morocco	*Saudi Arabia*
Nigeria	1986, 1989	*Nigeria*	Turkey
Oman	1986	*North Korea*	*Venezuela*
Pakistan	all years	*Pakistan*	Yugoslavia
Panama	1992, 1993	Peru	
Philippines	1985, 1986	*Philippines*	
Saudi Arabia	all except 1990, 1991, 1993	*Saudi Arabia*	
South Africa	all years	*South Africa*	
Sudan	1986	Sri Lanka	
Syria	1986, 1992	Sudan	
Thailand	1988, 1989	Syria	
Turkey	all except 1986	Thailand	
Venezuela	1990	*Venezuela*	
Viet Nam	1985, 1987, 1988, 1992		
Yugoslavia	1985–91		
Slovenia	1992, 1994, 1995		
Zimbabwe	1994		

Source: Brauer 2002b

Notes: For the Arms Control and Disarmament Agency (ACDA, 1997), 'all years' refers to all years 1985–95; Brzoska (1995) lists only African, Asian, Latin American and Middle Eastern nations, counting Turkey as European; Rana (1995) only lists producers of 'small arms'. Countries listed in *italic* appear on all three lists. For simplicity, Brauer designated countries as 'developing' when their per capita GNP was estimated as below US$9,700 in 1995, i.e. those countries not classified as 'high-income economies' by the World Bank (World Bank 1997). This excludes arms producers once considered 'developing', such as Israel, South Korea, Taiwan, Singapore, Spain and Portugal. East-Central and Southeast-Central European nations, i.e. erstwhile satellites and republics of the former Soviet Union that nowadays would appropriately be designated as 'developing' are also excluded that if there is a relationship between disarmament and development, it may be one that has to be constructed politically, not one that is pre-given by economic forces. It would appear from this survey that their conclusion remains relevant to the modern world.

An interesting observation is that while the evidence from military expenditure to growth is weak (even if the link is negative), the opposite link is very strong: the People's Republic of China and India, in particular, are engaged in an economic arms race of sorts because it is economic growth that, without question, generates the resources needed to feed the military. Japan managed to become a major military force, despite having a constitutional requirement to keep military spending below 1% of GDP – its economy grew so much that 1% represented a large resource. The lesson might be that if you want to have any hope of becoming (militarily) strong, invest in the economy. Once states are economically strong, there is too much at stake to risk it in war and they may also gain security from developed economies if they become too important to the world economy to allow them to be invaded. The best way to true security may actually be through economic development.

It seems unfortunate that after 25 years of work or so, the findings of the review should be so hedged. This is partly owing to the problems of getting reliable data, and possibly a hangover from Cold War debates that in some cases reflected political positions rather that the pursuit of quality research. However, it also reflects the fact that military spending and arms transfers, while more important than their share of resources might suggest, are still only a small part of any economy and can easily be swamped by other factors. As we get more post-Cold War data, we will hope to better distinguish the trends, and so provide more careful analyses of the contemporary world. Clearly, this is an important and urgent task.

Notes

1 This paper is based on work undertaken for Oxfam. We are grateful to Jurgen Brauer, Michael Brzoska, Katherine Nightingale, Donald Mclellan and Ron Smith for helpful comments.
2 This can be simply because of the different conventions, or attempts to 'massage' the figures using mechanisms such as double-bookkeeping, extra budgetary accounts, highly aggregated budget categories, military assistance and foreign exchange manipulation. In some developing countries, the military has a much wider remit (for example, they are involved in building projects with social outcomes, e.g. building roads, hospitals, etc., or take part in what would more normally be considered civilian police duties).
3 The problems of collecting military spending data are reflected in the copious footnotes accompanying the SIPRI Yearbook data. The most extreme case was Argentina in 1982, where the IISS military expenditure figure and that published by the IMF differed by 1,034%.
4 Even if data are comparable, the use of the exchange rate to put them into a common currency is not without its problems, as it will not reflect the different relative prices of the categories of military expenditure and the different compositions across countries. The Summers Heston dataset provides data for a cross-section of countries, which have been adjusted to take account of these problems, but in most cases researchers focus upon standardized data such as the share of military expenditure in gross domestic product (GDP) or gross national product (GNP). See pwt.econ.upenn.edu; Alan Heston, Robert Summers and Bettina Aten, Penn World Table Version 6.2, Center for International Comparisons of Production, Income and Prices at the University of Pennsylvania, September 2006.
5 The former is, of course, only a necessary condition for the latter and the starting point for any such analysis should really be some theoretical understanding of the links between the two. Similarly, it is important to recognize that military spending is only one aspect of militarism in a society and is only a measure of inputs rather than output.
6 Indeed, many poor countries, even those with civil wars, spend relatively little on the military. In particular, many African countries have low military burdens, but there are other obstacles to growth (Collier 2007).
7 For a recent example, see Dunne and Perlo-Freeman (2003).
8 The security web concept is an attempt to capture the impact of changes in the security environment. This is done by defining a security web – neighbours and other countries that are either allies or present a threat – and aggregating their military expenditures to form a security web variable.

Bibliography

Aizenman, Joshua and Reuven Glick, 'Military Expenditure, Threats and Growth', FRBSF Working Paper 2003 8, 2003
Ali, Hamid E., 'Military Expenditures and Inequality: Empirical Evidence from Global Data', *Defence and Peace Economics*, Vol. 18(6), January 2007

Aslam, Rabia, 'Measuring the Peace Dividend: Evidence from Developing Countries', *Defence and Peace Economics*, Vol. 18(1), February 2007

Ball, Nicole, 'Defense and Development: A Critique of the Benoit Study', *Economic Development and Cultural Change*, Vol. 31, 1983

Baran, Paul and Paul Sweezy, *Monopoly Capital*, London, Monthly Review Press, 1966

Benoit, Emile, *Defense and Growth in Developing Countries*, Boston, Heath and Lexington Books, 1973

——'Growth and Defense in Developing Countries', *Economic Development and Cultural Change*, Vol. 26, No. 2, January 1978

Biswas, Basudeb and Rati Ram, 'Military Expenditure and Economic Growth in the Less Developed Countries: An Augmented Model and Further Evidence', *Economic Development and Cultural Change*, Vol. 34, No. 2, January 1986

Brauer, Jurgen, 'Reviving or Revamping the 'Disarmament-for-Development' Thesis?', *Bulletin of Peace Proposals*, Vol. 21, No. 3, September 1990

——'Arms Production in Developing Nations: The Relation to Industrial Structure, Industrial Diversification, and Human Capital Formation', *Defence Economics*, Vol. 2, No. 2, April 1991

——'Military Expenditures and Human Development Measures', *Public Budgeting and Financial Management*, Vol. 8, No. 1, Spring 1996

——'Survey and Review of the Defense Economics Literature on Greece and Turkey: What Have We Learned?', *Defence and Peace Economics*, Vol. 13, No. 2, 2002a

——'The Arms Industry in Developing Nations: History and Post-Cold War Assessment', in Jurgen Brauer and J. Paul Dunne, eds, *Arming the South: The Economics of Military Expenditures, Arms Production and Trade in Developing Countries*, New York, Palgrave Macmillan, 2002b

Brauer, Jurgen and J. Paul Dunne, eds, *Arming the South: The Economics of Military Expenditures, Arms Production and Trade in Developing Countries*, New York, Palgrave Macmillan, 2002

——*Arms Trade and Economic Development: Theory, Policy, and Cases in Arms Trade Offsets*, Routledge, London, 2004

Brauer, Juergen and J. Paul Dunne, 'Arms Trade Offsets and Development', Discussion Papers 0504, University of the West of England, Department of Economics, 2006

Brzoska, Michael, 'Research Communication: The Military Related External Debt of Third World Countries', *Journal of Peace Research*, Vol. 20, No.3, 1983

——'The Financing Factor in Military Trade', *Defence and Peace Economics*, Vol. 5, 1994

——'Spread of Conventional Weapons Production Technology', in Sverre Lodgaard and Robert L. Pfaltzgraff, Jr (eds), *Arms and Technology Transfers: Security and Economic Considerations Among Importing and Exporting States*, New York and Geneva, United Nations Institute for Disarmament Research (UNIDIR), 1995

——'The Economics of Arms Imports After the End of the Cold War', *Defence and Peace Economics*, Vol. 15, Issue 2, 2004

——*Analysis of Recommendations for Covering Security Expenditures Within and Outside of Official Development Assistance (ODA)*, Bonn International Centre for Conversion (BICC), Research Paper No. 53, 2006

Cappelen, Adne, Olav Bjerkholt and Nils Petter Gleditsch, *Global Conversion from Arms to Development Aid: Macroeconomic Effects on Norway*, Oslo, PRIO, 1982

Chan, Steve, 'Military Expenditures and Economic Performance', in *World Military Expenditures and Arms Transfers*, US Arms Control and Disarmament Agency, US Government Printing Office, 1987

Chatterji, Manas, 'Regional Conflict and Military Spending in the Developing Countries', in Walter Isard and Charles Anderton, eds, *Economics of Arms Reduction and the Peace Process*, New York, North-Holland, 1992

Collier, Paul, 'Development and Conflict', Centre for the Study of African Economies, Department of Economics, University of Oxford, Oxford, 2004

——*The Bottom Billion*, Oxford, Oxford University Press, 2007

Collier, Paul and Anke Hoeffler, *Military Expenditure: Threats, Aid, and Arms Races*, Mimeograph, University of Oxford, Oxford, 2004

Cuaresma, Jesús Crespo and Gerhard Reitschuler, 'A Non-Linear Defence Growth Nexus? Evidence from the US Economy', *Defence and Peace Economics*, Vol. 15(1), February 2003

——'A Non-Linear Defence-Growth Nexus? Evidence from the U.S. Economy', *Defence and Peace Economics*, Vol. 15, No. 1, 2004

Deger, Saadet, 'Human Resources, Government Education Expenditure, and the Military Burden in Less Developed Countries', The Journal of Developing Areas, Vol. 20, No. 1, 1985

——*Military Expenditure in Third World Countries: the Economic Effects*, London, Routledge and Kegan Paul, 1986

Dunne, J. Paul, 'Economic Effects of Military Expenditure in Developing Countries: A Survey', in Nils Petter Gleditsch, Olav Bjerkholt, Ådne Cappelen, Ron P. Smith and J. Paul Dunne, eds, *The Peace Dividend*, Amsterdam, North-Holland, 1996

——'Problems of Post Conflict reconstruction in Africa: A Comparative Analysis of the Experience of Mozambique and Rwanda', *Economics of Peace and Security Journal*, Vol. 1, No. 2, 2006

Dunne, J. Paul and Fanny Coulomb, 'Peace, War and International Security: Economic Theories', Discussion Papers 0803, University of the West of England, Department of Economics, 2008

Dunne, J. Paul and Guy Lamb, 'Defence Industrial Participation: The Experience of South Africa', in Jurgen Brauer and J. Paul Dunne, eds, *Arms Trade and Economic Development: Theory Policy and Cases in Arms trade Offsets*, London, Routledge, 2004

Dunne, J. Paul and Nadir Mohammed, 'Military Spending in Sub-Saharan Africa: Evidence for 1967 85', *Journal of Peace Research*, Vol. 32, No. 3, 1995

Dunne, J. Paul and Sam Perlo-Freeman, 'The Demand for Military Spending in Developing Countries', *International Review of Applied Economics*, Vol. 17, No. 1, 2003

Dunne, J. Paul and Ron P. Smith, 'The Econometrics of Military Arms Races', in Keith Hartley and Todd Sandler, eds, *Handbook of Defence Economics*, Amsterdam, North-Holland, 2007

Frederiksen, Peter and Robert E. Looney, 'Defense Expenditures and Economic Growth in Developing Countries', *Armed Forces and Society*, Vol. 9, No. 4, 1983

Galvin, Hannah, 'The Impact of Defence Spending on the Economic Growth of Developing Countries: A Cross Section Study', *Defence and Peace Economics*, Vol. 14(1), February 2003

Gleditsch, Nils Petter, Olav Bjerkholt, Ådne Cappelen, Ron P. Smith and J. Paul Dunne, eds, *The Peace Dividend*, Amsterdam, North-Holland, 1996

Gleditsch, Nils Petter, Adne Cappelen and Olav Bjerkholt, *The Wages of Peace: Disarmament in a Small Industrialised Economy*, London, PRIO, Sage, 1994

Hartley, Keith, *Economic Aspects of Disarmament: Conversion as an Investment Process*, Geneva, UNIDIR, 1993

Hartley, Keith and Todd Sandler, eds, *Handbook of Defense Economics*, Amsterdam, Elsevier, 1995

—— *The Economics of Defense*, Cambridge, Cambridge University Press, 1995

IANSA, Oxfam and Saferworld, *Africa's Missing Billions*, Briefing Paper 107, Control Arms Campaign, 2007

Isard, Walter and Charles Anderton, eds, *Economics of Arms Reduction and the Peace Process*, New York, North-Holland, 1992

Joerding, Wayne, 'Economic Growth and Defence Spending Granger Causality', *Journal of Development Economics*, Vol. 21, 1986

Kaldor, Mary, 'Problems of Adjusting to Lower Levels of Military Spending in Developed and Developing Countries', Paper prepared for a World Bank Conference, Washington, DC, April 1991

—— *New and Old Wars: Organised Violence in a Global Era*, Cambridge, Polity Press, 2006

Knight, Malcolm, Norman Loayza and Delano Villanueva, 'The Peace Dividend: Military Spending Cuts and Economic Growth', *World Bank Policy Research Working Paper* No. 1577, 1996

Leontief, Wassily and Faye Duchin, *Military Spending: Facts and Figures, Worldwide Implications, and Future Outlook*, New York, Oxford University Press, 1983

Murdoch, James C. and Todd Sandler, 'Economic Growth, Civil Wars and Spatial Spillovers', *Journal of Conflict Resolution*, Vol. 46, No. 1, 2002

Nabe, Oumar, 'Military Expenditures and Industrialization in Africa', *Journal of Economic Issues*, Vol. 18, 1983

Omitoogun, Wuyi and Eboe Hutchful, *Budgeting for the Military Sector in Africa*, Oxford, Oxford University Press / SIPRI, 2006

Pieroni, Luca, 'Military Expenditure and Economic Growth', *Defence and Peace Economic*, 2008

Ram, Rati, 'Defense Expenditure and Economic Growth', in Keith Hartley and Todd Sandler (eds), *Handbook of Defense Economics*, Vol. I, Amsterdam: Elsevier Science, 1995

Ram, Rati, 'Defence Expenditure and Economic Growth: Evidence from Recent Cross-Country Panel Data', in Attiat F. Ott and Richard J. Cebula, eds, *The Elgar Companion to Public Economics: Empirical Public Economics*, Cheltenham, Edward Elgar, 2003

Rana, Swadesh, 'Small Arms and Intra-State Conflicts', Research Paper No. 34, United Nations Institute for Disarmament Research (UNIDIR), Geneva, March 1995

Richardson, Lewis Fry, *Arms and Insecurity: A Mathematical Study of Causes and Origins of War*, Pittsburgh, Boxwood Press, 1960

Rosh, Robert M., 'Third World Militarisation: Security Webs and the States They Ensnare', *Journal of Conflict Resolution*, Vol. 32, No. 4, 1988

Scheetz, Thomas, 'Military Expenditure and Development in Latin America', in Jurgen Brauer and J. Paul Dunne (eds), *Arming the South*, London, Palgrave, 2002

SIPRI, *SIPRI Yearbook of World Armament and Disarmament*, Stockholm: Stockholm International Peace Research Institute / Oxford University Press, various years.

Smaldone, Joseph P., 'African Military Spending: Defence versus Development?', *African Security Review*, Vol. 15, No. 4, 2006

Smith, Dan and Ron Smith, 'Military Expenditure, Resources and Development', University of London, Birkbeck College Discussion Paper No. 87, November 1980

Smith, Ron, 'Defence Expenditure and Economic Growth', in Gleditsch, Nils Petter, Goran Lindgren, Naima Mouhleb, Sjoerd Smit and Indra de Soysa, *Making Peace Pay: A Bibliography on Disarmament and Conversion*, Claremont, Regina Books, 2000

World Bank, *Expanding the Measure of Wealth*, Washington, DC, World Bank, 1997

Yakovlev, Pavel, 'Arms Trade, Military Spending and Economic Growth', *Defence and Peace Economics*, Vol. 18(4), 2007

22 Post-Cold War control of conventional arms

Sibylle Bauer

Introduction

'Hard realists' claim, with Colin Gray, that arms control is impossible when needed and not necessary when possible – referred to as the arms control paradox (Gray 1992). Even with the fairly mixed experience of the current decade, this tool of security policy arguably remains useful, although, and maybe because, its role and specific applications have evolved and expanded considerably. Arms control refers to restrictions upon the development, production, stockpiling, proliferation, transfer, testing, deployment and usage of weapons. In addition to these hard security aspects, the arms control debate and negotiations also comprise softer elements, such as confidence-building measures, transparency, information exchange and verification.

During the Cold War, arms control efforts focused on bilateral treaties limiting nuclear weapons and delivery systems between the two superpowers. There were also ground-breaking multilateral treaties designed to prohibit or limit the development, production, transfer and use of weapons of mass destruction (WMD). The Treaty on the Non-proliferation of Nuclear Weapons (NPT) was opened for signature in 1968 and entered into force in 1970, while the 1972 Biological and Toxin Weapons Convention (BWC) entered into force in 1975. The 1993 Chemical Weapons Convention entered into force in 1997 and thus after the end of the Cold War. While the BWC and CWC ban biological and chemical weapons for all UN Member States, the NPT allows a temporary exemption for the five permanent members of the UN Security Council (the P5) who all possessed nuclear weapons at the time the NPT negotiations were concluded. Article VI of the treaty requires all states parties to work towards eventual nuclear disarmament, but the time frame for doing so remains vague and discussion on this point has not advanced over the past 40 years. At the same time, the number of countries with nuclear weapons or nuclear weapon capabilities has increased, though advocates for the value of the NPT argue that this number has not increased by as much as it would have but for the Treaty. Efforts are also made to complement the three treaties, which were negotiated with state-run programmes in mind, by other measures aimed to meet threats posed by non-state actors (Anthony 2006).

Improving East-West relations towards the end of the Cold War enabled negotiations in the conventional area, most notably the 1990 Treaty on Conventional Armed Forces in Europe (CFE). Regional processes to control conventional arms have been more successful than global ones, but have also encountered difficulties in recent years. The original CFE Treaty, which entered into force two years later, established limits on key categories of conventional military equipment in Europe (from the Atlantic to the Urals). It also mandated the destruction of excess weaponry. While still considered 'by far the most extensive conventional arms control regime worldwide' (Lachowski 2008), the CFE has been in a major crisis. After a seven-year stalemate, the Russian Federation unilaterally suspended participation in the Treaty in December 2007, over a controversy regarding withdrawal of Russian forces and equipment from Moldova and Georgia to comply with commitments agreed at the Istanbul summit of

1999 (Lachowski 2008; Lachowski 2009). It should be kept in mind that the CFE originated in a period when the Soviet Union still existed and Yugoslavia had not disintegrated. Since then, an adaptation was negotiated but this process has lost momentum – or, one could argue, entered a dead end – due to the disagreements with Russia and entanglement with broader political and security issues (Lachowski and Post 2009). The Georgian war of August 2008 further exacerbated the dividing lines and created an even more difficult environment for advancing the arms control agenda. CFE-inspired sub-regional arms control in South-Eastern Europe, on the other hand, has remain functional, in spite of various challenges, not the least related to Kosovo (Lachowski 2008; Lachowski and Post 2009). Arms control agreements were also concluded in Central Asia during the 1990s, which have functioned as confidence-building measures and contributed to resolving border questions, facilitating co-ordination on security policy and creating a basis for closer economic co-operation (Trominov 2003). Whether European and Central Asian arms control models could be applied to other regions of the world is an open question.

The post-Cold War era achieved progress in prohibiting or limiting uses of certain weapons on humanitarian grounds, and two multilateral agreements banning entire conventional weapon categories – anti-personnel mines (APM) and cluster munitions. There has also been movement in international discussions on arms transfer control as a result of the Cold War ending. Up until the 1990s, arms transfer decisions were taken largely on the basis of military alliances, along the east-west divide. Since then, other considerations ranging from commercial interests to human rights and humanitarian law have come to the fore, and increased international deployment of European and other forces have changed the parameters of the debate. Moreover, threat perceptions and policy agendas have shifted and now focus on terrorism, failed and failing states, non-state actors, intra-state conflicts rather than inter-state conflicts, (potential) nuclear weapon states, and the proliferation of small arms and light weapons (SALW) and their role in fuelling and enabling armed conflicts around the world.

This chapter surveys key trends and developments in conventional arms control since the end of the Cold War and thus over the past 20 years, with a strong focus on the subject of this volume, the international arms trade. It looks at arms control as it relates to the production and transfer of conventional arms. The first section is dedicated to classic arms control developments, including inhumane weapons control and the UN Register of Conventional Arms, which aims at transparency and restrictions in transfers. Key international developments since the end of the Cold War include notably the initiative to negotiate an Arms Trade Treaty (ATT), and the 2001 Small Arms Programme of Action and follow-on process which comprehensively looks at the SALW issue, not just at transfers. Both processes are institutionally located within the UN. The chapter subsequently zooms in on arms transfer controls as one sub-area that has gained in importance in the post-Cold War period. An analysis of international trends and challenges in this area is followed by a survey of developments in arms transfer control in the Wassenaar Arrangement (the international export-control regime that deals with conventional arms), and the European Union (EU) as – of any multilateral body – it has by far advanced the furthest world-wide in terms of institutionalization, regulation and norm-building, both more broadly and for this specific area. It should be noted that the term transfer not only includes the commercial trade, but also government-to-government transfers and the ever-expanding range of relevant activities and transactions, such as brokering and transit.

International arms control processes

Arms control aims at stabilization and balance, whereas disarmament involves arms reduction or even elimination, but the two areas have been very closely linked in international negotiations. During the Cold War international arms control in the conventional area was largely limited to debates on transparency and achieved no agreements or results due to a linkage with the nuclear disarmament agenda on which there has been no movement. The end of the Cold War enabled not only transparency agreements (notably the UN Register of Conventional Arms, but also a dramatic rise in national and regional reporting), but also limited conventional arms control processes at the global level. The latter were initially limited to certain categories (landmines and cluster munitions) and linked to the international humanitarian law agenda, and aimed for their elimination. Since the 2000s, processes have been initiated which concern broader weapons categories. Their goal is not elimination, but rather establishment of rules for the use and spread of those types of weapons which are commonly accepted as essential to national and international security, based on the right to self-defence rooted in the UN Charter.

Inhumane weapons control

The Convention on the Prohibition of the Use, Stockpiling, Production and Transfer of Anti-personnel Mines (also known as the Ottawa Convention) was a major arms control and disarmament success as it for the first time bans a whole category of conventional weapons. This had previously only been achieved for WMDs. One key to the success of the APM treaty was to take the process outside the UN framework to bypass objections from Security Council members the People's Republic of China, Russia and the USA, and other countries such as India and Pakistan. This is at the same time a major weakness of the agreement, as key producers, users and possessors are missing in the list of signatories. (Another limitation being that only anti-personnel mines are prohibited, not anti-tank mines, for example, which can also harm civilians but have more military utility and against which it is, therefore, more difficult to generate sufficient support.) In December 1997, 122 states signed the Ottawa Convention. Following the 40th ratification the Convention entered into force in March 1999, and became binding international law on those who have ratified it. As of 2009, the Convention has 156 states parties.

The new Convention on Cluster Munitions (CCM), which was adopted in May 2008 and signed in Oslo in December 2008 by 94 countries, prohibits the use, production, stockpiling and transfer of cluster munitions. Some so-called smart cluster munitions are exempt. It has three things in common with the Ottawa Convention: it is a disarmament treaty that bans a whole category of weapons; it was taken out of the UN forums due to frustration over a lack of progress among states leading the process, and instead taken forward by a coalition of like-minded states; and a non-governmental organization (NGO) campaign played an important role, in this case the Cluster Munition Coalition (www.stopclustermunitions.org).

The Norwegian Government launched the Oslo process aimed to prohibit cluster munitions with the first global conference on cluster munitions held in Oslo in February 2007 – largely in response to the lack of progress in agreeing such a ban within the UN Conference on Disarmament. The Convention on Prohibitions or Restrictions on the Use of Certain Conventional Weapons which may be Deemed to be Excessively Injurious or to have Indiscriminate Effects (Convention on Certain Conventional Weapons, CCW, also known a the Inhumane Weapons Convention) entered into force in 1983, with five protocols adopted since. Protocol V of the CCW, which entered into force in 2006, addresses the humanitarian impact of explosive remnants of war, which encompasses cluster munitions, but does not include a ban. Protocol VI to the CCW on cluster munitions is still under negotiation. A major drawback of the CCM is that it thus far lacks the backing of precisely those states holding the majority of international cluster munitions stockpiles, which instead insist on keeping the negotiations within the framework of the CCW Convention.

Further progress in inhumane weapons control was achieved with the First CCW Review Conference of 1995, which resulted in a protocol that prohibits uses (although not production) of blinding lasers, which entered into force in 1998. The same Conference also added a revised protocol II which places new restrictions on the use, production and transfer of anti-personnel landmines (www.unog.ch/CCW).

Global norm building for arms transfers and production within the UN framework

Transparency in arms transfers has been discussed by the UN since the organization's establishment, but was not translated into concrete steps until the end of the Cold War (UN Secretary-General 1991; Wulf 1991). By the end of the 1980s, the global political climate had become more favourable to transparency-related initiatives. Transparency has become an increasingly important foreign policy objective as a confidence-building measure (CBM), primarily at a regional level – especially in the Organization for Security and Co-operation in Europe (OSCE). Within the OSCE, arms-related data, *inter alia* on arms transfers, have been exchanged among governments on a confidential basis.

Within the UN framework, transparency in arms has become widely accepted by governments as a desirable goal, although interpretations of transparency continue to differ widely. In 1991 the UN General Assembly established the UN Register of Conventional Arms (UN General Assembly 1991). Governments agreed to provide, on a voluntary basis, information about imports and exports of seven types of major conventional weapons in a standardized form. Additional background information regarding their military holdings, procurement through national production and relevant policies can also be submitted. The UN Register goes beyond the concept of intergovernmental transparency, as the submissions are publicly available. The UN Register is the first global mechanism where governments provide information about arms imports and exports to the public. In 2003 the UN Register was expanded to include lower calibre artillery and man-portable air defence systems (MANPADS), and states were additionally invited to provide background information on international transfers of SALW – as a result of which a substantial and increasing number of them has indeed provided such data (Holtom 2008, 2009).

Regional transparency mechanisms for arms transfers, most notably in the EU, have overtaken the UN process in terms of scope and level of transparency. Although set against the background of increased global transparency since the end of the Cold War, the transparency dynamic in the EU since the mid-1990s, the EU reporting system on arms exports and the wide availability of national reports are unique features (Bauer and Bromley 2004). Other regional transparency mechanisms focus on intergovernmental information exchanges rather than public transparency. A report by the Small Arms Survey and the Norwegian Initiative on Small Arms Transfers gives an overview of public reports of major arms exporters outside the EU, showing a broader trend of increased international reporting following the end of the Cold War, and provide an overview of regional transparency mechanisms set up in the ECOWAS in Africa, the OAS and Mercosur in Latin America and the OSCE in Europe (Haug et al. 2002).

It was the UN Register that prompted many EU governments to publish annually their first public statistics on exports of major conventional arms in the form of a national submission to the UN. While these documents were directed neither to the public nor to parliament, they nevertheless established a public reporting mechanism at the national level. Provision of public information in the UN context has created routine public reporting on arms exports in national bureaucracies, and thus contributed to an environment of enhanced national and EU transparency. None the less, the majority of EU governments did not produce a more comprehensive national report on arms exports until after the annual reporting system in the context of the EU Code of Conduct on Arms Exports of 1998 was established (www.sipri.org/contents/armstrad/atlinks_gov.html). Another indication of the linkage between regional and international processes is that the adoption of EU arms transfer criteria as a legally binding document in 2008 can in part be attributed to efforts to have a credible position in the ATT negotiations.

The title of the UN Programme of Action to Prevent, Combat and Eradicate the Illicit Trade in Small Arms and Light Weapons in All Its Aspects (PoA) of 2001 reflect the compromise outcome of two key controversies among Member States from the beginning of the process (UNODA). First, should the process be limited to addressing the illicit trade, or also establish rules for government-authorized transfers? Second, should it seek a legally binding agreement, or essentially be an awareness-raising and consensus-building exercise seeking to achieve substantial results in specific questions such as stockpile destruction? The UN has held one review conference in 2006 and Biannual Meetings of States (BMS) since 2001. Some progress was achieved at the third BMS in July 2008 by focusing on the less controversial areas of international co-operation and assistance, national capacity-building, tracing, brokering, stockpile management and surplus disposal. While the overall PoA implementation record is poor (Biting the Bullet 2003, 2006), its main achievement can be seen in raising the profile of the small arms issue. While each process has its own dynamics and specific promoting and impeding factors, the UN small arms process centred around the PoA has clearly contributed to the enabling environment for the expansion of the UN Register to SALW and a range of different national and regional SALW initiatives and processes (within the OSCE, ECOWAS, OAS, etc.). The discussion on legally binding rules for arms transfers, which has been a major point of contention, has been taken up within the broader ATT process (Holtom 2008).

Questions of scope and mandate were subject to controversy from the beginning of the process. A number of preparatory conference participants, including the EU, interpreted the mandate broadly to cover the legal arms trade, the logic being that illegal arms transfers generally start out as legal in the sense of being authorized by a state authority until they enter the black market. Therefore, it is argued that transparency in and controls of the legal arms trade must be improved in order to effectively address illicit trafficking. Countries reluctant to adopt such a broad mandate include UN Security Council members China and Russia (Bauer 2001a). A narrow interpretation would focus on enforcement of laws and government decisions, not on the broader factors contributing to illicit trafficking and a comprehensive view of arms flows. Parallel instruments such as the 2001 UN Firearms Protocol, which entered into force in 2005 and supplements the Transnational Crime Convention (UN General Assembly 2001), show how broad the range of issues and policy areas discussed within the arms control umbrella has become since the end of the Cold War. Addressing issues such as civilian possession and deliveries to non-state actors within the PoA has encountered fierce resistance from the US delegation due to the influence of the domestic pro-gun lobby, and insistence that the USA should be free to deliver to rebel groups (Bauer 2001b). The broader issue of how to regulate the legal trade has since been taken up in a separate, complementary ATT process.

Initiatives to negotiate an international arms trade treaty were formally taken up in the UN framework in 2006. The General Assembly adopted a resolution which requested that Member States submit their views on the 'feasibility, scope and draft parameters for a comprehensive, legally binding instrument establishing common international standards for the import, export and transfer of conventional arms', and mandated the Secretary-General to establish a Group of Governmental Experts (GGE) to examine these same issues (UN General Assembly 2006). After three sessions, in August 2008 the GGE proposed further discussion of issues arising from their deliberations within the UN framework (UN General Assembly 2008a). In October 2008 the General Assembly established a process to take forward these discussions through a series of meetings scheduled for 2009, and an open-ended working group (OEWG) took up its work in March 2009 (UN General Assembly 2008b). The statements made at the OEWG illustrate the broad gulf that still exists within the P5 and beyond.

It remains to be seen what the concrete results of the ATT process will be. While it should not be overloaded with expectations, this process for the first time creates an international forum specifically dedicated to the global arms trade. Within this come many fundamental issues related to specific interpretations of legitimate self-defence and questions of sovereignty and legitimate state authority. It should be kept in mind, though, that some international norms on arms transfers already exist: not only generic international treaty provisions, but specific UN arms embargoes. In a 2008 report, SIPRI and Uppsala University present a comprehensive analysis of the 27 UN arms embargoes that have been imposed since 1990 and assess their impact on arms flows to their targets or improving target behaviour (Fruchart et al. 2007). They conclude that the impact depends on the goal of the embargo: countering threats against global security, strengthening legitimate government authority, or achieving the peaceful political settlement of a violent armed conflict through conflict management. The analysis also distinguishes between impacts during three phases: threats to impose an embargo (and their credibility), implementation and post-embargo. The main finding is that 'the effectiveness of UN arms embargoes depends primarily on the capacity and will of UN member states, particularly the UNSC P5 states, arms-supplying states, transit and transhipment states, and states neighbouring embargoed targets' (Fruchart et al. 2007, 51). This highlights the importance of national transfer controls to give teeth to international norms.

Trends and developments in post-Cold War transfer controls

Arms transfer control constitutes a key element of arms control. It aims to control movements of both newly produced and surplus weapons and their components, but does not address existing stocks or their destruction. Transfer control is a preventive instrument that can help to reduce security threats posed by armed conflict and terrorist access to arms. It is also linked to the broader international agenda and efforts to prevent violations of human rights and humanitarian law, and to maximize development prospects. At the same time, though rarely discussed in political forums, arms control and technology access is also a function of power politics. The increase in arms producers has changed these dynamics somewhat.

Governments are motivated by a number of considerations to put transfer controls in place. First and foremost, they are an essential element of national and international security. Export controls are also required to be in compliance with commitments and obligations under international law as well as regional commitments such as the OSCE criteria for arms transfers (OSCE 1996). Functioning national export controls are not only a formal requirement for EU membership and the participation in international export control regimes, but are mandated by UN Security Council Resolution 1540 of May 2004 (UNSRC 1540).

UNSCR 1540 was adopted unanimously under Chapter VII of the UN Charter and is, then, binding on Member States. With regard to 'related materials' defined as 'materials, equipment and technology covered by relevant multilateral treaties and arrangements, or included on national control lists, which could be used for the design, development, production or use of nuclear, chemical and biological weapons and their means of delivery', 1540 obliges UN members to: 'establish, develop, review and maintain appropriate effective national export and trans-shipment controls over such items, including appropriate laws and regulations to control export, transit, trans-shipment and re-export and controls on providing funds and services related to such export and trans-shipment such as financing, and transporting that would contribute to proliferation, as well as establishing end-user controls; and establishing and enforcing appropriate criminal or civil penalties for violations of such export control laws and regulations'. This also has implications for conventional arms: while policies related to conventional weapons and WMD are distinct areas, there are many overlaps and connections – regarding the ministries/authorities and individual officials in charge, because export controls for military and dual-use items are often included in one piece of legislation, and last but not least because conventional dual-use items link the two areas legally, politically and technically.

Governments are also compelled to put transfer controls in place due to a self-interest to receive advanced technology. A country may limit its own ability to receive weapons if it is not considered able to control the end-use and prevent unauthorized re-export. In fact, the risk of diversion or undesirable re-export constitutes Criterion 7 of the EU Code of Conduct on Arms Exports. US extraterritorial re-export controls also function as a deterrent. Finally the image of the supplier country suffers with illicit trafficking, export scandals and transfers to controversial destinations.

Transfer control has undergone a major transformation in the post-Cold War period – with additional changes following the terrorist attacks of 11 September 2001, in particular the increased focus on non-state actors and terrorist threats. The Cold War rationale of transfer control was technology denial to the opposite bloc. This key function of export control was reflected in COCOM, the Coordinating Committee on Multilateral Export Controls, which sought to deny the Warsaw Pact access to Western technology. Hence, the first major shift after the Cold War was the move from a bloc-oriented to a more inclusive and co-operative approach reflected in the transformation of COCOM into the Wassenaar Arrangement in 1995, which includes many former Warsaw Pact countries.

With the exception of embargoes, (Western) governments now usually assess exports to all destinations on a case-by-case basis against agreed guidelines as opposed to ideological criteria. Economic considerations play a larger role in shaping export control policies. At the same time, a number of factors were pushing governments to consider more restrictive arms export policies: export control loopholes were illustrated in the 1991 Gulf War, which showed the 'boomerang effect' (i.e. armed forces in peace-keeping missions, for example, having to fight against weapons supplied by their own government), and by various export scandals and controversies – also relating to the use of weapons produced under licences granted in the past. The UN General Assembly, the P5 and regional organizations each agreed sets of guidelines for arms transfers in the early 1990s (Goldblat 2002, 241–6).

The second major shift is from a territorial focus to an end-use focus, i.e. the destination country is no longer the primary consideration, but the recipient within the destination country, considering *inter alia* risks of re-export and diversion to other end-users or end-uses. Determining the real end-use has arguably become the most difficult task of export licensing and enforcement officers.

This also includes a shift from a focus on state actors to a focus on non-state actors, especially terrorists, which is the background for UNSRC 1540. Counter-proliferation, counter-terrorism and export controls could overlap insofar as they seek to prevent the access of non-state actors to weapons and explosives. This second shift reflects broader developments, notably the increase in intra-state conflicts and increased terrorism concerns. This is also reflected in the type of weapons subject to particular scrutiny, such as MANPADS (Wassenaar Arrangement 2007a; OSCE 2008), or the modalities of the transfers, for example regarding air transport (Wassenaar Arrangement 2007b).

A third trend is the increased complexity regarding the type of items controlled, the reason for the controls and the type of activities subject to state control – export, import, transport, transit/trans-shipment, brokering, financing, etc. In principle, goods and technologies subject to control include those that were specially designed, developed or adapted for military use, and dual-use items which have both civil and military applications. Technological developments have increased the importance of dual-use items for military capacities (such as equipment and technology required for command, control, communication and reconnaissance (C3R). Another challenge are technology transfers, including in intangible form (through software up/downloads, e-mail, etc.) and technical assistance (e.g. the movement of technical experts, with or without laptops). These trends have been reinforced by globalization and companies operating world-wide. A large proportion of transfers today are intra-company, and international companies have transferred research facilities abroad. Also, unlisted items can be subject to control, the so-called catch-all for certain end-uses: for the conventional area, this can apply to items to be used in connection with listed item in embargoed destinations, or in connection with items that were illegally exported. This means that items become subject to control not because they are explicitly listed in a law or regulation, but if they are or may be intended for a certain end-use(r). Brokering and trans-shipment to hide diversion routes undermine efforts to identify the true end-user. The challenge of unlisted items reflects the second trend identified above.

As a fourth trend, one can identify the loosening of certain controls in trusted communities, possibly while strengthening other controls. More tailored controls seek to facilitate trade and economically and technologically competitive arms production, while minimizing the risk that military items are transferred to unauthorized recipients. This also involves placing more responsibility on companies.

These overall developments have reduced the control function of physical borders and increased the importance of long-term, preventive measures such as international co-operation and awareness-raising with industry. The post-Cold War period has seen the emergence of outreach, co-operation and assistance programmes. These have focused mostly on dual-use items that are relevant to WMD programmes, but to a lesser extent, and increasingly so, include a component addressing conventional arms. Part of the reason is that effective export controls in the conventional area have been more common and tend to be more a question of political will and policy than of technical capacity and know-how, while the opposite tends to be the case for dual-use export controls. There has also been a stronger emphasis on WMD concerns in export control assistance programmes, while until recently, small arms assistance programmes have focused more on combating illicit trafficking and stockpile destructions than on licensing procedures and export criteria. This is changing slowly with recent outreach efforts linked to the EU Code of Conduct on Arms Exports and the ATT.

The biggest donor in export control capacity building has been the USA with their Export Control and Related Border Security (EXBS) programme, which has about US$40m. per year at its disposal. The EU, which began allocating systematic funding for export control assistance in the dual-use area in 2004, in 2008 added a first (and still rather limited) conventional arms component of export control co-operation activities with non-EU countries. It is focused on EU Code outreach to candidate, accession and European Neighbourhood Policy countries and the ATT Joint Action (EU Council 2008a, 2009). Both EU initiatives constitute vehicles for co-operation and dialogue on export control issues if they are developed into structures and opportunities for co-operation and exchange rather than limited to one-off events.

Transfer control processes outside the UN framework

International export control regimes

The international export control regimes are broader than regional processes but are not, and are not intended to be, global. Rather, they constitute agreements among key suppliers, and have been accused of exclusivity. However, they increasingly play a role of setting standards for effective export control systems which since 2004 are required by the UN Security Council. They also conduct technical work from which smaller countries in particular benefit, for example establishing and updating control lists (though these can by definition never be purely technical decisions, as their definition and interpretation involve subjective and political elements). The regimes' standard setting function was reinforced by the inclusion of regime control lists in the restriction measures against the Democratic People's Republic of Korea (North Korea) (UNSRC 1718 of 2006) and against Iran (UNSRC 1737 of 2006), which make them globally applicable (Anthony and Bauer 2007).

A comprehensive control list for conventional arms and dual-use items was developed by the Wassenaar Arrangement.[1] The decision to establish this regime was taken by 33 states in

December 1995 at a meeting in Wassenaar, the Netherlands. The objective of the Arrangement is to promote transparency, exchange of information and exchange of views on transfers of an agreed range of items with a view to promoting responsibility in transfers of conventional arms and dual-use goods and technologies and to preventing 'destabilizing accumulations' of such items. The Arrangement was enlarged for the first time since its establishment with the 2004 admission of Slovenia. Six more countries were admitted to the Arrangement in 2005 (Croatia, Estonia, Latvia, Lithuania, Malta and South Africa, the latter expanding membership to the African continent for the first time). In addition to agreeing the control lists and exchanging information, participating states have also developed a number of documents and guidelines for specific policy, licensing and enforcement issues within export control (www.wassenaar.org).

Regional transfer control agreements: the EU approach

The EU has developed a unique approach to balancing trade facilitation and trade controls, which seeks to combine the principle of free movement of goods within the EU with security interests and other foreign policy considerations such as human rights and conflict prevention. An added complexity and distinct feature is the pillar system, which maintains competency on military and security issues within the EU Member States, while the Community regulates on a range of issues which include trade controls for dual-use items. These regulations are implemented by national governments.

Major changes regarding transfer controls of military equipment were prepared in 2008. At the end of 2008, agreement was reached between the European institutions to facilitate intra-Community defence transfers. The directive is expected to be published in the Official Journal in mid-2009, and thus enter into force. This is part of a package of measures that the European Commission proposed in December 2007 to support the development of a stronger and more competitive European defence industry, including proposals to reduce obstacles to cross-border trade in defence-related products within the EU (European Commission 2007b). (In contrast to the situation regarding dual-use goods, where a common primary legislation governs exports of listed items from the EU, each EU Member State to date uses national legislation to control exports of military items.) These proposals are not new, but go back to similar initiatives a decade earlier. At the time, the political framework and institutional set-up was not ripe for these to materialize. Instead, trade facilitation measures designed to support armaments co-operation were discussed in the so-called Letter of Intent (LOI) process, which only involved the EU's six biggest arms producers, and resulted in the Framework Agreement 'Concerning Measures to Facilitate the Restructuring and Operation of the European Defence Industry', which was signed in July 2000 and entered into force in 2001 after two countries ratified it (Bauer and Winks 2001). Many LOI elements were taken up in the new directive, which applies to all 27 Member States. Once in force, the directive will make individual licensing for exports of arms and components within the EU the exception (European Parliament 2008).

Already in 1998 the EU adopted a Code of Conduct on Arms Exports as a political agreement designed to set common standards across the EU for the export of military equipment (EU Council 1998). Under the Code, Member States have agreed to apply the following criteria to assess applications for licences for the export of military equipment:

- Respect for international commitment
- Respect for human rights (and international humanitarian law, added formally in 2008)
- Internal situation in recipient country
- Preservation of regional peace, security and stability
- National security of Member States and friendly and allied countries
- Behaviour of recipient *vis-à-vis* international community (including attitude to terrorism and respect for international law)

- Risk of diversion or undesirable re-export
- Recipient's economic and technical capacity

The eight criteria correspond to those agreed by the then 12 European Community members in 1991–92, but are each elaborated by means of several subcriteria. The Code's operative provisions outline reporting procedures as well as intergovernmental denial notification and consultation mechanisms in cases where governments hold different views when applying the EU criteria to a licence application. Governments are obliged to circulate detailed information on export denials to other EU Member States, including the reason for the refusal. If another Member State intends to grant an export licence for an 'essentially identical transaction', it must first consult the EU Member State(s) that previously denied such an export to explain the reasoning for its intention to grant a licence. The consulting government may still grant the licence, but must inform the consulted government(s) of the 'undercut' and explain its decision.

The Code's adoption should be seen against the background of an industrial restructuring process that internationalized arms production. In addition, changes in the international environment, particularly the end of the Cold War, were crucial for the emergence of European approaches to export controls. A key factor in reaching agreement on the EU Code of Conduct was that stronger competition, in the face of shrinking domestic and export markets, had increased the possibility of undercuts. At the same time, a number of factors were pushing governments to consider more restrictive arms export policies. Armed conflicts during the 1990s brought home how arms exports could have a negative impact on regional stability and security and might be used against the armed forces of the supplier states or their allies.

Since adoption, the Code has been transformed from a Council Declaration containing political commitments into a policy co-ordination tool far beyond its original scope. The development of what could be called a Code regime has been achieved through a process of dialogue, negotiation and review based on practical experience, as Member States have increasingly felt comfortable discussing arms export policy in the EU context and have gained more confidence in the Code as a policy tool. Information exchange, consultation and reporting procedures have become part of licensing officials' day-to-day routine. EU government officials meet regularly as the Council's Working Group on Arms Exports (COARM) to harmonize the Code's application and to narrow the scope for interpretation of the criteria and operative provisions.

EU governments have agreed a number of additional documents in the context of the EU Code. The 2003 Common Position on the control of arms brokering (EU Council 2003) contains a series of measures to be implemented at the national level. A Users' Guide to the EU Code further defines and interprets the terms and procedures of the original Code document (EU Council 2008c).

One of the main tools for assessing how states interpret and apply the EU Code is an annual report on the Code's implementation. The European Parliament has annually published a parliamentary report in response to the Council report. The Council's annual reports have become more comprehensive over the years. They contain an overview of COARM discussions, decisions and future priorities. The statistical annex has been expanded from one page to almost 400 pages, mainly because data are broken down by recipient country and category of military equipment, but also because of EU enlargement.

In December 2008 EU Member States transformed the 1998 EU Code of Conduct on Arms Exports from a Council Declaration into a Common Position (EU Council 2008b). This gives the agreement legal status and obliges governments to implement it nationally. The title of the document was also changed. It now defines Common Rules Governing Control of Exports of Military Technology and Equipment. The document broadens the scope of transactions covered by the agreement to include brokering, and makes a number of other amendments that strengthen the original agreement. The Common Rules apply to export licence applications for licences for physical exports, including those for licensed production in third countries, for brokering licences, for transit or trans-shipment licences, and for any intangible transfers of software and technology, where those exist in national export control systems.

In their analysis of the impact of the EU Code regime on actual exports, Bromley and Brzoska (2008) conclude that it has indeed had an effect on major conventional weapons exports from the EU, but limited to the human rights and armed conflict criteria. Also, while it has resulted in greater restrictiveness in terms of a reduction of exports to strong norm violators, they found little evidence of a harmonization of EU export decisions as a result of the EU Code. This question of harmonization is an issue that will need both further analysis and addressing at policy level, in particular against the background of the new directive on intra-Community transfers. The directive will require a number of legal adjustments of the national export control laws governing the export of military equipment. It will also create new enforcements demands for national authorities, as they will be required to enforce the licensing decisions and accompanying re-transfer conditions of another EU Member State, i.e. to prevent, detect, investigate and possibly prosecute any violations.

Conclusions

The end of the Cold War changed the dynamics, parameters, forms and key players of arms control efforts. First, the scope of issues, types of arms and choice of instruments within the arms control umbrella has widened considerably. Players have also diversified, not only with the shift from the superpowers being the key to arms control to a wide and global range of essential state actors, but the increased involvement of NGOs in promoting and shaping arms control and the need to focus also on non-state actors as addresses of arms control measures. Second, regional initiatives emerged for both transfers and classic arms limitation that are far advanced, notably in Europe. Third, transfer controls became a major area of success, which was a no-go during the Cold War. However, regional processes have advanced far beyond global ones. Fourth, there was real progress on prohibiting certain types of weapons on humanitarian grounds in international processes. The successful ban of anti-personnel landmines and the very recent agreement on the ban of cluster munitions have been milestones. This leads to the fifth point, the question of where these international processes take place – outside the UN or within the UN? This typically involves a trade-off: key countries are left out, but real progress is achieved, and there is always the hope that political pressure will turn them around. Finally, while WMD were the main focus of the Cold War, since then conventional arms have taken up more and more space on the international political agenda, in particular small arms. However, in recent years the WMD agenda has resurfaced, and the political and security agenda has been dominated by proliferation concerns and the prospect of a nuclear Iran. Verification is a key issue, although in trusted communities this is not the case. The key issue to success of the EU Code of Conduct is that it was placed in a sufficiently strong institutional, legal and political context. To end on a positive note, then, the outcome of the US elections have given rise to hopes that the US negotiating position, which has blocked or slowed down progress in a number of arms control processes, will change.

Note

1 Other international export control regimes are not directly relevant to this volume, which focuses on conventional arms. For further information on the Australia Group, the Nuclear Suppliers Group and the Missile Technology Control Regime, which deal with items that have applications for chemical, biological and nuclear weapons and carriers, see the websites of these regimes and the annual overviews of developments in the regimes documented in the SIPRI Yearbooks *Armaments, Disarmament and International Security*.

Bibliography

Anthony, Ian, 'Reflections on Continuity and Change in Arms Control', *SIPRI Yearbook 2006*, Oxford, Oxford University Press, 2006

Anthony, Ian and Sibylle Bauer, 'Controls on Security-Related International Transfers', *SIPRI Yearbook 2007*, Oxford, Oxford University Press, 2007

Bauer, Sibylle, 'EU Pushing for Firm Commitments at UN Small Arms Conference', *European Security Review*, No. 4, March 2001a, www.isis-europe.org/index.php?page=esr

——'EU Small Arms Policy after the UN Conference', *European Security Review*, No. 8, October 2001b, www.isis-europe.org/index.php?page=esr

Bauer, Sibylle and Mark Bromley, *The European Union Code of Conduct on Arms Exports: Improving the Annual Report*, SIPRI Policy Paper No. 8, Stockholm, SIPRI, November 2004, www.sipri.org

Bauer, Sibylle and Rachel Winks, 'The Institutional Framework for European Arms Policy Co-operation', in Claude Serfati et al., eds, *The Restructuring of the European Defence Industry — Dynamics of Change*, European Commission, Directorate General for Research / Office of Official Publications of the European Union, Luxembourg, 2001

Biting the Bullet, *Implementing the Programme of Action 2003*, 2003, www.saferworld.org.uk/publications.php/121/implementing_the_programme_of_action_2003

——*Reviewing Action on Small Arms 2006. Assessing the First Five Years of the Programme of Action*, 2006, www.iansa.org/un/review2006/redbook2006/index.htm

Bromley, Mark and Michael Brzoska, 'Towards a Common, Restrictive EU Arms Export Policy? The Impact of the EU Code of Conduct on Major Conventional Arms Exports', *European Foreign Affairs Review*, Vol. 13, No. 13, 2008

EU Council, 'Council Common Position on the Control of Arms Brokering', *Official Journal of the European Union*, no. L 156, 25 June 2003

——*EU Code of Conduct on Arms Exports*, 5 June 1998, www.consilium.europa.eu/uedocs/cmsUpload/08675r2en8.pdf

——Council Joint Action 2008/230/CFSP on 'Support for EU Activities in Order to Promote the Control of Arms Exports and the Principles and Criteria of the EU Code of Conduct on Arms Exports Among Third Countries', *Official Journal of the European Union*, no. L 75, 18 March 2008a

——'Council Common Position 2008/944/CFSP of 8 December 2008 Defining Common Rules Governing Control of Exports of Military Technology and Equipment', *Official Journal of the European Union*, no. L 335, 13 December 2008b

——'User's Guide to the European Union Code of Conduct on Arms Exports', Council doc. No. 7486/08, Brussels, 29 February 2008c, www.consilium.europa.eu

——'Council Decision 2009/42/CFSP of 19 January 2009 on Support for EU Activities in Order to Promote Among Third Countries the Process Leading Towards an Arms Trade Treaty, in the Framework of the European Security Strategy', *Official Journal of the European Union*, L17, 22 January 2009

European Commission, *Proposal for a Directive of the European Parliament and of the Council on Simplifying Terms and Conditions of Transfers of Defence-related Products Within the Community*, COM(2007) 765 final, Brussels, 5 December 2007a

——'Commission Proposes New Competitive Measures for Defence Industries and Markets', Press Release IP/07/1860, 5 December 2007b, europa.eu/rapid/pressReleasesAction.do?reference=IP/07/1860

European Parliament, Committee on the Internal Market and Consumer Protection, *Report on the Proposal for a Directive of the European Parliament and of the Council on Simplifying Terms and Conditions of Transfers of Defence-related Products Within the Community (COM(2007)0765 — C6-0468/2007 — 2007/0279(COD))*, European Parliament Session Document No. A6-0410/2008, 15 October 2008, www.europarl.europa.eu/oeil/FindByProcnum.do?lang=en&procnum=COD/2007/0279

Fruchart, Damien, Paul Holtom, Siemon Wezeman, Daniel Srandow and Peter Wallensteen (eds), *United Nations Arms Embargoes: Their Impact on Arms Flows and Target Behaviour*, Stockholm, SIPRI/Uppsala University, 2007, www.sipri.org

Goldblat, Jozef, *Arms Control: The New Guide to Negotiations and Agreements*, London, Sage / SIPRI and International Peace Research Institute Oslo (PRIO), 2002

Gray, Colin, *House of Cards. Why Arms Control Must Fail*, Ithaca, NY, 1992

Haug, Maria et al., *Shining a Light on Small Arms Exports: The Record of State Transparency*, Small Arms Survey Occasional Paper 4, Geneva and Oslo, Small Arms Survey and Norwegian Initiative on Small Arms Transfers, January 2002, www.nisat.org

Holtom, Paul, *Reporting Transfers of Small Arms and Light Weapons to the United Nations Register of Conventional Arms, 2007*, SIPRI Background Paper, Stockholm, February 2009

——'Combating the illicit trade in small and light weapons', *SIPRI Update: Global Security & Arms Control*, July–August 2008, www.sipri.org/contents/update/08/07/essay.html

Lachowski, Zdzislaw, 'Conventional Arms Control', *SIPRI Yearbook 2008*, Oxford, Oxford University Press, 2008

——*The CFE Treaty One Year After its Unilateral Suspension: a Forlorn Treaty*, SIPRI Policy Brief, January 2009

Lachowski, Zdzislaw and Svenja Post, 'Conventional Arms Control', *SIPRI Yearbook 2009*, Oxford, Oxford University Press, 2009 (forthcoming)

OSCE, 'Principles Governing Conventional Arms Transfers', *Programme for Immediate Action Series*, No. 3, DOC.FSC3/96, 1996, www.osce.org

——Forum for Security Cooperation Decision No. 5/08, 'Decision on Updating the OSCE Principles for Export Controls of Man-Portable Air Defence Systems', 26 May 2008, www.osce.org/fsc/documents.html

SIPRI, *SIPRI Yearbook*, Oxford, Oxford University Press, various annual editions

Trominov, Dmitri, 'Arms Control in Central Asia', in *Armament and Disarmament in the Caucasus and Central Asia*, SIPRI Policy Paper No. 3, 2003

UN General Assembly, *Transparency in Armament*, UN General Assembly Resolution A/RES/46/36L, 9 December 1991

——*Protocol Against the Illicit Manufacturing of and Trafficking in Firearms, Their Parts and Components and Ammunition, Supplementing the United Nations Convention Against Transnational Organized Crime*, UN General Assembly Resolution A/RES/55/255, 8 June 2001

——*Towards an Arms Trade Treaty: Establishing Common International Standards for the Import*, UN General Assembly Resolution A/RES/61/89, 18 December 2006

——*Report of the Group of Governmental Experts to Examine the Feasibility, Scope and Draft Parameters for a Comprehensive, Legally Binding Instrument Establishing Common International Standards for the Import, Export and Transfer of Conventional Arms*, UN General Assembly document A/63/334, 26 August 2008a

——*Towards an Arms Trade Treaty: Establishing Common International Standards for the Import, Export and Transfer of Conventional Arms*, UN General Assembly document A/C.1/63/L.39, 17 October 2008b

UN Secretary-General, *Report by the Secretary-General, Study on Ways and Means of Promoting Transparency in International Transfers of Conventional Arms*, UN document A/46/301, 9 September 1991

UNODA (UN Office for Diarmament Affairs), www.un.org/disarmament/convarms/SALW/Html/SALW-PoA-ISS_intro.shtml

Wassenaar Arrangement, 'Elements for Export Controls of Man-portable Air Defence Systems (MANPADS)', Vienna, December 2007a, www.wassenaar.org/publicdocuments/index.html

——'Best Practices to Prevent Destabilising Transfers of Small Arms and Light Weapons (SALW) Through Air Transport', Vienna, December 2007b, www.wassenaar.org/publicdocuments/index.html

Wulf, Herbert, 'United Nations Deliberations on the Arms Trade', in Ian Anthony, ed., *Arms Export Regulations*, Oxford, Oxford University Press/SIPRI, 1991

23 Insurgencies and the impact on arms procurement

Isaiah Wilson, III

These past 18-plus years have been testament to a tsunami of change in international defence and security affairs; nothing short of a revolutionary alteration of the *causus beli* and *modus operandi* of US intervention policy, and an equal number of tectonic disruptions and shifts in US strategic doctrinal thinking, the determination of core-essential-peripheral roles and missions, conduct of those missions, and the underpinning of US arms procurement and defence spending rationales.

The words of US Secretary of Defense Robert M. Gates express the change succinctly:

> Since September 2001, our Nation has been engaged in a multi-theater, long-term conflict against militant extremists who seek to erode the strength and will of the United States, our partners, and our allies through irregular and asymmetric means. As the Department of Defense continues to engage in ongoing operations, we must also prepare for our future challenges by learning from the past, building on the present, and taking advantage of opportunities to increase the effectiveness and efficiency of our institution.
>
> (Department of Defense 2009)

Preparing for our future challenges and the compound security dilemmas characterizing them is the penultimate test of national will and capacity, for today and the foreseeable future. The learning from the past, the building on the present, and the taking advantage of opportunities – and the crises born of and from the wake of the terrorist attacks of 11 September 2001, Afghanistan, and Iraq – has, frankly, been a painful and painstaking process. The growing pains of change continue within the US military services, across the interagency and intergovernmental and multinational communities. When it comes to the centre-stage challenge of insurgency and counter-insurgency perhaps the most painful and consequential of battles – the internal 'insurgency' raging within the US land forces (i.e. Army and Marine Corps) – becomes the debates and battles over the future of land campaigning for the purposes of war and peace in an era of protracted conflicts and how best to man, train, equip and employ the force.

This chapter will showcase some of the impacts and implications, twists and turns, of the events of 11 September 2001 and its progeny international internal conflicts (Afghanistan, Iraq, etc.) on US strategic doctrinal thinking, operational practices, and how insurgencies have altered the revolution in military affairs (RMA) debate and, as a consequence, has and will continue to shape and change future US arms procurement and defence spending.

Dawn of a new world (dis)-order

The first decade of this new post-11 September world order is already showing the limits of our past understanding of war, of peace, and of the limits of international (foreign) intervention in general. The strategic realities of the 21st century security environment defy all those factors that have, over the past two centuries, offered ends, ways and means of dividing our understanding of war from those of peace, as well as limiting our actions in each activity. In terms of our modern, 19th- and 20th-century notions of war, war could be – and was – defined as two kinds, unlimited (total) and limited, with both kinds equally limited to a particular conventional type of warfare prescribing to a very particular rule set for how warfare was to be conducted. This first decade of the new century shows a new array of challenges – and challengers – to this modern-age rule set.

Irregular threats, insurgency and questions in future force procurement

The recent past and, undeniably, the ongoing US interventions in Iraq and Afghanistan, vividly demonstrate(d) the consequences of failing to address adequately the dangers posed by insurgencies and failing states. The challenge sets are not a matter of the choosing, but more a collective of compounded threats. As Secretary of Defense Gates expressed in an article in *Foreign Affairs*:

> [T]errorist networks can find sanctuary within the borders of a weak nation and strength within the chaos of social breakdown. A nuclear-armed state could collapse into chaos and criminality. The most likely catastrophic threats to the US homeland – for example, that of a US city being poisoned or reduced to rubble by a terrorist attack – are more likely to emanate from failing states than from aggressor states.
>
> (Gates 2009)

Despite its characterization as an unconventional way of warfare, the challenge of insurgency is the age-old form of war; the ancient scourge and the present haunt of the international community in places like Iraq and Afghanistan.

The unique challenges of insurgency

> Insurgency and its tactics are as old as warfare itself. Joint doctrine defines an insurgency as an organized movement aimed at the overthrow of a constituted government through the use of subversion and armed conflict. Counterinsurgency is those political, economic, military, paramilitary, psychological, and civic actions taken by a government to defeat an insurgency.
>
> (Department of Defense 2001)

Since the end of the Cold War, although the aggregate number of interstate wars have declined, intrastate conflicts have both increased and internationalized, drawing US military forces into the burgeoning field of international humanitarian intervention (Dobbins et al. 2003). The most likely conflicts of the next 50 years or more will be wars of insurgency bringing with them irregular warfare tactics and techniques all within an expansive 'arc of instability' that currently encompasses much of the greater Middle East, parts of Africa, and Central and South Asia. Iraq is one node in this wider global insurgency, albeit now a centrally important one. To wage warfare to a sustainable win in these kinds of wars demands more than a military approach and more than a martial solution for – and definition of – 'victory'.

A counterinsurgency way of intervention – one that focuses on closing with those to be governed (the local populations) in ways that restore trust and confidence in those populations and rebuilds legitimacy between the government and the governed rather than merely on 'close-with-to-destroy' tactics and techniques – is the key to success. Final victory in these kinds of interventions lies in the legitimacy of ideas that are brought to a negotiation, more so than the material power that can be brought to bear to a fight by a government-in-residence, a foreign nation, or community of foreign nations taking part in the intervention.

Thinking anew to act anew: the force modernization debate

In a campaign speech at The Citadel, South Carolina on 23 September 1999, then Governor George W. Bush articulated a clear understanding of the evolving strategic environment, America's pre-eminence in technology and the role of the military. With regard to the strategic environment and revolution in technologies, he stated:

> We see the contagious spread of missile technology and weapons of mass destruction. We know that this era of car bombers and plutonium merchants and cyber terrorists and drug cartels and unbalanced dictators – all the unconventional and invisible threats of new technologies and old hatreds. These challenges can be overcome, but they cannot be ignored.
> (George W. Bush, speech 'A Period of Consequence', 1999)

The role of the military, in his words, was 'to deter wars – and win wars when deterrence fails', not to 'be permanent peacekeepers, dividing warring parties. This is not our strength or our calling' (G. W. Bush 1999).

In the aftermath of the events of 11 September, the Bush Administration was confronted with the very environment that the then Governor Bush had enunciated in his speech to The Citadel. The wars in Afghanistan and Iraq would soon unfold the strategic realities of fighting non-state actors and insurgencies. In each case, the Administration and the military had underestimated the follow-on phases of warfare that include stabilization and enabling civil authority, each of which often require confronting an insurgency. The preparation for both wars had focused largely on the military instrument of power and the technological capabilities that the military had developed over the course of 25 or more years; high-tech, machine-based warfare enabling the USA to execute rapid high-tech operations through technologically enabled shock-and-awe practices. What is all too painfully well known now, and confusingly opaque at that time, was just how 'indecisive' this RMA-driven and military-dominant approach to these 'New Wars' (Kaldor 2006) of the 21st century would prove to be. Neither the Administration nor the US military had a comprehensive understanding, strategy or doctrine to provide a framework for establishing the conditions for stable democratic governance after the initial kinetic operations had toppled hostile regimes, in both Afghanistan and Iraq. Operations were conducted with an over-reliance on technological capabilities, not to mention poor assumptions regarding what at that time was referred to as the post-conflict hostilities phases of the war (Phase-IV a) – what was, more accurately, the hydra-headed Iraqi insurgency.

Fighting to change, changing to fight

A popular and seminal debate has raged among military scholars and practitioners for at least the past 20 years; it is a discussion that continues to this day: are we experiencing a period of revolutionary change in geostrategic relations, a change that has brought about an RMA? The fact that we are even having the wide debate over the RMA is testament to at least a growing perception of a gap between war as we have known it and practised it in the 'past' and an older, pre-modern conception of war as reintroduced to us, particularly since 11 September 2001. For the purposes of this book, whether this tectonic rumble meets the prerequisites of a *bona fide* RMA is irrelevant. What counts is that the debate validates and legitimizes the notion that some sort of change is upon us, negatively impacting our war-waging and peace-winning effectiveness.

The revolution in military affairs

Today, most defence analysts agree: the Pentagon is in serious need of reform. Major acquisition programmes now have the largest cost overruns since the Government Accountability Office (GAO) started to record them. Today, the US defence budget is higher than at any point since the end of the Second World War, yet the size of the combat formations of the Army, Navy and Air Force are the smallest since 1946. Beyond the exponentially rising costs of modern defence acquisition and procurement – higher costs, or wages, that yield fewer and fewer defence 'wares' – lies the equally concerning forced modernization question of whether what we are buying is actually, and fully, what is needed to effectively deal with the challenges facing the country in the 21st century.

In his book *Breaking the Phalanx: A New Design for Landpower in the 21st Century*, Douglas MacGregor proposed a new design and operating concept for use of American military landpower and in so doing proposed the importance for a state-society to take proactive command and control over the forces of technological change in order to ensure an organizational and operationally effective (right and proper) array of forces available and way of warfare. The book's dust-jacket description summarizes the contribution of the work this way:

> Central to the proposal is the simple thesis that the US Army must take control of its future by exploiting the emerging revolution in military affairs. [A]nd while ground forces must be equipped with the newest Institute weapons, new technology will not fulfill its promise of shaping the battlefield to American advantage if new devices are merely grafted on to old organizations that are not specifically designed to exploit them. It is not enough to rely on the infusion of new, expensive technology into the American defense establishment to preserve America's strategic dominance in the next century. The work makes it clear that planes, ships, and missiles cannot do the job of defending America's global security issues alone. The United States must opt for reform and reorganization of the nation's ground forces and avoid repeating Britain's historic mistake of always fielding an effective army just in time to avoid defeat, but too late to deter an aggressor.
>
> (Douglas MacGregor, 1997)

Some have argued convincingly that the USA has a historical propensity for getting the calculus of change and continuity wrong (America's 'First Battles' phenomenon). The present, like the past, is a time of both continuity and change and must be understood as such. The military theorist and historian A. T. Mahan described the relationship between continuity and change: 'While many of the conditions of war vary from age to age with the progress of weapons, there are certain teachings in the school of history which remain constant ... [I]t is wise to observe things that are alike, it is also wise to look for things that differ' (Wilson 2007, 213).

So it is in the school of war. Distinguishing between true and justified rationales for affecting change in a society's military affairs from 'false labours' and determining in this fashion what demands adaptation and what things remain constant and deserve preservation are perhaps the key determinants in the success or failure of any military transformation. This is also the case for the war in Iraq.

The RMA approach takes a holistic approach in the study of modern warfare and military innovation, accounting for more than mere technological advancements in the tactics, techniques and procedures of war (battles and engagements). This holistic approach rightly accounts for (considers) the geopolitical, geo-economic, societal, operational and strategic factors that contribute critical pieces to the puzzle of modern warfare.

Modern RMA theorists seem to agree on the following definition offered by Andrew Krepinevich: '[RMA] occurs when applications of new technologies into a significant number of military systems combines with innovative operational concepts and organizational adaptation in a way that fundamentally alters the character of conflict. It does so by an order of magnitude or greater – in the combat potential and military effectiveness of armed forces' (Wilson 2007, 221).

The origins of modern armies drew upon larger, non-military developments in European societies. The following Michael Howard quotation succinctly describes this 17th- and

18th-century 'RMA' reinforcing the arguments made by Krepinevich, which emphasized the criticality of integrating new capabilities into new operational concepts and organizations:

> The growing capacity of European governments to control, or at least tap, the wealth of the community, and from it to create the mechanisms – bureaucracies, fiscal systems, armed forces – which enable them yet further to extend their control over the community, is one of the central developments in the historical era which, opening in the latter part of the seventeenth century, has continued to our time. In the eighteenth century, this process was to gather increasing momentum, but until then it was a very halting affair. Its progress can be traced as clearly as anywhere else in the gradual acquisition of state control over the means of making war – over that violent element in European society which ... had in the early seventeenth century virtually escaped from control and was feeding itself, so that the historian has to speak not so much of 'war', or 'wars' as of ... a melee.
>
> (Wilson 2007, 222)

Michael Howard's recipe for the makings of an RMA emphasized the importance of capturing the change within the state's controls over the means of making war, so as to avoid the degradation of warfare into violent chaotic melees of limited or no directed and controllable purposes – melee for the sake of melee.

The question of the day – our times – is whether or not the current debate within the US military over force modernization and procurements is on a path that will take the nation and its fighting forces where they need to go and how they need to go.

The case of Iraq

Returning to the case of Iraq, by late summer 2003 the US military had awoken to an insurgency. As one early voice on the faulty operational planning underpinning the war campaign stated, 'while the US military had its eyes and attention turned toward the Iraqi ports (for redeployment state-side), a growing insurgency had its eyes and attention already focused on the Iraqi people' (Packer 2003). In large part a result of over three decades of focus on conventional kinetic warfare, from the first post-Viet Nam version of Army Field Manual (FM) 100–105 in 1976, the US Army would attempt to quell the rising violence in Iraq through direct lethal combat operations (an 'anti-insurgency' approach). Indeed, in preparation for their deployment to Iraq, Army units continued to train on traditional machine-warfare tasks. To bring the point even more bluntly to light, in an interview conducted with the *New York Times* and *Washington Post*, then Major-General William Wallace, the V Corps commander leading coalition forces during the rapid march up country phases of OIF-1, stated that: '[T]he enemy we're fighting is a bit different than the one we war-gamed against, because of these paramilitary forces. We knew they were here, but we did not know how they would fight' (*Washington Post*, 27 March 2003).

In spite of clearly recognizing this dawn of a major shift (revolution?) in the military affairs of the war in Iraq, as late of 2006 the Quadrennial Defense Review (QDR) found that units continued to focus on cordoning off areas and conducting search-and-destroy operations.

Finally, after three-and-a-half years of battling the insurgency, in both Iraq and Afghanistan, and amid growing public disillusionment with the wars efforts, the US Army and US Marine Corps combined efforts in developing a new and comprehensive doctrine that would adopt the less-kinetic, British model of fighting an insurgency – a population-centric approach ... the *modus operandi* of classic counterinsurgency.[1]

In December 2005, then Lieutenant-General David Petreaus gathered a group of experienced Army and Marine Corps veterans of Afghanistan and Iraq to begin the new counterinsurgency doctrine. The resulting manual, FM 3–24/FMFM 3–24, offers the following as preamble for its offerings of a new, 'older' approach to fighting – and winning – against wars of insurgency.

> This manual is designed to fill a doctrinal gap. It has been 20 years since the US Army published a manual devoted to counterinsurgency operations, and 25 since the Marine Corps published its last such manual. With our Soldiers and Marines fighting insurgents in both Afghanistan and Iraq, it is thus essential that we give them a manual that provides principles and guidelines for counterinsurgency operations (COIN). Such guidance must be grounded in historical studies. However, it also must be informed by contemporary experiences.
>
> (Petreaus and Mattis 2006, 1)

Considering new roles and missions

In 2006 the US Department of Defense (DoD) in its latest National Military Strategy (NMS) identified four categories of threat that now define how the USA perceives the security dilemmas of the 21st century – threats that seek to erode, paralyze, marginalize and, in general, challenge US power and hegemony: traditional threats; irregular threats; disruptive threats; catastrophic threats.

The ongoing conflicts in Iraq and Afghanistan appear to be the bell-weathers of a peculiar era of persistent conflict marked by irregular threats posed by the asymmetrical tactics, techniques and practices of both traditional states, non-state actors and state-non-state consortia.

When thinking about the range of threats, it has become the common practice to imagine the range and buffet of security challenges as a spectrum, easily divisible between a 'high end' threat from the 'low end', – the conventional from the irregular, armoured divisions on one side, guerrillas toting AK-47s on the other (Gates 2009). The contemporary facts are undeniable, as the political scientist Colin Gray notes:

> [T]he categories of warfare are blurring and no longer fit into neat, tidy boxes. One can expect to see more tools and tactics of destruction – from the sophisticated to the simple – being employed simultaneously in hybrid and more complex forms of warfare.
>
> (Gates 2009)

The question at hand is whether these kinds of compound, irregular threats demand major adjustments in force procurement and, if so, to what degree and direction.

Overcoming the paradox of counterinsurgency

With more than 300 insurgencies fought since 1800, the current 'face' of battle in Iraq and Afghanistan is a familiar one. The puzzle dates back to the history of man, the state, and war (and peace), the implications of which were best captured and described centuries ago in the tale of King Pyrrhus and his leadership of the Hellenic city states in war against the Romans:

> The two armies separated; and we are told that Pyrrhus said to one who was congratulating him on his victory, 'If we are victorious in one more battle with the Romans, we shall be utterly ruined.' For he had lost a great part of the forces with which he came, and all his friends and generals except a few; moreover, he had no others whom he could summon from home, and he saw that his allies in Italy were becoming indifferent, while the army of the Romans, as if from a fountain gushing forth indoors, was easily and speedily filled up again, and they did not lose courage in defeat, nay, their wrath gave them all the more vigour and determination for the war.
>
> (Cf. the Demetrius, xxxvi.2–6, xxxvii)[2]

What explains the pyrrhic victory, this tendency of the stronger to lose to the weaker in wars of asymmetric ends, ways and means? This question is a crucial one, especially if defence and military experts are accurate in their projections of a next 50–100 years of these kinds of wars: wars of insurgency and counterinsurgency.

During the 19th century, states routinely defeated insurgent foes. Over the 20th century, though, this pattern reversed, with states increasingly less likely to defeat insurgents or avoid meeting at least some of their demands. In an effort to account for this pattern of outcomes in counterinsurgency wars, two defence and security studies scholars recently published their findings from a longitudinal comprehensive study of over 286 wars of insurgency taking place between 1800 and 2005 (Lyall and Wilson 2009). The study finds that higher levels of mechanization, along with external support for insurgents and the counterinsurgent's status as an occupier, are associated with an increased probability of state defeat.

The researchers go further, arguing that increasing mechanization within state militaries after the First World War was primarily responsible for this paradoxical shift.

> Unlike their nineteenth-century predecessors, modern militaries possess force structures that inhibit information collection among local populations. This not only complicates the process of sifting insurgents from noncombatants but increases the difficulty of selectively applying rewards and punishment among the fence-sitting population. Modern militaries may therefore inadvertently fuel, rather than deter, insurgencies.
>
> (Lyall and Wilson 2009, 1)

The implications are stark; the decisions and directions for future US procurement implied must be, and will be, determinative, even *revolutionary*. If, in fact, a hyper-prescription to a conventional, industrial, machine-based approach to warfare proves a key accelerant to war-loss as a counterinsurgent force, and the future shows more rather than fewer of these kinds of wars, then some degree of departure from the machinist approach is not only warranted, but perhaps essential to future success. Trade-offs of high-tech military-industrial complex main-stays such as heavy navy carriers, air force high-performance fighters, and even the US Army's Future Combat System (FCS) may be required for purchase of resources more appropriate to the counterinsurgent's warfare.

Of course, war is an organic thing; it has a life of its own, its own logic and always a vote. While the future may witness more wars of an irregular type – more insurgencies and war to counter them – this reality does not necessarily mean that there will be no more major theatre wars of a machine, high-tech type. As Secretary of Defense Gates acknowledges, the threat of conventional war is not ended, although the challenge to US convention, power and prowess may be more indirect:

> Other nations may be unwilling to challenge the United States fighter to fighter, ship to ship, tank to tank. But they are developing the disruptive means to blunt the impact of US power, narrow the USA's military options, and deny the US military freedom of movement and action. In the case of the People's Republic of China, Beijing's investments in cyberwarfare, antisatellite warfare, antiaircraft and antiship weaponry, submarines, and ballistic missiles could threaten the USA's primary means to project its power and help its allies in the Pacific: bases, air and sea assets, and the networks that support them. This will put a premium on the USA's ability to strike from over the horizon and employ missile defenses and will require shifts from short-range to longer-range systems, such as the next-generation bomber.
>
> (Gates 2009)

The traditional military industrial complex (MIC), in other words, need not tremble in expectation of a death of its future relevancy; on the contrary, the MIC may still yet prove more 'warranted' than ever before. That said, the machine way of war, preferred by the US military, and descriptive of the preferred 'American Way of War' (Weigley 1977) may need to make some major adjustments and accommodations and a foreboding counterinsurgency way of warfare. In spite of these projections and empirical facts that support them, the armed services – especially the land force communities (i.e. Army and Marine Corps) – are forming warring camps and drawing lines in the sand.

The battle within: the machinists versus the counterinsurgents

The 2008 National Defense Strategy is explicit in its assessment of the future global threat environment and the necessary directions of future US strategy and force development, concluding that although US predominance in conventional warfare is not unchallenged, it is sustainable for the medium term given current trends. In Secretary of Defense Gates's own words:

> It is true that the United States would be hard-pressed to fight a major conventional ground war elsewhere on short notice, but as I have asked before, where on earth would we do that? US air and sea forces have ample untapped striking power should the need arise to deter or punish aggression – whether on the Korean Peninsula, in the Persian Gulf, or across the Taiwan Strait. So although current strategy knowingly assumes some additional risk in this area, that risk is a prudent and manageable one.
>
> (Gates 2009)

Despite this recognition on the part of the Secretary of Defense of a changed and changing set of global security challenges that demand more investments in 'less-tech', manning, training and equipping for counterinsurgency operations and the like through trade-offs drawn from the high-tech, high end of the conflict spectrum, a debate – an inter-communal war – persists, and is building, between the US armed services and, perhaps more significantly, within the US land forces (the US Army more pointedly) over 'how' and 'with what' the Nation's armed forces will prepare themselves to fight and win America's wars and preferred 'peace.'

This intra-communal conflict is perhaps taking on its most stark, revealing and worrisome 'tribalism' within the US Army, the nation's principle land-campaigning service, over two interrelated arguments: whether the future logic of America's wars (interventions) will require more of an old-school grammar of machine-based, lethal/kinetic approaches (the major combat operations school of thought and practice), or demand a 'newer' (or much more ancient, depending on your point of view) grammar of a more indirect, hybridized, lower-tech / higher-ideational approach (the counterinsurgency school of thought and practice). The debate over the 'future' of the US Army's multi-year, multi-billion dollar high-tech system of systems, Future Combat System (FCS), provides the relevant real-world backdrop and a most revealing 'tale of the tape' between the contenders: the Machinists and the Counterinsurgents.

The US Army Future Combat System: programme origins and expectations

The FCS is a multi-year, multi-billion dollar programme at the heart of US Army force modernization. It is the Army's major research, development and acquisition programme, consisting of 14 manned and unmanned systems tied together by an extensive communications and information network. FCS is intended to replace such current systems as the M-1 Abrams tank and the M-2 Bradley infantry fighting vehicle.

In October 1999, then Chief of Staff of the Army (CSA) General Eric Shinseki introduced the Army's transformation strategy, which was intended to convert all of the Army's divisions (called Legacy Forces) into new organizations (called the Objective Force). General

Shinseki's intent was to make the Army lighter, more modular and – most importantly – more deployable.

General Shinseki's vision for the FCS was that it would consist of smaller and lighter ground and air vehicles – manned, unmanned and robotic – and would employ advanced offensive, defensive and communications/information systems to 'outsmart and outmanoeuvre heavier enemy forces on the battlefield' (Tiboni 2004).

FCS and counterinsurgency

For better or worse – by the looks of it, for worse – the future face of warfare and US armed intervention will be one of countering the complexities of insurgency. The need to prepare accordingly was articulated by Secretary of Defense Gates:

> As secretary of defense, I have repeatedly made the argument in favor of institutionalizing counterinsurgency skills and the ability to conduct stability and support operations. I have done so not because I fail to appreciate the importance of maintaining the USA's current advantage in conventional war fighting but rather because conventional and strategic force modernization programs are already strongly supported in the services, in Congress, and by the defense industry. The base budget for fiscal year 2009, for example, contains more than \$180 billion for procurement, research, and development, the overwhelming preponderance of which is for conventional systems.
>
> (Gates 2009)

The Army contends that the FCS is specifically designed for the 'Long War' and fighting insurgencies (Feickert 2007, 14). The US Army's experience in Iraq suggests that its strategy for making lightly armoured vehicles equally as survivable as the heavily armoured Abrams tank may not be feasible. To achieve comparable survivability, US combat vehicles would avoid being targeted by exploiting superior knowledge of enemy activities. Yet, the threat in Iraq has come primarily in urban settings from individually launched weapons, and the ability to identify attackers' locations may be beyond any technology now envisioned (CBO 2007, 8).

While most agree that the FCS network, as envisioned by the Army, should provide the Army with enhanced communications, intelligence and sensing capabilities, some argue that the Army is placing undue emphasis on theoretical FCS technological capabilities in making its case for FCS relevancy in counterinsurgency operations. Some suggest that effective counterinsurgency operations are characterized by cultural awareness, interpersonal relationships and security provided through human presence, and are less a function of superior technology and firepower.

Again, the earlier referenced Lyall and Wilson study not only questions the effectiveness of modern 'mechanized' militaries in waging a successful counterinsurgency campaigns, but moreover, that an over-prescription to an industrial approach to warfare – what the researchers call an 'industrial-age "lock-in"'– might in fact promote, if not actually accelerate, that industrial power's losing tendency as the counterinsurgent. The study maintains that modern mechanized forces are unsuitable for counterinsurgencies by design 'because their structures and associated tactics inhibit the construction of information networks among the local population' (Lyall and Wilson 2009, 72).

> Struggle to defeat insurgents because they rarely solve the "identification problem" – how to sort insurgents from the noncombatant population selectively. Built for direct combat, modern militaries are isolated from local populations by their technology and thus are "starved" of the information that would enable counterinsurgents to use their power selectively. As a result, these militaries often inadvertently swell insurgent ranks while dissuading

potential collaborators through the indiscriminate application of coercive and non-coercive power.

(Lyall and Wilson 2009, 75)

While certainly provocative, the questions and concerns this study and the larger body of scholarship it builds upon at a minimum demands a baldly honest consideration of the efficacy of high-tech approaches to US force modernization in the face of the core of the counter-insurgency dilemma: waging war in ways commensurate with and supportive of winning (and keeping) a legitimate, sustainable 'peace'.

A list of significant first and second steps

The DoD is exploring interagency issues and problems associated with key national security challenges, including co-operative security, stability operations, irregular warfare, and homeland defence and civil support. While these activities are certainly core mission areas for the DoD, they require substantial military and civilian interaction. Building a cohesive, whole-of-government approach to the nation's enduring security challenges is the new policy goal, with a move toward a more effective balanced approach to strategy and operations the end state.

Again, as Secretary of Defense Robert Gates articulates:

> The defining principle of the Pentagon's new National Defense Strategy is balance. The United States cannot expect to eliminate national security risks through higher defense budgets, to do everything and buy everything. The Department of Defense must set priorities and consider inescapable tradeoffs and opportunity costs.

(Gates 2009)

The failure to take nation-building (or stability and reconstruction) phases of intervention as seriously as initial combat operations has had serious consequences for the USA, for US national security policy and strategy focused on enhancing international efforts to stabilize and rebuild nations after conflict, and consequently for the global community in general. Since 2004, the US Government has made deliberate efforts to reorganize US intervention capacity and capabilities, particularly within the Departments of Defense and State. One of the major efforts to accomplish 'winning the peace' has been a Defense-State collaborative effort to develop common tasks and objectives for stability and reconstruction operations (SRO). In 2004 the Office of the Coordinator for Reconstruction and Stabilization (S/CRS) was formed in the Department of State, with the mission to lead, co-ordinate, and institutionalize US Government civilian capacity 'to prevent or prepare for post-strife, so as to reach a sustainable path toward peace, democracy, and a market economy' (Department of State 2005). Within the DoD perhaps even more substantial efforts have been undertaken to improve upon the effectiveness of US Government efforts in intervention policy.

By December 2005, the DoD had adopted a new revised concept of phased operations (i.e. campaigning), which acknowledged the need for greater interface with other civilian authorities and agencies placing greater emphasis on the 'stabilize and enable civilian authority' phases of intervention (Department of Defense 2006). In February 2005 President George W. Bush issued an Executive Directive – NSPD-44 – to the DoD ordering all DoD armed services to improve their SRO capacity and capabilities to levels commensurate with their traditional prowess at major combat operations (MCO) (White House 2005). In response, the DoD developed and issued DoD Directive 3000.05 to provide directive guidance concerning military support for stability, security, transition and reconstruction (SSTR) operations. DoD Directive 3000.05 states that stability operations are a 'core U.S. military mission that the Department of Defense shall be prepared to conduct and support' (Department of Defense

2005, 2). The new US Counterinsurgency Manual, FM 3–24/FMFM 3–24, has made all of the effective painful lessons gathered from experimenting with counterinsurgency concepts and techniques in Iraq approved, if still not yet fully accepted doctrine.

In spite of these notable efforts to reform and reorganize ('transform') for more effective US intervention policy, the discovery of a new and more effective concept of and operational approach to the challenges of post-industrial intervention remains far beyond the horizon. Anaemic funding and resource allocations to US Government agencies other than the DoD has contributed to continued failures to correct the impotency of US intervention efforts – as witnessed in degrading situations in Afghanistan and Iraq. The DoD continues to take the lion's share of defence budget appropriations and other resource authorizations. As a consequence, US intervention policy remains largely the endeavour of military intervention – which, again is increasingly proving wanting and short-shrift as adequate treatment to the crisis challenges of the 21st century. With a defining truth of successful counterinsurgency being 'no military solutions, only political ones', this imbalance will undoubtedly curtail the nation's ability to secure viable and sustainable victories. This worrisome stage may already be set in the case of Afghanistan.

Conclusion: back to the future?

> The Pentagon has to do more than modernize its conventional forces; it must also focus on today's unconventional conflicts – and tomorrow's.
>
> (Gates 2009)

The USA, for better or for worse, has come to the conclusion that the ultimate problem of contemporary international affairs is the 'pathological weakness of states', and the instability and threat that can, and often does, emanate from failed, failing, or misgoverned states.

We now understand that more often than not, internal conflict persists long after a military intervention has been mounted. We can now also better appreciate the complexity that comes with these sorts of protracted interventions: for how long can the intervener intervene? For how long must the intervener be willing and capable of intervening? While premature exit only leads to a catastrophic loss of what was gained and, more often than not, leads to return visits to the original crisis zone, staying beyond local and regional welcome can lead to equally unsavoury outcomes.

These new realities bring new demands regarding why, where and for what purposes the USA will intervene abroad. Countering insurgencies will clearly be at the centre of that future purpose. How the USA prepares to contend with these new challenges – how they modernize the force – will prove determinative of the nation's future successes or failings in countering insurgency.

Notes

1 According to the 2006 counterinsurgency operations (COIN) Manual, 'a counterinsurgency campaign is, as described in this manual, a mix of offensive, defensive, and stability operations, conducted along multiple lines of operation. It requires Soldiers and Marines to employ a mix of both familiar combat tasks and skills more often associated with nonmilitary agencies, with the balance between them varying depending on the local situation. Conducting a successful counterinsurgency campaign thus requires a flexible, adaptive force led by agile, well-informed, culturally astute leaders'.

2 Also see Plutarch, Life of Pyrrhus, 21:8.

Bibliography

Alywin-Foster, Nigel, 'Changing the Army for Counterinsurgency Operations', *Military Review*, November–December 2005

Arreguin-Toft, Ivan, *How the Weak Win Wars*, Cambridge, Cambridge University Press, 2005

Atkinson, Rick, 'General: A War Likely; Logistics, Enemy Force Reevaluation', *Washington Post*, 27 March 2003

Bartels, Larry, 'Pooling Disparate Observations', *American Journal of Political Science*, 40 (3), 1996

Beckett, Ian, *Modern Insurgencies and Counter-Insurgencies: Guerillas and their Opponents Since 1750*, London and New York, Routledge, 2001

Bert, Wayne, *The Reluctant Superpower: United States Policy in Bosnia, 1991–95*, New York, St Martin's Press, 1997

Betts, Richard, *Surprise Attack*, Washington, Brookings Institution, 1981

Biddle, Stephen, *Military Power: Explaining Victory and Defeat in Modern Battle*, Princeton, Princeton University Press, 2004

Blaufarb, Douglas, *The Counterinsurgency Era: U.S. Doctrine and Performance, 1950 to the Present*, New York, The Free Press, 1977

Bobbitt, Phillip, *The Shield of Achilles: War, Peace and the Course of History*, New York, Anchor, 2003

Brodie, Bernard, *War and Politics*, New York, Macmillan, 1973

Brown, Michael E., *The International Dimensions of Internal Conflict*, Cambridge, MA, MIT Press, 1996

Charters, David A., ed., *Peacekeeping and the Challenge of Civil Conflict Resolution*, Proceedings of the Sixth Annual Conflict Studies Conference, September 1992, University of New Brunswick, 1994

Clausewitz, Carl von, *On War*, ed. and translated by Michael Howard and Peter Paret, Princeton, Princeton University Press, 1984

Clifford, Bob, *The Marketing of Rebellion: Insurgents, Media and International Activism*, Cambridge, Cambridge University Press, 2005

Clutterbuck, Richard, *The Long War: Counterinsurgency in the Third World*, New York, Penguin Books, 1976

Congressional Budget Office (CBO), 'Budget Options', February 2007

Damrosch, Lori Fisler, ed., *Enforcing Restraint: Collective Intervention in Internal Conflicts*, New York, Council on Foreign Relations Press, 1993

Department of Defense, *Joint Publication 3–07.3: Joint Tactics, Techniques, and Procedures for Peacekeeping Operations*, Washington, US Department of Defense, 29 April 1994

——*Joint Doctrine for Military Operations Other than War* (Joint Publication 3–07), Washington, US Department of Defense, 16 June 1995

——*Joint Publication 1–02, Department of Defense Dictionary of Military and Associated Terms*, 12 April 2001 (as amended 17 October 2008), US Department of Defense

——'Military Support for Stability, Security, Transition, and Reconstruction (SSTR)', Department of Defense (DoD) Directive Number 3000.05, Washington, DC, Department of Defense, 2005

——Joint Publication 3.0, Joint Operations, 17 September 2006, Incorporating Change 1, 13 February 2008, US Department of Defense

——*Quadrennial Roles and Missions Review Report*, US Department of Defense, Washington, January 2009

Department of State, 'State Department Fact Sheet', Office of the Coordinator for Reconstruction and Stabilization (S/CRS), Washington, DC, Department of State, 2005, www.state.gov/documents/organization/43429.pdf

Dobbins, James, et al., *America's Role in Nation-Building: From Germany to Iraq*, Santa Monica, RAND, 2003

Dwyer, Jim, 'A Gulf Commander Sees a Longer Road', *New York Times*, 28 March 2003

Etzioni, Amitai, *From Empire to Community: A New Approach to International Relations*, New York, Palgrave Macmillan, 2004

Fearon, James and David Laitin, 'Ethnicity, Insurgency, and Civil War', *American Political Science Review*, 97 (1) 2003

Feickert, Andrew, 'The Army's Future Combat System (FCS): Background and Issues for Congress', CRS (Congressional Research Service) Report, US Library of Congress, updated 11 October 2007

Friedman, Thomas, *The Lexus and the Olive Tree: Understanding Globalization*, New York, Farrar, Straus and Giroux, 1999

Galula, David, *Counterinsurgency Warfare: Theory and Practice*, St Petersburg, FL, Hailer, 2005 (originally published 1964)

Gates, Robert, 'A Balanced Strategy: Reprogramming the Pentagon for a New Age', *Foreign Affairs*, January/February 2009

Grenier, John, *The First Way of War: American War Making on the Frontier, 1607–1814*, Cambridge, Cambridge University Press, 2005

Griffith, Samuel B., *On Guerrilla Warfare*, 2nd Edition, University of Illinois Press, 2000

Haass, Richard N., *Intervention: The Use of American Military Force in the Post-Cold War World*, Washington, The Carnegie Endowment for International Peace, 1994

Hashim, Ahmed, *Insurgency and Counter-Insurgency in Iraq*, Ithaca, Cornell University Press, 2006

Hoffmann, Stanley, 'The Politics and Ethics of Military Intervention', *Survival*, Vol. 37, No. 4, Winter 1995–96

Holbrooke, Richard, *To End a War*, New York, Random House, 1998

Howard, Michael, *War in European History*, Cambridge, MA, Oxford University Press, 2001

Kaldor, Mary, *New and Old Wars: Organized Violence in a Global Era*, London, Polity, 2006

Kalyvas, Stathis N., *The Logic of Violence in Civil War*, Cambridge, Cambridge University Press, 2006

Kilcullen, David, 'Countering Global Insurgency', *Small Wars Journal*, 2006, smallwarsjournal.com/documents/kilcullen.pdf

Klare, Michael and Peter Kornbluh, eds, *Low Intensity Warfare, Counterinsurgency, Proinsurgency and Antiterrorism in the Eighties*, New York, Random House, 1988

Krepinevich, Andrew, *The Army and Vietnam*, Baltimore, Johns Hopkins University Press, 1986

Lyall, Jason A. and Isaiah Wilson III, 'Rage Against the Machines: The Determinants of Success in Counterinsurgency', *International Organization*, January/February 2009

MacGregor, Douglas *Breaking the Phalanx: A New Design for Landpower in the 21st Century*, Westport, CT, Praeger, 1997

Mack, Andrew, 'Why Big Nations Lose Small Wars: The Politics of Asymmetric Conflict', *World Politics*, 27 (2), 1975

Mandel, Robert, *The Meaning of Military Victory*, Boulder, Lynne Reiner, 2006

Manwaring, Max and Jon Fishel, 'Insurgency and Counter-Insurgency: Towards a New Analytical Approach', *Small Wars and Insurgencies*, Winter 1992

Marks, Edward, 'Peace Operations: Involving Regional Organizations', *Strategic Forum*, No. 25, April 1995

Merom, Gil, *How Democracies Lose Small Wars*, Cambridge, Cambridge University Press, 2003

Nagl, John, *Learning to Eat Soup with a Knife: Counterinsurgency Lessons from Malaysia and Vietnam*, Chicago, University of Chicago Press, 2005

O'Neill, Bard E., *Insurgency and Terrorism: Inside Modern Revolutionary Warfare*, New York, Potomac Books, 2001

Osgood, Robert E., *Limited War: The Challenges to American Strategy*, Chicago, University of Chicago Press, 1957

Packer, George, *The Assassin's Gate: American in Iraq*, New York, Farrar, Straus and Giroux, 2003

Petreaus, David and Jim Mattis, 'Counterinsurgency (Final Draft)', Headquarters, Department of the Army, USA, December 2006, www.fas.org/irp/doddir/army/fm3-24.pdf

Pike, Douglas, *PAVN: People's Army of Vietnam*, Da Capo Reprint edition, 1991

Quinn, Dennis J., ed., *Peace Support Operations and the U.S. Military*, Washington, National Defense University Press, 1994

Ricks, Thomas, *Fiasco: The American Military Adventure in Iraq*, New York, Penguin, 2006

Sarkasian, Sam and William Scully, eds, *U.S. Policy and Low Intensity Conflict*, London, Transaction Press, 1981

Scales, Robert H., *Firepower in Limited War*, Washington, National Defense University Press, 1990

Shafer, Michael D., *Deadly Paradigms: The Failure of U.S. Counterinsurgency Policy*, Princeton, Princeton University Press, 1988

Shy, John and Thomas W. Collier, 'Revolutionary War', in Peter Paret, ed., *Makers of Modern Strategy: From Machiavelli to the Nuclear Age*, Princeton, Princeton University Press, 1986

Smoke, Richard, *War: Controlling Escalation*, Cambridge, MA, Harvard University Press, 1977

Taber, Robert, *The War of the Flea*, New York, Lyle Stuart, 1965

Thompson, Robert, *Defeating Communist Insurgency: The Lessons of Malaya and Vietnam*, New York, Praeger, 1966

Tiboni, Frank, 'Army's Future Combat Systems at the Heart of Transformation', Federal Computer Week, 9 February 2004

Urquhart, Brian, *A Life in Peace and War*, New York, Harper and Row, 1987

Waltz, Kenneth, *Man, the State, and War*, New York, Columbia University Press, 1959

Weigley, Russell F., *The American Way of Way: A History of United States Military Strategy*, Indiana University Press, 1977

White House, 'Statement on Presidential Directive on U.S. Efforts for Reconstruction and Stabilization', Washington, DC, White House, 2005, www.whitehouse.gov/release/2005/12/20051214.html

Williams, Michael, *Civil Military Relations and Peacekeeping*, Adelphi Paper 321, International Institute for Strategic Studies, London, 1998

Wilson, Isaiah, III, *Thinking Beyond War: Why America Fails to Win the Peace*, New York, Palgrave Macmillan, 2007

Wilson, Isaiah, III and James J. F. Forest, *The Politics of Defence: International and Comparative Perspectives*, London, Routledge, 2008

Woodward, Susan L., *Balkan Tragedy: Chaos and Dissolution After the Cold War*, Washington, The Brookings Institution Press, 1995

Zakaria, Fareed, *Fight for Freedom*, New York, W. W. Norton, 2003

24 Private military and security companies and the international trade in small arms and light weapons

Malcolm Hugh Patterson

Introduction: SALW, PMSCs and the state

Private military and security contractor or 'PMSC' is a broadly accepted initialism that denotes a range of service providers described in various categories and taxonomies (Wulf 2005; Mandel 2002; Kinsey 2006; Singer 2003). Over the last 20 years PMSCs have evolved to a point where they provide indispensable support for military forces fielded by a growing number of states and more advanced militaries in particular. They are most prominently integrated in the USA, which possesses the most sophisticated armed forces and cannot sustain a major campaign without these firms (Singer 2007, 3). PMSCs also play an expanding role in the delivery of a broad range and depth of logistic and security functions in support of both civilian government and non-government organizations (Vaux 2002, 14–6; van Brabant 2002). Much PMSC business involves tasks in unstable and violent places. Here and elsewhere these firms have exhibited both permissible and less than ethical behaviour in dealings that have involved small arms and light weapons (SALW). Perhaps unsurprisingly, allegations of PMSC misconduct have involved weaponry; and these firms have been trenchantly criticized as 'corporate mercenaries' by unsympathetic non-governmental organizations (NGOs) that target weapons proliferation (Campaign Against the Arms Trade 2006; War on Want 2007). Because small-arms related segments of the business have grown in the last two decades (Scahill 2007) it is timely to reflect on the relationship between this industry and the arms trade.

PMSCs are frequently presented as an affront to states' authority (Krahmann 2003; Leander 2005, 803–26; Wulf 2005). This is misleading. There has never been a clear divide between public and private resources in armed conflict and states have always employed both. The legitimate exercise of violence and related functions is undergoing a process of devolution from governments to others. Weberian principles of state control tend to be tenaciously valued, even as new and numerous agents move execution of matters of state further from their principals' hands. This evolution has generated problems of principal control but state authority is hardly facing extinction. PMSCs generally serve larger corporations, NGOs, intergovernmental organizations (IGOs) and states, the more successful companies having cultivated close working relations with influential governments. With few exceptions (Cockayne 2007; Stober 2007) the nature of the agency that results has been the subject of insufficient academic examination. In the context of the trade in SALW this association is particularly pertinent. This is because contemporary problems associated with SALW and the industry usually arise from profit-seeking by PMSCs in the service of states' purposes. This notion should be elevated to the level of a guiding principle, but it has instead been distorted by those who misperceive the state as losing control of fundamental responsibilities, rather than choosing to exercise a modern form of sovereign authority through agency. The consequence is that while these companies merit careful scrutiny, the goals of influential states (which are often their principals) rarely receive analyses which should be at least as exacting.

The point is readily illustrated. The top 10 arms exporters are mostly advanced states. In descending order these are the USA, Russia, Germany, France, the United Kingdom (UK),

Netherlands, Italy, Sweden, the People's Republic of China and the Ukraine (SIPRI 2008). Many are participants in individual, regional and wider responses to demands for small arms control. At the individual level the USA enjoys the status of the world's largest small arms exporter by value (Gabelnick, Haug and Lumpe 2006, 1) while the US state retains an Under-Secretary for Arms Control and International Security (Department of State 2008). At the regional level the Europeans collaborate in codes on arms exports (EU Council 1998); dual use goods and technologies (Wassenaar 2004); principles on the brokering of small arms and light weapons (OSCE 2000; OSCE 2004); and an agreement on Best Practice Guidelines for Exports of Small Arms and Light Weapons (Wassenaar 2002).

Yet, the effectiveness of European small arms control regimes remains questionable (Weidacher 2005; Amnesty International 2004). One would be prudent to exercise similar caution when contemplating the success of restraint upon US SALW proliferation. It is not possible even to procure accurate export figures from either the US Government or US producers (Gabelnick, Haug and Lumpe 2006, 4–7, 78). The Bush Administration permitted arms exports to notorious human rights violators in return for political advantage (Gabelnick, Haug and Lumpe 2006, 61). At the broader multi-lateral level, effective co-operation is also of limited value. The UN membership prefers a narrow focus, concentrating on the illicit trade through the UN Programme of Action to Prevent, Combat and Eradicate the Illicit Trade in Small Arms and Light Weapons in All its Aspects (United Nations 2001b); and the Protocol against the Illicit Manufacturing and Trafficking in Firearms, Their Parts and Components and Ammunition, supplementing the United Nations Convention against Transnational Organized Crime (United Nations 2001a). Other General Assembly Resolutions (United Nations 2006) and the posture of the UN's Department of Disarmament Affairs (UNDDA 2008) support this orientation. UN specialized agencies play various roles in addressing problems associated with SALW, but the degree of states' commitment exercised through the UN is sharply limited (Krause 2004, 24, 28). This qualification is consistent with states' resistance to conventional arms control measures more generally – a notable example being meagre state adherence to the goals of the UN 'Register of Conventional Arms' (Laurence, Wagenmakers and Wulf 2005).

Anti-proliferation efforts are of limited value because states consistently see it in their interests to overtly or covertly transfer small arms and encourage the trade whenever doing so serves their interests. Although a slightly tangential observation in the present context, it has been governments of states that in total killed more of their own citizens during the last century than were dispatched by either interstate or civil wars (Rummel 1994, 2–3). States have exercised sovereign authority to behave (or misbehave) in this homicidal fashion notwithstanding evolving humanitarian intervention doctrines (International Development Research Centre 2001) and evolving precepts of international criminal law (Rome Statute of the ICC, United Nations 1998). The point should not be overstated, but in each of the better-known examples of PMSC involvement in small arms and other conventional weapons transfers, it has been governments of states that have been the largest single influence in the creation of conditions in which these firms have evolved. And it has been governments that have chosen to purchase the services these companies provide. For example, the government of Papua-New Guinea freely contracted with Sandline and the Sierra Leone government-in-exile did likewise; while the authorities in Croatia and Bosnia-Herzegovina were doubtless pleased when the US Government allowed the American firm MPRI to assist both of them. Just as states favour particular arms brokers with their patronage (Stohl 2005), they also favour PMSCs which they believe will serve their purposes more or less reliably. These purposes may or may not be peaceable.

The conclusion to be drawn is that the modern state is evidently a violent hypocrite and its recurrent delinquency exhibits particular attributes that should attract further and incisive study. Compared with other international actors even small states are often relatively wealthy and frequent principals to PMSC agents when states seek objectives that extend from the laudable to the nefarious. This extensive spectrum of freedom is keenly prized and encroachment seldom tolerated. That explains why – however desirable – states are unlikely to co-ordinate a web of effective international, regional and individual state controls over PMSCs and arms trading (Makki et al. 2001, 3, 14). By the same token, states' mixed and often contradictory purposes explain the confusing heterogeneity in their conduct towards both PMSCs and the arms trade. A coherent understanding of the following issues is offered in that often volatile context.

PMSCs and SALW: seven issues

1 PMSCs, SALW and the occasional indeterminacy of contractor weaponry

One problem is the indeterminacy of weaponry employed in certain armed PMSC operations. This matter is not resolved through uncomplicated reliance on corporate adherence to states' requirements consistent with international agreements and norms. For example, the US Government is as modern as any and its armed forces are probably no less effective in administration and enforcement than most others. On the other hand, company personnel working for USA-based PMSCs face lethal risks to their welfare in places like Iraq and Afghanistan. They may not consider it in their interests to eschew what Steve Fainaru of the *Washington Post Foreign Service* described as 'prohibited' weapons (Fainaru 2007). In his example, 'Crescent Security' personnel at Tallil air base, Iraq were found in possession of fragmentation grenades and anti-armour weapons.

The US military had proscribed company possession of these weapons, yet the firm's employees saw fit to procure and possess them with an intention to use them in the dangerous circumstances of their employment. To company staff the possession of this equipment may have appeared prudent and sensible in their violent situation. They may even have been correct. However, the larger point is not that these personnel may have breached various contractual and legal obligations; significance in the present context lies in two facts: first, that the opinion of corporate agents regarding suitable weapons differed from requirements held by agencies of the US Government; and second, company employees were prepared to act upon this conviction. This is a classic variant of the principal / agent control dilemma, where the parties' intentions differ notwithstanding the precision with which their contracts may have been drawn. This would not occur or would be a different type of problem if the company's tasks had been carried out by the US military or Department of State.

The incident should not have been unexpected. The difficulty is that several of those virtues that states value when deploying contract personnel in violent circumstances are also those that create hazards regarding weaponry. That is to say, contractors deliver states a degree of political convenience where a state's uniform may prove unpopular in theatre; they carry greater expendability where the political consequences of injured or deceased military personnel may give pause to political decision-makers, or where the costs to the state of those injured or ill are likely to be less than soldiers who may enjoy more generous benefits for a longer period; and PMSCs are likely to lower the costs of state association where contractors (rather than troops) conduct themselves in an unsavoury fashion. For example, contractors may inflict violence that is not proportionate to their objectives; they may engage in sexual misconduct or other premeditated or opportunistic criminal enterprises; or more generally offend host state populations to the extent of provoking armed responses. Most of these hazards are notoriously common in many lawless and violent places and this was the case long before and after the evolution of the modern state in the middle of the 17th century. Governments today continue to balance what they see as desirable features of armed agents against the risks and consequences of losing an uncertain degree of control. Because that loss is difficult to quantify (especially where violence is likely), the bargain is inherently unstable.

2 PMSCs, SALW and international humanitarian law

A second matter concerns PMSC conduct in regard to weaponry and ammunition that conforms to international humanitarian norms. This concept will be familiar to those personnel amongst contractors who in earlier years served in states' militaries. Do private contractors meet their obligations without employing methods and means proscribed amongst states by international treaties, international customary law (Gillard, 2006) and at a corporate level, those more nebulous dictates of 'good corporate governance'? Do these companies evince desirable conduct where they are incorporated, where management is based, where recruitment is conducted, and where they train and then operate? Each may be a different location. Do they require tangible evidence of conformity to best practices by their sub-contractors? How do directors and company management address concerns voiced by critics and outsiders? Does management offer evidence that makes plain an observance of desirable practices? If this is the case, is reassuring behaviour the product of an ethical culture, or a response to state direction based on rules and norms considered binding or desirable by states in one or more of the above locations?

Concern over adherence to international humanitarian principles pertinent to small arms and contractors is not a matter of theory alone. There is an issue over PMSC use of non-standard ammunition by contractors working for Blackwater. The recently devised 'blended metal' projectile is sometimes termed 'armour piercing/limited penetration' (APLP), because it passes through steel sheeting but not flesh. On entering a human being the round allegedly shatters explosively, creating what the American *Army Times* called 'untreatable wounds' (Roos 2003; RBCD 2008). In Iraq that observation has apparently proved accurate. The blended metal round is a concept quite different to the expanding round proscribed for state parties' use in the 1899 Hague Declaration (IV, 3) Concerning Expanding Bullets (Hague Declaration). None the less, that treaty codified one element of the customary rule prohibiting the use of weapons that cause unnecessary suffering (Roberts and Guelff 2000, 63). Use of this ammunition would appear at least contentious in the context of this principle of international customary law.

Anecdotal evidence suggests that some units within modern military forces enjoy certain freedoms in their choice of weaponry and ammunition. Even so, one imagines that the US Government is likely to resist distribution of blended metal rounds amongst the bulk of its uniformed troops. Private firms that provide security or occasional paramilitary services are not branches of the US Government, although the USA retains international humanitarian responsibilities that it may not elude by simple commercial proxy. One person who has noted the APLP phenomenon is a member of the UN 'Working Group on the Use of Mercenaries' (OHCHR). Jose L. Gomes del Prado recently suggested that 'there are cases where PMSC employees have used ... experimental ammunition prohibited by international law' (del Prado 2008). This assertion appears to be a reference to the Army Times article. Del Prado's view may be debatable; less arguable is his forceful political posture and public hostility to Blackwater and similar firms. In the present climate, PMSCs, and Blackwater in particular, defend public profiles that are already vulnerable. Management would be wise to protect their interests by adherence to international norms attached to small arms, light weapons and the ammunition they choose for various tasks.

3 PMSCs, SALW, humanitarian principles and clandestine operations

Private military and security companies have played roles in state clandestine operations in the past and this continues to be the case today. In the UK context, private military operations were influenced by a formative predecessor. The explicitly titled 'British Mercenary Organisation' operated in Yemen on the side of the Royalist forces during the 1962–65 hostilities.

Clive Jones contends that this entity was the historical antecedent to more modern PMCs, which took form 30 years later or more (Jones 2004, 3–4, 223–7). On the other side of the Atlantic US history and culture differ considerably, but there is scant reason to imagine that the nature of covert US purposes is much different. US journalist Nir Rosen was a recent Fellow at the 'Center on Law and Security' at New York University School of Law. In early 2008 he addressed an audience at NYU on his return from a trip to the Middle East. He described how he had been informed by plausible sources that Blackwater personnel had recently been involved in offensive operations in Somalia. He alleged that other US contractors then in Iraq, including those from the company MVM, had also been involved in offensive armed operations.[1] Claims of this nature are credible.

For more than two years the George W. Bush Administration was involved in less than successful covert hostilities within the unfortunate state of Somalia (Salopek 2008). In Blackwater's case, that firm has contracts with the US Government that exceeded the value of US $1 billion by the end of 2006. That figure does not appear to include the value of the firm's classified contracts (TradingMarkets.com 2008). It appears quite conceivable that the US Government would exploit private sources of paramilitary labour in those more lethal aspects of the US 'war on terror'. And it would also appear that clandestine contractors do carry out violent Central Intelligence Agency (CIA) operations – for example, those conducted on the Afghan / Pakistani border (Young Pelton 2006). Just as most aspects of classified operations are spared the illuminating gaze of public scrutiny, this privilege is likely to extend to the nature of small arms and ammunition procured, carried, discharged, traded, distributed and otherwise dispersed by USA-based PMSCs involved in these operations. The general inference one may draw is that a cloak of secrecy attached to classified contractor operations makes it very difficult to determine whether PMSC conduct complies with international humanitarian principles relating to SALW.

4 PMSCs, SALW exports, dishonest employees and the negligent agent

Another matter concerns US Federal Government investigations of Blackwater in connection with several breaches of US firearms laws. In September 2007 the firm was investigated for alleged infringements of US export regulations in connection with firearms, night-vision scopes and armour (BBC News 2007). At that time the US Attorney's office in North Carolina, in association with Department of State and Pentagon auditors, concluded that there was sufficient evidence to charge Blackwater employees (Lee 2007). Two former employees had already pleaded guilty to firearms trafficking offences in early 2007 (Scott 2007). At the time of writing, the US Department of State's Directorate of Defense Trade Controls had also moved to fine the North Carolina firm for shipping inadequately licensed weapons to police training centres in Jordan and Iraq (Friedman 2008). The Department of Commerce was also conducting a review and federal officials had convened a grand jury to examine the company's arms shipments and decide whether further criminal charges were warranted (Friedman 2008). Curiously, Blackwater has been allowed to continue transfers of controlled exports under a system of heightened Department of State scrutiny (Baker 2008).

Although aspects of Blackwater's arms and other controlled exports have not been resolved, a general question arises over the effectiveness of the US regulatory and enforcement apparatus in dealing with SALW exporters which are also PMSCs, and this USA-based company in particular. Both queries are of particular concern because the USA has a statutory and administrative apparatus which at first blush appears to provide adequate licence and export controls (Caparini 2007). In light of the difficulties that have emerged at Blackwater, reasonable doubts lead one to wonder if the US Government would be wiser to experiment less often with arms exports in the hands of Blackwater and similar firms. It may instead be more far-sighted to rely on state bureaucracies and the US military for most of this work.

States' militaries have a certain advantage in that armed forces inevitably experience problems with service personnel trafficking in small arms and light weapons from time to time, but unlike PMSCs, armed forces usually employ dedicated criminal investigators who are competent to scrutinize such matters. These employees are trained to carry out their tasks in both their home states and the more hostile circumstances presented by a foreign conflict. For example, the US Army has a Criminal Investigation Command (US Army 2008). On the other hand, the US Government may prefer to allow PMSCs to retain an exporting role. If so, the Obama Administration might be prudent to consider a thorough alteration to the manner in which it manages moral hazards associated with SALW exports currently involving PMSCs.

5 PMSCs, SALW and the entrepreneurially minded agent

Unlike a state's armed forces, PMSCs are agents that may engage in inventive or unorthodox conduct in the pursuit of profit, while fulfilling a contract which involves commerce in arms. The 'Arms to Africa Affair' is a well-known example from a decade ago (Sandline, 2008). Sandline International was hired to assist the return to power of the then Sierra Leonean government-in-exile led by Ahmed Kabbah. The company was to act in co-operation with a Nigerian-led force to remove a junta and to that end purchased 30 tons of Bulgarian arms and apparently delivered them to Nigerian forces already deployed in Sierra Leone (O'Loughlin 2000). The problem for the company was that the UN Security Council had placed an embargo on arms transfers to Sierra Leone (United Nations 1997). The UK was subject to that prohibition and the UK Government was embarrassed by the actions of British nationals who held management positions in the company. Significantly, company representatives defended their actions vigorously. They emphasized that they had acted in good faith by informally notifying the UK Government of their actions through an allegedly co-operative High Commissioner in Sierra Leone.

Modern PMSCs are occasionally asserted to be unlikely to subvert the policies of those states in which they are based (Tickler 1987; Shearer 1997). This argument seems strongest where companies are led by nationals of more powerful states having global interests, and where PMSCs base their offices in these states' capitals. Likewise, the implications of an absence of patronage can be crucial. One reason for the decline of the South African firm Executive Outcomes (EO) was that the company did not enjoy the support of the black majority South African regime. Instead, EO attracted ideological hostility and eventually restrictive legislation (Regulation of Foreign Military Assistance Act 1998). British history has bequeathed a more benign legacy for UK-controlled or -influenced PMSCs. Even so, the Arms to Africa Affair was complicated by the willingness of an agent working for a government-in-exile to entertain considerable political risk in an attempt to fulfil its contract. The unanticipated consequences illustrate an undesirable degree of unpredictability when contemplating an outcome arising from a mix of arms dealing, entrepreneurial business, intrastate warfare and the competing goals of at least three governments: the Kabbah Sierra Leonean government-in-exile, the ECOWAS deployment led by the Nigerians and the UK Government then led by Tony Blair.

In the context of the Bulgarian small arms transfer the key issue is a mistaken perception as to the freedom that management of this PMSC imagined it enjoyed. It seems plausible to suggest that to Sandline executives an offer of assistance in putting down a junta combined lucrative business with sufficiently ethical conduct as they saw it. Management appears to have held the erroneous belief that keeping the UK Government informed through informal means would prove adequate political preparation when planning (albeit indirectly) to supply small arms to a belligerent. Company directors and executives did not appear to expect the political controversy that ensued over the UN Security Council resolution, its application to British nationals and their firm's supply of small arms. One should also add that state officials declined to prosecute company officers in the UK over allegations arising from their behaviour (BBC News 1998).

In hindsight, a repeat of an incident resembling the Arms to Africa Affair would seem unlikely. Yet it remains reasonable to imagine that other PMSC management may in future conduct politically contentious and diplomatically disruptive operations in the pursuit of profit. In different circumstances those operations may once again be judged by company executives as sufficiently ethical. That may, once again, involve actions apparently taken in good faith through informing selected actors while unwisely excluding others. Once again, senior management may conduct themselves on mistaken political assumptions which remain uncorrected while unidentified dilemmas emerge and intensify. Once more, this could easily continue up to that point at which escalating consequences shape the characteristics of another political scandal.

6 PMSCs, SALW and the corrupt agent

There have been claims of PMSC involvement in illicit weapons trading (Mathieu and Dearden 2006). Whether these are true or not, the possibility should not seem particularly startling. The nature of warfare today is in one sense no different to those struggles in recent and more distant history. Small arms and light weapons fill one category in a range of commodities that collectively form a familiar currency: diamonds and precious gems, addictive drugs, gold, lumber, oil, minerals, other extractive commerce and illicit currency transfers, and the labour required to move it all. As in the past, this trade is conducted by governments, warlords and criminals. The means also remain unchanged: diplomacy, conventional commerce, underground trade, violence and subterfuge. These in turn take on an assortment of recognizably sordid and time-proven forms to which modern government and business are no strangers (McCoy 1972).

There is no reason why those personnel who direct, manage and otherwise serve today's PMSCs should be considered immune to moral hazards arising from armed conflict. When exploiting the link between a capacity to inflict violence and a willingness to turn that capacity to a profit, management and employees in modern corporations are likely to grapple with temptations similar to those experienced by predecessors long past. Consider the chartered company of several centuries ago. Prominent English and Dutch examples do not bear comparison in several decisive aspects. The workforce in today's PMSC is in relative terms far better educated and much more efficiently organized. Employees enjoy vastly better information technology. They are financially, legally and commercially much more sophisticated. And when engaged in legitimate small arms transfers modern communications may alert PMSC staff to lucrative deals outside legal avenues.

By the same token one should avoid confusing modern PMSCs with those criminalized entities or loose affiliations of rogues who supply today's illicit markets. For example, the infamous Colonel Yair Klein and his company 'Spearhead Ltd' are believed to have trained employees of the drug cartel controlled by Gonzalo Rodriguez, the now deceased Colombian narco-baron. It seems that Klein later sold his talents to the even more appalling Revolutionary United Front in Sierra Leone (Silverstein 2000, 161; Singer 2003, 220). Security firms in South-Eastern Europe have been corrupted by organized crime and improper political affiliations (Associated Press 2005) and it seems that Eastern European criminals have tried to buy Scandinavian security firms (Axis Information and Analysis 2005). It is conceivable that corrupted firms could expand into international PMSC work where criminal dealings in SALW would almost certainly present lucrative opportunities.

In contrast, the more successful PMSC is likely to have built a reputation on favourable relations with the US and UK governments, among others. For management of these firms plausible corruption scenarios are likely to arise from more legitimate intentions. For example, a military training firm might be contracted to assist a South American government instruct its troops in a struggle against narco-insurgents. It is conceivable that several company employees may abruptly switch sides for vastly better pay. And they might take some modern and quite lethal small arms, light weapons and ammunition with them. They would certainly possess the skills to instruct others in the operation, maintenance and tactical applications. At the same time their ex-PMSC managers may have been honest; they may have acted in good faith and been guilty of no moral turpitude regarding either their past employees or newly irate clients. However, those former employees would be likely to embarrass their former PMSC management and create unpleasant circumstances for an increasingly apprehensive government.

A more ambiguous area concerns PMSC directors who wish to profit by assisting those illiberal men who exploit what is left of decaying states. There is some evidence that a few PMSCs have agreed to part ownership of foreign subsidiaries also owned by the leaders of these frail states. The PMSCs may generate healthy profits, but joint ownership in those circumstances suggests erasure of the line between public governance and private interests. In its place, the modern state becomes an armed fiefdom, supported by newly effective military and security advisers. Cullen suggests that this may have been the case with TeleServices and Alpha 5 in Angola (Cullen 2000).

A general principle one might apply is that even with honesty and good faith the public good of security is only furnished by a company as a means of securing the private good of increased shareholder wealth. As Brooks and Solomon succinctly put it, 'PMCs work for money, not idealism' (Brooks and Solomon 2000). Just so. That may be a defensible enough principle when contemplating the consequences of a trade in commodities less lethal than small arms and light weapons, but in resource-rich authoritarian states one often observes vestigial public policy machinery combined with limited public liberty and intolerant government. A recurrent problem in such states is a well-known relationship between arms transfers and worsening human rights abuses (Yanik 2006, 359). Within a frail or sub-functioning society, PMSC influence over state dealings in small arms and light weapons would appear likely to serve less than praiseworthy purposes.

7 PMSCs, SALW and the inappropriately violent agent

Since the US invasion of Iraq in March 2003 there have been persistent reports of contractors firing on Iraqi civilians and attacking their property without reasonable cause (Finer 2006; Jackman 2006). Alarmingly, in what Amnesty International has called 'rules free zones' (Amnesty International USA 2006) it seems there may have been scores of unlawful killings and other serious crimes of violence (Isenberg 2006, 12). Evidence suggests that the figure is at least what investigative journalist Robert Young Pelton has called 'a not insignificant number' (Young Pelton 2006, 114). In a comparison raised by industry critic Jeremy Scahill, from 2003 to early 2007 there were 64 US military personnel charged with what he termed 'murder-related' offences. Over that period there had been no similar charges brought (through any means) against armed US contractors (KPBS Radio 2007).

Amnesty has compiled an alarming list of allegations of contractor misconduct in both Afghanistan and Iraq (AIUSA 2006; Cowell, 2006) and the US 'Government Accountability Office' has identified frequent and violent incidents in Iraq between private security and the US military, particularly with convoys and at checkpoints (GAO 2005, 4). The creation of the Reconstruction Operations Center in October 2004 improved co-ordination of intelligence and contractor / military relations. None the less, friendly fire incidents where US forces have attacked private security employees have apparently been so numerous that contractors have not bothered to report them (Hartung 2006). In 2005 the Third Infantry Division was responsible for security in and around Baghdad. Its then Deputy Commander was Brigadier Karl R. Horst and he put the matter this way:

> These guys run loose in this country and do stupid stuff. There's no authority over them, so you can't come down on them hard when they escalate force … They shoot people, and someone else has to deal with the aftermath. It happens all over the place.
>
> (Finer 2005)

There is much anecdotal evidence of excessive and plainly criminal contractor violence involving small arms. For example, DynCorp whistleblowers who aired allegations of an apparently gratuitous murder by a work supervisor were promptly dismissed by their employer (Myers 2006). As of December 2008 it was not clear whether a past Blackwater employee now living in Seattle will face unlawful homicide charges in connection with what appears to have been the drunken shooting of an Iraqi Vice-Presidential bodyguard (Seattle Times 2008). The reader may also be familiar with the Nisoor Square incident, in which members of a Blackwater convoy shot and killed at least 17 civilians and wounded perhaps 24 others.

More than a year after the Nisoor Square violence the US Department of Justice launched criminal prosecutions of five or six of those involved (Thompson and Risen 2008). This is significant because the American military concluded that all of the killings were unjustified and potentially criminal, while an FBI investigation determined that 14 of the 17 homicides were unjustified (Johnston and Broder 2007). Contractors allegedly responsible for small-arms related violence sometimes face investigations carried out by their employers. That administrative action occurs in a climate tainted by an obvious conflict of interest (Swain 2005). This is unavoidable, regardless of the diligence and skill that honest company management might attempt to exercise in unenviable circumstances.[2]

While evidence of serious misconduct mounts, equally alarming has been the broad institutional failure by the US Government to identify and apply appropriate criminal laws or suitably amend and adapt those that exist (Human Rights First 2008). Simply repatriating those suspected of small-arms related misconduct is no answer where there exists no certainty that crucial forensic evidence will be collected in a timely fashion by competent technicians, that the location and interview of relevant witnesses will occur in ethical circumstances, and that evidence and witnesses will follow a suspect to a competent court located perhaps thousands of kilometres away. Nor is there reason to expect that jurisdiction, substantive law and due process will combine to achieve a just outcome in a state where the political climate and other dynamics have been fashioned to discourage precisely this result.

This is no more or less than a reflection of the invading forces' indifference to Iraqi welfare consistent with a broader pattern. The Iraq invasion and occupation has been well-known for a more general absence of accountability for human rights abuses (Jennings 2006). Where agencies of the US Government have behaved poorly, it is to be expected that the same government would spend five years discouraging the exercise of a genuinely effective criminal justice system that addresses the misconduct of its agents. Here, principal and agent share a common if disagreeable interest (Strobel 2008).

Conclusion: PMSCs, SALW and the state: the good, the bad and the simply useful

PMSCs are likely to expand in capacity and influence as states increasingly outsource aspects of military-related tasks while these firms extend their range and depth of capabilities. Many companies both large and small will continue to seek contracts with major states. Some will attempt to increase roles in peace-keeping-related deployments. Others will meet the needs of niche war participants in the reliable if competitive intra-state warfare market. A few will cover the field. Regardless of whether clients are large or small, PMSCs will continue to play familiar roles in the trade in SALW. They will provide advice on suitable purchases and desirable brokers (and they may be brokers). They will negotiate, assist in the organization of efficient payment, identify desirable forms of transport and appropriate stockpile sites, and train clients in SALW use, maintenance and field application.

Some researchers of SALW and PMSCs are employed by the more mercurial arms-promoting states. Others are funded by IGOs. Still more are financed by governments through less-direct sponsorship. It is not surprising that many evince a reluctance to identify those selfish reasons that explain why governments consistently act in bad faith over two issues: states' ineffective suppression of small arms proliferation; and states' reluctance to temper their increasingly well-funded enthusiasm for PMSCs. Debate on the latter, in particular, continues to be manoeuvred with surprising ease. Modern PMSCs may be put to constructive or less prudent purposes and despite shortcomings – particularly in effective criminal law – these firms have some legitimate roles to play. Modern states simultaneously guide, influence and benefit from a contractor phenomenon that has its antecedents in the earliest records of armed conflict. There have been attempts at newer forms of PMSC governance; some appear desirable (e.g. United Nations 2008). However, without recognition of the primacy of states' purposes it is inevitable that the symbiotic relationship between the arms trade and PMSCs will continue in an unpredictable and poorly controlled experiment. For reasons tied to their own advantage, states are likely to encourage discussion that continues to attach responsibility for problems to corporate actors, thereby obscuring the more pivotal role of state responsibility.

Notes

1 Nir Rosen spoke on 3 April 2008 at the Center on Law and Security / NYU School of Law Seminar entitled 'Privatizing Defense: Blackwater, Contractors and American Security'. MVM, Inc. company website (viewed 10 November 2008) at www.mvminc.com.
2 For one company's perspective on CENTCOM rules of engagement, the US Department of State and CPA Order – Memo 17, see Aegis, *Statement on Video Clip Compilation* (29 November 2005) at AMPMlist@yahoogroups.com (viewed 21 December 2005).

Bibliography

Aegis, *Statement on Video Clip Compilation*, 29 November 2005
'AIUSA to Highlight Emerging Problems with Private Military Contractors During 2006', Annual Report Release, *usnewswire.com*, 23 May 2006
Amnesty International, 'Undermining Global Security: The European Union's Arms Exports', February 2004, www.amnesty.org/en/library/asset/ACT30/003/2004/en/dom-ACT300032004en.html
Amnesty International USA, *Annual Report*, 23 May 2006, www.amnestyusa.org/annualreport
Associated Press, 'Private Security Companies in Southeastern Europe Often Linked with Organized Crime: Report', *Associated Press*, 14 September 2005
Axis Information and Analysis, www.axisglobe.com/news.asp?news=8158
Baker, Michael, 'State Department to Scrutinize Blackwater Exports', *Associated Press*, 17 December 2008
BBC News, 'Sandline Not to Face Prosecution', 31 May 1998
——— 'Blackwater Arms Smuggling Probe', 22 September 2007
Brooks, Douglas, and Hussein Solomon, 'From the Editor's Desk', *Conflict Trends*, June 2000
Campaign Against the Arms Trade, *Corporate Mercenaries*, 2006, www.caat.org.uk/issues/corporate-mercenaries.php
Caparini, Marina, 'Licensing Regimes for the Export of Military Goods and Services', in Chesterman, Simon and Chia Lehnardt, *From Mercenaries to Market* Oxford, Oxford University Press, 2007
Center on Law and Security / NYU School of Law, 'Privatizing Defense: Blackwater, Contractors and American Security', Seminar, 3 April 2008
Cockayne, James, 'Make or Buy? Principal-Agent Theory and the Regulation of Private Military Companies', in Chesterman, Simon and Chia Lehnardt, *From Mercenaries to Market* Oxford, Oxford University Press, 2007
Cowell, Alan, 'Rights Group Faults US for War Outsourcing', *New York Times*, 23 May 2006
Cullen, Patrick, 'Keeping the New Dog of War on a Tight Leash', *Conflict Trends*, June 2000
del Prado, Jose L. Gomes, 'Impact on Human Rights of Private Military and Security Companies' Activities', *Global Research*, 11 October 2008
Department of State (USA), www.state.gov (viewed 15 June 2009)
European Council, *EU Code of Conduct on Arms Exports*, 5 June 1998, www.consilium.europa.eu/uedocs/cmsUpload/08675r2en8.pdf
Fainaru, Steven, 'Cutting Costs, Bending Rules, and a Trail of Broken Lives', *Washington Post Foreign Service*, 29 July 2007, www.washingtonpost.com
Finer, Jonathan, 'Security Contractors in Iraq Under Scrutiny After Shootings', *Washington Post Foreign Service*, 10 September 2005, www.washingtonpost.com
——— 'State Department Contractors Kill 2 Civilians in North Iraq', *Washington Post*, 9 February 2006
Friedman, Daniel, 'Blackwater Could Face Sanctions for Improper Arms Shipments', *Congress Daily*, 7 November 2008, www.govexec.com/dailyfed/1108/110708cdpm1.thm

Gabelnick, Tamar, Maria Haug and Lora Lumpe, *A Guide to the US Small Arms Market, Industry and Exports, 1998 2004*, Occasional Paper, Small Arms Survey, Geneva, 2006

Gillard, Emanuela-Chiara, 'Private Military/Security Companies: the Status of their Staff and their Obligations under International Humanitarian Law and the Responsibilities of States in Relation to their Operations', *Swiss Initiative on PMCs/PSCs* Kusnacht Workshop, Swiss Department of Foreign Affairs, 16 January 2006

Government Accountability Office (GAO), *Rebuilding Iraq: Actions Needed to Improve Use of Private Security Providers*, Report to Congressional Committees GAO-05-737, July 2005

Hague Declaration (IV, 3) Concerning Expanding Bullets (1899) UKTS 32 (1907) Cd. 3751

Hartung, William D., *Soldiers Versus Contractors: Emerging Budget Reality*, World Policy Institute, 10 February 2006

Human Rights First, *Private Security Contractors at War: Ending the Culture of Impunity*, 2008, Executive Summary, www.humanrightsfirst.org/us_law/pmc/pages.asp?country=us&id=10&misc1=exec-sum

International Development Research Centre, *The Responsibility to Protect: Report of the International Commission on Intervention and States Sovereignty*, Ottawa, 2001

Isenberg, David, *A Government in Search of Cover: PMCs in Iraq*, British-American Security Information Council, March 2006

Jackman, Tom, 'US Contractor Fired on Iraqi Vehicles for Sport, Suit Alleges', *Washington Post*, 17 November 2006

Jennings, Kathleen M., *Armed Services: Regulating the Private Military Industry*, FAFO Report 532, New Security Program, Norway, 2006

Johnston, David and John M. Broder, 'FBI Says Guards Killed 14 Iraqis Without Cause', *New York Times*, 14 November 2007

Jones, Clive, *Britain and the Yemen Civil War, 1962 1965*, Brighton, Sussex Academic, 2004

KPBS Radio, 'These Days', Alan Ray interview of Jeremy Scahill and Doug Brooks, 2 May 2007, www.kpbs.org/radio/these_days?id=8189

Kinsey, Christopher, *Corporate Soldiers and International Security*, London, Routledge, 2006

Krahmann, Elke, 'Conceptualizing Security Governance', *Cooperation and Conflict*, Vol. 38 No. 1, 2003

Krause, Keith, 'Facing the Challenge of Small Arms: The UN and Global Security Governance', in R. M. Price and M. W. Zacher, *The United Nations and Global Security*, New York and Basingstoke, Palgrave Macmillan, 2004

Laurance, Edward J., Hendrik Wagenmakers and Herbert Wulf, 'Managing the Global Problems Created by the Conventional Arms Trade: An Assessment of the United Nations Register of Conventional Arms', *Global Governance*, Vol. 11, 2005

Leander, Anna, 'The Power to Construct International Security: On the Significance of Private Military Companies', *Millennium*, Vol. 33, No. 3, June 2005

Lee, Matthew, 'Feds Target Blackwater in Weapons Probe', *AP News*, 22 September 2007

McCoy, Alfred W., *The Politics of Heroin in South-East Asia*, New York, Harper and Colophon, 1972

Makki, Sami, Sarah Meek, Abdel-Fatau Musah, Michael Crowley and Damian Lilly, *Private Military Companies and the Proliferation of Small Arms: Regulating the Actors*, International Alert, Safer World and British American Security Information Council, August 2001

Mandel, Robert, *Armies Without States: The Privatization of Security*, Boulder, CO, Lynne Rienner, 2002

Mathieu, Fabien and Nicholas Dearden, *Corporate Mercenaries – The Threat of Private Military and Security Companies*, War on Want, 2006

MVM, Inc., www.mvminc.com

Myers, Lisa, 'Did Americans Fire on Iraqis for Sport?', *MSNBC.com*, 21 December 2006

'New Mercenary Law to Put Squeeze on Soldiers of Fortune', *Africa News*, 3 August 2005

Office of the United Nations Commissioner for Human Rights (OHCHR), www2.ohchr.org/english/issues/mercenaries/index.htm (accessed 10 December 2008)

Organization for Security and Co-operation in Europe (OSCE), *OSCE Document on Small Arms and Light Weapons*, Doc FSC.DOC/1/00, November 2000, www.grip.org/bdg/pdf/20001124-OSCE_SALW.pdf

——*OSCE Principles on the Control of Brokering in Small Arms and Light Weapons*, OSCE Ministerial Council, Sofia, 7 December 2004, Decision No. 7/04, www.osce.si/docs/mc-dec_7 04.pdf

O'Loughlin, Edward, 'Sandline Scandal Arms Shipment Reaches Forces', *The Independent*, 22 May 2000, www.independent.co.uk/news/world/africa/sandline-scandal-arms-shipment-reaches-forces-715976.html

RBCD, Performance Plus Ammunition, 2008, www.rbcd.net

Regulation of Foreign Military Assistance Act, No. 15 (1998)

Roberts, Adam and Richard Guelff, *Documents on the Laws of War*, 3rd edition, Oxford, Oxford University Press, 2000

Roos, John G., '1 Shot Killer: This 5.56mm Round Has All the Stopping Power You Need – But You Can't Use It', *The Army Times*, 1 December 2003

Rummel, Rudolph J., 'Power, Genocide and Mass Murder', *Journal of Peace Research*, Vol. 31, No.1, 1994

Salopek, Paul, 'Nobody is Watching', *Chicagotribune.com*, 24 November 2008, www.chicagotribune.com/news/nationworld/chi-shadow_war2nov24,0,4720127.story

Sandline, www.sandline.com/hotlinks/sierra_leone.html (accessed 2008)

Scahill, Jeremy, *Blackwater: The Rise of the World's Most Powerful Mercenary Army*, New York, Nation Books / Avalon, 2007

Scott, David, 'Blackwater Denies Arms Smuggling Allegations', *AP News*, 22 September 2007, www.thefreelibrary.com/Blackwater+denies+smuggling+allegations-a01610771779

Seattle Times, 'Seattle Man Could Face Charges in Blackwater Case', *Seattle Times*, 14 November 2008

Shearer, David, *Private Armies and Military Intervention*, Adelphi Paper No. 316, International Institute for Strategic Studies, London, 1997

Silverstein, Kenneth, *Private Warriors*, London, Verso Books, 2000

Singer, Peter W., *Corporate Warriors*, Ithaca and London, Cornell University Press, 2003

—— *Can't Win With 'Em, Can't Go to War Without 'Em: Private Military Contractors and Counterinsurgency*, Brookings Foreign Policy Paper Series No. 4, September 2007, www.brookings.edu/papers/2007/0927militarycontractors.aspx

SIPRI, *Ten Arms Exporters 2003–2007*, Stockholm International Peace Research Institute, 2008, www.sipri.org/googlemaps/at_top_20_exp_map.html

Stober, Jan, 'Contracting in War', in Thomas Jager and Gerhad Kummel, eds, *Private Military Companies: Chances, Problems, Pitfalls and Prospects*, Wiesbaden, VS Verlag, 2007

Stohl, Rachel, 'Fighting the Illicit Trafficking of Small Arms', *SAIS Review*, Vol. 25, No. 1, Winter 2005

Strobel, Warren P., 'Report: State Dept., Blackwater Cooperated to Neutralize Killings', McClatchy Newspapers / *bnd.com*, 16 December 2008, www.bnd.com/news/state/v-print/story540853.html

Swain, Jon, 'Making a Killing', *The Sunday Times Magazine*, 23 October 2005, www.timesonline.co.uk/article/0,2099-1824220,00.html

Thompson, Ginger and James Risen, '5 Guards Face Charges in Iraq Deaths', *New York Times*, 5 December 2008, www.nytimes.com/2008/12/06/washington/06blackwater.html?ref=middleeast

Tickler, Peter, *The Modern Mercenary: Dog of War or Soldier of Honour?* UK, Patrick Stephens Publishing, 1987

TradingMarkets.com, 'Blackwater's Aggressive, Entrepreneurial Culture Keeps its Business Growing', 17 May 2008, www.tradingmarkets.com/site/news/Stock%20News/1575255/

United Nations, UNSC Res 1132 (1997), United Nations Security Council, 8 October 1997

—— *Rome Statute of the International Criminal Court*, UN Doc. A/CONF. 183/9; 37 ILM 1002, 1998, 2187 UNTS 90

—— *Protocol against the Illicit Manufacturing and Trafficking in Firearms, Their Parts and Components and Ammunition, supplementing the United Nations Convention against Transnational Organized Crime*, UNGA RES 55/255, 31 May 2001a, Treaty and Protocols, www.unodc.org/documents/treaties/UNTOC/Publications/TOC%20Convention/TOCebook-e.pdf

—— 'UN Programme of Action to Prevent, Combat and Eradicate the Illicit Trade in Small Arms and Light Weapons in All its Aspects', UN Doc, A/CONF.192/15, 2001b, disarmament.un.org/cab/poa.html

—— UNGA A/RES/60/68, 6 January 2006

—— UNGA / UNSC A/63/467-S/2008/636 (6 October 2008), *Montreux Document on pertinent international legal obligations and good practices for States related to operations of private military and security companies during armed conflict*, 17 September 2008

United Nations Department of Disarmament Affairs (UNDDA), www.un.org/disarmament/convarms/SALW/Html/SALW-PoA-ISS_intro.shtml

US Army, Criminal Investigation Command, www.cid.army.mil/mission.html (accessed 2008)

van Brabant, Koenraad, *Humanitarian Action and Private Security Companies*, Humanitarian Practice Network, 2002, www.odihpn.org/report.asp?ID=2419

Vaux, Tony, 'European Aid Agencies and Their Use of Private Security Companies', in Tony Vaux, Chris Seiple, Greg Nakano and Koenraad van Brabant, *Humanitarian Action and Private Security Companies: Opening the Debate*, International Alert, London, 2002

Vaux, Tony, Chris Seiple, Greg Nakano and Koenraad van Brabant, *Humanitarian Action and Private Security Companies*, International Alert, www.internationalalert.org/pdf/pubsec/humanitarianaction.PDF

War on Want, *Getting Away with Murder*, 2007, www.caat.org.uk/issues/WoW_Mercenaries_Briefing.pdf

Wassenaar Arrangement/Best Practice Guidelines for Exports of Small Arms and Light Weapons, December 2002, www.wassenaar.org/docs/best_practice_salw.htm

Wassenaar Arrangement on Export Controls for Conventional Arms and Dual-Use Goods and Technologies, July 2004, www.wassenaar.org/introduction/howitworks.html

Weidacher, Reinhilde, *Behind a Veil of Secrecy: Military Small Arms and Light Weapons Production in Western Europe*, Occasional Paper, Small Arms Survey, Geneva, 2005

Wulf, Herbert, *Internationalizing and Privatizing War and Peace*, Hampshire (UK), Palgrave Macmillan, 2005

Yanik, Lerna K., 'Guns and Human Rights: Major Powers, Global Arms Transfers, and Human Rights Violations', *Human Rights Quarterly*, Vol. 28, No. 2, May 2006

Young Pelton, Robert, *Licensed to Kill*, New York, Crown, 2006

25 Future war

The shape of arms to come

Malcolm R. Davis[1]

Truly it is said that nothing dates so rapidly as yesterday's tomorrow.

(Gray 2005)

Introduction

As the quote from Gray correctly suggests, the future is never quite what you expect it to be (Gray 2005, 20). The terrorist attacks against the USA on 11 September 2001 seemed to reinforce the emerging threat posed by unconventional non-state adversaries – terrorists, insurgencies, warlords and international criminals – and accentuated for many what had been a perception of a declining relevance of major interstate warfare since the end of the Cold War in 1991. Ralph Peters argued that in future wars we would face warriors, not soldiers, describing them as:

> ... erratic primitives of shifting allegiance, habituated to violence, with no stake in civil order. Unlike soldiers, warriors do not play by our rules, do not respect treaties, and do not obey orders they do not like.

(Peters 1999, 32)

The growing awareness of such post-modern adversaries since the end of the Cold War represents one face of future warfare, but not a complete portrait. As the years progress from that fateful morning in New York City and Washington, our understanding of emerging trends in 21st century security dynamics suggests a different conception of future warfare to a narrow perspective characterized by the 'war on terror'. The risk of major power geopolitical competition in an emerging multi-polar world means that the prospect of large-scale interstate warfare should not be dismissed as irrelevant to the emerging security paradigm. The prospect of a broad spectrum of military challenges is inherently more difficult to prepare for than thinking about the future in much narrower terms, that focuses only on non-state threats to peace and stability.

In an address in May 2008, US Secretary of Defense Bob Gates, referred to 'thiswaritis' vs. 'nextwaritis' and argued that greater focus needed to be paid to winning today's wars against unconventional non-state adversaries, rather than preparing for potential future conflicts with major peer competitors (Gates 2008). History is littered with examples of states preparing and equipping for the wrong war and the wrong adversary, either because they failed to understand the forces shaping the security environment or because they became fixated on one sort of conflict and stripped away resources that could contribute to success in other types of conflict. Thus Gates's view that 'nextwaritis' should not be allowed to dominate planning and procurement, whilst certainly justified given the strategic requirement to ensure success in Iraq and Afghanistan, runs the risk if taken too far, that the US military will fail to adequately prepare for future wars against major state adversaries, which will be more likely in coming decades. It is the author's contention that given the finite (and likely shrinking) resources for funding military modernization, and the very long procurement cycles that now seem to be a permanent feature for developing major military capabilities, it is becoming vital to look beyond current conflicts and embrace a degree of 'nextwaritis'. Obviously there is a clear requirement to achieve success in current conflicts – failure in either Iraq or Afghanistan, and retreat from confronting terrorism, would have catastrophic strategic consequences. However, such a prioritization of goals should not lead to eventual strategic failure and military defeat in future wars, which could be very different from current operations in Afghanistan and Iraq.

Having some conception of what future war will be like will thus shape priorities in capability acquisition, and the future arms trade must match the strategic and military priorities of states in coming decades which will be confronted by a broad spectrum of military challenges. The dilemma posed by Gates's 'thiswaritis vs. nextwaritis' argument highlights strategic uncertainty and security complexity which characterizes the future security environment. Thus, the goal of this chapter is not a narrow focus on future weapons technology and its relationship to the international arms trade; instead it seeks to explore how the shape of arms to come will relate to an uncertain future security environment and to explore the likely character and conduct of future wars. In understanding this context and considering how radical new military capabilities may evolve through a process of military transformation, an assessment of the likely nature of the future arms trade can be developed.

The future strategic context

In 2009 the international system is no longer characterized by a USA-led 'unipolar moment', but by an emerging competitive multi-polar world in which resources will be increasingly constrained; US power will decline relative to rising powers such as the People's Republic of China and potentially a resurgent Russia (Altman 2009, 14); and a 'new security agenda' such as climate change, resource competition, demographics and societal breakdown will challenge the stability of a globalized international order (US National Intelligence Council 2008; US Joint Forces Command 2008). Gray argues persuasively that what had become an increasingly orthodox post Cold War perspective which suggested the obsolescence of major interstate war is not a fact, but merely a theory based on recent trends which are easily misinterpreted.

> The principal weaknesses of this particular grand narrative are: the unsound assumption that states, even the greatest among them, are in decline as significant players in international security politics; an unduly narrow view of the reasons why states have fought each other, and may well do so in the future; and finally, an unwise belief that a current trend, even if accurately interpreted represents history's last move.
>
> (Gray 2005, 139)

During the post Cold War interregnum of 1991–2001, some commentators sought to equate the increasingly visible threat posed by unconventional opponents and a perceived 'new security agenda' as indicative that the likelihood of major interstate conflict was on the wane (Smith 2006, 1–18, 267–9). The security environment has moved on and a narrow focus only on such challenges is insufficient as a basis for truly understanding the future security environment. Although international terrorism will clearly remain an enduring global threat, the international system has changed significantly from the early 1990s, or indeed that which existed in 2001. The suggestion that traditional interstate warfare is being replaced by unconventional 'post-modern' conflicts, waged in part or full by irregular non-state adversaries, does not adequately consider current geopolitical and security trends that will shape the security environment of the future, and thus determine the character and conduct of future war (Kagan 2008, 10–2). Notions of a coming anarchy of failed states, in which militias, warlords and terrorists exploit chaos to gain power against helpless captive populations certainly have relevance (Kaplan 2001, 43–50), but should not be seen to fully describe a complex and uncertain security environment. A more useful approach is to suggest a spectrum of conflict comprising both symmetrical and asymmetrical threats between a range of actors including state and non-state opponents. This is not about sitting on intellectual fences, but instead reflects real change in the international system which challenges narrower perspectives on the future of warfare. Interstate war between major actors can, and probably will, occur in the first half of the 21st century for a variety of reasons that are becoming increasingly apparent as this new security environment evolves.

However, surely the forces of globalization would act as a constraint on the use of force between states, as would the established norms and values of international law, and the stabilizing presence of multilateral organizations such as the United Nations? The role of globalization as a 'great stabiliser' is commonly promoted as evidence of the obsolescence of interstate war (Friedman 2007, 585–95). By participating in a globalized international order, state actors have little to gain and much to lose by the resort to use of force against each other. Instead, the maintenance of stability promotes greater opportunity for all states to benefit from globalization to achieve security, wealth and influence. The key national interests of individual states are subsumed by the good of all, and war as a tool for achieving policy ends becomes unthinkable.

Such a comforting assumption is open to challenge. Think of the globalized international system that is emerging as a vast machine. When the machine is well maintained, and fed a continuous supply of resources and information it will more than likely run smoothly. However, if events occur which interrupt the flow of resources and information, or if errors creep into its mechanism, then the machine becomes increasingly unstable and prone to failure. Globalization will work well for those able to fully exploit it, and certainly the promise of mutual benefit to all participants of a globalized international order does reinforce an incentive towards stability rather than conflict. However, globalization, whilst acting as a means towards wealth, security and stability, can at the same time act as a conduit for insecurity and crisis. As in the simile with the vast machine, if resources fail to be acquired to sustain a globalized order, or if information and processes input into the system acts to cumulatively unbalance it – the 2008 global financial crisis is an excellent example – globalization begins to cause insecurity and instability rather than shield actors from it. At this point, there would be a tendency for states to ensure their national interests are protected through a return to realist approaches to international affairs. Furthermore, the assumption that critical national interests are overshadowed by a need to preserve a globalized order is false. States go to war to protect such interests, irrespective of the presence of a globalized international order. It is unlikely that China would choose to allow Taiwan its independence rather than embarking on the use of force (even at the risk of war with the USA), for fear of disrupting globalized trade. As pervasive as globalization is, it is not above those critical national interests that states will shed blood and treasure to defend.

Furthermore, vast areas of the planet lack 'connectivity' to the globalized core, either through deliberate choice, or through lack of technological foundation. These regions lie in what Barnett refers to as 'the non-integrating gap' (Barnett 2004, 121–54). Cultural resistance to the spread of globalization is more apparent within this region, given the perception by many of its inhabitants of globalization as merely a new form of Western cultural imperialism. In this way, globalization may act to promote conflict rather than ensure peace and stability. Forces opposed to modernity such as international terrorist networks like al-Qa'ida will exploit globalization to access their opponent's soft and open societies, whilst seeking to gain popular support through supporting cultural resistance to the spread of markets, and the breakdown of borders between civilizations. Likewise, competitor states seeking to generate strategic blows can undertake non-military operations such as trade war that uses a globalized international system as access to the adversary's societal core (Liang and Xiangsui 1999, 3). Finally, globalization generates an effect of immediacy leading to the effects of a crisis being rapidly transmitted across the globe, be it via information links, open borders or through financial disruption. If the machine breaks, it breaks rapidly.

A key feature of the security environment in the 21st century is the rapid redistribution of global power and replacement of a unipolar order with a multi-polar world, which looks increasingly likely to be competitive rather than co-operative in nature. There is a rapid, accelerating transfer of power from the old global centre of the West – Europe and the USA – to the new global core in the East – China, India and potentially Russia, as well as rapidly developing states in East Asia (Altman 2009, 2–3). As these states develop, their appetite for resources will grow. It is the issue of resources – energy, food, water and arable land – that addresses the question of why war, including traditional interstate war, might occur in the future (Klare 2002, 13–8). Of greatest significance certainly in the first half of the 21st century will be competition over access to and control of energy resources – in particular fossil fuels – to sustain the rapid economic growth, which in the case of rising powers such as China, is inherently linked to regime security and survival (Friedman 2007, 574). In exploring the impact of resource competition on future international security, Klare states:

> ... what we are seeing is the emergence of a new geography of conflict – a global land-scape in which competition over vital resources is becoming the governing principle behind the disposition and use of military power.
>
> (Klare 2002, 214)

It is concerns over a looming decline in production globally that leads to a growing spectre of 'Peak Oil' in which:

> ... exaggerated reserves (proven and unproven), a declining rate of oil discovery, and peaking production in mature fields will combine to tighten supplies, perhaps more rapidly than can be fully compensated for by unconventional oil supplies ... [leading to] a significant, prolonged and continuing contraction in [oil] production (and significantly raised prices) beginning by the 2020s.
>
> (Elhefnawy 2008, 37–66)

The Pentagon's 'Joint Operating Environment 2008' report alludes to the threat of Peak Oil, stating:

> The implications for future conflicts are ominous. If the major developed and developing states do not undertake a massive expansion of [oil] production and refining capabilities, a severe energy crunch is inevitable.
>
> (US Joint Forces Command 2008, 17)

The challenge of Peak Oil is that as oil production declines globally, the shift in power between the old centre and new core will accelerate. As the price increases as production declines, leading key oil-producing states, such as those in the Organization of Petroleum Exporting Countries (OPEC) will achieve greater global political leverage and higher economic revenue. This will result in these states enjoying increasing strategic power and influence, as well as greater military potential (King 2008, 6–9; Campbell and Laherrere 1998, 78–83). Current trends suggest that the future security environment will see a concentration of power in the hands of key oil and natural gas producers, including potential regional and global competitors such as Iran and Russia. Naturally, there will be a greater focus by the USA, the EU, China, Japan and India, which are all heavily dependent on distant oil reserves, on ensuring unconstrained access to critical supplies. Indeed, China's military development is in part about ensuring the ability to prevent an independent Taiwan, and in part about having the means to project military power to ensure access to and, if necessary, control over key maritime Sea Lanes of Communication (SLOCs) along which runs its oil lifeline. Future competition between states over access to resource-rich areas that previously were uneconomical to exploit – such as the Arctic – may lead to increasing tension, conflict and even war (US National Intelligence Council 2008, 41–7).

Even if new alternative energy technologies are developed in a timely fashion – perhaps by the 2030s – it is likely that global implementation of these technologies to sustain increasing energy demand in national grids and to support rapidly expanding global transportation infrastructure will lag behind the maturation of alternative energy technology. The key dilemma that will challenge the international system in coming years is how to sustain economic growth, which is essential to a stable globalized international system, through a continued reliance on fossil fuels, until this 'implementation lag' can be overcome, whilst meeting the longer-term challenge posed by climate change (Elhefnawy 2008, 46–8). When new sources of clean energy are available and can be implemented widely, the instability caused by declining oil production and the concentration of economic, political and military power through key actors having a monopoly on those declining resources could enter a new phase, as the source of their wealth disappears. It is the OPEC states that will ultimately be the losers in the long term, if their economies remain dependent on oil wealth (US National Intelligence Council 2008, 46). Those states that can rapidly transfer and implement alternative energy technologies by the middle of the 21st century will enjoy a very significant geopolitical advantage.

Sharpening trends towards demographic change have direct bearing on resource insecurity. The ageing of the Western world generates long-term security pressures in terms of resources, social change and cultural change (Wood 1994, 192, 197–204). The developing world – with rapidly growing populations of predominantly young people – have a legitimate requirement for resources such as water, food, arable land, access to technology, medicine and education (de Blij 2007, 96). The lack of such resources – likely to be exacerbated by the gradually increasing effects of climate change over the course of the 21st century – will lead to increasing flows of economic and environmental migrants and refugees to regions on the globe where the resources remain. This will act to generate domestic, economic and social challenges for states, mostly in the developed world, which must manage what becomes a largely unstoppable tide of cultural change. It is the disparity in wealth, health and quality of life between the developed and the developing world that feeds into the growth of this problem, and allows extremist groups to generate a rapidly growing base for support, and then exploit cultural and ethnic diasporas to export their beliefs into the open societies of the developed world. The end result is the risk of growing cultural, religious and ethnic divisions within societies, greater demand on limited resources to sustain increasing populations and, ultimately, changes in a society's culture that are reflected in changes to their strategic culture.

The re-emergence of ideological competition – dismissed as largely irrelevant with the collapse of Soviet Communism at the end of the Cold War – is once again increasingly apparent in the 21st century security discourse. The events of 11 September 2001 and the threat posed by international terrorism from networked entities such as al-Qa'ida is an enduring challenge. Al-Qa'ida highlights an Islamist fundamentalist ideology that directly threatens both Western liberal democratic systems and values, as well as those of secular Islamic states (Gunaratna 2002, 92–3). However, it is the potential for ideological competition between Western liberal democracies and increasingly powerful authoritarian capitalist states – specifically China and Russia – which adds an unexpected and complicating factor to the future security environment, and which reinforces the potential for military competition in a more traditional sense.

Both China and Russia represent successful authoritarian states embracing the Meiji Japanese perspective of 'rich country, strong army' (Kagan 2008, 24). The growing success of such authoritarian capitalist states is characterized by a combination of their strong nationalism, increasing financial power through rapidly growing market economies, access to resources, and undisputed authoritarianism. Such states represent an alternative ideological path that will appeal to a wide variety of states, which are under pressure from liberal democracies that promote development through democratization. Whilst both states have serious internal security challenges that must resolved in the future, the current success of China and Russia demonstrate that there are alternative paths to national development besides the traditional Westminster or Jeffersonian tradition. Azar Gat suggests that the rise of China and Russia as authoritarian capitalist states represents a return to the international system that existed prior to the Cold War, and suggests a new 'second world' structure is emerging.

> They [China and Russia] could establish a powerful authoritarian capitalist order that allies political elites, industrialists, and the military; that is nationalist in orientation; and that participates in the global economy on its own terms, as imperial Germany and imperial Japan did in the 1930s.
>
> (Gat 2007, 62)

Talk of a new Cold War between the West and Russia (most notable since the 2008 Russia–Georgia war) is certainly premature. Suggestions of an inevitable confrontation with a rising China remain highly debatable. However, the success of such states in combining capitalism and authoritarianism could generate ideological tensions, especially if international faith in democratic capitalist states were shaken. Gat's analysis goes on to note that:

> … the liberal political and economic consensus is vulnerable to unforeseen developments, *such as a crushing economic crisis that could disrupt the global trading system* [emphasis added by author] … Were the West to be hit by such upheavals, support for liberal democracy in Asia, Latin America, and Africa where adherence to that model is more recent, incomplete, and insecure could be shaken.
>
> (Gat 2007, 66)

The devastating global financial crisis, which began in 2008 and continued into 2009, reinforces Gat's argument, which challenges the notion of inevitability of Western liberal, democratic traditions. In a key point, Gat states:

> … the near total dominance of liberal-democracy since the Soviet Union's collapse will be short-lived and a universal democratic peace is still far off … Beijing, Moscow and their future followers might well be on antagonistic terms with the democratic countries, with all the potential for suspicion, insecurity and conflict that this entails.
>
> (Gat 2007, 67)

In summary, the future of war is a broad spectrum of many different types of conflict. The challenge posed by unconventional non-state adversaries, epitomized by groups such as al-Qa'ida, the Taliban, Hezbollah and Hamas, represent one face of future warfare. Such adversaries will not go away, and will confront both Western liberal democracies and secular Islamic states in coming decades. The new security agenda that highlights a range of challenges posed by climate change, resource depletion and competition, demographics and social insecurity is also a key factor in shaping the security environment. Finally, recent trends towards a multi-polar international order tend to suggest a return of traditional geopolitics, and with it, an increasing likelihood of interstate war if critical interests are challenged, or if the basis for a stable globalized international system is undermined. In considering how war might be fought in this highly challenging future security environment, understanding a process of military transformation which is currently underway by many of the major state actors highlights likely risks and opportunities facing states in preparing for the shape of arms and warfare to come.

Future warfare – going beyond the RMA

The perception of future war that emerged from the 1991 Gulf War suggested a radical departure from previous conflicts. Future war would be fast, decisive, precise and much more calibrated and controllable than in previous wars. Military advantage would not be driven so much by mass, but technological edge and concentration of precision force in the right place and at the right time to deliver the right effect. The concept devised to explain the radical change in the approach to the use of force was the revolution in military affairs (RMA). Krepinevich in a seminal article, 'From Cavalry to Computer', argued that an RMA occurs when:

> ... the application of new technologies into a significant number of military systems combines with innovative operational concepts and organizational adaptation in a way that fundamentally alters the character and conduct of conflict. It does so by producing a dramatic increase – often an order of magnitude or greater – in the combat potential and military effectiveness of armed forces.

> (Krepinevich 1994, 30)

It could be argued that a perception of 'revolutionary change' was an illusion because the capabilities deployed during the 1991 Gulf War had in many instances emerged as a process of evolutionary change dating back to the Viet Nam War in the 1960s and the Yom Kippur War (October War) of 1973. What was new was that the 1991 Gulf War was the first war to be shown on global television networks, 24 hours a day, seven days a week, and thus smart bombs and cruise missiles, satellites and, ironically, stealth aircraft, were more visible to the broader population than ever before. The popular perception was of something new and radically different from previous conflicts. After the conclusion of hostilities on 28 February 1991, debate over the 'lessons learned' led to a perception of the notion of an information-led RMA that would drive the future shape of armed forces. There was a tendency to use the 1991 Gulf War as a 'template' for all future conflicts, and procurement priorities, doctrinal change and organizational development emerged from this template. The combination of advanced intelligence, surveillance and reconnaissance (ISR) capabilities, precision strike systems, and networked command and control promoted new approaches to the use of force that emphasized a greater degree of precision in the application of military effects, rather than brute indiscriminate force. New concepts such as 'effects-based operations' suggested that advances in ISR, as well as command and control would allow RMA-based forces to get inside an adversary's decision cycle or 'OODA loop' (Hammond 2001, 4–5).[2] This would allow such forces to out-think and out-fight – to 'lock out' – an adversary to the point whereby it would lack the means and will to fight. Modern warfare could thus be nuanced and precisely calibrated to generate 'effect' rather than blunt destruction. The perceived significance of the information-led RMA of the 1990s was that it allowed not only change in the way force was used, which implied doctrinal innovation, but new types of structures – organizational transformation – to fully utilize modern military power in a digital age.

Ultimately, the information led RMA was superseded by the concept of military transformation during the years of the George Bush Sr Administration. Transformation can be very broadly defined as:

> ... a process that shapes the changing nature of military competition and cooperation through new combinations of concepts, capabilities, people and organizations that exploit our nation's advantages and protect against our asymmetric vulnerabilities to sustain our strategic position, which helps underpin peace and stability in the world.

> (Blaker 2007, 23)

At the heart of transformation was the application of technological advance in areas such as computers, communications, command and control that would lead to an emphasis on developing network-centric warfare (NCW) as the basis of future military operations. The concept of NCW, in which sensors, command and control and strike capabilities were 'networked' via common datalinks, would give military forces the means to exploit an ability to mass firepower rather than forces, as well as 'self synchronize' (manoeuvre in the most efficient means possible) and operate in a highly mobile and dispersed manner (Hooker et al. 2005, 21). The NCW paradigm gained huge prominence as a foundation for transformation (Alberts et al. 2000, 88). The benefits of NCW were only achievable through the use of digital datalinks between ISR systems and decision-makers at the command and control level who could exploit a common operating picture of the battlespace to cue precision strike capabilities (McMaster 2008, 565). Although building this 'sensor to shooter link' was at the heart of NCW, more significant was how military forces sought to use transformation at a strategic level as a proactive process that sought to shape the global security environment in a manner that benefited the USA and its key allies. Transformation was designed to prevent the rise of potential adversaries to a position whereby they could challenge the military pre-eminence of the USA (Blaker 2007, 25).

The common thread running through transformation is a reliance on technological innovation to achieve certainty in understanding the battlespace, and acting decisively and rapidly to out-fight and out-think the adversary (McMaster 2003, 9–11). Whilst transformation might inform one particular approach to the use of force, optimized for the high-intensity combined arms battle, recent US operational experience suggests extreme caution before supporting notions that combinations of ISR, command and control and precision strike capabilities offer the possibility of lifting 'the fog of war' and removing 'friction' from war (Owens 2000, 119, 136–8, 146–7). There seems little evidence of dominant battlespace knowledge (DBK) being achieved, let alone exploited, in the war in Iraq from the end of the main conflict phase in April 2003 through to the present, in a manner that delivers rapid success. In contrast to the technological nirvana suggested by advocates of transformation, the potential for long-term strategic success in Iraq has demanded an increase in the numbers of ground forces through 'the Surge'. More importantly is recognition of the importance of addressing Iraq's national political and societal infrastructure, whilst winning the hearts and minds of its people. In other words, for all its technological wizardry, transformation has failed to supplant strategy in war.

Different strategic cultures imply that notions of transformation, whilst relevant to an idealized 'Western way of war', do not suggest a notion of 'future war' in a more general sense. The timeless nature of war, identified by Clausewitz, emphasizes the inevitability of friction, the persistence of fog of war, and the challenge of overcoming a lack of knowledge of an opponent's intent, history, politics and culture in order to achieve success (McMaster 2008, 569). It is these factors that can prevent effective development of strategy. A failure to formulate effective strategy will ultimately contribute to defeat at a military level, and strategic failure to achieve policy objectives (Murray 2008, 561–2). McMaster argues against an over-reliance on transformation as a basis for preparing for future war (McMaster 2008, 565). He notes that future wars are unlikely to be symmetrical in nature, and future adversaries, whether non-state groups or hostile state opponents, are not likely to fight the USA on its own terms or in a manner that suits a 'Western way of war' epitomized by military transformation.

The shape of arms to come and the future of the arms trade

The vision of future war painted by transformation advocates – the war we would prefer to fight – is not likely to be the reality of future war. Future wars are likely to involve ruthless and potent adversaries – both state and non-state – which fully utilize a range of asymmetric means to counter the military-technological advantages (Schnaubelt 2007, 96). The future of war is unlikely to revisit the experience of seeing inferior '3GW' forces flung mindlessly against superior information-enabled forces, as happened in the 1991 Gulf War (Hammes 2004, 252–4, 257–60). Opponents understand the significance of the classic lesson from Sun Tzu: 'one who knows the enemy and knows himself will not be endangered in a hundred engagements' (Sun Tzu 1994, 179). Sun Tzu's axiom highlights the importance of identifying and attacking an adversary's vulnerabilities, whilst protecting vulnerabilities in one's own side. Furthermore, finding the asymmetric edge over an opponent is as relevant from low-intensity intra-state 'ragged war' through to the largest high-intensity interstate wars, and even at the level of nuclear war.

In considering the impact of transformation, it is the author's contention that a degree of caution should be maintained in relying on technological 'silver bullets' to shape thinking about the future of war. However, technological advance and warfare are inextricably and undeniably integrated, and denial of the potential advantages of new technological approaches to war is as misguided as placing blind faith in such future possibilities. The reality is that technological change will remain a constant of military affairs, as it always has been. A range of future military capabilities are on the horizon that will offer radical new approaches to the use of force to the side best able to exploit such technologies for military effect. In a consideration of the future of war, the key challenge is that the spread of technology cannot be controlled and our future opponents are more likely to exploit military transformation to erode any military-technological advantage held currently by the USA and its allies (US National Intelligence Council 2008, 29–36).

In the 2003 Iraq War, the use of 'Blue Force Tracker' – in effect a battlefield radio that combined GPS information and digital datalinks to transmit data rather than just voice – allowed the USA and its coalition partners to understand the battlespace rapidly and with greater fidelity, and thus enjoy a very significant advantage in undertaking combined arms manoeuvre operations (Cordesman 2003, 240–5). Here is a technology that marries communications and navigation to geospatial information, to provide a picture of the location of friendly and hostile units on the battlespace in real time. It allows a friendly force to fully exploit the principles of military force and manoeuvre, to concentrate effect against an adversary's tactical and operational centre of gravity, and act inside the decision cycle of the opponent. Transformation proponents argue that NCW systems like Blue Force Tracker, if employed in large numbers throughout the battlespace, allow networked forces to gain a knowledge edge and apply precision firepower at the right place and right time, reducing the enemy's means to resist attack. Though Blue Force Tracker proved invaluable to coalition forces, it failed to compensate for the failure of strategy, which emerged after the main combat phase was concluded, and did not prevent Iraqi forces from exploiting tactical surprise to launch (largely ineffectual) attacks during the main combat phase (Zuccino 2004)

A heavy reliance on NCW systems like Blue Force Tracker is likely to emerge as a vulnerability for US and allied forces in future conflicts. The fragile technological foundations that are essential to sustain NCW are increasingly likely to be attacked from the outset of a conflict. This may be achieved through acquiring a range of electronic warfare, GPS jamming, counter-space systems and information warfare capabilities, which will become increasingly available on the arms market (Department of Defense 2008, 20–1). Such 'Counter-C^2' measures suggest that future war may see conflict within the electromagnetic and information dimensions to either preserve or remove a 'knowledge edge'. Both sides will seek to exploit advanced information and electronic warfare (I&EW) capabilities, which can identify opponents' I&EW systems and neutralize them before they can be employed. Such conflict within the electromagnetic and information dimensions of warfare could radically reshape the character and conduct of war, by opening up completely new realms of operations, such as Cyberspace.

In considering how the arms trade may change to match future warfare, the potential for information warfare – aka 'Cyberwar' – suggests the future shape of arms may need not just datalinks, but entirely new conceptual understanding of how radical forms of military force might be employed (Arquilla and Ronfeldt 1997, 30–2, 43–5). Cyberwar is waged within a virtual, man-made realm – Cyberspace – and can reach into the heart of open, information-based societies and unleash attacks on critical information infrastructure, which can generate a form of informational and electronic devastation that is quite unique. Dependence on information systems by most of the developed world creates strategic vulnerability to adversary cyber attack. Future cyberwar capabilities are likely to proliferate on the arms trade more rapidly than traditional forms of military capability because access to information technology and expertise in the techniques of cyberwar attack and defence are easily acquired through the commercial sector. The 'market' for cyberwar is unregulated, with little in the way of legal prohibitions to prevent the spread of capability and expertise. Small groups, individuals with a grudge or for hire, and major state actors can and will exploit cyberwar during future conflicts, and potentially prior to a recognizable outbreak of hostilities in the traditional sense.

Waging the information and electro-magnetic battle is likely to encompass development of Directed Energy Weapons (DEW), which will radically change the character and conduct of future war. The development of High Power Microwave (HPM) systems will allow the generation of rapid destructive – though likely non-lethal – effects at militarily useful ranges. Microwave weapons are designed to burn out an opponent's electronic systems, including command and control networks and ISR capabilities over a wide area (Beason 2005, 100–1; Walling 2001, 90–103) and are likely to appear in operational service with the USA, China, Russia and states within Western Europe within the next 10 years (Warwick 2009, 46–51).[3]

Space-based military capabilities are proliferating as more states exploit the space environment for military purposes. Space has been militarized since the beginning of the space age in the early 1960s, but there is an increasing likelihood of 'weaponization' occurring in coming years. China's anti-satellite (ASAT) test on 11 January 2007 represented a clear step towards weaponization (Milowicki and Johnson-Freese 2008, 4). China has clearly stated a requirement to counter an adversary's critical space capabilities, including command and control, communications, and ISR satellites. It is developing a range of ground-based and space-based ASAT systems for precisely that purpose, and the January 2007 test demonstrated that China could 'hold at risk' satellites in low Earth orbit (LEO)[4] (Department of Defense 2008, 27–8; Wortzel 2008, 112–37). Furthermore, the nature of ASATs makes it extremely difficult to implement, verify and monitor any arms control agreement prohibiting such capabilities, as the January 2007 Chinese test demonstrates. Any satellite could be used as an ASAT simply by colliding it with a target. Although the open sale of ASAT capabilities on the arms market seems unlikely, the sale of 'Space Denial' capabilities, such as GPS jamming systems and satellite communications interception is likely to occur more easily. Furthermore, China's ASAT capability demonstrated the ability to adapt existing ballistic missile technology to the ASAT role, should they chose to do so (Kaiser 2008, 314). The solution to countering the emerging challenge posed by future ASAT capabilities may be a greater emphasis on investing in large numbers of low-cost small satellites, launched on demand by commercial space-launch capabilities. By embracing 'the small and many' rather than being dependent on 'the large, expensive and few' it would be much more difficult for future adversaries equipped with ASATs to quickly neutralize an opponent's critical space capabilities. Because small satellites are significantly lower-cost than traditional satellites, they thus open up the use of space to a wider range of actors. Indeed, becoming a 'spacepower' may not even demand a costly investment in the complete range of space capabilities at a national level. States and even non-state actors can already exploit commercial satellite capabilities for communications, navigation and ISR at low cost. Small satellites offer a broader range of states the ability of acquiring an indigenous space capability for military or non-military purposes at much lower cost and over reduced time in the future.

Advanced information warfare, counter-space and DEW capabilities contribute towards a steady erosion of US and Western military advantage over coming decades, and future wars are not going to be as one-sided as a result. However, preserving the knowledge edge is only part of the challenge facing the USA and its allies. In considering the prospect of future war, there seems little likelihood of direct military threats to the USA or Western Europe; and the USA in particular, but also many of its key allies, emphasizes expeditionary capabilities, which rely on maritime forces. A major challenge facing expeditionary forces will be to counter attempts by adversaries to deny access through a range of military measures. Anti-ship cruise missile (ASCM) and anti-ship ballistic missile (ASBM) systems (Fisher 2008), shore-based missiles, and quiet submarines equipped with torpedoes and mines will threaten expeditionary naval forces at very long range. The challenge posed by these systems is significant and, whilst the notion that expeditionary naval forces cannot survive is misleading and over-stated, anti-access capabilities will be in increasing demand in coming years. Even non-state actors are likely to seek such capabilities. During the 2006 Lebanon War, an Israeli naval vessel, the INS Hanit, was successfully attacked by Hezbollah with an Iranian-supplied anti-ship missile launched from shore, suggesting that even non-state actors may increase their ability to exploit more traditional military capabilities (Kainikara and Parkin 2007, 51).

The Western air power edge seems also likely to be eroded. For example, stealth technology has existed since the late 1970s and has allowed the USA to enjoy a significant advantage in air power in recent conflicts. Stealth aircraft can penetrate an adversary's air defences without being detected, giving them a significant advantage over non-stealth aircraft and laying open less sophisticated adversaries to the sort of offensive air operations seen during the 1991 Gulf War, the 1999 Kosovo Conflict and the 2003 Iraq War (Meilinger 1997, 66). However, there will be increasingly a 'stealth vs. counter-stealth' duel as a result of the development of more sophisticated integrated air defence systems (IADS) that can detect even advanced stealth aircraft at longer range using a range of passive sensor technologies (Sweetman 2006). By eroding the effectiveness of stealth through investment in counter-stealth sensors, future adversaries may prevent opponents that are heavily dependent on stealth aircraft from using their air power effectively in a conflict. Such counter-stealth capabilities would be in high demand by those states that feel at greatest risk from adversaries equipped with stealth aircraft or missiles. The sale of counter-stealth sensors when combined with advanced 'double digit' surface-to-air missiles (SAMs) would offer a cost-effective means to counter Western air power in future conflicts.

One of the most notable trends since the early 1990s has been the development of unmanned systems. The battlespace of the future is likely to see large numbers of unmanned systems performing a wide variety of roles and tasks. Unmanned systems will not be confined to supporting roles, but will deliver firepower against future adversaries on a much more extensive scale than is currently seen with armed Predator and Reaper UAVs over Afghanistan. For example, naval forces could exploit the reach, stealth and persistence of large numbers of unmanned systems in the maritime environment as a highly mobile, very stealthy expeditionary sensor grid, allowing a task force to rapidly gain an understanding of the battlespace, whether it is on the open ocean, or operating in the littoral.

In thinking about how to use unmanned systems, one approach might be the use of 'swarming'. The concept of swarming is not new, but dates back to the battles of Alexander in 329BC (Edwards 2006, 179). Modern concepts of swarming are based on ensuring superior situational awareness, exploiting stealth, utilizing standoff capability, and attacking an adversary through encirclement and simultaneity from multiple axes. Swarm attacks can be 'pulsed' – short, sharp attacks, followed by a retreat, and then subsequent attacks to throw an adversary off balance. The principles of swarming are ideally suited to small, high speed, stealthy unmanned systems which can exploit surprise to deliver rapid attacks within the decision cycle of an adversary. It is already evident that potential adversaries exploit swarming in military operations, so there is no reason to expect that such attacks will not be faced in future operations, most notably in the maritime environment (Haghshenass 2006). The potential for swarming attacks to overwhelm traditional approaches to maritime operations suggests that one response to the threat posed by naval swarm attacks is to defend with a counter-swarm. Success in undertaking a manoeuvrist approach in modern naval warfare may ironically depend on waging attritional battles between competing swarms of high-speed, unmanned systems in the air, and on or under the sea, whilst manned platforms act as command and control nodes, and wage an information battle to detect and disable the opponent's command and control system to deny them information dominance. Emerging capabilities in miniature munitions and directed energy weapons will reinforce the future potential of realizing this military capability.

In thinking radically about future warfare, bold ideas are the most engaging. The development of micro autonomous systems and technology (MAST) and the application of nanotechnology could lead to the future battlespace being flooded with large numbers of micro-platforms that emulate insects or birds to move from location to location, all networked and able to act as a 'sensor cloud', or able to deliver lethal payloads against targets in an overwhelming, but largely invisible force (Fulghum 2009, 24). MAST technology goes some way towards realizing Libicki's concept of 'Fire Ant Warfare', which could transform the face of future war (Libicki 1997, 198–201). Such technologies, whilst technologically challenging now, may exploit commercial developments in robotics and microelectronics to become available to a broader range of users in the same way that information technology – once only available to high-level government and military agencies – is now literally available to all as mobile phones, iPods or laptop computers. Commercial applications for low-cost robotic systems would drive the proliferation of technology and expertise, and promote rapid innovation in the application of robotics in the battlespace. There is no real possibility that a monopoly on such future capabilities could be maintained by one or a small number of actors. The spread of such technologies from civilian to military environments is inevitable in coming decades. Such possibilities suggest that the arms trade of 2030 may be unrecognizable in comparison to what exists today!

Finally, it is important to consider the future shape of weapons of mass destruction (WMD). The international non-proliferation regime to prevent the spread of nuclear weapons looks weak at best, with India and Pakistan having confirmed their nuclear status in 1998, the Democratic People's Republic of Korea (North Korea) having broken out of the 1967 Nuclear Non-Proliferation Treaty (NPT) in 2003, and Iran seemingly set to follow suit, with estimates that the current Iranian nuclear programme will enable it to acquire a nuclear weapon well before 2015. Levite warns of coming nuclear 'anarchy' as one possibility of a failure to restore the NPT regime (Levite 2009, 27). A failure to prevent the unravelling of global norms against nuclear proliferation suggests that other states may respond to Iran and North Korea's acquisition of nuclear capabilities in kind, and a chain of 'wildfire' proliferation may lead to a rapid increase in the number of nuclear weapons states. Nor has the proliferation of chemical and biological weapons been constrained by arms control agreements, such as the 1992 Chemical Weapons Convention and the 1972 Biological and Toxin Weapons Convention, with numerous states now possessing significant chemical and biological warfare (CBW) capabilities. The development of future CBW capabilities looks set to continue. The development of 'Novichok' fourth-generation chemical agents (FGA), initially by the Soviet Union and subsequently by the Russian Federation, are five-to-eight times as lethal as VX, and are based on commercial precursors not banned under the CWC. Such weapons set a dangerous precedent, which risks greater proliferation of new 'novel' chemical agents (Mirzayanov 1995, 23). Likewise, research and development into genetic engineering and biotechnology holds open the prospect of radically new and much more deadly biological weapons, which are genetically designed to be highly usable on the battlefield for tactical purposes, including bioregulator-based agents (Dando 1999, 53–60). The future of chemical and biological weapons capabilities may, thus, see a renewed threat of such weapons not only appearing in the arsenals of some states, but also becoming sought after by weak states seeking a low-cost means of deterring or defeating a more powerful opponent.

Conclusion

The nature of the future arms trade will be driven by its customer's requirements – the armed forces of the world's major actors. The broad range of security challenges that shape the future of war will suggest that the arms trade will match the nature of this strategic context. Current trends in the international security environment suggest both a continuing challenge from a range of unconventional adversaries, and a return of traditional geopolitical competition between major state actors as the 'Unipolar Moment' is replaced by a competitive multipolar world. A range of security challenges – both traditional as well as the 'new security agenda' – suggest that the future security environment will be characterized by accelerating change, strategic uncertainty and security complexity.

Transformation correctly suggests an imperative for maintaining a technological edge against a range of perceived likely opponents – both state and non-state. Conversely, those future adversaries will seek the means to undermine this edge, either by fighting in a manner that denies the USA and its allies the opportunity to exploit advanced capabilities to full effect, or by acquiring asymmetric capabilities that counter any perceived technological edge. The emergence of a multi-polar world and the rise of powerful new actors suggest that coming decades will see an intensified contest to challenge the traditional military-technological advantage held by the USA and its allies. The arms trade will naturally accelerate this process by allowing accelerating proliferation of advanced military capabilities and, more broadly, technologies that will sustain the growing military power of rising actors. The future of the arms trade will reflect this inherent competition and the multi-faceted nature of the security environment. In tomorrow's arm's bazaars, expect to see RPGs and AK-47s alongside advanced information warfare capabilities, unmanned systems and anti-access capabilities. Very much the baroque arsenal for the 21st century!

Notes

1 The comments in this chapter represent the personal views of the author and in no way reflect the official policy of the Australian Government, the Australian Department of Defence, or the Royal Australian Navy.
2 The OODA Loop concept was suggested by Col. John Boyd, and describes a continuous decision cycle comprising Observe, Orientate, Decide and Act as a means explaining military decision-making.
3 DEW generates effect at the Speed of Light, or ~ 186,000 miles (~300,000 km) per second.
4 Low Earth orbit extends from 100 miles up to 800 miles above the Earth.

Bibliography

Alberts, David S., John T. Garstka, Frederick P. Stein, *Network Centric Warfare – Developing and Leveraging Information Superiority*, 2nd Edition (Revised), Washington, CCRP Publications, 2000

Altman, Roger C., 'The Great Crash, 2008', *Foreign Affairs*, Vol. 88, No. 1, January/February 2009

Arquilla, John and David Ronfeldt, 'Cyberwar is Coming', in John Arquilla and David Ronfeldt, eds, *In Athena's Camp – Preparing for Conflict in the Information Age*, Santa Monica, RAND, 1997

Barnett, Thomas, *The Pentagon's New Map: War and Peace in the Twenty First Century*, New York, Putnam's, 2004

Beason, Doug, *The E Bomb*, Cambridge, Da Capo Press, 2005

Blaker, James R., *Transforming Military Force: The Legacy of Arthur Cebrowski and Network Centric Warfare*, Westport, Praeger Security International, 2007

Campbell, Colin J. and Jean H. Laherrere, 'The End of Cheap Oil', *Scientific American*, March 1998

Cordesman, Anthony H., *The Iraq War: Strategy, Tactics and Military Lessons*, Washington, CSIS, 2003

Dando, Malcolm, *Biotechnology Weapons and Humanity*, Amsterdam, Harwood Academic Publishers, 1999

De Blij, Harm, *Why Geography Matters: Three Challenges Facing America*, Oxford, Oxford University Press, 2007

Department of Defense, *Annual Report to Congress: Military Power of the People's Republic of China 2008*, US Department of Defense, June 2008, www.defenselink.mil/pubs/pdfs/China_Military_Report_08.pdf

Edwards, Sean J. A., *Swarming and the Future of Warfare*, Santa Monica, RAND, 2006

Elhefnawy, Nader, 'The Impending Oil Shock', in *Survival*, Vol. 50, No. 2, April–May 2008

Fisher, Richard D., 'Strait shooter: PLA expands and upgrades missile arsenal', *Jane's Intelligence Review*, October 2008

Friedman, Thomas L., *The World is Flat: A Brief History of the Twenty-First Century*, New York, Picador, 2007

Fulghum, David A., 'Bugging the Bugs', *Aviation Week and Space Technology*, Vol. 170, No. 2, January 2009

Gat, Azar, 'The Return of Authoritarian Great Powers', *Foreign Affairs*, July/August 2007

Gates, Robert, 'Speech by U.S. Secretary of Defense', May 2008, www.defenselink.mil/speeches/speech.aspx?speechid=1240

——'Speech by U.S. Secretary of Defense', September 2008, www.defenselink.mil/speeches/speech.aspx?speechid=1279

Gray, Colin S., *Another Bloody Century: Future Warfare*, London, Weidenfeld and Nicholson, 2005

Gunaratna, Rohan, *Inside Al Qaeda: Global Network of Terror*, Carlton North, Scribe Publications, 2002

Haghshenass, Fariborz, 'Iran's Doctrine of Asymmetric Naval Warfare', Policy Watch No. 1179, December 2006, www.washingtoninstitute.org

Hammes, Thomas, *The Sling and the Stone: On War in the 21st Century*, St Paul, Zenith Press, 2004

Hammond, Grant T., *The Mind of War: John Boyd and American Security*, Washington, Smithsonian Institution Press, 2001

Hooker, Richard D., Jr, H. R. McMaster and Dave Grey, 'Getting Transformation Right', *Joint Forces Quarterly*, Issue 38, 3rd Quarter 2005, www.amnesty.org/en/library/asset/ACT30/003/2004/en/dom-ACT300032004en.html

Kagan, Robert, *The Return of History and the End of Dreams*, New York, Alfred Knopf, 2008

Kainikara, Sanu and Russell Parkin, *Pathways to Victory: Observations from the 2006 Israel-Hezbollah Conflict*, Canberra, Air Power Development Centre, 2007

Kaiser, Stefan A., 'Viewpoint: Chinese Anti-satellite Weapons: New Power Geometry and New Legal Policy', *Astropolitics*, Vol. 6 (3), January 2008

Kaplan, Robert D., *The Coming Anarchy: Shattering the Dreams of the Post Cold War*, New York, Vintage Books, 2001

King, Neil, 'Peak Oil: A Survey of Security Concerns', September 2008, www.cnas.org/node/182

Klare, Michael T., *Resource Wars: The New Landscape of Global Conflict*, New York, Owl Books, 2002

Krepinevich, Andrew F., 'Cavalry to Computer: The Pattern of Military Revolution', *The National Interest*, No. 37, Fall 1994

Levite, A. E., *Heading for the Fourth Nuclear Age*, Carnegie Endowment for International Peace, Winter 2009, www.carnegieendowment.org/publications/index.cfm?fa=view&id=22655&prog=zgp&proj=znpp

Liang, Q. and W. Xiangsui, 'Unrestricted Warfare', 1999, www.terrorism.com/documents/TRC-Analysis/unrestricted.pdf

Libicki, Martin C., 'The Small and the Many', in John Arquilla and David Ronfeldt, eds, *In Athena's Camp: Preparing for Conflict in the Information Age*, Santa Monica, RAND, 1997

McMaster, H. R., 'Crack in the Foundation: Defense Transformation and the Underlying Assumption of Dominant Knowledge in Future War', 2003, www.au.af.mil/au/awc/awcgate/army-usawc/mcmaster_foundation.pdf

——'Learning from Contemporary Conflicts to Prepare for Future War', *Orbis*, Vol. 52, No. 4, Fall 2008

Meilinger, Philip S., Col. (USAF), 'Air Targeting Strategies: An Overview', in Richard P. Hallion, ed., *Air Power Confronts an Unstable World*, London, Brasseys, 1997

Milowicki, Gene. V. and Joan Johnson-Freese, 'Strategic Choices: Examining the United States Military Response to the Chinese Anti-Satellite Test', in *Astropolitics*, Vol. 6 (1), January 2008

Mirzayanov, Vil S., 'Dismantling the Soviet/Russian Chemical Weapons Complex', in Amy E. Smithson, Vil S. Mirzayanov, Roland LaJoie and Michael Krepon, eds, *Chemical Weapons Disarmament in Russia: Problems and Prospects*, Washington, Stimson Center, 1995

Murray, Williamson, 'History, War, and Future', *Orbis*, Vol. 52, No. 4, Fall 2008

Owens, William, ed., *Lifting the Fog of War*, New York, Farrar, Straus and Giroux, 2000

Peters, Ralph, *Fighting for the Future: Will America Triumph?*, Mechanicsburg, Stackpole Books, 1999

Schnaubelt, Christopher M., 'Whither the RMA?', *Parameters*, Autumn 2007

Smith, Rupert, *The Utility of Force: The Art of War in the Modern World*, London, Penguin Books, 2006

Sun Tzu, *The Art of War*, translated by Ralph D. Sawyer, Boulder, Westview Press, 1994

Sweetman, Bill, 'The Future of Advanced Stealth: Worth the Cost?', *Jane's Defence Weekly*, July 2006

US Joint Forces Command, *The Joint Operating Environment 2008: Challenges and Implications for the Future Joint Force*, United States Joint Forces Command, November 2008, us.jfcom.mil/sites/J5/j59/default.aspx

US National Intelligence Council, *Global Trends 2025: A Transformed World*, US National Intelligence Council, November 2008, www.dni.gov/nic/NIC_2025_project.html

Walling, Eileen M., 'High Power Microwaves and Modern Warfare', in William C. Martel, ed., *The Technological Arsenal: Emerging Defense Capabilities*, Washington, Smithsonian Institution Press, 2001

Warwick, Graham, 'Electric Charge; Efficiency Drive; Next Light', *Aviation Week and Space Technology*, Vol. 170, No. 2, January 2009

Wood, William B., 'Crossing the Line: Geopolitics of International Migration', in George J. Demko and William B. Wood, eds, *Reordering the World: Geopolitical Perspectives on the 21st Century*, Oxford, Westview Press, 1994

Wortzel, Larry M., 'The Chinese People's Liberation Army and Space Warfare', *Astropolitics*, Vol. 6 (2), May 2008

Zuccino, David and Mike Bowden, *Thunder Run: Three Days with Tusker Brigade in the Battle for Baghdad*, Atlantic Books, 2004

Selected reading

Reference volumes

Defence Intelligence Organisation (DIO), *Defence Economic Trends in the Asia-Pacific*, Canberra, Australian Government Publishing Service, various annual editions
DeRouen, Karl and Paul Bellamy, eds, *International Security and the United States: An Encyclopedia*, Westport, Praeger Security International, 2007
IISS, *The Military Balance*, London, International Institute for Strategic Studies, various annual editions
Israel's Leading Enterprises, Israel, Dun and Bradstreet, various annual editions
Middle East Strategic Balance, Tel-Aviv, The Jaffee Center for Strategic Studies, Tel-Aviv University, various editions
SIPRI, *SIPRI Yearbook*, Stockholm, Stockholm International Peace Research Institute, various annual editions

Books and monographs

Alberts, David S., John J. Garstka and Frederick P. Stein, *Network Centric Warfare: Developing and Leveraging Information Superiority*, 2nd Edition (revised), Washington, CCRP Publications, 2000
Alic, John et al., *Beyond Spin-off: Military and Commercial Technology in a Changing World*, Cambridge, MA, Harvard Business School Press, 1992
Allen, Kenneth and Jonathan Pollack, *China's Air Force Enters the 21st Century*, Santa Monica: RAND, 1995
Anderson, Lisa, *The State and Social Transformation in Tunisia and Libya, 1830–1980*, Princeton, Princeton University Press, 1996
Anthony, Ian, ed., *Arms Export Regulations*, Oxford, Oxford University Press/SIPRI, 1991
Arquilla, John and David Ronfeldt, eds, *In Athena's Camp: Preparing for Conflict in the Information Age*, Santa Monica, RAND, 1997
Arnett, Eric, ed., *Military Capacity and the Risk of War: China, India, Pakistan and Iran*, New York: Oxford University Press/ SIPRI, 1997
Arreguin-Toft, Ivan, *How the Weak Win Wars*, Cambridge, Cambridge University Press, 2005
Ashton, Nigel, *King Hussein of Jordan: A Political Life*, New Haven, CT, Yale University Press, 2008
Ball, Desmond, *Signals Intelligence in the Post-Cold War Era: Developments in the Asia-Pacific Region*, Singapore, Institute of Southeast Asian Studies, 1993
——*Burma's Military Secrets: Signals Intelligence (SIGINT) from the Second World War to Civil War and Cyber Warfare*, Bangkok, White Lotus, 1998
Baran, Paul and Paul Sweezy, *Monopoly Capital*, London, Monthly Review Press, 1966
Barnett, Thomas, *The Pentagon's New Map: War and Peace in the Twenty First Century*, New York, Putnam's, 2004
Bauer, Sibylle and Mark Bromley, *The European Union Code of Conduct on Arms Exports: Improving the Annual Report*, SIPRI Policy Paper No. 8, Stockholm, SIPRI, November 2004
Beason, Doug, *The E Bomb*, Cambridge, Da Capo Press, 2005
Beckett, Ian, *Modern Insurgencies and Counter-Insurgencies: Guerillas and their Opponents Since 1750*, London and New York, Routledge, 2001
Bell, Coral, *The End of the Vasco da Gama Era: The Next Landscape of World Politics*, Lowy Institute Paper No. 21, Lowy Institute, Sydney, 2007
Benoit, Emile, *Defense and Growth in Developing Countries*, Boston, Heath/Lexington Books, 1973
Bert, Wayne, *The Reluctant Superpower: United States Policy in Bosnia, 1991–95*, New York, St Martin's Press, 1997
Betts, Richard, *Surprise Attack*, Washington, Brookings Institution, 1981
Biddle, Stephen, *Military Power: Explaining Victory and Defeat in Modern Battle*, Princeton, Princeton University Press, 2004
Bischak, Greg, ed., *Towards a Peace Economy in the United States: Essays on Military Industry, Disarmament and Economic Conversion*, New York, St Martin's Press, 1991
Bitzinger, Richard A., *The Globalization of Arms Production: Defense Markets in Transition*, Washington, Defense Budget Project, 1993

——— *Towards a Brave New Arms Industry?*, Adelphi Paper No. 356, International Institute for Strategic Studies, London, 2003

Blaker, James, *Transforming Military Force: The Legacy of Arthur Cebrowski and Network Centric Warfare*, Westport, Praeger Security International, 2007

Blank, Stephen, *The Dynamics of Russian Weapons Sales to China*, Carlisle, US Army War College, 1997

Blaufarb, Douglas, *The Counterinsurgency Era: U.S. Doctrine and Performance, 1950 to the Present*, New York, The Free Press, 1977

Bobbitt, Philip, *The Shield of Achilles: War, Peace, and the Course of History*, New York, Anchor Books, 2003

Brauer, Jurgen and J. Paul Dunne, eds, *Arming the South: The Economics of Military Expenditures, Arms Production and Trade in Developing Countries*, New York, Palgrave Macmillan, 2002

——— *Arms Trade and Economic Development: Theory, Policy, and Cases in Arms Trade Offsets*, London, Routledge, 2004

Briody, Dan, *The Halliburton Agenda*, New Jersey, John Wiley, 2004

Brodet, David, Moshe Yustman and Maurice Teubal, eds, *Industrial-Technological Policy for Israel*, Jerusalem, Jerusalem Institute for Israeli Studies, 1990

Brown, Michael E., *The International Dimensions of Internal Conflict*, Cambridge, MA, MIT Press, 1996

Brzoska, Michael and Peter Lock, eds, *Restructuring of Arms Production in Western Europe*, Oxford, Oxford University Press, 1992

Brzoska, Michael and Thomas Ohlson, *Arms Transfers to the Third World 1971–85*, Oxford, Oxford University Press, 1987

Buzan, Barry, *An Introduction to Strategic Studies, Military Technology and International Relations*, London, Macmillan, 1987

Cappelen, Adne, Olav Bjerkholt and Nils Petter Gleditsch, *Global Conversion from Arms to Development Aid: Macroeconomic Effects on Norway*, Oslo, PRIO, 1982

Chapman, Gary and Joel Yudken, *Briefing Book on the Military-Industrial Complex*, Washington, Council for a Livable World Education Fund, December 1992

Chesterman, Simon and Chia Lehnardt, *From Mercenaries to Market*, Oxford, Oxford University Press, 2007

Cleveland, William L., *A History of Modern Middle East*, 2nd edition, Oxford, Westview, 2000

Clifford, Bob, *The Marketing of Rebellion: Insurgents, Media and International Activism*, Cambridge, Cambridge University Press, 2005

Clutterbuck, Richard, *The Long War: Counterinsurgency in the Third World*, New York, Penguin Books, 1976

Cogan, Charles G., *The Third Option: The Emancipation of European Defence 1989–2000*, Westport and London, Praeger, 2001

Cohen, Mitchell, *Zion and State: Nation, Class and the Shaping of Modern Israel*, New York, Columbia University Press, 1992

Cohen, Stephen P., *India: Emerging Power*, New Delhi, Oxford University Press, 2001

——— *The Indian Army: Its Contribution to the Development of a Nation*, New Delhi, Oxford University Press, 1990

Collier, Paul, *The Bottom Billion*, Oxford, Oxford University Press, 2007

Collier, Paul and Anke Hoeffler, *Military Expenditure: Threats, Aid, and Arms Races*, Oxford, Mimeograph, University of Oxford, 2004

Cooper, Robert, *The Breaking of Nations*, New York, Atlantic Books, 2004

Cordesman, Anthony H., *Iran's Military Forces in Transition: Conventional Threats and Weapons of Mass Destruction*, Westport, CT, Praeger, 1999

——— *A Tragedy of Arms: Military and Security Developments in the Maghreb*, Westport, Praeger, 2002

——— *The Iraq War: Strategy, Tactics and Military Lessons*, Washington, CSIS, 2003

Cordesman, Anthony and Ahmed Hashim, *Iran: Dilemmas of Dual Containment*, Boulder, Westview, 1997

Costigan, Sean S. and Ann R. Markusen, eds, *Arming the Future: A Defense Industry for the 21st Century*, New York, Council on Foreign Relations Press, 1999

Damrosch, Lori Fisler, ed., *Enforcing Restraint: Collective Intervention in Internal Conflicts*, New York, Council on Foreign Relations Press, 1993

Dando, Malcolm, *Biotechnology Weapons and Humanity*, Amsterdam, Harwood Academic Publishers, 1999

De Blij, Harm, *Why Geography Matters: Three Challenges Facing America*, Oxford, Oxford University Press, 2007

Dobbins, James et al., *America's Role in Nation-Building: From Germany to Iraq*, Santa Monica, RAND, 2003

Dumas, Lloyd and Marek Thee, eds, *Making Peace Possible: The Promise of Economic Conversion*, Oxford, Pergamon Press, 1989

Edwards, Sean J. A., *Swarming and the Future of Warfare*, Santa Monica, RAND, 2006

Eisenstadt, Michael, *Iranian Military Power: Capabilities and Intentions*, Policy, Paper No. 42, The Washington Institute for Near East Policy, Washington, 1996

Elsner, Wolfram, ed., *Arms, War, and Terrorism in the Global Economy Today-Economic Analyses and Civilian Alternatives*, New Brunswick, NJ, Transaction Publishers, 2007

Engdahl, F. William, *A Century of War: Anglo American Oil Politics and the New World Order*, London, Pluto Press, 2004

Etzioni, Amitai, *From Empire to Community: A New Approach to International Relations*, New York, Palgrave Macmillan, 2004

Feldman, Shai and Yiftah Shapir, eds, *The Middle East Military Balance 2000–2001*, Israel, Jaffee Center for Strategic Studies, 2001

Fontanel, Jacques and Manas Chatterji, eds, *War, Peace and Security*, Bingley, Emerald, 2009

Friedman, Thomas, *The World is Flat: A Brief History of the Twenty-First Century*, New York, Picador, 2007

Fromkin, David, *A Peace to End All Peace: The Fall of the Ottoman Empire and the Creation of the Modern Middle East*, New York, Henry Holt and Company, 1989

Fruchart, D. et al., *United Nations Arms Embargoes: Their Impact on Arms Flows and Target Behaviour*, Stockholm, SIPRI/ Uppsala University, 2007

Gansler, Jacques, *Defense Conversion: Transforming the Arsenal of Democracy*, Cambridge, MA, MIT Press, 1995

Gennady, Chufrin, ed., *Russia and Asia: The Emerging Security Agenda*, Stockholm, SIPRI, 1999

Giroux, Henry, *The University in Chains: Confronting the Military Industrial Academic Complex*, Boulder, CO, Paradigm, 2007

Gleditsch, Nils Petter, Adne Cappelen and Olav Bjerkholt, *The Wages of Peace: Disarmament in a Small Industrialised Economy*, London, PRIO/Sage, 1994

Gleditsch, Nils Petter, Goran Lindgren, Naima Mouhleb, Sjoerd Smit and Indra de Soysa, *Making Peace Pay: A Bibliography on Disarmament and Conversion*, Claremont, Regina Books, 2000

Gleditsch, Nils Petter, Olav Bjerkholt, Ådne Cappelen, Ron P. Smith and J. Paul Dunne, eds, *The Peace Dividend*, Amsterdam, North-Holland, 1996

Goldblat, Jozef, *Arms Control: The New Guide to Negotiations and Agreements*, London, Sage/SIPRI and International Peace Research Institute Oslo (PRIO), 2002

Goldman, Emily and Tom Mahnken, eds, *The Information Revolution in Asia*, New York, Palgrave Macmillan, 2004

Gray, Colin S., *House of Cards. Why Arms Control Must Fail*, Ithaca, NY, 1992

—— *Another Bloody Century: Future Warfare*, London, Weidenfeld and Nicholson, 2005

Green, Michael, *Arming Japan: Defense Production, Alliance Politics, and the Postwar Search for Autonomy*, New York, Columbia University Press, 1995

Grenier, John, *The First Way of War: American War Making on the Frontier, 1607–1814*, Cambridge, Cambridge University Press, 2005

Guay, Terrence, *At Arm's Length*, London, Macmillan, 1998

Gunaratna, Rohan, *Inside Al Qaeda: Global Network of Terror*, Carlton North, Scribe Publications, 2002

Haass, Richard N., *Intervention: The Use of American Military Force in the Post-Cold War World*, Washington, The Carnegie Endowment for International Peace, 1994

Hallion, Richard P., ed., *Air Power Confronts an Unstable World*, London, Brasseys, 1997

Hamilton, Daniel S., ed., *Transatlantic Transformations: Equipping NATO for the 21st Century*, Washington, John Hopkins University, 2004

Hammes, Thomas, *The Sling and the Stone: On War in the 21st Century*, St Paul, Zenith Press, 2004

Hammond, Grant T., *The Mind of War: John Boyd and American Security*, Washington, Smithsonian Institution Press, 2001

Hartley, Keith, *Economic Aspects of Disarmament: Conversion as an Investment Process*, Geneva, UNIDIR, 1993

Hartley, Keith and Todd Sandler, *The Economics of Defense*, Cambridge, Cambridge University Press, 1995

Hartley, Keith and Todd Sandler, eds, *Handbook of Defense Economics*, Amsterdam: Elsevier, 1995

—— *Handbook of Defence Economics*, Amsterdam, North-Holland, 2007

Hartung, William D. and Frida Berrigan, *Militarization of U.S. Africa Policy, 2000 to 2005: A Fact Sheet*, Arms Trade Resource Centre, Axis of Influence-World Policy Institute: Research Project, 2005, www.worldpolicy.org/projects/ arms/reports/AfricaMarch2005.html

Hashim, Ahmed, *Iranian National Security Policies under the Islamic Republic: New Defense Thinking and Growing Military Capabilities*, Occasional Paper No. 2, The Henry L. Stimson Center, 1994

—— *Insurgency and Counter-Insurgency in Iraq*, Ithaca, Cornell University Press, 2006

Haug, Maria et al., *Shining a Light on Small Arms Exports: The Record of State Transparency*, Small Arms Survey Occasional Paper 4, Geneva and Oslo, Small Arms Survey and Norwegian Initiative on Small Arms Transfers, January 2002

Higgs, Robert, ed., *Arms Politics and the Economy: Historical and Contemporary Perspectives*, New York, Holmes and Meier, 1990

Howard, Michael, *War in European History*, Cambridge, MA, Oxford University Press, 2001

Hrebenar, Ronald, *Japan's New Party System*, 3rd edition, Boulder, CO, Westview Press, 2000

Hudson, Michael C., *Arab Politics: The Search for Legitimacy*, New Haven, CT, Yale University Press, 1977

Hughes, Christopher, *Japan's Re-emergence as a 'Normal' Military Power*, Adelphi Paper 368 69, London, International Institute for Strategic Studies, 2005

Huldt, Bo and Masako Ikegami, eds, *The Strategic Yearbook on East Asian Security*, Swedish National Defence College and the Finnish Defence University, 2008

Huntington, Samuel, *The Third Wave: Democratization in the Late Twentieth Century*, Norman, University of Oklahoma Press, 1993

Huxley, Tim and Susan Willett, *Arming East Asia*, Adelphi Paper 329, International Institute of Strategic Studies, London, 1999

Ikegami-Andersson, Masako, *The Military-Industrial Complex: The Cases of Sweden and Japan*, Aldershot, Dartmouth Publishing Company, 1992

Isard, Walter and Charles Anderton, eds, *Economics of Arms Reduction and the Peace Process*, New York, North-Holland, 1992

Jager, Thomas and Gerhad Kummel, eds, *Private Military Companies: Chances, Problems, Pitfalls and Prospects*, Wiesbaden, VS Verlag, 2007

James, Andrew, *The Defence Industry and Globalisation: Challenging Traditional Structures*, Stockholm, Defence Research Establishment, 2001

Ji, You, *The Armed Forces of China*, Sydney, London and New York, Allen and Unwin/I. B. Tauris, 1999

Jones, Clive, *Britain and the Yemen Civil War, 1962–1965*, Brighton, Sussex Academic, 2004

Kagan, Robert, *The Return of History and the End of Dreams*, New York, Alfred Knopf, 2008

Kainikara, Sanu and Russell Parkin, *Pathways to Victory: Observations from the 2006 Israel-Hezbollah Conflict*, Canberra, Air Power Development Centre, 2007

Kaldor, Mary, *New and Old Wars: Organised Violence in a Global Era*, Cambridge, Polity Press, 2006

Kalyvas, Stathis N., *The Logic of Violence in Civil War*, Cambridge, Cambridge University Press, 2006

Kaplan, David E. and Andrew Marshall, *The Cult at the End of the World: The Incredible Story of Aum*, London, Arrow, 1996

Kaplan, Robert D., *The Coming Anarchy: Shattering the Dreams of the Post Cold War*, New York, Vintage Books, 2001

Kavic, Lorne J., *India's Quest for Security: Defence Policies, 1947–1965*, Berkeley: University of California Press, 1967

Keohane, Daniel, *Europe's New Defense Agency*, London, Center for European Reform, 2004

Kinsey, Christopher, *Corporate Soldiers and International Security*, London, Routledge, 2006

Kiss, Yudit, *The Defence Industry in East-Central Europe: Restructuring and Conversion*, Oxford, Oxford University Press, 1998

Klare, Michael T., *Resource Wars: the New Landscape of Global Conflict*, New York, Owl Books, 2002

Klare, Michael and Peter Kornbluh, eds, *Low Intensity Warfare, Counterinsurgency, Proinsurgency and Antiterrorism in the Eighties*, New York, Random House, 1988

Klieman, Aharon, *Double-Edged Sword: Israel Defence Exports as an Instrument of Foreign Policy*, Tel-Aviv, Am Oved, 1992

Klieman, Aharon and Reuven Pedatzur, *Rearming Israel: Defense Procurement through the 1990s*, Tel-Aviv, Jaffee Center for Strategic Studies, 1991

Kosiak, Steven M., *Cost of the Wars in Iraq and Afghanistan, and Other Military Operations through 2008 and Beyond*, Washington, Center for Strategic and Budgetary Assessments, 2008

Krause, Keith, *Arms and the State: Patterns of Military Production and Trade*, Cambridge, Cambridge University Press, 1995

Krepinevich, Andrew, *The Army and Vietnam*, Baltimore, Johns Hopkins University Press, 1986

Kwak Tae-hwan and Seung-ho Joo, eds, *North Korea's Second Nuclear Crisis and Northeast Asian Security*, Hampshire and Burlington, Ashgate, 2007

Lansford, Tom and Blagovest Tashev, eds, *Old Europe: New Europe and the US: Renegotiating Transatlantic Security in the Post 9/11 Era*, Hampshire, Ashgate, 2005

Laurance, Edward J., *The International Arms Trade*, New York, Lexington, 1992

Lifshitz, Yaacov, *The Economics of Producing Defense*, Boston: Kluwer Academic Publishers, 2003

Lorell, Mark A. et al., *Going Global? U.S. Government Policy and the Defense Aerospace Industry*, Santa Monica, RAND, 2002

Lovering, John, *Global Arms Economy*, London, Pluto, 2000

MacMillan, Margrate, *Paris 1919: Six Months that Changed the World*, New York, Random House, 2002

Mandel, Robert, *Armies Without States. The Privatization of Security*, Boulder, CO, Lynne Rienner, 2002

——— *The Meaning of Military Victory*, Boulder, CO, Lynne Reiner, 2006

Markusen, Ann and Sean Costigan, eds, *Arming the Future: A Defense Industry for the Twenty-First Century*, New York, Council on Foreign Relations Press, 1999

Markusen, Ann, Peter Hall, Scott Campbell and Sabina Dietrick, *The Rise of the Gunbelt*, Oxford, Oxford University Press, 1991

Markusen, Ann and Joel Yudken, *Dismantling the Cold War Economy*, New York: Basic Books, 1992

Marshall, Andy W., *Problems of Estimating Military Power*, Santa Monica: RAND, 1966

Martel, William C., ed., *The Technological Arsenal: Emerging Defense Capabilities*, Washington, Smithsonian Institution Press, 2001

Martin, Stephen, ed., *The Economics of Offsets: Defence Procurement and Countertrade*, Amsterdam, Harwood Academic Publishers, 1996

McCoy, Alfred W., *The Politics of Heroin in South-East Asia*, New York, Harper and Colophon, 1972

Merom, Gil, *How Democracies Lose Small Wars*, Cambridge, Cambridge University Press, 2003

Morgenthau, Hans, *Politics Among Nations: The Struggle for Power and Peace*, New York, Alfred A. Knopf, 1948

Nagl, John, *Learning to Eat Soup with a Knife: Counterinsurgency Lessons from Malaysia and Vietnam*, Chicago, University of Chicago Press, 2005

O'Neill, Bard E., *Insurgency and Terrorism: Inside Modern Revolutionary Warfare*, New York, Potomac Books, 2001

Omitoogun, Wuyi and Eboe Hutchful, *Budgeting for the Military Sector in Africa*, Oxford, Oxford University Press/SIPRI, 2006

Oros, Andrew, *Normalizing Japan: Politics, Identity, and the Evolution of Security Practice*, Stanford, Stanford University Press, 2008

Ott, Attiat F. and Richard J. Cebula, eds, *The Elgar Companion to Public Economics: Empirical Public Economics*, Cheltenham, Edward Elgar, 2003

Owens, William, ed., *Lifting the Fog of War*, New York, Farrar, Straus and Giroux, 2000

Packer, George, *The Assassin's Gate: American in Iraq*, New York, Farrar, Straus and Giroux, 2003

Pearson, Frederic S. and John Sislin, *Arms and Ethnic Conflict*, Lanham, MD, Rowman and Littlefield, 2001

Peri, Joram and Amnon Neubach, *The Military-Industrial Complex in Israel*, Tel-Aviv, International Center for Peace in the Middle East, 1984

Peters, Ralph, *Fighting for the Future: Will America Triumph?* Mechanicsburg, Stackpole Books, 1999

Pierre, Andrew J., ed., *Cascade of Arms: Controlling Conventional Weapons Proliferation in the 1990s*, Washington, Brookings Institution, 1997

Pollack, Jonathan D., ed., *Korea: The East Asian Pivot*, Newport, Naval War College Press, 2004

Porter, Michael E., *The Competitive Advantage of Nations*, New York, The Free Press, 1990

Prabhakar, Lawrence S., Joshua Ho and Sam Bateman, eds, *The Evolving Maritime Balance of Power in The Asia-Pacific*, Singapore, World Scientific Publisher, 2006

Price, R. M. and M. W. Zacher, *The United Nations and Global Security*, New York and Basingstoke, Palgrave Macmillan, 2004

Quinn, Dennis J., ed., *Peace Support Operations and the U.S. Military*, Washington, National Defense University Press, 1994

Rao, P. V. R., *India's Defence Policy and Organisation Since Independence*, New Delhi, The United Services Institution of India, 1977

Renwick, Neil, *Japan's Alliance Politics and Defence Production*, Basingstoke, Hampshire, Macmillan, 1995

Ricks, Thomas, *Fiasco: The American Military Adventure in Iraq*, New York, Penguin, 2006

Rosen, Stephen P., *Societies and Military Power: India and Its Armies*, Ithaca, Cornell University Press, 1996

Samuels, Richard, *'Rich Nation, Strong Army': National Security and the Technological Transformation of Japan*, New York, Cornell University Press, 1994

Sandler, Todd and Keith Hartley, *The Economics of Defence*, Cambridge, Cambridge University Press, 1995

——— *The Political Economy of NATO*, New York, Cambridge University Press, 1999

Sarkasian, Sam and William Scully, eds *U.S. Policy and Low Intensity Conflict*, London, Transaction Press, 1981

Sawyer, Ralph D., *Sun Tzu, The Art of War*, Boulder, Westview Press, 1994

Scahill, Jeremy, *Blackwater: The Rise of the World's Most Powerful Mercenary Army*, New York, Nation Books/Avalon, 2007

Scales, Robert H., *Firepower in Limited War*, Washington, National Defense University Press, 1990

Seale, Patrick, *Asad: The Struggle for the Middle East*, Berkeley, CA, University of California Press, 1990

Serfati, Claude et al., eds, *The Restructuring of the European Defence Industry: Dynamics of Change*, European Commission, Directorate General for Research / Office of Official Publications of the European Union, Luxembourg, 2001

Shafer, Michael D., *Deadly Paradigms: The Failure of U.S. Counterinsurgency Policy*, Princeton, Princeton University Press, 1988

Shearer, David, *Private Armies and Military Intervention*, Adelphi Paper No. 316, International Institute for Strategic Studies, London, 1997

Shlaim, Avi, *Lion of Jordan: The Life of King Hussein in War and Peace*, New York, Knopf, 2008

Silverstein, Kenneth, *Private Warriors*, London, Verso Books, 2000

Singer, Peter W., *Corporate Warriors*, Ithaca and London, Cornell University Press, 2003

Singh, Jasjit, *India's Defence Spending: Assessing Future Needs*, New Delhi, Knowledge World, 2001

Singh, Ravinder Pal, ed., *Arms Procurement Decision Making, Volume 1: China, India, Israel, Japan, South Korea and Thailand*, Stockholm, SIPRI, 1998

Smith, Ron, *Military Economics: The Interaction of Power and Money*, Basingstoke, Palgrave Macmillan, 2009

Smith, Ron and Dan Smith, *The Economics of Militarism*, London, Pluto Press, 1983

Smith, Rupert, *The Utility of Force: The Art of War in the Modern World*, London, Penguin Books, 2006

Smithson, Amy et al., *Chemical Weapons Disarmament in Russia: Problems and Prospects*, Washington, Stimson Center, 1995

Spillman, Kurt R. and Joachim Krause, *Kosovo: Lessons Learned for International Cooperative Security*, Bern and New York, Peter Lang, 2000

Steyn, Hannes, Richard van de Walt and Jan van Loggernberg, *Armament and Disarmament South Africa's Nuclear Experience*, Pretoria, Network Publications, 2003

Subrahmanyam, K., *Perspectives in Defence Planning*, New Delhi, Abhinav, 1972

Susman, Gerald and Sean O'Keefe, eds, *The Defense Industry in the Post-Cold War Era: Corporate Strategies and Public Policy Perspectives*, Oxford, Elsevier, 1998

Taylor, Trevor, *Defence, Technology and International Integration*, London, Francis Pinter, 1982

Tickler, Peter, *The Modern Mercenary: Dog of War or Soldier of Honour?* London, Patrick Stephens Publishing, 1987

van Creveld, Martin, *Technology and War: From 2000 BC to the Present*, New York, Free Press/Macmillan, 1989

——— *The Transformation of War*, New York, Free Press/Macmillan, 1991

Vaux, Tony, Chris Seiple, Greg Nakano and Koenraad van Brabant, *Humanitarian Action and Private Security Companies: Opening the Debate*, London, International Alert, 2002

Wang Gungwu and Yongnian Zheng, eds, *China and the New International Order*, London, Routledge, 2008

Waters, Gary, Desmond Ball and Ian Dudgeon, *Australia and Cyber-warfare*, Canberra, ANU E Press, Australian National University, 2008

Weatherby, Joseph, *The Middle East and North Africa: A Political Primer*, New York, Longman, 2002

Weatherby, Joseph et al., *The Other World: Issues and Politics of the Developing Word*, 6th edition, New York, Pearson Longman, 2009

Wheeler, Winslow, *Wastrels of Defense: How Congress Sabotages U.S. Security*, Annapolis, MD, Naval Institute Press, 2004

Williams, Michael, *Civil Military Relations and Peacekeeping*, Adelphi Paper 321, International Institute for Strategic Studies, London, 1998

Wilson, Isaiah, III, *Thinking Beyond War: Why America Fails to Win the Peace*, New York, Palgrave Macmillan, 2007

Wilson, Isaiah, III and James J. F. Forest, *The Politics of Defence: International and Comparative Perspectives*, London, Routledge, 2008

Woodward, Susan L., *Balkan Tragedy: Chaos and Dissolution After the Cold War*, Washington, The Brookings Institution Press, 1995

Wulf, Herbert, *Internationalizing and Privatizing War and Peace*, Basingstoke, Palgrave Macmillan, 2005

Young Pelton, Robert, *Licensed to Kill*, New York, Crown, 2006

Zakaria, Fareed, *Fight for Freedom*, New York, W. W. Norton, 2003

Zuccino, David and Mike Bowden, *Thunder Run: Three Days with Tusker Brigade in the Battle for Baghdad*, Atlantic Books, 2004

Articles/working papers

Aalto, Erkki, Daniel Keohane, Christian Mölling and Sophie de Vaucorbeil, *Towards a European Defence Market*, Chaillot Paper 113, Paris: European Union Institute for Security Studies, 2008

Abu-Qarn, A. S. and Abu-Bader, S., 'Structural Break in Military Expenditures: Evidence for Egypt, Israel, Jordan and Syria', *Peace Economics, Peace Science and Public Policy*, 14(1), 2008

Aizenman, Joshua and Reuven Glick, 'Military Expenditure, Threats and Growth', FRBSF Working Paper 2003-8, 2003

Ali, Hamid E, 'Military Expenditures and Inequality: Empirical Evidence from Global Data', *Defence and Peace Economics*, Vol. 18(6), January 2007

Altman, Roger C., 'The Great Crash, 2008', *Foreign Affairs*, Vol. 88, No. 1, Jan./Feb. 2009

Alywin-Foster, Nigel, 'Changing the Army for Counterinsurgency Operations', *Military Review*, November–December 2005

Amnesty International, 'Undermining Global Security: The European Union's Arms Exports', February 2004

Arbatov, Alexei, *Russian Military Policy Adrift*, Carnegie Briefing Paper, Vol. 8, Issue 6, Carnegie Moscow Center, Moscow, November 2006, www.carnegie.ru/en/pubs/briefings/brifing%2011_06%20E.pdf

Aslam, Rabia, 'Measuring the Peace Dividend: Evidence from Developing Countries', *Defence and Peace Economics*, Vol. 18(1), Feb. 2007

Balakrishnan, Kogila, 'Defense Industrialization in Malaysia: Development Challenges and the Revolution in Military Affairs', *Security Challenges*, Summer 2008

Ball, Desmond, 'Arms and Affluence: Military Acquisitions in the Asia-Pacific Region', *International Security*, Vol. 18, No. 3, Winter 1993/94

——*Developments in Signals Intelligence and Electronic Warfare in Southeast Asia*, Working Paper No. 290, Strategic and Defence Studies Centre, Australian National University, Canberra, December 1995

——*The New Submarine Combat Information System and Australia's Emerging Information Warfare Architecture*, Working Paper No. 359, Strategic and Defence Studies Centre, Australian National University, Canberra, May 2001

——'China Pursues Space-based Intelligence Gathering Capabilities', *Jane's Intelligence Review*, Vol. 15, No. 12, December 2003

——'Intelligence Collection Operations and EEZs: The Implications of New Technology', *Marine Policy*, No. 28, 2004

Ball, Desmond and Euan Graham, *Japanese Airborne SIGINT Capabilities*, Working Paper No. 353, Strategic and Defence Studies Centre, Australian National University, Canberra, December 2000

Ball, Nicole, 'Defense and Development: A Critique of the Benoit Study', *Economic Development and Cultural Change*, Vol. 31, 1983

Bartels, Larry, 'Pooling Disparate Observations', *American Journal of Political Science*, 40 (3), 1996

Bauer, Sibylle, 'EU Pushing for Firm Commitments at UN Small Arms Conference', *European Security Review*, No. 4, March 2001, www.isis-europe.org/index.php?page=esr

——'EU Small Arms Policy after the UN Conference', *European Security Review*, No. 8, October 2001, www.isis-europe.org/index.php?page=esr

Becher, Klaus, Gordon Adams and Burkard Schmitt, *European and Transatlantic Defence-Industrial Strategies*, ESF Working Paper No. 10, January 2003

Benoit, Emile, 'Growth and Defense in Developing Countries', *Economic Development and Cultural Change*, Vol. 26, No. 2, January 1978

Berger, Thomas, 'From Sword to Chrysanthemum: Japan's Culture of Anti-Militarism', *International Security*, Vol. 17, No. 4, 1993

Berglas, Eithan, 'Defence and the Economy: The Israeli Experience', Discussion Paper 83.01, 1983, The Maurice Falk Institute for Economic Research, Jerusalem

Biswas, Basudeb and Rati Ram, 'Military Expenditure and Economic Growth in the Less Developed Countries: An Augmented Model and Further Evidence', *Economic Development and Cultural Change*, Vol. 34, No. 2, January 1986

Bitzinger, Richard A., 'The Globalization of the Arms Industry: The Next Proliferation Challenge', *International Security*, Fall 1994

Brauer, Jurgen, 'Reviving or Revamping the "Disarmament-for-Development" Thesis?', *Bulletin of Peace Proposals*, Vol. 21, No. 3, September 1990

——'Arms Production in Developing Nations: The Relation to Industrial Structure, Industrial Diversification, and Human Capital Formation', *Defence Economics*, Vol. 2, No. 2, April 1991

——'Military Expenditures and Human Development Measures', *Public Budgeting and Financial Management*, Vol. 8, No. 1, Spring 1996

——'Survey and Review of the Defense Economics Literature on Greece and Turkey: What Have We Learned?', *Defence and Peace Economics*, Vol. 13, No. 2, 2002

Bromley, Mark, 'The Europeanisation of Arms Export Policy in the Czech Republic, Slovakia, and Poland', *European Security*, Vol. 2, No. 16, 1997

Bromley, Mark and Michael Brzoska, 'Towards a Common, Restrictive EU Arms Export Policy? The Impact of the EU Code of Conduct on Major Conventional Arms Exports', *European Foreign Affairs Review*, Vol. 13, No. 3, 2007

Bromley, Mark and Catalina Perdomo, *CBMs in Latin America and the Effect of Arms Acquisitions by Venezuela*, Real Instituto Elcano Working Paper No. 41, September 2005

Brunton, Bruce G., 'Institutional Origins of the Military Industrial Complex', *Journal of Economic Issues*, Vol. 22, June 1988

Brzoska, Michael, 'The Reporting of Military Expenditures', *Journal of Peace Research* Vol. 18, No. 3, 1981
——'Research Communication: The Military Related External Debt of Third World Countries', *Journal of Peace Research*, Vol. 20, No. 3, 1983
——'The Financing Factor in Military Trade', *Defence and Peace Economics*, Vol. 5, 1994

Carson, Iain, 'Transformed? A Survey of the Defense Industry', *The Economist*, 20 July 2002

Chin Kin Wah, *Defence Spending in Southeast Asia*, Singapore, Institute for Southeast Asian Studies, 1987

Clapham, Christopher, 'Rethinking African States', *African Security Review*, Vol. 10 (3), 2001, www.iss.co.za/Pubs/ASR/10N03/Clapham.html

Copson, Raymond W., Kerry Dumbaugh and Michelle Lan, *China and Sub-Saharan Africa*, Congressional Research Service (CRS) Report RL133055, 2008, www.fas.org/sgp/crs/row/index.html

Cornish, Paul, 'European Security: The End of the Architecture and New NATO', *International Affairs*, Vol. 72, 1996

Crook, John R., 'Continuing Efforts to Curtail Iranian Nuclear Program', *The American Journal of International Law*, Vol. 100, No. 4, October 2006

Cuaresma, Jesus Crespo and Gerhard Reitschuler, 'A Non-Linear Defence Growth Nexus? Evidence from the US Economy', *Defence and Peace Economics*, Vol. 15(1), February 2003

Cullen, Patrick, 'Keeping the New Dog of War on a Tight Leash', *Conflict Trends*, June 2000

Deger, Saadet and R. Smith, 'Military Expenditure and Growth in Less Developed Countries', *Journal of Conflict Resolution*, Vol. 27, No. 2, 1983

del Prado, Jose L. Gomes, 'Impact on Human Rights of Private Military and Security Companies' Activities', *Global Research*, 11 October 2008

De Vestel, Pierre, *Defence Markets and Industries in Europe: Time for Political Decisions?* Chaillot Paper 21, Western European Union, Paris, November 1995

Dibb, Paul, 'Force Modernization in Asia: Towards 2000 and Beyond', Canberra, Australian National University, 1997
——'The Revolution in Military Affairs and Asian Security', *Survival*, Vol. 39, No. 4, Winter 1997–98

Dunne, J. Paul, 'The Changing Military Industrial Complex in the UK', *Defence Economics*, Vol. 4, No. 2, March 1993
——'The Making of Arms in South Africa', *Economics of Peace and Security Journal*, Vol. 1, No. 1, January 2006
——'Problems of Post Conflict reconstruction in Africa: A Comparative Analysis of the Experience of Mozambique and Rwanda', *Economics of Peace and Security Journal*, Vol. 1, No. 2, 2006

Dunne, J. Paul, Maria Garcia-Alonso, Paul Levine and Ron Smith, 'Determining the Defence Industrial Base', *Defence and Peace Economics*, Vol. 18, No. 3, 2007
——'Managing Asymmetric Conflict', *Oxford Economic Papers*, Vol. 58, 2006

Dunne, J. Paul and Nadir Mohammed, 'Military Spending in Sub-Saharan Africa: Evidence for 1967–85', *Journal of Peace Research*, Vol. 32, No. 3, 1995

Dunne, J. Paul and Sam Perlo-Freeman, 'The Demand for Military Spending in Developing Countries', *International Review of Applied Economics*, Vol. 17, No. 1, 2003

Elbadawi, Ibrahim and Nicholas Sambanis, 'Why Are There So Many Civil Wars in Africa? Understanding and Preventing Violent Conflict', *Journal of African Economics*, December 2000, siteresources.worldbank.org/DEC/Resources/warsinAfrica.pdf, 2000

Elhefnawy, Nader, 'The Impending Oil Shock', *Survival*, Vol. 50, No. 2, April–May 2008

Erickson, Jennifer L., *The Arms Trade Treaty: The Politics behind the UN Process*, Working Paper, Research Unit, European and Atlantic Security, German Institute for International and Security Affairs, Berlin, FG3-WP 09, July 2007

Fearon, James and David Laitin, 'Ethnicity, Insurgency, and Civil War', *American Political Science Review*, 97 (1) 2003

Frederiksen, Peter and Robert E. Looney, 'Defense Expenditures and Economic Growth in Developing Countries', *Armed Forces and Society*, Vol. 9, No. 4, 1983

Gabelnick, Tamar, Maria Haug and Lora Lumpe, *A Guide to the US Small Arms Market, Industry and Exports, 1998–2004*, Occasional Paper, Small Arms Survey, Geneva, 2006

Galvin, Hannah, 'The Impact of Defence Spending on the Economic Growth of Developing Countries: A Cross Section Study', *Defence and Peace Economics*, Vol. 14(1), February 2003

Gansler, Jaques S., 'Transforming the US Defence Industrial Base', *Survival*, Vol. 35, No. 4, Winter 1993
——'US Defence Industrial Policy', *Security Challenges*, Vol. 3, No. 2, June 2007

Gat, Azar, 'The Return of Authoritarian Great Powers', *Foreign Affairs*, July/August 2007

Gilby, Nicholas, 'Corruption and the Arms Trade: The U.K. Ministry of Defence and the Bribe Culture', *Economics of Peace and Security Journal*, Vol. 3, No. 1, 2008

Golan, Galia, 'Gorbachev's Difficult Time in the Gulf', *Political Science Quarterly*, 107(2), Summer 1992

Gray, Colin S., 'The Arms Race Phenomenon', *World Politics*, Vol. 24, No. 1, 1972

Haghshenass, Fariborz, 'Iran's Doctrine of Asymmetric Naval Warfare', www.washingtoninstitute.org, Policy Watch No. 1179, December 2006

Halperin, Ariel, 'Force Buildup and Economic Growth', *Economic Quarterly*, Vol. 131, 1987

Hartley, Keith, 'Defence Industrial Policy in a Military Alliance', *Journal of Peace Research*, Vol. 43, No. 4, 2006
——'European Defense Industrial Policy and the United Kingdom's Defence Industrial Base', *Economics of Peace and Security Journal*, Vol. 3, No. 1, 2008

Hartung, William D., *Soldiers Versus Contractors: Emerging Budget Reality*, World Policy Institute, 10 February 2006

Hoffmann, Stanley, 'The Politics and Ethics of Military Intervention', *Survival*, Vol. 37, No. 4, Winter 1995–96

Hooker, Richard D., Jr, H. R. McMaster and Dave Grey, 'Getting Transformation Right', *Joint Forces Quarterly*, Issue 38, 3rd Quarter 2005, www.amnesty.org/en/library/asset/ACT30/003/2004/en/dom-ACT300032004en.html

Howorth, J., 'Britain, France and the European Defence Initiative', *Survival*, Vol. 42, 2000

Huxley, Tim, 'Singapore and Malaysia: A Precarious Balance?', *Pacific Review*, Vol. 4, No. 3, 1991

Ikenberry, John, 'The Rise of China and the Future of the West: Can the Liberal System Survive', *Foreign Affairs*, January/February 2008

James, Andrew D., 'The Transatlantic Defence R&D Gap: Causes, Consequences and Controversies', *Defence and Peace Economics*, Vol. 17, No. 3, June 2006

Ji, You, 'Adding Offensive Teeth to the PLA Air Force', *Issues & Studies*, Vol. 35, No. 2, 1999

———'The Anti-Secession Law and the Risk of War in the Taiwan Strait', *Contemporary Security Policy*, Vol. 27, No. 2, 2006

Kaiser, Stefan A., 'Viewpoint: Chinese Anti-satellite Weapons: New Power Geometry and New Legal Policy', *Astropolitics*, Vol. 6 (3), January 2008

Kapur, S. Paul, 'Ten Years of Instability in a Nuclear South Asia', *International Security*, Vol. 33 (2), Fall 2008

Kilcullen, David, 'Countering Global Insurgency', *Small Wars Journal*, 2006, smallwarsjournal.com/documents/kilcullen.pdf

Knight, Malcolm, Norman Loayza and Delano Villanueva, *The Peace Dividend: Military Spending Cuts and Economic Growth*, World Bank Policy Research Working Paper No. 1577, 1996

Krahmann, Elke, 'Conceptualizing Security Governance', *Cooperation and Conflict*, Vol. 38, No. 1, 2003

Krepinevich, Andrew F., 'Cavalry to Computer: The Pattern of Military Revolution', *The National Interest*, No. 37, Fall 1994

Ladwig, Walter C., III, 'A Cold Start for Hot Wars? An Assessment of the Indian Army's New Limited War Doctrine', *International Security*, Vol. 32 (3), Winter 2007/08

Lamb, Guy, *Beyond 'Shadow Boxing' and 'Lip Service'*, Occasional Paper 135, Institute for Security Studies, April 2007, www.iss.co.za

Laurance, Edward J., Hendrik Wagenmakers and Herbert Wulf, 'Managing the Global Problems Created by the Conventional Arms Trade: An Assessment of the United Nations Register of Conventional Arms', *Global Governance*, Vol. 11, 2005

Leander, Anna, 'The Power to Construct International Security: On the Significance of Private Military Companies', *Millennium*, Vol. 33, No. 3, June 2005

Lebovic, James and Ahmad Ishaq, 'Military Burden, Security Needs, and Economic Growth in the Middle East', *Journal of Conflict Resolution*, 31, 1987

Liang, Q. and W. Xiangsui, 'Unrestricted Warfare', 1999, www.terrorism.com/documents/TRC-Analysis/unrestricted.pdf

Lovering, John, 'Military Expenditure and the Restructuring of Capitalism: The Military Industry in Britain', *Cambridge Journal of Economics*, Vol. 14, No. 4, December 1990

Luckham, Robin, 'Africa: Arming the State', *New Internationalist*, Vol. 139, September 1984, www.newint.org/issue139/military.htm

Lyall, Jason A. and Isaiah Wilson III, 'Rage Against the Machines: The Determinants of Success in Counterinsurgency', *International Organization*, Jan./Feb. 2009

Mack, Andrew, 'Why Big Nations Lose Small Wars: The Politics of Asymmetric Conflict', *World Politics*, 27 (2), 1975

Manwaring, Max and Jon Fishel, 'Insurgency and Counter-Insurgency: Towards a New Analytical Approach', *Small Wars and Insurgencies*, Winter 1992

Marks, Edward, 'Peace Operations: Involving Regional Organizations', *Strategic Forum*, No. 25, April 1995

Markusen, Ann, 'The Economics of Defence Industry Mergers and Divestiture', *Economic Affairs*, Vol. 17, No. 4, December 1997

Mathieu, Fabien and Nicholas Dearden, *Corporate Mercenaries: The Threat of Private Military and Security Companies*, War on Want, 2006

McCoy, Clifford, 'Myanmar's Losing Military Strategy', *Asia Times*, 7 October 2006, www.atimes.com/atimes/Southeast_Asia/HJ07Ae01.html

McMaster, H. R., 'Learning from Contemporary Conflicts to Prepare for Future War', *Orbis*, Vol. 52, No. 4, Fall 2008

Menon, Rajan, 'The Strategic Convergence between Russia and China', *Survival*, Vol. 39, No. 2, 1997

Merom, Gil, 'Israel's National Security and the Myth of Exceptionalism', *Political Science Quarterly*, 114(3), Autumn 1999

Milowicki, Gene. V. and Joan Johnson-Freese, 'Strategic Choices: Examining the United States Military Response to the Chinese Anti-Satellite Test', in *Astropolitics*, Vol. 6 (1), January 2008

Mintz, Alex and Huang Chi, 'Guns versus Butter: The Indirect Link', *American Journal of Political Science*, 35 (3), August 1991

Mintz, Alex and Randolph Stevenson, 'Defense Expenditures, Economic Growth, and the Peace Dividend: A Longitudinal Analysis of 103 Countries', *Journal of Conflict Resolution*, 39 (2), 1995

Moore, James, 'An Assessment of the Iranian Military Rearmament Program', *Comparative Strategy*, Vol. 13, No. 4, 1994

Murray, Williamson, 'History, War, and Future', *Orbis*, Vol. 52, No. 4, Fall 2008

Niksch, Larry A., *North Korea's Nuclear Weapons Program*, Congressional Research Service, Library of Congress, Washington, 5 October 2006

Noh, Hoon, *South Korea's 'Cooperative Self-Reliant Defense': Goals and Directions*, KIDA Paper No. 10, Seoul, Korea Institute for Defense Analyses, April 2005

Nye, Joseph S. and William A. Owens, 'America's Information Edge', *Foreign Affairs*, Vol. 75, No. 2, March–April 1996

Pant, Harsh V., 'India in the Asia-Pacific: Rising Ambitions with an Eye on China', *Asia-Pacific Review*, Vol. 14 (1), May 2007

Perlo-Freeman, Sam and Elizabeth Sköns, *The Private Military Services Industry*, SIPRI Insights on Peace and Security, No. 1, September 2008

Quandt, William. B., 'Camp David and Peacemaking in the Middle East', *Political Science Quarterly*, 101(3), 1986

Rangsimaporn, Paradorn, 'Russia's Debate on Military-Technological Cooperation with China', *Asian Survey*, May/June 2006

Rosh, Robert M., 'Third World Militarisation: Security Webs and the States They Ensnare', *Journal of Conflict Resolution*, Vol. 32, No. 4, 1988

Rummel, Rudolph J., 'Power, Genocide and Mass Murder', *Journal of Peace Research*, Vol. 31, No.1, 1994

Sadeh, Sharon, 'Israel's Beleaguered Defense Industry', *Middle East Review of International Affairs*, Vol. 5, No. 1, 2001

Schnaubelt, Christoper M., 'Whither the RMA?' *Parameters*, Autumn 2007

Sholam, Danny, 'Chemical and Biological Weapons in Egypt', *The Non Proliferation Review*, Spring 1998, cns.miis.edu/pubs/npr/vol05/53/shoham53.pdf

Singer, Peter W., *Can't Win With 'Em, Can't Go to War Without 'Em: Private Military Contractors and Counterinsurgency*, Brookings Foreign Policy Paper Series No. 4, September 2007, www.brookings.edu/papers/2007/0927militarycontractors.aspx

Smaldone, Joseph P, 'African Military Spending: Defence versus Development?' *African Security Review*, Vol. 15, No. 4, 2006

Smith, Dan and Ron Smith, *Military Expenditure, Resources and Development*, University of London, Birkbeck College Discussion Paper No. 87, November 1980

Smith, Ron and Paul Dunne, 'Is Military Spending a Burden? A Marxo-Marginalist Response to Pivetti', *Cambridge Journal of Economics*, Vol. 18, 1994

Sorbara, Mark J., 'Oil Security: The United States and Maritime Security in the Gulf of Guinea', *Petroleum Africa*, July 2007

Srinivas, V. N., 'Trends in Defence Expenditure', *Air Power Journal*, Vol. 3, No. 1, Spring 2006

Stavriankakis, Anna, 'Licensed to Kill: The United Kingdom's Arms Export Licensing Process', *Economics of Peace and Security Journal*, Vol. 3, No. 1, 2008

Steinberg, Demitri, 'Trends in Soviet Military Expenditures', *Soviet Studies*, Vol. 42, No. 4, October 1990

Stohl, Rachel, 'Fighting the Illicit Trafficking of Small Arms', *SAIS Review*, Vol. 25, No. 1, Winter 2005

Story, Ian and You Ji, 'China's Aircraft Carrier Ambitions: Seeking Truth from Rumours', *The Naval War College Review*, Vol. LVII, No. 1, 2003

Strategic Comments, 'Singapore's Military Modernization', *Strategic Comments*, Vol. 13, Issue 10, December 2007

Tan, Andrew T. H., *Force Modernisation Trends in Southeast Asia*, Working Paper No. 59, Institute of Defence and Strategic Studies (IDSS), Singapore, January 2004

Tinchieri, Lucca, 'Is the 1998 Code of Conduct on Arms Exports Adequate to Support the EU's Promotion of Human Rights?' *Hamburger Beiträge*, No. 149, Hamburg, Institut für Friedensforschung und Sicherheitspolitik, 2008

Tishler, Asher and Ze'ev Rotem, 'Factors Explaining the International Success of the Israeli Defence Industry', *Economic Quarterly*, No. 3, 1995

Tsai, Ming-yen, 'Russian-Chinese Military Ties: Development and Implications', *Journal of Russia Studies*, No. 5, 2005

van Brabant, Koenraad, *Humanitarian Action and Private Security Companies*, Humanitarian Practice Network, 2002

Wallner, D., 'Estimating Non-Transparent Military Expenditures: The Case of China (PRC)', *Defense and Peace Economics*, Vol. 8, 1997

Waltz, Susan, 'Islamist Appeal in Tunisia', *The Middle East Journal*, 40(4), 1986

Weidacher, Reinhilde, *Behind a Veil of Secrecy: Military Small Arms and Light Weapons Production in Western Europe*, Occasional Paper, Small Arms Survey, Geneva, 2005

Wortzel, Larry M., 'The Chinese People's Liberation Army and Space Warfare', *Astropolitics*, Vol. 6 (2), May 2008

Yakovlev, Pavel, 'Arms Trade, Military Spending and Economic Growth', *Defence and Peace Economics*, Vol. 18(4), 2007

Yanik, Lerna K., 'Guns and Human Rights: Major Powers, Global Arms Transfers, and Human Rights Violations', *Human Rights Quarterly*, Vol. 28, No. 2, May 2006

Conference papers/proceedings

Bennett, Bruce, 'The Emerging Ballistic Missile Threat: Global and Regional Ramification', paper presented at the Airpower Conference, Yonsei University, Seoul, June 1999

Chapman, John, *Will the EU Get Tough on Opening Up National Defense Procurements?*, paper presented at The New Defense Agenda, Brussels, 18 April 2005

Fisher, Richard D., Jr, 'PLAAF Equipment Trends', paper presented at the National Defense University Conference on PLA and Chinese Society in Transition, 30 October 2001, www.ndu.edu/inss/China_Center/RFischer.htm

Tellis, Ashley J., *Future Fire: Challenges Facing Indian Defense Policy in the New Century*, paper presented at the India Today Conclave, New Delhi, 13 March 2004, www.ceip.org/files/pdf/futurefire.pdf

Official reports/documents

Amnesty International USA, *Annual Report*, 23 May 2006 www.amnestyusa.org/annualreport

Archick, Kristin and Paul Gallis, *NATO and the European Union*, CRS (Congressional Research Service) Report, US Library of Congress, RS32342, January 2008

Asia-Pacific Economic Update, Honolulu, United States Pacific Command, January 2000

BAE Systems, *Annual Report 2007*, www.baesystems.com

'Below the Radar: U.S. military programs with Latin America, 1997–2007', joint publication from the Center for International Policy, the Latin America Working Group Education Fund, and the Washington Office on Latin America, March 2007

Central Intelligence Agency, *The Acquisition of Technology Relating to Weapons of Mass Destruction and Advanced Conventional Munitions*, unclassified report to Congress, July 2003, www.cia.gov/library/reports/archived-reports-1/jan_jun2003.htm

Corporate Mercenaries, Campaign Against the Arms Trade, 2006, www.caat.org.uk/issues/corporate-mercenaries.php

CSIS, *The Future of the Transatlantic Defense Community: Final Report of the CSIS Commission on Transatlantic Security and Industrial Cooperation in the Twenty-first Century*, Washington, Center for Strategic and International Studies (CSIS), January 2003

Department of Defense (USA), *Annual Report on the Military Power of the People's Republic of China*, report to Congress Pursuant to the FY2000 National Defense Authorization Act, 12 July 2002, US Department of Defense, www.defenselink.mil/news/Jul2002/d20020712china.pdf

——*Quadrennial Defense Review 2006*, 3 February 2006

——*100 Companies Receiving the Largest Dollar Volume of Prime Contract Awards, Fiscal Year 2006*, Washington, US Department of Defense, 2007

——*Annual Report to Congress: Military Power of the People's Republic of China 2008*, US Department of Defense, June 2008, www.defenselink.mil/pubs/pdfs/China_Military_Report_08.pdf

Department of State (USA), *Joint Statement on the Merida Initiative: A New Paradigm for Security Cooperation*, Department of State, 22 October 2007

EDA, *Defense Data of EDA Participating Member States in 2007*, Brussels, European Defense Agency, 12 December 2008

EU Council, *EU Code of Conduct on Arms Exports*, EU Council, 5 June 1998, www.consilium.europa.eu/uedocs/cmsUpload/08675r2en8.pdf

Government Accountability Office, *Rebuilding Iraq: Actions Needed to Improve Use of Private Security Providers*, Report to Congressional Committees GAO-05-737, July 2005

Grimmett, Richard F., *Conventional Arms Transfers to Latin America: US Policy*, CRS (Congressional Research Service) Report, US Library of Congress, 97–512 F, 5 August 1997

——*Military Technology and Conventional Weapons Expenditure Countries: The Wasseenaar Arrangement*, CRS (Congressional Research Service) Report, US Library of Congress, RS20517, 29 September 2006

——*Conventional Arms Trade and Developing Nations, 1999–2006*, CRS (Congressional Research Service) Report, US Library of Congress, RL34187, 26 September 2007

——*Conventional Arms Transfers to Developing Nations, 2000–2007*, CRS (Congressional Research Service) Report, US Library of Congress, RL34723, 23 October 2008

Hartley, Keith and Andrew Cox, *The Costs of Non-Europe in Defence Procurement*, Executive Summary, study carried out for the Commission of the European Communities DG III, Brussels, 1992

Hartung, William D. and Frida Berrigan, *Militarization of U.S. Africa Policy, 2000 to 2005: A Fact Sheet*, Arms Trade Resource Centre, Axis of Influence-World Policy Institute: Research Project, 2005, www.worldpolicy.org/projects/arms/reports/AfricaMarch2005.html

International Development Research Centre, *The Responsibility to Protect: Report of the International Commission on Intervention and States Sovereignty*, Ottawa, 2001

Israel Defense Sales Directory 2007/8, Tel-Aviv, Ministry of Defence, 2007

The Kargil Review Committee Report, *From Surprise to Reckoning*, New Delhi, Sage Publications, 1999

Klepsch, Egon (rapporteur), *Report drawn on Behalf of the Politcal Affairs Committee on European Cooperation in Arms Procurement*, Doc. No. 83/78, European Communities, European Parliament, Strasbourg, 8 May 1978

Ministry of Defence (India), *Annual Report*, 2007–8

Ministry of Defence (Japan), *Defense of Japan 2007*, Tokyo, Ministry of Defence, 2007

Ministry of Defence (UK), *Defence Industrial Policy*, MoD Policy Paper No. 5, London, Ministry of Defence, October 2002

Ministry of National Defence (Republic of Korea), *Defense White Paper 2006*, Ministry of National Defence, 2006

Perry, William J., *The Perry Report*, US State Department, 12 October 1999

Rumsfeld, Donald H., *Executive Summary of the Report to the Commission to Assess the Ballistic Missile Threat to the United States*, 15 July 1998

Serfati, Claude, ed., *Government-Companies Relations in the Arms Industry: Between Change and Stability?*, Brussels, Office for Official Publications of the European Communities, 2000

Serfati, Claude, Michael Brzoska, Björn Hagelin, Elisabeth Sköns and Wim Smit, eds, *The Restructuring of the European Defence Industry: Dynamics of Change*, Luxembourg, Office for Official Publications of the European Communities, 2000

United States Joint Forces Command, *The Joint Operating Environment 2008: Challenges and Implications for the Future Joint Force*, United States Joint Forces Command, November 2008, us.jfcom.mil/sites/J5/j59/default.aspx

US ACDA (Arms Control and Disarmament Agency), *World Military Expenditures and Arms Transfers 1995*, dosfan.lib.uic.edu/acda/wmeat95/wmeatcov.htm

US Congress, *North Korea Advisory Group Report to the Speaker of the U.S. House of Representatives*, November 1999

——*Merida Initiative to Combat Illicit Narcotics and Reduce Organized Crime Authorization Act of 2008*, 11 June 2008

US National Intelligence Council, *Global Trends 2025: A Transformed World*, US National Intelligence Council, November 2008, www.dni.gov/nic/NIC_2025_project.html

World Military Expenditures and Arms Transfers, US Arms Control and Disarmament Agency, US Government Printing Office, 1987

Journals, news agencies and newspapers

These are some of the sources on the global arms trade which the contributing writers have found useful in the preparation of their chapter articles

Africa News
The Age (Melbourne)
Agence France-Presse
Air Force News
Air Forces Monthly
Air Power Journal
Asia Times, www.atimes.com
Asian Defence Journal
Asian Wall Street Journal
Asia-Pacific Defence Reporter
Associated Press
Australian Financial Review
Aviation Week and Space Technology
Bangkok Post (Thailand)
BBC News, news.bbc.co.uk
Channel News Asia, www.channelnewsasia.com
Daily Telegraph
Defence Industry Daily, www.defenseindustrydaily.com
Defense News
The Economist
Flight International
Forbes.com, www.forbes.com
The Hindu
The Independent
India Abroad
India Post
India Today
Indian Express
Jane's Defense Weekly
Jane's Intelligence Review
Jane's International Defense Review
The Japan Times
Korea Times
Latin American Security & Strategic Review (LASSR)
Los Angeles Times
Miami Herald
Military Technology
Moscow Defence Brief, mdb.cast.ru/mdb/5 2002/ff/atd
The Nation (Thailand)
Naval Forces
New Straits Times (Malaysia)
New York Times
Press Trust of India
Reuters
Seattle Times
Straits Times (Singapore)
Strategy Page, www.strategypage.com
Sydney Morning Herald
The Tribune
Unmanned Vehicles
USA Today
Voice of America
Washington Post
Washington Times
Xinhua

Index

28316067R00230

Printed in Great Britain
by Amazon